Rationalism in politics

Michael Oakeshott was born December 11, 1901, at Chelsfield, Kent, England. He attended St. George's School, Harpenden, from 1912 to 1920 and was a Scholar of Gonville and Caius College, Cambridge, from 1920 to 1923, taking the History Tripos, Parts I and II in 1922–23. He held a graduate studentship from 1923 to 1926 when he became a Fellow of Gonville and Caius College, and began a period of study at Tübingen and Marburg. From 1929 to 1951 he was Official Fellow and Lecturer in History, Gonville and Caius College, and from 1933 to 1950, University Lecturer in History.

He served in the British Army in England, France, and Germany from 1942 to 1945. Returning to Cambridge, he founded *The Cambridge Journal* in 1947. He became a Fellow of Nuffield College, Oxford, in 1950–51, and then Professor of Political Science, The London School of Economics and Political Science, in 1951, a post he held until his official retirement in 1967. He became a Fellow of the British Academy in 1966.

He died December 19, 1990 at his home in Acton, Dorset, and is buried in the parish churchyard at neighboring Langton Matravers.

MICHAEL JOSEPH OAKESHOTT

Rationalism in politics and other essays

MICHAEL OAKESHOTT

Foreword by Timothy Fuller

NEW AND EXPANDED EDITION

Liberty Fund

Indianapolis

This book is published by Liberty Fund, Inc., a foundation established to encourage study of the ideal of a society of free and responsible individuals.

The cuneiform inscription that serves as the design motif for our endpapers is the earliest-known written appearance of the word "freedom" (*ama-gi*), or "liberty." It is taken from a clay document written about 2300 B.C. in the Sumerian city-state of Lagash.

Frontispiece photo by Ken Abbott, 2954 Shady Hollow West, Boulder, CO 80302.

LIBRARY OF CONGRESS CATALOGING-IN-PUBLICATION DATA

Oakeshott, Michael Joseph, 1901–1990
  Rationalism in politics and other essays / Michael Oakeshott.—New and expanded ed.
    p.   cm.
  Includes bibliographical references and index.
  ISBN 0-86597-094-7 (hardcover). —ISBN 0-86597-095-5 (pbk.)
  1. Political science—Philosophy. 2. Rationalism. I. Title.
JA71.024   1991
320—dc20
                               91-6951
                                CIP

12 11 10 09 08 07 06 05 04 03 C 7 6 5 4 3
11 10 09 08 07 06 05   P 8 7 6 5

To C.S.

Contents

• Indicates essay is new to this edition.

Preface to the first edition

Of these essays, composed during the last twelve years, seven were first published elsewhere. Each was written for a different occasion, but they seem to me to go together well enough to be put together. They are all concerned with doing, understanding and explaining; with different modes of these activities and with their relations to one another. And, although they do not compose a settled doctrine, they disclose a consistent style or disposition of thought. The essay on poetry is a belated retraction of a foolish sentence in *Experience and Its Modes*.

M.O.

1962

Oakeshott's rationalism in politics today

TIMOTHY FULLER

The publication of *Rationalism in Politics* in 1962 was a major event in contemporary political philosophy, accelerating Michael Oakeshott's advance to the forefront of contemporary political philosophers. This new edition adds six essays, five previously published, and the never before published "Political Discourse," each of which is consistent with the themes and the disposition of the original edition of *Rationalism in Politics*.

The essays now are arranged thematically rather than chronologically, for two reasons: to emphasize the consistency of Michael Oakeshott's thinking in this book with the arguments of *Experience and Its Modes* (1933) and *On Human Conduct* (1975), and to incorporate the additions in a coherent manner into the whole. It is important, however, to remember what kind of "whole" *Rationalism in Politics* is. Professor Oakeshott's own retrospective judgment, twenty-eight years on, was that the book remains a set of *essays*, "modest intellectual adventures in which a human circumstance is explored, understood and distinguished as an arrangement of related characteristics composing a coherent 'character', rather than an inquiry designed to extrapolate a non-circumstantial, definitive 'nature'." In short, Oakeshott, like Montaigne who inspires the style of *Rationalism in Politics*, does not try to subjugate experience in an intellectual scheme. He "essays" to understand himself in relation to the circumstances of his time as he understands them, asking his readers to accept the invitation to respond out of their own reflections in conversation.

Parts One and Two establish Oakeshott's understanding of the uses and misuses of reason as they show themselves both in the conduct of politics and in the academic study of the history of politics.

Part Three provides a substantial introduction to the importance of Hobbes in the theoretical analysis of modern political life and his influence on Oakeshott's own thinking about politics. In Part Four, Oakeshott turns his attention to the issues of politics as illuminated by the theoretical foundation laid in the earlier parts. Part Five elucidates his understanding of the perennial human predicament and the possibility, through the poetic voice, of transposing the apparent curses of the human condition into blessings.

The reader will note some stylistic elements in *Rationalism in Politics* which have led to perceptions that Oakeshott wrote in an antiquarian, local, peculiarly British way. These opinions say much about his earlier readers who couldn't comprehend his political philosophy, differing as it did from the dominant liberalism of postwar thinking. The stylistic elements in *Rationalism in Politics*—often felicitous, unusual, and complex—do not define Oakeshott's aim.

This new edition of *Rationalism in Politics* is the best place to begin exploring Oakeshott's thought. These essays disclose aspects of the full range of his reflections. One must then also consult *Experience and Its Modes* and *On Human Conduct* to see the thematic consistency in Oakeshott's thought and the systematic exposition of his ideal of civil association.

The initial American reception of *Rationalism in Politics* was colored by some reviewers' ignorance of his earlier work, and among others by a progressivist attitude that distrusted thinkers loosely

defined as "pessimistic," "traditionalist," "Burkean," or "conservative." A generation later, conservatism is more respectable, and, to
a degree, Oakeshott's prominence has risen accordingly among
many who formerly ignored or discounted him. They can now see
that he combines a commitment to individual liberty with a
profound grasp of the historic achievements of European civilization. His skeptical conservatism, however, remains difficult to
transform into programmatic activism. And his conception of philosophizing differs from some other schools of political philosophy
in the Anglo-American world.

Oakeshott shares with traditional philosophy the skepticism
that a great deal of what passes for knowledge is puffed-up nonsense, revealing itself for what it is whenever someone tries to "put
it into practice." One can safely say that many Soviet, Eastern European, and Chinese citizens today know by hard experience what
"rationalism in politics" is all about. It was more courageous to attack in 1962 (or in 1947, when the title essay "Rationalism in Politics" first appeared) what today is fashionably attacked by many.
Contemporary world history dramatically illustrates the breakdown
of the claims made for rationalism and ideology in the twentieth
century. Oakeshott, from his earliest writings, shows remarkable
insight and prescience about this, not because he made predic-
tions, but because he kept his eye fixed on the seductive tempta-
tions of pridefulness endemic in the human condition.

Political life dramatically displays this human condition. In political life we conduct ourselves in terms of wished-for conditions
that we think "ought to be" but that are "not yet." This world of the
incessantly wished-for arises through the expression of individual
opinions that can easily conflict. Often, those engaged in practical
activity imagine there can be a state of affairs which, once attained,
will bring to an end the necessity to desire anything more. The pur-
veyors of plans for a Tower of Babel ever lurk on the street corners
and in the alley ways of political life.

Actually, Oakeshott's work *is* a teaching about the limits of politics and the disillusioning effects of the effort to find the meaning
of life there. A number of early reviewers of *Rationalism in Politics*

believed Oakeshott to be uninterested in argument, clarity, or, finally, political philosophy itself. He was incorrectly taken to mean
that it is pointless to seek meaning in life. Clearly, this does not
follow logically, and it does not, in fact, accurately describe
Oakeshott's position. What it does reveal is how deeply politicized
political philosophy has become in our time.

There is a categorical difference, Oakeshott believes, between
philosophy and politics. Philosophy, which seeks understanding for
its own sake, cannot be reduced to politics, and politics, which
must ever seek to preserve and to change, cannot be transposed into philosophy.[1] Political life has its own character. If Oakeshott does
not flatter that life, neither does he despise it. Politics he accepts, as
did Aristotle, as an independent mode of human activity, needing
no speculative master to put it right. This is not to say that politics
cannot go astray. The "rationalists" Oakeshott seeks to refute in the
present volume insist on ideologies or technocratic schemes of social engineering to guide the decisions of political life, overriding
the practical sense of affairs to be found in experienced politicians.
Philosophy, in opposing ideology as its caricature, neither forgets
nor denies the impossibility of success in controlling and directing
the political life to a predefined goal. The very structure of *Rationalism in Politics* as a collection of essays is part of Oakeshott's stance
against the modern quest for a science of social life.

The world, Oakeshott argues, is what we understand it to be.
We are always engaged in interpreting a world of interpreted experience, actively participating in shaping our world even as we learn
its already present characteristics. We can enjoy no fixed, permanent condition, and all intellectual constructs suggesting this possibility are misleading. We are born and grow up in an already
ongoing world, learning its features from those who have already
acquired an understanding of it. Gradually, we discover that we
must make sense out of it for ourselves. We are cast into a world to
which we did not seek entry, but we are dependent upon it in order

---

[1] For further discussion on this point see the first essay of Oakeshott's *On Human Conduct*,
pp. 27–29, and also his debate with D. D. Raphael in *Political Studies*, Volumes XII, XIII
(see bibliography of this book).

to move independently within it. We each must seek to understand in our own way what others already seem to understand, and in so doing we inevitably alter what we are seeking to understand. Hence, in altering it in order to understand it, we will never get to the end of the process of understanding it. Nothing is defined with finality for one's reflective intelligence. We must learn for ourselves what it means to be human.

But if the world is necessarily in continuous alteration, imagining its perfection as the attainment of the unalterable is a mistake. The intensity of the desire for completion is unfulfillable and yet by that very fact drives onward the practical life. Every circumstance is the harbinger of further circumstance. Life is a predicament, not a journey. We cannot accumulate and bank our successful decisions; past success does not guarantee future success; what is brought into being by our ingenuity has not the power to become immortal; what we have won, we can also lose.

This is the world of human freedom as Oakeshott understands it: Freedom is an inherent feature of human existence, present as soon as a human being is present. Freedom is not to be seen only as a condition eventually to be won, but as a perpetually present feature of conscious existence. Tyranny is bogus just because it tries to repress what cannot be repressed in human existence: the necessity for every human being to act out of his own response to the world. When human beings gain liberation from tyranny, they are not being given their freedom, for no one has special possession of it or the authority to dispense or withhold it; they are being acknowledged as having freedom.

This condition of freedom can appear as either a blessing or a curse. There is no doubt, however, that whatever different individuals make out of their freedom, they cannot eliminate it without eliminating themselves. The desire of some, in effect, to eliminate themselves as selves and thus escape the condition of freedom is chimerical. Thus, Oakeshott's counsel is to enjoy and to explore our opportunities and to beware of those who would offer us "relief" from the ordeal of being free.

Oakeshott characteristically sees the human condition as an adventure to be welcomed. The ordeal of consciousness is also a great opportunity, and he admires those who, whether humble or exalted, poor or rich, ordinary or brilliant, in different ways achieve a sense of themselves and a style that shows their success in achieving individual humanity. There are no collective achievements in these matters. We are to each other not role models but additions to the variety of human possibilities to be enjoyed.

In short, Oakeshott's nonteleological view of a human life is integral to what he thinks it means to be free and individual. We are free, he says, in interpreting and responding to our circumstances through the use of our intelligence, and we may do well or badly in this. And we are individual because we cannot deduce from another's life what we must do, suggestive though the lives of others may be. That there are those who fail to do well in the undertaking is among the mysteries of a complex human condition. There is no "rational solution" or formula for resolving this human diversity into a simple, unitary achievement.

Governing, in this essentially nonpolitical and nonrationalist vision, does not require a prior theory to get going. A farmer, he used to say in lectures to undergraduates, is not first an agricultural theorist, and politicians do not start out by theorizing politics. Here he harked back to Aristotle's view that the political scientist begins by examining the existing state of affairs and by finding out what its practitioners opine. The first task, in other words, is to understand what is going on in any activity that excites one's intellectual curiosity, and to try to understand it as it presents itself before presuming to pronounce upon it. If the farmer or the politician have learned their tasks by apprenticeship, they might then devise abstract descriptions of what they have learned, but the description must be an abridgement, derived from conversancy with the activity itself, and it cannot substitute for the activity itself.

Politics springs "neither from instant desires, nor from general principles, but from the existing traditions of behaviour themselves."[2] These arrangements to which politicians attend reflect the

---

[2] "Political Education," p. 56.

current state of long evolving combinations of desires and principles. They reflect manners of living, ways of life, composed over time by the myriad choices of individuals in learning to associate with each other. Practices evolve through which desires and principles are integrated in a concrete way, rendering civil association concrete and humanly possible.

There is no logically necessary direction to be pursued in such an arrangement, no self-evidently right "intimation" of further steps to be taken among all the intimations that appear. Oakeshott employs the word *intimation* specifically to avoid the thought of a "logically implied" direction. We cannot know ahead of our judgments and decisions what it is "necessary" to do. If we could, our anxieties over judgments and decisions would cease. Contingency is unavoidable: One event touches another but why they do so will always be, in some irreducible degree, inexplicable.[3] Just as we cannot specify a final perfecting and unifying goal, but we may minimize the chance for disaster "if we escape the illusion that politics is ever anything more than the pursuit of intimations; a conversation, not an argument."[4]

Some object to emphasizing intimations and conversation, seeing them as a denial of the rough, coercive, often violent character of political life. Oakeshott has been accused of aestheticism, and of failing to appreciate the necessity of struggle to achieve creativity in practice. But Oakeshott's point emanates from an attitude toward political life that is both well informed and philosophically detached. He knows perfectly well what goes on in political life, but he sees in it a self-deluding tendency that he refuses to honor.

Like St. Augustine, Oakeshott can see the political order as the humanly available remedy for human insufficiencies without overrating its achievement. And from Aristotle, who showed us that human beings, although possessing the capacity to become morally

---

[3] In "The Activity of Being an Historian," in this volume, and in *On History and Other Essays* (Oxford: Blackwell, 1983), he gives detailed analyses of this point which, together with "Rationalism in Politics," "Rational Conduct," the first essay in *On Human Conduct*, and the criticism of the historical mode of knowing in *Experience and Its Modes* (Cambridge: Cambridge University Press, 1933), constitute something approaching a critical philosophy of the limits of the social sciences.

[4] "Political Education," p. 58.

virtuous, do not automatically (by natural processes) become virtuous, Oakeshott derives the lesson that we humans must learn everything and go on learning as long as we live. Politics and government are "necessary evils."

Political action ever hovers between pursuing perfection as the crow flies and declining into cynical grasping after power for its own sake. The Tower of Babel offers itself in many outwardly attractive guises, promising to overleap the limits of the human condition.

Thus, Oakeshott concludes, the turning of conversation into argument risks forgetting the limits of politics.[5] If he cannot eradicate this risk, Oakeshott can still remind us of its perils. To meditate on the temporality and mortality of all human things is to dampen our misplaced enthusiasms which, horrifyingly in the twentieth century, have produced the ultimate caricatures of "enlightenment" and the "dignity of man."

Fortunately, to dispel illusions is not to kill the human spirit; the latter arises from its own ashes. Nevertheless, sensible people will avoid recipes for ash heaps. There is something of a mystery about how we shall reacquire this good sense. Oakeshott thinks it has to do with long training for governance through many generations, and with an education that is not imbued with false hopes of perfection through "scientific policy-making." "Government . . . does not begin with a vision of another, different and better world, but with the observation of the self-government practised even by men of passion in the conduct of their enterprises . . . the intimations of government are to be found in ritual, not in religion or philosophy; in the enjoyment of orderly and peaceable behaviour, not in the search for truth or perfection."[6]

These reflections are preparatory to genuine moral achievements, those possible for an individual whose regard for others grows out of understanding, through experience and reflection,

---

[5] The primacy of conversationality to a human and humane life is nowhere more powerfully evoked than in "The Voice of Poetry in the Conversation of Mankind," and in his essays on education in *The Voice of Liberal Learning.*

[6] "On Being Conservative," p. 428.

what it means to be human. Oakeshott derives this also from that great, often misunderstood, English political thinker, Hobbes, who counseled us to learn to read in ourselves "not this or that particular man; but mankind," and to remember that "much laughter at the defects of others, is a sign of pusillanimity. For of great minds, one of the proper works is, to help and free others from scorn; and compare themselves only with the most able."[7]

Like Hobbes, Oakeshott, in seeking to understand the universal human predicament, acquires confidence out of the humility of honest human self-recognition. It is an aristocratic acknowledgment of the democracy of the human condition, not to be confused with democratic regimes that may or may not be respectful of freedom and diversity. Coupled with recognition of the astonishing diversity of human conduct, this protects against the politics of perfectionism and uniformity, those pervasive, damaging weapons of modern faithlessness.

Oakeshott expresses confidence, not despair. It is a confidence that human intelligence can continue to use its resources; that intelligence is not exhausted; that we actually can maintain an even keel in practice. The responsibility to do so falls to each generation in turn. No generation can be known to be the final one, and, in any case, to act as if it were is implicitly to claim what we do not and cannot know. Like Socrates and Montaigne, Oakeshott finds the courage to face mortality openly, and, in so doing, like them, he finds a release from despair, entering upon what can be termed a kind of nondogmatic faith in the power of the human spirit.

---

[7] Thomas Hobbes, *Leviathan*, edited with an introduction by Michael Oakeshott (Oxford: Basil Blackwell, 1960), pp. 6, 36.

Bibliography

Principal works by Michael Oakeshott

Experience and Its Modes (Cambridge University Press, 1933, reprinted 1966; paperback edition, Cambridge 1986). Ultimately indispensable for a full understanding of Oakeshott's philosophical outlook, this is the foundation from which all of his subsequent thought develops and to which he has remained faithful in spirit, if not always in detail.

The Social and Political Doctrines of Contemporary Europe (Cambridge University Press, 1939). A collection of texts illustrating the doctrines of Representative Democracy, Catholicism, Communism, Fascism, and National Socialism through Oakeshott's skeptical eye.

On Human Conduct (Oxford: Clarendon Press, 1975; paperback edition, Oxford, 1990). This is the work Oakeshott himself considers the definitive statement of his political philosophy. It is modeled on Hobbes's *Leviathan* and *De Cive*, offering a systematic exposition of the ideal of civil association implicit in modern European history, and the nature of the historical opposition to it.

Hobbes on Civil Association (University of California Press and Basil Blackwell, 1975). Collects most of his essays on Hobbes. Two of them, including the famous Introduction to *Leviathan*, are included in the present volume.

On History and Other Essays (Oxford: Basil Blackwell and New York: Barnes & Noble, 1983). Contains three papers on the nature of historical knowledge, plus "The Rule of Law," to be read in conjunction with his theory of political authority and civil association in the second essay of *On Human Conduct*, and "The Tower of Babel," the second essay he has published with this title, the first appearing in *Rationalism in Politics*. It retells the biblical story as it pertains to our time.

The Voice of Liberal Learning: Michael Oakeshott on Education, edited with an introduction by Timothy Fuller (Yale University Press, 1989; paperback edition, Yale, 1990). Offers six essays on learning and teaching, evoking the education Oakeshott finds fit for potential subscribers to his ideal civil association.

The following two works provide virtually complete bibliographical information on works by Michael Oakeshott through 1976.

"A Bibliography of Michael Oakeshott" compiled by W. H. Greenleaf for *Politics and Experience: Essays Presented to Professor Michael Oakeshott on the Occasion of His Retirement*, edited by Preston King and B. C. Parekh (Cambridge University Press, 1968). Most of Oakeshott's writings to 1968 are listed.

"Bibliographical Note" by Josiah Lee Auspitz for *Political Theory*, Volume 4, Number 3, August 1976, pp. 295–301. Auspitz has also compiled, but not published, a list of minor writings of Oakeshott not included here.

Selected secondary works

Josiah Lee Auspitz, "Individuality, Civility, and Theory: The Philosophical Imagination of Michael Oakeshott" in *Political Theory*, Volume 4, Number 3, 1976, pp. 261–94. An excellent introduction to the intention of Oakeshott's political philosophy, it is part of an issue wholly devoted to assessing Oakeshott's political ideas.

Wendell John Coats, Jr., "Michael Oakeshott's Critique of Rationalism in Politics" and "Michael Oakeshott as Liberal Theorist" in *The Activity of Politics and Related Essays* (Selinsgrove: Susquehanna University Press and London & Toronto: Associated University Presses, 1989), pp. 34–41 and 42–57, respectively. Acute expositions placing Oakeshott within the tradition of classical liberalism.

Charles Covell, *The Redefinition of Conservatism* (New York: St. Martin's Press, 1985). Examines Oakeshott's impact on contemporary British conservative thought.

Maurice Cowling, *Religion and Public Doctrine in Modern England*, Volume 1 (Cambridge University Press, 1980). Locates Oakeshott in debates on public doctrine in England that began in the nineteenth century.

Richard E. Flathman, *The Practice of Political Authority* (University of Chicago Press, 1980). A critique of Oakeshott's theory of political authority.

Paul Franco, *The Political Philosophy of Michael Oakeshott* (Yale University Press, 1990). The only complete and current exposition so far published, superseding W. H. Greenleaf's *Oakeshott's Philosophical Politics* (London: Longman's Green, 1966). Franco compares Oakeshott to other contemporary political philosophers and provides current bibliographical information.

Richard B. Friedman, "Oakeshott on the Authority of Law" in *Ratio Juris*, Volume 2, Number 1, March 1989, pp. 27–40. A fine analysis of Oakeshott's theory of the rule of law and of the dialectic of liberty and authority.

Timothy Fuller, "Authority and the Individual in Civil Association: Oakeshott, Flathman and Yves Simon" in NOMOS, Volume 29, *Authority Revisited*, edited by Roland Pennock and John Chapman (New York University Press, 1987), pp. 131–51. Examines Oakeshott's theory of authority in relation to two alternative views of authority, one liberal-democratic and one Thomistic.

Robert Grant, *Oakeshott* (London: Claridge Press, 1990). An informed, short exposition of Oakeshott's work as a whole that includes a brief biographical chapter.

Shirley Robin Letwin, "Morality and Law" in *Ratio Juris*, Volume 2, Number 1, March 1989, pp. 55–65. Argues that Oakeshott's idea of the rule of law is superior to that of either legal positivists or normative theorists.

John Liddington, "Oakeshott: Freedom in a Modern European State" in *Conceptions of Liberty in Political Philosophy*, edited by Zbigniew Pelczynski and John Gray (New York: St. Martin's Press, 1984), pp. 289–320. An appreciative but critical analysis of Oakeshott's distinction between form and substance in conduct.

Kenneth Minogue, "Michael Oakeshott" in *Contemporary Political Philosophers*, edited by Anthony de Crespigny and Kenneth Minogue (New York: Dodd, Mead & Company, 1975), pp. 120–46. Captures both the spirit and wit of Oakeshott's philosophical enterprise.

D. D. Raphael, "Professor Oakeshott's *Rationalism in Politics*" in *Political Studies*, Volume XII, Number 2, June 1964, pp. 202–15; Michael Oakeshott, "Rationalism in Politics: A Reply to Professor Raphael" in *Political Studies*, Volume XIII, Number 2, 1965, pp. 89–92; D. D. Raphael, "Rationalism in Politics: A Note on Professor Oakeshott's Reply" in *Political*

Studies, Volume XIII, Number 3, 1965, pp. 395–7. An enlightening debate over *Rationalism in Politics* and one of the few occasions when Oakeshott has responded directly and publicly to his critics.

Jeremy Rayner, "The Legend of Oakeshott's Conservatism: Sceptical Philosophy and Limited Politics" in *Canadian Journal of Political Science*, Volume 18, No. 2, 1985, pp. 313–338. Shows Oakeshott's skepticism to be the key to understanding his position in the classical liberal tradition.

Michael Williams, "Liberalism and Two Conceptions of the State" in *Liberalism Reconsidered*, edited by Douglas MacLean and Claudia Mills (Totowa: Rowman and Allenheld, 1983), pp. 117–29. Analyzes Oakeshott's offer of a conservative liberalism.

Rationalism in politics

PART ONE

Reason and the conduct of political life

Rationalism in politics

Les grands hommes, en apprenant aux
faibles à réfléchir, les ont mis sur la route
de l'erreur.
                                    VAUVENARGUES,
                        Maxims et Réflexions, 221

ONE

The object of this essay is to consider the character and pedigree of the most remarkable intellectual fashion of post-Renaissance Europe. The Rationalism with which I am concerned is modern Rationalism. No doubt its surface reflects the light of rationalisms of a more distant past, but in its depth there is a quality exclusively its own, and it is this quality that I propose to consider, and to consider mainly in its impact upon European politics. What I call Rationalism in politics is not, of course, the only (and it is certainly not the most fruitful) fashion in modern European political thinking. But it is a strong and a lively manner of thinking which, finding support in its filiation with so much else that is strong in the intellectual composition of contemporary Europe, has come to colour the ideas, not merely of one, but of all political persuasions, and to flow over every party line. By one road or another, by conviction, by its supposed inevitability, by its alleged success, or even quite unreflectively, almost all politics today have become Rationalist or near-Rationalist.

The general character and disposition of the Rationalist are, I think, not difficult to identify. At bottom he stands (he always

5

stands) for independence of mind on all occasions, for thought free from obligation to any authority save the authority of 'reason'. His circumstances in the modern world have made him contentious: he is the *enemy* of authority, of prejudice, of the merely traditional, customary or habitual. His mental attitude is at once sceptical and optimistic: sceptical, because there is no opinion, no habit, no belief, nothing so firmly rooted or so widely held that he hesitates to question it and to judge it by what he calls his 'reason'; optimistic, because the Rationalist never doubts the power of his 'reason' (when properly applied) to determine the worth of a thing, the truth of an opinion or the propriety of an action. Moreover, he is fortified by a belief in a 'reason' common to all mankind, a common power of rational consideration, which is the ground and inspiration of argument: set up on his door is the precept of Parmenides—judge by rational argument. But besides this, which gives the Rationalist a touch of intellectual equalitarianism, he is something also of an individualist, finding it difficult to believe that anyone who can think honestly and clearly will think differently from himself.

But it is an error to attribute to him an excessive concern with *a priori* argument. He does not neglect experience, but he often appears to do so because he insists always upon it being his own experience (wanting to begin everything *de novo*), and because of the rapidity with which he reduces the tangle and variety of experience to a set of principles which he will then attack or defend only upon rational grounds. He has no sense of the cumulation of experience, only of the readiness of experience when it has been converted into a formula: the past is significant to him only as an encumbrance. He has none of that *negative capability* (which Keats attributed to Shakespeare), the power of accepting the mysteries and uncertainties of experience without any irritable search for order and distinctness, only the capability of subjugating experience; he has no aptitude for that close and detailed appreciation of what actually presents itself which Lichtenberg called *negative enthusiasm*, but only the power of recognizing the large outline which a general theory imposes upon events. His cast of mind is gnostic, and the sagacity of Ruhnken's rule, *Oportet quaedam nescire*, is lost upon him. There are some minds which give us the sense that they have passed through an elaborate education which was designed to initiate them into the traditions and achievements of their civilization; the immediate impression we have of them is an impression of cultivation, of the enjoyment of an inheritance. But this is not so with the mind of the Rationalist, which impresses us as, at best, a finely-tempered, neutral instrument, as a well-trained rather than as an educated mind. Intellectually, his ambition is not so much to share the experience of the race as to be demonstrably a self-made man. And this gives to his intellectual and practical activities an almost preternatural deliberateness and self-consciousness, depriving them of any element of passivity, removing from them all sense of rhythm and continuity and dissolving them into a succession of climacterics, each to be surmounted by a *tour de raison*. His mind has no atmosphere, no changes of season and temperature; his intellectual processes, so far as possible, are insulated from all external influence and go on in the void. And having cut himself off from the traditional knowledge of his society, and denied the value of any education more extensive than a training in a technique of analysis, he is apt to attribute to mankind a necessary inexperience in all the critical moments of life, and if he were more self-critical he might begin to wonder how the race had ever succeeded in surviving. With an almost poetic fancy, he strives to live each day as if it were his first, and he believes that to form a habit is to fail. And if, with as yet no thought of analysis, we glance below the surface, we may, perhaps, see in the temperament, if not in the character, of the Rationalist, a deep distrust of time, an impatient hunger for eternity and an irritable nervousness in the face of everything topical and transitory.

Now, of all worlds, the world of politics might seem the least amenable to rationalist treatment—politics, always so deeply veined with both the traditional, the circumstantial and the transitory. And, indeed, some convinced Rationalists have admitted defeat here: Clemenceau, intellectually a child of the modern Rationalist tradition (in his treatment of morals and religion, for example), was anything but a Rationalist in politics. But not all have admitted defeat. If we except religion, the greatest apparent victories of Rationalism have been in politics: it is not to be expected that whoever is prepared to carry his rationalism into the conduct of life will hesitate to carry it into the conduct of public affairs.[1]

But what is important to observe in such a man (for it is characteristic) is not the decisions and actions he is inspired to make, but the source of his inspiration, his idea (and with him it will be a deliberate and conscious idea) of political activity. He believes, of course, in the open mind, the mind free from prejudice and its relic, habit. He believes that the unhindered human 'reason' (if only it can be brought to bear) is an infallible guide in political activity. Further, he believes in argument as the technique and operation of 'reason'; the truth of an opinion and the 'rational' ground (not the use) of an institution is all that matters to him. Consequently, much of his political activity consists in bringing the social, political, legal and institutional inheritance of his society before the tribunal of his intellect; and the rest is rational administration, 'reason' exercising an uncontrolled jurisdiction over the circumstances of the case. To the Rationalist, nothing is of value merely because it exists (and certainly not because it has existed for many generations), familiarity has no worth, and nothing is to be left standing for want of scrutiny. And his disposition makes both destruction and creation easier for him to understand and engage in, than acceptance or reform. To patch up, to repair (that is, to do anything which requires a patient knowledge of the material), he regards as waste of time; and he always prefers the invention of a new device to making use of a current and well-tried expedient. He does not recognize change unless it is a self-consciously induced change, and consequently he falls easily into the error of identifying the customary and the traditional with the changeless. This is aptly illustrated by the rationalist attitude towards a tradition of ideas. There is, of course, no question either of retaining or improving such a tradition, for both these involve an attitude of submission. It must be destroyed. And to fill its place the Rationalist puts some-

[1] A faithful account of the politics of rationalism (with all its confusions and ambivalences) is to be found in H.J. Blackham, *Political Discipline in a Free Society*.

thing of his own making—an ideology, the formalized abridgment of the supposed substratum of rational truth contained in the tradition.

The conduct of affairs, for the Rationalist, is a matter of solving problems, and in this no man can hope to be successful whose reason has become inflexible by surrender to habit or is clouded by the fumes of tradition. In this activity the character which the Rationalist claims for himself is the character of the engineer, whose mind (it is supposed) is controlled throughout by the appropriate technique and whose first step is to dismiss from his attention everything not directly related to his specific intentions. This assimilation of politics to engineering is, indeed, what may be called the myth of rationalist politics. And it is, of course, a recurring theme in the literature of Rationalism. The politics it inspires may be called the politics of the felt need; for the Rationalist, politics are always charged with the feeling of the moment. He waits upon circumstance to provide him with his problems, but rejects its aid in their solution. That anything should be allowed to stand between a society and the satisfaction of the felt needs of each moment in its history must appear to the Rationalist a piece of mysticism and nonsense. And his politics are, in fact, the rational solution of those practical conundrums which the recognition of the sovereignty of the felt need perpetually creates in the life of a society. Thus, political life is resolved into a succession of crises, each to be surmounted by the application of 'reason'. Each generation, indeed, each administration, should see unrolled before it the blank sheet of infinite possibility. And if by chance this *tabula rasa* has been defaced by the irrational scribblings of tradition-ridden ancestors, then the first task of the Rationalist must be to scrub it clean; as Voltaire remarked, the only way to have good laws is to burn all existing laws and to start afresh.[2]

Two other general characteristics of rationalist politics may be observed. They are the politics of perfection, and they are the politics of uniformity; either of these characteristics without the other

[2] Cf. Plato, *Republic*, 501A. The idea that you can get rid of a law by burning it is characteristic of the Rationalist, who can think of a law only as something written down.

denotes a different style of politics. The essence of rationalism is their combination. The evanescence of imperfection may be said to be the first item of the creed of the Rationalist. He is not devoid of humility; he can imagine a problem which would remain impervious to the onslaught of his own reason. But what he cannot imagine is politics which do not consist in solving problems, or a political problem of which there is no 'rational' solution at all. Such a problem must be counterfeit. And the 'rational' solution of any problem is, in its nature, the perfect solution. There is no place in his scheme for a 'best in the circumstances', only a place for 'the best'; because the function of reason is precisely to surmount circumstances. Of course, the Rationalist is not always a perfectionist in general, his mind governed in each occasion by a comprehensive Utopia; but invariably he is a perfectionist in detail. And from this politics of perfection springs the politics of uniformity; a scheme which does not recognize circumstance can have no place for variety. 'There must in the nature of things be one best form of government which all intellects, sufficiently roused from the slumber of savage ignorance, will be irresistibly incited to approve,' writes Godwin. This intrepid Rationalist states in general what a more modest believer might prefer to assert only in detail; but the principle holds —there may not be one universal remedy for all political ills, but the remedy for any particular ill is as universal in its application as it is rational in its conception. If the rational solution for one of the problems of a society has been determined, to permit any relevant part of the society to escape from the solution is, *ex hypothesi*, to countenance irrationality. There can be no place for preferences that is not rational preference, and all rational preferences necessarily coincide. Political activity is recognized as the imposition of a uniform condition of perfection upon human conduct.

The modern history of Europe is littered with the projects of the politics of Rationalism. The most sublime of these is, perhaps, that of Robert Owen for 'a world convention to emancipate the human race from ignorance, poverty, division, sin and misery'—so sublime that even a Rationalist (but without much justification) might think it eccentric. But not less characteristic are the diligent search of the present generation for an innocuous power which may safely be made so great as to be able to control all other powers in the human world, and the common disposition to believe that political machinery can take the place of moral and political education. The notion of founding a society, whether of individuals or of States, upon a Declaration of the Rights of Man is a creature of the rationalist brain, so also are 'national' or racial self-determination when elevated into universal principles. The project of the so-called Re-union of the Christian Churches, of open diplomacy, of a single tax, of a civil service whose members 'have no qualifications other than their personal abilities', of a self-consciously planned society, the Beveridge Report, the Education Act of 1944, Federalism, Nationalism, Votes for Women, the Catering Wages Act, the destruction of the Austro-Hungarian Empire, the World State (of H. G. Wells or anyone else), and the revival of Gaelic as the official language of Eire, are alike the progeny of Rationalism. The odd generation of rationalism in politics is by sovereign power out of romanticism.

TWO

The placid lake of Rationalism lies before us in the character and disposition of the Rationalist, its surface familiar and not unconvincing, its waters fed by many visible tributaries. But in its depths there flows a hidden spring, which, though it was not the original fountain from which the lake grew, is perhaps the pre-eminent source of its endurance. This spring is a doctrine about human knowledge. That some such fountain lies at the heart of Rationalism will not surprise even those who know only its surface; the superiority of the unencumbered intellect lay precisely in the fact that it could reach more, and more certain, knowledge about man and society than was otherwise possible; the superiority of the ideology over the tradition lay in its greater precision and its alleged demonstrability. Nevertheless, it is not, properly speaking, a philosophical theory of knowledge, and it can be explained with agreeable informality.

Every science, every art, every practical activity requiring skill of any sort, indeed every human activity whatsoever, involves knowledge. And, universally, this knowledge is of two sorts, both of which are always involved in any actual activity. It is not, I think, making too much of it to call them two sorts of knowledge, because (though in fact they do not exist separately) there are certain important differences between them. The first sort of knowledge I will call technical knowledge or knowledge of technique. In every art and science, and in every practical activity, a technique is involved. In many activities this technical knowledge is formulated into rules which are, or may be, deliberately learned, remembered, and, as we say, put into practice; but whether or not it is, or has been, precisely formulated, its chief characteristic is that it is susceptible of precise formulation, although special skill and insight may be required to give it that formulation.[3] The technique (or part of it) of driving a motor car on English roads is to be found in the Highway Code, the technique of cookery is contained in the cookery book, and the technique of discovery in natural science or in history is in their rules of research, of observation and verification. The second sort of knowledge I will call practical, because it exists only in use, is not reflective and (unlike technique) cannot be formulated in rules. This does not mean, however, that it is an esoteric sort of knowledge. It means only that the method by which it may be shared and becomes common knowledge is not the method of formulated doctrine. And if we consider it from this point of view, it would not, I think, be misleading to speak of it as traditional knowledge. In every activity this sort of knowledge is also involved; the mastery of any skill, the pursuit of any concrete activity is impossible without it.

These two sorts of knowledge, then, distinguishable but inseparable, are the twin components of the knowledge involved in every concrete human activity. In a practical art, such as cookery, nobody supposes that the knowledge that belongs to the good cook is confined to what is or may be written down in the cookery book; technique and what I have called practical knowledge combine to make

---

[3] G. Polya, *How to Solve It.*

skill in cookery wherever it exists. And the same is true of the fine arts, of painting, of music, of poetry; a high degree of technical knowledge, even where it is both subtle and ready, is one thing; the ability to create a work of art, the ability to compose something with real music qualities, the ability to write a great sonnet, is another, and requires, in addition to technique, this other sort of knowledge. Again, these two sorts of knowledge are involved in any genuinely scientific activity.[4] The natural scientist will certainly make use of the rules of observation and verification that belong to his technique, but these rules remain only one of the components of his knowledge; advance in scientific discovery was never achieved merely by following the rules.[5] The same situation may be observed also in religion. It would, I think, be excessively liberal to call a man a Christian who was wholly ignorant of the technical side of Christianity, who knew nothing of creed or formulary, but it would be even more absurd to maintain that even the readiest knowledge of creed and catechism ever constituted the whole of the knowledge that belongs to a Christian. And what is true of cookery, of painting, of natural science and of religion, is no less true of politics: the knowledge involved in political activity is both technical and practical.[6] Indeed, as in all arts which have men as their plastic material, arts such as medicine, industrial management, diplomacy, and the art of military command, the knowledge involved in political activity is pre-eminently of this dual character. Nor, in these arts, is it correct to say that whereas technique will tell a man (for example, a doctor) *what* to do, it is practice which tells him *how* to do it—the 'bed-side manner', the appreciation of the individual with whom he has to deal. Even in the *what*, and above all in diagnosis, there lies already this dualism of technique and practice: there is no knowl-

---

[4] Some excellent observations on this topic are to be found in M. Polanyi, *Science, Faith and Society.*

[5] Polya, for example, in spite of the fact that his book is concerned with heuristic, suggests that the root conditions of success in scientific research are, first, 'to have brains and good luck', and secondly, 'to sit tight and wait till you get a bright idea', neither of which are technical rules.

[6] Thucydides puts an appreciation of this truth into the mouth of Pericles. To be a politician and to refuse the guidance of technical knowledge is, for Pericles, a piece of folly. And yet the main theme of the Funeral Oration is not the value of technique in politics, but the value of practical and traditional knowledge, ii, 40.

edge which is not 'know how'. Nor, again, does the distinction between technical and practical knowledge coincide with the distinction between a knowledge of means and a knowledge of ends, though on occasion it may appear to do so. In short, nowhere, and pre-eminently not in political activity, can technical knowledge be separated from practical knowledge, and nowhere can they be considered identical with one another or able to take the place of one another.[7]

Now, what concerns us are the differences between these two sorts of knowledge; and the important differences are those which manifest themselves in the divergent ways in which these sorts of knowledge can be expressed and in the divergent ways in which they can be learned or acquired.

Technical knowledge, we have seen, is susceptible of formulation in rules, principles, directions, maxims—comprehensively, in propositions. It is possible to write down technical knowledge in a book. Consequently, it does not surprise us that when an artist writes about his art, he writes only about the technique of his art. This is so, not because he is ignorant of what may be called aesthetic element, or thinks it unimportant, but because what he has to say about *that* he has said already (if he is a painter) in his pictures, and he knows no other way of saying it. And the same is true when a religious man writes about his religion[8] or a cook about cookery. And it may be observed that this character of being sus-

---

[7] Duke Huan of Ch'i was reading a book at the upper end of the hall; the wheelwright was making a wheel at the lower end. Putting aside his mallet and chisel, he called to the Duke and asked him what book he was reading. 'One that records the words of the Sages,' answered the Duke. 'Are those Sages alive?' asked the wheelwright. 'Oh, no,' said the Duke, 'they are dead.' 'In that case,' said the wheelwright, 'what you are reading can be nothing but the lees and scum of bygone men.' 'How dare you, a wheelwright, find fault with the book I am reading. If you can explain your statement, I will let it pass. If not, you shall die.' 'Speaking as a wheelwright,' he replied, 'I look at the matter in this way; when I am making a wheel, if my stroke is too slow, then it bites deep but is not steady; if my stroke is too fast, then it is steady, but it does not go deep. The right pace, neither slow nor fast, cannot get into the hand unless it comes from the heart. It is a thing that cannot be put into words [rules]; there is an art in it that I cannot explain to my son. That is why it is impossible for me to let him take over my work, and here I am at the age of seventy still making wheels. In my opinion it must have been the same with the men of old. All that was worth handing on, died with them; the rest, they put in their books. That is why I said that what you were reading was the lees and scum of bygone men.' *Chuang Tzu.*

[8] St François de Sales was a devout man, but when he writes it is about the technique of piety.

ceptible of precise formulation gives to technical knowledge at least the appearance of certainty: it appears to be possible to be certain about a technique. On the other hand, it is a characteristic of practical knowledge that it is not susceptible of formulation of this kind. Its normal expression is in a customary or traditional way of doing things, or, simply, in practice. And this gives it the appearance of imprecision and consequently of uncertainty, of being a matter of opinion, of probability rather than truth. It is, indeed, a knowledge that is expressed in taste or connoisseurship, lacking rigidity and ready for the impress of the mind of the learner.

Technical knowledge can be learned from a book; it can be learned in a correspondence course. Moreover, much of it can be learned by heart, repeated by rote, and applied mechanically: the logic of the syllogism is a technique of this kind. Technical knowledge, in short, can be both taught and learned in the simplest meanings of these words. On the other hand, practical knowledge can neither be taught nor learned, but only imparted and acquired. It exists only in practice, and the only way to acquire it is by apprenticeship to a master—not because the master can teach it (he cannot), but because it can be acquired only by continuous contact with one who is perpetually practising it. In the arts and in natural science what normally happens is that the pupil, in being taught and in learning the technique from his master, discovers himself to have acquired also another sort of knowledge than merely technical knowledge, without it ever having been precisely imparted and often without being able to say precisely what it is. Thus a pianist acquires artistry as well as technique, a chess-player style and insight into the game as well as a knowledge of the moves, and a scientist acquires (among other things) the sort of judgement which tells him when his technique is leading him astray and the connoisseurship which enables him to distinguish the profitable from the unprofitable directions to explore.

Now, as I understand it, Rationalism is the assertion that what I have called practical knowledge is not knowledge at all, the assertion that, properly speaking, there is no knowledge which is not technical knowledge. The Rationalist holds that the only element of *knowledge* involved in any human activity is technical knowledge, and that what I have called practical knowledge is really only a sort of nescience which would be negligible if it were not positively mischievous. The sovereignty of 'reason', for the Rationalist, means the sovereignty of technique.

The heart of the matter is the pre-occupation of the Rationalist with certainty. Technique and certainty are, for him, inseparably joined because certain knowledge is, for him, knowledge which does not require to look beyond itself for its certainty; knowledge, that is, which not only ends with certainty but begins with certainty and is certain throughout. And this is precisely what technical knowledge appears to be. It seems to be a self-complete sort of knowledge because it seems to range between an identifiable initial point (where it breaks in upon sheer ignorance) and an identifiable terminal point, where it is complete, as in learning the rules of a new game. It has the aspect of knowledge that can be contained wholly between the two covers of a book, whose application is, as nearly as possible, purely mechanical, and which does not assume a knowledge not itself provided in the technique. For example, the superiority of an ideology over a tradition of thought lies in its appearance of being self-contained. It can be taught best to those whose minds are empty; and if it is to be taught to one who already believes something, the first step of the teacher must be to administer a purge, to make certain that all prejudices and preconceptions are removed, to lay his foundation upon the unshakable rock of absolute ignorance. In short, technical knowledge appears to be the only kind of knowledge which satisfies the standard of certainty which the Rationalist has chosen.

Now, I have suggested that the knowledge involved in every concrete activity is never solely technical knowledge. If this is true, it would appear that the error of the Rationalist is of a simple sort —the error of mistaking a part for the whole, of endowing a part with the qualities of the whole. But the error of the Rationalist does not stop there. If his great illusion is the sovereignty of technique, he is no less deceived by the apparent certainty of technical knowledge. The superiority of technical knowledge lay in its appearance of springing from pure ignorance and ending in certain and complete knowledge, its appearance of both beginning and ending with certainty. But, in fact, this in an illusion. As with every other sort of knowledge, learning a technique does not consist in getting rid of pure ignorance, but in reforming knowledge which is already there. Nothing, not even the most nearly self-contained technique (the rules of a game), can in fact be imparted to an empty mind; and what is imparted is nourished by what is already there. A man who knows the rules of one game will, on this account, rapidly learn the rules of another game; and a man altogether unfamiliar with 'rules' of any kind (if such can be imagined) would be a most unpromising pupil. And just as the self-made man is never literally *self*-made, but depends upon a certain kind of society and upon a large unrecognized inheritance, so technical knowledge is never, in fact, self-complete, and can be made to appear so only if we forget the hypotheses with which it begins. And if its self-completeness is illusory, the certainty which was attributed to it on account of its self-completeness is also an illusion.

But my object is not to refute Rationalism; its errors are interesting only in so far as they reveal its character. We are considering not merely the truth of a doctrine, but the significance of an intellectual fashion in the history of post-Renaissance Europe. And the questions we must try to answer are: What is the generation of this belief in the sovereignty of technique? Whence springs this supreme confidence in human 'reason' thus interpreted? What is the provenance, the context of this intellectual character? And in what circumstances and with what effect did it come to invade European politics?

THREE

The appearance of a new intellectual character is like the appearance of a new architectural style; it emerges almost imperceptibly, under the pressure of a great variety of influences, and it is a misdirection of inquiry to seek its origins. Indeed, there are no origins; all that can be discerned are the slowly mediated changes, the shuffling and reshuffling, the flow and ebb of the tides of inspiration, which issue finally in a shape identifiably new. The ambition of the historian is to escape that gross abridgment of the process which gives the new shape a too early or too late and a too precise definition, and to avoid the false emphasis which springs from being over-impressed by the moment of unmistakable emergence. Yet that moment must have a dominating interest for those whose ambitions are not pitched so high. And I propose to foreshorten my account of the emergence of modern Rationalism, the intellectual character and disposition of the Rationalist, by beginning it at the moment when it shows itself unmistakably, and by considering only one element in the context of its emergence. This moment is the early seventeenth century, and it was connected, *inter alia*, with the condition of knowledge—knowledge of both the natural and the civilized world—at that time.

The state of European knowledge at the beginning of the seventeenth century was peculiar. Remarkable advances had already been achieved, the tide of inquiry flowed as strongly as at any other period in our history, and the fruitfulness of the presuppositions which inspired this inquiry showed no sign of exhaustion. And yet to intelligent observers it appeared that something of supreme importance was lacking. 'The state of knowledge,' wrote Bacon, 'is not prosperous nor greatly advancing.'[9] And this want of prosperity was not attributable to the survival of a disposition of mind hostile to the sort of inquiry that was on foot; it was observed as a hindrance suffered by minds already fully emancipated from the presuppositions (though not, of course, from some of the details) of Aristotelian science. What appeared to be lacking was not inspiration or even methodical habits of inquiry, but a consciously formulated technique of research, an art of interpretation, a method whose rules had been written down. And the project of making good this want was the occasion of the unmistakable emergence of the new intellectual character I have called the Rationalist. The dominating

[9] Bacon, *Novum Organum* (Fowler), p. 157.

figures in the early history of this project are, of course, Bacon and Descartes, and we may find in their writings intimations of what later became the Rationalist character.

Bacon's ambition was to equip the intellect with what appeared to him necessary if certain and demonstrable knowledge of the world in which we live is to be attained. Such knowledge is not possible for 'natural reason', which is capable of only 'petty and probable conjectures', not of certainty.[10] And this imperfection is reflected in the want of prosperity of the state of knowledge. The *Novum Organum* begins with a diagnosis of the intellectual situation. What is lacking is a clear perception of the nature of certainty and an adequate means of achieving it. 'There remains,' says Bacon, 'but one course for the recovery of a sound and healthy condition—namely, that the entire work of understanding be commenced afresh, and the mind itself be from the very outset not left to take its own course, but guided at every step.'[11] What is required is a 'sure plan', a new 'way' of understanding, an 'art' or 'method' of inquiry, an 'instrument' which (like the mechanical aids men use to increase the effectiveness of their natural strength) shall supplement the weakness of the natural reason: in short, what is required is a formulated technique of inquiry.[12] He recognizes that this technique will appear as a kind of hindrance to the natural reason, not supplying it with wings but hanging weights upon it in order to control its exuberance;[13] but it will be a hindrance of hindrances to certainty, because it is lack of discipline which stands between the natural reason and certain knowledge of the world. And Bacon compares this technique of research with the technique of the syllogism, the one being appropriate to the discovery of the truth of things while the other is appropriate only to the discovery of the truth of opinions.[14]

The art of research which Bacon recommends has three main characteristics. First, it is a set of rules; it is a true technique in

[10] *Ibid.*, p. 184.
[11] *Ibid.*, p. 182.
[12] *Ibid.*, p. 157.
[13] *Ibid.*, p. 295.
[14] *Ibid.*, p. 168.

that it can be formulated as a precise set of directions which can be learned by heart.[15] Secondly, it is a set of rules whose application is purely mechanical; it is a true technique because it does not require for its use any knowledge or intelligence not given in the technique itself. Bacon is explicit on this point. The business of interpreting nature is 'to be done as if by machinery',[16] 'the strength and excellence of the wit (of the inquirer) has little to do with the matter',[17] the new method 'places all wits and understandings nearly on a level'.[18] Thirdly, it is a set of rules of universal application; it is a true technique in that it is an instrument of inquiry indifferent to the subject-matter of the inquiry.

Now, what is significant in this project is not the precise character of the rules of inquiry, both positive and negative, but the notion that a technique of this sort is even possible. For what is proposed—infallible rules of discovery—is something very remarkable, a sort of philosopher's stone, a key to open all doors, a 'master science'. Bacon is humble enough about the details of this method, he does not think he has given it a final formulation; but his belief in the possibility of such a 'method' in general is unbounded.[19] From our point of view, the first of his rules is the most important, the precept that we must lay aside received opinion, that we must 'begin anew from the very foundations'.[20] Genuine knowledge must begin with a purge of the mind, because it must begin as well as end in certainty and must be complete in itself. Knowledge and opinion are separated absolutely; there is no question of ever winning true knowledge out of 'the childish notions we at first imbibed'. And this, it may be remarked, is what distinguishes both Platonic and Scholastic from modern Rationalism: Plato is a rationalist, but the dialectic is not a technique, and the method of Scholasticism always had before it a limited aim.

The doctrine of the *Novum Organum* may be summed up, from

---

[15] *Ibid.*, p. 168.

[16] *Ibid.*, p. 182.

[17] *Ibid.*, p. 162.

[18] *Ibid.*, p. 233.

[19] *Ibid.*, p. 331.

[20] *Ibid.*, p. 295.

our point of view, as the sovereignty of technique. It represents, not merely a preoccupation with technique combined with a recognition that technical knowledge is never the whole of knowledge, but the assertion that technique and some material for it to work upon are all that matters. Nevertheless, this is not itself the beginning of the new intellectual fashion, it is only an early and unmistakable intimation of it: the fashion itself may be said to have sprung from the exaggeration of Bacon's hopes rather than from the character of his beliefs.

Descartes, like Bacon, derived inspiration from what appeared to be the defects of contemporary inquiry; he also perceived the lack of a consciously and precisely formulated technique of inquiry. And the method propounded in the *Discours de la Méthode* and the *Regulae* corresponds closely to that of the *Novum Organum*. For Descartes, no less than for Bacon, the aim is certainty. Certain knowledge can spring up only in an emptied mind; the technique of research begins with an intellectual purge. The first principle of Descartes is 'de ne reçevoir jamais aucune chose pour vraie que je ne la connusse évidemment être telle, c'est-à-dire d'éviter soigneusement la précipitation et la prévention', 'de bâtir dans un fonds qui est tout à moi'; and the inquirer is said to be 'comme un homme qui marche seul et dans les ténèbres'.[21] Further, the technique of inquiry is formulated in a set of rules which, ideally, compose an infallible method whose application is mechanical and universal. And thirdly, there are no grades in knowledge, what is not certain is mere nescience. Descartes, however, is distinguished from Bacon in respect of the thoroughness of his education in the Scholastic philosophy and in the profound impression that geometrical demonstration had upon his mind, and the effect of these differences in education and inspiration is to make his formulation of the technique of inquiry more precise and in consequence more critical. His mind is oriented towards the project of an infallible and universal method or research, but since the method he propounds is mod-

---

[21] *Discours de la Méthode*, ii.

elled on that of geometry, its limitation when applied, not to possibilities but to things, is easily apparent. Descartes is more thorough than Bacon in doing his scepticism for himself and, in the end, he recognizes it to be an error to suppose that the method can ever be the sole means of inquiry.[22] The sovereignty of technique turns out to be a dream and not a reality. Nevertheless, the lesson his successors believed themselves to have learned from Descartes was the sovereignty of technique and not his doubtfulness about the possibility of an infallible method.

By a pardonable abridgment of history, the Rationalist character may be seen springing from the exaggeration of Bacon's hopes and the neglect of the scepticism of Descartes; modern Rationalism is what commonplace minds made out of the inspiration of men of discrimination and genius. *Les grands hommes, en apprenant aux faibles à réfléchir, les ont mis sur la route de l'erreur.* But the history of Rationalism is not only the history of the gradual emergence and definition of this new intellectual character; it is, also, the history of the invasion of every department of intellectual activity by the doctrine of the sovereignty of technique. Descartes never became a Cartesian; but, as Bouillier says of the seventeenth century, 'le cartésianisme a triomphé; il s'est emparé du grand siècle tout entier, il a pénétré de son esprit, non seulement la philosophie, mais les sciences et les lettres ellesmêmes'.[23] It is common knowledge that, at this time, in poetry and in drama, there was a remarkable concentration on technique, on rules of composition, on the observance of the *bienséances* of literature, which continued unabated for nearly two centuries. A stream of books flowed from the presses on the 'art of poetry', the 'art of living', the 'art of thinking'. Neither religion, nor natural science, nor education, nor the conduct of life itself escaped from the influence of the new Rationalism; no activity was immune, no society untouched.[24]

---

[22] *Ibid.*, vi.

[23] *Histoire de la philosophie cartésienne*, i, 486.

[24] One important aspect of the history of the emergence of Rationalism is the changing connotation of the word 'reason'. The 'reason' to which the Rationalist appeals is not, for example, the Reason of Hooker, which belongs still to the tradition of Stoicism and of Aquinas. It is a faculty of calculation by which men conclude one thing from another and discover fit

The slowly mediated changes by which the Rationalist of the seventeenth century became the Rationalist as we know him today, are a long and complicated story which I do not propose even to abridge. It is important only to observe that, with every step it has taken away from the true sources of its inspiration, the Rationalist character has become cruder and more vulgar. What in the seventeenth century was *'L'art de penser'* has now become *Your mind and how to use it, a plan by world-famous experts for developing a trained mind at a fraction of the usual cost.* What was the *Art of Living* has become the *Technique of Success*, and the early and more modest incursions of the sovereignty of technique into education have blossomed into *Pelmanism.*

The deeper motivations which encouraged and developed this intellectual fashion are, not unnaturally, obscure; they are hidden in the recesses of European society. But among its other connections, it is certainly closely allied with a decline in the belief in Providence: a beneficient and infallible technique replaced a beneficient and infallible God; and where Providence was not available to correct the mistakes of men it was all the more necessary to prevent such mistakes. Certainly, also, its provenance is a society or a generation which thinks what it has discovered for itself is more important than what it has inherited,[25] an age over-impressed with its own accomplishment and liable to those illusions of intellectual grandeur which are the characteristic lunacy of post-Renaissance Europe, an age never mentally at peace with itself because never reconciled with its past. And the vision of a technique which puts all minds on the same level provided just the short-cut which would attract men in a hurry to appear educated but incapable of appreciating the concrete detail of their total inheritance. And, partly

means of attaining given ends not themselves subject to the criticism of reason, a faculty by which a world believed to be a machine could be disclosed. Much of the plausibility of Rationalism lies in the tacit attribution to the new 'reason' of the qualities which belong properly to the Reason of the older intellectual tradition. And this ambiguity, the emergence of the new connotation out of the old, may be observed in many of the writers of the early seventeenth century—in, for example, the poetry of Malherbe, an older contemporary of Descartes, and one of the great progenitors of the sovereignty of technique in literature.

[25] This was certainly true of the age of Bacon. And Professor Bernal now tells us that more has been found out at large and in detail about nature and man in the thirty years after 1915 than in the whole of history.

under the influence of Rationalism itself, the number of such men has been steadily growing since the seventeenth century.[26] Indeed it may be said that all, or almost all, the influences which in its early days served to encourage the emergence of the Rationalist character have subsequently become more influential in our civilization.

Now, it is not to be thought that Rationalism established itself easily and without opposition. It was suspect as a novelty, and some fields of human activity—literature, for example—on which at first its hold was strong, subsequently freed themselves from its grasp. Indeed, at all levels and in all fields there has been continuous criticism of the resistance to the teachings of Rationalism. And the significance of the doctrine of the sovereignty of technique becomes clearer when we consider what one of its first and profoundest critics has to say about it. Pascal is a judicious critic of Descartes, not opposing him at all points, but opposing him nevertheless, on points that are fundamental.[27] He perceived, first, that the Cartesian desire for certain knowledge was based upon a false criterion of certainty. Descartes must begin with something so sure that it cannot be doubted, and was led, as a consequence, to believe that all genuine knowledge is technical knowledge. Pascal avoided this conclusion by his doctrine of probability: the only knowledge that is certain is certain on account of its partiality; the paradox that probable knowledge has more of the whole truth than certain

---

[26] Not so very long ago, I suppose, the spectators at horse-races were mostly men and women who knew something at first-hand about horses, and who (in this respect) were genuinely educated people. This has ceased to be so, except perhaps in Ireland. And the ignorant spectator, with no ability, inclination or opportunity to educate himself, and seeking a short-cut out of his predicament, demands *a book*. (The twentieth century vogue in cookery books derives, no doubt, from a similar situation.) The authors of one such book, *A Guide to the Classics, or how to pick the Derby winner*, aware of the difference between technical and complete knowledge, were at pains to point out that there was a limit beyond which there were no precise rules for picking the winner, and that some intelligence (not supplied by the rules themselves) was necessary. But some of its greedy, rationalistic readers, on the look-out for an infallible method, which (like Bacon's) would place their small wits on a level with men of genuine education, thought they had been sold a pup—which only goes to show how much better they would have spent their time if they had read St Augustine or Hegel instead of Descartes: *je ne puis pardonner à Descartes.*
[*A Guide to the Classics, or how to pick the Derby winner* was co-authored by Oakeshott and Guy Griffith. It was first published in 1936 by Faber & Faber. It was reissued in a revised edition in 1947 under the title *A New Guide to the Derby, How to pick the winner.* —T.F.]
[27] *Pensées* (Brunschvicg), i, 76.

knowledge. Secondly, Pascal perceived that the Cartesian *raisonne-ment* is never in fact the whole source of the knowledge involved in any concrete activity. The human mind, he asserts, is not wholly dependent for its successful working upon a conscious and formulated technique; and even where a technique is involved, the mind observes the technique 'tacitement, naturellement et sans art'. The precise formulation of rules of inquiry endangers the success of the inquiry by exaggerating the importance of method. Pascal was followed by others, and indeed much of the history of modern philosophy revolves round this question. But, though later writers were often more elaborate in their criticism, few detected more surely than Pascal that the significance of Rationalism is not its recognition of technical knowledge, but its failure to recognize any other: its philosophical error lies in the certainty it attributes to technique and in its doctrine of the sovereignty of technique; its practical error lies in its belief that nothing but benefit can come from making conduct self-conscious.

FOUR

It was, of course, improbable that politics should altogether escape the impress of so strong and energetic an intellectual style as that of the new Rationalism. But what, at first sight, is remarkable is that politics should have been earlier and more fully engulfed by the tidal wave than any other human activity. The hold of Rationalism upon most departments of life has varied in its firmness during the last four centuries but in politics it has steadily increased and is stronger now than at any earlier time. We have considered already the general intellectual disposition of the Rationalist when he turns to politics; what remains to be considered are the circumstances in which European politics came to surrender almost completely to the Rationalist and the results of the surrender.

That all contemporary politics are deeply infected with Rationalism will be denied only by those who choose to give the infection another name. Not only are our political vices rationalistic, but so also are our political virtues. Our projects are, in the main, rationalist in purpose and character; but, what is more significant, our whole attitude of mind in politics is similarly determined. And those traditional elements, particularly in English politics, which might have been expected to continue some resistance to the pressure of Rationalism, have now almost completely conformed to the prevailing intellectual temper, and even represent this conformity to be a sign of their vitality, their ability to move with the times. Rationalism has ceased to be merely one style in politics and has become the stylistic criterion of all respectable politics.

How deeply the rationalist disposition of mind has invaded our political thought and practice is illustrated by the extent to which traditions of behaviour have given place to ideologies, the extent to which the politics of destruction and creation have been substituted for the politics of repair, the consciously planned and deliberately executed being considered (for that reason) better than what has grown up and established itself unselfconsciously over a period of time. This conversion of habits of behaviour, adaptable and never quite fixed or finished, into comparatively rigid systems of abstract ideas, is not, of course, new; so far as England is concerned it was begun in the seventeenth century, in the dawn of rationalist politics. But, while formerly it was tacitly resisted and retarded by, for example, the informality of English politics (which enabled us to escape, for a long time, putting too high a value on political action and placing too high a hope in political achievement—to escape, in politics at least, the illusion of the evanescence of imperfection), that resistance has now itself been converted into an ideology.[28] This is, perhaps, the main significance of Hayek's *Road to Serfdom* —not the cogency of his doctrine, but the fact that it is a doctrine. A plan to resist all planning may be better than its opposite, but it belongs to the same style of politics. And only in a society already deeply infected with Rationalism will the conversion of the traditional resources of resistance to the tyranny of Rationalism into a self-conscious ideology be considered a strengthening of those re-

---

[28] A tentative, and therefore not a fundamentally damaging, conversion of this sort was attempted by the first Lord Halifax.

sources. It seems that now, in order to participate in politics and expect a hearing, it is necessary to have, in the strict sense, a doctrine; not to have a doctrine appears frivolous, even disreputable. And the sanctity, which in some societies was the property of a politics piously attached to traditional ways, has now come to belong exclusively to rationalist politics.

Rationalist politics, I have said, are the politics of the felt need, the felt need not qualified by a genuine, concrete knowledge of the permanent interests and direction of movement of a society, but interpreted by 'reason' and satisfied according to the technique of an ideology: they are the politics of the book. And this also is characteristic of almost all contemporary politics: not to have a book is to be without the one thing necessary, and not to observe meticulously what is written in the book is to be a disreputable politician. Indeed, so necessary is it to have a book, that those who have hitherto thought it possible to get on without one, have had, rather late in the day, to set about composing one for their own use. This is a symptom of the triumph of technique which we have seen to be the root of modern Rationalism; for what the book contains is only what it is possible to put into a book—rules of a technique. And, book in hand (because, though a technique can be learned by rote, they have not always learned their lesson well), the politicians of Europe pore over the simmering banquet they are preparing for the future; but, like jumped-up kitchen-porters deputizing for an absent cook, their knowledge does not extend beyond the written word which they read mechanically—it generates ideas in their heads but no tastes in their mouths.

Among the other evidences of Rationalism in contemporary politics, may be counted the commonly admitted claim of the 'scientist' as such (the chemist, the physicist, the economist or the psychologist) to be heard in politics; because, though the knowledge involved in a science is always more than technical knowledge, what it has to offer to politics is never more than a technique. And under this influence, the intellect in politics ceases to be the critic of political habit and becomes a substitute for habit, and the life of a society loses its rhythm and continuity and is resolved into a succession of problems and crises. Folk-lore, because it is not technique, is identified with nescience, and all sense of what Burke called the partnership between present and past is lost.[29]

There is, however, no need to labour the point that the most characteristic thing about contemporary politics is their rationalist inspiration; the prevailing belief that politics are easy is, by itself, evidence enough. And if a precise example is required we need look no further for it than the proposals we have been offered for the control of the manufacture and use of atomic energy. The rationalist faith in the sovereignty of technique is the presupposition both of the notion that some over-all scheme of mechanized control is possible and of the details of every scheme that has so far been projected: it is understood as what is called an 'administrative' problem. But, if Rationalism now reigns almost unopposed, the question which concerns us is, What are the circumstances that promoted this state of affairs? For the significance of the triumph lies not merely in itself, but in its context.

Briefly, the answer to this question is that the politics of Rationalism are the politics of the politically inexperienced, and that the outstanding characteristic of European politics in the last four centuries is that they have suffered the incursion of at least three types of political inexperience—that of the new ruler, of the new ruling class, and of the new political society—to say nothing of the incursion of a new sex, lately provided for by Mr Shaw. How appropriate rationalist politics are to the man who, not brought up or educated to their exercise, finds himself in a position to exert political initiative and authority, requires no emphasis. His need of it is so great that he will have no incentive to be sceptical about the possibility of a magic technique of politics which will remove the handicap of his lack of political education. The offer of such a technique will seem to him the offer of salvation itself; to be told that the necessary knowledge is to be found, complete and self-contained, in a book, and to be told that this knowledge is of a sort that can be learned by heart quickly and applied mechanically, will seem, like

[29] A poetic image of the politics of Rationalism is to be found in Rex Warner's book, *The Aerodrome*.

salvation, something almost too good to be true. And yet it was this, or something near enough to be mistaken for it, which he understood Bacon and Descartes to be offering him. For, though neither of these writers ventures upon the detailed application of his method to politics, the intimations of rationalist politics are present in both, qualified only by a scepticism which could easily be ignored. Nor had he to wait for Bacon and Descartes (to wait, that is, for a general doctrine of Rationalism); the first of these needy adventurers into the field of politics was provided for on his appearance a century earlier by Machiavelli.

It has been said that the project of Machiavelli was to expound a *science* of politics, but this, I think, misses the significant point. A science, we have seen, is concrete knowledge and consequently neither its conclusions, nor the means by which they were reached, can ever, as a whole, be written down in a book. Neither an art nor a science can be imparted in a set of directions; to acquire a mastery in either is to acquire an appropriate connoisseurship. But what can be imparted in this way is a technique, and it is with the technique of politics that Machiavelli, as a writer, is concerned. He recognized that the technique of governing a republic was somewhat different from that appropriate to a principality, and he was concerned with both. But in writing about the government of principalities he wrote for the *new* prince of his day, and this for two reasons, one of principle and the other personal. The well-established hereditary ruler, educated in a tradition and heir to a long family experience, seemed to be well enough equipped for the position he occupied; his politics might be improved by a correspondence course in technique, but in general he knew how to behave. But with the new ruler, who brought to his task only the qualities which had enabled him to gain political power and who learnt nothing easily but the vices of his office, the *caprice de prince*, the position was different. Lacking education (except in the habits of ambition), and requiring some short-cut to the appearance of education, he required a book. But he required a book of a certain sort; he needed a crib: his inexperience prevented him from tackling the affairs of State unseen. Now, the character of a crib is that its author must have an educated man's knowledge of the language, that he must prostitute his genius (if he has any) as a translator, and that it is powerless to save the ignorant reader from all possibility of mistake. The project of Machiavelli was, then, to provide a crib to politics, a political training in default of a political education, a technique for the ruler who had no tradition. He supplied a demand of his time; and he was personally and temperamentally interested in supplying the demand because he felt the 'fascination of what is difficult'. The new ruler was more interesting because he was far more likely than the educated hereditary ruler to get himself into a tricky situation and to need the help of advice. But, like the great progenitors of Rationalism in general (Bacon and Descartes), Machiavelli was aware of the limitations of technical knowledge; it was not Machaivelli himself, but his followers, who believed in the sovereignty of technique, who believed that government was nothing more than 'public administration' and could be learned from a book. And to the new prince he offered not only his book, but also, what would make up for the inevitable deficiencies of his book—himself: he never lost the sense that politics, after all, are diplomacy, not the application of a technique.

The new and politically inexperienced social classes which, during the last four centuries, have risen to the exercise of political initiative and authority, have been provided for in the same sort of way as Machiavelli provided for the new prince of the sixteenth century. None of these classes had time to acquire a political education before it came to power; each needed a crib, a political doctrine, to take the place of a habit of political behaviour. Some of these writings are genuine works of political vulgarization; they do not altogether deny the existence or worth of a political tradition (they are written by men of real political education), but they are abridgments of a tradition, rationalizations purporting to elicit the 'truth' of a tradition and to exhibit it in a set of abstract principles, but from which, nevertheless, the full significance of the tradition inevitably escapes. This is pre-eminently so of Locke's *Second Treatise of Civil Government*, which was as popular, as long-lived and as valuable a political crib as that greatest of all cribs to a religion,

Paley's *Evidences of Christianity*. But there are other writers, like
Bentham or Godwin, who, pursuing the common project of providing for the political inexperience of succeeding generations, cover
up all trace of the political habit and tradition of their society with
a purely speculative idea: these belong to the strictest sect of Rationalism. But, so far as authority is concerned, nothing in this
field can compare with the work of Marx and Engels. European politics without these writers would still have been deeply involved in
Rationalism, but beyond question they are the authors of the most
stupendous of our political rationalisms—as well they might be, for
it was composed for the instruction of a less politically educated
class than any other that has ever come to have the illusion of exercising political power. And no fault can be found with the mechanical manner in which this greatest of all political cribs has been
learned and used by those for whom it was written. No other technique has so imposed itself upon the world as if it were concrete
knowledge; none has created so vast an intellectual proletariat, with
nothing but its technique to lose.[30]

The early history of the United States of America is an instructive chapter in the history of the politics of Rationalism. The situation of a society called upon without much notice to exercise political initiative on its own account is similiar to that of an individual
or a social class rising not fully prepared to the exercise of political
power; in general, its needs are the same as theirs. And the similarity is even closer when the independence of the society concerned
begins with an admitted illegality, a specific and express rejection
of a tradition, which consequently can be defended only by an appeal to something which is itself thought not to depend upon tradition. Nor, in the case of the American colonists, was this the whole
of the pressure which forced their revolution into the pattern of Rationalism. The founders of American independence had both a tra-

---

[30] By casting his technique in the form of a view of the course of events (past, present and
future), and not of 'human nature', Marx thought he had escaped from Rationalism; but
since he had taken the precaution of first turning the course of events into a doctrine, the
escape was an illusion. Like Midas, the Rationalist is always in the unfortunate position of
not being able to touch anything, without transforming it into an abstraction; he can never
get a square meal of experience.

dition of European thought and a native political habit and experience to draw upon. But, as it happened, the intellectual gifts of
Europe to America (both in philosophy and religion) had, from the
beginning, been predominantly rationalistic: and the native political habit, the product of the circumstances of colonisation, was
what may be called a kind of natural and unsophisticated rationalism. A plain and unpretending people, not given over-much to reflection upon the habits of behaviour they had in fact inherited,
who, in frontier communities, had constantly the experience of setting up law and order for themselves by mutual agreement, were
not likely to think of their arrangements except as the creation of
their own unaided initiative; they seemed to begin with nothing,
and to owe to themselves all that they had come to possess. A civilization of pioneers is, almost unavoidably, a civilization of self-consciously self-made men, Rationalists by circumstance and not by reflection, who need no persuasion that knowledge begins with a
tabula rasa and who regard the free mind, not even as the result of
some artificial Cartesian purge, but as the gift of Almighty God, as
Jefferson said.

Long before the Revolution, then, the disposition of mind of the
American colonists, the prevailing intellectual character and habit
of politics, were rationalistic. And this is clearly reflected in the
constitutional documents and history of the individual colonies.
And when these colonies came 'to dissolve the political bands which
have connected them with another', and to declare their independence, the only fresh inspiration that this habit of politics received
from the outside was one which confirmed its native character in
every particular. For the inspiration of Jefferson and the other
founders of American independence was the ideology which Locke
had distilled from the English political tradition. They were disposed to believe, and they believed more fully than was possible for
an inhabitant of the Old World, that the proper organization of a
society and the conduct of its affairs were based upon abstract
principles, and not upon a tradition which, as Hamilton said, had
'to be rummaged for among old parchments and musty records'.
These principles were not the product of civilization; they were nat-

ural, 'written in the whole volume of human nature'.[31] They were to be discovered in nature by human reason, by a technique of inquiry available alike to all men and requiring no extraordinary intelligence in its use. Moreover, the age had the advantage of all earlier ages because, by the application of this technique of inquiry, these abstract principles had, for the most part recently, been discovered and written down in books. And by using these books, a newly made political society was not only not handicapped by the lack of a tradition, but had a positive superiority over older societies not yet fully emancipated from the chains of custom. What Descartes had already perceived, 'que souvent il n'y a pas tant de perfection dans les ouvrages composés de plusieurs pièces et faits de la main de divers maîtres qu'en ceux anquels un seul a travaillé', was freshly observed in 1777 by John Jay—'The Americans are the first people whom Heaven has favoured with an opportunity of deliberating upon, and choosing the forms of government under which they should live. All other constitutions have derived their existence from violence or accidental circumstances, and are therefore probably more distant from their perfection. . . .'[32] The Declaration of Independence is a characteristic product of the *saeculum rationalisticum*. It represents the politics of the felt need interpreted with the aid of an ideology. And it is not surprising that it should have become one of the sacred documents of the politics of Rationalism, and, together with the similar documents of the French Revolution, the inspiration and pattern of many later adventures in the rationalist reconstruction of society.

The view I am maintaining is that the ordinary practical politics of European nations have become fixed in a vice of Rationalism, that much of their failure (which is often attributed to other

---

[31] There is no space here to elucidate the exceedingly complicated connections between the politics of 'reason' and the politics of 'nature'. But it may be observed that, since both reason and nature were opposed to civilization, they began with a common ground; and the 'rational' man, the man freed from the idols and prejudices of a tradition, could, alternatively, be called the 'natural' man. Modern Rationalism and modern Naturalism in politics, in religion and in education, are alike expressions of a general presumption against all human achievement more than about a generation old.

[32] Of course both 'violence' and 'accidental circumstances' were there, but being present in an unfamiliar form they were unrecognized.

and more immediate causes[33]) springs in fact from the defects of the Rationalist character when it is in control of affairs, and that (since the rationalist disposition of mind is not a fashion which sprang up only yesterday) we must not expect a speedy release from our predicament. It is always depressing for a patient to be told that his disease is almost as old as himself and that consequently there is no quick cure for it, but (except for the infections of childhood) this is usually the case. So long as the circumstances which promoted the emergence of rationalist politics remain, so long must we expect our politics to be rationalist in disposition.

I do not think that any or all of the writers whom I have mentioned are responsible for our predicament. They are the servants of circumstances which they have helped to perpetuate (on occasion they may be observed giving another turn to the screw), but which they did not create. And it is not to be supposed that they would always have approved of the use made of their books. Nor, again, am I concerned with genuinely philosophical writing about politics; in so far as that has either promoted or retarded the tendency to Rationalism in politics, it has always been through a misunderstanding of its design, which is not to recommend conduct but to explain it. To explore the relations between politics and eternity is one thing; it is something different, and less commendable, for a practical politician to find the intricacy of the world of time and contingency so unmanageable that he is bewitched by the offer of a quick escape into the bogus eternity of an ideology. Nor, finally, do I think we owe our predicament to the place which the natural sciences and the manner of thinking connected with them has come to take in our civilization. This simple diagnosis of the situation has been much put about, but I think it is mistaken. That the influence of the genuine natural scientist is not necessarily on the side of Rationalism follows from the view I have taken of the character of any kind of concrete knowledge. No doubt there are scientists

[33] War, for example. War is a disease to which a rationalist society has little resistance; it springs easily from the kind of incompetence inherent in rationalist politics. But it has certainly increased the hold of the Rationalist disposition of mind on politics, and one of the disasters of war has been the new customary application to politics of its essentially rationalist vocabulary.

deeply involved in the rationalist attitude, but they are mistaken when they think that the rationalist and the scientific points of view necessarily coincide. The trouble is that when the scientist steps outside his own field he often carries with him only his technique, and this at once allies him with the forces of Rationalism.[34] In short, I think the great prestige of the natural sciences has, in fact, been used to fasten the rationalist disposition of mind more firmly upon us, but that this is the work, not of the genuine scientist as such, but of the scientist who is a Rationalist in spite of his science.

FIVE

To this brief sketch of the character, and the social and intellectual context of the emergence of Rationalism in politics, may be added a few reflections. The generation of rationalist politics is by political inexperience out of political opportunity. These conditions have often existed together in European societies; they did so in the ancient world, and that world at times suffered the effects of their union. But the particular quality of Rationalism in modern politics derives from the circumstance that the modern world succeeded in inventing so plausible a method of covering up lack of political education that even those who suffered from that lack were often left ignorant that they lacked anything. Of course, this inexperience was never, in any society, universal; and it was never absolute. There have always been men of genuine political education, immune from the infection of Rationalism (and this is particularly so of England, where a political education of some sort has been much more widely spread than in some other societies); and sometimes a dim reminder of the limitations of his technique has penetrated even the mind of the Rationalist. Indeed, so impractical is a *purely* rationalist politics, that the new man, lately risen to power, will often be found throwing away his book and relying upon his general

---

[34] A celebrated scientist tells us: 'I am less interested than the average person in politics because I am convinced that all political principles today are makeshifts, and will ultimately be replaced by principles of scientific knowledge.'

experience of the world as, for example, a business man or a trade union official. This experience is certainly a more trustworthy guide than the book—at least it is real knowledge and not a shadow—but still, it is not a knowledge of the political traditions of his society, which, in the most favourable circumstances, takes two or three generations to acquire.

Nevertheless, when he is not arrogant or sanctimonious, the Rationalist can appear a not unsympathetic character. He wants so much to be right. But unfortunately he will never quite succeed. He began too late and on the wrong foot. His knowledge will never be more than half-knowledge, and consequently he will never be more than half-right.[35] Like a foreigner or a man out of his social class, he is bewildered by a tradition and a habit of behaviour of which he knows only the surface; a butler or an observant house-maid has the advantage of him. And he conceives a contempt for what he does not understand; habit and custom appear bad in themselves, a kind of nescience of behaviour. And by some strange self-deception, he attributes to tradition (which, of course, is pre-eminently fluid) the rigidity and fixity of character which in fact belongs to ideological politics. Consequently, the Rationalist is a dangerous and expensive character to have in control of affairs, and he does most damage, not when he fails to master the situation (his politics, of course, are always in terms of mastering situations and surmounting crises), but when he appears to be successful; for the price we pay for each of his apparent successes is a firmer hold of the intellectual fashion of Rationalism upon the whole life of society.

Without alarming ourselves with imaginary evils, it may, I think, be said that there are two characteristics, in particular, of political Rationalism which make it exceptionally dangerous to a society. No sensible man will worry greatly because he cannot at once hit upon a cure for what he believes to be a crippling complaint; but if he sees the complaint to be of a kind which the passage of time must make more rather than less severe, he will have a more

---

[35] There is a reminiscence here of a passage in Henry James, whose study of Mrs Headway in *The Siege of London* is the best I know of a person in this position.

substantial cause for anxiety. And this unfortunately appears to be so with the disease of Rationalism.

First, Rationalism in politics, as I have interpreted it, involves an identifiable error, a misconception with regard to the nature of human knowledge, which amounts to a corruption of the mind. And consequently it is without the power to correct its own short-comings; it has no homeopathic quality; you cannot escape its errors by becoming more sincerely or more profoundly rationalistic. This, it may be observed, is one of the penalties of living by the book; it leads not only to specific mistakes, but it also dries up the mind itself: living by precept in the end generates intellectual dishonesty. And further, the Rationalist has rejected in advance the only external inspiration capable of correcting his error; he does not merely neglect the kind of knowledge which would save him, he begins by destroying it. First he turns out the light and then complains that he cannot see, that he is 'comme un homme qui marche seul et dans les ténèbres'. In short, the Rationalist is essentially ineducable; and he could be educated *out* of his Rationalism only by an inspiration which he regards as the great enemy of mankind. All the Rationalist can do when left to himself is to replace one rationalist project in which he has failed by another in which he hopes to succeed. Indeed, this is what contemporary politics are fast degenerating into: the political habit and tradition, which, not long ago, was the common possession of even extreme opponents in English politics, has been replaced by merely a common rationalist disposition of mind.

But, secondly, a society which has embraced a rationalist idiom of politics will soon find itself either being steered or drifting towards an exclusively rationalist form of education. I do not mean the crude purpose of National Socialism or Communism of allowing no education except a training in the dominant rationalist doctrine, I mean the more plausible project of offering no place to any form of education which is not generally rationalistic in character.[36] And when an exclusively rationalist form of education is fully estab-

[36] Something of this sort happened in France after the Revolution; but it was not long before sanity began to break in.

lished, the only hope of deliverance lies in the discovery by some neglected pedant, 'rummaging among old parchments and musty records', of what the world was like before the millennium overtook it.

From the earliest days of his emergence, the Rationalist has taken an ominous interest in education. He has a respect for 'brains', a great belief in training them, and is determined that cleverness shall be encouraged and shall receive its reward of power. But what is this education in which the Rationalist believes? It is certainly not an initiation into the moral and intellectual habits and achievements of his society, an entry into the partnership between present and past, a sharing of concrete knowledge; for the Rationalist, all this would be an education in nescience, both valueless and mischievous. It is a training in technique, a training, that is, in the half of knowledge which can be learnt from books when they are used as cribs. And the Rationalist's affected interest in education escapes the suspicion of being a mere subterfuge for imposing himself more firmly on society, only because it is clear that he is as deluded as his pupils. He sincerely believes that a training in technical knowledge is the only education worth while, because he is moved by the faith that there is no knowledge, in the proper sense, except technical knowledge. He believes that a training in 'public administration' is the surest defence against the flattery of a demagogue and the lies of a dictator.

Now, in a society already largely rationalist in disposition, there will be a positive demand for training of this sort. Half-knowledge (so long as it is the technical half) will have an economic value; there will be a market for the 'trained' mind which has at its disposal the latest devices. And it is only to be expected that this demand will be satisfied; books of the appropriate sort will be written and sold in large quantities, and institutions offering a training of this kind (either generally or in respect of a particular activity) will spring up.[37] And so far as our society is concerned, it is now long

[37] Some people regard this as the inevitable result of an industrial civilization, but I think they have hit upon the wrong culprit. What an industrial civilization needs is genuine skill; and in so far as our industrial civilization has decided to dispense with skill and to get along with merely technical knowledge it is an industrial civilization gone to the bad.

since the exploitation of this demand began in earnest; it was already to be observed in the early nineteenth century. But it is not very important that people should learn the piano or how to manage a farm by a correspondence course; and in any case it is unavoidable in the circumstances. What is important, however, is that the rationalist inspiration has now invaded and has begun to corrupt the genuine educational provisions and institutions of our society: some of the ways and means by which, hitherto, a genuine (as distinct from a merely technical) knowledge has been imparted have already disappeared, others are obsolescent, and others again are in process of being corrupted from the inside. The whole pressure of the circumstances of our time is in this direction. Apprenticeship, the pupil working alongside the master who in teaching a technique also imparts the sort of knowledge that cannot be taught, has not yet disappeared; but it is obsolescent, and its place is being taken by technical schools whose training (because it can be a training only in technique) remains insoluble until it is immersed in the acid of practice. Again, professional education is coming more and more to be regarded as the acquisition of a technique,[38] something that can be done through the post, with the result that we may look forward to a time when the professions will be stocked with clever men, but men whose skill is limited and who have never had a proper opportunity of learning the *nuances* which compose the tradition and standard of behaviour which belong to a great profession.[39] One of the ways in which this sort of knowledge has hitherto been preserved (because it is a great human achievement, and if it is not positively preserved it will be lost) and transmitted is a family tradition. But the Rationalist never understands that it takes about two generations of practice to learn a profession; indeed, he does everything he can to destroy the possibility of such an education, believing it to be mischievous. Like a man whose only

[38] Cf. James Boswell, *The Artist's Dilemma*.

[39] The army in wartime was a particularly good opportunity of observing the difference between a trained and an educated man; the intelligent civilian had little difficulty in acquiring the technique of military leadership and command, but (in spite of the cribs provided: *Advice to Young Officers*, etc.) he always remained at a disadvantage beside the regular officer, the man educated in the feelings and emotions as well as the practices of his profession.

language is Esperanto, he has no means of knowing that the world did not begin in the twentieth century. And the priceless treasure of great professional traditions is, not negligently but purposefully, destroyed in the destruction of so-called vested interests. But perhaps the most serious rationalist attack upon education is that directed against the Universities. The demand for technicians is now so great that the existing institutions for training them have become insufficient, and the Universities are in process of being procured to satisfy the demand. The ominous phrase, 'university trained men and women', is establishing itself, and not only in the vocabulary of the Ministry of Education.

To an opponent of Rationalism these are local, though not negligible, defeats, and, taken separately, the loss incurred in each may not be irreparable. At least an institution like a University has a positive power of defending itself, if it will use it. But there is a victory which the Rationalist has already won on another front from which recovery will be more difficult because, while the Rationalist knows it to be a victory, his opponent hardly recognizes it as a defeat. I mean the circumvention and appropriation by the rationalist disposition of mind of the whole field of morality and moral education. The morality of the Rationalist is the morality of the self-conscious pursuit of moral ideals, and the appropriate form of moral education is by precept, by the presentation and explanation of moral principles. This is presented as a higher morality (the morality of the free man: there is no end to the clap-trap) than that of habit, the unselfconscious following of a tradition of moral behaviour; but, in fact, it is merely morality reduced to a technique, to be acquired by training in an ideology rather than an education in behaviour. In morality, as in everything else, the Rationalist aims to begin by getting rid of inherited nescience and then to fill the blank nothingness of an open mind with the items of certain knowledge which he abstracts from his personal experience, and which he believes to be approved by the common 'reason' of mankind.[40] He will defend these principles by argument, and they will compose a co-

[40] Of this, and other excesses of Rationalism, Descartes himself was not guilty. *Discours de la Méthode*, iii.

herent (though morally parsimonious) doctrine. But, unavoidably, the conduct of life, for him, is a jerky, discontinuous affair, the solution of a stream of problems, the mastery of a succession of crises. Like the politics of the Rationalist (from which, of course, it is inseparable), the morality of the Rationalist is the morality of the self-made man and of the self-made society: it is what other peoples have recognized as 'idolatry'. And it is of no consequence that the moral ideology which inspires him today (and which, if he is a politician, he preaches) is, in fact, the desiccated relic of what was once the unselfconscious moral tradition of an aristocracy who, ignorant of ideals, had acquired a habit of behaviour in relation to one another and had handed it on in a true moral education. For the Rationalist, all that matters is that he has at last separated the ore of the ideal from the dross of the habit of behaviour; and, for us, the deplorable consequences of his success. Moral ideals are a sediment; they have significance only so long as they are suspended in a religious or social tradition, so long as they belong to a religious or a social life.[41] The predicament of our time is that the Rationalists have been at work so long on their project of drawing off the liquid in which our moral ideals were suspended (and pouring it away as worthless) that we are left only with the dry and gritty residue which chokes us as we try to take it down. First, we do our best to destroy parental authority (because of its alleged abuse), then we sentimentally deplore the scarcity of 'good homes', and we end by creating substitutes which complete the work of destruction. And it is for this reason that, among much else that is corrupt and unhealthy, we have the spectacle of a set of sanctimonious, rationalist politicians, preaching an ideology of unselfishness and social service to a population in which they and their predecessors have done their best to destroy the only living root of moral behaviour; and opposed by another set of politicians dabbling with the project of

---

[41] When Confucius visited Lao Tzu he talked of goodness and duty. 'Chaff from the winnower's fan,' said Lao Tzu, 'can so blear the eyes that we do not know if we are looking north, south, east or west; at heaven or at earth. . . . All this talk of goodness and duty, these perpetual pin-pricks, unnerve and irritate the hearer; nothing, indeed, could be more destructive of inner tranquillity.' *Chuang Tzu.*

converting us from Rationalism under the inspiration of a fresh rationalization of our political tradition.

"Rationalism in Politics" first appeared in *Cambridge Journal*, Volume I, 1947.

Political education[1]

The two former occupants of this Chair, Graham Wallas and Harold Laski, were both men of great distinction; to follow them is an undertaking for which I am ill-prepared. In the first of them, experience and reflection were happily combined to give a reading of politics at once practical and profound; a thinker without a system whose thoughts were nevertheless firmly held together by a thread of honest, patient inquiry; a man who brought his powers of intellect to bear upon the inconsequence of human behaviour and to whom the reasons of the head and of the heart were alike familiar. In the second, the dry light of intellect was matched with a warm enthusiasm; to the humour of a scholar was joined the temperament of a reformer. It seems but an hour ago that he was dazzling us with the range and readiness of his learning, winning our

[1] First delivered as an Inaugural Lecture at the London School of Economics, this piece was commented upon from various points of view. The notes I have now added, and a few changes I have made in the text, are designed to remove some of the misunderstandings it provoked. But, in general, the reader is advised to remember that it is concerned with understanding or explaining political activity which, in my view, is the proper object of political education. What people project in political activity, and different styles of political conduct, are considered here, first merely because they sometimes reveal the way in which political activity is being understood, and secondly because it is commonly (though I think wrongly) supposed that explanations are warrants for conduct.

sympathy by the fearlessness of his advocacy and endearing himself to us by his generosity. In their several ways, ways in which their successor cannot hope to compete with them, these two men left their mark upon the political education of England. They were both great teachers, devoted, tireless, and with sure confidence in what they had to teach. And it seems perhaps a little ungrateful that they should be followed by a sceptic; one who would do better if only he knew how. But no one could wish for more exacting or more sympathetic witnesses of his activities than these two men. And the subject I have chosen to speak about today is one which would have their approval.

ONE

The expression 'political education' has fallen on evil days; in the wilful and disingenuous corruption of language which is characteristic of our time it has acquired a sinister meaning. In places other than this, it is associated with that softening of the mind, by force, by alarm, or by the hypnotism of the endless repetition of what was scarcely worth saying once, by means of which whole populations have been reduced to submission. It is, therefore, an enterprise worth undertaking to consider again, in a quiet moment, how we should understand this expression, which joins together two laudable activities, and in doing so play a small part in rescuing it from abuse.

Politics I take to be the activity of attending to the general arrangements of a set of people whom chance or choice have brought together. In this sense, families, clubs, and learned societies have their 'politics'. But the communities in which this manner of activity is pre-eminent are the hereditary co-operative groups, many of them of ancient lineage, all of them aware of a past, a present, and a future, which we call 'states'. For most people, political activity is a secondary activity—that is to say, they have something else to do besides attending to these arrangements. But, as we have come to understand it, the activity is one in which every member of the group who is neither a child nor a lunatic has some part and some responsibility. With us it is, at one level or another, a universal activity.

I speak of this activity as 'attending to arrangements', rather than as 'making arrangements', because in these hereditary co-operative groups the activity is never offered the blank sheet of infinite possibility. In any generation, even the most revolutionary, the arrangements which are enjoyed always far exceed those which are recognized to stand in need of attention, and those which are being prepared for enjoyment are few in comparison with those which receive amendment: the new is an insignificant proportion of the whole. There are some people, of course, who allow themselves to speak

> As if arrangements were intended
> For nothing else but to be mended,

but, for most of us, our determination to improve our conduct does not prevent us from recognizing that the greater part of what we have is not a burden to be carried or an incubus to be thrown off, but an inheritance to be enjoyed. And a certain degree of shabbiness is joined with every real convenience.

Now, attending to the arrangements of a society is an activity which, like every other, has to be learned. Politics make a call upon knowledge. Consequently, it is not irrelevant to inquire into the kind of knowledge which is involved, and to investigate the nature of political education. I do not, however, propose to ask what information we should equip ourselves with before we begin to be politically active, or what we need to know in order to be successful politicians, but to inquire into the kind of knowledge we unavoidably call upon whenever we are engaged in political activity and to get from this an understanding of the nature of political education.

Our thoughts on political education, then, might be supposed to spring from our understanding of political activity and the kind of knowledge it involves. And it would appear that what is wanted at this point is a definition of political activity from which to draw some conclusions. But this, I think, would be a mistaken way of going about our business. What we require is not so much a definition of politics from which to deduce the character of political education, as an understanding of political activity which includes a recognition of the sort of education it involves. For, to understand an activity is to know it as a concrete whole; it is to recognize the activity as having the source of its movement within itself. An understanding which leaves the activity in debt to something outside itself is, for that reason, an inadequate understanding. And if political activity is impossible without a certain kind of knowledge and a certain sort of education, then this knowledge and education are not mere appendages to the activity but are part of the activity itself and must be incorporated in our understanding of it. We should not, therefore, seek a definition of politics in order to deduce from it the character of political knowledge and education, but rather observe the kind of knowledge and education which is inherent in any understanding of political activity, and use this observation as a means of improving our understanding of politics.

My proposal, then, is to consider the adequacy of two current understandings of politics, together with the sort of knowledge and kind of education they imply, and by improving upon them to reach what may perhaps be a more adequate understanding at once of political activity itself and the knowledge and education which belong to it.

TWO

In the understanding of some people, politics are what may be called an empirical activity. Attending to the arrangements of a society is waking up each morning and considering, 'What would I like to do?' or 'What would somebody else (whom I desire to please) like to see done?', and doing it. This understanding of political activity may be called politics without a policy. On the briefest inspection it will appear a concept of politics difficult to substantiate; it does not look like a possible manner of activity at all. But a near approach to it is, perhaps, to be detected in the politics of the proverbial oriental despot, or in the politics of the wall-scribbler and the vote-catcher. And the result may be supposed to be chaos modified by whatever consistency is allowed to creep into caprice. They are the politics attributed to the first Lord Liverpool, of whom Acton said, 'The secret of his policy was that he had none', and of whom a Frenchman remarked that if he had been present at the creation of the world he would have said, '*Mon Dieu, conservons le chaos*'. It seems, then, that a concrete activity, which may be described as an approximation to empirical politics, is possible. But it is clear that, although knowledge of a sort belongs to this style of political activity (knowledge, as the French say, not of ourselves but only of our appetites), the only kind of education appropriate to it would be an education in lunacy—learning to be ruled solely by passing desires. And this reveals the important point; namely, that to understand politics as a purely empirical activity is to misunderstand it, because empiricism by itself is not a concrete manner of activity at all, and can become a partner in a concrete manner of activity only when it is joined with something else—in science, for example, when it is joined with hypothesis. What is significant about this understanding of politics is not that some sort of approach to it can appear, but that it mistakes for a concrete, self-moved manner of activity what is never more than an abstract moment in any manner of being active. Of course, politics are the pursuit of what is desired and of what is desired at the moment; but precisely because they are this, they can never be the pursuit of merely what recommends itself from moment to moment. The activity of desiring does not take this course; caprice is never absolute. From a practical point of view, then, we may decry the *style* of politics which approximates to pure empiricism because we can observe in it an approach to lunacy. But from a theoretical point of view, purely empirical politics are not something difficult to achieve or proper to be avoided, they are merely impossible; the product of a misunderstanding.

THREE

The understanding of politics as an empirical activity is, then, inadequate because it fails to reveal a concrete manner of activity at all. And it has the incidental defect of seeming to encourage the thoughtless to pursue a *style* of attending to the arrangements of their society which is likely to have unfortunate results; to try to do something which is inherently impossible is always a corrupting enterprise. We must, if we can, improve upon it. And the impulse to improve may be given a direction by asking, 'What is it that this understanding of politics has neglected to observe?' What (to put it crudely) has it left out which, if added in, would compose an understanding in which politics are revealed as a self-moved (or concrete) manner of activity? And the answer to the question is, or seems to be, available as soon as the question is formulated. It would appear that what this understanding of politics lacks is something to set empiricism to work, something to correspond with specific hypothesis in science, an end to be pursued more extensive than a merely instant desire. And this, it should be observed, is not merely a good companion for empiricism; it is something without which empiricism in action is impossible. Let us explore this suggestion, and in order to bring it to a point I will state it in the form of a proposition: that politics appear as a self-moved manner of activity when empiricism is preceded and guided by an ideological activity. I am not concerned with the so-called ideological *style* of politics as a desirable or undesirable manner of attending to the arrangements of a society; I am concerned only with the contention that when to the ineluctable element of empiricism (doing what one wants to do) is added a political ideology, a self-moved manner of activity appears, and that consequently this may be regarded in principle as an adequate understanding of political activity.

As I understand it, a political ideology purports to be an abstract principle, or set of related abstract principles, which has been independently premeditated. It supplies in advance of the activity of attending to the arrangements of a society a formulated end to be pursued, and in so doing it provides a means of distinguishing between those desires which ought to be encouraged and those which ought to be suppressed or redirected.

The simplest sort of political ideology is a single abstract idea, such as Freedom, Equality, Maximum Productivity, Racial Purity, or Happiness. And in that case political activity is understood as the enterprise of seeing that the arrangements of a society conform to or reflect the chosen abstract idea. It is usual, however, to recognize the need for a complex scheme of related ideas, rather than a single idea, and the examples pointed to will be such systems of ideas as: 'the principles of 1789', 'Liberalism', 'Democracy', 'Marxism', or the Atlantic Charter. These principles need not be considered absolute or immune from change (though they are frequently so considered), but their value lies in their having been premeditated. They compose an understanding of *what* is to be pursued independent of *how* it is to be pursued. A political ideology purports to supply in advance knowledge of what 'Freedom' or 'Democracy' or 'Justice' is, and in this manner sets empiricism to work. Such a set of principles is, of course, capable of being argued about and reflected upon; it is something that men compose for themselves, and they may later remember it or write it down. But the condition upon which it can perform the service assigned to it is that it owes nothing to the activity it controls. 'To know the true good of the community is what constitutes the science of legislation,' said Bentham; 'the art consists in finding the means to realize that good.' The contention we have before us, then, is that empiricism can be set to work (and a concrete, self-moved manner of activity appear) when there is added to it a guide of this sort: desire and something not generated by desire.

Now, there is no doubt about the sort of knowledge which political activity, understood in this manner, calls upon. What is required, in the first place, is knowledge of the chosen political ideology—a knowledge of the ends to be pursued, a knowledge of what we want to do. Of course, if we are to be successful in pursuing these ends we shall need knowledge of another sort also—a knowledge, shall we say, of economics and psychology. But the common characteristic of all the kinds of knowledge required is that they may be, and should be, gathered in advance of the activity of attending to the arrangements of a society. Moreover, the appropriate sort of education will be an education in which the chosen political ideology is taught and learned, in which the techniques necessary for success are acquired, and (if we are so unfortunate as to find ourselves empty-handed in the matter of an ideology) an education in the skill of abstract thought and premeditation necessary to compose one for ourselves. The education we shall need is one which enables us to expound, defend, implement, and possibly invent a political ideology.

In casting around for some convincing demonstration that this understanding of politics reveals a self-moved manner of activity, we should no doubt consider ourselves rewarded if we could find an example of politics being conducted precisely in this manner. This at least would constitute a sign that we were on the right track. The defect, it will be remembered, of the understanding of politics as a purely empirical activity was that it revealed, not a manner of activity at all, but an abstraction; and this defect made itself manifest in our inability to find a *style* of politics which was anything more than an approximation to it. How does the understanding of politics as empiricism joined with an ideology fare in this respect? And without being over-confident, we may perhaps think that this is where we wade ashore. For we would appear to be in no difficulty whatever in finding an example of political activity which corresponds to this understanding of it: half the world, at a conservative estimate, seems to conduct its affairs in precisely this manner. And further, is it not so manifestly a possible style of politics that, even if we disagree with a particular ideology, we find nothing technically absurd in the writings of those who urge it upon us as an admirable style of politics? At least its advocates seem to know what they are talking about: they understand not only the manner of the activity but also the sort of knowledge and the kind of education it involves. 'Every schoolboy in Russia,' wrote Sir Norman Angel, 'is familiar with the doctrine of Marx and can recite its catechism. How many British schoolboys have any corresponding knowledge of the principles enunciated by Mill in his incomparable essay on Liberty?' 'Few people,' says Mr E. H. Carr, 'any longer contest the thesis that the child should be educated *in* the official ideology of his country.' In short, if we are looking for a sign to indicate that the understanding of politics as empirical activity preceded by ideological activity is an adequate understanding, we can scarcely be mistaken in supposing that we have it to hand.

And yet there is perhaps room for doubt: doubt first of all whether in principle this understanding of politics reveals a self-moved manner of activity; and doubt, consequentially, whether what have been identified as examples of a *style* of politics corresponding exactly to this understanding have been properly identified.

The contention we are investigating is that attending to the arrangements of a society can begin with a premeditated ideology, can begin with independently acquired knowledge of the ends to be pursued.[2] It is supposed that a political ideology is the product of intellectual premeditation and that, because it is a body of principles not itself in debt to the activity of attending to the arrangements of a society, it is able to determine and guide the direction of that activity. If, however, we consider more closely the character of a political ideology, we find at once that this supposition is falsified. So far from a political ideology being the quasi-divine parent of political activity, it turns out to be its earthly stepchild. Instead of an independently premeditated scheme of ends to be pursued, it is a system of ideas abstracted from the manner in which people have been accustomed to go about the business of attending to the arrangements of their societies. The pedigree of every political ideology shows it to be the creature, not of premeditation in advance of political activity, but of meditation upon a manner of politics. In short, political activity comes first and a political ideology follows after; and the understanding of politics we are investigating has the disadvantage of being, in the strict sense, preposterous.

Let us consider the matter first in relation to scientific hypothesis, which I have taken to play a role in scientific activity in some respects similar to that of an ideology in politics. If a scientific hypothesis were a self-generated bright idea which owed nothing to scientific activity, then empiricism governed by hypothesis could be considered to compose a self-contained manner of activity; but this certainly is not its character. The truth is that only a man who is

---

[2] This is the case, for example, with Natural Law; whether it is taken to be an explanation of political activity or (improperly) as a guide to political conduct.

already a scientist can formulate a scientific hypothesis; that is, an hypothesis is not an independent invention capable of guiding scientific inquiry, but a dependent supposition which arises as an abstraction from within already existing scientific activity. Moreover, even when the specific hypothesis has in this manner been formulated, it is inoperative as a guide to research without constant reference to the traditions of scientific inquiry from which it was abstracted. The concrete situation does not appear until the specific hypothesis, which is the occasion of empiricism being set to work, is recognized as itself the creature of knowing how to conduct a scientific inquiry.

Or consider the example of cookery. It might be supposed that an ignorant man, some edible materials, and a cookery book compose together the necessities of a self-moved (or concrete) activity called cooking. But nothing is further from the truth. The cookery book is not an independently generated beginning from which cooking can spring; it is nothing more than an abstract of somebody's knowledge of how to cook: it is the stepchild, not the parent of the activity. The book, in its turn, may help to set a man on to dressing a dinner, but if it were his sole guide he could never, in fact, begin: the book speaks only to those who know already the kind of thing to expect from it and consequently how to interpret it.

Now, just as a cookery book presupposes somebody who knows how to cook, and its use presupposes somebody who already knows how to use it, and just as a scientific hypothesis springs from a knowledge of how to conduct a scientific investigation and separated from that knowledge is powerless to set empiricism profitably to work, so a political ideology must be understood, not as an independently premeditated beginning for political activity, but as knowledge (abstract and generalized) of a concrete manner of attending to the arrangements of a society. The catechism which sets out the purposes to be pursued merely abridges a concrete manner of behaviour in which those purposes are already hidden. It does not exist in advance of political activity, and by itself it is always an insufficient guide. Political enterprises, the ends to be pursued, the arrangements to be established (all the normal ingredients of a political ideology), cannot be premeditated in advance of a manner of attending to the arrangements of a society; *what* we do, and moreover what we want to do, is the creature of *how* we are accustomed to conduct our affairs. Indeed, it often reflects no more than a discovered ability to do something which is then translated into an authority to do it.

On August 4, 1789, for the complex and bankrupt social and political system of France was substituted the Rights of Man. Reading this document we come to the conclusion that somebody has done some thinking. Here, displayed in a few sentences, is a political ideology: a system of rights and duties, a scheme of ends—justice, freedom, equality, security, property, and the rest—ready and waiting to be put into practice for the first time. 'For the first time?' Not a bit of it. This ideology no more existed in advance of political practice than a cookery book exists in advance of knowing how to cook. Certainly it was the product of somebody's reflection, but it was not the product of reflection in advance of political activity. For here, in fact, are disclosed, abstracted and abridged, the common law rights of Englishmen, the gift not of independent premeditation or divine munificence, but of centuries of the day-to-day attending to the arrangements of an historic society. Or consider Locke's *Second Treatise of Civil Government*, read in America and in France in the eighteenth century as a statement of abstract principles to be put into practice, regarded there as a preface to political activity. But so far from being a preface, it has all the marks of a postscript, and its power to guide derived from its roots in actual political experience. Here, set down in abstract terms, is a brief conspectus of the manner in which Englishmen were accustomed to go about the business of attending to their arrangements—a brilliant abridgment of the political habits of Englishmen. Or consider this passage from a contemporary continental writer: 'Freedom keeps Europeans in unrest and movement. They wish to have freedom, and at the same time they know they have not got it. They know also that freedom belongs to man as a human right.' And having established the end to be pursued, political activity is represented as the realization of this end. But the 'freedom' which can be pursued is not an independently premeditated 'ideal' or a dream; like scientific hypothesis, it is something which is already intimated in a concrete manner of behaving. Freedom, like a recipe for game pie, is not a bright idea; it is not a 'human right' to be deduced from some speculative concept of human nature. The freedom which we enjoy is nothing more than arrangements, procedures of a certain kind: the freedom of an Englishman is not something exemplified in the procedure of *habeas corpus*, it *is*, at that point, the availability of that procedure. And the freedom which we wish to enjoy is not an 'ideal' which we premeditate independently of our political experience, it is what is already intimated in that experience.[3]

On this reading, then, the systems of abstract ideas we call 'ideologies' are abstracts of some kind of concrete activity. Most political ideologies, and certainly the most useful of them (because they unquestionably have their use), are abstracts of the political traditions of some society. But it sometimes happens that an ideology is offered as a guide to politics which is an abstract, not of political experience, but of some other manner of activity—war, religion, or the conduct of industry, for example. And here the model we are shown is not only abstract, but is also inappropriate on account of the irrelevance of the activity from which it has been abstracted. This, I think, is one of the defects of the model provided by the Marxist ideology. But the important point is that, at most, an ideology is an abbreviation of some manner of concrete activity.

We are now, perhaps, in a position to perceive more accurately the character of what may be called the ideological *style* of politics, and to observe that its existence offers no ground for supposing that the understanding of political activity as empiricism guided solely by an ideology is an adequate understanding. The ideological style of politics is a confused style. Properly speaking, it is a traditional manner of attending to the arrangements of a society which has been abridged into a doctrine of ends to be pursued, the abridgment (together with the necessary technical knowledge) be-

---

[3] Cf. 'Substantive law has the first look of being gradually secreted in the interstices of procedure.' Maine, *Dissertations on Early Law and Customs, Early Law and Customs*, p. 389.

ing erroneously regarded as the sole guide relied upon. In certain circumstances an abridgment of this kind may be valuable; it gives sharpness of outline and precision to a political tradition which the occasion may make seem appropriate. When a manner of attending to arrangements is to be transplanted from the society in which it has grown up into another society (always a questionable enterprise), the simplification of an ideology may appear as an asset. If, for example, the English manner of politics is to be planted elsewhere in the world, it is perhaps appropriate that it should first be abridged into something called 'democracy' before it is packed up and shipped abroad. There is, of course, an alternative method: the method by which what is exported is the detail and not the abridgment of the tradition and the workmen travel with the tools—the method which made the British Empire. But it is a slow and costly method. And, particularly with men in a hurry, *l'homme à programme* with his abridgment wins every time; his slogans enchant, while the resident magistrate is seen only as a sign of servility. But whatever the apparent appropriateness on occasion of the ideological style of politics, the defect of the explanation of political activity connected with it becomes apparent when we consider the sort of knowledge and the kind of education it encourages us to believe is sufficient for understanding the activity of attending to the arrangements of a society. For it suggests that a knowledge of the chosen political ideology can take the place of understanding a tradition of political behaviour. The wand and the book come to be regarded as themselves potent, and not merely the symbols of potency. The arrangements of a society are made to appear, not as manners of behaviour, but as pieces of machinery to be transported about the world indiscriminately. The complexities of the tradition which have been squeezed out in the process of abridgment are taken to be unimportant: the 'rights of man' are understood to exist insulated from a manner of attending to arrangements. And because, in practice, the abridgment is never by itself a sufficient guide, we are encouraged to fill it out, not with our suspect political experience, but with experience drawn from other (often irrelevant) concretely understood activities, such as war, the conduct of industry, or Trade Union negotiation.

FOUR

The understanding of politics as the activity of attending to the arrangements of a society under the guidance of an independently premeditated ideology is, then, no less a misunderstanding than the understanding of it as a purely empirical activity. Wherever else politics may begin, they cannot begin in ideological activity. And in an attempt to improve upon this understanding of politics, we have already observed in principle what needs to be recognized in order to have an intelligible concept. Just as scientific hypothesis cannot appear, and is impossible to operate, except within an already existing tradition of scientific investigation, so a scheme of ends for political activity appears within, and can be evaluated only when it is related to, an already existing tradition of how to attend to our arrangements. In politics, the only concrete manner of activity detectable is one in which empiricism and the ends to be pursued are recognized as dependent, alike for their existence and their operation, upon a traditional manner of behaviour.

Politics is the activity of attending to the general arrangements of a collection of people who, in respect of their common recognition of a manner of attending to its arrangements, compose a single community. To suppose a collection of people without recognized traditions of behaviour, or one which enjoyed arrangements which intimated no direction for change and needed no attention,[4] is to suppose a people incapable of politics. This activity, then, springs neither from instant desires, nor from general principles, but from the existing traditions of behaviour themselves. And the form it takes, because it can take no other, is the amendment of existing arrangements by exploring and pursuing what is intimated in them. The arrangements which constitute a society capable of political activity, whether they are customs or institutions or laws or

---

[4] E.g. a society in which law was believed to be a divine gift.

diplomatic decisions, are at once coherent and incoherent; they compose a pattern and at the same time they intimate a sympathy for what does not fully appear. Political activity is the exploration of that sympathy; and consequently, relevant political reasoning will be the convincing exposure of a sympathy, present but not yet followed up, and the convincing demonstration that now is the appropriate moment for recognizing it. For example, the legal status of women in our society was for a long time (and perhaps still is) in comparative confusion, because the rights and duties which composed it intimated rights and duties which were nevertheless not recognized. And, on the view of things I am suggesting, the only cogent reason to be advanced for the technical 'enfranchisement' of women was that in all or most other important respects they had already been enfranchised. Arguments drawn from abstract natural right, from 'justice,' or from some general concept of feminine personality, must be regarded as either irrelevant, or as unfortunately disguised forms of the one valid argument; namely, that there was an incoherence in the arrangements of the society which pressed convincingly for remedy. In politics, then, every enterprise is a consequential enterprise, the pursuit, not of a dream, or of a general principle, but of an intimation.[5] What we have to do with is something less imposing than logical implications or necessary consequences: but if the intimations of a tradition of behaviour are less dignified or more elusive than these, they are not on that account less important. Of course, there is no piece of mistake-proof apparatus by means of which we can elicit the intimation most worth while pursuing; and not only do we often make gross errors of judgment in this matter, but also the total effect of a desire satisfied is so little to be forecast, that our activity of amendment is often found to lead us where we would not go. Moreover, the whole enterprise is liable at any moment to be perverted by the incursion of an approximation to empiricism in the pursuit of power. These are features which can never be eliminated; they belong to the character of political activity. But it may be believed that our mistakes of under-

[5] See *The Pursuit of Intimations*, p. 66.

standing will be less frequent and less disastrous if we escape the illusion that politics is ever anything more than the pursuit of intimations; a conversation, not an argument.

Now, every society which is intellectually alive is liable, from time to time, to abridge its tradition of behaviour into a scheme of abstract ideas; and on occasion political discussion will be concerned, not (like the debates in the *Iliad*) with isolated transactions, nor (like the speeches in Thucydides) with policies and traditions of activity, but with general principles. And in this there is no harm; perhaps even some positive benefit. It is possible that the distorting mirror of an ideology will reveal important hidden passages in the tradition, as a caricature reveals the potentialities of a face; and if this is so, the intellectual enterprise of seeing what a tradition looks like when it is reduced to an ideology will be a useful part of political education. But to make use of abridgment as a technique for exploring the intimations of a political tradition, to use it, that is, as a scientist uses hypothesis, is one thing; it is something different, and something inappropriate, to understand political activity itself as the activity of amending the arrangements of a society so as to make them agree with the provisions of an ideology. For then a character has been attributed to an ideology which it is unable to sustain, and we many find ourselves, in practice, directed by a false and a misleading guide: false, because in the abridgment, however skilfully it has been performed, a single intimation is apt to be exaggerated and proposed for unconditional pursuit and the benefit to be had from observing what the distortion reveals is lost when the distortion itself is given the office of a criterion; misleading, because the abridgment itself never, in fact, provides the whole of the knowledge used in political activity.

There will be some people who, though in general agreement with this understanding of political activity, will suspect that it confuses what is, perhaps, normal with what is necessary, and that important exceptions (of great contemporary relevance) have been lost in a hazy generality. It is all very well, it may be said, to observe in politics the activity of exploring and pursuing the intimations of a tradition of behaviour, but what light does this throw upon a political crisis such as the Norman Conquest of England, or the establishment of the Soviet *régime* in Russia? It would be foolish, of course, to deny the possibility of serious political crisis. But if we exclude (as we must) a genuine cataclysm which for the time being made an end of politics by altogether obliterating a current tradition of behaviour (which is *not* what happened in Anglo-Saxon England or in Russia),[6] there is little to support the view that even the most serious political upheaval carries us outside this understanding of politics. A tradition of behaviour is not a fixed and inflexible manner of doing things; it is a flow of sympathy. It may be temporarily disrupted by the incursion of a foreign influence, it may be diverted, restricted, arrested, or become dried-up, and it may reveal so deep-seated an incoherence that (even without foreign assistance) a crisis appears. And if, in order to meet these crises, there were some steady, unchanging, independent guide to which a society might resort, it would no doubt be well advised to do so. But no such guide exists; we have no resources outside the fragments, the vestiges, the relics of its own tradition of behaviour which the crisis has left untouched. For even the help we may get from the traditions of another society (or from a tradition of a vaguer sort which is shared by a number of societies) is conditional upon our being able to assimilate them to our own arrangements and our own manner of attending to our arrangements. The hungry and helpless man is mistaken if he supposes that he overcomes the crisis by means of a tin-opener: what saves him is somebody else's knowledge of how to cook, which he can make use of only because he is not himself entirely ignorant. In short, political crisis (even when it seems to be imposed upon a society by changes beyond its control) always appears *within* a tradition of political activity; and 'salvation' comes from the unimpaired resources of the tradition itself. Those societies which retain, in changing circumstances, a lively sense of their own identity and continuity (which are without that

[6] Cf. the passage from Maitland quoted on p. 173. The Russian Revolution (what actually happened in Russia) was not the implementation of an abstract design worked out by Lenin and others in Switzerland: it was a modification of *Russian* circumstances. And the French Revolution was far more closely connected with the *ancien régime* than with Locke or America.

hatred of their own experience which makes them desire to efface it) are to be counted fortunate, not because they possess what others lack, but because they have already mobilized what none is without and all, in fact, rely upon.

In political activity, then, men sail a boundless and bottomless sea; there is neither harbour for shelter nor floor for anchorage, neither starting-place nor appointed destination. The enterprise is to keep afloat on an even keel; the sea is both friend and enemy; and the seamanship consists in using the resources of a traditional manner of behaviour in order to make a friend of every hostile occasion.[7]

A depressing doctrine, it will be said—even by those who do not make the mistake of adding in an element of crude determinism which, in fact, it has no place for. A tradition of behaviour is not a groove within which we are destined to grind out our helpless and unsatisfying lives: *Spartam nactus es; hanc* exorna. But in the main the depression springs from the exclusion of hopes that were false and the discovery that guides, reputed to be of superhuman wisdom and skill, are, in fact, of a somewhat different character. If the doctrine deprives us of a model laid up in heaven to which we should approximate our behaviour, at least it does not lead us into a morass where every choice is equally good or equally to be deplored. And if it suggests that politics are *nur für die Schwindelfreie*, that should depress only those who have lost their nerve.

FIVE

The sin of the academic is that he takes so long in coming to the point. Nevertheless, there is some virtue in his dilatoriness; what

---

[7] To those who seem to themselves to have a clear view of an immediate destination (that is, of a condition of human circumstance to be achieved), and who are confident that this condition is proper to be imposed upon everybody, this will seem an unduly sceptical understanding of political activity; but they may be asked where they have got it from, and whether they imagine that 'political activity' will come to an end with the achievement of this condition? And if they agree that some more distant destination may then be expected to disclose itself, does not this situation entail an understanding of politics as an open-ended activity such as I have described? Or do they understand politics as making the necessary arrangements for a set of castaways who have always in reserve the thought that they are going to be 'rescued'?

he has to offer may, in the end, be no great matter, but at least it is not unripe fruit, and to pluck it is the work of a moment. We set out to consider the kind of knowledge involved in political activity and the appropriate sort of education. And if the understanding of politics I have recommended is not a misunderstanding, there is little doubt about the kind of knowledge and the sort of education which belongs to it. It is knowledge, as profound as we can make it, of our tradition of political behaviour. Other knowledge, certainly, is desirable in addition; but this is the knowledge without which we cannot make use of whatever else we may have learned.

Now, a tradition of behaviour is a tricky thing to get to know. Indeed, it may even appear to be essentially unintelligible. It is neither fixed nor finished; it has no changeless centre to which understanding can anchor itself; there is no sovereign purpose to be perceived or invariable direction to be detected; there is no model to be copied, idea to be realized, or rule to be followed. Some parts of it may change more slowly than others, but none is immune from change. Everything is temporary. Nevertheless, though a tradition of behaviour is flimsy and elusive, it is not without identity, and what makes it a possible object of knowledge is the fact that all its parts do not change at the same time and that the changes it undergoes are potential within it. Its principle is a principle of *continuity*: authority is diffused between past, present, and future; between the old, the new, and what is to come. It is steady because, though it moves, it is never wholly in motion; and though it is tranquil, it is never wholly at rest.[8] Nothing that ever belonged to it is completely lost; we are always swerving back to recover and make something topical out of even its remotest moments: and nothing for long remains unmodified. Everything is temporary, but nothing is arbitrary. Everything figures by comparison, not with what stands next to it, but with the whole. And since a tradition of behaviour is not susceptible of the distinction between essence and acci-

[8] The critic who found 'some mystical qualities' in this passage leaves me puzzled: it seems to me an exceedingly matter-of-fact description of the characteristics of any tradition—the Common Law of England, for example, the so-called British Constitution, the Christian religion, modern physics, the game of cricket, shipbuilding.

dent, knowledge of it is unavoidably knowledge of its detail: to know only the gist is to know nothing. What has to be learned is not an abstract idea, or a set of tricks, not even a ritual, but a concrete, coherent manner of living in all its intricateness.

It is clear, then, that we must not entertain the hope of acquiring this difficult understanding by easy methods. Though the knowledge we seek is municipal, not universal, there is no shortcut to it. Moreover, political education is not merely a matter of coming to understand a tradition, it is learning how to participate in a conversation: it is at once initiation into an inheritance in which we have a life interest, and the exploration of its intimations. There will always remain something of a mystery about how a tradition of political behaviour is learned, and perhaps the only certainty is that there is no point at which learning it can properly be said to begin. The politics of a community are not less individual (and not more so) than its language, and they are learned and practised in the same manner. We do not begin to learn our native language by learning the alphabet, or by learning its grammar; we do not begin by learning words, but words in use; we do not begin (as we begin in reading) with what is easy and go on to what is more difficult; we do not begin at school, but in the cradle; and what we say springs always from our manner of speaking. And this is true also of our political education; it begins in the enjoyment of a tradition, in the observation and imitation of the behaviour of our elders, and there is little or nothing in the world which comes before us as we open our eyes which does not contribute to it. We are aware of a past and a future as soon as we are aware of a present. Long before we are of an age to take interest in a book about our politics we are acquiring that complex and intricate knowledge of our political tradition without which we could not make sense of a book when we come to open it. And the projects we entertain are the creatures of our tradition. The greater part, then—perhaps the most important part—of our political education we acquire haphazard in finding our way about the natural-artificial world into which we are born, and there is no other way of acquiring it. There will, of course, be more to acquire, and it will be more readily acquired, if we have the good fortune to be born into a rich and lively political tradition and among those who are well educated politically; the lineaments of *political* activity will earlier become distinct: but even the most needy society and the most cramped surroundings have some political education to offer, and we take what we can get.

But if this is the manner of our beginning, there are deeper recesses to explore. Politics are a proper subject for academic study; there is something to think about and it is important that we should think about the appropriate things. Here also, and everywhere, the governing consideration is that what we are learning to understand is a political tradition, a concrete manner of behaviour. And for this reason it is proper that, at the academic level, the study of politics should be an historical study—not, in the first place, because it is proper to be concerned with the past, but because we need to be concerned with the detail of the concrete. It is true that nothing appears on the present surface of a tradition of political activity which has not its roots deep in the past, and that not to observe it coming into being is often to be denied the clue to its significance; and for this reason genuine historical study is an indispensable part of a political education. But what is equally important is not what happened, here to there, but what people have thought and said about what happened: the history, not of political ideas, but of the manner of our political thinking. Every society, by the underlinings it makes in the book of its history, constructs a legend of its own fortunes which it keeps up to date and in which is hidden its own understanding of its politics; and the historical investigation of this legend—not to expose its errors but understand its prejudices—must be a pre-eminent part of a political education. It is, then, in the study of genuine history, and of this quasi-history which reveals in its backward glances the tendencies which are afoot, that we may hope to escape one of the most insidious current misunderstandings of political activity—the misunderstanding in which institutions and procedures appear as pieces of machinery designed to achieve a purpose settled in advance, instead of as manners of behaviour which are meaningless when separated from their context: the misunderstanding, for example, in which Mill convinced himself that something called 'Representative Government' was a 'form' of politics which could be regarded as proper to any society which had reached a certain level of what he called 'civilization'; in short, the misunderstanding in which we regard our arrangements and institutions as something more significant than the footprints of thinkers and statesmen who knew which way to turn their feet without knowing anything about a final destination.

Nevertheless, to be concerned only with one's own tradition of political activity is not enough. A political education worth the name must embrace, also, knowledge of the politics of other contemporary societies. It must do this because some at least of our political activity is related to that of other people's, and not to know how they go about attending to their own arrangements is not to know the course they will pursue and not to know what resources to call upon in our own tradition; and because to know only one's own tradition is not to know even that. But here again two observations must be made. We did not begin yesterday to have relations with our neighbours; and we do not require constantly to be hunting outside the tradition of our politics to find some special formula or some merely *ad hoc* expedient to direct those relations. It is only when wilfully or negligently we forget the resources of understanding and initiative which belongs to our tradition that, like actors who have forgotten their part, we are obliged to gag. And secondly, the only knowledge worth having about the politics of another society is the same kind of knowledge as we seek of our own tradition. Here also, *la verité reste dans les nuances*; and a comparative study of institutions, for example, which obscured this would provide only an illusory sense of having understood what nevertheless remains a secret. The study of another people's politics, like the study of our own, should be an oecological study of a tradition of behaviour, not an anatomical study of mechanical devices or the investigation of an ideology. And only when our study is of this sort shall we find ourselves in the way of being stimulated, but not intoxicated, by the manners of others. To range the world in order to select the 'best' of the practices and purposes of others (as the eclectic Zeuxis is said to have tried to compose a figure more beautiful than Helen's by putting together features each notable for its perfection) is a corrupting enterprise and one of the surest ways of losing one's political balance; but to investigate the concrete manner in which another people goes about the business of attending to its arrangements may reveal significant passages in our own tradition which might otherwise remain hidden.

There is a third department in the academic study of politics which must be considered—what, for want of a better name, I shall call a philosophical study. Reflection on political activity may take place at various levels: we may consider what resources our political tradition offers for dealing with a certain situation, or we may abridge our political experience into a doctrine, which may be used, as a scientist uses hypothesis, to explore its intimations. But beyond these, and other manners of political thinking, there is a range of reflection the object of which is to consider the place of political activity itself on the map of our total experience. Reflection of this sort has gone on in every society which is politically conscious and intellectually alive; and so far as European societies are concerned, the inquiry has uncovered a variety of intellectual problems which each generation has formulated in its own way and has tackled with the technical resources at its disposal. And because political philosophy is not what may be called a 'progressive' science, accumulating solid results and reaching conclusions upon which further investigation may be based with confidence, its history is specially important: indeed, in a sense, it has nothing but a history, which is a history of the incoherencies philosophers have detected in common ways of thinking and the manner of solution they have proposed, rather than a history of doctrines and systems. The study of this history may be supposed to have a considerable place in a political education, and the enterprise of understanding the turn which contemporary reflection has given to it, an even more considerable place. Political philosophy cannot be expected to increase our ability to be successful in political activity. It will not help us to distinguish between good and bad political projects; it has no power to guide or to direct us in the enterprise of pursuing the intimations of our tradition. But the patient analysis of the general ideas which have come to be connected with political activity—in so far as it succeeds in removing some of the crookedness from our thinking and leads to a more economical use of concepts, is an activity neither to be overrated nor despised. But it must be understood as an explanatory, not a practical, activity, and if we pursue it, we may hope only to be less often cheated by ambiguous statement and irrelevant argument.

Abeunt studia in mores. The fruits of a political education will appear in the manner in which we think and speak about politics and perhaps in the manner in which we conduct our political activity. To select items from this prospective harvest must always be hazardous, and opinions will differ about what is most important. But for myself I should hope for two things. The more profound our understanding of political activity, the less we shall be at the mercy of plausible but mistaken analogy, the less we shall be tempted by a false or irrelevant model. And the more thoroughly we understand our own political tradition, the more readily its whole resources are available to us, the less likely we shall be to embrace the illusions which wait for the ignorant and the unwary: the illusion that in politics we can get on without a tradition of behaviour, the illusion that the abridgment of a tradition is itself a sufficient guide, and the illusion that in politics there is anywhere a safe harbour, a destination to be reached or even a detectable strand of progress. 'The world is the best of all possible worlds, and *everything* in it is a necessary evil.'[9]

THE PURSUIT OF INTIMATIONS

[1] This expression, as I hoped I had made clear, was intended as a description of what political activity actually is in the circumstances indicated, namely, in the 'hereditary, co-operative groups, many of them of ancient lineage, all of them aware of a past, a present, and a future, which we call "states" '. Critics who find this to

---

[9] [This quote comes from the Preface to F. H. Bradley's *Appearance and Reality.* —T.F.]

be so specialized a description that it fails altogether to account for some of the most significant passages in modern political history are, of course, making a relevant comment. But those who find this expression to be meaningless in respect of every so-called 'revolutionary' situation and every essay in so-called 'idealistic' politics may be asked to think again, remembering that it is neither intended as a description of the motives of politicians nor of what they believe themselves to be doing, but of what they actually succeed in doing.

I connected with this understanding of political activity two further propositions: first, that if true, it must be supposed to have some bearing upon how we study politics, that is, upon political education; secondly, that if true, it may be supposed to have some bearing upon how we conduct ourselves in political activity—there being, perhaps, some advantage in thinking and speaking and arguing in a manner consonant with what we are really doing. The second of these propositions I do not think to be very important.

[2] It has been concluded that this understanding of political activity reduces it to 'acting on hunches', 'following intuitions' and that it 'discourages argument of any sort'. Nothing I have said warrants this conclusion. The conclusion I myself drew in this connection was that, if this understanding of political activity were true, certain forms of argument (e.g. arguments designed to determine the correspondence of a political proposal with Natural Law or with abstract 'justice') must be considered either irrelevant or as clumsy formulations of other and relevant inquiries, and must be understood to have a merely rhetorical or persuasive value.

[3] It has been suggested that this understanding of political activity provides no standard or criterion for distinguishing between good and bad political projects or for deciding to do one thing rather than another. This, again, is an unfortunate misreading of what I said: 'everything figures, not with what stands next to it, but with the whole'. Those who are accustomed to judge everything in relation to 'justice', or 'solidarity', or 'welfare' or some other abstract 'principle', and know no other way of thinking and speaking, may perhaps be asked to consider how, in fact, a barrister in a Court of

Appeal argues the inadequacy of the damages awarded to his client. Does he say, 'This is a glaring injustice', and leave it at that? Or may he be expected to say that the damages awarded are 'out of line with the general level of damages currently being awarded in libel actions'? And if he says this, or something like it, is he to be properly accused of not engaging in argument of any sort, or of having no standard or criterion, or of merely referring to 'what was done last time'? (Cf. Aristotle, *Analytica Priora*, II. 23.) Again, is Mr N. A. Swanson all at sea when he argues in this fashion about the revolutionary proposal that the bowler in cricket should be allowed to 'throw' the ball: 'the present bowling action has evolved as a sequence, from underarm by way of round-arm to over-arm, by successive legislation of unorthodox actions. Now, I maintain that the "throw" has no place in this sequence . . .'? Or, is Mr G. H. Fender arguing without a standard or criterion, or is he merely expressing a 'hunch', when he contends that the 'throw' *has* a place in this sequence and should be permitted? And is it so far-fetched to describe what is being done here and elsewhere as 'exploring the intimations' of the total situation? And, whatever we like to say in order to bolster up our self-esteem, is not this the manner in which changes take place in the design of anything, furniture, clothes, motor-cars and societies capable of political activity? Does it all become much more intelligible if we exclude circumstance and translate it into the idiom of 'principles', the bowler, perhaps, arguing his 'natural right' to throw? And, even then, can we exclude circumstance: would there ever be a question of the right to throw if the right to bowl over-arm had not already been conceded? At all events, I may perhaps be allowed to reiterate my view that moral and political 'principles' are abridgments of traditional manners of behaviour, and to refer specific conduct to 'principles' is not what it is made to appear (*viz.* referring it to a criterion which is reliable because it is devoid of contingency, like a so-called 'just price').

[4] It has been asserted that in politics there is no 'total situation': 'why should we presuppose that, inside the territory we call Britain . . . there is only one society, with one tradition? Why should not there be two societies . . . each with its own way of life?' In the

understanding of a more profound critic this might be a philosophical question which would require something more than a short answer. But in the circumstances it is perhaps enough to say: first, that the absence of homogeneity does not necessarily destroy singleness; secondly, what we are considering here is a legally organized society and we are considering the manner in which its legal structure (which in spite of its incoherencies cannot be supposed to have a competitor) is reformed and amended; and thirdly, I stated (on p. 56) what I meant by a 'single community' and my reasons for making this my starting-place.

[5] Lastly, it has been said that, since I reject 'general principles', I provide no means for detecting incoherencies and for determining what shall be on the agenda of reform. 'How do we discover what a society [sic] intimates?' But to this I can only reply: 'Do you want to be told that in politics there is, what certainly exists nowhere else, a mistake-proof manner of deciding what should be done?' How does a scientist, with the current condition of physics before him, decide upon a direction of profitable advance? What considerations passed through the minds of medieval builders when they detected the inappropriateness of building in stone as if they were building in wood? How does a critic arrive at the judgment that a picture is incoherent, that the artist's treatment of some passages is inconsistent with his treatment of others?

J. S. Mill (*Autobiography*, OUP pp. 136–7, 144–5), when he abandoned reference to general principle either as a reliable guide in political activity or as a satisfactory explanatory device, put in its place a 'theory of human progress' and what he called a 'philosophy of history'. The view I have expressed in this essay may be taken to represent a further stage in this intellectual pilgrimage, a stage reached when neither 'principle' (on account of what it turns out to be: a mere index of concrete behaviour) nor any general theory about the character and direction of social change seem to supply an adequate reference for explanation or for practical conduct.

"Political Education" first appeared as a short book published by Bowes and Bowes in 1951. The appendix "The Pursuit of Intimations" was new in the original 1962 edition of *Rationalism in Politics*.

Political discourse

Politics may be identified, in the first place, as a practical activity concerned with making a response to situations of a certain sort: political situations.

A political situation may be identified, first, as a condition of things recognized to have sprung, not from natural necessity, but from human choices or actions, and to which more than one response is possible. Thus, politics may be said to be the activity of responding to conditions of things already recognized to be the product of choices.

Secondly, a political situation may be said to be a 'public', not a 'private', situation. This does not carry us very far, because 'public' and 'private' are what they are believed to be: what falls within each of these realms is a matter of local opinion. Nevertheless, if there is to be political activity a distinction of some sort must be made between 'public' and 'private'. And since what belongs to the 'public' realm is usually taken to be what it is believed a ruler or a government should take cognizance of, a political situation may be identified as a contingent situation to which a ruler or a government (and not a private person, as such) is expected to respond.

Two of the ingredients of political activity are then: a situation of a certain sort and a response to it by somebody recognized to have the authority to respond to it.

Such situations may be of various magnitudes. They may be generated by a specific action (like the seizure of the Suez Canal), or by an observed tendency in local human conduct (like the aggressive expansionist disposition of the French revolutionary government). They may be generated by a specific belief (like Zionism, or the belief that women should have the vote, or that Ireland should have 'Home Rule'), or by more general beliefs (like the belief that the threat of nuclear war is insufferable, or that the economy of Britain is stagnant). And, obviously, the response looked for will correspond to the magnitude of the situation discerned.

Now, none of these situations, not even the simplest imaginable, bears its significance on its surface. Each is a contingent event or complex of events, the product of human sentiments, choices and actions; and each requires interpretation. And since what is sought in politics is a response to it, this interpretation will be diagnostic and prognostic, and not explanatory. Thus, even the situation to be attended to is the product of deliberation in which it is recognized, identified, interpreted, given an intelligible character, or a least a name. And this introduces a third ingredient into political activity; namely, the ingredient of deliberation or reflection.

Deliberation is necessary before an identifiable political situation can even appear. But it is required, also, in the choice of the response to be made to the situation; for a political situation is one to which there is no *necessary* response.

Sometimes this response may be what may be called a response of 'principle': the conclusion, for example, that 'honor' requires us to do *this*. And, in this case, the deliberation will take the form of reflection designed to elicit the 'principle' which should be operative.

But, more often, deliberation about the response to be made will be concerned with two distinguishable considerations: first, reflection about the consequences of a proposed response; and secondly reflection about the relation of these consequences to beliefs about better and worse conditions of things.

First, every political decision is designed to achieve or to avoid some more or less specific condition of things; and before it is chosen its merits as a response to the particular situation must, in some manner or other, have been considered. The question to be answered is: will a decision to do *this* now achieve what I want to achieve or avoid what I want to avoid?

But, in addition to this, what has to be considered is the reverberations which the decision to act in this way may set going elsewhere, and their propensity to limit or to nullify the condition of things designed to be achieved. A decision to do *this* rather than *that* is a choice made in relation to all the consequences of doing *this* or *that*, in so far as they can be foreseen. Thus, every political decision is inherently complex—a response, not merely to a specified situation, but to the current *continuum* of political circumstances.

Secondly, no response to any situation is possible without some relevant beliefs about better and worse conditions of things. To reflection designed to discover the probable consequences of what it is proposed to do must be added reflection about those consequences in terms of better and worse.

These, then, are the considerabilities of political activity: a political situation, a person or persons recognized to have the authority to respond to it, and deliberation in which *this* response is chosen in preference to *that*.

Now, political discourse appears when, in connection with political activity, words are spoken or written and heard or read. The speakers may be many or few; the theatre and the audience may be large or small. The utterances may compose an oration, or they may be a contribution to a debate or a conversation; they may be designed to serve different ends, they may be appropriate to different audiences, and they may have different logical structures.

If he who speaks has also the authority to act, his utterances may be designed to evoke courage or compliance in his audience, or they may be argumentative utterances. If they are argumentative, they may be designed to justify an action performed or to persuade the audience to approve of what it is proposed to do. And the argument may be designed to reveal the course of deliberation in which the proposal was chosen in preference to others, or it may be designed to conceal it, or some parts of it.

Others will address themselves to those in authority or to those who (in respect of their position or numbers) may be able to influence them. And their design may be to encourage or to support, to criticize or to question, to persuade those in authority to consider other proposals or to take other decisions, to elicit an account of what has been done or to demand a defence of it.

In short, political discourse includes a great variety of different sorts of utterance, and in this paper I am going to confine myself to what may be called argumentative discourse, and further to that sort of argumentative discourse which purports to reveal (and not conceal) deliberation about response to political situations.

Now, all pieces of political discourse, even the most informal, make use of general abstract ideas. Indeed, it would be impossible to diagnose a political situation, to formulate a response to it, or to consider the probable consequences of this response and their propensities for good or ill, without recourse to some general ideas about human conduct.

Many of these ideas belong to the common stock of ideas we use in thinking or talking about any practical situation and what should be done in response to it; others have a more exclusive reference to political situations. But wherever they come from, they compose what may be called a general vocabulary of political discourse. From time to time words are added to this vocabulary, and other words fall into disuse.

The sort of words I am thinking of, the words apt to appear in any piece of political discourse are, for example: necessary, cause, effect, consequence, natural, rational, traditional, organic, contingent, useful, desirable; purpose, function, development, opportunity, intention; right, duty, just, unjust; public, private, common, social, civil, constitutional, legal; authority, power, privilege, rule, violence; principal, agent, representative, responsible, voluntary, consent, freedom, independence; adult, individual, group, church, association, class, people, nation, race; alliance, allegiance, interest, party, pressure, struggle, stagnant; revolutionary, democratic, reactionary, liberal, progressive, underdeveloped, welfare; imperial, colonial, neo-colonial; leader, elite, bureaucracy, tyranny, parliamentary, Fascist, totalitarian, tribal, Jewish, Afro-Asian; war, peace, unity, diversity, etc. These words are not all the same part of speech; and, of course, in different connections they may have different meanings. Some of them may also belong to vocabularies of explanation.

But it often happens that a selection from these words is put together to compose a special vocabulary in terms of which political situations are identified and responses to them formulated, recommended, criticized or defended. Indeed, the argument of most pieces of political discourse makes use of a special vocabulary of this sort, and it often carries specialization further by imposing a particular and exclusive meaning upon some of the words.

Every piece of political discourse, then, may be said to be the recognition of a political situation and the defence or recommendation of a response to it in terms of a special vocabulary understood to be related to political activity. And it seems not inappropriate to speak of such special vocabularies as 'ideologies'. At least that is what I shall call them.

Where the idioms come from which compose these 'ideologies' and how they come to be collected together, I am not going to enquire: what I want to consider is their place in political discourse.

A political 'ideology', in this sense, is an invitation to interpret political situations and to think about what is desirable and undesirable in a certain manner, and an invitation to consider some consequences of political decisions and actions to be more important than others. It allows a certain range of observations and a certain range of proposals to be made. For these terms of political deliberation do not themselves divulge the character of the situation or the response to be made to it; that is the product of the deliberation. Nor can they be thought of as the 'cause' of a decision or an action; actions are never 'caused' by beliefs of this sort. They merely point in certain directions and make it more difficult to look in other directions. An 'ideology', as a vocabulary of beliefs in terms of which to conduct political discourse, may have internal tensions and discrepancies; it may be composed of few and simple, or of many and complex beliefs; its invitations (like others) may be precise ('Come to lunch tomorrow') or they may be indefinite ('Nice to see you some time'). This will be reflected in the discourse. But this vocabulary of general beliefs remains an adjunct to political reasoning; it is merely a means of talking what is alleged to be sense about political situations.

This may be illustrated as follows. In some circumstances, all the participants in current political discourse may be said to share a common political 'ideology'. This was pretty well the case in Republican Rome. But it does not mean that we are unable to distinguish the speech of one politician from that of another, or that there never was any disagreement about the response to be made to a given situation. A substantial 'ideological' agreement did not forbid the recommendation of divergent choices about what to do. But it did make it easier than might otherwise have been the case for a ruler to defend his decisions convincingly: he knew in advance the words, the expressions, the reasons and the sentiments which would be likely to impress his audience.

The situation within any of the states of modern Europe has, since the sixteenth century, been somewhat different from this. Here, divergencies of general beliefs related to politics, divergencies which sometimes compose firmly outlined 'ideologies', have imposed upon political deliberation a confusion and upon political discourse a complexity unknown, for example, to Republican Rome.

Here is an instance of this from English history: When the House of Commons met in January 1689 to consider the flight of James II to France, the overwhelming majority believed him to be no longer King. The problem was how to elucidate this belief in a manner that would be convincing to all Englishmen: it was a problem of discourse. The document produced, notorious for its equivocations and inconsistencies, was designed to interpret the situation in a manner which would satisfy each of the current and conflicting beliefs about the office of King of England and to point to a single response. It stated that James II, having endeavoured to subvert the constitution of the kingdom by breaking the original contract between king and people, and, by the advice of Jesuits and other wicked persons, having violated the fundamental laws, and having withdrawn himself from the kingdom, had abdicated the government, and that the throne had thereby become vacant. This sentence bears witness to the 'ideological' diversity of the times; it attempted to satisfy all the components of that diversity.

Political discourse in modern European states has, then, for a very long time been distinguished on account of the variety of special vocabularies of belief in which it is conducted. Each of the current vocabularies directs attention to different considerations in identifying political situations and in assessing the important consequences of decisions, and each suggests different beliefs about what is, in general, desirable and undesirable. In this manner they impose conditions upon political deliberation and discourse, and upon the kinds of choice to be made in response to emergent situations.

But this variety of vocabulary is not as great as it might appear at first sight. These 'ideologies', in respect of the content of the beliefs which compose them, often show only marginal differences. They may be expected to overlap one another and they often do so. There is, at least, nothing to forbid commerce between them. And if we were to consider the provenance and pedigree of these general ideas we should be able to account for the commerce which often takes place between these 'ideologies'. Few of them are incapable of change; it is often possible to translate the terms of one into the terms of another; but, generally speaking, it is impossible to deliberate on political situations or to participate in political discourse without having some command over one of the special political vocabularies current in contemporary Europe. And these vocabularies have, of course, now spread themselves about the whole world.

So far, I have been considering the beliefs which compose a vocabulary of political discourse in respect of their content. I have recognized 'ideologies' as idioms of deliberation and discourse. Thus, 'liberalism' is seen to be different from 'syndicalism' in virtue of having a different vocabulary of beliefs in which to interpret political situations, and so on.

But there is something else to be considered. Besides its vocabulary of beliefs every piece of political discourse has a logical design. This logical design appears, unavoidably, in the logical status given to the conclusion reached in the discourse. An argument, for example, which ends with *Quod erat demonstrandum* is an argument of a different logical design from one which (like the argument of a prosecuting counsel in a court of law) ends in some quite different manner. But although the logical design of an argument is revealed in the logical status of its conclusion, it derives from the logical status given to the beliefs which compose its vocabulary of discourse. For example, an argument which ends appropriately with *Quod erat demonstrandum*, does so because the logical status of axiom has been given to at least one of the beliefs contained in its vocabulary of discourse.

Thus, political 'ideologies' may be considered either as vocabularies of beliefs, which invite political discourse to take certain directions and to reach certain conclusions, or as composed of beliefs which, because of the logical status given to them, impose a certain logical design upon political discourse and impose a certain logical status upon its conclusions. And I want now to consider some of the different kinds of logical design which have been imposed in this manner upon political deliberation and discourse in the history of European politics.

There is one sort of logical design for political discourse which is both the commonest and the most difficult to describe, so I will begin by giving an example of it.

In 432 B.C., according to Thucydides, Pericles made a speech in which he advised the Athenian Assembly (with whom the decision rested) that the time had come to make a stand against Sparta. The Spartans had recently expressed a desire that peace should be preserved, but Pericles interpreted this as a ruse to gain time in order to complete preparations for war. And, in any case, they had announced certain conditions. 'They order us', said Pericles, 'to raise the siege of Potidea; they warn us not to interfere in Aegina; they require us to revoke the decree excluding the Megarians from Athenian territory.' 'I hope,' he went on, 'that none of you will think that we go to war over a trifle if we refuse to revoke the Megara decree . . . . If you give way on this, you will instantly be met with further demands because you will be thought to have been frightened into obedience, and in the end you will find yourselves overpowered by the Spartans without a blow having been struck.' Look at what has happened elsewhere as a result of believing in the pacific intentions of Sparta.

Moreover, he continued, the Athenian resources for war are not inferior to those of Sparta. There will be dangers to be faced. We may not be able to defend Attica. But our navy is strong and well-prepared, and that should be the pivot of our strategy. And we are not without allies whose help may be depended upon. The time has come to resist; we can be defeated only by our own blunders. Did not our fathers successfully resist the Medes with resources far inferior to what we now have? My advice is that you refuse the Spartan demands and prepare yourself for the almost unavoidable battle. If you listen to those who recommend acquiescence, you will not escape war; you will only have to fight in a worse situation and not one of your own choosing.

Now, it will be noticed that this speech deals expressly or by implication with all the considerations we have seen to belong to political discourse. It diagnoses the situation; it makes a proposal about what the response to it should be; it recommends this proposal by considering a large number of the consequences likely to follow from acting upon it; it balances the merits of this proposal against those of at least one other proposal; and it assumes agreement about the general conditions of things to be preferred.

Our concern is with the logical design of this kind of political discourse. And in this matter we cannot do better than to listen to Aristotle, whose *Rhetoric* is the classic treatment of this subject.

Aristotle recognized this sort of political discourse as a kind of reasoning which, without the aid of axioms, is designed to recommend what to do and what not to do in a contingent situation where there are possible alternative actions.

The situation having been recognized and the proposal made, the argument is directed to considering the consequences likely to follow from acting on the proposal. This entails a forecast of the response which the action will be likely to meet from anyone whom it affects, directly or indirectly.

The materials out of which such an argument is constructed, says Aristotle, are probabilities, signs and examples. Probabilities are contingencies which usually happen; signs are events which are usually antecedent or concomitant to other events; examples are situations alleged to be significantly similar to the situation in question and about which more is known.

If the reasoning takes a syllogistic form (which it need not), it will be an *enthymeme*; that is, a syllogism in which the major premise is a maxim and in which one at least of the minors may be suppressed as a matter of common knowledge or agreement. A maxim is a general statement relating to what is usually to be expected in human conduct, or to what is normally agreed to be desirable.

Arguments constructed out of these materials cannot be refuted by showing that their major premise is not certainly true or by showing that the conclusion is uncertain, because such arguments do not pretend to be dialectical demonstration. Indeed, strictly speaking, they cannot be 'refuted' at all. They may be resisted by arguments of the same sort which, on balance, are found to be more convincing. Conclusions based upon what is likely to happen because it usually happens, may be rebutted by showing that the probability is less strong than is alleged, or that some other expectation is more likely to be fulfilled. Conclusions which rely upon signs (which in political arguments are always fallible signs, not necessary causes), may be rebutted by showing that the connection between the sign and what it is alleged to signify is less strong than is supposed. Conclusions which rely upon examples may be rebutted by showing that the alleged similarity is absent or exaggerated, or that the alleged analogy (if it is an analogy, and not a similarity, that is alleged) is far-fetched, or by the production of negative in-

stances or of other examples of an opposite tendency and of superi-
or cogency or number.

The beliefs which compose the vocabulary of this kind of political discourse are, then, given the logical status of maxims or of materials from which maxims may be constructed. Its argument is
concerned with contingencies, not necessities; with probabilities
and expectations, not with demonstrable certainties; with conjectures, not proofs; with surmises and guesses, not with calculations.
It is reasoning designed to persuade to decision and action where
proof or disproof of the propositions contained in the proposal is
impossible to provide.

But, Aristotle continues, this kind of political discourse is
designed to persuade, also, about the good or the harm to be expected to follow, or not to follow, from a proposed course of action.
Like all advice to do or not to do things, political advice is concerned with *eudaimonia*, human happiness, what promotes it and
what is hostile to it. Here, however, *eudaimonia* is not understood
to be a simple, universal, unchanging condition of things, but to be
composed of the complex, changing conditions of things, often circumstantially discrepant from one another, which we are usually
disposed to agree to be desirable. These, says Aristotle, may be
called the 'admitted goods' of the society. Thus, the logical status of
all value judgements in political discourse of this sort is also that of
maxims—general statements about what are usually believed to be
preferable conditions of things.

Moreover, since all the 'admitted goods' of a society cannot necessarily be equally secured on any one occasion, it will fall to this
kind of political discourse to show that more of these 'goods' will be
secured, and fewer will be prejudiced, if *this* proposal is followed in
preference to any other; or to show why, in these circumstances,
this 'good' should be secured at the expense of *that*. And the form
such an argument must take is a weighing of *pros* and *cons* and
conjecture about likely consequences of action.

Here, then, is political discourse of a certain logical design; it is
argument to persuade but without being able to prove. And it gets
this design from the logical status given to the beliefs which com-

pose its vocabulary of discourse—the status of maxims or the components of maxims: beliefs generally held to be true, and values generally held to be important.

This, perhaps, is the commonest logical design to be found in political discourse. It is the design of all political speeches which have come down to us from the ancient world; it is the design of most parliamentary utterances during the last five centuries; it is the design of all State Papers—nowhere more exactly reflected than, for example, in Sir Eyre Crowe's 1907 Memorandum on German foreign policy.

But it is no secret that political discourse of this logical design has been thought to be profoundly unsatisfactory, no matter what refinement is achieved in the choice of maxims, examples and signs. And the defect which has been discerned in it is, precisely, the uncertainty of its conclusions and its immersion in imperfectly predictable contingency. Can we not do better than these surmises and conjectures, shots in the dark and actions recommended because they are marginally preferable to others?

A yearning of this sort may, perhaps, be reflected in the ancient practice of consulting oracles in matters of great political importance and in taking the auspices before venturing upon action. To have the advice or the approval of the all-knowing gods (it was thought) would be to enjoy a measure of certainty which human deliberation is unable to supply. But the pronouncements of oracles were often ambiguous and the good-will of the gods was not above suspicion. As Machiavelli remarks, however punctilious the Romans were in ascertaining the auspices, 'when they saw a good reason why certain things should be done, they did them anyhow, whether the auspices were favorable or not.' Consequently, the desire for certainty in place of conjecture in political affairs—and, indeed, in all practical affairs—turned in other directions in search of satisfaction.

Now, what are we asking for if we seek the emancipation of political deliberation from conjecture and opinion about the probable consequences of actions and about the contingent desirability of different conditions of things? We are asking for political discourse of a different logical design from that which belongs to the deliberations of Pericles and that which Aristotle examined in the *Rhetoric*. We are asking for demonstrative political discourse. We are seeking a kind of argument capable of proving or disproving the 'correctness' of political proposals. In short, we are asking for *apodeictic* political discourse.

And there are at least two different conditions in which it has been believed that political discourse could acquire this character: (1) Demonstrative political discourse could appear, it has been thought, if there were known principles or axioms of absolute certainty and of universal application to which any political proposal could be referred in order to determine its merits. (2) Or it could appear, if we possessed categorical information about human conduct, human circumstances, the course of events, and what is sometimes called the conditions of political society which would enable us to predict, instead of conjecturing, the consequences of different decisions before they were acted upon, and which would enable us to prove the 'correctness' of our judgements about what is desirable and undesirable to be done or to be endured on any occasion.

In short, it has been believed that demonstrative political discourse could spring either from an 'ideology' whose component beliefs were given the logical status of axioms, or from an 'ideology' whose component beliefs were given the logical status of categorically informative statements about human beings and the course of events.

Plato is the father of demonstrative political discourse in the first of these versions. He understood political activity to be the pursuit of human excellence or *dikaiosune*, and that the idea of 'justice' provides a universal and unchanging standard by which the merit of all human actions may be determined. He recognized knowledge of the idea 'justice' as genuine knowledge released from the uncertainties and relativities of *doxa*; and as the necessary and sufficient condition of political discourse, which thus could become demonstrative argument governed by an 'ideology' composed of a single idea given the status of axiom.

The strength of Plato's position is obvious. He recognized that if political discourse was to be demonstrative it must escape from having to balance one 'admitted good' against another in deciding upon a response to a political situation, because this can never reach a demonstrative conclusion. What is desirable must be simple, universal and unchanging. The image of political discourse which never left Plato's mind was that of a man with an utterly reliable measuring-rod in his hand: political argument was setting political proposals against a single, unambiguous, universally valid measure, and judging them according to this measure. And this, as Isocrates perceived, was why Plato was so careful, in the Socratic dialogues, to reduce all virtues to one virtue, *dikaiosune*. The possibility of conflict between moral ideals must be removed if political discourse were to become demonstrative.

The design of demonstrative political discourse is to be able to prove the 'correctness' or the 'incorrectness' of a proposal to respond to a political situation in a certain manner. This may be done only if contingency is removed from the situation, because so long as it remains in the situation it must reappear in the response. Plato proposed to do this by interpreting every political situation, not as an emergent event or complex of events, but as an ideal divergence from an ideal 'justice', and by recognizing every political decision, not as a decision to do something, but as a decision to ascertain the divergence. For him, a political situation was constituted by its 'injustice', and a political decision was the recognition of this injustice.

But these conditions, although they elicit demonstrative argument, make it impossible for the argument to address itself to any concrete political situation whatever. Demonstrative argument can be concerned only with the relations between abstract ideas, between *dikaiosune* and *democracy*, for example. But as soon as argument concerns itself with any contingent emergent situation (with what to do about a subject city in revolt, for example) it must relapse from proof into undemonstrative argument. It is impossible to have the same sort of knowledge of a contingent situation as one may purport to have about *dikaiosune*.

Indeed, Plato himself recognized this. He does not attempt to deduce the details of the life and education of the Guardians from the axiom of 'justice', because this would be impossible; he merely tries to persuade us that 'just' rule will be the probable consequence of rulers of this sort. Or again, he saw that in politics it would be necessary to win the compliance, by persuasion, of those incapable of appreciating proof, and he suggested that this could be done by telling them a convincing story. But, since he thought this might be done once and for all, it never qualified his rejection of the notion of politics as an activity permanently related to contingencies of this or any other sort, or his confidence in the possibility of demonstrative political argument.

In the enterprise of constructing a demonstrative kind of political discourse upon an 'ideology' of axioms, Plato has had many followers; but the only other writer I know who has embraced this project and explored it with comparable intrepidity is Rousseau.

The problem of how to achieve infallibly correct political decisions, how to make infallibly just laws, how to be ruled by a mistake-proof will, devoid of contingency, is one to which Rousseau continually returns. But the nemesis which overtook Plato, overtook Rousseau also. A mistake-proof *volonté général* is substituted for deliberative discourse (which must always be liable to error), but it is found to have no instructions whatever for interpreting any actual political situation or about the response to be made to it.

The other more moderate followers of Plato in this enterprise have been betrayed by their moderation. They did not discern that the logical condition of demonstrative political discourse of this kind is the exclusion of diverse and potentially conflicting axioms. Instead of a single comprehensive axiom (like *dikaiosune* or an infallible *volonté général*) they sought refuge in a collection of alleged axioms—the 'natural' rights of man, or a 'natural' law composed of a variety of precepts—and thus they defeated themselves.

In the bastard logical design of their discourse, propositions, which are no more than maxims, have imposed upon them the character of axioms, a character they could not sustain. For it could not be denied that there might be circumstances in which one alleged 'natural' right should have a priority over another, or in which one alleged precept of 'natural' law should be given precedence over another, and in arguing this priority or precedence political discourse must descend from demonstration to concern itself with contingencies and relativities. Where there are a number of reputed axioms, casuistry makes its appearance, and casuistry can never be demonstrative argument. It may be thought possible to demonstrate one's 'natural' rights as indisputable axioms of conduct; but it can never be possible to prove the 'correctness' of a proposal for the temporary sacrifice of, for example, 'freedom of movement' to 'freedom from want'. Such a proposal may be recommended, perhaps convincingly, in an undemonstrative argument, and it will often be the task of political discourse to argue such proposals; but they can never be proved.

The current looser forms of this kind of political discourse, which appear to set up beliefs, like that of the right of 'national self-determination', as axioms, fail even more obviously to be demonstrative. For, while such beliefs may be recognized as belonging to what Aristotle called the 'admitted goods', which in political discourse have always to be balanced with one another in an argument which takes the form of weighing the *pros* and *cons* in the context of a particular set of circumstances, they are utterly unable to maintain their alleged character as axioms. And even if there were recognized to be one good of such supreme worth that all others were insignificant beside it, the proposition in which this good is stated would remain a maxim. A single good can have the character of an axiom only when it is regarded, like Plato's *dikaiosune*, as including all other goods.

But the failure of an 'ideology' of reputed axioms to generate demonstrative political discourse does not exhaust the possibilities. There is a second well-explored version of this enterprise to be considered. Here the demonstrative character of political discourse is made to spring, not from an 'ideology' composed of axioms, but from an 'ideology' composed of propositions understood to contain categorical information about human beings, human circumstances and the course of events.

These propositions, it is recognized, must contain genuine and verifiable information in respect to all those matters which in undemonstrative political discourse are regarded as matters of opinion and conjecture. That is to say, they must contain information, which is beyond doubt, about human conduct, about the future course of events and about what is good or evil, or what is better or worse, in all conditions of human circumstances. Two examples may serve to show what is required and how it may be supplied.

Political decisions may be based upon prophecy, such as the celebrated prophecies of Merlin about the future course of events in medieval England. Here, prophecy was not regarded as astute conjecture; it was understood to convey absolutely reliable information about what was going to happen, and therefore (it might be thought) information upon which 'correct' political decisions could be taken. Unfortunately, the information was scrappy; where the prophet was silent nothing was known with comparable certainty. And, in the absence of other indisputable information, deliberation about political decisions must relapse into ordinary undemonstrative discourse. Moreover, where there is a prophetic utterance, it relates merely to a future event; it does not supply the politician or ruler with a uniquely 'correct' response to the current situation. It does not even suggest, much less demonstrate, what should be done now in order that a preferred condition of things may be made to emerge; and it supplies no means of deciding what constitutes better or worse conditions of things. In short, mere prophecy and the information it contains (although it may be absolutely reliable information) does not provide what is required to generate demonstrative political deliberations.

But a second example shows how these defects may be remedied. Jeanne d'Arc listened to the 'voices' which informed her, not in the guarded and ambiguous tones usual in political orcles but in an exact utterance precisely what should be done in a particular contingent circumstance. The injunctions of these 'voices' were not regarded as the recommendations of an astute political advisor, good at guessing how things are likely to turn out; they were recognized as the injunctions of a deity who knew very well how things would turn out if they were obeyed and who could not be supposed to recommend anything but what was the best. The 'correctness' of these injunctions was a function of the authority from whom they came. If their 'correctness' had been doubted, the doubt could properly have been silenced by referring to this authority and by pointing both to his omniscience in respect of all those considerations which appear in the deliberations of ordinary mortals and to his infallibility as a judge of good and evil. That is to say, the 'correctness' of these injunctions was, in all respects, demonstrable in advance, and in no respect did it wait for verification by the event. The deliberation was demonstrative because it was the deliberation of an omniscient and benevolent deity.

Here, then, is the paradigm case of demonstrative political deliberation based, not upon axioms, but upon information; the case in which all the necessary conditions are satisfied. And the version of the enterprise to construct demonstrative political discourse which we are now concerned with may be recognized as an attempt to reproduce these conditions, but without invoking divine omniscience.

These being the *desiderata*, it is not surprising that it came to be believed that the most satisfactory form which these informative propositions about human beings, human circumstances and the future course of events, could assume was that of 'laws' of human conduct, or 'laws' of social change or development, analogous to the 'laws' reputed to have been discerned by, for example, biologists or geneticists.

If information of this sort were available, it seemed possible that the diagnosis of political situations, the consideration of the consequences of political decisions and their propensities for good or evil would be finally emancipated from opinion and conjecture. And it was even believed that, in virtue of information of this kind, such a mastery over human circumstances would be achieved that decisions could be taken which would have no consequences but those they were designed to have.

Now, this was the project of Karl Marx and his associates. And it is easy to see why he recognized it as the exclusion of what he called 'ideology' from politics. 'Ideological' beliefs, for Marx, were what *doxai* were for Plato, uncertain opinions, corrupted by partiality and relativity and representing a 'false consciousness' of the world. But the propositions of Marx's 'science of the history of society' were declared not to be, in this sense, 'ideological' because they were alleged to be the results of research and enquiry and to be capable of verification before they were used to diagnose political situations or to formulate political proposals. Nevertheless, they compose what I have called an 'ideology'; that is, a vocabulary of beliefs in terms of which political deliberation and discourse may be carried on. And they are beliefs which have been given a certain logical status.

Of course, Marx and his associates were not alone in exploring the possibility of this particular version of demonstrative political discourse: this enterprise had been on the agenda of European thought for many centuries. In all its essentials it is a form of gnosticism, and in modern times it has had many followers.

The intellectual superiority of Marx over Merlin is that what he purported to supply was not mere scraps of information about future events, but information of a comprehensive and generalized kind, including information alleged to enable us to distinguish 'scientifically' between better and worse conditions of things. And the superiority of Marx over Joachim de Fiore is that his information purported to derive, not from divine inspiration, but from research and enquiry which had reached conclusions capable of being verified and which had been verified.

Let us, briefly, consider the process in which he attempted to establish the 'laws' of human conduct and social change which were to compose this 'science of the history of society' and which were to constitute the vocabulary of ideas for a demonstrative kind of political deliberation. It was a process which has its counterpart in all enterprises of this sort.

Marx had very hazy notions about the character of the explanatory 'laws' in which natural scientists are accustomed to express the regularities they observe. But he did understand that they concerned relations, not between concrete situations or events, but between abstractions. And in seeking such 'laws' in respect of men and human societies he settled upon two major abstractions. The first was: men as merely physical beings subsisting in relation to a merely physical world; and this relation he identified as that of satisfying wants by using tools. The second was: 'societies' as merely organizations of 'tool using'. These abstractions gave him the ideal situation or *continuum*, the internal structure of which he was to explore. In exploring it several other useful abstractions appeared, such as the 'conditions of production', 'class', 'capital', 'labor', and so on, whose ideal relations to one another could be understood as examples of the operation of general 'laws'. These abstract ideas were the terms of the equations in which these 'laws' were expressed.

But to display, in this manner, the relationships between abstract ideas, and to display ideal situations as composed of these relationships, obviously falls far short of anything like a 'science of the history of society'. It yields no informative propositions whatever about the world of concrete human activities, nor any propositions relevant to deliberation and discourse about concrete contingent situations. Before a 'science of the history of society' could appear two great changes had to be imposed upon the material Marx had collected.

The abstract terms of this ideal world of 'tool using' and its organization had, first, to be made concrete by being identified with concrete historical situations. 'Capitalism', for example, had to be translated from being a term in an equation into an actual situation in a history of 'tool using' and its organization; and 'class' had to be translated from an hypothetical relationship to an ideal process of purely physical 'production' into an historical emergence. And the 'laws', which had hitherto been equations showing the necessary relationships between abstractions, had to be translated into 'laws' capable of explaining the historic appearance of different 'tool using' situations and of predicting those to appear in the future. These translations were effected by Marx without, it would seem, his knowing what he was doing. Nor is this surprising, because there is evidence which suggests that he was unaware that they were translations. Of course, they have no semblance of validity; but, what is more important is that they were not enough to accomplish his purpose. More was required before a 'science of the history of society' could appear.

The alleged 'laws' explanatory of the historic changes and development of 'tool using' and its organization had, secondly, to be shown to be the 'laws' explanatory of all human activities, politics among them. 'Capitalism', for example, must be shown to be a concept as cogent in the explanation of religious, moral, legal, artistic, or political change as it was alleged to have been found cogent for this explanation of changes in 'tool using' and its organization. And it was as clear to Marx and his associates, as it is clear to us, that some reasoned defence of this view of things is required. They produced two arguments.

In the first, 'tool using' is agreed not to be the sole activity of human beings and the organization of 'tool using' is agreed not to be the sole organization of human societies. But it was asserted that all other human activities and organizations are subordinate to the activity of 'tool using' and its organization, either because they 'derived' from it and were in some unexplained manner dependent upon it, or because they were subsequent to it in the historic order of the appearance of human activities. In this argument (if it can be called an argument) it seems as if Marx intended to present the relation between 'tool using' and other human activities as itself explicable in terms of a 'law' belonging to a 'science of the history of society': the relation of changes in religious belief, for example, to changes in 'tool using' techniques being understood as examples of a general explanatory 'law' analogous to the 'laws' alleged to explain the changes in 'tool using' techniques themselves. And, obscure as this notion is, its obscurity does not conceal the *petitio principii* upon which it rests: what the argument is designed to prove is assumed to be true.

The second argument is dialectical. It begins with an alleged axiom—that matter is primary because it is the cause of all sensations. From this, it is argued that the 'laws' explanatory of material changes are the primary 'laws' explanatory of all changes in human activities. But 'tool using' and its organization, it is asserted, is 'material' activity because it is concerned directly with the physical world. Hence, the 'laws' explanatory of changes in 'tool using' and its organization are the primary explanatory 'laws' of all other human activities. Other human activities may conceivably have 'laws' of their own, but if so they are subordinate to the 'laws' explanatory of 'tool using' and its organization, perhaps, in a manner analogous to the subordination of the 'laws' of physiology to those of chemical change where every physiological process is understood as a chemical process; that is, they related to different degrees of abstraction.

The difficulty with this argument is, of course, that the major premise is far from being self-evidently true, that at least one of the minor premises is certainly false, and that the conclusion does not follow. It is safe to say that no conclusion whatever with regard to the relationship between different human activities can be drawn from the proposition that matter is primary and mind is derivative.

It may be said, then, that Marx's design for a 'science of the history of society' is hopelessly ramshackle; each of the steps in which it was constructed is logically indefensible and the conclusion is without any vestige of validity.

But even if it had been successful, if reliable 'laws' of social change had been established, it would still not have furnished us with informative propositions in terms of which political deliberation and discourse could be carried on, much less terms in which they could become demonstrative. For all political deliberation, all deliberation about what to do or what not to do, entails beliefs about what is better and worse. All argument designed to recommend an action is designed to show, not only that *these* will be its consequences, but also that they are to be preferred to any other. And no distinction between better and worse conditions of things can be derived from the sort of information provided by explanatory 'laws' of human conduct or social change. Explanatory 'laws' can themselves provide no prescriptions.

This difficulty, also, was recognized by Marx and by others bent upon this enterprise, for they made some efforts to circumvent it.

But the design of all these circumventions is self-defeating. Prescription cannot be assimilated to explanation by showing that all judgements of better and worse are themselves examples of the operation of general explanatory 'laws' of human conduct. And that is all they ever attempted to show. 'Laws' which explain the generation or appearance of 'admitted good' in the history of a society are not more prescriptive than any other explanatory laws.

The project of Karl Marx is an individual adventure within the larger enterprise of exploring the possibility of demonstrative political discourse based upon an 'ideology' composed of categorically informative propositions about human beings and the course of events. It is interesting in itself; but for us its main interest is that the obstructions which frustrated it are, in principle, obstructions which must frustrate every undertaking of this sort. Explanatory 'laws' of social change cannot generate political deliberation capable of reaching 'correct' political decisions, or political discourse capable of proving decisions to be 'correct' or 'incorrect'.

The disappointment of the hope of achieving demonstrative political deliberation with the aid of an 'ideology' composed of explanatory 'laws' of social change or development is one of the great traumatic experiences of the early twentieth century. This hope cannot be said to have evaporated, the relics of it still linger; but I do not think I misjudge the situation if I detect a slackening of the impulse. Nobody believes such 'laws' to be obtainable; and no sensible person has ever believed that, if such 'laws' were obtainable, they would be capable of generating demonstrative political discourse.

But the larger hope of, somehow, emancipating political deliberation from mere opinion and conjecture has not evaporated: it has merely turned, in search of satisfaction, in other and somewhat less ambitious directions. In its current form, this hope expresses itself in the search for information which (although it is not expected to be in the form of 'laws' of social change) is expected to provide 'correct' diagnoses of political situations, 'correct' prediction of the consequences of human actions and 'correct' political decisions.

This enterprise is pursued, now, by many different methods: in the so-called comparative study of social organizations, governments and instruments of government; in the elucidation of ideal types—'democracies', 'police states', 'one-party governments', 'totalitarian regimes'; in the search for what is common and essential to typical situations—such as, 'war', 'revolution', 'rapidly developing economies', 'stable societies', and so on, in the collection of statistics and in the calculation of probabilities. And this enterprise has come to describe itself as 'the end of ideologies'.

Now, it is not for me, or for anyone else, to say that it cannot produce any information relevant to the diagnosis of political situations, or to forecasting the consequences of actions. Indeed, it must be expected to produce some information relevant to these undertakings. But, without going further, three things may be said of it.

First, the more generalized this information is (that is to say, the more it tends to satisfy the intellectual urge to explain), the less it will provide anything relevant to political deliberation or discourse; and the more it is concerned with specific and local conditions, the more it is likely to provide us with the kind of information useful in political deliberation.

Secondly, whatever it contributes to political deliberation and discourse it can never succeed in emancipating them from opinion and conjecture, or in transforming them from the weighing of *pros* and *cons* into demonstration. No recognition of a political situation in terms of an ideal type can dispense us from the necessity of considering the respects in which it diverges from the type; for it is these divergences which constitute the situation for the politician. No such recognition is itself capable of prescribing a response to it, much less a uniquely 'correct' response. Nor can prescription ever derive wholly from the prediction, however accurate, of the consequences of actions. Prescription always entails judgements about what is better or worse, and these are always *doxai*, for they always relate to contingent situations.

Thirdly, this enterprise, which identifies itself as 'the end of ideologies' in political discourse, is, in fact, nothing of the sort. When Marx announced the end of 'ideological' political discourse, he understood himself to be proclaiming the end of undemonstrative political discourse and its replacement by discourse governed by a vocabulary of 'scientifically' validated political beliefs. And, no doubt, these latest opponents of 'ideological' discourse have a similar conception of their enterprise. If this is so, they will suffer the same kind of frustration as that which overtook the enterprise of Marx and others. The information they design to supply could not turn political discourse into a demonstration; at most it could provide a vocabulary of beliefs in terms of which some marginally more reliable maxims might be formulated. These are not at all to be despised: they are what every politician has sought ever since the emergence of political activity. But maxims are not axioms, nor are they categorically informative propositions about human conduct.

If I appear to express a certain dissatisfaction with political discourse which designs to demonstrate the 'correctness' of what it recommends, I would not like it to be thought that, on that account, I consider this kind of political discourse to be mere error.

All political discourse is designed to persuade, and allegedly demonstrative political discourse must be recognized as discourse which designs to persuade by purporting to prove. And since there are certainly conditions in which it may achieve its design, it must be recognized, not as mere error, but as discourse appropriate to a certain sort of audience. But that is another matter which would lead us far afield.

This essay has been concerned with explanation—explaining how and why some enterprises in respect of political discourse are logically self-defeating. But I would like to end on a practical note, a matter which (because it concerns contingencies) I do not pretend to be anything but a matter of opinion.

Public affairs are important enough for it to be impossible not to wish that we could argue our proposals and defend our decisions in a demonstrative manner; and it is only to be expected that a way of doing so should have been sought. But, while acknowledging these attempts as intelligible and even laudable, it would be unwise not to recognize the damage they may do in politics.

We are not likely to be deceived by a man who claims to be able to prove the 'correctness' of what he proposes; but we are apt to be over-impressed by one who talks about his proposals in a manner which implies that their unique appropriateness is demonstrable. And this is common enough: the naive attribution of the status of axioms to what are nothing more than opinions is the vice of much contemporary political argument.

Further, a craving for demonstrative political argument may corrupt us by suggesting that we have not got to make choices, sometimes on little more than the courage of our convictions, or by suggesting that we can pass off the responsibility for making these choices upon some axiom or 'law' for which, in turn, we have no responsibility.

And, what is equally important, this craving for demonstrative political argument may make us discontented with ordinary political discourse which, because it is not demonstrative, we may be tempted to regard as a species of unreason. This would be a disastrous error. It is an error, because discourse which deals in conjectures and possibilities and the weighing of circumstantial *pros* and *cons* is reasoning, and it is the only sort of reasoning appropriate to practical affairs. In this matter Aristotle and Isocrates are better guides than Plato and Marx. And it would be disastrous, because it would tend to bring political discourse into such disrepute that we would become inclined to do without it altogether—to give up reflection and argument because they could not be demonstrative. Or it might discourage the only sort of intellectual effort capable of improving the quality of our political discourse. I mean the effort to understand our 'principles' and our 'admitted goods' in such a way as to recognize each as a choice we have made for ourselves on our own moral responsibility, and in such a way that each is given its due and none becomes a tyrant; the effort to address ourselves to real and not imaginary situations; and the effort to support our proposals with relevant arguments in which conjectures are not confused with certainties nor opinion with demonstrable truth.

'Political Discourse' is published here for the first time.

PART TWO

Dissecting rationalism

Rational conduct

The word *rational* has been strangely
abused of late times.
COLERIDGE
Aids to Reflection

The word *Reason*, and the epithets connected with it—*Rational*
and *Reasonable*—have enjoyed a long history which has be-
queathed to them a legacy of ambiguity and confusion. Like mir-
rors, they have reflected the changing notions of the world and of
human faculty which have flowed over our civilization in the last
two thousand years; image superimposed upon image has left us
with a cloudy residue. Any man may be excused when he is puzzled
by the question how he ought to use these words, and in particular
how he ought to use them in relation to human conduct and to
politics; for, in the first place, these words come before us as attributes of 'argument', and what is puzzling is the analogy in which
they are applied to 'conduct'. The philosopher may succeed in dis-
entangling the confusion which springs from merely crooked thinking, and the historian in telling the story of the ambiguity and in
making sense of it without the help of those adventitious aids, the
categories of truth and error. My purpose here is to seek a satisfactory way of using the word *Rational* in connection with conduct,
and to explore some of the territory which opens up in the process:
the impulse is both philosophical and historical.

ONE

I will begin with the assumption that when we speak of human behaviour and the management of our affairs as 'rational', we mean to commend it. 'Rational conduct' is something no man is required to be ashamed of. It is usually held that something more than 'rationality' is required in order to make conduct either endearing or saintly, or to make the management of affairs a dazzling success; but, generally speaking, it belongs to our tradition to find 'rationality' a laudable quality, or, at least, to find irrationality something proper to be avoided. We are, then, to consider an idea which in relation to human conduct implies commendation. Our civilization, it is true, has acquired a parallel vocabulary in which 'rational' is a word of denigration, but the spring of this rebound was an opposition to a narrowing of human sympathies, a restriction of what was thought admirable and proper to be done which had become reflected in the word, rather than a denial of all standards of propriety.

Secondly, I shall assume that the word 'rational', when used in connection with human conduct, refers, in the first place, to a manner of behaving and only derivatively to an action in respect of what it achieves or of the success with which it accomplishes what was intended. Thus, to behave 'rationally' is to behave 'intelligently', and whether such behaviour is pragmatically successful will depend upon circumstances other than its 'rationality'. This, again, coincides with usage; a 'lunatic', whose behaviour we recognize as 'irrational', is not always unsuccessful in achieving his designs, and we know that, even in argument, a correct conclusion may be reached in spite of false reasoning.

Ever since the eighteenth century we have had presented to us a variety of forms of behaviour or projects of activity, each recommended on account of its 'rationality'. There have been 'rational educaton', 'rational agriculture', 'rational diet', 'rational dress', to say nothing of 'rational religion', and 'rational spelling'. The segregation of the sexes in education, eating meat and drinking intoxicants were, for example, held to be 'irrational'. One famous protagonist of rational dress asserted that a shirt-collar which did not leave space for the insertion of a loaf of bread was irrationally restrictive of the flow of air to the body; and the wearing of a hat has frequently been said to be 'irrational'. But the expression 'rational dress' was applied, in particular, in Victorian times, to an extraordinary garment affected by girls on bicycles, and to be observed in the illustrations of the *Punch* of the period. Bloomers were asserted to be the 'rational dress' for girl cyclists. And as a means to putting straight our own ideas of 'rationality' we could do worse than to consider what was being thought by those who asserted the 'rationality' of this garment.[1]

There is little doubt about what they were thinking of in the first place. They were concentrating their attention upon the activity of *propelling* a bicycle. The things to be considered, and to be related to one another, were a bicycle of a certain design and the structure of the human body. All considerations other than these were dismissed because they were believed to be of no account in determining the 'rationality' of the dress to be designed. And, in particular, the designers were decided not to take account of current prejudice, convention or folklore, concerning feminine dress; from the standpoint of 'rationality' these must be considered only as limiting circumstances. Consequently, the first step in the project of designing a 'rational' dress for this purpose must be a certain emptying of the mind, a conscious effort to get rid of preconceptions. Of course knowledge of a certain sort would be required— knowledge of mechanics and anatomy—but the greater part of a man's thoughts would appear as an encumbrance in this enterprise, as a distraction from which it was necessary to avert the attention. If one were an investor anxious to employ a designer on this project, one might do well to consider a Chinese, for example, rather than an Englishman, because he would be less distracted by irrelevant considerations; just as the South American republics applied to Bentham for a 'rational' constitution. The 'rationality' sought by these Victorian designers was, then, an eternal and a

---

[1] Whether Mrs Bloomer herself made this assertion, or whether it was made by others on behalf of her invention, I do not know.

universal quality; something rescued from the world of mere opinion and set in a world of certainty. They might make mistakes; and if they were not mistakes in mechanics and anatomy (which would be unlikely), they would be the mistakes of a mind not firmly enough insulated from preconception, a mind not yet set free. Indeed, they did make a mistake; impeded by prejudice, their minds paused at bloomers instead of running on to 'shorts'—clearly so much more complete a solution of their chosen problem. Or was it a mistake? Perhaps it was, instead, some dim recognition of a more profound understanding of 'rationality' which made them stop there. We must consider the possibility later on.

Now, the questions we may ask ourselves are, why were bloomers thought to be a 'rational' form of dress for girl cyclists? And why was this way of going about things considered to be pre-eminently 'rational'? In general the answers to these questions are, first, Because they were adapted to circumstances—bloomers were a successful solution of the specific problem set; if the bicycle to be propelled had been of a different design (if, for example, arms and not legs had been the propelling limb) the clothing considered 'rational' would have been of a different design. And secondly, Because the solution sprang (or seemed to spring) solely from the reflective consideration of the problem set—bloomers were a 'rational' form of dress because the act of designing them (or the act of wearing them) sprang from an antecedent act of independent reflective effort, undistracted by 'irrelevant' considerations. Here, in short, was an example of the much advertised 'rational method' in action.

TWO

The view we are to consider[2] takes *purpose* as the distinctive mark of 'rationality' in conduct: 'rational' activity is behaviour in which an independently premeditated end is pursued and which is determined solely by that end. This end may be an external result to be achieved, or it may be the enjoyment of the activity itself. To play a

[2] Professor Ginsberg in *Reason and Unreason in Society* gives an account of the view I am considering here.

game in order to win (and perhaps to win a prize), and to play it for its own sake, for the enjoyment of it, are both purposive activities. Further, 'rational' conduct is behaviour *deliberately* directed to the achievement of a *formulated* purpose and is governed solely by that purpose. There may be other, perhaps unavoidable, consequences or results springing from the conduct, but these must be regarded as extraneous, fortuitous and 'irrational' because they are unwanted and no part of the design. Bloomers were not designed to shock Victorian sensibility, to amuse or to distract, but to provide a form of dress precisely suitable for cycling. The designers did not say to themselves, 'Let us invent something amusing'; nor, on the other hand, did they think that the 'absurdity' of their creation was in any degree a qualification of its 'rationality': indeed, 'absurdity' is so much a common feature of all the works of designers inspired by this notion of 'rationality' that it could normally be taken as a sign of success. 'Rational' conduct will, then, usually, have not only a specific end, but also a simple end; for when the end is in fact complex, activity can be efficiently directed towards its achievement only when, either the complexity is presented as a series of simple ends (the achievement of one leading on to the achievement of the next and so to the final end), or where the simple components of the complex end are seen to be related to the specific components of the activity. Hence, in 'rational behaviour', the necessity of a strict formulation of the end to be pursued; the decision of the designer of bloomers to confine his attention to mechanics and anatomy and to neglect all other considerations. 'Rational' activity is activity in search of a certain, a conclusive answer to a question, and consequently the question must be formulated in such a way that it admits of such an answer.

Now, the deliberate direction of activity to the achievement of a specific end can be successful only when the necessary means are available or procurable and when the power exists of detecting and appropriating from the means which are available those which are necessary. Consequently, there will be in 'rational' conduct, not only a premeditated purpose to be achieved, but also a separately premeditated selection of the means to be employed. And all this requires reflection and a high degree of detachment. The calculated choice of end and means both involves and provides a resistance to the indiscriminate flow of circumstances. One step at a time is the rule here; and each step is taken in ignorance of what the next is to be. The 'rationality' of conduct, then, on this view of it, springs from something that we do *before* we act; and activity is 'rational' on account of its being generated in a certain manner.

A further determination of this so-called 'rational' conduct may be found in the kinds of behaviour it excludes or opposes itself to. First, merely capricious conduct will be excluded; conduct, that is, which has no end settled in advance. Secondly, it will oppose itself to merely impulsive conduct—conduct from which there is absent the necessary element of reflective choice of means to achieve the desired end. Thirdly, this 'rational' conduct is in permanent opposition to conduct which is not governed by some deliberately accepted rule or principle or canon and which does not spring from the explicit observance of a formulated principle. Further, it excludes conduct which springs from the unexamined authority of a tradition, a custom or a habit of behaviour. For, although achievement of a purpose may be embedded in a merely traditional mode of conduct, the purpose itself is not disentangled, and a man may remain true to the tradition while being wholly ignorant of any propositional formulation of the end pursued. For example, certain procedures in the House of Commons may, in fact, achieve certain specific purposes, but since they were not expressly designed to achieve these purposes their character as means to ends often remains hidden and unformulated. And lastly, I think that activity in pursuit of an end for which the necessary means are known to be absent may fairly be said to be excluded; behaviour of this sort is not 'rational'.

Let us explore the matter a little more deeply. But it must be made clear, before we begin, that what we are considering is presented to us as, taken by itself, a possible (and a valuable) *mode of conduct*, a manner of behaviour, and not merely a manner of thinking about behaviour. It may be admitted that human beings do not often achieve this mode of conduct; and it may be agreed, without detriment to the view we are considering, that the usual behaviour

of the major part of mankind does not appear to be of this character, but is something very much less disciplined. But the view we
are to investigate is that this is a possible mode of conduct, that
concrete activity can spring up in this manner and that on account
of it springing up in this manner it may be called 'rational'. What,
then, we may inquire, are the assumptions of this view, and what
is the validity of these assumptions?

It would appear that the first assumption is that men have a
power of reasoning about things, of contemplating propositions
about activities, and of putting these propositions in order and
making them coherent. And it is assumed, further, that this is a
power independent of any other powers a man may have, and something from which his activity can *begin*. And activity is said to be
'rational' (or 'intelligent') on account of being preceded by the exercise of this power, on account of a man having 'thought' in a certain manner before he acted. 'Rational' conduct is conduct springing from an antecedent process of 'reasoning'. In order that a man's
conduct should be wholly 'rational', he must be supposed to have
the power of first imagining and choosing a purpose to pursue, of
defining that purpose clearly and selecting fit means to achieve it;
and this power must be wholly independent, not only of tradition
and of the uncontrolled relics of his fortuitous experience of the
world, but also of the activity itself to which it is a preliminary. And
for a number of men to enjoy wholly 'rational' conduct together, it
must be supposed that they have in common a power of this sort
and that the exercise of it will lead them all to the same conclusions
and issue in the same form of activity.

There are, of course, various well-known but crude formulations of this supposition but we need not concern ourselves with
them. The power in question has been hypostatized and given a
name; it is called 'Reason'. And it has been supposed that the
human mind must contain in its composition a native faculty of
'Reason', a light whose brightness is dimmed only by education, a
piece of mistake-proof apparatus, an oracle whose magic word is
truth. But if this is going further than is either wise or necessary,
what does seem unavoidable (if there is to be this power) is the sup-

position that a man's mind can be separated from its contents and its activities. What needs to be assumed is the mind as a neutral instrument, as a piece of apparatus. Long and intensive training may be necessary in order to make the best use of this piece of machinery; it is an engine which must be nursed and kept in trim. Nevertheless, it is an independent instrument, and 'rational' conduct springs from the exercise of it.

The mind, according to this hypothesis, is an independent instrument capable of dealing with experience. Beliefs, ideas, knowledge, the contents of the mind, and above all the activities of men in the world, are not regarded as themselves mind, or as entering into the composition of mind, but as adventitious, posterior acquisitions of the mind, the results of mental activity which the mind might or might not have possessed or undertaken. The mind may acquire knowledge or cause bodily activity, but it is something that may exist destitute of all knowledge, and in the absence of any activity; and where it has acquired knowledge or provoked activity, it remains independent of its acquisition or its expression in activity. It is steady and permanent, while its filling of knowledge is fluctuating and often fortuitous. Further, it is supposed that this permanent mental instrument, though it exists from birth, is capable of being trained. But what is called a 'trained mind' is, like the schoolboy's tears over a proposition in Euclid, a *consequence* of learning and activity, and is not a *conclusion* from it. Hence, mental training may take the form either of a purely functional exercise (like gymnastics), or of an exercise which incidentally gets us somewhere, like running to catch a bus. The mind may be trained by 'pelmanism' or by learning Latin grammar. Lastly, it is supposed that the mind will be most successful in dealing with experience when it is least prejudiced with already acquired dispositions or knowledge: the open, empty or free mind, the mind without disposition, is an instrument which attracts truth, repels superstition and is alone the spring of 'rational' judgment and 'rational' conduct. Consequently, the purely formal exercise of the mind will normally be considered a superior sort of training to the mixed exercise which involves a particular 'knowledge how' and unavoidably leaves behind some relic of acquired disposition. And the first training of a mind already infected with a disposition will be a process of purification, of getting rid of accumulated special knowledge and skill— a process of re-establishing virginal detachment. Childhood is, unfortunately, a period during which, from the lack of a trained mind, we give admittance to a whole miscellany of beliefs, dispositions, knowledge not in the form of propositions; the first business of the adult is to disencumber his mental apparatus of these prejudices. This, then, is 'intelligence', the 'rational' part of man; and human activity is to be counted 'rational' if and when it is preceded and caused by the exercise of this 'intelligence'.

THREE

Now, it may appear that what I am describing is a fanciful view of things, held only by a few eccentrics who need not be taken seriously and whose assertions should not be taken *au pied de la lettre*. But this is not so. It is a view, a theory, which has a respectable place in the history of philosophy; and philosophers have done much to encourage the ordinary man to think in this manner. It is true that many who speak in a way which leads us to suppose that they hold some such theory would disclaim the theory while preserving the manner of speech; but these should be asked to explain what they mean. As a point of view this is common enough; it is shared, for example, by all the cruder advocates of mental training in place of education. It gives meaning to the common assertion that such and such an action or measure is 'logical', and that because it is 'logical' it should be performed or set on foot. To this view belongs the principle of *la carrière ouverte aux talents*, the notion that the members of the Civil Service should 'have no qualifications other than their personal abilities', and the suggestion that we should teach children how to use the English language but without encumbering their minds with English literature.[3] The view we are considering is not, I think, an invention of my own; it has ad-

---

[3] C. D. Darlington, *The Conflict of Science and Society.*

herents in every department of life. It sees 'rationality' in conduct as the product of a determinate, independent instrument, and asserts that the 'rational' way of going about things is to go about them under the sole guidance of this instrument.

The appearance which conduct would tend to assume if it conformed to this notion of 'rationality' is not in any doubt. Activity would be bent towards the performance of actions in pursuit of preconceived and formulated ends, actions determined wholly by the ends sought and from which fortuitous and unwanted consequences had, so far as possible, been excluded. Its aim would be, first, to establish a proposition, to determine a purpose to be pursued, secondly, to determine the means to be employed to achieve that (and no other) end, and, thirdly, to act. Human behaviour would appear to be broken up into a series of problems to be solved, purposes to be achieved and a series of individual actions performed in pursuit of these ends. The unprejudiced consideration of every project would take place of policy, precedent and prescription would be avoided (so far as possible) in determining enterprise, and the man who had a formula would come to oust the man who had none.

Now, it is necessary to be guarded in speaking of the sort of activity which might be supposed to spring up in response to the ideal of 'rational' conduct we have before us, because what we are considering is not, in fact, a way of behaving, but a theory of behaviour. And since, as I hope to show, it is an erroneous theory, a misdescription of human behaviour, it is impossible to produce any clear and genuine example of behaviour which fits it. If this is 'rational' behaviour, then it is not merely undesirable; it is in fact impossible. Men do not behave in this way, because they cannot. No doubt those who have held this theory have thought that they were describing a possible form of behaviour; and by calling it 'rational', they recommended it as desirable: but they were under an illusion. No doubt, also, wherever this theory is current, behaviour will *tend* to conform to the pattern it suggests; but it will not succeed. The practical danger of an erroneous theory is not that it may persuade people to act in an undesirable manner, but that it may confuse activity by putting it on a false scent. But it is with the theory itself that we are concerned.

FOUR

It is no secret that this view of 'rationality' in conduct leaves something to be desired. Criticism has fastened upon many of the details, and some of it has been cogent enough to make necessary extensive repairs to the theory. I do not myself wish to direct attention to defect in detail, but to what seems to me to be the main short-coming. And I believe that when the precise character of the theory is perceived, it will be seen to collapse under the weight of its own imperfections. My view is that this is not a satisfactory notion of *rational* conduct because it is not a satisfactory account of any sort of conduct.

Let us begin with the idea of 'the mind' or 'intelligence' which is at the centre of this theory. The notion is: that first there is something called 'the mind', that this mind acquires beliefs, knowledge, prejudices—in short, a filling—which remain nevertheless a mere appendage to it, that it causes bodily activities, and that it works best when it is unencumbered by an acquired disposition of any sort. Now, this mind I believe to be a fiction; it is nothing more than an hypostatized activity. Mind as we know it is the offspring of knowledge and activity; it is composed entirely of thoughts. You do not first have a mind, which acquires a filling of ideas and then makes distinctions between true and false, right and wrong, reasonable and unreasonable, and then, as a third step, causes activity. Properly speaking the mind has no existence apart from, or in advance of, these and other distinctions. These and other distinctions are not acquisitions; they are constitutive of the mind. Extinguish in a man's mind these and other distinctions, and what is extinguished is not merely a man's 'knowledge' (or part of it), but the mind itself. What is left is not a neutral, unprejudiced instrument, a pure intelligence, but nothing at all. The whole notion of the mind as an apparatus for thinking is, I believe, an error; and it is the error at the root of this particular view of the nature of 'rationality' in conduct. Remove that, and the whole conception collapses.

But further, and following from this, it is an error to suppose that conduct could ever have its spring in the sort of activity which is misdescribed by hypostatizing a 'mind' of this sort; that is, from the power of considering abstract propositions about conduct. That such a power exists is not to be doubted; but its prerequisite is conduct itself. This activity is not something that can exist in advance of conduct; it is the result of reflection upon conduct, the creature of a subsequent analysis of conduct. And this goes, not only for conduct in the narrow sense, but for activity of every sort, for the activity of the scientist, for example, or of the craftsman, no less than for the activity in politics and in the ordinary conduct of life. And consequently it is preposterous, in the strict meaning of the word, to maintain that activity can derive from this kind of thinking, and it is unwise to recommend that it should do so by calling activity 'rational' only when it appears to have this spring. *Doing* anything both depends upon and exhibits knowing how to do it; and though part (but never the whole) of knowing how to do it can subsequently be reduced to knowledge in the form of propositions (and possibly to ends, rules and principles), these propositions are neither the spring of the activity nor are they in any direct sense regulative of the activity.

The characteristic of the carpenter, the scientist, the painter, the judge, the cook, and of any man in the ordinary conduct of life, and in his relations with other people and with the world around him, is a knowledge, not of certain propositions about themselves, their tools, and the materials in which they work, but a knowledge of how to decide certain questions; and this knowledge is the condition of the exercise of the power to construct such propositions. Consequently, if 'rationality' is to represent a desirable quality of an activity, it cannot be the quality of having independently premeditated propositions about the activity before it begins. And this applies to propositions about the end or purpose of an activity no less than to any other kind of proposition. It is an error to call an activity 'rational' on account of its end having been specifically determined in advance and in respect of its achieving that end to the exclusion of all others, because there is in fact no way of determining an end for activity in advance of the activity itself; and if there were, the spring of activity would still remain in knowing how to act in pursuit of that end and not in the mere fact of having formulated an end to pursue. A cook is not a man who first has vision of a pie and then tries to make it; he is a man skilled in cookery, and both his projects and his achievements spring from that skill. 'Good' English is not something that exists in advance of how English is written (that is to say, English literature); and the knowledge that such and such is a sloppy, ambiguous construction, or is 'bad grammar', is not something that can be known independently and in advance of knowing how to write the language.

My view is, then, that this project of finding a mode of conduct which, in this sense, is 'rational' is misconceived. The instrumental mind does not exist, and if it did it would always lack the power to be the spring of any concrete activity whatever.

Nevertheless, it is undeniable that men for long enough have deliberately tried to behave in this sense 'rationally'. They have believed that 'rational' conduct of this sort has a pre-eminent virtue. They have been conscious often of a failure to divest themselves of the encumbrance of other springs of action, but they have been pleased with themselves whenever they have believed that they had attended only to the voice of this 'reason'. And I think, perhaps, what helps to explain the illusion is the false but plausible theory of education which makes it seem not an illusion. We may be agreed that it is preposterous to suppose an activity can spring from the premeditation of propositions about the activity, but we are apt to believe that in order to teach an activity it is necessary to have converted our knowledge of it into a set of propositions—the grammar of a language, the rules of research, the principles of experiment and verification, the canons of good workmanship—and that in order to learn an activity we must begin with such propositions. It would be foolish, of course, to deny that this device has a pedagogic value. But it must be observed that, not only are these rules, etc., these propositions about the activity, an abridgment of the teacher's concrete knowledge of the activity (and therefore posterior to the activity itself), but learning them is never more than the meanest part of education in an activity. They can be taught, but they are not the only things that can be learned from a teacher. To work alongside a practised scientist or craftsman is an opportunity not only to learn the rules, but to acquire also a direct knowledge of how he sets about his business (and, among other things, a knowledge of how and when to apply the rules); and until this is acquired nothing of great value has been learned. But it is only when we think of this as of no account in comparison with the learning of the rules themselves, or when we reject it as not teaching in the proper sense, or not properly knowledge, that the character of learning an activity seems to support the view that activity itself can spring from independently premeditating propositions about it.

But anyone who attempts to explain the lure of this 'rationality' must venture deep into the hidden history of European mental dispositions, particularly in the last four centuries. No doubt it is idle to fix upon specific causes, but I think it will be found that three circumstances have contributed greatly to the attraction which this 'rationality' has for us. First, there has been a laudable conviction that mental honesty, disinterestedness, absence of prejudice, are intellectual virtues of the highest value. But this conviction has unfortunately been combined, in a strange confusion of mind, with the belief that disinterestedness is possible only to a mind which is wholly self-moved[4]—that is, a mind devoid of acquired disposition. To value intellectual honesty and at the same time to identify it with activity specifically determined to be 'honest', and not to recognize it as an acquired skill of which there are various idioms each with its appropriate circumstances, is the first step towards this unfortunate ideal of 'rationality'.

Secondly, there has been a passionate desire for certainty —about matters of belief and conduct—which has been combined with the conviction that certainty is possible only in respect of something we have been 'given', and not in respect of anything we

[4] It would be difficult to find a more persuasive account of this doctrine than that contained in Spinoza's *Ethics*.

have ascertained, that certainty is a gift of grace, not a reward of work. Certainty, it seemed, must be something with which we must *begin*; and only propositional knowledge, independent of activity, seemed to offer it. The craving for this sort of mistake-proof certainty is not, I think, so creditable as the desire for intellectual honesty: indeed, I think the instrumental mind may be regarded as, in some respects, the relic of a belief in magic.

And thirdly, there has been in many departments of life, and particularly in politics, a growing ignorance of how to go about things and a more frequent appearance of situations which, because they seem to be 'new', find us unprepared with a ready means of dealing with them. When in politics you do not know how to behave, you will tend to cry down the value and necessity of this sort of knowledge, and to cry up the value and necessity of a free and open mind supposed to be endowed with the capacity of knowing in advance of activity. An example of this is to be found in the French political reformers of the time of Louis XIV. The state of France, they were convinced, was desperate; but there, hidden in the traditions of French government, were institutions, ways of doing things, long fallen into desuetude, to which the reformers could and did appeal. They possessed knowledge of how affairs had been conducted, and this knowledge determined their proposals. The state of Europe, also, was desperate. But here such knowledge was absent; Europe, so far as they knew, never had been organized. And since what was needed had to be invented (as they thought) *de novo*, their plans for European peace were presented as creatures of pure intelligence. The difference between the plans of the Abbé de St Pierre for France and his plans for Europe is remarkable. Knowledge of how to behave, of course, is never wholly absent; at this time of day (or even at that) the human race has something to call upon, and in fact calls upon it. There is no danger that anyone will succeed in achieving a purely 'rational' politics in this sense. But the resort of mankind to such genuine knowledge as it has, is often hindered by this unhappy attachment to a false ideal of freedom of mind and an abstract and attenuated 'rationality'. And politics is a field of activity peculiarly subject to the lure of this 'rational' ideal. If you start being merely 'intelligent' about a boiler or an electrical generator you are likely to be pulled up short by an explosion; but in politics all that happens is war and chaos, which you do not immediately connect with your error. The doctrinaire in politics is not a man, the spring of whose activity is independent propositional knowledge about an end to be pursued, but a man who fails to recognize what the true spring is. Usually he is a man who, having rejected as worthless the current knowledge of how to behave in politics, falls back upon his knowledge of how to behave in other activities (which is not always a good guide) while erroneously supposing that he has fallen back upon knowledge independent of any activity and provided by some potentially infallible 'intelligence'.

To the firm believer in this idea of 'rationality', the spectacle of human behaviour (in himself and in others) departing from its norm may be expected to confirm his suspicion that 'rational' conduct of this sort is difficult, but not to shake his faith in its possibility and desirability. He will deplore the unregulated conduct which, because it is externally unregulated, he will think of as 'irrational'. But it will always be difficult for him to entertain the notion that what he identified as 'rational' conduct is in fact impossible, not because it is liable to be swamped by 'insane and irrational springs of wickedness in most men', but because it involves a misrepresentation of the nature of human conduct. He will readily admit that he has been the victim of an illusion; but the exact character of the illusion will elude him. An interesting example of this is afforded by J. M. Keynes's essay, *My Early Beliefs*,[5] where a candid attempt to supersede what he detected as a too narrow idea of 'rationality' in behaviour is ruined by a failure to carry out a similar reform in the idea of 'irrationality'. In the end, Keynes still retains the idea of 'rational' conduct as that which springs from an independently premeditated purpose, and he modifies his original exclusive attachment to such conduct by admitting that much of what it excludes (which he identifies as 'vulgar passions', 'volcanic and even wicked impulses', 'spontaneous outbursts') is valuable

[5] J. M. Keynes, *Two Memoirs*.

while nevertheless remaining 'irrational'. This is a confused position; and from confusion of this sort a fresh attempt to determine the meaning of 'rationality' in conduct is not likely to spring. Both this, and the current despair of the possibility of rational conduct (the current 'irrationalism'), must be put on one side if we are to make any advance.

FIVE

Let us return to the activity of the designers of Victorian 'rational dress', and to the activity of those who wore it because they believed themselves to be behaving 'rationally' by doing so. We have supposed (not without some grounds) that what they *thought* they were doing was to design a garment suited to a particular purpose, the purpose of *propelling* a bicycle. They premeditated their purpose, and they selected a precise and narrow purpose in order to premeditate it without distraction; and they applauded their activity as 'rational' because of the manner in which they went about their enterprise. The result was 'rational' because it achieved a set and premeditated purpose and because it sprang from this prior act of theorizing. But we have observed that there were elements in the situation which might lead us to doubt whether what they *thought* they were doing (and on account of which they attributed 'rationality' to their conduct) properly coincided with what they were in fact doing. Why did their enterprise pause at 'bloomers' and not pass on to 'shorts'? The answer that they merely made a mistake, that this stopping-place represents a failure of 'rationality', is too easy. Their invention may be taken to indicate, not that they failed in their chosen enterprise, but that they were guided in fact by considerations which they believed themselves to have escaped and on account of this escape were behaving 'rationally'. Bloomers are not the answer to the question, What garment is best adapted to the activity of *propelling* a bicycle of a certain design? but to the question, What garment combines within itself the qualities of being well adapted to the activity of propelling a bicycle and of being suitable, all things considered, for an English girl to be seen in when riding a bicycle in 1880? And, unknown to themselves, it was the project of answering this question which moved the designers. But if we credit them with a belief in the idea of 'rationality' which we have found to be unsatisfactory, then we may suppose that they would regard activity in pursuit of this purpose as wanting in 'rationality'. It is true that the activity would spring from a premeditated end, and consequently would have some flavour of 'rationality' about it; but it would be a very different sort of activity from what they were accustomed to call 'rational'. It would be an activity in principle indistinguishable from that of *any* dress designer. In the first place, this is a question that *clearly* could not be answered by 'pure intelligence'; it demands something more than the instrumental mind. This, of course, is true also of the first question, the question we supposed to be actually in the mind of the designer; but its truth was obscured because it seemed that in order to answer this first question the operation called for was primarily an emptying of the mind. Here, however, something much more positive is required. No capitalist with any sense would think of entrusting the enterprise to a Chinese; his ignorance of English taste, tradition, folklore and prejudice in respect of women's clothing would be a hopeless handicap. And though there is, here, a premeditated end to be pursued, it is an exceedingly complex end; there is a tension within the purpose itself—anatomical and mechanical principles pulling one way, perhaps, and social custom another. It is a question which admits of no *certain* answer, because it involves an assessment of opinion; and it is one which cannot be answered once and for all, because the problem is tied to place and time. In short, this is hardly a 'rational' question in the sense of 'rationality' we have so far been considering. And yet, I think it is the question which the designers of 'rational dress' were, in fact, trying to answer, and which they succeeded in answering when they produced bloomers.[6]

---

[6] Readers of Tolstoy's *Anna Karenina* will remember the discussion between Levin and Sviajsky about 'rational' agriculture. For Sviajsky 'rational' agriculture consists wholly in the introduction of machinery, proper methods of accounting, etc. But Levin sees at once that something has been forgotten: it is not 'rational' to give complicated machinery for the use of peasants who do not know how to use it and who have a contempt for it. What is 'rational' in Germany is not 'rational' in Russia. You must educate your peasant and adapt the level of your technical improvements to the level of his education. Levin knows (but he

Here we have reached something more like a piece of concrete human activity, and our question must be, In what respect can this be considered 'rational' activity? The unregenerate believer in the idea or 'rationality' which we have seen fit to reject, will reply that it is 'rational' because it is activity springing from a premeditated purpose, though the purpose here is neither simple nor capable of being premeditated by mere 'intelligence'; its independence of the activity is at least doubtful. He will contend that nothing has yet been said which destroys the old criterion; this is 'rational' activity because it is premeditated, 'reasoned' activity. And, although our original supposition was that the end achieved by the dress-designers was not in fact premeditated by them (what they set themselves was something much narrower than what they achieved), it would be wise to give him his point, because there seems, so far, no reason why it should not have been premeditated. But the point is good only because we have not yet achieved a concrete view of human activity; we are still dealing with abstractions, though not with such narrow abstractions as the high and dry believer in the instrumental mind.

SIX

Now, if we consider the concrete activity of an historian, a cook, a scientist, a politician or any man in the ordinary conduct of life, we may observe that each is engaged upon answering questions of a certain sort, and that his characteristic is that he knows (or thinks he knows) the way to go about finding the answer to that sort of question. But the questions which he knows to belong to his sort of activity are not known to be such in advance of the activity of trying to answer them: in pursuing these questions, and not others, he is not obeying a rule or following a principle which comes from outside the activity, he is pursuing an activity which, in general, he knows how to pursue. It is the activity itself which defines the ques-

does not know how to explain) that an activity consists in knowing how to behave; Sviajsky does not know this, and represents a typical 'rationalist' position. *Anna Karenina*, Pt. III, Chs. 27, 28; Pt. IV, Ch. 3.

tions as well as the manner in which they are answered. It is, of course, not impossible to formulate certain principles which may seem to give precise definition to the kind of question a particular sort of activity is concerned with; but such principles are derived from the activity and not the activity from the principles. And even if a man has some such propositional knowledge about his activity, his knowledge of his activity always goes far beyond what is contained in these propositions. It is clear, then, that the activity of these men (and I would say all other activity also) is something that comes first, and is something into which each one gradually finds his way: at no time is he wholly ignorant of it; there is no identifiable beginning. Of course, the activity in general does not exist in advance of the activities which compose it; it consists wholly in knowing how to tackle problems of a certain sort. But it does exist in advance of the specific engagement a particular scientist or cook may have undertaken. How, then (if this is as clear as I think it is), do we get the illusion that the activity of these and other men could spring from and be governed by an end, a purpose or by rules independent of the activity itself and capable of being reflected upon in advance, with the possible corollary that, in respect of this spring and government, it should be called 'rational'.

Each man engaged in a certain kind of activity selects a particular question and engages himself to answer this question. He has before him a particular project: to determine the weight of the moon, to bake a sponge cake, to paint a portrait, to disclose the mediations which comprise the story of the Peninsular War, to come to an agreement with a foreign power, to educate his son—or whatever it may be. And, with the normal neglect with which a man engaged upon a particular task treats what is not immediately before him, he supposes that his activity springs from and is governed solely by his project. No man engaged in a particular task has in the forefront of his attention the whole context and implications of that engagement. Activity is broken up into actions, and actions come to have a false appearance of independence. And further, this abstraction of view is normally increased when what we observe is somebody else's activity. Every trade but our own seems to be comprised wholly of tricks and abridgments. There is, then, no mystery how it can come to be supposed that an activity may spring from an independently determined purpose to be pursued: the mistake arises from endowing a whole activity with the character of a single action when it is abstracted from the activity to which it belongs, from endowing, for example, the activity of cooking with the character of making a particular pie when the maker is assumed not to be a cook.

But if our cook or scientific practitioner were to consider the implications of his particular actions he would rapidly reach two conclusions. First, he would observe that, in pursuing his particular project, his actions were being determined not solely by his premeditated end, but by what may be called the traditions of the activity to which his project belonged. It is because he knows how to tackle problems of this sort that he is able to tackle this particular problem. He would observe, in other words, that the spring and government of his actions lay in his *skill*, his knowledge of how to go about his business, his participation in the concrete activity in relation to which his particular engagement is an abstraction. And though his participation in this concrete activity (the activity of being a cook or a scientist) may on some occasions appear to take the form of the application of a rule or the pursuit of a purpose, he would see at once that this rule or this purpose derived from the activity and not vice versa, and that the activity itself could never as a whole be reduced to the pursuit of an end or the application of a rule determined in advance of the activity.

But if his first observation is that, whatever the appearances to the contrary, no actual engagement can ever spring from or be governed by an independently premeditated end—the problems put down for solution or the project selected for pursuit—and that if this were all there was, his particular activity could never begin, his second observation will be more radical: he will observe that it is impossible even to project a purpose for activity in advance of the activity itself. Not only is his participation in the concrete activity which is involved in the solution of this sort of problem the source of his power to *solve* his particular problem and is the spring of the activity which goes to solve it, but also it is his participation in this concrete activity which presents the problem itself. Both the problems and the course of investigation leading up to their solution are already hidden in the activity, and are drawn out only by a process of abstraction. It is necessary to possess a knowledge of how to go about it (that is, to be already within an activity) before you embark upon a particular project, but it is equally necessary to have the same sort of knowledge in order to formulate a project. A particular action, in short, never begins in its particularity, but always in an idiom or a tradition of activity. A man who is not already a scientist cannot even formulate a scientific problem; what he will formulate is a problem which a connoisseur will at once recognize *not* to be a 'scientific' problem because it is incapable of being considered in a 'scientific' manner. Similarly, a connoisseur in historical inquiry will at once recognize that a question such as, Was the French Revolution a mistake? is a non-historical question.

We have come back, then, to the conclusions we reached earlier on, but in a more radical form. Activity springing from and governed by an independently premeditated purpose is impossible; the power of premeditating purpose, of formulating rules of conduct and standards of behaviour in advance of the conduct and activity itself is not available to us. To represent the spring and government of activity thus is to misrepresent it. To suggest that activity ought to be of this character and to try to force it into this pattern, is to corrupt it without being able to endow it with the desired character. To speak of such conduct as 'rational' conduct is meaningless because it is not conduct at all but only an emaciated shadow of conduct. And it may be remarked also that if we agree it to be foolish to call conduct 'rational' on account of its being wholly determined by an independently premeditated purpose, we must agree further that it should not be called 'rational' in respect of it achieving its purpose, in respect (that is) of its *success*. The achievement of a desired result is not the mark of 'rationality' in conduct because, as we have seen, it is only by a process of neglect and abstraction that conduct can be supposed to spring from the desire to achieve a specific result.

SEVEN

So far our conclusions appear to be mainly negative, but the process of exploration has I think disclosed what I take to be a more profitable view of 'rationality' in conduct. If the 'rationality' of conduct does not lie in something that has taken place in advance of the conduct—in the independent premeditation of a purpose or of a rule to be applied—if the 'rationality' of conduct is not something contributed to the conduct from some source outside the idiom of the conduct concerned, it would appear that it must be a quality or a characteristic of the conduct itself.

All actual conduct, all specific activity springs up within an already existing idiom of activity. And by an 'idiom of activity' I mean a knowledge of how to behave appropriately in the circumstances. Scientific activity is the exploration of the knowledge scientists have of how to go about asking and answering scientific questions; moral activity is the exploration of the knowledge we have of how to behave well. The questions and the problems in each case spring from the knowledge we have of how to solve them, spring from the activity itself. And we come to penetrate an idiom of activity in no other way than by practising the activity; for it is only in the practice of an activity that we can acquire the knowledge of how to practise it. We begin with what we *know*—as scientists, with what we know of how a scientist works; as moral beings, with what we know about how to behave well—and if we knew nothing we could never begin. Gradually, and by a variety of means, we improve and extend our first knowledge of how to pursue the activity. Among such means (though in a subordinate position, because it obviously depends upon the achievement of a certain level in our knowledge of how to pursue the activity) is the analysis of the activity, the definition of the rules and principles which seem to inhere in it and in reflection upon these rules and principles. But these rules and principles are mere abridgments of the activity itself; they do not exist in advance of the activity, they cannot properly be said to govern it and they cannot provide the impetus of the activity. A complete mastery of these principles may exist alongside a complete inability to pursue the activity to which they refer. For the pursuit of the activity does not consist in the application of these principles; and even if it did, the knowledge of how to apply them (the knowledge actually involved in pursuing the activity) is not given in a knowledge of them.

If, then, it is agreed that the only significant way of using the word 'rational' in relation to conduct is when we mean to indicate a quality or characteristic (and perhaps a desirable quality or characteristic) of the activity itself, then it would appear that the quality concerned is not mere 'intelligence', but *faithfulness to the knowledge we have of how to conduct the specific activity we are engaged in*. 'Rational' conduct is acting in such a way that the coherence of the idiom of activity to which the conduct belongs is preserved and possibly enhanced. This, of course, is something different from faithfulness to the principles or rules or purposes (if any have been discovered) of the activity; principles, rules and purposes are mere abridgments of the coherence of the activity, and we may easily be faithful to them while losing touch with the activity itself. And it must be observed that the faithfulness which characterizes 'rationality' is not faithfulness to something fixed and finished (for knowledge of how to pursue an activity is always in motion); it is a faithfulness which itself contributes to (and not merely illustrates) the coherence of the activity. And the implications of this view are: first, that no conduct, no action or series of actions, can be 'rational' or 'irrational' out of relation to the idiom of activity to which they belong; secondly, that 'rationality' is something that lies always *ahead*, and not *behind*, but yet it does not lie in the success with which a desired result or a premeditated end is achieved; and thirdly, that an activity as a whole (science, cooking, historical investigation, politics or poetry) cannot be said either to be 'rational' or 'irrational' unless we conceive all idioms of activity to be embraced in a single universe of activity. Let us consider where this view gets us.

EIGHT

How does it apply to the activity we call 'science'? Scientific activity is not the pursuit of a predetermined end; nobody knows where it will reach. There is no achievement, prefigured in our minds, which we can set up as a criterion by which to judge current achievements or in relation to which current engagements are a means. Its coherence does not spring from there being an over-all purpose which can be premeditated. Individual investigators may, and usually do, premeditate particular purposes, set themselves particular problems. Nevertheless, as we have seen, their activity does not spring from these purposes and is not governed by them: they arise as abstractions out of knowing how to conduct a scientific inquiry, and are never *independently* premeditated. Nor does the coherence of scientific activity lie in a body of principles or rules to be observed by the scientist, a 'scientific method'; such principles and rules no doubt exist, but they also are only abridgments of the activity which at all points goes beyond them, and goes beyond them, in particular, in the connoisseurship of knowing how and when to apply them. Its coherence lies nowhere but in the way the scientist goes about his investigation, in the traditions of scientific inquiry. These traditions are not fixed and finished, and they are not to be identified with merely current scientific opinion, or with an identifiable 'method'; they are the guide in every piece of scientific investigation and at the same time they are being extended and enlarged wherever scientists are at work. And because these traditions are not a finished achievement which can be completely prefigured in the mind of the scientist before he begins his activity (such as a 'method' might be supposed to be), conformity with them cannot properly be spoken of as itself the over-all purpose in science.

Now, the view I am recommending is that the conduct of a scientist may properly be called 'rational' in respect of its faithfulness to the traditions of scientific inquiry. And the 'irrational' scientist is not the man whose activity springs from some source other than the independent premeditation of a purpose (no man's activity could spring from this source), nor is he the man whose activity is ungoverned by pre-established rules and principles (for there are no such rules and principles), nor again is he the man who makes no observations, who achieves no results, who has nothing to show for his activity: the 'irrational' scientist is in fact, the scientific crank and the eccentric. And he is identified not by his departure from merely current scientific opinion, but by his unfaithfulness to the whole tradition of scientific inquiry, by his ignorance of how to set about a scientific investigation—an ignorance which is displayed not in the results of his activity, but in the course of his activity itself, in the questions he asks as well as in the sort of answers he is satisfied to give. And if we consider the matter I think we shall find that this, as often as not, is how we are accustomed to use the word 'rational' in this connection, though we are not always as clear as we should be about what we have excluded when we do use it in this manner.

NINE

Now, some people in general sympathy with this view of the matter will nevertheless suspect that scientific activity is a special case and that what may be true there is not true elsewhere. Consequently, in conclusion, I must try to show the relevance of this view of things to what may be called the general moral or social conduct of human beings: for I do not admit that scientific activity is, in this respect, a special case. And if there is an appearance of dogmatism in what I have got to say, that is because I have already disclosed the arguments which have persuaded me.

Human conduct, in its most general character, is energy; it is not caused by energy, it does not express or display energy, it is energy. As energy, it may appear as appetite or desire—not, of course, as undifferentiated want, but as a certain mode of want. But here again, desire is not the cause of activity; desire is being active in a certain manner. A man, that is, does not first have a 'desire' which then causes him to become active or which manifests itself in activity: to say that he has a desire for something is only another way of saying that he is being active in a certain manner—

e.g. the manner of activity involved in reaching out his hand to turn off the hot water, in making a request (such as, 'Please pass me the Dictionary' or 'Which is the way to the National Gallery?'), in looking up the times of the trains to Scotland, in contemplating with pleasure a meeting with a friend. These activities are not activities which presuppose and express or exhibit or give evidence of an antecedent state of desire; they are themselves the characteristic activities of desiring.

Now, activities of desiring are not separated and detached from one another, and the objects upon which desire is centred do not come and go at random or follow one another fortuitously. To say that a man has a character or a disposition is to say, among other things, that his activities of desiring compose a more or less coherent whole. A fresh activity of desiring appears nowhere except within an already organized whole; it does not come from the outside with the presentation of an object, but is a differentiation within an existing idiom of activity. And our knowledge of that idiom is, in the first place, our skill in managing the activity of desiring. We do not first have a desire and then set about discovering how to satisfy it; the objects of our desires are known to us in the activity of seeking them.

Social life—the life of human beings—is to know that some directions of the activity of desiring are approved and others disapproved, that some are right and others wrong. That there may be principles, or even rules, which may be seen to underlie this approval and disapproval, is not improbable; the searching intellect will always find principles. But this approval and disapproval does not spring from these principles or from a knowledge of them. They are merely abridgments, abstract definitions, of the coherence which approvals and disapprovals themselves exhibit. Nor may approval and disapproval be thought of as an additional activity, governed by an independently predetermined end to be achieved. An independently predetermined end has no more place in moral activity than it has in scientific. Approval and disapproval, that is, is not a separate activity which supervenes upon the activity of desiring, introducing norms of conduct from some external source; they are inseparable from the activity of desiring itself. Approval and disapproval are only an abstract and imperfect way of describing our unbroken knowledge of how to manage the activity of desiring; of how to behave. In short, moral judgment is not something we pronounce either before, or after, but in our moral activity.

Human activity, then, is always activity with a pattern; not a superimposed pattern, but a pattern inherent in the activity itself. Elements of this pattern occasionally stand out with a relatively firm outline; and we call these elements, customs, traditions, institutions, laws, etc. They are not, properly speaking, *expressions* of the coherence of activity, or expressions of approval and disapproval, or of our knowledge of how to behave—they *are* the coherence, they are the substance of our knowledge of how to behave. We do not first decide that certain behaviour is right or desirable and then express our approval of it in an institution; our knowledge of how to behave well is, at this point, the institution. And it is because we are not always as clear about this as we should be that we sometimes make the mistake of supposing that institutions (particularly political institutions) can be moved around from place to place as if they were pieces of machinery instead of idioms of conduct.

Now, it might be supposed that the positive problem of social conduct (that is, human conduct) is how to secure the satisfaction of approved desires; and this, indeed, is a more reasonable way of describing it than the usual negative manner—how to prevent activity taking undesirable directions. Nevertheless, this again is not a separate problem. We do not first have a desire, then approve it, and then seek out a way of adjusting it to other approved desires and a way of satisfying it. This would make sense only if we imagined that in approval and disapproval and in finding out means of satisfaction we already had a desire fully before us and were calling upon some authority outside the activity itself to settle the question of its propriety; but to imagine this is to imagine an error. What is here set down as a linear process is in fact a single whole which is never wanting of any of its parts.

So far I have emphasized the coherence of moral activity, and it is proper to do this first because moral activity begins (if it can be said to begin anywhere) in coherence. We begin with a knowledge of how to behave—not, of course, a perfect knowledge, or a knowledge which is an endowment from another world, but a knowledge which is coeval with the activity of desiring. And what I have attributed to the activity is a set in a certain direction, a current, something that may be called a prevailing sympathy. The movement in the activity does not spring from the application of some external force, and the direction is not determined by a pre-established end; it is necessary to have recourse to such ideas as these only if we have fallen into the initial error of supposing, first, an activity which begins from rest (a 'knowledge' which springs from sheer ignorance), and secondly, an activity with no direction in particular (a 'knowledge' in which truth and error, or right and wrong, are still waiting to be distinguished). But it is time to consider the things which may clog the movement or compromise the direction; to consider our ignorance of how to behave.

That moral activity should play upon the margins of current moral achievement, appealing from contemporary incoherence to the coherence of a whole moral tradition, is as normal as the activity which merely gyrates around the pivot of contemporary coherence; they are alike exhibitions of a knowledge of how to behave. In neither is the movement clogged or the direction of the movement compromised. But a genuine clog and compromise is not impossible, and it is a sufficiently common occurrence to merit being taken into account in considering the nature of moral activity. The condition may be described comprehensively as a loss of confidence in the traditional direction of moral activity, which carries with it a failure of impetus in the activity itself, and is both a symptom and a condition of a breakdown in the effectiveness of moral education (the handing on of knowledge of how to behave).[7] It is unnecessary to investigate the possible occasions of the emergence of this condition; though it is remarkable how trivial are some of the apparent causes—an earthquake, a plague, a war, or a mechanical invention, each appears to have had the power of disrupting (more or

---

[7] It seems that it was for a situation of this sort that Mencius prescribed.

less seriously) the current of moral activity, to have had the power of dispersing it into fortuitous eddies and of leading it to lose itself in random inundations of the countryside. But it is worth noting that this is a circumstance which has no exact parallel in the history of scientific activity—though in principle there is nothing in science which makes it immune from such a malady, and it may even now be sickening for an attack.

In general, the remedy for such a condition must, of course, be treatment which will result in a revival of confidence and a renewal of impetus. And, in general again, such treatment must make use of what is still unimpaired in the sufferer. The notion that a knowledge of how to behave can be permanently replaced by something else just as good, and the notion that the patient must be allowed (or even encouraged) to die in order that he may start life again on new and firmer foundations, will be entertained only by those who are wholly ignorant of the nature of moral activity. The remedy usually favoured in these cases is a transfusion of a specially rich mixture of ideals, principles, rules and purposes. And there are two conditions in which this remedy may have the desired result: first, if the ideals, principles, etc., are themselves drawn from the ailing moral tradition, or (shall we say) from the same blood-group as the patient; and secondly, if the patient can assimilate the transfusion and transform it in his own arteries from knowledge of propositions about good behaviour into a knowledge of how to behave. The first of these conditions is easily satisfied: the only principles and ideals available are in fact abridgments of the lost knowledge of how to behave. They may be presented as something more imposing— as gifts straight from the gods—and a superstitious reverence may be accorded them on account of this appearance; but it is doubtful whether this indulgence in illusion will increase the chances of the cure being effective. The second condition is more difficult to satisfy. To turn the dry bones of a morality into a living thing is by no means easy—indeed, it is utterly impossible if the sum total of our knowledge is anatomical. There is, in fact, no way in which a knowledge of how to behave can be made to spring solely from a knowledge of propositions about good behaviour. In the end, the cure depends upon the native strength of the patient; it depends upon the unimpaired relics of his knowledge of how to behave.

We have considered briefly moral activity in health and in disease: our question now is, Where in all this is 'rational' conduct? It is commonly believed (as we have seen) that there is something pre-eminently 'rational' in conduct which springs (or appears to spring) from the independent premeditation of a purpose or a rule of behaviour, and that it is 'rational' on account of the antecedent process of premeditation and on account of the success with which the purpose is achieved. And if we were to accept this view it would appear that moral conduct would be pre-eminently 'rational' when it was being treated for a diseased condition. But even this is rather more than may properly be concluded; the most that may, in fact, be claimed is that conduct is specially 'rational' when it is being cured of a disease and when the success of the treatment depends upon the illusion that the curative property of the substance injected derives from its being uncontaminated with the character of the diseased moral tradition—an illusion similar to that of the man who thinks he has found a new and independent way of living when he is really only spending his inherited capital. Of course, reflection upon the principles and ends in conduct may serve other than remedial purposes; it has a pedagogic and perhaps even a prophylactic use: the important point, however, is that it is never more than a device.

But we have seen fit to reject this whole view of the matter. This conduct may be 'rational', but if so the marks of its 'rationality' have been misconceived. Everywhere we come back to the conclusion that concrete activity is knowing how to act; and that if 'rationality' is to be properly attributed to conduct, it must be a quality of the conduct itself. On this principle, practical human conduct may be counted 'rational' in respect of its faithfulness to a knowledge of how to behave well, in respect of its faithfulness to its tradition of moral activity. No action is by itself 'rational', or is 'rational' on account of something that has gone on before; what makes it 'rational' is its place in a flow of sympathy, a current of moral activity. And there is no ground here upon which we may exclude *a priori* any type of action. An impulsive action, a 'spontaneous outburst', activity in obedience to a custom or to a rule, and an action which is preceded by a long reflective process may, alike, be 'rational'. But it is neither 'rational' nor 'irrational' on account of these or in default of these or of any similar characteristics. 'Rationality' is the certificate we give to any conduct which can maintain a place in the flow of sympathy, the coherence of activity, which composes a way of living. This coherence is not the work of a faculty called 'Reason' or of a faculty called 'Sympathy', it springs neither from a separately inspired moral sense nor from an instrumental conscience. There is, in fact, no external harmonizing power, insulated from the elements enjoying and in search of harmony. What establishes harmony and detects disharmony, is the concrete mind, a mind composed wholly of activities in search of harmony and throughout implicated in every achieved level of harmony.

And here again, it may be pointed out that this is how we are accustomed to use the word 'rational', though we do not always perceive the implications of using it in this way. When a court of law has to decide whether on a particular occasion a man used 'reasonable care', what the court is concerned with is not some abstractly 'rational' amount of care, the same in all circumstances and on all occasions, nor is it inquiring into the length and cogency of a process of reflection which may have gone on in the recesses of the man's mind before he acted—it is concerned to come to a conclusion about the action itself, to decide whether the man on the occasion used the knowledge of how to behave which he could be supposed to possess. And the decision is reached only by considering what the man actually did, and not what he may have thought before he acted. 'Reasonable care' is not something that can be known in advance and with certainty. It is the degree of care which an English jury (or judge) would expect to be exercised in given circumstances by an Englishman of ordinary knowledge, foresight and alertness. The jury or the judge is on this occasion the voice of the current of moral activity. They represent something; but they do not represent anything beyond the knowledge of how to behave well which belongs to our way of living. In short, human conduct

may be said to be 'rational' when it exhibits the sort of 'intelligence'
appropriate to the idiom of activity concerned.

"Rational Conduct" first appeared in *Cambridge Journal*, Volume IV, 1950.

The new Bentham

Jeremy Bentham died on June 6th, 1832. According to his wish, his body was preserved for the obscure purposes of science; but his ideas, quickly forgotten by his unappreciative countrymen, enjoyed a merely oblique, though extensive, survival in the views of the few men whom he influenced directly and in certain reforms and tendencies towards reform in the legal system of England. What was mortal survived; what was immortal was buried and forgotten. But now, one hundred years later, though there is no suggestion that this grotesque skeleton were better underground, there is more than one suggestion that what was so thoughtlessly buried might be unearthed. Indeed, this business of exhumation has already begun. It remains to be seen, however, whether what comes to the surface is merely a corpse—a spiritual corpse to be set beside the still unburied skeleton—or a regenerate Bentham, a man with a new life and a new meaning. Nobody gets out of his grave exactly as he was put in, but unless there is some phœnix quality in the mind of Bentham, unless he was buried alive by his contemporaries, mere exhumation will do neither him nor us any good. My business is, then, to consider this attempt to rehabilitate Jeremy Bentham, to consider the skill with which it is being performed, and to consider whether the result is something alive and with a meaning for present consciousness, or just one more of these embalmed corpses with too many of which the world is already cumbered.

But first let us consider for a moment the Bentham who was buried, the old, unregenerate Bentham. At his death, to those who did not know him and to the many who did, Bentham was, I suppose, little more than a figure of fun; an eccentric old gentleman who wrote much and published little. But to his intimates, to the 'School' which in later years he gathered round himself, he was a master, 'the great critical thinker of his age and country'. And by many others he was recognised as a figure of importance in the history of their time. Moreover, among those who have left us their thoughts on the subject, there seems to have been a considerable agreement with regard to the character of his genius. By his friends he was known as a man of acute feeling; an affectionate man, extraordinarily sensitive to the pleasure and pain of others, 'passionately fond of flowers' and with a peculiar sympathy for animals. He was a man overflowing with benevolence towards the human race; the hero of Fénelon come to life. Further, it was recognised that, as far as his intellectual activity was concerned, 'the field of practical abuses' was his field. His genius, as he says himself, was for legislation. Bentham 'combined what had not yet been done, the spirit of the Philanthropic with that of the Practical. He did not declaim about abuses; he went at once to their root; he did not idly penetrate the sophistries of Corruption; he smote Corruption herself. He was the very Theseus of legislative reform—he not only pierced the Labyrinth—he destroyed the Monster'. And the great benefit which he conferred upon his age and country lay in 'the example which he set of treating law as no peculiar mystery, but a simple piece of practical business, wherein means were to be adapted to ends, as in any other of the arts of life'. He was 'the man who found Jurisprudence a gibberish and left it a science'. And he achieved this end because he combined with a considerable knowledge of English law a considerable contempt for its precedents, its prejudices and its irrationality. But Bentham was not, for his contemporaries, merely a reformer of the law and of jurisprudence; he was 'the great critical thinker of his age and country': and the lesson of his life was 'to show that speculative philosophy, which to the superficial appears a thing so remote from the business of life and the outward interests of men, is in reality the thing on earth which most influences them'. Bentham not only reformed the law so that (as Dicey says) 'the history of legal reform in England in the nineteenth century is the story of the shadow cast by one man, Bentham', but he 'introduced for the first time precision of thought into moral and political philosophy'. And finally, according to the view which has been repeated by every writer on Bentham since Mill's astonishing essay appeared in 1838, 'it was not his *options* but his *method*, that constituted the novelty and the value of what he did'. Bentham founded not a doctrine but a method; the 'method of detail', 'of testing wholes by separating them into their parts', the method of 'exhaustive classification'. He was primarily and predominantly a master of detailed analysis, the inventor of a method of thought destined to revolutionize every department of intellectual interest.

But the defects, no less than the merits, of Bentham's genius were recognized by his contemporaries. Mill, who at the age of fifteen 'embraced Benthamism as a religion', later conceived some doubts about the competence of his master's philosophy to explain all things in heaven and earth. And particularly, Bentham's genius appeared to suffer from the fact that his life was 'secluded in a peculiar degree, by circumstances and character, from the business and intercourse of the world'. In English philosophy it had become (and to some extent still remains) a tradition to separate experience from reflection, and Mill saw Bentham as a master of reflection whose experience was peculiarly and fatally restricted. 'He had neither internal experience, nor external; the quiet, even tenor of his life, and his healthiness of mind, conspired to exclude him from both'. And consequently 'he was not a great philosopher, but he was a great reformer in philosophy'. And besides this defect, others saw in Bentham a man who 'did not appear to have entered very deeply into the metaphysical grounds of his opinions', a superficial thinker, a man 'who enumerates, classifies the facts, but does not account for them', a man whose thinking stops short of the satisfaction of thought. It is true that to Mill Bentham was a man who 'always knew his own premises'. But on this point Mill seems to have been misled by Bentham's contempt for established authorities, particularly the acknowledged authorities of Jurisprudence, into thinking that his master was 'critical' in a more profound sense. A hundred men are contemptuous of all the obvious and established authorities for one man who really begins to think for himself, for one who is an independent thinker; and Bentham certainly was not that one.

This, then, is the old Bentham, the traditional Bentham to whom all the old books (including the eleven volumes of the 'Collected Works') introduce us. Other writers during the last thirty years have extended the picture. Some, like Leslie Stephen and M. Halévy, have shown us the connection between Bentham and his predecessors and contemporaries; others, like Professor Phillipson and Mr. Atkinson, have given us a more detailed view of some special aspect of Bentham's work. But, in the main, what they have had to say has not seriously modified, though it has considerably extended, the story told by Mill and other of Bentham's contemporaries. But the new, regenerate Bentham, revealed to us in half-a-dozen recently published books, appears to differ radically from the old. We are given a new view of Bentham's life and character, and we are given a new view of the range and significance of his ideas. The real Bentham, we are told, did not live the restricted life of the legendary Bentham; and the real Bentham was a man of far more universal genius than his contemporaries ever supposed. It is, however, impossible here to discuss this rehabilitation in all its aspects, and I have chosen instead to consider it as it is attempted in the work of two writers: Mr. C. W. Everett, of Columbia University, who besides editing one of Bentham's hitherto unpublished works, has given us a new view of the life and character of Bentham[1];

[1] C. W. Everett. *Bentham's Comments on the Commentaries*, edited with an Introduction (Oxford, 1928). *The Education of Jeremy Bentham* (Columbia University Press, Humphrey Milford, 1931).

and Mr. C. K. Ogden, who has given us a new view of Bentham's ideas.[2]

A new biography may be new because it is based upon new discoveries or because it ventures upon a new interpretation of material already well-known. And it may be said at once that the novelty of Mr. Everett's work on the early life of Bentham depends in the main (though not entirely) upon certain discoveries he has made during the last three years while examining the voluminous collection of Bentham MSS. in the British Museum and in University College, London. He has undertaken, on the strength of these discoveries, to refute biographically the traditional view (derived from Mill) that Bentham was incomplete 'as a representative of universal human nature', and to show us a Bentham less cut-off from the world, less untouched by hope and fear, desire and disappointment, than the old Bentham appeared to be. Not one of Bentham's English school, he remarks, had known him before the age of sixty; and this incomplete acquaintance with the early life and fortunes of their master led them to misconceive his character, to think him less experienced than he actually was. His early love for Mary Dunkly was unknown to them, they were imperfectly acquainted with his strained relations with his father, and his intimate and affectionate relations with his younger brother Samuel. They knew only a Bentham passionately devoted to the reform of the law: they were ignorant of Bentham the lover, the man of the world, the man of moods, of gaiety and melancholy, the man who had a disappointment to forget, and the man who had difficult questions of personal conduct to answer. And Mr. Everett has been able to show us this new Bentham directly and vividly in the hitherto unpublished letters to his brother Samuel. Henceforward, whatever defects may be found in Bentham's philosophy, it is no longer possible to account for them by referring to the 'secluded' character of his life.

But this fresh account of Bentham's early life does not stop there, with a mere amplification of our knowledge of the facts, it ventures upon a new interpretation of the old material, the bio-

[2] C. K. Ogden, *Bentham's Theory of Legislation*, with an Introduction and Notes (Kegan Paul, 1931).

graphical material to be found in the last two volumes of Bentham's
collected works. This interpretation is sometimes a little uncertain
and indefinite, but so far as it goes it is admirably performed. We
are given a picture of Bentham's early life and activities less encum-
bered than is usually the case with the detail of his later theories,
his ethical, legal and political opinions. Indeed, this is perhaps the
first biography of Bentham written by a man whose interest lies in
biography rather than in law or philosophy; and from this, I think,
it derives its great merits. The book is short, boldly conceived, simply planned and executed in a manner at once thorough and unpre-
tentious. As a biography its only defect is, I think, a tendency to
over-simplification: certain events in Bentham's life are singled out
and made to appear more 'decisive' than is the case in any man's
life. Bentham's attendance at Blackstone's lectures, his friendship
with Lord Shelburn, his meeting with Dumont at Lansdowne
House—these no doubt were important events, but too much can
be made of them as absolute 'turning-points'. In this, and in some
other matters, Mr. Everett seems to me to have been insufficiently
critical, to have relied too much upon the appearance of things.
And this relatively uncritical attitude has resulted in a partial failure to formulate clearly and unambiguously, and to place in the
foreground, the real point of the biography. And it has resulted also, I think, in an actual misunderstanding of certain aspects of
Bentham's genius. For what, in effect, we are shown is not a Bentham who is a mere reformer of the law, a speculative thinker, a
man whose work looks forward into the nineteenth century, an early democrat, but Bentham the *philosophe*, the creature of the eighteenth century, the native of France rather than England, the companion in thought of Helvetius, Diderot, Voltaire and d'Alembert,
the last of the believers in Benevolent Despotism. And, when this
view is grasped firmly, when its implications are fully appreciated,
not only is a new Bentham revealed, but the two 'major problems' of
Bentham's life (which Mr. Everett states but solves only perfunctori-
ly) are at once resolved;—Why was Bentham's genius recognized
more fully on the Continent, in North and South America and in
Russia, than in England? And why did Bentham write so much

and publish so little? Indeed, they disappear as problems because they become what we should expect, and not what puzzles us.

Now, the character of the *philosophe* is both peculiar and interesting; and, taken as a whole, it is so foreign to the English character that it does not surprise us that Bentham was so little regarded in his own country and so greatly respected outside it, wherever this *philosophe* civilization had developed and established itself. There are, I suppose, three prime elements in this character, and all were highly developed in Bentham. First, an age of *philosophisme* implies a peculiar confidence in knowledge, indiscriminate knowledge; it implies an hydroptic thirst for information about the present world, its composition and its laws, and about human nature, its needs and desires. The *philosophe* believes in knowledge in a way which we find difficult to understand—we who have long ago lost this confidence. And he can exist only when there is a certain rude copiousness about the supply of knowledge which permits no suggestion of a limit. His is an inventive, ingenious, mildly perplexed and easily satisfied mind; there is vitality but no discrimination. All knowledge appears equally significant; and there is so much to be learned that there is neither time nor inclination to stay and learn anything profoundly. One thing leads to another before it has itself been exhausted; and when every suggestion is followed, it is impossible to follow one suggestion far. It is true that the world of knowledge, after a visitation of *philosophisme*, somewhat resembles a September orchard after a plague of wasps, but to the *philosophe* himself his life appears an endless intellectual adventure; he is entirely ignorant of the senseless depredation his lack of discrimination involves, and he is unconscious of his vulgarity. And, if he is fortunate, the disenchantment which, it would seem, must overtake such a way of living, can be avoided.

But secondly, besides this belief in encyclopædic knowledge, the *philosophe* is remarkable for his general credulity. He does not know what it is to be perplexed; he only knows what it is to be ignorant. And he is protected from the dilemmas of doubt by a tough hide of self-confidence. Appearing to doubt everything and to be engaged upon the construction of a new world from the bottom up, he is really the most credulous of men. There is plenty of audacity and some courage in his thought, but little freedom and no candour. He does not, it is true, begin from the same place and with the same prejudices as his less enlightened contemporaries, nevertheless he begins with a whole miscellany of presuppositions which he has neither the time, the inclination nor the ability to examine. There is, in short, little or nothing in common between the *philosophe* and the philosopher. For the *philosophe* the world is divided between those who agree with him and 'fools'; 'science' is contrasted with superstition, and superstition is identified with whatever is established, generally believed or merely felt.

And thirdly, besides his thirst for knowledge and his naïve cast of mind, the *philosophe* is a rationalist, in the restricted sense that he believes that what is made is better than what merely grows, that neatness is better than profusion and vitality. The genius of the *philosophe* is a genius for rationalization, for *making* life and the business of life rational rather than for *seeing* the reason for it, for inculcating precise order, no matter at what expense, rather than for apprehending the existence of a subtle order in what appears to be chaotic.

There is, of course, much that is admirable in this type of mind; but it will be seen at once that its justification lies solely in the present appreciation of life and the world which it achieves, and not in any contribution to knowledge it has to offer to later generations. If it gives no present enjoyment to those who possess it, it is idle to look for other achievements. It can make no serious contribution to our store of knowledge; it denies the traditions of the past and attempts to fasten no new traditions on the future. What was important to the eighteenth century *philosophes* was not what they learned or discovered, not the knowledge they acquired, but merely the sense of life which the pursuit of knowledge engendered. And what is important to us is not the discoveries they made—these, for the most part, were negligible—but the general view of life by means of which they succeeded in making themselves at home in the world. The *philosophes* were the initiators of innumerable practical reforms, but in no direction did they achieve any real extension of knowledge; their minds were replete with half-conceived ideas. *Philosophisme*, that is, is a backwater so far as the main stream of European scholarship, philosophy and scientific research is concerned. The character of Voltaire's biblical criticism, for example, is entirely misconceived if it is considered as an attempt to make a serious contribution to the historical study of the Bible.

Now, the view I wish to suggest is that Bentham was, in all respects, a typical eighteenth century *philosophe*, and that for this reason his reputation was greater on the Continent than in England. And for this view Mr. Everett supplies much of the evidence we require. First, Bentham was moved by this peculiar, indiscriminate activity which belongs to *philosophisme*, and which accounts for his having completed so little of what he began. 'I am still persuaded, my dear Bentham,' writes George Wilson in 1787, 'that you have for some years been throwing away your time. . . . Your history, since I have known you, has been to be always running from a good scheme to a better. In the meantime, life passes away and nothing is completed'. Chemistry, the law, education, engineering, prison reform, psychology, economics—these were a few of the interests which served to supply material for his 'unnatural, unexampled appetite for innovation'. Never for a moment was his mind occupied with one thing to the exclusion of all others. And it is not surprising that, 'for this sake of expedition', Bentham should desire '5 or 6 pupils who were initiated in my principles to whom I could give as many parts of my plan to execute under my eyes'. In his undergraduate days at Oxford the study of chemistry had much engaged Bentham's attention; and along with chemistry, of course, went astronomy. But for Bentham, as for more than one of his brother *philosophes* on the Continent, the science which appeared more important than any other was the science of government, for by means of this the whole human race was to be rescued from superstition. To create a science of politics, to apply the scientific method to the field of law, to unite law and science, to discover some means for measuring accurately political satisfactions—these were his ambitions. And in pursuit of this end, two things appeared to Bentham's *philosophe* mind to be necessary: first, a clean start; secondly, a code, something made, organized and definite, as distinct from what had merely grown. The clean start he found, or he imagined, in Russia; though of course he did not stay there long enough to achieve anything significant. Russia was virgin soil for the legislator; it appeared to be in the condition which the eighteenth century *philosophes* believed the human mind to be at birth, a *tabula rasa*. And secondly, the organization and rationalization of law implied in a code was what engaged Bentham's attention more nearly to the exclusion of other interests throughout the whole of his life. It was natural for a *philosophe* to hate the English common law and to be suspicious of judge-made law, for in both there is an element of uncertainty; on account of both English law can never be an artistic whole. But, in his contempt of the first, Bentham seems to have forgotten that law must change, that law is an expression of what is and not of what ought to be; he forgot, in short, what all the benevolent despots forgot. And his suspicion of the second was based upon a misconceived theory of knowledge. He appears to have believed that thought is always and expressly dominated by the circumstances of its generation, that there can be no thought independent of the psychological situation. The whole of every judgment, he believed, depends upon the psychical state of the individual who judges and derives from this its truth or falsehood. Such an opinion involves, of course, at once universal scepticism and self-contradiction; but Bentham was aware of neither of these implications. And in this matter, as in many others, he would have been on safer ground had he maintained his opinion as a mere prejudice instead of attempting to establish it as a principle. It is all very well to see Bentham's influence everywhere in the legislation of the nineteenth century, but when we consider how extreme his views about English law actually were, what must be noticed is, not the number of his isolated suggestions which have been put into practice, but the total rejection which his fundamental principles have suffered.

My view is, then, that the value of Mr. Everett's biography lies in what it suggests rather than in any specific interpretation of Bentham's life and mind which it offers. It suggests a Bentham different from the old, traditional Bentham, who was created by the liberal writers of the nineteenth century. In it Bentham is seen to belong to his century—the eighteenth century—and his environment. We are shown a living Bentham, a complete man, and not the mere thinker with which we have so long been obliged to content ourselves. And it remains to be seen whether, when this study is carried into Bentham's later life, yet another Bentham will appear. But, thus far, whatever his democratic sympathies, whatever specific modernity some of his suggestions show, what we have is Bentham the *philosophe*. And I venture to think that he remained a *philosophe* to the end.

It is now time to turn from this, to the other side of the attempt to rehabilitate Bentham; from Mr. Everett to Mr. Ogden. This new edition of the *Theory of Legislation* is a reprint, with a few verbal alterations, of Hildreth's translation (originally published in 1864) of parts of the three volumes prepared by Dumont from Bentham's half-French and half-English manuscripts and published in Paris in 1802 under the title of *Traités de législation Civile et Pénale, etc.* Hildreth's was not the first translation; an earlier was published in 1830. And it is not the most recent; Mr. C. M. Atkinson prepared a fresh, and on the whole better, translation with notes which was published in 1914. Setting aside, however the need for this reprint, what are important for us now are Mr. Ogden's *Introduction* and his *Notes*. For it is in these that the attempt is made to give a new range and significance to Bentham's ideas.

The *Introduction* is divided into three parts. First there is a discussion of Bentham's genius and ideas generally, secondly a few pages on the *Theory of Legislation* itself, and thirdly, some consideration of the relations of Bentham and Dumont. And something of interest has been found to say on all these topics. I shall deal, however, only with the first. Nobody denies Bentham's importance in the history of English law and legislation and it would be difficult to exaggerate that importance; and the discussion of the Bentham-Dumont relationship is in the main of merely historical and biographical interest. What is important for us is the thesis which Mr. Ogden undertakes to defend in the first part. 'It is that Bentham's merits, in spite of his great and deserved influence on the nineteenth century, are only now coming to be fully realized; that with every decade after the centenary of his death (1932) the significance of his achievement will become more obvious; and that fifty years from to-day he will stand out as one of the greatest figures in European thought, along with Réamur, Leibnitz, Newton, Malthus and Helmholtz. . . .

'The grounds for the view that the full recognition of Bentham's work is still to come are as follows:

1. His theory of Language and Linguistic Fictions.

2. His contribution to the problem of an International Language.

3. His insight into the Psychology of Value, in conformity with the most recent tendency of Criticism.

4. His proposals for the Codification of nearly every legal system in the world, and particularly the Constitutions of South America.

5. His services to International Law.

6. His work on the Foundations of Humanitarianism and Public Health'.

Now, it cannot be denied that this estimate of Bentham's genius and importance creates a considerable revolution in the current view. And the question for us is, how far can it be maintained?

With regard to Mr. Ogden's thesis, three general observations may be made. First, he somewhat naïvely remarks that 'of course any estimate of Bentham must depend to a large extent upon our interests and our general approach'. Thus, if we are interested in what interested Bentham, he will be important; if not, not. And since Mr. Ogden is most interested in the theory of language, this is the most important aspect of Bentham's work. Secondly, the criterion of importance which Mr. Ogden suggests is this: wherever in a writer who died a hundred years ago any ideas (however random, disconnected and undeveloped) appear which 'anticipate the modern view' of the matter, that writer is important. What makes a long-dead writer important are 'the echoes of modernity which reverberate through the fabric of his system'. And, whatever we may think of this criterion, since Bentham was a *philosophe*, a man with an inventive mind, a man of innumerable 'ideas' none of which he worked out fully, it is not difficult, if we adopt it, to represent him as 'a giant in the history of English thought'. Indeed, if these are our 'interests', and this our 'general approach', Bentham will have few competitors for the place of first importance; though if what we are after is modernity, I should have thought that, so far from being modern, at least one half of the grounds which are advanced to substantiate this claim on behalf of Bentham belong to the last century. And thirdly, Mr. Ogden everywhere asserts Bentham's importance, provides us with numerous quotations from present-day writers who also assert his importance, but nowhere is this importance actually shown and brought home to us. We are promised much, a bold thesis is proposed, but little or nothing is fulfilled.

The view is, then, that Bentham's chief interest lay, not in 'the law as it ought to be' (as Bentham himself seems to have thought) but in Orthology; and that his importance in the history of thought lies in his contribution, not to legal reform, but to the 'science of symbolism'. In this field Bentham was 'a century ahead of his times', and he omitted to publish his writings on this subject merely because 'he had little hope of being understood'. But it must be said at once that considerably more and better evidence than Mr. Ogden offers us must be produced before this view can be established. That Bentham had this interest has always been known, and it was an interest he had in common with many of his contemporary *philosophes;* but unless we are to consult merely our own interests as the criterion of what is important and of what interested Bentham most, there seems no reason at all for not believing that the established view of Bentham as primarily interested in the law and as performing his most important services in that field, is not merely established but also true.

The notion of an International Language from which the irrationalities and complexities (and subtleties) of all existing languages should have been removed, is one which would naturally appeal to the *philosophe*. Whatever has merely grown is for that reason abhorrent to him. And it does not surprise us to find Bentham engaged, for a while, with this notion. But whether, on this account, he is to be considered 'one of the greatest figures in European thought' appears to me doubtful, if not ridiculous.

And again, with regard to Bentham's psychology, all he has to offer us is one or two half-formulated doctrines developed for the purpose of jurisprudence. And the fact that there is to be found in Bentham's works a 'remarkable anticipation of the modern account of appetency' will scarcely persuade us that he was a great psychologist. When we consider the state of flux in which the science of psychology is at the present time, the fact that in Bentham there are to be found, disconnected and undeveloped, some of the ideas which for one school of psychologists appear, for the moment, true, cannot be considered very significant or important. And, in any case, although Mr. Ogden loudly announces Bentham the great innovator in psychology, no evidence is produced to show that such a Bentham exists outside his eager imagination.

Bentham's services to International Law are neither extensive nor striking; and Mr. Ogden says nothing to alter this view. Indeed when we consider what Bentham might have done, having regard to the state in which international law then was and to the real character of Bentham's genius we are surprised that what he has to say is so commonplace and devoid of significance. Of the whole of Bentham's *Principles of International Law* (a very brief work), only the last part, *A Plan for an Universal Peace* (which has nothing to do with international law itself), is of the least interest to-day. No amount of rehabilitation will make Bentham rank as one of the great publicists of international law. And what has Mr. Ogden to say to the contrary? Merely that 'the very term *international* was his own creation'. But first, if it were, it would constitute no very staggering contribution; and secondly, does he suppose that Bentham had never heard of *jus inter gentes*? We shall be hearing next that Bentham is the greatest English theologian, on the strength of a couple of Voltarian anti-religious tracts.

Mr. Ogden's *Notes* are designed, for the most part, neither to elucidate Bentham's meaning, nor (like the notes in Mr. Atkinson's edition of the *Theory of Legislation*) to elucidate points of law and legal history, but to drive home the thesis of the *Introduction*, that is, 'to provide the student with references to the more important recent literature of the subject, partly in relation to psychology'. Thus, his first note is on the Principle of Utility, and the question proposed is, 'To what extent has the intervening century illuminated or invalidated (Bentham's) main position?' But the writer of the note seems unaware of the magnitude of the question he undertakes to dispose of in half a page, and unaware also of the destructive criticism of the last century which the utilitarian moral theory has not managed to survive. He is satisfied with a reference to Sidgwick and to Dr. Broad and the remark that 'there the matter rests' —which, of course, it does not. Other notes approach Bentham's most casual remarks with a pathetic seriousness, as if everything he wrote were full of 'echoes of modernity'. When Bentham, with a charming eighteenth century carelessness, observes that 'the occupations of a savage after he has supplied himself with physical necessaries, the only ones he knows, are soon described', the note directs us to the latest works on anthropology for 'the modern treatment of these subjects'. Some of these *Notes*, however, are more relevant, and the most useful are those which refer us to other passages in Bentham's works and those which elucidate some historical question.

In short, this attempt to represent Bentham as a greater Orthographist than psychologist, and as a more significant figure in both of these fields than in the field of law and jurisprudence, must be considered to have failed. It has failed because there is no evidence to support it and because it rests upon a false criterion of significance and upon the mere predilections of the writer who makes it. Bentham was an ingenious man, and if we look hard enough we shall certainly find in his works some 'remarkable anticipations' of fairly modern views. But what of it? Does that make him a giant? A thinker like Bentham does not trouble to discriminate or confine himself; he skims the cream. He is not listened to in his own day because he is ahead of his time; but, when it is all over, he has nothing to hand on to his successors save a few random suggestions and a few inventions more ingenious than sound. And this, I think, is the character of Bentham's genius whenever it applied itself outside the law.

Bentham as a thinker belonged essentially to the eighteenth century, and this fact has been obscured by writers on Bentham because they are determined to direct their attention away from what Bentham actually thought and the eighteenth century presuppositions of his thought, towards the so-called after-effects or consequences of his thought. What has practical consequence is, almost always, the idea itself served from the grounds and reasons which lie in the mind of the thinker, the mere *obiter dictum*. Cremation, contraception, co-education, this or that reform of the law, may be advocated for a hundred different reasons, and what is influential is, usually, the bare advocacy of the view. But when we come to consider what a man actually thought, it is not these bare ideas which are important, but the grounds and reasons for them which he believed to be cogent, the *ratio decidendi*. And in the case of Bentham, these grounds and reasons were all typical of eighteenth century thought, and nearly all fallacious. For Bentham, so far from having thought out his first principles, had never given them a moment's consideration. He had studied closely the work of Locke, Hume, Condillac and Helvetius. And while he was a thinker rather than a reader when it came to dealing with the law, he remained always a reader and not a thinker with regard to the philosophical first principles which lay behind. No man with so little interest in or aptitude for philosophy has ever taken so large a place in the history of philosophy as Bentham. It is safe to say that, so far as philosophy is concerned, there is nothing in the whole of Bentham's works which is original either in conception or exposition: both his ideas and the words and phrases in which he expresses them are derived almost entirely from the half-dozen philosophical writers whom he had studied. The principle of pleasure and pain comes from Helvetius, sympathy and antipathy from Hume, utility from any one of a dozen writers; his theory of knowledge is derived entirely from Locke and Hume; and wherever he ventures beyond what others had already thought out—as for example in his formulation of the principle of utility—he becomes at once confused and self-contradictory. Utilitarianism as Bentham left it is nothing more than a chaos of precise ideas. No man was ever more at the mercy of traditional doctrines in philosophy than Bentham. He belongs in these matters to the eighteenth century, and is an example of that not uncommon character in England—a man revolutionary in almost all practical matters, but dependent, unoriginal and cluttered up with prejudice in matters of speculation.

The principle of utility performed wonders in the reform of the law, or rather wonders were performed in its name, but this was possible only because the inherent fallacies which lie at the root of his principle were unappreciated or neglected. The principle, for the purpose of reform, was a mere *obiter dictum*; its *ratio decidendi* was ignored or forgotten. But if we wish to discover Bentham's quality as a thinker, we shall turn from these *obiter dicta* to their *rationes decidendi*, and we shall find these, for the most part, pointing us back into the eighteenth century, and moreover disfigured with the most naïve blunders.

And when we turn from his doctrines to his method, we find something admirably suited to Bentham's schemes for reforming the law, but (as a serious contribution to thought) something so naïve and childish that it is difficult to understand how it could ever have been selected as the finest product of the genius of any man who achieved so much as Bentham achieved in the way of practical reform. Bentham's method is based, of course, upon his view that 'in the whole human race, considered at all periods of its history, the knowledge of particulars has preceded that of generals'. But it is not the mere fact that Bentham was the simplest and most unconstrained nominalist in the history of English thought which is fatal to his reputation as a philosopher, but the fact that he assumed nominalism to be the only possible theory of knowledge, and was neither interested nor troubled to think about the matter.[3] His

---

[3] On this point Mr. Ogden has a characteristically wild remark. 'That such a man,' he says 'should be content to hand over his most profound and considered achievements without comment to posterity, is merely evidence that he had little hope of being understood by anyone who had lived but one contemporary life. Even fifty years later, we find Vaihinger delaying the publication of his work *The Philosophy of As-If* till 1911, on the ground that

method is based throughout upon presuppositions which he had never so much as considered. Analysis and synthesis, data and generalization, materials and conclusions, the bricks and the building —this was Bentham's crude and unconsidered conception of the character of knowledge. Thought, for him, as for most of the English philosophers at that time, was merely decaying sensation; and what could not be explained otherwise could always be accounted for by the principle of Association.

It appears, then, that Mill's estimate of Bentham's genius is, with certain reservations, more accurate than the view with which we are now presented. Mr. Everett has certainly proved to us that Bentham's life and character were somewhat different from what we had been led to suppose; thanks to him we are now in possession of a fuller knowledge of both than was at the disposal of Mill or any of the intimates of Bentham during his later years. But so far as the interpretation of his mind and genius goes, we have little advantage over Mill. And if it now appears that Mill was wrong in believing that this 'method' of Bentham's was so original and so significant, that he was wrong in thinking that Bentham's utilitarianism was good enough as a theory of law, though not sufficiently comprehensive as a theory of morals, his *Essay* on Bentham still remains the best short account of the work and genius of his master. Bentham is a great and important figure in the history of English law, but there appears to me no doubt at all that if we follow the direction in which Mr. Ogden points, and look in Bentham for a man whose main interest and most important work was in Orthology, psychology, logic and philosophy, rather than in 'the law as it ought to be' and in jurisprudence, we shall end with an entirely false view of Bentham's genius.

such an extension of nominalism would be ridiculed in official circles'. In the first place, there is no proof that Bentham delayed publication for the same reason as Vaihinger—that is mere conjecture. Secondly, it is stupid conjecture when we consider the extreme carelessness of Bentham with regard to the publication of any of his works: with Bentham it was not a policy so much as negligence. And thirdly, whereas when Vaihinger was writing the predominant fashion in philosophy was Idealism and a man might well wonder whether a nominalist theory would get a hearing, in Bentham's day in England nominalism was a fashion, a prejudice, a universal assumption. Bentham's nominalism so far from being revolutionary was merely insipid conventionalism.

Bentham's life and work abound in remarkable contrasts: a man without any real interest in speculative thought for its own sake, and yet a 'hermit'; a man who shrank from the world, the practice of the law and the compromises of politics, and yet one whose beneficial influence was felt entirely in these practical matters; a man who by force, cunning and ridicule killed many of the fallacies which dominated legal and political theory, yet one whose arguments were, in most cases, misconceived, and whose own thought was riddled with the most naïve fallacies; a man who spent his life talking about first principles, but who never once got beyond a consideration of what is secondary and dependent. The lesson of his life is not, as Mill thought, to show how speculative philosophy enters into and influences practical life, but to show that what in speculation is always the most influential in practical life is something half-thought out, something hazy, indefinite and confused. It is not the philosopher, the victim of thought, who influences our practical conduct of life, but the philosophaster, the *philosophe*. The significance of Bentham as a reformer of the law and as the first English writer on jurisprudence of any importance, is immense. But as a philosopher, as a thinker, he is negligible. 'It is the fashion of youth,' wrote Hegel, 'to dash about in abstractions: but the man who has learnt to know life steers clear of the abstract "either-or", and adheres to the concrete'. And Bentham (says Mill) was 'a boy to the end'.

"The New Bentham" was first published in *Scrutiny*, Volume I, 1932, and is new to this edition of *Rationalism in Politics*.

The activity of being
an historian

ONE

Activities emerge naïvely, like games that children invent for themselves. Each appears, first, not in response to a premeditated achievement, but as a direction of attention pursued without premonition of what it will lead to. How should our artless ancestor have known what (as it has turned out) it is to be an astronomer, an accountant, or an historian? And yet it was he who, in play, set our feet on the paths that have led to these now narrowly specified activities.[1] For, a direction of attention, as it is pursued, may hollow out a character for itself and become specified in a 'practice'; and a participant in the activity comes to be recognized not by the results he achieves but by his disposition to observe the manners of the 'practice'. Moreover, when an activity has acquired a certain firmness of character, it may present itself as a puzzle, and thus provoke reflection; for, there may come a point at which we not only wish to acquire and exercise the skill which constitutes the activity,

[1] Cf. Plato, *Laws*, 672B.

151

but may wish also to discern the logic of the relation of this activity (as it has come to be specified) to others and to ascertain its place on the map of human activity.

What we now understand as the activity of being an historian was generated in this manner. Beginning in a direction of attention naïvely pursued, it has achieved the condition of a specific activity whose participants are known by their faithfulness to the 'practice' that has emerged. And during the last two hundred years or so this activity has been much reflected upon.

Reflection has taken two directions. First, what has been sought is a satisfactory general description of the activity of being an historian as it has come to establish itself. The assumption here is that the activity is itself an historical emergence and that the degree of specification it has now achieved is sufficient to identify it as a coherent manner of thinking about the world. And the fruits of such an inquiry would be the disclosure of the kind of intelligibility that historical thinking, in its present condition, imparts to the world, and the manner in which this activity can be distinguished from others which (in the process of emergence) it has succeeded in separating itself from. This, no doubt, is a difficult inquiry; but it is one that seems capable of yielding some conclusions.

The second direction of inquiry may be said to spring (but not necessarily) from the first. Assuming a satisfactory description of the current condition of the activity of being an historian has been achieved, the questions asked are: Does this condition intimate (or, must we not on general grounds assume) the possibility of further specification which would not merely modify in detail the present specification of the activity but would generate its definitive character? And if so, what is this character? And since I propose to concern myself very little with this line of inquiry, I should, perhaps, say a word about it before putting it on one side. Briefly, the notion appears to be this: the activity of being an historian is that of understanding the past; but, since the current manner of doing this leaves the past incompletely intelligible, there must (in principle) be another manner of understanding the past which, because it is free from this defect, may be regarded as the consummation to which 'history' in its present condition points. And, although there may be others yet unproposed, the most favoured candidate has, for some time, been an inquiry designed to make past events intelligible by revealing them as examples of general laws. I do not myself understand how this line of thought could lead to profitable conclusions; but at least it is clear that it rests upon far from self-evidently true presuppositions, and whether or not it may turn out to be profitable will depend upon our satisfying ourselves that they are warranted. Moreover, it should be observed that what is being sought here is not merely a demonstration that historical thinking in its present condition must, in principle, leave the past incompletely intelligible, but a manner of thinking about the past which is at once superior to 'history' in its present condition and is capable of taking its place.

T W O

I propose, then, to consider the manner and achievements of current reflection about the present condition of the activity of being an historian; the reflection, that is, which seeks a general description of the activity as it has come to establish itself, and to determine the kind of intelligibility it imparts to the world.

The historian is understood, in the first place, to be distinguished on account of the direction of his attention; he is concerned with the past. He is interested in the world around him considered as evidence for a world that is no longer present; and we recognize his activity as one of inquiring into 'the past' and making statements about it. Nevertheless, we recognize, also, that to inquire into the past and to make statements about it is an exceedingly commonplace activity and one that we engage in every day of our lives: it is represented, for example, in the activity of remembering, and in so simple an inquiry as, 'Where did you get that hat?' Consequently, if we are interested, we cast around in order to discern some special characteristics which will serve to distinguish the activity of an historian from that of others who share with him an interest in 'the past'. And many who have reflected upon this subject have reached a conclusion something like this:

Whoever pays attention to the past and asks questions or makes statements about it must be understood to be participating in some measure in the activity which is the pre-eminent concern of an historian. All statements about the past are, in some sense, 'historical' statements. But an historian is distinguished by reason of the care he takes to verify his statements. 'History' emerges as a specific activity out of a general and unspecified interest in the past whenever there is a genuine concern for 'truth'; and an 'historical' event is any happening which we are warranted in believing (in virtue of its being a conclusion to a certain method of inquiry) took place in the manner described.[2] Thus, the activity of inquiring into and making statements about the past appears as a hierarchy of attitudes towards the past. At the head of this scale of attitudes stands 'the historian', specified by his care for 'truth', his technical skill in eliciting 'truth', and perhaps also by a propensity to regard some observations about the past, and some events, as more significant than others. In this manner his activity is differentiated, not only from the informal inquiries about the past which every man from time to time, in the course of business or pleasure, engages in, but also from the activity (for example) of an annalist or a chronicler, whose utterances spring from inquiries recognized to be less extended and less critical than those of an historian.

This general account of the matter has much to commend it. At least, it recognizes 'the historian' (in virtue of a 'practice') to be engaged in a specific activity. No doubt it is an incomplete account; and no doubt, also, it is philosophically naïve. But it has the virtue of not forbidding further investigation: indeed, it may be observed to point to two directions of further inquiry. For its incompleteness and philosophical naïvety lie, not in the formulation of the problem as one of ascertaining the *differentia* of 'historical' research, but only in the conclusions reached.

---

[2] Thus, Cicero distinguished the 'historical' from the 'imagined' past, the one being concerned with 'truth' and the other with 'pleasure'.

It urges us, first, to be more exact in our understanding of the details of the 'practice' of 'the historian'. And in response to this suggestion, attempts have been made to elicit a heuristic of historical investigation and to reduce the 'practice' of 'the historian' to a set of rules. But, as reflection might have warned us would be the case, this has not turned out a very profitable enterprise. And I do not propose to pursue it here.

There is, however, another direction of inquiry which this formulation of the problem suggests: it provokes us to consider whether the activity of being an historian may be more exactly specified in terms of the *kind* of question he asks and the *kind* of statement he makes about the past. And since in this direction of inquiry there remains a yet unfulfilled promise of profit, I propose to consider where it has led us and what further conclusions it is capable of yielding.

Investigators who have followed this path have already reached certain conclusions. They have observed, for example, that inquiry into the past may take the form of asking what *must* have happened, or what *might* have happened, or what *did* happen; and, for the most part, they have concluded that an *historian* is distinguished by an exclusive concern with what *did* happen. Or, again, a distinction has been drawn between the 'natural' world and the 'human' world; and it has been concluded that the events with which an historian is concerned are those which may be imputed to human actions and those which (though they belong to the 'natural' world, like earthquakes and climatic changes) we are warranted in believing to have conditioned or determined specific human conduct. And, as a refinement of this, Collingwood considered that the *res gestae* of 'history' are not *any* human actions, but only 'reflective' actions; that is, actions which spring from a purpose pursued. Further, it has been suggested that an attitude towards the past which provokes an inquiry into the 'origins' of some feature of the present world is an attitude foreign to an historian. In the same manner, the very recent past has been considered inappropriate for 'historical' investigation. And (a last example) some inquirers into the activity of the 'historian' have concluded that he is not concerned with the moral rightness and wrongness of human actions and that statements of moral approval or disapproval, of praise or condemnation, are out of place in his writings.

Now, all these suggestions may be recognized as attempts to determine more exactly the *kind* of questions it is appropriate for 'the historian' to ask, and the *kind* of statements it is appropriate for him to make about the past. They are attempts to distinguish a specifically 'historical' attitude towards 'the past' from other current or possible attitudes and thus to specify more precisely the activity of being an historian. Each suggestion is supported by some show of reasoning. The questions excluded from the concern of 'the historian' are identified either as questions inherently impossible to answer, or as questions which his evidence or his technique does not equip 'the historian' to answer; or they are excluded for some other reason. And, so far, there is much to be said for this manner of gradually elucidating the activity of 'the historian'; it has the virtues of moderation and empiricism.

Nevertheless, there remains something unsatisfactory about this procedure of piecemeal exclusion. Even if the reasoning which supports each exclusion were more cogent than it often is, the absence of attachment to a comprehensive view of the situation gives to each the indelible appearance of arbitrariness. Each remains a separate exclusion (or prohibition), supported by *ad hoc* reasoning which is apt to be either misconceived or inadequate because it is unrelated to any conspectus of the *kind* of inquiry and the *kind* of utterance appropriate to an 'historical' investigation of the past. In short, the current manner of exploring the activity of 'the historian' sets us a task: to discern the logic of these piecemeal attempts to delineate the field of historical inquiry.

The imperfectly considered assumptions of the current view appear to be something like this. It is believed that among the different kinds of statement that may be made about the past, it is possible to detect and to specify certain kinds, or even a certain kind which it is the peculiar province of 'the historian' to make. It is believed that there are many statements we, quite properly, make about the past which (even though they cannot be denied to be in some sense 'true') are, nevertheless, not 'historical' statements. It is believed that an 'historical' event is not any happening which we have warrant for thinking took place, but a happening of a peculiar sort which reveals itself in answer to a certain kind of question. Our task is to elucidate these assumptions so that the view of the activity of 'the historian' which they entail may be more fully disclosed and perhaps more firmly based.

THREE

It is proper to begin with our attitudes towards the world around us, because inquiring into 'the past' is the exhibition of a certain attitude towards the components of this world. Every happening that we see taking place before our eyes, if we attend to it at all, arouses a response. And every happening is capable of arousing a variety of responses. For example, I may observe the demolition of an old building, and my response may be merely a movement of self-preservation—to get out of the way of débris. It may, however, be a more complicated response. I may recognize what is happening as an act of vandalism, and suffer anger or depression; or I may understand it as evidence of progress, and be elated on that account; or indeed, the whole scene may be contemplated without *arrière pensée*, as a picture, an image whose design is a delight to the eyes. In short, to attend to what is happening before us is always to make something of it for ourselves. Seeing is recognizing what we see as *this* or *that*. And if I have a companion I may make a statement about what I am seeing whose idiom reveals the manner in which I am attending to it and understanding it.

Everything that goes on before our eyes is, then, eligible for a vast variety of interpretations. But, in general, it seems that our responses to the world are of two kinds. Either we may regard the world in a manner which does not allow us to consider anything but what is immediately before our eyes and does not provoke us to any conclusions; or we may look upon what is going on before us as evidence for what does not itself appear, considering, for example, its causes or its effects. The first of these responses is simple and unvarying; and I shall call it the response of *contemplation*. It is pre-eminently the response of the artist and the poet, for whom the world is composed, not of events recognized as signs or portents, but of causeless 'images' of delight which provoke neither approval nor disapproval, and to which the categories 'real' and 'fictitious' are alike inapplicable. The second response, however, is capable of internal variety; and in it two main idioms may be distinguished, which I shall call, respectively, the *practical* and the *scientific* response.

First, we may recognize what is happening in respect of its relation to ourselves, our fortunes, desires and activities. This is the commonest kind of response; we absolve ourselves from it with difficulty, and relapse into it easily. I call it a *practical* response, and its partner is the perception of a *practical* event.

From birth we are active; not to be active is not to be alive. And what concerns us first about the world is its habitableness, its friendliness or hostility to our desires and enterprises. We want to be at home in the world, and (in part) this consists in being able to detect how happenings will affect ourselves and in having some control over their effects.

This service is performed, in the first place, by our senses. In 'seeing', 'hearing', 'tasting', 'touching', we become acquainted with what is happening: and, at the same time, we place a certain interval between ourselves and what is happening, giving ourselves an opportunity to act in what we judge to be an appropriate manner. 'Seeing' places the greatest space-time interval between ourselves and events; 'hearing', a smaller, but still useful interval; in 'tasting' the interval is further contracted; and in 'touching' it is reduced to almost nothing at all.

But in order to understand the world in relation to ourselves we make use of certain conceptual distinctions. We recognize events as friendly or hostile, things as edible or poisonous, useful or useless, cheap or expensive, and so on. And most, if not all, these distinctions are examples of the recognition, in practical life, of what may be called 'cause' and 'effect'. For, in practical life, to recognize an event as a 'cause' is to understand it as a sign that other events are likely to follow: to understand an event as friendly is to expect it to be followed by other events of a certain kind; to recognize a commodity as 'cheap' is to recognize it as a signal of other events to come. And the ability to recognize events as, in this sense, 'causes' at once gives us a greatly enhanced mastery over the world; it enables us to anticipate events that have not yet taken place and thus gives us an added opportunity of controlling their impact upon ourselves.

Moreover, it is to this practical attitude towards the world that our judgments of approval and disapproval and our moral appraisals and imputations belong. The categories of 'right' and 'wrong', 'good' and 'bad', 'justice' and 'injustice' etc. relate to the organization and understanding of the world in respect of its relationship to ourselves, in respect (that is) of its habitableness. 'Hero' and 'villain' may be crude categories, but their place is in the world of practical activity. And in condemning 'vice' and applauding 'virtue' we express our beliefs about what is desirable and what is undesirable in human conduct and character.

The practical attitude, then, admits us to a world of discourse; but it is not the only world of discourse available to us. It has a partner and an alternative in what I have called the *scientific* attitude. In this, we are concerned, not with happenings in their relation to ourselves and to the habitableness of the world, but in respect of their independence of ourselves. In short, the attitude here is what we vulgarly call an 'objective' attitude; and this 'objectivity' is reflected in the idiom of the statements we make about the happenings we observe. While the hunter recognizes animals as dangerous or friendly (denoting some as specifically 'man-eating'), while the house-wife distinguishes commodities in respect of their price, while the cook knows things in respect of their taste, and while the moralist expresses himself in statements of approval or disapproval, the categories of the scientist arrange things in a different manner —not at all as they affect him or his fortunes, but as they are in their independence of himself.

The general character of the scientist's concern with the world appears in his notion of 'cause' and 'effect'. When the practical man recognizes an event as a 'cause' he recognizes it as a *sign* that some other event may be expected to follow; and the ground of his recognition is his experience of the world in relation to himself. For the scientist, on the other hand, 'cause' is a much more precise and more restricted notion; and 'cause' in his sense is so difficult to determine that it lacks practical usefulness. It is the necessary and sufficient conditions of a hypothetical situation. 'Cause' and 'effect', that is, denote general and necessary relations and not merely a relation which it has proved practically useful to observe.

The contrast between the practical and the scientific responses to the world may be illustrated as follows: When we are concerned with things in their relation to ourselves and to the habitableness of the world, it is appropriate to say that 'seeing' puts things at a greater distance from ourselves than 'hearing'. And consequently we recognize that it is greater handicap to be blind than to be deaf. But when we are concerned with things in respect of their independence of ourselves, we say, instead, that the speed of light is greater than the speed of sound. 'Light' and 'sound' are, so to speak, the 'scientific' equivalents of the practical activities of 'seeing' and 'hearing'.

Or again, if I say: 'I am hot,' I shall be recognized to be speaking in the idiom of practice. I am making a statement about the world in relation to myself, and the manner in which it is made will certainly convey either satisfaction or dissatisfaction. If I say: 'It is a hot day', I am still making a statement about the world in relation to myself. Its reference is more extended, but the remark is unmistakably in the practical idiom. If I say: 'The thermometer on the roof of the Air Ministry stood at 90°F. at 12 noon G.M.T.' I may not have emancipated myself completely from the practical attitude, but at least I am capable of being suspected of making a statement, not about the world in relation to myself but about the world in respect of its independence of myself. And when, finally, I say: 'The boiling point of water is 100° Centigrade', I am making a statement which may be recognized to have achieved the idiom of 'science'. The situation described is hypothetical, and the observation is not about the world in relation to myself.

In both the practical and the scientific responses, then, the world appears as a world of 'facts'; 'truth' and 'error' are relevant categories, though in the one case it is 'practical' truth and in the other 'scientific'. And in both these attitudes we are provoked to look for what is not present: events are the 'effects' of 'causes' and the portents of events to come. On the other hand, the attitude of contemplation discloses to us a world of mere 'images' which provoke neither inquiry nor speculation about the occasion and conditions of their appearance, but only delight in their having appeared.

FOUR

We have been considering events as they take place before our eyes; and we have concluded that these are capable of a variety of interpretation, and what we see is relative to how we look. And, further, we have agreed that the historian is concerned with 'the past'. What we must now observe is that 'the past' is a construction we make for ourselves out of the events which take place before our eyes. Just as the 'future' appears when we understand the present events as evidence for what is about to happen, so what we call 'the past' appears when we understand current happenings as evidence for what has already happened. In short (to confine ourselves to our immediate concern) 'the past' is a consequence of understanding the present world in a particular manner.

Consider: what we have before us is a building, a piece of furniture, a coin, a picture, a passage in a book, a legal document, an inscription on stone, a current manner of behavior or a memory. Each of these is a present event. And one reponse (though not of course the only possible response) to these events is to understand them as evidence for events that have already taken place. There is, indeed, nothing in the present world which is incapable of being regarded in this manner; but also there is nothing which can be regarded *only* in this manner.

'The past', then, is a certain way of reading 'the present'. But in addition to its being a reading of the world in which present events are understood as evidence for events that have already taken place, it is a reading which may denote a variety of attitudes towards these past events. And (if we are to be guided by the utterance of those who have spoken and written about past events) the three most important attitudes available to us may be called the *practical*, the *scientific* and the *contemplative*. And there is a manner of speaking about past events which is appropriate to each of these attitudes.

First, if we understand a past event merely in relation to ourselves and our own current activities, our attitude may be said to be a 'practical' attitude.

This, for example, is the attitude of a practising lawyer to a past event which he concludes to have taken place by understanding a present event (a legal document before him) as evidence for something that has already happened. He considers the past event solely in relation to its present consequences and he says to his client: 'under this will you may expect to inherit £1,000'; or, 'we must take Counsel's opinion on the validity of this contract'. And further, of course, he is interested only in past events which *have* present practical consequences.

Now, just as our commonest attitude towards what we see taking place before us is a practical attitude, so our commonest attitude to what we conclude (on the evidence of a present experience) to have already taken place is a practical attitude. Usually, we interpret these past happenings in relation to ourselves and to our current activities. We read the past backwards from the present or from the more recent past, we look in it for the 'origins' of what we perceive around us, we make moral judgments about past conduct, we call upon the past to speak to us in utterance related to the present; and what appears is a practical past. And the questions we ask, and the statements we make about the past, are those that are appropriate to our practical attitude. They are statements such as these:

You are looking very well: where did you go for your holiday?
The summer of 1920 was the finest in my experience.
He died too soon.

King John was a bad King.

The death of William the Conqueror was accidental.

It would have been better if the French Revolution had never taken place.

He dissipated his resources in a series of useless wars.

The Pope's intervention changed the course of events.

The evolution of Parliament.

The development of industrial society in Great Britain.

The Factory Acts of the early nineteenth century culminated in the Welfare State of the twentieth century.

The loss of markets for British goods on the Continent was the most serious consequence of the Napoleonic Wars.

The effect of the Boer War was to make clear the necessity for radical reform in the British Army.

The next day the Liberator addressed a large meeting in Dublin.

Here, in each of these statements, as we shall see, the idiom is that of practice.

Secondly, our attitude to what we conclude to have happened in the past may be, generally speaking, what I have called a 'scientific' attitude. Here, we are concerned, not with past events in relation to ourselves and to the habitableness of the world, but in respect of their independence of ourselves. The practical response is the response of a partisan, of one sort or another; in the scientific response what appears is the past unassimilated to ourselves, the past for its own sake.

But while the word 'scientific' may properly be used, in a general way, to denote an interest in past events in respect of their independence of ourselves, it is necessary to make two qualifications. First, the concern of 'the scientist' with necessary and sufficient conditions will be reflected in the idiom in which he speaks about the past. And a model of the kind of statement he will be disposed to make is to be found in this sentence from Valéry: 'all the revolutions of the nineteenth century had as their necessary and sufficient conditions the centralized constitutions of power, thanks to which . . . a minimum strength and duration of effort can deliver an entire nation at a single stroke to whoever undertakes the adventure.' In short, if we give a stricter meaning to the word 'science', what appears is not merely statements in which the past remains unassimilated to the present, but also statements in which events are understood to exemplify general laws. And secondly, if we speak still more strictly, there can in fact be no 'scientific' attitude towards the past, for the world as it appears in scientific theory is a timeless world, a world, not of actual events, but of hypothetical situations.

Lastly, our attitude—and consequently the manner in which we recognize past happenings and the utterances we make about them—may be what I have called a 'contemplative' attitude. This is illustrated in the work of a so-called 'historical' novelist, for whom the past is neither practical nor scientific 'fact', but a storehouse of mere images. For example, in Tolstoy's *War and Peace* Napoleon is an image about whom it is as irrelevant to ask: Where was he born? Was he really like that? Did he in fact do this, or say that? Where was he in the intervals when he was not on the stage? as it would be to ask similar questions about Shakespeare's Orsino, Duke of Illyria in *Twelfth Night*. But here a qualification is necessary. Since 'the past', as such, cannot appear in 'contemplation' (this attitude being one in which we do not look for what does not immediately appear), to 'contemplate' past events is, properly speaking, a dependent activity in which what is contemplated are not past events but present events which (on account of some *other* attitude towards the present) have been concluded to have taken place. To remember, and to contemplate a memory, are two different experiences; in the one past and present are distinguished, in the other no such distinction is made. In short, just as when an object of use (a ship or a spade) is 'contemplated' its usefulness is neglected, so when what in another attitude would be recognized as a past event is 'contemplated', its pastness is ignored.

What we call 'past events' are, then, the product of understanding (or having understood) present occurrences as evidence for happenings that have already taken place. The past, in whatever manner it appears, is a certain sort of reading of the present. Whatever attitudes present events are capable of provoking in us may also be provoked by events which appear when we regard present events as evidence for other events—that is, by what we call 'past' events. In short, there is not one past because there is not one present: there is a 'practical' past, a 'scientific' past and a (specious) 'contemplative' past, each a universe of discourse logically different from either of the others.

FIVE

Now, among those who regard present events as evidence for events that have already taken place, 'the historian' is taken to be supreme. And properly so. For, although the practical man often finds it useful to take this attitude towards the present, and although both the scientist (in a general way) and the poet are each capable of doing so (or of making use of the results of others having done so), 'the historian' never does anything else. The activity of the historian is pre-eminently that of understanding present events—the things that are before him—as evidence for past happenings. His attitude towards the present is one in which the past *always* appears. But in order to understand his activity fully, the question we must ask ourselves is: Can we discern in the attitude of 'historians' towards the past and in the kind of statements they are accustomed to make about it, any characteristics that warrant us to conclude that, besides a 'practical' past, a 'scientific' past and a (specious) 'contemplative' past, there is a specifically 'historical' past?

There is one difficulty which seems to stand in the way of our inquiry, but which may be disposed of at once; it is, in fact, a fictitious difficulty. The practical manner of understanding the past is as old as the human race. To understand everything (including what we believe to have happened in the past) in relation to ourselves is the simplest and least sophisticated manner of understanding the world. And the contemplative attitude towards what are otherwise recognized as past events is, also, generally speaking, primordial and universal. Circumstances may hinder it; and even in people accustomed to it, it may get over-laid and pushed aside in favour of some other attitude. But the great poetic sagas of European and Eastern peoples show that from very early times what in other idioms of observation are known as past events have been recognized not as 'facts' but as 'images' of contemplation. The questions that are appropriate and those that are inappropriate to be asked about Jude the Obscure are the same as those that are respectively appropriate and inappropriate to be asked about Homer's Ulysses or Roland and Oliver. In short, when we consider the kind of statements men have been accustomed to make about the past, there is no doubt that the vast bulk of them is in the practical or the artistic idiom. Consequently, if we go to writers who have been labelled 'historians' (because they have displayed a sustained interest in past events) and ask, what kind of statement are they accustomed to make about the past, we shall find a great preponderance of practical and contemplative statements. And this observation seems to take the wind out of the sails of our inquiry. For where, it will be asked, are we to go to find out what it is to be an historian but to the practice of those who have displayed a sustained interest in the past? And if we go there, the answer ready for us seems to be: History is a miscellany of utterances about the past in which the practical and the contemplative idiom is predominant. And unless we are prepared to erect an imaginary character called, for no good reason, 'the historian', there remains nothing more to be said.

However, this difficulty need not disconcert us. There are, indeed, two considerations which enable us to avert this collapse of our inquiry. First, it must be remembered that in considering 'history' we are considering an activity which (like many others) has emerged gradually and has only recently begun to acquire a specific character. We easily recognize that the activity of being an astronomer, and the statements we expect from those whom we understand to be engaged in astronomy, are in many respects different from what they were when the activity was less exactly specified than it now is. We do not regard all the different kinds of statement (or even all the different kinds of 'true' statement) that have been made about the stars as proper to be made by the man whom we recognize to be 'an astronomer'; indeed, we exclude many of these statements as clearly foreign to what we now recognize as the activity of being an astronomer. And although we have been more hesitant in applying the same reasoning to the activity of being an historian, the two activities are, in this respect, similar to one another. Moreover, inquiry has disclosed in considerable detail the process in which the activity of being an historian has become specified. It is a process (similar to that in which the 'natural scientist' as we now understand him emerged) in which new techniques for the critical treatment of sources of information have been developed, and in which general organizing concepts have been generated, criticized, experimented with and rejected or reformulated.[3] And in neither of these respects has there been unbroken progress; valuable achievements have often been forgotten or allowed to lapse, only to be recovered again when a turn in the fortunes of historiography has recalled them. And again, the activity of being an historian has been dispersed over a variety of circumstantially separated fields of study, and often a closer specification of the activity has been achieved in some fields before it has appeared (often by a process of diffusion) in others. Thus, it is generally true to say that the pioneers of specification have been biblical and ecclesiastical historians, and advances made in these fields have gradually spread to others. And, for example, the rapid and remarkable achievements of historians of the Middle Ages during the last eighty years were often made possible only by the application of the earlier technical achievements of the historians of the ancient world. In short, although we may hope to discern in it some special characteristics, we are not looking for the necessary and sufficient conditions of the activity of being an historian. The activity is what it has become and our present analysis begins and ends with what has been achieved.

[3] In one of his notebooks (Add. 5436, 62), quoted in H. Butterfield, *Man on His Past* (p. 98), Acton observes: 'Expressions like: the growth of language, physiology of the State, national psychology, the mind of the Church, the development of Platonism, the continuity of law—questions which occupy half the mental activity of our age—were unintelligible to the eighteenth century—to Hume, Johnson, Smith, Diderot.' But it is not less true to say that the last eighty years have seen the rejection of most, if not all, of these concepts; they have again become unintelligible.

And secondly, if we study the utterances of those who have displayed a sustained interest in the past, especially those of recent writers, we shall find, in addition to practical and contemplative statements, statements in what appears to be another idiom. And since this other kind of statement is, generally speaking, found *only* in the writings of those whom we are now accustomed to recognize as 'historians' we may think it profitable to consider whether they do not provide a hint of an attitude towards the past which, being neither specifically practical, nor scientific, nor contemplative, may properly be called 'historical'.

SIX

Now, with these considerations in mind we are perhaps in a better position to tackle the question, what is the activity of being an historian? with greater expectation of reaching a reasoned conclusion.

We have observed, first, that 'the historian' is one who understands the events of the world before him as evidence for events that have already taken place. Other sorts of inquiries do this also; 'the historian' is unique in never doing any else. But, what sort of statements does he make about the past thus revealed? What is the character of these statements about the past which 'historians' (but not other kinds of writers about the past) sometimes (but not always) make?

Their first characteristic is that they are *not* designed to assimilate the past to a present, either of fact or desire: the attitude towards the past is *not* what I have called a practical attitude.

The practical man reads the past backwards. He is interested in and recognizes only those past events which he can relate to present activities. He looks to the past in order to explain his present world, to justify it, or to make it a more habitable and a less mysterious place. The past consists of happenings recognized to be contributory or non-contributory to a subsequent condition of things, or to be friendly or hostile to a desired condition of things. Like the gardener, the practical man distinguishes, in past happenings, between weeds and permissible growths; like the lawyer, he distinguishes between legitimate and illegitimate children. If he is a politician, he approves whatever in the past appears to support his political predilections and denounces whatever is hostile to them. If he is a moralist he imposes upon the past a moral structure, distinguishing virtue and vice in human character, right and wrong in human action, approving the one and condemning the other. If his point of observation gives him a wide view, he perceives in the more profound movements of events those that are malign and those that are beneficent. If he is governed by a favourite project, the past appears as a conflict of events and actions relative to that project. In short, he treats the past as he treats the present, and the statements he is disposed to make about past actions and persons are of the same kind as those he is disposed to make about a contemporary situation in which he is involved.

But in the specifically 'historical' attitude (as represented in the kind of statements about the past I have in mind as peculiar to historical writers), the past is *not* viewed in relation to the present, and is *not* treated as if it were the present. Everything that the evidence reveals or points to is recognized to have its place; nothing is excluded, nothing is regarded as 'non-contributory'. The place of an event is not determined by its relation to subsequent events.[4] What is being sought here is neither a justification, nor a criticism nor an explanation of a subsequent or present condition of things. In 'history' no man dies too soon or by 'accident'; there are no successes and no failures and no illegitimate children. Nothing is approved, there being no desired condition of things in relation to which approval can operate; and nothing is denounced. This past is without the moral, the political or the social structure which the practical man transfers from *his* present to *his* past. The Pope's intervention did not change the course of events, it *was* the course of events, and consequently his action was not an 'intervention'. X did not die 'too soon'; he died when he did. Y did not dissipate his resources in a series of useless wars: the wars belong to the actual course of events, not some imaginary illegitimate course of events.

---

[4] Compare Maitland's attitude to a legal document with that of the practising lawyer.

It was not 'the Liberator' who addressed the meeting in Dublin; it was Daniel O'Connell. In short, there is to be found an attitude towards the past which is discernibly different from the 'practical' attitude; and since this attitude is characteristic (though, of course, with some qualifications) of those whom we are accustomed to call 'historians' because of their sustained and exclusive interest in the past, its counterpart may be called the specifically 'historical' past. And further, on this reading of the situation, statements in the practical idiom about the past must be recognized, not as 'untrue' statements (because there is nothing to exclude them from being true within their own universe of discourse: if anyone died 'accidentally', William the Conqueror certainly did; and, so far as Charles V's policy was concerned, the Pope *did* intervene), but merely as 'non-historical' statements about the past.

This distinction between the 'practical' and the 'historical' past may be re-enforced by a further observation. The attention of the practical man is directed to the past by the miscellany of present happenings which, on account of his current interests, ambitions and directions of activity, are important to him, or by the present happenings which chance puts in his way or in which the vicissitudes of his life happen to involve him. That is to say, the materials of which he may ask the question, What evidence does it supply about the past? come to him either by chance or in an uncriticized choice. In short, his evidence, what he begins with, is something he merely accepts from the happenings around him; he neither looks for it, nor rejects anything that is offered. But with the historian this is not so. His inquiry into the past is not determined by chance encounters with current happenings. He collects for himself a world of present experiences (documents etc.), which is determined by considerations of appropriateness and completeness. It is from *this* world of present experiences that the 'historical' past springs.

In this reading of it, then, the activity of 'the historian' may be said (in virtue of its emancipation from a practical interest in the past) to represent an interest in past events for their own sake, or in respect of their independence of subsequent or present events.

In short, it may be recognized as what I have called, in a general sense, a 'scientific' attitude towards the past. And on this account we are not surprised to observe that what, generally speaking, may be called a 'scientific' attitude towards the world, and an 'historical' attitude towards the past, have emerged together, and with some interdependence, in modern Europe. For, the specification of the activity of being a 'scientist' and the specification of the activity of being an 'historian' were both achieved in a process of emancipation from the primordial and once almost exclusive practical attitude of mankind. Nor, again, is it surprising that, for example, an inquiry into the stars emancipated from a practical interest and partnered by statements about them in the 'scientific' idiom and not the practical idiom,[5] should have appeared somewhat in advance of a similar emancipation in respect of inquiry into the past. The past choices and actions of mankind are so supremely eligible to be regarded and spoken about as if they were present, and the past is so important a component in practical activity, that to free oneself from this attitude must be recognized as an immensely difficult achievement—far more difficult than the parallel achievements of not *always* understanding the world before us only in relation to our current desires and enterprises.

Nevertheless, the observation of this general affinity between a 'scientific' attitude towards the world and an 'historical' attitude towards the past has been an occasion of stumbling. It provoked a disposition to think it proper that wherever the activity of being a scientist led (as that activity became more narrowly specified), the activity of being an historian should follow. And, in particular, the concern of the scientist with general causes and with necessary and sufficient conditions was taken as a model which 'the historian' should follow as best he could. What was forgotten was that the condition of these concerns of the 'scientist' was their application

[5] By a 'scientific' inquiry into the stars I do not, of course, mean either an inquiry unprovoked by a desire for useful information (in connection with navigation, for example), or an inquiry by its character excluded from providing such information; I mean an inquiry in which the stars are not regarded (as they once were) as interesting on account of their power to determine or reveal human destiny. Indeed, an attitude towards the stars in which they are understood in respect of their independence of ourselves is a condition of any inquiry which could produce useful information (e.g. in navigation).

to hypothetical situations, a condition which should at once have been recognized as separating his activity from any that could be properly attributed to an 'historian'. However, the intoxication of the historian with the more specific (as distinct from the general) concerns of the scientist, was short lived; it lasted little more than a hundred years. And, paradoxically, it must be regarded as a belated intrusion of a practical attitude into an activity which was already in process of specifying itself by means of an emancipation from this interest. For the enterprise of distinguishing general causes in respect of past events is now to be recognized as an attempt to assimilate once more (but in a new and apparently more profitable manner) the past to the present and the future, an attempt to make the past speak to the present, and consequently as a relapse in the direction of practice.

In the 'historian's' understanding of events, just as none is 'accidental', so none is 'necessary' or 'inevitable'. What we can observe him doing in his characteristic inquiries and utterances is, not extricating general causes or necessary and sufficient conditions, but setting before us the events (in so far as they can be ascertained) which mediate one circumstance to another. A scientist may detect a set of conditions which compose the necessary and sufficient conditions of a hypothetical situation denoted by the expression 'combustion' or 'oxidation'; when these are present, and nothing else is present to hinder their operation, combustion takes place. But 'the historian', although he sometimes writes of the outbreak of war as a 'conflagration', nevertheless leaves us in no doubt that he knows of no set of conditions which may properly be called the necessary and sufficient conditions of war. He knows only a set of happenings which, when fully set out, make the outbreak of *this* war seem neither an 'accident', nor a 'miracle', nor a necessary event, but merely an intelligible occurrence. This, for example, is what de Tocqueville does in *L'Ancien Régime:* the French Revolution is come upon, and its character is exhibited, not as the necessary and inevitable consequence of preceding events, but as an intelligible convergence of human choices and actions.

Or, consider this passage from Maitland:

The theory that land in the last resort is held of the King
becomes the theory of our law at the Norman Conquest. It is
assumed in Doomsday Book . . . quietly assumed as the basis
of the survey. On the other hand we can say with certainty
that before the Conquest this was not the theory of English
law. Towards such a theory English law had been tending for
a long while past, very possibly the time was fast
approaching when the logic of the facts would have generated
this idea; the facts, the actual legal relationships, were such
that the wide principle 'all land held in the last resort of the
King' would not greatly disturb them. Still this principle had
not been evolved. It came to us from abroad; but it came in
the guise of a quiet assumption; no law forced it upon the
conquered country; no law was necessary; in Normandy lands
were held of the Duke, the Duke again held of the King; of
course it was the same in England; no other system was
conceivable. The process of confiscation gave the Conqueror
abundant opportunity for making the theory true in fact; the
followers whom he rewarded with forfeited lands would of
course hold of him; the great English landowners, whose
lands were restored to them, would of course hold of him. As
to the smaller people, when looked at from a point of view
natural to a Norman, they were already tenants of the great
people, and when the great people forfeited their rights, there
was but a change of lords. This assumption was sometimes
true enough, perhaps in other cases quite false; in many
cases it would seem but the introduction of a new and
simpler terminology; he who formerly was a *landowner*
personally bound to a lord, became a land tenant holding
land of a lord. There was not legislation, and I believe no
chronicler refers to the introduction of this new theory. As to
the later lawyers, Glanvil and Bracton, they never put it into
words. They never state as a noteworthy fact that all land is
held of the King: *of course* it is.

Here what is being disclosed is a process of change. Maitland is not
concerned with general causes or with necessary and sufficient conditions. He shows us a happening (in this case, a manner of think-

ing about land); and in order to make it intelligible he shows us how events converged to provoke this happening.

Briefly, then, and without supposing it to be the last word on this difficult subject, it seems that there is an attitude towards the past, which has emerged gradually and in the face of many hindrances, in which past events are understood as 'facts' and not mere 'images', are understood in respect of their independence of subsequent events or present circumstances or desires, and are understood as having no necessary and sufficient conditions. That is, there is an attitude towards the past, which provokes a specific kind of inquiry and utterance, but is neither a practical, nor a scientific, nor a contemplative attitude. There may be few inquirers into the past who persevere in this attitude without any relapse into other attitudes; but when we find this attitude adhered to consistently we recognize it as a noteworthy achievement. And the propriety of denoting it as a specifically 'historical' attitude rests upon two observations. First, although this attitude is not *always* exhibited in the inquiries and utterances of writers we are accustomed to call 'historians', it is exhibited *only* by such writers. And secondly, the activity of being an historian is not a gift bestowed suddenly upon the human race, but an achievement. It has emerged gradually from a miscellany of activities in which present events are understood as evidence for past happenings; and what seems to have been thrown up in this process of specification is an attitude of the kind I have described.

Nevertheless, it must be acknowledged that it imparts to the past, and so the world, a peculiarly tentative and intermediate kind of intelligibility, and we may find ourselves provoked to look beyond it. It exhibits an elementary 'scientific' character, and thus often seems to point to a more comprehensively 'scientific' understanding of the world in which past events are recognized as examples of general laws. But while the pursuit of this more strictly 'scientific' understanding is enticing, and might (for a while) divert attention from what we now recognize as the enterprise in 'historical' understanding, the difficulties it would encounter (both in making its conceptual structure coherent and in the acquisition of appropriate information) would be great; and it is not easy to see how (even if it achieved conclusions of some sort) the one could ever be shown to supersede the other.

SEVEN

My contention has been that, in current reflection, the enterprise of specifying more exactly the character of 'history' has taken the course of excluding 'the historian' from certain kinds of inquiry and certain kinds of utterance, but that, in default of a concerted understanding of what at present it is to be an historian, we are unable to judge the cogency of these exclusions or the appropriateness of the reasoning with which each is supported. And, whatever the defects of the view of the activity of an historian I have put before you, it at least has the merit of allowing us to do what we were not able to do before. (Whether it enables us to do it correctly is, of course, another matter.) For it now appears that most, if not all, the exclusions which current reflection has suggested are designed to insulate the activity of 'the historian' more conclusively from what I have called a 'practical' attitude towards past events; indeed, this has been the effect of nearly all the technical achievements of historiography during the last two hundred years. And because, in the piecemeal method of determining the character of 'historical' inquiry, this has been lost sight of (or has never properly appeared), the exclusions have often been imperfectly specified and have often been supported by irrelevant reasoning.

For example, the suspicion we have of the notion of historical inquiry as an inquiry into 'origins' turns out to be a proper suspicion, but not for the reasons usually given. 'The historian' is disposed to decline the search for 'origins', not because the expression 'origin' is ambiguous (opening the door to a confusion between a 'cause' and a 'beginning'), or because 'origins' are beyond the reach of discovery, or because they are of insignificant interest, but because to inquire into 'origins' is to read the past backwards and thus assimilate it to subsequent or present events. It is an inquiry which looks to the past to supply information about the 'cause' or the 'beginning' of an already specified situation. And governed by this restricted purpose, it recognizes the past only in so far as it is represented in this situation, and imposes upon past events an arbitrary teleological structure. It is, for example, the practising lawyer, and not Maitland, who is disposed to regard inquiry into the past as a search for 'origins'. In short, such expressions as 'the origins of the French Revolution', 'the origins of Christianity', or 'the origins of the Tory Party' denote a backward reading of the past and the incursion of a practical attitude into what purports to be an 'historical' inquiry. Instead of provoking the inquirer to discover the manner in which one concrete situation is mediated into another, it provokes him merely to an abstract view of the past, the counterpart of the abstraction he has chosen to investigate.

Further, we have been warned to be sceptical about the possibility of genuine historical inquiry into the events of the recent past; and we have been warned of the qualified 'historical' character that we should expect of 'official' inquiries into the past. Here also, the view of 'history' I have suggested reinforces these warnings; indeed it extends their scope. But at the same time it transforms, rather than merely confirms, the reasoning with which they are usually supported. A variety of reasons is given for believing that inquiring into the recent past, and 'official' inquiry into the past, cannot be expected to achieve the status of 'historical' investigation. It is said that recent events are particularly difficult to get into focus, that the survival of prejudice hinders detachment and that the evidence to be mastered is at once vast in bulk and at the same time often frustratingly incomplete. And it is said that 'official' inquiring into the past is liable to be qualified by the presence of interests other than that of the discovery of the 'truth'. And all this is well observed. But the real ground of our scepticism is the observation that the past always comes to us, in the first place, in the idiom of practice and has to be translated into the idiom of 'history', and that it is specially difficult for 'the historian' to perform his task of translation when change of circumstances, the passage of time, or the intrusion of indifference has done little or nothing to assist him. Just as it is easier to 'contemplate' an object which uselessness and irrelevance to current enterprises insulates and puts a frame round, and just as it is easier to see the joke when it is not against oneself, so it will be easier (other things being equal) to make 'history' out of a past which does not positively provoke a nonhistorical attitude.

Moreover, this reading of the situation not only puts our scepticism upon firmer ground; it also enlarges its scope in two directions. First, it becomes clear that a wide sympathy for all the persons and interests engaged in a situation (that is to say, mere absence of bias) can never, by itself, turn a 'practical' account of the situation into an 'historical' account: we are dealing here with two discrete universes of discourse. And secondly, it appears that it is not only the recent past that it is difficult to see 'historically'; it is any period or situation that circumstantially provokes a practical interest. Not so long ago what are called 'the middle ages' of Europe were pre-eminent in provoking a practical attitude; it was exceedingly difficult not to assimilate the events of those times, in one way or another, to later times and to the present. Indeed, the expression 'middle ages' (like the expressions 'ancient', 'modern', 'renaissance', 'enlightened', 'gothic', etc.) began life as 'practical' not 'historical' expressions, and have only recently begun to acquire a limited 'historical' usefulness.[6] The study of the middle ages began under the shadow of the political destruction of the institutions of feudal society, and it was a long time before it escaped from this shadow. And there is much to be said for the belief that the seventeenth century past of England, and perhaps the Norman past of Ireland, are, at the present time, less easy for us to insulate from a practical (political or religious) attitude, and more difficult for us to view 'historically', than almost any other period of our past. An 'historical' attitude towards the Duke of Alva is, even now, difficult to achieve in Belgium; and it is still not easy for Spanish writers to translate the Iberian civilization of the Moors into the idiom of 'history'; that is to

[6] It is worth recalling Huisinga's observation that these and similar expressions (e.g. 'Carolingian', 'feudal', 'christian', 'humanist') in historical writing are not to be regarded as hypotheses to be proved or foundations upon which large structures may be built, but as terms to be used lightly for whatever particle of intelligibility or illumination they may contain.

say, not to write about it as if it were an intrusion, illegitimate and regrettable. In short, when the true ground of the difficulty of writing near-contemporary 'history' is made to appear, it reveals itself as the ground of a much wider field of difficulties in the 'historical' investigation of the past.[7]

But the recommendation to the historian to exclude moral judgment (not, of course, the description of conduct in, generally speaking, moral terms) from his utterance affords the best example both of the usefulness and the defects of our current manner of specifying the activity of 'the historian'. On the view of the activity I have suggested, the exclusion of expressions of moral approval and condemnation and of expressions which purport to determine the moral value of conduct in the past, is confirmed; but the reasoning with which this exclusion is usually supported is seen to be, for the most part, misconceived or irrelevant. Various reasons are given. We are told that the moral assessment of past conduct involves the application either of absolute moral standards (about which nevertheless there is no agreement), or of the standards current when and where the actions were performed (and in this case the inquirer is merely concerned to elicit what a moralist of the time *would* have said; whereas he would be much better employed in eliciting what was in fact said, and thus make his inquiry a 'history' of moral opinions), or of the standards of some other place and time, the present time, for example (and 'historically' there seems no more reason to choose one time and place as our point of reference rather than another, and the whole activity is revealed as arbitrary and redundant). And we are told, further, that since the moral goodness and badness of conduct relates to the motives of actions and since motives are always hidden in the recesses of the soul, evidence will

---

[7] 'The fact that the political struggles, so to call them, of modern history being part of the same in which we are ourselves engaged, affects the value of the history both ways. It increases our concern, while at the same time it blinds and distorts our view. To what an extent it is likely to do this latter may be concluded from the fact that, even as regards ancient history and times long past, if there is any resemblance between the politics then and now, we seem scarcely able to look fairly at them. A certain degree of remoteness, then, in the objects of history is desirable, though not always effective against prejudice similar to our prejudice now, and quite necessary against the actual mixture of our present prejudiced views of things with the history: we want it for every reason to stand well off from us'. John Grote, in *Cambridge Essays*, 1856, p. 111.

always be lacking to pronounce moral judgments of this sort about either past or present conduct. But this argument would only exclude moral imputations, not moral appraisals, from the writings of 'the historian'; whereas the intention was to exclude both. The truth is, however, that the ground for excluding moral judgment from 'historical' inquiry and utterance is not the difficulty of agreeing upon a standard to apply, nor the alleged absence of evidence, but the observation that to pronounce upon the moral value of conduct, and the imposition of a moral structure upon the past, represents the incursion of a practical interest into the investigation of the past. And, as we have seen, when this interest intrudes there is room for no other. The investigator of the past who appears as an advocate in the cause of good behaviour succeeds only in setting before us a practical past. When we judge the *moral* value of past conduct, just as when we judge the value or usefulness of past conduct from any other point of view ('useless' wars, for example), we are treating it as if it were present; and no other reason than this need be given for the exclusion of moral judgment from the activity of 'the historian'. In short, to inquire into the moral value of past conduct is to relapse into a practical attitude towards the past, and if relapse were allowed at this point, it could not properly be disallowed at any other.

It seems, then, that our current manner of specifying the activity of 'the historian' has resulted in a number of observations which, taken together, have gone some way towards delineating the activity. But when the logic of these separate observations is considered, it not only provides a means of confirming or rejecting them, but it also suggests modifications and extensions which put our specification on firmer ground.

EIGHT

There are many conclusions which seem to follow from this reading of the activity of being an historian. It would appear that the task of 'the historian' cannot properly be described as that of recalling or of re-enacting the past; that, in an important sense, an 'historical'

event is something that never happened and an 'historical' action
something never performed; that an 'historical' character is one
that never lived. The idiom of happening is always that of practice,
and the record of happening is usually in the idiom of practice; and
'practice' and 'history' are two logically distinct universes of discourse. The task of 'the historian' is, thus, to create by a process of
translation; to understand past conduct and happening in a manner in which they were never understood at the time; to translate
action and event from their practical idiom into an historical idiom.
But, instead of pursuing any of these conclusions of detail, I wish
to end with a more general observation on the present difficulty of
being an historian.

We have come to believe that (in the same manner as other activities) the activity of being an historian has now achieved some
measure of specification; and perhaps this is so. But while we have
learnt to recognize some of the enemies of the 'historical' attitude
towards the past, we have still far to go in defeating them. If I interpret correctly current reflection on this subject, we consider ourselves (in an intellectual effort spread over nearly a hundred years)
to have struggled out of the *cul de sac* into which historical inquiry
wandered under the guidance of 'science'; and we have come to recognize what I have called the 'practical' attitude to the past as the
chief undefeated enemy of 'history' (although there is still both hesitation and confusion about this). But we recognize, also, that it is a
very difficult enemy to defeat. In this engagement, one of our difficulties springs from our perception that a practical attitude towards the past, and the use of a practical idiom in speaking about
the past, certainly cannot be dismissed as merely illegitimate. Who
are we to forbid it? On what grounds should the primordial activity
of making ourselves at home in the world by assimilating *our* past
to *our* present be proscribed? This, perhaps, is no great difficulty; it
is surmounted when we recognize that the practical past (including
moral judgments about past conduct) is not the enemy of mankind,
but only the enemy of 'the historian'. But we are left with the more
serious difficulty that springs from the fact that the practical idiom

has imposed itself for so long upon *all* inquiry into the past that its hold cannot readily be loosened, and the fact that we live in an intellectual world which, because of its addiction to 'practice', is notably hostile to 'history'.

Nor should we encourage ourselves with false hopes; with the belief that an 'historical' attitude towards the past is now more common than it used to be, the belief (as it is said) that this is in some relevant sense a peculiarly historically-minded age. This, I think, is an illusion. Certainly the disposition of our time is to regard the events that take place before our eyes as evidence for past events, to understand them as 'effects' and to turn to the past to discover their 'causes'; but this disposition is joined with another no less strong, the propensity to assimilate the past to the present. Our predominant interest is not in 'history' but only in retrospective politics. And the past is now more than ever a field in which we exercise our moral and political opinions, like whippets in a meadow on Sunday afternoon. And even our theorists (from whom something better might have been expected) are bent rather upon elucidating the tie between past and present than upon pointing out that what matters is the *kind* of 'present', and that it is precisely the task of 'the historian' to loosen the tie between the past and the 'practical' present.

The 'historian' adores the past; but the world today has perhaps less place for those who love the past than ever before. Indeed, it is determined not to allow events to remove themselves securely into the past; it is determined to keep them alive by a process of artificial respiration or (if need be) to recall them from the dead so that they may deliver their messages. For it wishes only to learn from the past and it constructs a 'living past' which repeats with spurious authority the utterances put into its mouth. But to the 'historian' this is a piece of obscene necromancy: the past he adores is dead. The world has neither love nor respect for what is dead, wishing only to recall it to life again. It deals with the past as with a man, expecting it to talk sense and have something to say apposite to its plebeian 'causes' and engagements. But for the 'historian', for whom the past is dead and irreproachable, the past is feminine. He loves it as a mistress of whom he never tires and whom he never expects to talk sense. Once it was religion which stood in the way of the appearance of the 'historical' past; now it is politics; but always it is this practical disposition.

'History', then, is the product of a severe and sophisticated manner of thinking about the world which has recently emerged from the naïve interest in what surrounds us on account of its intimations of what is no longer present. It represents neither an aesthetic enjoyment, nor a 'scientific' recognition, nor a practical understanding. Like these, it is a dream; but it is a dream of another sort. There is a past, that of legend and saga, which is a drama from which all that is casual, secondary and unresolved has been excluded; it has a clear outline, a unity of feeling and in it everything is exact except place and time. There is a past in which contingencies have been resolved by being recognized as products of necessary and sufficient conditions and as examples of the operation of general laws. And there is a past in which every component is known and is intelligible in respect of its relation to a favoured present. But the 'historical' past is of another sort than these. It is a complicated world, without unity of feeling or clear outline: in it events have no over-all pattern or purpose, lead nowhere, point to no favoured condition of the world and support no practical conclusions. It is a world composed wholly of contingencies and in which contingencies are intelligible, not because they have been resolved, but on account of the circumstantial relations which have been established between them: the historian's concern is not with causes but with occasions. It is a picture drawn on many different scales, and each genuine piece of historical writing has a scale of its own and is to be recognized as an independent example of historical thinking. The activity of being an historian is not that of contributing to the elucidation of a single ideal coherence of events which may be called 'true' to the exclusion of all others; it is an activity in which a writer, concerned with the past for its own sake and working to a chosen scale, elicits a coherence in a group of contingencies of similar magnitudes. And if in so new and so delicate an enterprise he finds himself tempted into making concessions to the idiom of legend, that perhaps is less damaging than other divergencies.

"The Activity of Being an Historian" first appeared in *Historical Studies I*, edited by T. D. Williams, in 1958.

The study of 'politics' in a university
AN ESSAY IN APPROPRIATENESS

The shape of the education offered in a university, like everything else, is subject to change. Those changes which have been engendered within a university by the emergence of some branch of study claiming to be in a condition to take its place beside the others already being pursued by undergraduates have usually been well enough managed. Of course, mistakes have been made, and changes which were distortions have been allowed to take place, but no great damage has been suffered from this cause. The sponsors of a new 'subject' of undergraduate study (and I am not here concerned with anything else) have usually not mistaken the sort of qualities they must claim on its behalf if they were to expect to launch it successfully; and in the early stages of its voyage they have been content to heave the lead every inch of the way. It was in this manner that schools of natural science, of modern history, of modern languages, of English literature and of economics made their appearance in English universities, and studies such as international law and genetics established themselves. Their inception was sometimes eased by the benevolence of a patron content to endow what had been approved; but on every occasion what was admitted to the undergraduate curriculum was something which had already been pursued as an academic study for a generation or more before the proposal was made.

In recent times, however, the shape of university education has been modified by changes springing from a different source. Benefactors with favourite projects of their own, a persuasive and energetic body of evangelists with a patron in their pockets, a profession set upon winning the status of a university study for its *mystique*, or even a government have made proposals designed to modify this shape. And though some of these proposals have turned out to be less disastrous than might have been forecast, they have not, on the whole, been so well managed. Greed, or the desire to appear abreast of the times, have often supervened to destroy both judgment and proper inquiry, and the shape of a university education has suffered some ill-considered and some destructive changes.

'Politics' found its way into English university education in a somewhat tortuous manner, quite unlike the simple and naïve manner in which it entered American university education. Proper consideration was not altogether lacking; there seemed to be something in existing arrangements to which it could appropriately be attached; generous and opinionated benefactors were not absent; persuasive and energetic evangelists often played their part. It was supported by distinguished and sometimes scholarly sponsors; ancient (though, alas, irrelevant) precedent and continental practice (not very closely observed) was cited in its favour; the disposition of the times flattered it. The entry was affected unobtrusively and under a number of different names, which made it appear eligible for whatever interpretation its professors and teachers might be disposed to put upon it. And in these unusual circumstances it is not surprising that, alongside the engagement to teach 'politics' to undergraduates, there should be (rather late in the day) an inquiry about what is to be taught. Confidence has not been lacking, but it has often been an irrevelant confidence in political opinions or in the existence of a suitable body of information to be imparted. And the inquiry itself has not always been well-directed; it has been too easily silenced whenever a likely formula has been devised. 'Politics', we have been told, is 'the study of political behaviour', or 'the study of power in society', or 'the study of political institutions and political theory'; but there has been an ominous silence about the manner in which this study is to be conducted.

This condition of things I find to be unsatisfactory, and I propose to reopen this inquiry and to set it going in a somewhat different direction. The question I propose to consider is: What study under the plausible name of 'Politics' is an appropriate component of a university education? And I propose to explore this theme by considering first the character of a university education in general.

ONE

We have a small stock of ideas at our disposal on this topic. We know that university education is after-school education; and we talk of it as 'advanced' or 'further' or 'higher' or 'specialized' education, education for adults, and so on. But these are all vague ideas, and if they were all we had we might have to confess that 'university' education is not very different from any other sort of education. This, indeed, is what some people believe to be the case. They are content with the distinction between 'elementary' and 'advanced', they think that advanced studies are characterized by greater detail and the requirement of more developed mental powers, and that consequently a 6th Form in a school begins to approximate to a university, and that a technical college is something like a university.

I do not, myself, believe any of this to be the case. I believe that university education is a specific sort of education, in some ways distinguished by its *elementary* character; and that although it is not the only sort of education and cannot take the place of any other sort, it is both important and unique. And I believe, consequently, that every component of a university education is properly a component in virtue of having a certain character or propensity.

Education I will take to be the process of learning, in circumstances of direction and restraint, how to recognize and make something of ourselves. Unavoidably, it is a two-fold process in which we enjoy an initiation into what for want of a better word I will call a 'civilization', and in doing so discover our own talents and aptitudes in relation to that civilization and begin to cultivate and to use them. Learning to make something of ourselves in no context in particular is an impossibility; and the context appears not only in what is learned but also in the conditions of direction and restraint which belong to any education.

Some people think of a civilization as a stock of things like books, pictures, musical instruments and compositions, buildings, cities, landscapes, inventions, devices, machines and so on—in short, as the results of mankind having impressed itself upon a 'natural' world. But this is an unduly restricted (indeed, an exceedingly primitive) understanding of that 'second nature' (as Hegel called it) which is the context of our activity. The world into which we are initiated is composed, rather, of a stock of emotions, beliefs, images, ideas, manners of thinking, languages, skills, practices and manners of activity out of which these 'things' are generated. And consequently it is appropriate to think of it not as a stock but as a capital; that is, somthing known and enjoyed only in use. For none of these is fixed and finished; each is at once an achievement and a promise. This capital has been accumulated over hundreds of years. And in use it earns an interest, part of which is consumed in a current manner of living and part reinvested.

From another point of view, however, a civilization (and particularly ours) may be regarded as a conversation being carried on between a variety of human activities, each speaking with a voice, or in a language of its own; the activities (for example) represented in moral and practical endeavour, religious faith, philosophic reflection, artistic contemplation and historical or scientific inquiry and explanation. And I call the manifold which these different manners of thinking and speaking compose, a conversation, because the relations between them are not those of assertion and denial but the conversational relationships of acknowledgment and accommodation.

If, then, we recognize education as an initiation into a civilization, we may regard it as beginning to learn our way about a material, emotional, moral and intellectual inheritance, and as learning to recognize the varieties of human utterance and to participate in the conversation they compose. And if we consider education as a process in which we discover and begin to cultivate ourselves, we may regard it as learning to recognize ourselves in the mirror of this civilization.

I do not claim universality for this image of education; it is merely the image (or part of it) which belongs to our civilization. But it is impossible to escape this sort of contingency, and we must take it as the context of our inquiry if anything relevant to our situation is to be said.

This education begins in the nursery where, for the most part, a child is learning to become at home in the natural-artificial world into which it was born. Here it is learning to use and to rely upon its senses and its limbs, to control its voice, to recognize its emotions, to suffer and overcome frustrations and to accommodate itself to others. It learns to speak, to play with words and at the same time to use and to understand the symbolic language of practical life. Here everything, or almost everything, is play. The product is insignificant; it is the activity it entails that matters. What is learned is all invested in the child itself; though, of course, being a child is having the command of a capital of pleasure and pain which earns an interest in the family life. And here, also, education has no specific orientation; it is not yet significantly concerned with individual talents and aptitudes, though these may show themselves early.

During school-days this sort of nursery education continues. To begin with, reading is from books designed to teach the recognition of words; writing is an exercise in calligraphy rather than a significant composition; there is the endless repetition of playing scales and pieces designed to improve dexterity; foreign languages appear merely as saying the same things only in other words; arithmetic is an exercise in handling figures.

But gradually and imperceptibly a transformation takes place, or begins to take place; a transformation for which story-telling, singing, drawing, dancing and social intercourse (that is, activities which unavoidably have some significant product, however transitory) have paved the way. *What* is read begins to be significant and to afford an entrance into literature; instrumental music becomes less a thing of the hand and eye than of the ear; and even foreign languages begin to appear as organizations of thoughts incapable of literal translation. In short, the intellectual capital of a civilization begins to be enjoyed and even used while the dexterities by which it is known and recognized are still imperfectly acquired. Or, perhaps, we have no more than a glimpse of how it might be enjoyed or used.

However, there is so much information to be gathered from so many different sources that, in school days, the intellectual inheritance appears much more like a stock of ideas, beliefs, perceptions, images and so on, than a capital. We acquire much that we do not know how to use, and much that we never think of in terms of use, that is, of investment to generate something valuable on its own account. Learning here is borrowing raw material the possible uses of which remain concealed. Or, to put it another way, most of what is learned is immediately and automatically reinvested in the ability to learn so that it appears to have no specific communicable or shareable product.

School-education, then, is not merely early education or simple education; it has a specific character. It is learning to speak before one has anything significant to say; and what is taught must have the qualities of being able to be learned without necessarily being understood, and of not being positively hurtful or nonsensical when learned in this way. Or, it may be said, what is taught must be capable of being learned without any previous recognition of ignorance: we do not begin to learn the multiplication tables because it suddenly dawns upon us that we do not know the sum of nine 8s, nor the dates of the Kings of England because we know we do not know when Edward I came to the throne: we learn these things at school because we are told to learn them. And further, school-education is without specific orientation; it is not yet concerned with individual talents and aptitudes, and if these show themselves (as they may) the design in school-education is not to allow them to take charge. At school we are, quite properly, not permitted to follow our own inclinations.

But our 'school-days' are now a longer period than they used to be; never less than ten years and for some fourteen and fifteen years. And before they come to an end, features of 'specialization' (as it is called) have begun to make their appearance in education. This I believe to be a mistake. But one can perceive the illusion of those who have imposed this mistake upon school-education, and one can discern the misapplied pressures which have encouraged it. What it entails, however, is that the area of delusive overlap between this level of education and other levels has been increased and what belongs properly to school-days is unfortunately curtailed in favour of a kind of 'specialization' which belongs neither to a vocational education nor to a university education and which stands in the way of both; namely, a 'specialization' in which the range of study is arbitrarily restricted without either an increase in depth or any specific orientation. Or, if there is an orientation, giving this school-specialization a turn in a 'vocational' direction, then it conflicts with the commendable English tradition that professional education should be seriously undertaken from its beginning and should not be preceded by a sort of pantomime: to learn a profession is to learn how to *do* something and the best preparation for this is not to learn how to act as if you were doing it.

Leaving school is, then, a momentous occasion. It is the signal for the appearance of a new attitude towards the capital we have inherited. Nevertheless, education continues, and it is apt to branch out in two different directions—which I shall call 'vocational' education and 'university' education. And these represent two different and to some extent complementary attitudes towards the capital which composes a civilization. They are two different kinds of education.

From one point of view, a civilization may be regarded as a collection of skills which together make possible and define a current manner of living. Learning one of these skills—that of a lawyer, a doctor, an accountant, an electrician, a farmer, a motor-mechanic or a commercial traveller—is borrowing an appropriate quantum of the total capital and learning to use it in such a manner that it earns an interest—an interest which, in principle, may be either expended in current consumption or reinvested to produce improvements in the skill itself. Each of these skills has an intellectual content, and many have a component of physical dexterity. A purely physical dexterity (pushing a barrow in Covent Garden comes near to this) is not a skill; it entails a negligible call upon the capital which composes a civilization, and the interest it earns (which is minimal) is all dispersed in current consumption. On the other hand, a skill with a large intellectual content is one which makes a considerable call upon capital (an emblem of which is the length of time required to learn it), and it is capable of earning a large unconsumed interest.

'Vocational' education is that in which these skills are acquired; and in this sort of education a civilization has the naïve appearance of the things known and the skills practised which are entailed in a current manner of living. This manner of living is never, of course, fixed and finished; but it has some sort of general direction of contemporary movement depending upon these skills and others which may spring from them. Nor is it ever absolutely coherent: it is composed of skills which are on their way out and those which are on their way in; with us, heraldry and the hand-loom lie side by side with animal genetics and the computer.

Now, in respect of what is taught and learned in this 'vocational' kind of education, some observations may be made. For most people it is an education in *one* skill. The skill may be complicated and may have a considerable intellectual content, or it may be simple and easily learned. But it is, essentially, a highly specialized education, and not only on account of its concentration upon a single skill. For, learning here means acquiring a specific body of knowledge and being able to move about within it with ease and confidence and to use it. The sort of familiarity which a carpenter or a builder may have with his tools and his materials often goes far beyond anything that is achieved, with *his* tools and materials, by an historian of the Papacy or a classical scholar; but there is a reason for this, namely, that his is a strictly circumscribed body of knowledge which does not significantly look outside itself. The design of a 'vocational' education is to be concerned with current practice and always with what is believed to be known. How it came to be known, what errors and imperfections it has left behind are no more significant than the practices of a sixteenth century printer are to a twentieth century linotype operator. The significant principle of specialization in this sort of education derives not only from the fact that most learners are concerned to acquire only one skill, but from its being concerned to impart to the learner what may be called the current achievement of a civilization in respect of a skill or practice needed in the contemporary world. In short, a 'vocational' education, while it does not absolutely forbid it, is not concerned with that level of learning at which what is learned is capable of earning an unconsumed interest: it makes no provision for teaching people how to be ignorant; knowledge here is never the recognition of something absent.

And here I want to introduce a distinction which I propose to use later on: the distinction between a 'language' (by which I mean a manner of thinking) and a 'literature' or a 'text' (by which I mean what has been said from time to time in a 'language'). It is the distinction, for example, between the 'language' of poetic imagination and a poem or a novel; or between the 'language' or manner of thinking of a scientist and a text-book of geology or what may be called the current state of our geological knowledge.

Now, what is being studied in a 'vocational' education is a 'literature' or a 'text' and not a 'language'. What is being acquired is a knowledge of what has been authoritatively said and not a familiarity with the manner of thinking which has generated what has been said. For example, in this sort of education what is learned is not how to think in a scientific manner, how to recognize a scientific problem or proposition or how to use the 'language' of science, but how to use those products of scientific thought which contribute to our current manner of living. Or, if this distinction seems to be too rigid, then it may be said that in a 'vocational' education what is learnt is not a 'living' language with a view to being able to speak it and say new things in it, but a 'dead' language; and it is learnt merely for the purpose of reading a 'literature' or a 'text' in order to acquire the information it contains. The skill acquired is the skill of using the information, not of speaking the 'language'.

Further, 'vocational' education is learning one of the skills of current life. Generally speaking only those skills which are currently practised are taught. This, where the skill is an ancient skill, sometimes entails drawing upon long accumulated capital; but in most cases it means drawing only upon capital accumulated in the last hundred years, or fifty, or even twenty: for the electrical engineer the world began the day before yesterday. In other words, a 'vocational' education is education to fit a man to fill a specific place in a current manner of living, or to satisfy a current demand. And consequently, it is not utterly far-fetched (as it would be in the case of school-education and, as we shall see, of a university education) to attempt to determine the number of persons who are needed to be trained in any particular skill if a current manner of living is to be sustained.

Now, as I understand it, university education is something entirely different from both school and 'vocational' education. It differs in respect of what is taught (and the criterion for determining what is appropriate to be taught), and in respect of how it is taught; and where it is a specialized education (which it need not be, but a 'vocational' education must be), the principle of specialization is different from that which is characteristic of 'vocational' education. Or, if that seems too dogmatic, then, I may say that I think that there *is* a sort of education which is clearly different from both school and 'vocational' education, and I think it is the sort which for centuries has been the concern of what we have hitherto called universities. And, to put it briefly, a university education is unlike either a school or a 'vocational' education because it is an education in 'languages' rather than 'literatures', and because it is concerned with the use and management of explanatory languages (or modes of thought) and not prescriptive languages. While a school-boy may be a passionate reader and may acquire from some books a store of information and from others a knowledge of himself and of how to behave, at a university he will be invited to seek something different from, perhaps, these same books. And he will come to understand that some books whose information is out-of-date or whose prescriptive utterances (if any) are unreliable—Gibbon or Stubbs, Dicey, Bagehot, Clark-Maxwell, Adam Smith—and are therefore worthless in a 'vocational' education, nevertheless have something to offer appropriate to a university education.

First, a university is an association of persons, locally situated, engaged in caring for and attending to the whole intellectual capital which composes a civilization. It is concerned not merely to keep an intellectual inheritance intact, but to be continuously recovering what has been lost, restoring what has been neglected, collecting together what has been dissipated, repairing what has been corrupted, reconsidering, reshaping, reorganizing, making more intelligible, reissuing and reinvesting. In principle, it works undistracted by practical concerns; its current directions of interest are not determined by any but academic considerations; the interest it earns is all reinvested.

This engagement is not, of course, confined to universities; many who are not members of one of these associations take part in it. But nowhere else is it undertaken in the manner I have described (that is, continuously and exhaustively) except in a university. And when universities have been negligent of this engagement, there has been nothing comparable to take their place. For the essence is that it is a co-operative enterprise, in which different minds, critical of one another, are engaged; and that it concerns not merely that part of our intellectual capital which has been accumulated in the last fifty or a hundred years, and not merely those items which have some immediate and practical contemporary relevance. And consequently, in a society (such as ours) which has a high standard of practical relevance, universities have often to be defended. And the usual defence is either to show that they also contribute (as least obliquely) to the prosecution of current undertakings, or to claim for them the status of an 'amenity'—that is, a piece of costly nonsense protected by our sentimental attachment from designed and immediate destruction but not so well protected against the imposition upon them of alien directions of activity.

Secondly, in a university this intellectual capital appears not as an accumulated result, an authoritative doctrine, a reliable collection of information, or a current condition of knowledge, but as a variety of modes of thinking or directions of intellectual activity, each speaking with a voice, or in a 'language' of its own, and related to one another conversationally—that is, not as assertion or denial, but as oblique recognition and accommodation. Science, for example, in a university, is not an encyclopædia of information or the present state of our 'physical' knowledge: it is a current activity, an explanatory manner of thinking and speaking being explored. And the same is true of mathematics, of philosophy and of history: each is an idiom of thought, a 'language' neither dead nor used simply to convey results, but in constant process of being explored and used. Doctrines, ideas, theories, which are used elsewhere to yield practical profits or to keep going a practical manner of living (like the Mendelian theory of biological inheritance, the molecular structure of matter, or Parkinson's law), in a university are recognized as temporary achievements whose value is their reinvestment value, and reinvestment here is being used in the exploration of the 'language', the explanatory manner of thinking and speaking, to which they properly belong.

Thirdly, a university is a place, not merely of learning and research, but of education. And what distinguishes the education it offers is, first of all, the character of the place itself. To study in a university is not like studying under a learned private scholar, nor is it like being taken on the grand tour by a lively and well-informed tutor. Each of these would be an education, but neither is a university education. Nor again, is it like being given the run of a first-class library. University education is the sort of education that may be enjoyed by having the run of a place where the activities I have described are going on and are going on in the manner I have described. And this distinguishes it, at once, from any other kind of education—school-education, the education available in a place of specialized 'vocational' training, in a polytechnic where a variety of skills are taught, in a specialized research institute which offers a few places for pupils, and that provided by a private scholar, engaged in one of these activities, who takes a pupil, as Döllinger took the young Acton. To be no more than a recognized spectator is to enjoy the opportunity of a kind of education which a different sort of place does not and cannot give, and which universities have offered in varying degrees ever since medieval times when they were places of 'chivalric' disputation between Masters and Doctors and undergraduates were spectator-learners of a mystery. In short, there appears in a university what cannot (or cannot so easily) appear elsewhere, the image of a civilization as a manifold of different intellectual activities, a conversation between different modes of thinking; and this determines the character of the education it offers.

Finally, a university is an association of persons engaged in formal teaching. In this respect it is distinguished by the engagements of the teachers. As teachers, they may be either better or worse than those elsewhere; but they are different because they are themselves learners engaged in learning something other than what they undertake to teach. They are not people with a set of conclusions, facts, truths, dogmas, etc., ready to impart or with a well-tried doctrine to hand out; nor are they people who make it their main business to be familiar with what may be called 'the current state of knowledge' in their department of study: each is a person engaged in the activity of exploring a particular mode of thought in particular connections.

Nevertheless, *what* they teach is not what they themselves are in process of learning, nor is it what they may have learned or discovered yesterday. As scholars they may live on what are called the 'frontiers of knowledge', but as teachers they must be something other than frontiersmen. Nor, again, is what they teach exactly the activity in which they are themselves engaged: their pupils are not exactly apprentices to an activity. A scientist, an historian or a philosopher does not teach his pupils to be scientists, historians, or philosophers. That is to say, his engagement as a teacher is not merely to educate possible successors to himself—though some of his pupils may turn out to be this. What a university teacher has, and what (because he is not distracted by considerations of immediate usefulness or contemporary appropriateness) he may impart, is familiarity with the modes of thought, the 'languages' which, from one point of view, compose the whole intellectual capital of a civilization. What a university has to offer is not information but practice in thinking; and not practice in thinking in no manner in particular but in specific manners each capable of reaching its own characteristic kind of conclusions. And what undergraduates may get at a university, and nowhere else in such favourable circumstances, is some understanding of what it is to think historically, mathematically, scientifically or philosophically, and some understanding of these not as 'subjects', but as living 'languages' and of those who explore and speak them as being engaged in explanatory enterprises of different sorts.

Going further, a university may be recognized as an association of teachers of this sort whose activity reflects some beliefs about how this sort of teaching may best be carried on. And the most important of these beliefs (now, alas, somewhat eroded) is that the proper way to impart a mode of thinking (that is, a 'language') is in conjunction with the study of an appropriate 'literature' or 'text': the belief that learning to think scientifically is best achieved by studying, not some so-called 'scientific method,' but some particular branch of science; and learning to think historically is to be achieved, not by studying something called 'the historical method', but by observing and following an historian at work upon a particular piece or aspect of the past. This (but only to the unwary) may suggest an approximation of university to 'vocational' education, but that this is an illusion is revealed when we observe that in a university education a 'text' is understood, not as an organization of information but as the paradigm of a 'language'. Consequently, with the recognition in a university that 'languages' may be most appropriately studied in conjunction with 'literatures' goes the recognition that some 'literatures' (that is, some branches of scientific study, some periods or passages of history, some legal systems, some philosophical writers) are in a more appropriate condition to be studied, or offer a clearer paradigm of the 'language' concerned, and that it is these 'literatures' or 'texts', and for these reasons, that the undergraduate is encouraged to read: chemistry rather than solar physics; the history of medieval England rather than of contemporary Java: Roman Law rather than Hittite or Celtic; Aristotle, Hume or Kant rather than Democritus, Leibnitz, Rickert or Bergson. And this is a convenient and appropriate way of determining what is to be studied because it leaves room for change and it indicates a criterion by which a branch of learning is to be judged in respect of undergraduate study—a criterion which is purely pædagogic and has nothing whatever to do with vocational or other extraneous considerations, such as the current academic interest of scholars, which may be in an entirely unsuitable condition for undergraduate pursuit.

From this enterprise of teaching undergraduates something about the intellectual capital of our civilization there has emerged, in general, two marginally different manners of setting it out for undergraduate study. Two sorts of 'specialized' study have established themselves. In the one (perhaps best represented by 'Greats'), a variety of modes of thinking—e.g. historical, philosophical, poetic, legal, and perhaps scientific—are studied, but in connection with 'literatures' or 'texts' in the Greek and Latin tongues or having place in the world of classical antiquity. In the other (represented by Schools of Modern History, of Mathematics, of Natural Science etc.), a single 'language', or mode of thought, is studied in connection with whatever 'literatures' or 'texts' there may be available in a suitable condition from time to time—e.g. the Constitutional History of Medieval England, Chemistry, Physics, Geology, etc., the English Law of Property, the poetry of sixteenth-century England, and so on. What determines the choice of these 'literatures' rather than others is their appropriateness to represent modes of thought; and this is recognized to depend upon their current condition, and (of course) their appropriateness for study by undergraduates who had received a certain sort of school-education.

This, then, is what I understand by university education. It is not something nebulous or indistinct, but something clear, unmistakable and distinct from every other sort of education. To be an undergraduate is to enjoy the 'leisure' which is denoted by thinking without having to think in the pragmatic terms of action and talking without having to speak in terms of prescription or practical advice—the 'leisure', in short, which distinguishes the peculiar academic engagement of explanation. And the belief that it is valuable, even for those who are to pass their lives in practical occupations of one sort or another and for whom (in that connection) a 'vocational' education may also be appropriate, to spend three years in which attention (so far as their studies are concerned) is expressly abstracted from prescriptive manners of thinking in order to concentrate it, not merely upon explanations, but upon the understanding of explanatory enterprises, is the belief in which the whole specific character of a university education is abridged. And anyone who wishes to impose a different character upon university education will not only be transforming the character of universities but will also have taken a decisive step in a direction which points to the removal from the scene of this kind of education.

TWO

Now, it may be supposed that, under the name of 'politics' (or some equivalent word), there is something appropriate to be taught and learned in each of the three kinds or levels of education I have mentioned—school, 'vocational' and university education. Politics, in fact, is talked and written about, studied and taught in a variety of manners which readily distinguish themselves from one another. We may, indeed, find that our present circumstances are not free from confusion, 'politics' being taught (for example) in universities in a manner more appropriate to some other kind of education; but (with this sketch of the respective characters of these sorts of education before us) it should not be impossible to discern the kind of political study appropriate to each.

In respect of school-education there is, I think, little difficulty in determining what in general is appropriate to be taught in this connection. It is, in the first place, something suitable to be learned by everybody, for one of the principles of school-education is that it is without significant orientation. And further, it is something that may be learned without the point of learning it being evident to the learner, and something that if learned in this way is not positively harmful or nonsensical. In the thoughts of the teacher it may be either a propædeutic (like Greek grammar to the reading of Greek poetry) or it may compose a stock of information considered to have some general usefulness on its own account; but in the thoughts of the learner it need not have any more attachment to a specific usefulness than geometry, algebra or physical geography. In short, what is appropriate is something which offers an introduction to an aspect of a civilization (the civilization which is the pupils' inheritance) understood as a stock of ideas, beliefs, images, practices, etc., rather than as a capital. And this, surely, was the character of 'civics' as it used to be taught in schools and is the character of its successor in our school education, namely, 'current affairs': an introduction to the current activities of governments and to the relevant structures and practices with some attention to the beliefs and opinions which may be held to illuminate them. Not, perhaps, a very inspiring study, and in its more desiccated passages (e.g., the duties of a town clerk, the House of Commons at work, and the pronouncements of a Kennedy, a Krushchev or a Castro) unlike Greek irregular verbs in holding out no evident promise of better things to come. Nevertheless, it is capable of defence as part of a school-education on the ground that, with us, politics is everybody's business; and because this sort of study is no more misleading than many other school studies (like economics and history) are bound to be. At least it is something to modify the mystery of the world as it appears in the newpapers, and it entails nothing to prohibit a more profound interest in public affairs such as occasionally (along with county cricket, space travel and church brasses) makes its appearance among school-boys. The interest it serves is an interest in public affairs.

Nor, I think, is there any greater difficulty in determining the character of what may be called a professional or 'vocational' education in politics, that is, an education designed specifically for those who are called upon or who wish to engage in political activity. A 'vocational' education (in the sense in which I am using the expression) may appear when three general conditions are satisfied, and it is apt to appear, in some form or other, whenever these conditions are satisfied. First, there must be a specific skill generally recognized to be entailed in a current manner of living; secondly, there must be something in connection with this skill which is capable of being taught, although it may also require practice which cannot formally be taught before the skill itself can be effectively exercised; and thirdly, there must be people who desire to exercise this skill and therefore desire to be educated in it. And it may plausibly be supposed that all these conditions are satisfied in respect of what we recognize as political activity—that is, activity concerned with governing and the instruments of government. Politics is unmistakably one of the skills entailed in our current manner of living. And not only are there people who engage in it professionally (politicians, party managers, agents and their assistants), but, as in respect of other professional skills (only more so), there are occasional participants or the servants of participants (like government or Trade Union officials) to whom the knowledge which is the stock-in-trade of the professional is also relevant. Indeed, the particular style of politics which has now imposed itself upon the world calls for and accommodates large numbers of these occasional participants, to say nothing of the political commentators and entertainers who have become a feature of our life and who require this information in their daily business. In these circumstances a 'vocational' education in politics has to be recognized as appropriate to a larger, more miscellaneous and consequently less precisely determined set of students than is the case in some (but not in all) other avocations. And if we hesitate to follow those who find it to be an appropriate 'vocational' education for every citizen in a 'democracy', or for a sufficient number to leaven the whole, then it may perhaps be recognized as a 'vocational' education appropriate to those who are, or who wish to be, politically self-conscious. But this does not entail any modification of its character as a 'vocational' education which here, as elsewhere, is an education designed to impart a body of reliable knowledge necessary in the successful exercise of a more or less particularized practical activity. And if the knowledge imparted here is used by some continuously and by others intermittently, by some professionally and by others incidentally, this does not distinguish it from (for example) the knowledge imparted in a professional legal education which is a necessary part of the equipment not only of those who practise the law as a profession but also of many who are engaged in many other businesses and occupations. And lastly, whatever doubts we may have about its extent, reliability and coherence (and whatever else we may think it desirable for a participator in politics to know), it would be absurdly captious to take the view that, in connection with politics, there is no information about current practices and current manners of thinking and speaking such as is the characteristic knowledge imparted in a 'vocational' education, or that this knowledge is incapable of being taught. Indeed, there is a vast quantity of this information, and much of it is so obscurely situated that it requires the persistence of a beaver to discover it and the mind of a chancery barrister to put it in order. On the face of it there is no reason why one should not undertake to teach politics as one might undertake to teach plumbing, 'home-making', librarianship, farming or how to run a bassoon factory; and this teaching is, in fact, undertaken.

And, to confirm this view, there already exists an extensive political literature (both books and periodicals), not devoid of general interest and capable of answering the curiosity of the unengaged, but satisfying the specification of a literature appropriate to a 'vocational' education. It is concerned with current practice; it is designed to convey the sort of information about the conduct of public affairs (what to do and how to do it) which anyone called upon or volunteering to participate needs to know; and the authors of it (by reason of their skill and knowledge) are frequently invited to perform the services of political architects or to act as consultants in the conduct of administration or of foreign affairs.

In this unsophisticated literature the properties of political and administrative devices such as federalism, second chambers, committees of inquiry, public corporations, taxes on capital, sumptuary laws, concentrations of power, etc., are dispassionately examined; the behaviour of voters is studied; the organization and propensities of different political parties are investigated; pressure groups, 'establishments' and *élites* are detected; policies are scrutinized in respect of their formation and consequences; the relative efficiency of different administrative areas of the various methods of communication in current use are considered; and a vast array of information about the current politics of other countries is collected and marshalled ready for those who have to take (or who want to take) decisions or make judgments about the conduct of foreign affairs. And at a somewhat lower level, there are handbooks designed for the guidance and instruction of the inferior ranks of administrators. Of course, all this outdistances in intellectual content (and sometimes in unengaged general interest) the technical literature concerned, for example, with building houses or growing tomatoes; but the disproportion is not overwhelming, and in design and purport all these technical literatures are indistinguishable from one another.

Moreover, technical literatures, even those in the highest class (like those of law or medicine), are apt to have their popular counterparts; and there seems little to stand in the way of the appearance of a vulgar counterpart to this literature of political inquiry and instruction. A little book on *How to Restore old Cottages* may be flanked on the bookstalls by one on *How to Restore old Monarchies;* an article on 'A face-lift for the kitchen: new and exciting materials' in a *Do It Yourself* magazine will be followed by others on 'Dos and Don'ts in making a Revolution', 'How to win an Election' and 'What you should know about Public Corporations'. Indeed, writings of this kind (with perhaps less obvious titles) have been available for more than a century.

Now, the contemplation of all these investigations has generated the vision of a modern 'science' of government and administration, a growing body of what is believed to be well-tested information, daily becoming more comprehensive, about the operation and reliabilty of the various processes, projects, policies, materials and devices available in current political and administrative activity 'to solve the political and governmental problems which confront mankind'.

The descriptions we have of this so-called 'master science'[1] do not present it as an enterprise in which events are understood in terms of the operation of general laws, but (more modestly) as 'a systematic, organized, teachable body of knowledge' springing from the study of political ideas, of the constitutions and processes of governments, of the structure and operation of political parties and groups, of the generation of public policy and opinion and of the relations between states.[2] From this knowledge it is designed to elicit a 'body of rational principles' concerning political activity and the administration of public affairs. And when we consider what we are told about 'the hopes and expectations reposed in this master science', the design in collecting together this body of knowledge and the design in teaching it, we are left in no doubt that it is intended to be the material of an education in political and administrative activity. The 'authentic aims' of this science are: 'to study the moral problems of mankind in order to establish the principles of collective morality'; to formulate 'the principles which should inspire political organization and action'; 'to throw light on political ideas and political action in order that the government of man may be improved'; 'to throw some light on the great problems of our time: such as the problem of avoiding war, of increasing international peace and security, of extending freedom, of assisting the development of backward countries, of preventing the exploitation of native races, of using government as a means of raising living standards and promoting prosperity, of banishing ignorance, squalor, destitution and disease through the social services, of increasing welfare, happiness and the dignity of mankind'; 'to solve the political and governmental problems which confront mankind'; 'to assuage the maladies and struggles and conflicts of men in society'; 'to show the nations how to achieve peace and se-

---

[1] W.A. Robson, *The University Teaching of the Social Sciences—Political Sciences*, UNESCO, 1954; H. J. Blackham, *Political Discipline in a Free Society*.

[2] This is sometimes generalized as the study of the manifestations, processes, scope, results and moral basis of 'power in society'.

curity'. And the design in teaching this science is to equip the student 'to comprehend the important political issues of the day'; 'to participate effectively in political discussion, to grasp the important questions of policy, to withstand the flattery of the demagogue, to resist the lies of the dictator or the promises of the imposter, to distinguish between propaganda and truth, to bring informed criticism to bear on public authorities, or to appreciate the criteria by which government action can be appraised'; and 'to give the voter an intelligent interest in the government of his country' without which 'democracy cannot work effectively'. In short, what is described here is unmistakably a 'vocational' education in politics; not a training appropriate only to a would-be official (though there is much here which is specially appropriate to those who engage professionally in politics or administration), but an education designed for participants in one of the skills which sustain our current manner of living, designed to improve the quality of their participation, and defended on account of 'the burning practical importance' of the problems with which this skill is concerned. It is an education with the same sort of design as that of a farmer or a medical practitioner, but (it is alleged) of unmistakably greater importance.

But avoiding flights of fancy, exaggerated expectations and a certain incoherence between what is set for study and the conclusions designed to be reached, it is difficult to disagree with the proposition that the serious inquiries I have mentioned, whose virtue is to investigate current political ideas and practices in a manner relevant to their use in political and administrative activity, intimate a body of knowledge capable of being taught and appropriate to be taught in a 'vocational' education in politics. The current state of our knowledge about voting habits, about the organization of the Conservative Party, about the President of the U.S.A., about the propensities of Trade Unions, and about the structure, control and administration of Public Corporations are as tangible pieces of information as the current state of our knowledge about the properties of the materials and devices used in domestic plumbing. And why should a voter, a political entertainer, a politician, a political agent or a local government official know less about his business than a doctor, a solicitor or a librarian?

Moreover, the other main aspect of political activity is, on the evidence, not less susceptible of similar treatment. Politics has always been three-quarters talk, and not to know to use the current vocabulary of politics is a serious hindrance to anyone who, either as an amateur or as a professional, wishes to participate in the activity. The language of politics is the language of desire and aversion, of preference and choice, of approval and disapproval, of praise and blame, of persuasion, injunction, accusation and threat. It is the language in which we make promises, ask for support, recommend beliefs and actions, devise and commend administrative expedients and organize the beliefs and opinions of others in such a manner that policy may be effectively and economically executed; in short, it is the language of every-day, practical life. But men engaged in political activity (like others engaged in business or in the promotion of a religion), in order to make their opinions and actions more attractive, are apt to recommend them in the idiom of general ideas; and in order to make the opinions and actions of others less attractive are apt to denigrate them in terms of general ideas. In this manner (and often by appropriating words and expressions originally designed for a wholly different use) the current vocabulary of politics has made its appearance. It contains such words and expressions as these: Democratic, liberal, equal, natural, human, social, arbitrary, constitutional, planned, integrated, communist, provocative, feudal, conservative, progressive, capitalist, national, reactionary, revolutionary, fascist, privileged, private, public, socialist; open, closed, acquisitive, affluent, responsible and irresponsible societies; the international order, party, faction, welfare and amenity. It is a complicated vocabulary, and to teach its use is clearly appropriate to a 'vocational' education in politics. And here, also, there is a literature whose virtue (if not design) is to teach the use of this vocabulary. Books are produced every day which are concerned to teach us how to think politically and to provide an education for those whose business or pleasure it is to speak the current language of politics. Indeed, an expression has been invented (or seconded) to specify this literature; it is the so-called literature of 'political theory'; and 'political theories' (in this usage) are appropriately qualified by adjectives such as 'democratic', 'socialist', 'conservative', 'liberal', 'progressive'—that is, by adjectives which themselves belong to the current vocabulary of politics and are designed to indicate the political colour of the theories.

A 'vocational' education in politics, then, is not a merely imagined possibility; the skills it is designed to impart are among the most frequently (and most unskilfully) practised in our current manner of living, and the words and ideas it is designed to familiarize us with are those most frequently used in public discussion: there is unmistakably appropriate material for composing a curriculum for such an education. And whatever the limitations of the 'science' of government to be imparted in this education, I am not among those who believe that it must be nugatory because it lacks the imposing generalizations of some other sciences. It can without difficulty sustain its character as a compendium of reliable information useful for those engaged in political activity.[3] And when we consider the relative complexity of this skill, the mixture of amateurism and professionalism which political and administrative activity among us provokes, and the absence of settled professional standards, it is not at all surprising, either that the curriculum of such an education should still lack authoritative definition, or that the institutions offering such an education should (outside the USA, Russia and China) remain comparatively few.

But there is another reason why the appearance of the possibility of a 'vocational' education in politics provoked, in this country, no great efflorescence of educational institutions to exploit it. For when, at long last, observation and reflection on current political activity had generated a body of information about government and administration, and when professional political skill ceased to be the exclusive business of Kings and hereditary ruling classes, when (in short) government ceased to be a mystery, and after a suitable

---

[3] This, however, is the most that can be said for it. The larger claims made on behalf of this 'master science' rest either upon the moral prejudices of those who make them (and which we cannot all be expected to share), or upon a naïve ethical naturalism.

interval had elapsed, politics *eo nomine* began to be taught in our universities; and the manner in which it was taught was that which is appropriate to a 'vocational' education. Unsuspecting undergraduates, most of whom had no thought of becoming professional politicians or administrators, but in a few of whom there was perhaps a vague desire to be politically self-conscious coupled with an inability to do it for themselves, found imposed upon them a curriculum of study of unimaginable dreariness in which they learned the structures of the current constitutions of the world and whose anatomical studies were enlivened only by some idle political gossip and some tendentious speculation about current policy. As a 'vocational' education in politics it was, of course, worthless; and yet the information it offered, and the manner in which it was offered, could have no conceivable interest to anyone except those whose heads were full of the enterprise of participating in political activity or to persons with the insatiable curiosity of a concierge. It merely provided a spurious academic focus for whatever political interest there might be about, and it was saved from manifest academic disgrace by the intrusion of a little genuine historical study. Together with this went the study of some notable books (like Plato's *Republic*, Hobbes's *Leviathan*, Rousseau's *du Contrat Social*, Mill's essay on *Liberty* and Bosanquet's *Philosophical Theory of the State*) and some less notable tracts, believed to be in some sense 'about politics' and therefore assumed to have a political 'ideal', or programme, or policy, or device to recommend. And the manner in which they were studied was designed to elicit and criticize this programme: they were recognized, in short, as books of 'political theory'.[4] Indeed, I can describe the manner in which these books were read only as a mixture between the manner in which one might read an out-of-date text-book on naval architecture and the manner in which one might study a current election manifesto. The result was that we were alive only to the political quaintness (or enormity) of these books, and our attention was narrowed down to

---

[4] And we had commentaries, like Hobhouse's *Metaphysical Theory of the State* (and later Crossman on *Plato Today* and Popper on *The Open Society and its Enemies*), to encourage us in this recognition.

listening either for the political *faux pas* or for the echoes of political modernity.

Some, of course, escaped. There were individuals who never surrendered to it; those universities in which 'politics' had long had its place as an occasion for historical or philosophical study were in some degree fortified against it; and, in any case, English universities are far less deeply compromised than those in America. But this regrettable disposition—regrettable because it conflicted with the most deeply rooted traditions of university education—set a course for 'politics' in those universities in which it established itself as an independent 'subject' of undergraduate study, a course from which divergence has been difficult even where it has been desired.

It was, no doubt, long ago agreed that this was a manner of studying politics (now perhaps to be found only in American textbooks) not entirely appropriate in a university; and many improvements have been made. But these improvements have, for the most part, been directed not to doing something else more appropriate in a university education, but to doing better what had been ill-done before. We have added the study of operation to the study of structure; we have added political parties, pressure groups, civil services, local authorities and public corporations to the study of the constitutions of governments; we have uncovered obscure passages in political organization; we have heard the call of political sociology; we have explored what can only be called the curiosities of politics; and we have tried to elicit information of more general interest by comparing one set of structures with another. In short, we have been neither idle nor unadventurous; but, in the main, we have continued to work at the same level of information as the pioneers of political study in universities—a level appropriate only to a 'vocational' education. And in respect of these classics of political reflection, our pupils are still encouraged to read them in order to discover the injunctions about political conduct they are believed to contain and in order to reflect upon the appropriateness to us of these injunctions; and they are still written about in this manner. The search for anything in the present teaching of 'politics' in our universities (wherever that teaching has firmly established itself) which separates it decisively and unmistakably from what is appropriate to what I have called a 'vocational' education in politics, anything which carries us beyond the study of 'literatures' as repositories of information to the study of a 'language' or a manner of thinking, is not very rewarding. Indeed, the most comprehensive recent description of the teaching of 'politics' in universities (from which I have already quoted) accepts without misgiving or apology this 'vocational' or participatory study as appropriate to a university education. No doubt, there is a certain amount of confusion, but there is little inclination to look in any other direction.

Now, I may be told I have overlooked two directions of movement both of which point to a manner of study which, it may be alleged, has gone some way to emancipate the teaching of 'politics' in a university from this 'vocational' disposition and to give it what is somewhat naïvely called a 'liberal' character. First, it will be said, we are no longer content to observe and to impart the miscellaneous results of our observation; we have out-grown political anatomy. Instead, we 'analyse' (blessed word) and teach the art of analysis, we compare (no less blessed word) and teach the science of making comparisons, we make ideal models, we construct hypotheses, we formulate the problems of the future and seek solutions. And this (or some of it) may, no doubt, be counted to us as merit: nobody can say we are simple-minded in our study of politics. But none of it has served (or is even designed) to set us on to some other questions than the essentially 'vocational' questions: How does it work? How can it be improved? Is it democratic? and so on. And much of it (because it has come to be concerned with imaginary 'systems' and 'processes', 'powers', 'establishments' and *élites*, stereotypes of one sort or another) diverts our attention from the often irregular character of political organizations and events, and thus makes our 'vocational' education less good than it might be. In short, and in spite of these complexities and subtleties which have given to our original naïvety a touch of sophistication, we are still disposed to teach 'politics' in universities as a kind of staff-duties course in politics.

But secondly, it will be said, in spite of our rather lamentable tendency to urge our pupils to acquaint themselves with the patterns and structures of current politics (that is, with the contents of political 'texts') and to provide for their needs by engaging experts on an ever increasing number of these 'texts', experts in the political 'systems' of India and Iraq, of Ghana and Indonesia, we do make a notable attempt to teach them how to use a 'language', namely, the language of politics. The difference between ourselves and the pioneers of 'politics' in universities, it will be said, is that for us the study of the dull and doubtful detail of political structures and operations is designed as a means of teaching our pupils how to think politically. In short we have begun to recognize that 'politics' in a university is appropriately concerned with the study of a 'language' and with 'literatures' only as paradigms of this 'language'. Yet, when we consider the efforts made to persuade our pupils to acquaint themselves with as large as possible a number of these 'texts', our disposition to recognize the 'authority' of those who are themselves engaged in political activity (or who have retired from it) and our recognition that there is a problem of 'bias' in teaching 'politics' in a university (all of which can relate only to a 'vocational' political education), we may perhaps doubt the truth of this claim. But, even assuming this difference between ourselves and the pioneers is well observed, something else is needed to distinguish our enterprise from that of a 'vocational' education in politics. All that is being alleged here is that we offer a 'vocational' education superior to that which used to be offered.

To be brief, the difference lies in the nature of the 'languages' concerned. To teach the language of current politics is an essential part of a 'vocational' education in politics, because skill in using this language, and being familiar with the manners of thinking it represents, is an essential part of political activity. But this is not a language of the same kind as the 'languages' which I have suggested it is the distinctive feature of a university education to put before undergraduates. These 'languages'—the 'languages' of history, of philosophy, of science and of mathematics—are all of them *explanatory* languages; each of them represents a specific mode of

explanation. But the language of politics is not a language of explanation, any more than the languages of poetry or moral conduct are
languages of explanation. There is no specifically 'political' explanation of anything: the word 'politics' stands for holding certain kinds
of beliefs and opinions, making certain kinds of judgments, performing certain kinds of actions, and thinking in terms of certain
practical, not explanatory, considerabilities. If there is a manner of
thinking and speaking that can properly be called 'political', the appropriate business of a university in respect of it is not to use it, or
to teach the use of it, but to explain it—that is, to bring to bear
upon it one or more of the recognized modes of explanation. If the
expression 'political activity' stands for something which plausibly
offers itself to be understood and to be explained, the questions a
teacher of 'politics' in a university should ask himself are: In what
manner do I design to explain it? Into what explanatory 'language'
or 'languages' should I translate it? What 'languages' of explanation
may an undergraduate find himself learning to use and to manage
in connection with politics?

Now, I believe that, if we put behind us the alluring but inappropriate 'vocational' enterprise of teaching the use and management of the language of politics, the study of 'politics' at a university may afford an undergraduate the opportunity of acquainting
himself with two different manners of understanding, two modes of
thought, two explanatory 'languages', namely, the 'languages' of
history and of philosophy. What falls outside these is, I think, one
or other of these manners of thinking disguised in some not very
elegant fancy dress. Each of these manners of thinking is a genuine
mode of explanation: each operates with clear criteria of relevance;
each is capable of reaching conclusions appropriate to itself; in
each it may be said that this or that is an error, but also (and more
significantly) that this or that is out of character; and statements
made in these 'languages' do not pretend to have injunctive force.
Thus, the appropriate engagement of an undergraduate student of
'politics' at a university will be to be taught and to learn something
about the modes of thought and manners of speaking of an historian and a philosopher, and to do this in connection with politics,

while others (in other Schools) are doing it in other connections. While one undergraduate may acquire some insight into the manner in which an historian thinks and speaks and understands and explains in connection with the English wool trade in the fifteenth century, or in connection with the Papacy in the sixteenth century (these being the chosen 'texts'), another, in a School of 'Politics', may do the same thing in connection with a political party, the House of Commons, Machiavelli's *Prince* or the Haldane Report. And while an undergraduate in a School of Philosophy may study Kant's *Critique of Pure Reason* (and if he does so in a university manner it is not merely to acquaint himself with Kant's conclusions but to understand Kant's problems and to acquire the connoisseurship which can recognize a philosophical argument), so an undergraduate in a School of 'Politics' may read Hobbes's *Leviathan* or Hegel's *Philosophy of Right* and hope to learn from his study something about the philosophical mode of thinking. And if it should turn out that politics is an appropriate occasion for acquiring a familiarity with other authentic languages of explanation, then the opportunity may properly be taken.[5] But it is only in this manner that a study of 'politics' unmistakably distinguished from a 'vocational' study, and one that can sustain a place in a specifically university kind of education, can appear.

The main hindrance to its doing so is the 'vocational' disposition with which 'politics' has come to establish itself in a university education and which it has never succeeded in throwing off. I do not think this disposition among university teachers of 'politics' is commonly the result of profound reflection, although some are held to it with a passionate attachment which they have tried their hands at defending. It springs, rather, from their being themselves primarily interested in politics in the vulgar sense and in the problems of administration, from their being impressed with the infor-

---

[5] It is true that for more than a century the possibility of a genuinely explanatory 'science' of politics has been explored. But since nobody is likely to claim that anything in a condition even remotely suitable to be put before an undergraduate as an occasion for his acquiring a familiarity with a scientific mode of thinking has appeared, I have not thought it necessary to consider what our situation would be if this enterprise had been more fruitful. Nor (except perhaps in America) has anyone attempted to teach such a 'science' to undergraduates.

mation about political and administrative activity believed to be available, and from an inability to understand why this information should not be imparted as a university education to undergraduates, or, indeed, what else there is plausibly to teach under the head of 'politics'. Their mistaken disposition, as university teachers, does not spring from the direction in which their own studies have taken them, but from their desire to teach undergraduates what they themselves are interested in, regardless of its inappropriateness.[6] They understand their problem as university teachers to be the problem of raising the study of politics above the level of 'current affairs' and to give it a respectable intellectual content. But they rarely understand that this can be done only by recognizing that the word 'politics' in a university education signifies, not a 'subject' of study, but a library of 'texts' which, in this kind of education, is merely the occasion for learning how to handle and manage some of the 'languages' of explanation.

And if it is said that the manner in which 'politics' is taught in universities has not forbidden a connection with history and philosophy, the reply must be that the connection is often resented as a diversion from the proper concerns of 'political science', and that wherever it has been made it has been apt to be corrupting rather than emancipating. 'History' appears, not as a mode of explanation, but merely as some conclusions of allegedly 'historical' writers believed to account for the present structure or to forecast the future

---

[6] It will, of course, be understood that I am not objecting to dons being concerned with politics. It is long since academics began to take an interest in the activity of governing and the instruments of government, and among the circumstances which in England (and perhaps also in America) have, in recent times, promoted this sort of interest is the fact that many academics, seconded during two wars to government offices, have found there a virgin (but not unsuspected) world and have felt the impulse to explore it. Moreover, the study of politics is not a novelty in European and American universities: it is said that the earliest European professorship in 'politics', founded at Uppsala in the seventeenth century, was the Chair of 'Statesmanship and Eloquence' (doing and talking, the inseparable components of political activity); and something called 'political science', constructed on various analogies and offering conclusions of various degrees of abstraction, has been pursued for more than a century. But if every don were to teach undergraduates what he himself is interested in, and if every professional chair were held to entail or to authorize a counterpart to itself in undergraduate education, there would be little in these days to distinguish a university from a mad-house. And if the contention is that undergraduates in significant numbers want to devote a large part of their university days learning what (it is alleged) will prepare them for a more intelligent participation in politics, the answer is that (except for the few who mistake a university for a place of 'vocational' education and who want to 'go in' for politics or to become administrators) this is not true; and in any case it is irrelevant.

prospect of (for example) a political party, or to provide evidence relating to the origin or the efficiency of an administrative device. 'History' is patronizingly admitted so long as it remains in the 'background' (whatever that may mean). And 'philosophy' appears, not as a manner of thinking but as a misused word to identify what is believed to be a certain kind of interest in politics. Merely to extend our studies backwards a little way into the past in order to account for a piece of political conduct is not 'doing' history; it is indulging in a piece of retrospective politics which makes certain that the historical mode of thinking never properly appears. And when in the writings of Plato or Hobbes or Rousseau or Hegel or Mill what is being looked for is the political disposition of these writers, when expressions like 'natural law', 'general will', 'freedom', 'the rule of law', 'justice', or 'sovereignty', which, philosophically speaking, are explanatory concepts, whose explanatory value might have been explored, are turned (as the politician turns everything he touches) into prescriptive concepts, and when what is reflected upon is merely their injunctive force, all chance is lost of learning something about the philosophical mode of thought. When, in this manner, a philosophical argument is turned into a so-called 'political theory' and it is thought appropriate to give it a political label, calling it 'democractic', conservative', 'liberal', 'progressive', or 'reactionary', a 'vocational' education in politics may be seen to have reimposed itself; and the opportunity has been lost of understanding that a philosopher is never concerned with a condition of things but only with a manner of explanation, and of recognizing that the only thing that matters in a philosophical argument is its coherence, its intelligibility, its power to illuminate and its fertility. And when we ask our pupils to display their attainments by discussing such questions as Was Mill a democrat? or, Has the House of Lords outlived its usefulness? or, Would not Ghana do better with a Presidential system of government than a Parliamentary? or, Is Great Britain heading for a One-Party State? we may suspect that a not very high class 'vocational' education in politics is at work.

We have far to go; and having got off on the wrong foot, progress towards a proper university education connected with politics is not likely to be very rapid. But there are two precepts which, if followed, would take us in what I believe to be the proper direction.

First, in a School of 'Politics' we should never use the language of politics; we should use only the explanatory 'languages' of academic study. Of course, the words which compose our vocabulary of politics may be uttered, but only in order to inquire into their use and meaning, in order to take them to pieces and write them out in the long-hand of historical or philosophical explanation. They should never be given the appearance of being themselves explanatory words and expressions. And we should recognize that this so-called 'political theory' is itself a form of political activity, and therefore not itself to be taught, but to be explained, historically or philosophically.

And secondly, since in a university we should regard ourselves as supervising, not the study of 'texts' understood as organizations of information, but the study of the use of explanatory 'languages' in connection with appropriate 'texts', these 'texts' should be chosen with care and for the relevant (pædagogic) reasons. As things are at present, any but the proper criteria are applied. A part of the world has only to be often in the newspapers, a state has only to be new or powerful, an administrative device has only to be considered interesting or administratively important by the pundits, and its claim to be chosen as a 'text' for undergraduate study in a university is believed to be irrefutable. But these, instead of being the best reasons for choosing it, are the worst; they are political, not pædagogic reasons. For example, it appears to me that the place which the politics of contemporary Russia has come to occupy in undergraduate study is indefensible except in the irrelevant terms of a 'vocational' political education. We know incomparably less about what goes on in Russian politics than in the politics of any other country in the world, bar perhaps China. Even in a 'vocational' political education this 'text' would be suspect: to set it for study would be inviting superficial and useless learning—systems instead of realities, mechanical models in place of concrete behaviour—and it would be justified only on account of the power and political importance of the Russian state and therefore the desirability of teach-

ing something about it, however inadequate. But in a university education these are not significant considerations; what matters there
is that the material should be in a suitable condition for the enterprise of teaching undergraduates how to think historically. And
this, unquestionably, is not the condition of current Russian politics. Why should a School of 'Politics' go out of its way to choose for
undergraduate study particularly obscure and corrupt 'texts', 'texts'
suitable only for the most skilful emandators, when well-edited
'texts', like the politics of France, or Sweden, or the USA, or Spain
(to say nothing of Great Britain), are available?

An academic study appears only when an activity is isolated
and when it is in a fit condition to be an occasion for explanatory
modes of thought. There are large tracts of the human past—arts
and literatures, laws and customs, happenings in the world, the
thoughts that men have entertained, their inventions and devices—
which are eligible for this kind of study. Physical and chemical operations wherever they take place, the properties of numbers, the
habits and customs of remote peoples, the structure and composition of the earth, and our own moral ideas, may be disengaged from
our approval and disapproval and may be studied from some other
standpoint than that of usefulness in the pursuit of our own practical enterprises. Even the study of the scarce opportunities the world
offers for satisfying our wants may be detached from considerations
of public or private policy. Each, it is true, contains an invitation
other than the invitation to explain; but it is an invitation we may
easily decline. In respect of current politics (our own or that of
neighbouring peoples), however, this is more difficult; it is not unmistakably promising material for the enterprise of explanation. It
is too difficult for most people to turn their backs upon the enterprise of participating and of thinking in the 'vocational' idiom of
participation; it is too easy to confuse injunction and explanation;
it is too attractive to neglect philosophy for finding reasons for holding favourite political opinions, and to avoid doing history for ourselves in favour of making use of the convenient conclusions of historians. Politics offers the most difficult of all 'literatures', the most
difficult of all collections of 'texts', in connection with which to learn

to handle and manage the languages of explanation: the idiom of the material to be studied is ever ready to impose itself upon the manner in which it is studied. Nevertheless, if we recognize what we should be doing at a university, the difficulty may itself be an attraction; if we recognize that our proper business is not with politics at all but with teaching, in connection with politics, how to manage the 'languages' of history and philosophy and how to distinguish them and their different sorts of utterance.

"The Study of Politics in a University" was first published in the original edition of *Rationalism in Politics*.

PART THREE

On Hobbes

Introduction to *Leviathan*

'We are discussing no trivial subject, but
how a man should live.'
—PLATO,
Republic, 352D.

ONE: BIOGRAPHICAL

Thomas Hobbes, the second son of an otherwise undis-
tinguished vicar of Westport, near Malmesbury, was born in
the spring of 1588. He was educated at Malmesbury where he became an exceptional scholar in Latin and Greek, and at Oxford
where in the course of five years he maintained his interest in classical literature and became acquainted with the theological contro-
versies of the day, but was taught only some elementary logic and
Aristotelian physics.

In 1608 he was appointed tutor (and later became secretary) to
the son of William Cavendish, first Earl of Devonshire. For the
whole of his adult life Hobbes maintained a close relationship with
the Cavendish family, passing many of his years as a member of the
household either at Chatsworth or in London. In these circumstances he came to meet some of the leading politicians and literary
men of his day, Bacon and Jonson among them. The year 1610 he
spent in France and Italy with his charge, getting a first glimpse of
the intellectual life of the continent and returning with a determination to make himself a scholar. The next eighteen years, passed

mostly at Chatsworth, were the germinating period of his future intellectual interests and activities. There is little record of how precisely they were spent, and the only literary product of this period of his life was the translation of Thucydides, published in 1629: but there can be no doubt that philosophy occupied his mind increasingly.

On the death of the second Earl of Devonshire in 1628, Hobbes accepted the position of tutor to the son of Sir Gervase Clinton, with whom he stayed three years, two of which were spent on the continent. It was at this time that Hobbes discovered for himself the intellectual world of mathematics and geometry, a world so important to the continental philosophers of his time, but of which hitherto he had been entirely ignorant. The discovery gave renewed impetus and fresh direction to his philosophical reflections, and from then philosophy dominated his mind.

In 1631 Hobbes returned to the Cavendish household as tutor to the new earl, with whom he made his third visit to the continent (1634–7). It was on this visit that he met Galileo in Florence and became acquainted with the circle of philosophers centred round Mersenne in Paris, and particularly with Gassendi. And on his return to England he completed in 1640 (but did not publish until 1650) his first important piece of philosophical writing, the *Elements of Law*. He was fifty-two years old, and he had in his head the plan of a philosophy which he desired to expound systematically.

The next eleven years were spent in Paris, free for a while from extraneous duties. But instead of embarking at once on the composition of the most general part of his philosophy—his philosophy of nature—he wrote *De Cive*, an exposition of his political philosophy, which was published in 1642. Paris for Hobbes was a society for philosophers; but in 1645 it became the home of the exiled court of Charles, Prince of Wales, and Hobbes was appointed tutor to the prince. His mind still ran on the philosophy of politics, and in 1651 his masterpiece, *Leviathan*, was published.[1]

---

[1] The texts of Hobbes's works referred to are, with the exceptions of *Leviathan* and the *Elements of Law*, those published in the *English Works of Thomas Hobbes*, edited by

In 1652 he returned to England, took up his place (which he was never again to leave) in the household of the Earl of Devonshire, and set about the composition of the rest of his philosophical system. In 1655 was published *De Corpore*, and in 1658 *De Homine*. He had still twenty years to live. They were years of incessant literary activity and of philosophical, mathematical, theological and political controversy. After the Restoration he was received at Court, and he spent much of his time in London. In 1675, however, perceiving that he must soon retire from the world, he retired to Chatsworth. He died in the winter of 1679 at the age of ninety-one.

TWO: THE CONTEXT OF *LEVIATHAN*

Leviathan is the greatest, perhaps the sole, masterpiece of political philosophy written in the English language. And the history of our civilization can provide only a few works of similar scope and achievement to set beside it. Consequently, it must be judged by none but the highest standards and must be considered only in the widest context. The masterpiece supplies a standard and a context for the second-rate, which indeed is but a gloss; but the context of the masterpiece itself, the setting in which its meaning is revealed, can in the nature of things be nothing narrower than the history of political philosophy.

Reflection about political life may take place at a variety of levels. It may remain on the level of the determination of means, or it may strike out for the consideration of ends. Its inspiration may be directly practical, the modification of the arrangements of a political order in accordance with the perception of an immediate benefit; or it may be practical, but less directly so, guided by general ideas. Or again, springing from an experience of political life, it may seek a generalization of that experience in a doctrine. And reflection is apt to flow from one level to another in an unbroken

Molesworth, 11 volumes, 1839 (referred to as *E.W.*), and in the *Opera Latina*, edited by Molesworth, 5 volumes, 1845 (referred to as *O.L.*). References to *Leviathan* (*L.*) are to the pages of the Clarendon Press reprint (1909) of the edition of 1651. References to the *Elements of Law* are to the edition by Tönnies, Cambridge, 1928.

movement, following the mood of the thinker. Political philosophy may be understood to be what occurs when this movement of reflection takes a certain direction and achieves a certain level, its characteristic being the relation of political life, and the values and purposes pertaining to it, to the entire conception of the world that belongs to a civilization. That is to say, at all other levels of reflection on political life we have before us the single world of political activity, and what we are interested in is the internal coherence of that world; but in political philosophy we have in our minds that world and another world, and our endeavour is to explore the coherence of the two worlds together. The reflective intelligence is apt to find itself at this level without the consciousness of any great conversion and without any sense of entering upon a new project, but merely by submitting itself to the impetus of reflection, by spreading its sails to the argument. For, any man who holds in his mind the conceptions of the natural world, of God, of human activity and human destiny which belong to his civilization, will scarcely be able to prevent an endeavour to assimilate these to the ideas that distinguish the political order in which he lives, and failing to do so he will become a philosopher (of a simple sort) unawares.

But, though we may stumble over the frontier of philosophy unwittingly and by doing nothing more demonstrative than refusing to draw rein, to achieve significant reflection, of course, requires more than inadvertence and more than the mere acceptance of the two worlds of ideas. The whole impetus of the enterprise is the perception that what really exists is a single world of ideas, which comes to us divided by the abstracting force of circumstances; is the perception that our political ideas and what may be called the rest of our ideas are not in fact two independent worlds, and that though they may come to us as separate text and context, the *meaning* lies, as it always must lie, in a unity in which the separate existence of text and context is resolved. We may begin, probably we must begin, with an independent valuation of the text and the context; but the impetus of reflection is not spent until we have restored in detail the unity of which we had a prevision. And, so far, philosophical reflection about politics will be nothing other than the intellectual restoration of a unity damaged and impaired by the normal negligence of human partiality. But to have gone so far is already to have raised questions the answers to which are not to be found in any fresh study of what is behind us. Even if we accept the standards and valuations of our civilization, it will be only by putting an arbitrary closure on reflection that we can prevent the consideration of the meaning of the general terms in which those standards are expressed; good and evil, right and wrong, justice and injustice. And, turning, we shall catch sight of all that we have learned reflected in the *speculum universitatis*.

Now, whether or not this can be defended as a hypothetical conception of the nature of political philosophy, it certainly describes a form of reflection about politics that has a continuous history in our civilization. To establish the connections, in principle and in detail, directly or mediately, between politics and eternity is a project that has never been without its followers. Indeed, the pursuit of this project is only a special arrangement of the whole intellectual life of our civilization; it is the whole intellectual history organized and exhibited from a particular angle of vision. Probably there has been no theory of the nature of the world, of the activity of man, of the destiny of mankind, no theology or cosmology, perhaps even no metaphysics, that has not sought a reflection of itself in the mirror of political philosophy; certainly there has been no fully considered politics that has not looked for its reflection in eternity. This history of political philosophy is, then, the context of the masterpiece. And to interpret it in the context of this history secures it against the deadening requirement of conformity to a merely abstract idea of political philosophy.

This kind of reflection about politics is not, then, to be denied a place in our intellectual history. And it is characteristic of political philosophers that they take a sombre view of the human situation: they deal in darkness. Human life in their writings appears, generally not as a feast or even as a journey, but as a predicament; and the link between politics and eternity is the contribution the political order is conceived as making to the deliverance of mankind.

Even those whose thought is most remote from violent contrasts of dark and light (Aristotle, for example) do not altogether avoid this disposition of mind. And some political philosophers may even be suspected of spreading darkness in order to make their light more acceptable. Man, so the varied formula runs, is the dupe of error, the slave of sin, of passion, of fear, of care, the enemy of himself or of others or of both—

O miseras hominum mentes, O pectora caeca

—and the civil order appears as the whole or a part of the scheme of his salvation. The precise manner in which the predicament is conceived, the qualities of mind and imagination and the kinds of activity man can bring to the achievement of his own salvation, the exact nature and power of civil arrangements and institutions, the urgency, the method and the comprehensiveness of the deliverance —these are the singularities of each political philosophy. In them are reflected the intellectual achievements of the epoch or society, and the great and slowly mediated changes in intellectual habit and horizon that have overtaken our civilization. Every masterpiece of political philosophy springs from a new vision of the predicament; each is the glimpse of a deliverance or the suggestion of a remedy.

It will not, then, surprise us to find an apparently contingent element in the ground and inspiration of a political philosophy, a feeling for the exigencies, the cares, the passions of a particular time, a sensitiveness to the dominant folly of an epoch: for the human predicament is a universal appearing everywhere as a particular. Plato's thought is animated by the errors of Athenian democracy, Augustine's by the sack of Rome, and what stirs the mind of Hobbes is 'grief for the present calamities of my country', a country torn between those who claimed too much for Liberty and those who claimed too much for Authority, a country given over into the hands of ambitious men who enlisted the envy and resentment of a 'giddy people' for the advancement of their ambitions.[2,3] And not

---

[2] *E.W.*, II, i–xxiv.

[3] *L.*, pp. 3, 274, 549. Hobbes had also in mind the situation in late sixteenth-century France.

being surprised at this element of particularity, we shall not allow it to mislead us into supposing that nothing more is required to make a political philosopher than an impressionable political consciousness; for the masterpiece, at least, is always the revelation of the universal predicament in the local and transitory mischief.[4]

If the unity of the history of political philosophy lies in a pervading sense of human life as a predicament and in the continuous reflection of the changing climate of the European intellectual scene, its significant variety will be found in three great traditions of thought. The singularities of political philosophies (like most singularities) are not unique, but follow one of three main patterns which philosophical reflection about politics has impressed upon the intellectual history of Europe. These I call traditions because it belongs to the nature of a tradition to tolerate and unite an internal variety, not insisting upon conformity to a single character, and because, further, it has the ability to change without losing its identity. The first of these traditions is distinguished by the master-conceptions of Reason and Nature. It is coeval with our civilization; it has an unbroken history into the modern world; and it has survived by a matchless power of adaptability all the changes of the European consciousness. The master-conceptions of the second are Will and Artifice. It too springs from the soil of Greece, and has drawn inspiration from many sources, not least from Israel and Islam. The third tradition is of later birth, not appearing until the eighteenth century. The cosmology it reflects in its still unsettled surface is the world seen on the analogy of human history. Its master-conception is the Rational Will, and its followers may be excused the belief that in it the truths of the first two traditions are fulfilled and their errors find a happy release. The masterpiece of political philosophy has for its context, not only the history of political philosophy as the elucidation of the predicament and deliverance of mankind, but also, normally, a particular tradition in that history; generally speaking it is the supreme expression of its own tradition. And, as Plato's *Republic* might be chosen as the repre-

[4] *L.*, p. 271.

sentative of the first tradition, and Hegel's *Philosophie des Rechts* of the third, so *Leviathan* is the head and crown of the second.

Leviathan is a masterpiece, and we must understand it according to our means. If our poverty is great, but not ruinous, we may read it not looking beyond its two covers, but intent to draw from it nothing that is not there. This will be a notable achievement, if somewhat narrow. The reward will be the appreciation of a dialectical triumph with all the internal movement and liveliness of such a triumph. But *Leviathan* is more than a *tour de force*. And something of its larger character will be perceived if we read it with the other works of Hobbes open beside it. Or again, at greater expense of learning, we may consider it in its tradition, and doing so will find fresh meaning in the world of ideas it opens to us. But finally, we may discover in it the true character of a masterpiece—the still centre of a whirlpool of ideas which has drawn into itself numberless currents of thought, contemporary and historic, and by its centripetal force has shaped and compressed them into a momentary significance before they are flung off again into the future.

THREE: THE MIND AND MANNER

In the mind of a man, the σύνολον of form and content alone is actual; style and matter, method and doctrine, are inseparable. And when the mind is that of a philosopher, it is a sound rule to come to consider the technical expression of this unity only after it has been observed in the less formal version of it that appears in temperament, cast of mind and style of writing. Circumstantial evidence of this sort can, of course, contribute nothing relevant to the substantiation of the technical distinctions of a philosophy; but often it has something to contribute to the understanding of them. At least, I think this is so with Hobbes.

Philosophy springs from a certain bent of mind which, though different in character, is as much a natural gift as an aptitude for mathematics or a genius for music. Philosophical speculation requires so little in the way of a knowledge of the world and is, in comparison with some other intellectual pursuits, so independent of book-learning, that the gift is apt to manifest itself early in life. And often a philosopher will be found to have made his significant contribution at an age when others are still preparing themselves to speak or to act. Hobbes had a full share of the *anima naturaliter philosophica*, yet it is remarkable that the beginning of his philosophical writing cannot be dated before his forty-second year and that his masterpiece was written when he was past sixty. Certainly there is nothing precocious in his genius; but are we to suppose that the love of reasoning, the passion for dialectic, which belong to the gift for philosophy, were absent from his character in youth? Writers on Hobbes have been apt to take a short way with this suggestion of a riddle. The life of Hobbes has been divided into neat periods, and his appearance as a philosopher in middle life has been applauded rather than explained. Brilliant at school, idle at the university, unambitious in early life, later touched by a feeling for scholarship and finally taking the path of philosophy when, at the age of forty, the power of geometric proof was revealed to him in the pages of *Euclid*: such is the life attributed to him. It leaves something to be desired. And evidence has been collected which goes to show that philosophy and geometry were not coeval in Hobbes's mind, evidence that the speculative gift was not unexercised in his earlier years.[5] Yet it remains true that when he appears as a philosophical writer, he is already adult, mature in mind; the period of eager search of tentative exploration, goes unreflected in his pages.

The power and confidence of Hobbes's mind as he comes before us in his writings cannot escape observation. He is arrogant (but it is not the arrogance of youth), dogmatic, and when he speaks it is in a tone of confident finality: he knows everything except how his doctrines will be received. There is nothing half-formed or undeveloped in him, nothing in progress; there is no promise, only fulfilment. There is self-confidence, also, a Montaigne-like self-confidence; he has accepted himself and he expects others to accept him on the same terms. And all this is understandable when we appreci-

[5] L. Strauss, *The Political Philosophy of Hobbes.*

ate that Hobbes is not one of those philosophers who allow us to see the workings of their minds, and that he published nothing until he was fifty-four years old. There are other, more technical, reasons for his confidence. His conception of philosophy as the establishment by reasoning of hypothetical causes saved him from the necessity of observing the caution appropriate to those who deal with facts and events.[6] But, at bottom, it springs from his maturity, the knowledge that before he spoke he was a match for anyone who had the temerity to answer back. It belonged to Hobbes's temperament and his art, not less than to his circumstances, to hold his fire. His long life after middle age gave him the room for change and development that others find in earlier years; but he did not greatly avail himself of it. He was often wrong, especially in his light-hearted excursions into mathematics, and he often changed his views, but he rarely retracted an opinion. His confidence never deserted him.

But if the first impression of Hobbes's philosophical writing is one of maturity and deliberateness, the second is an impression of remarkable energy. It is as if all the lost youth of Hobbes's mind had been recovered and perpetuated in this pre-eminently youthful quality. One of the more revealing observations of Aubrey about him is that 'he was never idle; his thoughts were always working'. And from this energy flow the other striking characteristics of his mind and manner—his scepticism, his addiction to system and his passion for controversy.

An impulse for philosophy may originate in faith (as with Erigena), or in curiosity (as with Locke), but with Hobbes the prime mover was doubt. Scepticism was, of course, in the air he breathed; but in an age of sceptics he was the most radical of them all. His was not the elegiac scepticism of Montaigne, nor the brittle net in which Pascal struggled, nor was it the methodological doubt of Descartes; for him it was both a method and a conclusion, purging and creative. It is not the technicalities of his scepticism (which we must consider later) that are so remarkable, but its ferocity. A me-

[6] L., p. 554.

dieval passion overcomes him as he sweeps aside into a common abyss of absurdity both the believer in eternal truth and the industrious seeker after truths; both faith and science. Indeed, so extravagant, so heedless of consequences, is his scepticism, that the reader is inclined to exclaim, what Hobbes himself is said to have exclaimed on seeing the proof of the forty-seventh theorem in *Euclid*, 'By God, this is impossible'. And what alone makes his scepticism plausible is the intrepidity of Hobbes himself; he has the nerve to accept his conclusions and the confidence to build on them. Both the energy to destroy and the energy to construct are powerful in Hobbes.

A man, it is generally agreed, may make himself ridiculous as easily by a philosophical system as by any other means. And yet, the impulse to think systematically is, at bottom, nothing more than the conscientious pursuit of what is for every philosopher the end to be achieved. The passion for clearness and simplicity, the determination not to be satisfied with anything inconsequent, the refusal to relieve one element of experience at the cost of another, are the motives of all philosophical thinking; and they conduce to system. 'The desire of wisdom leadeth to a kingdom'. And the pursuit of system is a call, not only upon fine intelligence and imagination, but also, and perhaps pre-eminently, upon energy of mind. For the principle in system is not the simple exclusion of all that does not fit, but the perpetual re-establishment of coherence. Hobbes stands out, not only among his contemporaries, but also in the history of English philosophy, as the creator of a system. And he conceived this system with such imaginative power that, in spite of its relatively simple character, it bears comparison with even the grand and subtle creation of Hegel. But if it requires great energy of mind to create a system, it requires even greater not to become the slave of the creation. To become the slave of a system in life is not to know when to 'hang up philosophy', not to recognize the final triumph of inconsequence; in philosophy, it is not to know when the claims of comprehension outweigh those of coherence. And here also the energy of Hobbes's mind did not desert him. When we come to consider the technicalities of his philosophy we shall observe a moderation that, for example, allowed him to escape an atomic philosophy, and an absence of rigidity that allowed him to modify his philosophical method when dealing with politics; here, when we are considering informally the quality of his mind, this ability appears as resilience, the energy to be perpetually freeing himself from the formalism of his system.

Thinking, for Hobbes, was not only conceived as movement, it was felt as movement. Mind is something agile, thoughts are darting, and the language of passion is appropriate to describe their workings. And the energy of his nature made it impossible for him not to take pleasure in controversy. The blood of contention ran in his veins. He acquired the lucid genius of a great expositor of ideas; but by disposition he was a fighter, and he knew no tactics save attack. He was a brilliant controversialist, deft, pertinacious and imaginative, and he disposed of the errors of scholastics, Puritans and Papists with a subtle mixture of argument and ridicule. But he made the mistake of supposing that this style was universally effective, in mathematics no less than in politics. For brilliance in controversy is a corrupting accomplishment. Always to play to win is to take one's standards from one's opponent, and local victory comes to displace every other consideration. Most readers will find Hobbes's disputatiousness excessive; but it is the defect of an exceptionally active mind. And it never quite destroyed in him the distinction between beating an opponent and establishing a proposition, and never quite silenced the conversation with himself which is the heart of philosophical thinking. But, like many controversialists, he hated error more than he loved truth, and came to depend overmuch on the stimulus of opposition. There is sagacity in Hobbes, and often a profound deliberateness; but there is no repose.

We have found Hobbes to possess remarkable confidence and energy of mind; we must consider now whether his mind was also original. Like Epicurus, he had an affectation for originality. He rarely mentions a writer to acknowledge a debt, and often seems over-sensitive about his independence of the past in philosophy. Aristotle's philosophy is 'vain', and scholasticism is no more than a 'collection of absurdities'. But, though he had certainly read more than he sometimes cared to admit—it was a favourite saying of his that if he had read as much as other men he should have known no more than other men—he seems to have been content with the reading that happened to come his way, and complained rather of the inconvenience of a want of conversation at some periods in his life than a lack of books. He was conscious of being a self-taught philosopher, an amateur, without the training of a Descartes or the background of a Spinoza. And this feeling was perhaps strengthened by the absence of an academic environment. One age of academic philosophy had gone, the next was yet to come. The seventeenth century was the age of the independent scholar, and Hobbes was one of these, taking his own way and making his own contacts with the learned world. And his profound suspicion of anything like authority in philosophy reinforced his circumstantial independence. The guidance he wanted he got from his touch with his contemporaries, particularly in Paris; his inspiration was a native sensitiveness to the direction required of philosophy if it were to provide an answer to the questions suggested by contemporary science. In conception and design, his philosophy is his own. And when he claimed that civil philosophy was 'no older than my own book *De Cive*',[7] he was expressing at once the personal achievement of having gone afresh to the facts of human consciousness for his interpretation of the meaning of civil association, and also that universal sense of newness with which his age appreciated its own intellectual accomplishments. But, for all that, his philosophy belongs to a tradition. Perhaps the truth is that Hobbes was as original as he thought he was, and to acknowledge his real indebtedness he would have required to see (what he could not be expected to see) the link between scholasticism and modern philosophy which is only now becoming clear to us. His philosophy is in the nature of a palimpsest. For its author what was important was what he wrote, and it is only to be expected that he should be indifferent to what is already there; but for us both sets of writing are significant.

[7] *E.W.*, I, ix.

Finally, Hobbes is a *writer*, a self-conscious stylist and the master of an individual style that expresses his whole personality; for there is no hiatus between his personality and his philosophy. His manner of writing is not, of course, foreign to his age; it belongs to him neither to write with the informality that is the achievement of Locke, nor with the simplicity that makes Hume's style a model not to be rejected by the philosophical writer of today. Hobbes is elaborate in an age that delighted in elaboration. But, within the range of his opportunities, he found a way of writing that exactly reflected his temperament. His controversial purpose is large on every page; he wrote to convince and to refute. And that in itself is a discipline. He has eloquence, the charm of wit, the decisiveness of confidence and the sententiousness of a mind made up: he is capable of urbanity and of savage irony. But the most significant qualities of his style are its didactic and its imaginative character. Philosophy in general knows two styles, the contemplative and the didactic, although there are many writers to whom neither belongs to the complete exclusion of the other. Those who practice the first let us into the secret workings of their minds and are less careful to send us away with a precisely formulated doctrine. Philosophy for them is a conversation, and, whether or not they write it as a dialogue, their style reflects their conception. Hobbes's way of writing is an example of the second style. What he says is already entirely freed from the doubts and hesitancies of the process of thought. It is only a residue, a distillate that is offered to the reader. The defect of such a style is that the reader must either accept or reject; if it inspires to fresh thought, it does so only by opposition. And Hobbes's style is imaginative, not merely on account of the subtle imagery that fills his pages, nor only because it requires imagination to make a system. His imagination appears also as the power to create a myth. *Leviathan* is a myth, the transposition of an abstract argument into the world of the imagination. In it we are made aware at a glance of the fixed and simple centre of a universe of complex and changing relationships. The argument may not be the better for this transposition, and what it gains in vividness it may pay for in illusion. But it is an accomplishment of art that Hobbes, in the history of political philosophy, shares only with Plato.

FOUR: THE SYSTEM

In Hobbes's mind, his 'civil philosophy' belonged to a system of philosophy. Consequently, an enquiry into the character of this system is not to be avoided by the interpreter of his politics. For, if the details of the civil theory may not improperly be considered as elements in a coherence of their own, the significance of the theory as a whole must depend upon the system to which it belongs, and upon the place it occupies in the system.

Two views, it appears, between them hold the field at the present time. The first is the view that the foundation of Hobbes's philosophy is a doctrine of materialism, that the intention of his system was the progressive revelation of this doctrine in nature, in man and in society, and that this revelation was achieved in his three most important philosophical works, *De Corpore, De Homine* and *De Cive*. These works, it is suggested, constitute a continuous argument, part of which is reproduced in *Leviathan*; and the novel project of the 'civil philosophy' was the exposition of a politics based upon a 'natural philosophy', the assimilation of politics to a materialistic doctrine of the world, or (it is even suggested) to the view of the world as it appeared in the conclusions of the physical sciences. A mechanistic-materialist politics is made to spring from a mechanistic-materialist universe. And, not improperly, it is argued that the significance of what appears at the end is determined at least in part by what was proved or assumed at the beginning. The second view is that this, no doubt, was the intention of Hobbes, but that 'the attempt and not the deed confounds him'. The joints of the system are ill-matched, and what should have been a continuous argument, based upon a philosophy of materialism, collapses under its own weight.

Both these views are, I think, misconceived. But they are the product not merely of inattention to the words of Hobbes; it is to be feared that they derive also from a graver fault of interpretation, a

false expectation with regard to the nature of a philosophical system. For what is expected here is that a philosophical system
should conform to an architectural analogue, and consequently
what is sought in Hobbes's system is a foundation and a super-
structure planned as a single whole, with civil philosophy as the top
storey. Now, it may be doubted whether any philosophical system
can properly be represented in the terms of architecture, but what
is certain is that the analogy does violence to the system of Hobbes.
The coherence of his philosophy, the system of it, lies not in an
architectonic structure, but in a single 'passionate thought' that
pervades its parts.[8] The system is not the plan or key of the labyrinth of the philosophy; it is, rather, a guiding clue, like the thread
of Ariadne.[9] It is like the music that gives meaning to the movement of dancers, or the law of evidence that gives coherence to the
practice of a court. And the thread, the hidden thought, is the continuous application of a doctrine about the nature of philosophy.
Hobbes's philosophy is the world reflected in the mirror of the philosophic eye, each image the representation of a fresh object, but
each determined by the character of the mirror itself. In short, the
civil philosophy belongs to a philosophical system, not because it is
materialistic but because it is philosophical; and an enquiry into
the character of the system and the place of politics in it resolves
itself into an enquiry into what Hobbes considered to be the nature
of philosophy.

For Hobbes, to think philosophically is to reason; philosophy is
reasoning. To this all else is subordinate; from this all else derives.
It is the character of reasoning that determines the range and the
limits of philosophical enquiry; it is this character that gives coherence, system, to Hobbes's philosophy. Philosophy, for him, is the
world as it appears in the mirror of reason; civil philosophy is the
image of the civil order reflected in that mirror. In general, the
world seen in this mirror is a world of causes and effects: cause and

---

[8] Confucius said, 'T'zu, you probably think that I have learned many things and hold them
in my mind.' 'Yes,' he replied, 'is that not true?' 'No,' said Confucius; 'I have one thing that
permeates everything.'—Confucius, *Analects*, XV, 2. *L.*, p. 19.
[9] *E.W.*, II, vi.

effect are its categories. And for Hobbes reason has two alternative
ends: to determine the conditional causes of given effects, or to determine the conditional effects of given causes.[10] But to understand
more exactly what he means by this identification of philosophy
with reasoning, we must consider three contrasts that run through
all his writing: the contrast between philosophy and theology (reason and faith), between philosophy and 'science' (reason and empiricism) and between philosophy and experience (reason and sense).

Reasoning is concerned solely with causes and effects. It follows, therefore, that its activity must lie within a world composed of
things that are causes or the effects of causes. If there is another
way of conceiving this world, it is not within the power of reasoning
to follow it; if there are things by definition causeless or ingener-
able, they belong to a world other than that of philosophy. This at
once, for Hobbes, excludes from philosophy the consideration of the
universe as a whole, things infinite, things eternal, final causes and
things known only by divine grace or revelation: it excludes what
Hobbes comprehensively calls theology and faith. He denies, not the
existence of these things, but their rationality.[11] This method of cir-
cumscribing the concerns of philosophy is not, of course, original
in Hobbes. It has roots that go back to Augustine, if not further,
and it was inherited by the seventeenth century (where one side of
it was distinguished as the heresy of Fideism: both Montaigne and
Pascal were Fideists) directly from its formulation in the Averroism
of Scotus and Occam. Indeed, this doctrine is one of the seeds in
scholasticism from which modern philosophy sprang. Philosophical
explanation, then, is concerned with things caused. A world of such
things is, necessarily, a world from which teleology is excluded; its
internal movement comprises the impact of its parts upon one another, of attraction and repulsion, not of growth or development. It
is a world conceived on the analogy of a machine, where to explain
an effect we go to its immediate cause, and to seek the result of a
cause we go only to its immediate effect.[12] In other words, the

[10] *E.W.*, I, 65–6, 387.
[11] *L.*, p. 80; *E.W.*, I, 10, 410.
[12] *E.W.*, II, xiv.

mechanistic element in Hobbes's philosophy is derived from his rationalism; its source and authority lie, not in observation, but in reasoning. He does not say that the natural world is a machine; he says only that the rational world is analogous to a machine. He is a scholastic, not a 'scientific' mechanist. This does not mean that the mechanistic element is unimportant in Hobbes; it means only that it is derivative. It is, indeed, of the greatest importance, for Hobbes's philosophy is, in all its parts, pre-eminently a philosophy of *power* precisely because philosophy is reasoning, reasoning the elucidation of mechanism and mechanism essentially the combination, transfer and resolution of forces. The end of philosophy itself is power—*scientia propter potentiam*.[13] Man is a complex of powers; desire is the desire for power, pride is illusion about power, honour opinion about power, life the unremitting exercise of power and death the absolute loss of power. And the civil order is conceived as a coherence of powers, not because politics is vulgarly observed to be a competition of powers, or because civil philosophy must take its conceptions from natural philosophy, but because to subject the civil order to rational enquiry unavoidably turns it into a mechanism.

In the writings of Hobbes, philosophy and science are not contrasted *eo nomine*. Such a contrast would have been impossible in the seventeenth century, with its absence of differentiation between the sciences and its still unshaken hold on the conception of the unity of human knowledge. Indeed, Hobbes normally uses the word science as a synonym for philosophy; rational knowledge is scientific knowledge. Nevertheless, Hobbes is near the beginning of a new view of the structure and parts of knowledge, a change of view which became clearer in the generation of Locke and was completed by Kant. Like Bacon and others before him, Hobbes has his own classification of the *genres* of knowledge,[14] and that it is a classification which involves a distinction between philosophy and what we have come to call 'science' is suggested by his ambiguous atti-

---

[13] *E.W.*, I, xiv; *O.L.*, I, 6.
[14] *L.*, p. 64.

tude to the work of contemporary scientists. He wrote with an unusually generous enthusiasm of the great advances made by Kepler,
Galileo and Harvey; 'the beginning of astronomy', he says 'is not to
be derived from farther time than from Copernicus';[15] but he had
neither sympathy nor even patience for the 'new or experimental
philosophy', and he did not conceal his contempt for the work of
the Royal Society, founded in his lifetime. But this ambiguity
ceases to be paradoxical when we see what Hobbes was about,
when we understand that one of the few internal tensions of his
thought arose from an attempted but imperfectly achieved distinction between science and philosophy. The distinction, well known
to us now, is that between knowledge of things as they appear and
enquiry into the fact of their appearing, between a knowledge (with
all the necessary assumptions) of the phenomenal world and a theory of knowledge itself. Hobbes appreciated this distinction, and his
appreciation of it allies him with Locke and with Kant and separates him from Bacon and even Descartes. He perceived that his
concern as a philosopher was with the second and not the first of
these enquiries; yet the distinction remained imperfectly defined in
his mind. But that philosophy meant for Hobbes something different from the enquiries of natural science is at once apparent when
we consider the starting-place of his thought and the character of
the questions he thinks it necessary to ask. He begins with sensation; and he begins there, not because there is no deceit or crookedness in the utterances of the senses, but because the fact of our
having sensations seems to him the only thing of which we can be
indubitably certain.[16] And the question he asks himself is, what
must the world be like for us to have the sensations we undoubtedly
experience? His enquiry is into the cause of sensation, an enquiry
to be conducted, not by means of observation, but by means of reasoning. And if the answer he proposes owes something to the inspiration of the scientists, that does nothing to modify the distinction

---

[15] *E.W.*, I, viii.

[16] It will be remembered that the brilliant and informal genius of Montaigne had perceived
that our most certain knowledge is what we know about ourselves, and had made of this a
philosophy of introspection.

between science and philosophy inherent in the question itself. For the scientist of his day the world of nature was almost a machine, Kepler had proposed the substitution of the word *vis* for the word *anima* in physics; and Hobbes, whose concern was with the rational world (by definition also conceived as the analogy of a machine), discovered that some of the general ideas of the scientists could be turned to his own purposes. But these pardonable appropriations do nothing to approximate his enquiry to that of Galileo or Newton. Philosophy is reasoning, this time contrasted, not with theology, but with what we have come to know as natural science. And the question, What, in an age of science, is the task of philosophy? which was to concern the nineteenth century so deeply, was already familiar to Hobbes. And it is a false reading of his intention and his achievement which finds in his civil philosophy the beginning of sociology or a science of politics, the beginning of that movement of thought that came to regard 'the methods of physical science as the proper models for political'.[17]

But the contrast that finally distinguishes philosophy and reveals its full character is that between philosophy and what Hobbes calls experience. For in elucidating this distinction Hobbes shows us philosophy coming into being, shows it as a thing generated and relates it to its cause thereby establishing it as itself a proper subject of rational consideration. The mental history of a man begins with sensation, 'for there is no conception in a man's mind, which hath not at first, totally, or by parts, been begotten upon the organs of sense'.[18] Some sensations, perhaps, occupying but an instant, involve no reference to others and no sense of time. But commonly, sensations, requiring a minimum time of more than a single instant, and reaching a mind already stored with the relics of previous sensations, are impossible without that which gives a sense of time—memory.[19] Sensation involves recollection, and a man's experience is nothing but the recollected after-images of sensations. But from his power to remember man derives anoth-

[17] J. S. Mill, *Autobiography*, p. 165.
[18] *L.*, p. 11.
[19] *E.W.*, I, 393.

er power, imagination, which is the ability to recall and turn over in the mind the decayed relics of past sensation, the ability to experience even when the senses themselves have ceased to speak. Moreover imagination, though it depends on past sensations, is not an entirely servile faculty; it is capable of compounding together relics of sensations felt at different times. Indeed, in imagination we may have in our minds images not only of what we have never actually seen (as when we imagine a golden mountain though we have seen only gold and a mountain), but even of what we could never see, such as a chimera. But imagination remains servile in that 'we have no transition from one imagination to another whereof we never had the like before in our senses'.[20] Two things more belong to experience; the fruits of experience. The first is History, which is the ordered register of past experiences. The second is prudence, which is the power to anticipate experience by means of the recollection of what has gone before. 'Of our conceptions of the past, we make a future'.[21] A full, well-recollected experience gives the 'foresight' and 'wisdom' that belong to the prudent man, a wisdom that springs from the appreciation of those causes and effects that time and not reason teaches us. This is the end and crown of experience. In the mind of the prudent or sagacious man, experience appears as a kind of knowledge. Governed by sense, it is necessarily individual, a particular knowledge of particulars. But, within its limits, it is 'absolute knowledge';[22] there is no ground upon which it can be doubted, and the categories of truth and falsehood do not apply to it. It is mere, uncritical 'knowledge of fact': 'experience concludeth nothing universal'.[23] And in all its characteristics it is distinguished from philosophical knowledge, which (because it is reasoned) is general and not particular, a knowledge of consequences and not of facts, and conditional and not absolute.

Our task now is to follow Hobbes in his account of the generation of rational knowledge from experience. In principle, experience

[20] *L.*, p. 18.
[21] *E.W.*, IV, 16.
[22] *L.*, p. 64.
[23] *E.W.*, IV, 18.

(except perhaps when it issues in history) is something man shares with animals and has only in a greater degree: memory and imagination are the unsought mechanical products of sensation, like the movements that continue on the surface of water after what disturbed it has sunk to rest. In order to surmount the limits of this sense-experience and achieve reasoned knowledge of our sensations, we require not only to have sensations, but to be conscious of having them; we require the power of introspection. But the cause of this power must lie in sense itself, if the power is to avoid the imputation of being an easy *deus ex machina*. Language satisfies both these conditions: it makes introspection possible, and springs from a power we share with animals, the physical power of making sounds. For, though language 'when disposed of in speech and pronounced to others'[24] is the means whereby men declare their thoughts to one another, it is primarily the only means by which a man may communicate his own thoughts to himself, may become conscious of the contents of his mind. The beginning of language is giving names to after-images of sensations and thereby becoming conscious of them; the act of naming the image is the act of becoming conscious of it. For, 'a name is a word taken at pleasure to serve as a mark that may raise in our minds a thought like some thought we had before'.[25]

Language, the giving of names to images, is not itself reasonable, it is the arbitrary precondition of all reasoning:[26] the generation of rational knowledge is by words out of experience. The achievement of language is to 'register our thoughts', to fix what is essentially fleeting. And from this achievement follows the possibility of definition, the conjunction of general names, proposition and rational argument, all of which consist in the 'proper use of names in language'. But, though reasoning brings with it knowledge of the general and the possibility of truth and its opposite, absurdity,[27] it

---

[24] *E.W.*, I, 16.
[25] *E.W.*, I, 16.
[26] This is why introspection that falls short of reasoning is possible. *E.W.*, I, 73.
[27] Since truth is of propositions its opposite is a statement that is absurd or nonsensical. Error belongs to the world of experience and is a failure in foresight. *L.*, p. 34.

can never pass beyond the world of names. Reasoning is nothing else but the addition and subtraction of names, and 'gives us conclusions, not about the nature of things, but about the names of things. That is to say, by means of reason we discover only whether the connections we have established between names are in accordance with the arbitrary convention we have established concerning their meanings'.[28] This is at once a nominalist and a profoundly sceptical doctrine. Truth is of universals, but they are names, the names of images left over from sensations; and a true proposition is not an assertion about the real world. We can, then, surmount the limits of sense-experience and achieve rational knowledge; and it is this knowledge, with its own severe limitations, that is the concern of philosophy.

But philosophy is not only knowledge of the universal, it is a knowledge of causes. Informally, Hobbes describes it as 'the natural reason of man flying up and down among the creatures, and bringing back a true report of their order, causes and effects'.[29] We have seen already how, by limiting philosophy to a knowledge of things caused (because reasoning itself must observe this limit) he separates it from theology. We have now to consider why he believed that the essential work of reasoning (and therefore of philosophy) was the demonstration of the cause of things caused. Cause for Hobbes is the means by which anything comes into being. Unlike any of the Aristotelian causes, it is essentially that which, previous in time, brings about the effect. A knowledge of cause is, then, a knowledge of how a thing is generated.[30] But why must philosophy be a knowledge of this sort? Hobbes's answer would appear to be, first, that this sort of knowledge can spring from reasoning while it is impossible to mere experience, and, secondly, that since, *ex hypothesi*, the data of philosophy are effects, the only possible enlargement of our knowledge of them must consist in a knowledge of their causes. If we add to the experience of an effect a knowledge of

[28] *O.L.*, V, 257.
[29] *E.W.*, I, xiii.
[30] *E.W.*, VII, 78.

its generation, a knowledge of its 'constitutive cause',[31] we know everything that may be known. In short, a knowledge of causes is the pursuit in philosophy because philosophy is reasoning.[32]

The third characteristic of philosophical knowledge, as distinguished from experience, is that it is conditional, not absolute. Hobbes's doctrine is that when, in reasoning, we conclude that the cause of something is such and such, we can mean no more than that such and such is a possible efficient cause, and not that it is the actual cause. There are three criteria by which a suggested cause may be judged, and proof that the cause actually operated is not among them. For reasoning, a cause must be 'imaginable', the necessity of the effect must be shown to follow from the cause, and it must be shown that nothing false (that is, not present in the effect) can be derived.[33] And what satisfies these conditions may be described as an hypothetical efficient cause. That philosophy is limited to the demonstration of such causes is stated by Hobbes on many occasions; it applies not only to the detail of his philosophy, but also to the most general of all causes, to body and motion. For example, when he says that the cause or generation of a circle is 'the circumduction of a body whereof one end remains unmoved', he adds that this gives 'some generation [of the figure], though perhaps not that by which it was made, yet that by which it might have been made'.[34] And when he considers the general problem of the cause of sensations, he concludes, not with the categorical statement that body and motion are the only causal existents, but that body (that is, that which is independent of thought and which fills a portion of space) and motion are the hypothetical efficient causes of our having sensations. If there were no body there could be no motion, and if there were no motion of bodies there could be no sensation; *sentire semper idem et non sentire ad idem recidunt.*[35] From beginning to end there is no suggestion in Hobbes

[31] *E.W.*, II, xiv.

[32] Hobbes gives the additional reason that a knowledge of causes is useful to mankind. *E.W.*, I, 7–10.

[33] *Elements of Law*, Appendix II, §1, 168.

[34] *E.W.*, I, 6, 386–7.

[35] *O.L.*, I, 321.

that philosophy is anything other than conditional knowledge, knowledge of hypothetical generations and conclusions about the names of things, not about the nature of things.[36] With these philosophy must be satisfied, though they are but fictions. Indeed, philosophy may be defined as the establishment by reasoning of true fictions. And the ground of this limitation is, that the world being what it is, reasoning can go no further. 'There is no effect which the power of God cannot produce in many several ways,'[37] verification *ad oculos* is impossible because these causes are rational not perceptible, and consequently the farthest reach of reason is the demonstration of causes which satisfy the three rational criteria.

My contention is, then, that the system of Hobbes's philosophy lies in his conception of the nature of philosophical knowledge, and not in any doctrine about the world. And the inspiration of his philosophy is the intention to be guided by reason and to reject all other guides: this is the thread, the hidden thought, that gives it coherence, distinguishing it from Faith, 'Science' and Experience. It remains to guard against a possible error. The lineage of Hobbes's rationalism lies, not (like that of Spinoza or even Descartes) in the great Platonic-Christian tradition, but in the sceptical, late scholastic tradition. He does not normally speak of Reason, the divine illumination of the mind that unites man with God; he speaks of reasoning. And he is not less persuaded of its fallibility and limitations than Montaigne himself.[38] By means of reasoning we certainly pass beyond mere sense-experience, but when imagination and prudence have generated rational knowledge, they do not, like drones, perish; they continue to perform in human life functions that reasoning itself cannot discharge. Nor, indeed, is man, in Hobbes's view, primarily a reasoning creature. This capacity for general hypothetical reasoning distinguishes him from the

---

[36] *L.*, pp. 49–50.

[37] *E.W.*, VII, 3. It may be observed that what is recognized here is the normally unstated presupposition of all seventeenth-century science: the Scotist belief that the natural world is the creation *ex nihilo* of an omnipotent God, and that therefore categorical knowledge of its detail is not deducible but (if it exists) must be the product of observation. Characteristically adhering to the tradition, Hobbes says that the only thing we can know of God is his omnipotence.

[38] *L.*, p. 34.

animal, but he remains fundamentally a creature of passion, and it is by passion not less than by reasoning that he achieves his salvation.[39]

We have considered Hobbes's view of philosophy because civil philosophy, whatever else it is, is philosophy. Civil philosophy, the subject of *Leviathan,* is precisely the application of this conception of philosophy to civil association. It is not the last chapter in a philosophy of materialism, but the reflection of civil association in the mirror of a rationalistic philosophy. But if the *genus* of civil philosophy is its character as philosophy, its *differentia* is derived from the matter to be considered. Civil philosophy is settling the generation or constitutive cause of civil association. And the kind of hypothetical efficient cause that civil philosophy may be expected to demonstrate is determined by the fact that civil association is an artifact: it is artificial, not natural. Now, to assert that civil association is an artifact is already to have settled the question of its generation, and Hobbes himself does not begin with any such assertion. His method is to establish the artificial character of civil association by considering its generation. But in order to avoid false expectations it will be wise for us to anticipate the argument and consider what he means by this distinction between art and nature.

Hobbes has given us no collected account of his philosophy of artifice; it is to be gathered only from scattered observations. But when these are put together, they compose a coherent view. A work of art is the product or effect of mental activity. But this in itself does not distinguish it securely from nature, because the universe itself must be regarded as the product of God's mental activity, and what we call 'nature' is to God an artifact;[40] and there are products of human mental activity which, having established themselves, become for the observer part of his natural world. More firmly defined, then, a work of art is the product of mental activity considered

[39] *L.,* p. 98.
[40] *L.,* p. 5.

from the point of view of its cause. And, since what we have to consider are works of human art, our enquiry must be into the kind of
natural human mental activity that may result in a work of art; for
the cause of a work of art must lie in nature; that is, in experience.
It would appear that the activities involved are willing and reasoning. But reasoning itself is artificial, not natural; it is an 'acquired'
not a 'native' mental activity,[41] and therefore cannot be considered
as part of the generation of a work of art.[42] We are left, then, with
willing, which, belonging to experience and not reasoning, is undoubtedly a natural mental activity. The cause (hypothetical and efficient, of course) of a human work of art is the will of a man. And
willing is 'the last desire in deliberating', deliberating being mental
discourse in which the subject is desires and aversions.[43] It is a
creative activity (not merely imitative), in the same way as imagination, working on sensations, creates a new world of hitherto separated parts. Both will and imagination are servile only in that their
products must be like nature in respect of being mechanisms; that
is, complexes of cause and effect.[44] Moreover, will creates not only
when it is single and alone, but also in concert with other wills.
The product of an agreement between wills is no less a work of art
than the product of one will. And the peculiarity of civil association, as a work of art, is its generation from a number of wills. The
word 'civil', in Hobbes, means artifice springing from more than
one will. Civil history (as distinguished from natural history) is the
register of events that have sprung from the voluntary actions of
man in commonwealths.[45] Civil authority is authority arising out
of an agreement of wills, while natural authority (that of the father
in the family) has no such generation and is consequently of a different character.[46] And civil association is itself contrasted on this

---

[41] *L.*, p. 29.

[42] The expression 'natural reason' is not absent from Hobbes's writings, but it means the
reasoning of individual men contrasted with the doubly artificial reasoning of the artificial
man, the Leviathan, e.g., *L.*, pp. 5, 42, 233, 242; *E.W.*, I, xiii.

[43] *L.*, p. 38.

[44] *L.*, p. 8.

[45] *L.*, p. 64.

[46] *L.*, p. 153.

account with the appearance of it in mere natural gregarious-ness.[47]

Now, with this understanding of the meaning of both 'civil' and 'philosophical', we may determine what is to be expected for a civil philosophy. Two things may be expected from it. First, it will exhibit the internal mechanism of civil association as a system of cause and effect and settle the generation of the parts of civil association. And secondly, we may expect it to settle the generation, in terms of an hypothetical efficient cause, of the artifact as a whole; that is, to show this work of art springing from the specific nature of man. But it may be observed that two courses lie open to anyone, holding the views of Hobbes, who undertakes this project. Philosophy, we have seen, may argue from a given effect to its hypothetical efficient cause, or from a given cause to its possible effect. Often the second form of argument is excluded; this is so with sensations, when the given is an effect and the cause is to seek. But in civil philosophy, and in all reasoning concerned with artifacta, both courses are open; for the cause and the effect (human nature and civil association) are both given, and the task of philosophy is to unite the details of each to each in terms of cause and effect. Hobbes tells us[48] that his early thinking on the subject took the form of an argument from effect (civil association) to cause (human nature), from art to nature; but it is to be remarked that, not only in *Leviathan*, but also in all other accounts he gives of his civil philosophy, the form of the argument is from cause to effect, from nature to art. But, since the generation is rational and not physical, the direction from which it is considered is clearly a matter of indifference.

FIVE: THE ARGUMENT OF *LEVIATHAN*

Any account worth giving of the argument of *Leviathan* must be an interpretation; and this account, because it is an interpretation, is not a substitute for the text. Specific comment is avoided; but the

[47] *L.*, p. 130.
[48] *E.W.*, II, vi, xiv.

implicit comment involved in selection, emphasis, the alteration of the language and the departure from the order of ideas in the text, cannot be avoided.

The nature of man is the predicament of mankind. A knowledge of this nature is to be had from introspection, each man reading himself in order to discern in himself, mankind. Civil philosophy begins with this sort of knowledge of the nature of man.[49]

Man is a creature of sense. He can have nothing in his mind that was not once a sensation. Sensations are movements in the organs of sense which set up consequent movements in the brain; after the stimulus of sense has spent itself, there remain in the mind slowly fading relics of sensations, called images or ideas. Imagination is the consciousness of these images, we imagine what was once in the senses but is there no longer. Memory is the recollection of these images. A man's experience is the whole contents of his memory, the relics of sensations available to him in recollection. And Mental Discourse is images succeeding one another in the mind. This succession may be haphazard or it may be regulated, but it always follows some previous succession of sensations. A typical regulated succession of images is where the image of an effect calls up from memory the image of its cause. Mental discourse becomes Prudence or foresight when, by combining the recollection of the images of associated sensations in the past with the present experience of one of the sensations, we anticipate the appearance of the others. Prudence is natural wisdom. All these together may be called the *receptive* powers of a man. Their cause is sensation (into the cause of which we need not enquire here), and they are nothing other than movements in the brain.[50]

But, springing from these there is another set of movements in the brain, which may be called comprehensively the *active* powers

---

[49] Man is a mechanism; but a mechanism may be considered at different levels of abstraction. For example, the working of a watch may be described mathematically in terms of quantities, or in the mechanical terms of force and inertia, or in terms of its visible parts, springs and cogs. And to choose one level does not deny the possibility of the others. In selecting introspection as the sort of knowledge of man required in civil philosophy, Hobbes is doing no more than to choose what he considers to be the relevant level of abstraction.

[50] *L.*, chs. i–iii.

of a man; his emotions or passions. These movements are called voluntary to distinguish them from involuntary movements such as the circulation of the blood. Voluntary activity is activity in response to an idea, and therefore it has its beginning in imagination. Its undifferentiated form is called Endeavour, which, when it is towards the image from which it sprang is called Desire or Appetite, and when it is away from its originating image is called Aversion. Love corresponds to Desire; Hate to Aversion. And whatever is the object of a man's desire he calls Good, and whatever he hates he calls Evil. There is, therefore, nothing good or evil as such; for different men desire different things, each calling the object of his desire good, and the same man will, at different times, love and hate the same thing. Pleasure is a movement in the mind that accompanies the image of what is held to be good, pain one that accompanies an image held to be evil. Now, just as the succession of images in the mind is called Mental Discourse (the end of which is Prudence), so the succession of emotions in the mind is called Deliberation, the end of which is Will. While desire and aversion succeed one another without any decision being reached, we are said to be deliberating; when a decision is reached, and desire is concentrated upon some object, we are said to will it. Will is the last desire in deliberating. There can, then, be no final end, no *summum bonum*,[51] for a man's active powers; human conduct is not teleological, it is concerned with continual success in obtaining those things which a man from time to time desires, and success lies not only in procuring what is desired, but also in the assurance that what will in the future be desired will also be procured. This success is called Felicity, which is a condition of movement, not of rest or tranquillity. The means by which a man may obtain this success are called, comprehensively, his Power; and therefore there is in man a perpetual and restless desire for power, because power is the *conditio sine qua non* of Felicity.[52]

[51] There is, however, a *summum malum*, and it is death; its opposite, being alive, is only a 'primary good'. *L.*, p. 75; *O.L.*, II, 98.
[52] *L.*, chs. vi, xi.

The receptive and the active powers of man derive directly from the possession of the five senses; the senses are their efficient cause. And since we share our senses with the animals, we share also these powers. Men and beasts do not have the same images and desires; but both alike have imagination and desire. What then, since this does not, differentiates man from beast? Two things: religion and the power of reasoning. Both these are at once natural and artificial: they belong to the nature of man because their generation is in sense and emotion, but they are artificial because they are the products of human mental activity. Religion and reasoning are mankind's natural inheritance of artifice.

The character of reasoning and its generation from the invention of speech has already been described. Here it need only be added that, just as Prudence is the end-product of imagination and Felicity of emotion, so Sapience is the end-product of reasoning; and Sapience is a wealth of general hypothetical conclusions or theorems, found out by reasoning, about the causes and consequences of the names of sensations.[53]

The seed of religion, like that of reasoning, is in the nature of man, though what springs from that seed, a specific set of religious beliefs and practices, is an artifact. The generation of religion is the necessary defect of Prudence, the inexperience of man. Prudence is foresight of a probable future based upon recollection, and insight into a probable cause also based upon recollection. Its immediate emotional effect is to allay anxiety and fear, fear of an unknown cause or consequence.[54] But since its range is necessarily limited, it has the additional effect of increasing man's fear of what lies beyond that limit. Prudence, in restricting the area in the control of fear, increases the fear of what is still to be feared; having some foresight, men are all the more anxious because that foresight is not complete. (Animals, having little or no foresight, suffer only the lesser evil of its absence, not the greater of its limitation.) Religion is the product of mental activity to meet this situation. It springs

[53] *L.*, chs. iv, v.
[54] For Hobbes, fear is aversion from something believed to be hurtful. *L.*, p. 43.

from prudent fear of what is beyond the power of prudence to find out,[55] and is the worship of what is feared because it is not understood. Its contradictory is Knowledge; its contrary is Superstition, worship springing from fear of what is properly an object of knowledge. The perpetual fear that is the spring of religion seeks an object on which to concentrate itself, and calls that object God. It is true that perseverance in reasoning may reveal the necessity of a First Cause, but so little can be known about it that the attitude of human beings towards it must always be one of worship rather than knowledge. And each man, according to the restriction of his experience and the greatness of his fear, renders to God worship and honour.[56]

The human nature we are considering is the internal structure and powers of the individual man, a structure and powers which would be his even if he were the only example of his species: we are considering the character of the solitary. He lives in the world of his own sensations and imaginations, desires and aversions, prudence, reason and religion. For his thoughts and actions he is answerable to none but himself. He is conscious of possessing certain powers, and the authority for their exercise lies in nothing but their existence, and that authority is absolute. Consequently, an observer from another world, considering the character of our solitary, would not improperly attribute to him a natural freedom or right of judgement in the exercise of his powers of mind and body for the achievement of the ends given in his nature.[57] In the pursuit of felicity he may make mistakes, in his mental discourse he may commit errors, in his reasoning he may be guilty of absurdity, but a denial of the propriety of the pursuit would be a meaningless denial of the propriety of his character and existence. Further, when our solitary applies his powers of reasoning to find out fit means to at-

---

[55] L., p. 82. The limitations of reasoning also produce fear, a rational fear of what is beyond the power of reason to discern.

[56] L., ch. xii.

[57] Freedom, for Hobbes, can be properly attributed only to a body whose motion is not hindered. L., p. 161. And the 'right' derives, of course, not from the authority of a natural law, but from the character of the individual as an *ens completum*.

tain the ends dictated by his emotional nature, he may, if his reasoning is steady, light upon some general truths or theorems with regard to the probable consequences of his actions. It appears, then, that morally unfettered action (which may be called a man's natural right to exercise his natural powers), and the possibility of formulating general truths about the pursuit of felicity, are corollaries of human nature.

Two further observations may be made. First, in the pursuit of felicity certain habits of mind and action will be found to be specially serviceable, and these are called Virtues. Other habits will hinder the pursuit, and these are called Defects. Defects are misdirected virtues. For example, prudence in general is a virtue, but to be overprudent, to look too far ahead and allow too much care for the future, reduces a man to the condition of Prometheus on the rock (whose achievements by night were devoured by the anxieties of the day), and inhibits the pursuit.[58] And the pre-eminently inhibiting defect from which human beings may be observed to suffer is Pride. This is the defect of Glory, and its other names are Vanity and Vain-glory. Glory, which is exultation in the mind based upon a true estimate of a man's powers to procure felicity, is a useful emotion; it is both the cause and effect of well-grounded confidence. But pride is a man's false estimate of his own powers, and is the forerunner of certain failure. Indeed, so fundamental a defect is pride, that it may be taken as the type of all hindrances to the achievement of felicity.[59] Secondly, it may be observed that death, the involuntary cessation of desire and the pursuit which is the end of desire, is the thing of all others the most hateful; it is the *summum malum*. And that which men hate they also fear if it is beyond their control. Prudence tells a man that he will die, and by taking thought the prudent man can sometimes avoid death by avoiding its probable occasions, and, so far, the fear of it will be diminished. But death will outdistance the fastest runner; in all its forms it is something to be feared as well as hated. Yet it is to be

[58]*L.*, p. 82.
[59]*L.*, pp. 44, 88.

feared most when it is most beyond the control of prudence: the death to be most greatly feared is that which no foresight can guard against—sudden death.[60] It would appear, then, that Pride is the type of all hindrances to the achievement of felicity, and death the type of all Aversion.

Now, the element of unreality in the argument so far is not that the solitary, whose character we have been considering, is an abstraction and does not exist (he does exist and he is the real individual man), but that he does not exist alone. This fact, that there is more than one of his kind, must now be recognized; we must turn from the nature of man to consider the natural condition of man. And it is at this point that the predicament of mankind becomes apparent; for, apart from mortality, the character of the solitary man presents nothing that could properly be called a predicament.

The existence of others of his kind, and the impossibility of escaping their company, is the first real impediment in the pursuit of felicity; for another man is necessarily a competitor. This is no mere observation, though its effects may be seen by any candid observer; it is a deduction from the nature of felicity. For, whatever appears to a man to belong to his felicity he must strive for with all his powers, and men who strive for the possession of the same object are enemies of one another. Moreover, he who is most successful will have the most enemies and be in the greatest danger. To have built a house and cultivated a garden is to have issued an invitation to all others to take it by force, for it is against the common view of felicity to weary oneself with making what can be acquired by less arduous means. And further, competition does not arise merely when two or more happen to want the same thing, for when a man is among others of his kind his felicity is not absolute but comparative; and since a large part of it comes from a feeling of superiority, of having more than his fellow, the competition is es-

---

[60] In *Leviathan* death itself is taken to be the greatest evil; the refinement about sudden death is an interpretation of the view that appears in the *De Cive* and elsewhere that the greatest evil is *violent* death at the hands of another. This not only terminates the pursuit of felicity, but does so in a manner shameful to the victim; it convicts him of inferiority.

sential, not accidental. There is, at best, a permanent potential enmity between men, 'a perpetual contention for Honour, Riches and Authority'.[61] And to make matters worse, each man is so nearly the equal of each other man in power, that superiority of strength (which might set some men above the disadvantage of competition: the possibility of losing) is nothing better than an illusion. The natural condition of man is one of the competition of equals for the things (necessarily scarce because of the desire for *superiority*)[62] that belong to felicity. But equality of power, bringing with it, not only equality of fear, but also equality of hope, will urge every man to try to outwit his neighbour. And the end is open conflict, a war of all against all, in which the defects of man's character and circumstances make him additionally vulnerable. For, if pride, the excessive estimate of his own powers, hinders a man in choosing the best course when he is alone, it will be the most crippling of all handicaps when played upon by a competitor in the race. And in a company of enemies, death, the *summum malum*, will be closer than felicity. When a man is among men, pride is more dangerous and death more likely.[63]

But further, the relationship between these self-moved seekers after felicity is complicated by an ambiguity. They are enemies but they also need one another. And this for two reasons: without others there is no recognition of superiority and therefore no notable felicity; and many, perhaps most of the satisfactions which constitute a man's felicity are in the responses he may wring from others. The pursuit of felicity, in respect of a large part of it, is a procedure of bargaining with others in which one seeks what another has got and for which he must offer a satisfaction in return.

The predicament may now be stated precisely. There is a radical conflict between the nature of man and the natural condition of mankind: what the one urges with hope of achievement, the other makes impossible. Man is solitary; would that he were alone. For the sweetness of all he may come by through the efforts of others, is

[61] *L.*, p. 547.
[62] *L.*, p. 130.
[63] *L.*, ch. xiii.

made bitter by the price he must pay for it, and it is neither sin nor depravity that creates the predicament; nature itself is the author of his ruin.

But, like the seeds of fire (which were not themselves warm) that Prometheus brought mankind, like the first incipient movements (hardly to be called such) that Lucretius, and after him Hobbes, supposes to precede visible movement, the deliverance lies in the womb of nature. The saviour is not a visitor from another world, nor is it some god-like power of Reason come to create order out of chaos; there is no break either in the situation or in the argument. The remedy of the disease is homeopathic.[64]

The precondition of the deliverance is the recognition of the predicament. Just as, in Christian theory, the repentance of the sinner is the first indispensable step towards forgiveness and salvation, so here, mankind must first purge itself of the illusion called pride. So long as a man is in the grip of this illusion he will hope to succeed tomorrow where he failed today; and the hope is vain. The purging emotion (for it is to emotion that we go to find the beginning of deliverance) is fear of death. This fear illuminates prudence; man is a creature civilized by fear of death. And what is begun in prudence is continued in reasoning; art supplements the gifts of nature.

For, as reasoning may find out truths for the guidance of a man in his pursuit of felicity when he is alone, so it is capable of uncovering similar truths in respect of his competitive endeavour to satisfy his wants. And since what threatens to defeat every attempt to procure felicity in these circumstances is the unconditionally competitive character of the pursuit (or, in a word, war), these truths found out by reason for avoiding this defeat of all by all may properly be called the articles of Peace. Such truths, indeed, have been uncovered, and they are all conditions qualifying the competitive pursuit of felicity which, if they are observed by all, will enhance the certainty, if not the magnitude of the satisfaction of each. They are sometimes called the 'laws of nature', but this is a misnomer except

---

[64] *L.*, p. 98.

in special circumstances (to be considered later) when they are recognized to be the commands of a God or of a civil sovereign. Properly speaking, they are only theorems, the product of reasoning about
what conduces to the optimum satisfaction of human wants.[65] And
they are fruitless until they are transformed from mere theorems
into maxims of human conduct and from maxims into laws; that
is, until they are recognized as valid rules of conduct of known jurisdiction, to be subscribed to by all who fall within that jurisdiction and to which penalties for non-subscription have been annexed and power to enforce them provided. But this transformation
also lies within the scope of human art. Such rules of conduct are
neither more nor less than the product of an agreement to recognize them as rules, and human beings endowed with the faculty of
speech may not only communicate their thoughts to one another
but also make agreements; indeed, their association is solely in
terms of agreements. In short, moved by fear of ill-success in procuring the satisfaction of their wants, instructed by the conclusions of reasoning about how this ill-success may be mitigated and
endowed with the ability to set these conclusions to work, human
beings enjoy the means of escaping from the predicament of mankind.

The substantial conclusions of human reasoning in this matter
Hobbes sums up in a maxim: *do not that to another, which thou
wouldest not have done to thyself.*[66] But, more important than
this, is its formal message, namely, that where there is a multitude
of men each engaged in unconditional competition with the others
to procure the satisfaction of his own wants, and of roughly equal
power to obtain each what he seeks, they may succeed in their respective endeavours only when its unconditionality is abated. The
abrogation of the competition is, of course, impossible; there can be
no common or communal felicity to which they might be persuaded
to turn their attention. But this race in which each seeks to come
first and is also unavoidably and continuously fearful of not doing

---

[65] *L.*, 122, 205.
[66] *L.*, p. 121.

so, must have some rules imposed upon it if it is not to run everyone into the ground. And this can be done only in an agreement of those concerned.

Now, in the day-to-day transactions in which human beings seek the satisfaction of their wants this message of reason may often be listened to and acted upon. They make *ad hoc* agreements about procedures of bargaining, they enter into formal relationships, they even make and accept promises about future actions and often keep them. And although such arrangements cannot increase the magnitude of their felicity they may make its pursuit less chancy. But this abatement of uncertainty is at best marginal and at worst delusive. These *ad hoc* formal relationships of mutual agreement between assignable persons are evanescent; remotely they may reflect generally accepted theorems about rational conduct, but as rules they are the products of specific and temporary agreements between the persons concerned. And further, they are always liable to be undermined by the substantial relationship of competitive hostility. And even if such agreements contain penalty clauses for the non-observance of the conditions they impose upon the conduct of a transaction, these (in the absence of an independent means of enforcing them) add nothing to the certainty of the sought-for outcome. And this is particularly the case where a promise to respond in the future is made by one who has already received a conditional benefit: the abatement of uncertainty it purports to offer depends upon the expectation of its being fulfilled, that is, upon whether or not it is in the interest of the respondent to keep his promise when the time comes to do so. And this, in Hobbes's view, must always be insufficiently certain for a reasonable man to bank upon it. In short, these *ad hoc* devices to increase the certainty of the satisfaction of wants, when taken alone, are themselves infected with uncertainty; where there is a present and substantial agreement about mutual interests they may be a convenience, where this is absent they provide merely an illusion of security.

What, then, is lacking here, and what is required for a 'constant and lasting' release from the impediments which frustrate the common pursuit of individual felicity, is settled and known rules of conduct and a power sufficient to coerce those who fall within their jurisdiction to observe them. How may this condition of things be imagined to be 'caused' or 'generated'? First, it can be the effect only of an agreement among the human beings concerned. It is human beings associated in a particular manner, and all human association is by agreement. Secondly, it can be the effect of only a particular kind of agreement; namely, one in which a number of men, neither small nor unmanageably large, associate themselves in terms of a covenant to authorize an Actor to make standing rules to be subscribed to indifferently in all their endeavours to satisfy their wants and to protect the association from the hostile attentions of outsiders, and to endow this Actor with power sufficient to enforce these conditions of conduct and to provide this protection. Or, if this is not the only imaginable cause of the desiderated condition of peace and security, then at least it is a possible cause.[67]

Such a covenant requires careful specification if it is to be shewn not itself to inhibit the pursuit of felicity and not to conflict with the alleged characters of those who enter into it. And it is susceptible of various descriptions. It may, in general, be recognized as an agreement of many to submit their wills every one to the will of an Actor in respect of 'all those things which concern the common peace and safety'.[68] More precisely it may be identified as an agreement in which each participator surrenders his natural right to 'govern himself' (or, 'to be governed by his own reason')[69] which derives from his natural right to the unconditional pursuit of his own felicity. But if so, the character of this surrender must be specified: it must be not a mere laying down of this right, but a giving up of it to another. The right of each to 'govern himself' (that is, to determine the conditions upon which he may pursue his felicity) is transferred to an Actor; that is, to one authorized in the agreement to exercise it. But who must this Actor be? Not a natural person, one among those who covenant to surrender their right to govern

[67] *L.*, ch. xvii.
[68] *L.*, p. 131.
[69] *L.*, p. 99.

themselves, for that would be merely to place the government of their conduct in the hands of one moved only by his appetite to satisfy his own wants. The Actor is an artificial man who represents or 'bears the person' of each of those who, by agreeing among themselves to do so, creates him and authorizes all his actions. What is created and authorized in this covenant is an Office which, although it may be occupied by one or by more than one office-holder, remains single and sovereign in all its official actions and utterances. Thus, the condition of peace and security is said to be the effect of 'a covenant of every man with every man, in such manner, as if every man should say to every man, *I authorize and give up my right of governing myself, to this man, or to this assembly of men, on this condition, that thou give up thy right to him, and authorize all his actions in like manner'.*[70] Or again, it may be recognized as a covenant in which the covenanters agree among themselves 'to confer all their strength and power upon one [artificial] man', thus providing the power to enforce recalcitrants to submit to the will and the judgement of an office-holder authorized to deliberate and to decide upon the conditions to be observed by all in their several adventures in pursuit of felicity. And here it is a covenant not merely to transfer a right (which could notionally be affected in a single once-for-all pronouncement), but to be continuously active in supplying the power required to exercise it—for the Office can have no such resources of its own.

This covenant, then, purports to create an artifact composed of a sovereign Ruler authorized and empowered by covenanters who thereby become 'united in one person', transform themselves into Subjects and thus release themselves from the condition of war of all against all. This artifact is called a Commonwealth or *civitas*.

This is Hobbes's account of the hypothetical efficient cause of civil association. There are refinements I have not mentioned and, no doubt, also, difficulties; but the rest of the civil philosophy consists of an exhibition of this artifact as a system of internal causes and effects, joining where necessary parts of its structure to partic-

[70] *L.*, p. 131.

ular features of the predicament from which it is designed to rescue mankind. This may be conveniently considered under four heads: (1) the constitution of the sovereign authority, (2) the rights and 'faculties' of the sovereign authority, (3) the obligations and liberties of subjects, (4) the civil condition.

(1) The recipient of the transferred rights, whatever its constitution, is a single and sovereign authority. But this Office may be occupied by one or by many, and if by more than one either by some or by all. Thus a civil authority may have a monarchical, an artistocratic (or oligarchical) or a democratic constitution. Which it is to be, is solely a matter of which is most likely to generate the peace for which civil association is instituted. The advantages of monarchy are obvious. But if the Office is occupied by an assembly of men, this cannot be because such an assembly is more likely to 'represent' the variety of opinion among subjects, for a ruler is not the interpreter of the various wants of his subjects but the custodian of their will for peace. However, no kind of constitution is without its defects. Reason gives no conclusive answer, but tells us only that the main consideration is not wise but authoritative rule.[71]

(2) The rights of the occupant of the sovereign office are those which the covenanters confer upon him.[72] They are the right to rule and the right to enjoy the support of those who, in the agreement, have created themselves Subjects. These rights are both limited and unconditional. The covenanters have not surrendered their right to pursue felicity; they have surrendered only their right each to do this unconditionally, or (which is the same thing) on conditions which each decides for himself. But the rights with which they have endowed the sovereign are not retractable, and since he is not himself a party to any agreement he does not 'bear their persons' on condition that he observes the terms of an agreement. Nor may any man exclude himself from the condition of Subject, on the grounds that he did not himself assent to the covenant, without declaring himself an 'outlaw' and forfeiting the protection of the sovereign.

---

[71] *L.*, ch. xix.
[72] *L.*, ch. xviii.

The right to rule is the right to be the sole judge of what is necessary for the peace and security of subjects.

The business of ruling is the exercise of this right. And the most important part of it is to make rules for the conduct of Subjects.[73] In a *civitas* the sovereign is the sole legislative authority; nothing is law save what he declares to be law, and it is law solely in virtue of that declaration. A law, in Hobbes's understanding of it, is a command, the expression of the Will of the Sovereign. Not every command of the sovereign is law, but only those commands which prescribe a rule of conduct to be subscribed to indifferently by all Subjects.

In general, the contents of civil law corresponds to the theorems which natural reason has uncovered about what conduces to peaceful relationships between human beings. In certain circumstances (with which we are not now concerned) these theorems may properly be called 'natural laws' and the legal virtue or validity of the declarations of a civil sovereign may be thought to derive, at least in part, from their correspondence with these 'natural laws'; but here the civil sovereign has nothing but theorems of natural reason to guide him and the legal validity of the rules he makes lies solely in their being his commands. In short, in civil association the validity of a law lies neither in the wisdom of the conditions it imposes upon conduct, nor even in its propensity to promote peace, but in its being the command of the sovereign and (although this is obscure) in its being effectively enforced. There may be unnecessary laws and even laws which increase rather than diminish contention, and these are to be deplored, but no valid law can, strictly speaking, be 'unjust'. 'Just' conduct is identifiable only in terms of law and in civil association there is none but civil law. And if, as Hobbes suggests, the law which identifies the conditions upon which a man may rightfully call anything his own and upon which he may recognize the rights of others in this respect is the most important branch of civil law, this is because in each man coming to know

---

[73] *L.*, p. 137, ch. xxvi.

what he may call his own and in being protected in his enjoyment of it the most fruitful cause of human contention is abated.[74]

Together with the right to make laws goes the right to interpret them, to administer them and to punish those who do not observe them. All law requires interpretation; that is, decision about what it means in contingent circumstances. This decision must be authoritative. And, in Hobbes's view, laws lose all their virtue if their observance is not enforced by inescapable penalties. This 'faculty' of the civil sovereign is exercised in courts of law presided over by himself or his agents. The sovereign's relationship to civil law is that as its maker he is *legibus solutus* (having unconditional authority to make or to repeal), but in respect of his judicial office he is bound by the law as it is. He may pardon some offences.[75]

Besides the sole right to make, repeal, interpret, administer and enforce rules, the sovereign is the judge of what is necessary for the peace and security of his subjects in respect of threats to the association coming from without: the right to negotiate, make war, conclude peace, levy taxes to defray the expenses of war and raise an army of volunteers of such dimensions as he shall think fit. He has the right to choose his own counsellors and agents, and he is himself the commander-in-chief of such military force as the association disposes.[76]

Lastly, the civil sovereign, although he cannot dictate the beliefs of his subjects, has the right to inspect and to govern all expressions of opinion or doctrine among his subjects (especially those addressed to large audiences) in relation to their propensity to promote or to disrupt the peace of the association. This censorship is not directly concerned with the truth or falsity of the opinions uttered, but 'a doctrine repugnant to peace, can no more be true, than peace and concord can be against the law of nature'.[77]

It should be noted that the office of Sovereign has no rights of 'lordship'; its *dominium* is solely *regale*.

[74] *L.*, pp. 111, 137.
[75] *L.*, p. 137.
[76] *L.*, pp. 137–8.
[77] *L.*, p. 136, ch. xlii.

(3) Civil Subjects are persons who, in a mutual agreement, have transferred the right of each to govern himself to a sovereign Actor; they have covenanted with one another to authorize all his actions, each to avouch every such action as his own, to submit their judgements and wills to his judgement and will in all that concerns their peace and security, to obey his commands and to pledge all their strength and power to support the exercise of his authority. Thus, in a mutual agreement, they have each and all undertaken an obligation. Each in agreement with all others has bound himself in advance to a specified course of conduct in relation to one another and in relation to a ruler and his acts of ruling. In what respect may a civil Subject be said to be free?[78]

Freedom means the absence of external impediment to movement; and a man, whose movement is the performance of actions he has willed to perform, is properly said to be free when 'in those things, which by his strength and wit he is able to do, [he] is not hindered to do what he has willed to do'.[79] Human freedom is a quality of conduct itself, not of will. To find no external stop in doing what he has a will to do is to be a free man.

Cives, however, are subject to artificial impediments which stand in the way of their doing what they wish to do; namely, civil laws and the penalties which attach to not observing them, even the penalty of death, which is a stop to all conduct. They are in a situation of being compelled to do what they may not wish to do. And in this respect their freedom is curtailed.

But, it may be observed, first, that this situation is one of their own choosing; they may have chosen it out of fear of the alternative (the perpetual and unregulated obstruction of their actions by others), but this does not make the covenant any the less a free action. Whatever impediments they suffer on this account have been authorized by themselves. And further, their covenant was an act designed to emancipate them from certain external impediments to the pursuit of felicity, and if it were to be conscientiously

[78] *L.*, ch. xxi.
[79] *L.*, p. 161.

observed by all there would be a net gain of freedom; fewer and less disastrous impediments to their willed actions.

More to the point, however, are the following considerations. Civil authority, the regulation of human conduct by law, does not and cannot prescribe the whole of any man's conduct. Apart from the fact that rules can be observed only in choosing to perform actions which they do not themselves prescribe, there is always an area of the conduct of civil Subjects which, on account of the silence of the law, they are free to occupy on their own terms; to do and to forebear each at his own discretion. And the 'greatest liberty' of civil subjects derives from the silences of the law.[80] Furthermore, civil subjects enjoy a freedom which Hobbes calls their 'true freedom', which derives from the precise form of the covenant; in specifying their obligations the covenant specifies also a freedom. Each covenanter has surrendered his right to govern himself and has undertaken to *authorize* the actions of the sovereign ruler as if they were his own. The terms of the covenant exclude, and are designed to exclude, any undertaking to surrender rights which cannot be given up without a man risking the loss of all that he designed to protect in making the covenant; that is, his pursuit of felicity and even his life.[81] Thus, the covenanter authorizes the sovereign to arraign him before a court for an alleged breach of the law, but he has no obligation to accuse himself without the assurance of pardon. And although, if convicted, he authorizes the infliction upon himself of the lawful penalty, even the penalty of death, he is not obliged to kill himself or any other man. And it is in the enjoyment of all those rights which he has not surrendered that the 'true freedom' of the Subject lies. Finally, although he cannot himself retract the authorization he has given, he retains the right to protect himself and his interests by such strength as he may have if the authorized ruler is no longer able to protect him.[82]

(4) The civil condition is an artifact. And since it is human beings associated in terms of the authorization of the decisions and

[80] *L.*, pp. 162, 168.
[81] *L.*, p. 167.
[82] *L.*, p. 170.

the actions of a single Sovereign, Hobbes calls it an Artificial Man. It is association articulated in terms of settled and known laws which define the conditions of a 'just' relationship between its members. And since 'justice', strictly speaking, is a function of having rules which cannot be breached with impunity, and since in default of a *civitas* there are no rules with penalties annexed to them but only unconditional competition for the satisfaction of wants together with some theorems about how this competition might become more fruitful from which nothing more than general maxims of prudent conduct may be rationally derived, 'justice' and the civil condition may be said to be coeval.

But if human beings may find in civil association a condition of 'peace' in which the frustrations and anxieties of an unconditional competition between men for the satisfaction of wants are relieved, these are not the only anxieties they suffer and this is not the only 'peace' they seek. They are dimly aware of inhabiting a world in which nothing happens without a cause and they think and speak of this world, metaphorically, as the 'natural kingdom of God', the first or master cause of all that happens being identified as the will of this God. But they are acutely aware of their ignorance of the efficient causes of occurrences and of their consequent inability to move about this world with confidence, assured of achieving the satisfaction of their wants. They are gnawed by an anxiety, distinguishable from that which arises from their lack of power to compete unconditionally with their fellows, and they seek relief not only in a *pax civilis* but in a *pax dei*. They attribute to this God nothing but what is 'warranted by natural reason', they acknowledge his power (indeed his omnipotence), they do not (or should not) dishonour him by disputing about his attributes, and they address him in utterances of worship—and all this in a design to ingratiate themselves with what they cannot control and thus abate their anxieties. In the civil condition this worship may be in secret and thus of no concern to the civil sovereign, or by private men in the hearing of others and thus subject to the conditions of civility. But since a civil association is a many joined in the will and authorized actions of a Sovereign authority it must display this unity in the worship of this God. He is to be recognized and honoured in a public *cultus* and in utterances and gestures determined by the civil Sovereign. In a *civitas* the *pax dei* is an integral part of the *pax civilis*.[83]

Now, even an attentive reader might be excused if he supposed that the argument of *Leviathan* would end here. Whatever our opinion of the cogency of the argument, it would appear that what was projected as a civil philosophy had now been fulfilled. But such is not the view of Hobbes. For him it remains to purge the argument of an element of unreality which still disfigures it. And it is not an element of unreality that appears merely at this point; it carries us back to the beginning, to the predicament itself, and to get rid of it requires a readjustment of the entire argument. It will be remembered that one element of unreality in the conception of the condition of nature (that is, in the cause of civil association) was corrected as soon as it appeared; the natural man was recognized to be, though solitary, not alone. But what has remained so far unacknowledged is that the natural man is, not only solitary and not alone, but is also the devotee of a positive religion; the religion attributed to him was something less than he believed. How fundamental an oversight this was we shall see in a moment; but first we may consider the defect in the argument from another standpoint. In the earlier statement, the predicament was fully exhibited in its universal character, but (as Hobbes sees it) the particular form in which it appeared to his time, the peculiar folly of his age, somehow escaped from that generality; and to go back over the argument with this in the forefront of his mind seemed to him a duty that the civil philosopher owed to his readers. The project, then, of the second half of the argument of *Leviathan* is, by correcting an error in principle, to show more clearly the local and transitory mischief in which the universal predicament of mankind appeared in the seventeenth century. And both in the conception and in the execution of this project, Hobbes reveals, not only his sensitiveness to the exi-

[83] *L.*, ch. xxi.

gencies of his time, but also the medieval ancestry of his way of thinking.

The Europe of his day was aware of three positive religions: Christianity, the Jewish religion and the Moslem. These, in the language of the Middle Ages, were *leges*,[84] because what distinguished them was the fact that the believer was subject to a *law*, the law of Christ, of Moses or of Mahomet. And no traditionalist would quarrel with Hobbes's statement that 'religion is not philosophy, but law'.[85] The consequence in civil life of the existence of these 'laws' was that every believer was subject to two laws—that of his *civitas* and that of his religion: his allegiance was divided. This is the problem that Hobbes now considers with his accustomed vigour and insight. It was a problem common to all positive religions, but not unnaturally Hobbes's attention is concentrated upon it in relation to Christianity.[86]

The man, then, whose predicament we have to consider is, in addition to everything else, a Christian. And to be a Christian means to acknowledge obligation under the *law* of God. This is a real obligation, and not merely the shadow of one, because it is a real law—a command expressing the will of God. This law is to be found in the Scriptures. There are men who speak of the results of human reasoning as Natural Laws, but if we are to accept this manner of speaking we must beware of falling into the error of supposing that they are laws because they are rational. The results of natural reasoning are no more than uncertain theorems,[87] general conditional conclusions, unless and until they are transformed into laws by being shown to be the will of some authority. If, in addition to being the deliverance of reasoning, they can be shown to be the will and command of God, then and then only can they properly be called laws, natural or divine; and then and then only can they be said to create obligation.[88] But, as a matter of fact, all the theorems

---

[84] Cf. the *De Legibus* of William of Auvergne, Bishop of Paris, d. 1249.
[85] *E.W.*, VII, 5.
[86] *L.*, ch. xxxii.
[87] *E.W.*, IV, 285.
[88] *L.*, p. 122; *E.W.*, IV, 285.

of reasoning with regard to the conduct of men in pursuit of felicity are to be found in the Scriptures, laid down as the commands of God. Now, the conclusion of this is, that no proper distinction can be maintained between a Natural or Rational and a Revealed law. All law is revealed in the sense that nothing is law until it is shown to be the command of God by being found in the Scriptures. It is true that the Scriptures may contain commands not to be discovered by human reasoning and these, in a special sense, may be called revealed; but the theorems of reasoning are laws solely on account of being the commands of God, and therefore their authority is no different from that of the commands not penetrable by the light of reasoning. There is, then, only one law, Natural and Divine; and it is revealed in Scripture.

But Scripture is an artifact. It is, in the first place, an arbitrary selection of writings called canonical by the authority that recognized them. And secondly, it is nothing apart from interpretation. Not only does the history of Christianity show that interpretation is necessary and has been various, but any consideration of the nature of knowledge that is not entirely perfunctory must conclude that 'no line is possible between what has come to men and their interpretation of what has come to them'.[89] Nothing can be more certain than that, if the law of God is revealed in Scripture, it is revealed only in an interpretation of Scripture.[90] And interpretation is a matter of authority; for, whatever part reasoning may play in the process of interpretation, what determines everything is the decision, *whose* reasoning shall interpret? And the far-reaching consequences of this decision are at once clear when we consider the importance of the obligations imposed by this law. Whoever has the authority to determine this law has supreme power over the conduct of men, 'for every man, if he be in his wits, will in all things yield to that man an absolute obedience, by virtue of whose sentence he believes himself to be either saved or damned'.[91]

---

[89] Hort, *The Way, the Truth and the Life*, p. 175.
[90] *L.*, ch. xxxiii.
[91] *E.W.*, II, 283–97.

Now, in the condition of nature there are two possible claim-
ants to this authority to settle and interpret Scripture and thus determine the obligations of the Christian man. First, each individual
man may claim to exercise this authority on his own behalf. And
this claim must at once be admitted. For, if it belongs to a man's
natural right to do whatever he deems necessary to procure felicity,
it will belong no less to this right to decide what he shall believe to
be his obligations under the law natural and divine. In nature every
man is 'governed by his own reason'.[92] But the consequences of this
will be only to make more desperate the contentiousness of the condition of nature. There will be as many 'laws' called Christian as
there are men who call themselves Christian; and what men did formerly by natural right, they will do now on a pretended obligation
to God. A man's actions may thus become conscientious, but conscience will be only his own good opinion of his actions.[93] And to
the secular war of nature will be added the fierceness of religious
dispute. But secondly, the claim to be the authority to settle and
interpret the Scriptures may be made on behalf of a special spiritual authority, calling itself, for the purpose, a church. And a claim of
this sort may be made either by a so-called universal church (when
the claim will be to have authority to give an interpretation to be
accepted by all Christians everywhere), or by a church whose authority is limited to less than the whole number of Christians. But,
whatever the form of the claim, what we have to enquire into is the
generation of the authority. Whence could such an authority be derived? We may dispose at once of the suggestion that any spiritual
authority holds a divine commission to exercise such a faculty.
There is no foundation in history to support such a suggestion;
and even if there were, it could not give the necessary ground for
the authority. For, such an authority could only come about by a
transfer of natural right as a consequence of a covenant; this is the
only possible cause of any authority whatever to order men. But we
have seen already that a transfer of rights as a consequence of a

[92] *L.*, p. 99.
[93] *L.*, p. 224.

covenant does not, and could not, generate a special spiritual authority to interpret scripture; it generates infallibly a civil society. A special spiritual authority for settling the law of God and Nature, cannot, then, exist; and where it appears to exist, what really exists is only the natural authority of one man (the proper sphere of which is that man's own life) illegitimately extended to cover the lives of others and masquerading as something more authoritative than it is; in short, a spiritual tyranny.

There is in the condition of nature, where Christians are concerned, a law of nature; and it reposes in the Scriptures. But what the commands of this law are no man can say except in regard to himself alone; the public knowledge of this law is confined to the knowledge of its bare existence.[94] So far, then, from the law of nature mitigating the chaos of nature, it accentuates it. To be a 'natural' Christian adds a new shadow to the darkness of the predicament of the condition of nature, a shadow that will require for its removal a special provision in the deliverance.

The deliverance from the chaos of the condition of nature as hitherto conceived is by the creation of a civil association or Commonwealth; indeed, the condition of nature is the hypothetical efficient cause of a Commonwealth. And when account is taken of this new factor of chaos, the deliverance must be by the creation of a Christian Commonwealth; that is, a civil association composed of Christian subjects under a Christian sovereign authority. The creation of this requires no new covenant; the natural right of each man to interpret Scripture and determine the law of God on his own behalf will be transferred with the rest of his natural right, for it is not a separable part of his general natural right. And the recipient of the transferred right is the artificial, sovereign authority, an authority which is not temporal *and* spiritual (for, '*Temporal* and *Spiritual* government are but two names brought into the world to make men see double, and mistake their lawful sovereign'),[95] but single and supreme. And the association represented in his person

[94] *L.*, p. 275.
[95] *L.*, p. 306.

is not a state *and* a church, for a true church (unlike the so-called churches which pretended their claims to be independent spiritual authorities in the condition of nature) is 'a company of men professing Christian Religion, united in the person of one Sovereign'. It cannot be a rival spiritual authority, setting up canons against laws, a spiritual power against a civil, and determining man's conduct by eternal sanctions,[96] because there is no generation that can be imagined for such an authority and its existence would contradict the end for which society was instituted. And if the Papacy lays claim to such an authority, it can at once be pronounced a claim that any other foreign sovereign might make (for civil associations stand in a condition of nature towards one another), only worse, for the Pope is a sovereign without subjects, a prince without a kingdom: 'if a man consider the original of this great Ecclesiastical Dominion, he will easily perceive, that the Papacy, is no other, than the *ghost* of the deceased *Roman Empire*, sitting crowned on the grave thereof: For so did the Papacy, start up on a sudden out of the ruins of that great Heathen Power'.[97]

It remains to consider what it means to be a Christian sovereign and a Christian subject. The chief right of the sovereign as Christian is the right to settle and interpret Scripture and thus determine authoritatively the rules that belong to the Law of God and Nature. Without this right it is impossible for him to perform the functions of his office. For, if he does not possess it, it will be possessed either by no one (and the chaos and war of nature will remain) or by someone else who will then, on account of the pre-eminent power this right gives, wield a supremacy both illegitimate and destructive of peace. But it is a right giving immense authority, for the laws it determines may be *called* God's laws, but are in fact the laws of the sovereign. With this right, the sovereign will have the authority to control public worship,[98] a control to be exercised in such a way as to oblige no subject to do or believe anything that

---

[96] *L.*, p. 214.
[97] *L.*, p. 457.
[98] *L.*, p. 136, ch. xlii.

might endanger his eternal salvation.[99] He may suppress organized superstition and heresy,[100] because they are destructive of peace; but an inquisition into the private beliefs of his subjects is no part of his right. And, as with other rights of sovereignty, he may delegate his right of religious instruction to agents whom he will choose, or even (if it be for the good of the society) to the Pope;[101] but the authority thus delegated is solely an authority to instruct, to give counsel and advice, and not to coerce.[102] But if the sovereign as Christian has specific rights, he has also obligations. For in the Christian Commonwealth there exists a law to which the sovereign is, in a sense, obliged. What had previously been merely the rational articles of peace, have become (on being determined in Scripture) obligatory rules of conduct. The sovereign, of course, has no obligations to his subjects, only functions; but the law of God is to him (though he has made it himself), no less than to his subjects, a command creating an obligation. And iniquity, which in a heathen sovereign could never be more than a failure to observe the conclusions of sound reasoning, in the Christian sovereign becomes a breach of law and therefore a sin, punishable by God.

The subject as Christian has a corresponding extension of his obligation and right. The rule of his religion, as determined by the authoritative interpretation of scripture, creates no new and independent obligations, but provides a new sanction for the observation of all his obligations. The articles of peace are for him no longer merely the conclusions of reasoning legitimately enforced by the sovereign power; they are the laws of God. To observe the covenant he has made with his fellows becomes a religious obligation as well as a piece of prudential wisdom. The freedom of the Christian subject is the silence of the law with regard to his thoughts and beliefs; for if it be the function of the sovereign to suppress controversy, he has no right to interfere with what he cannot in fact control and what if left uncontrolled will not endanger peace. 'As for the inward

[99] *L.*, ch. xliii.
[100] *L.*, p. 453.
[101] *L.*, pp. 421, 427.
[102] *L.*, p. 384.

thought and *belief* of men, which human governors take no notice of (for God only knoweth the heart), they are not voluntary, nor the effect of the laws, but of the unrevealed will and of the power of God; and consequently fall not under obligation'.[103] It is a darkly sceptical doctrine upon which Hobbes grounds toleration.

The argument is finished: but let no one mistake it for the book. The skeleton of a masterpiece of philosophical writing has a power and a subtlety, but they are not to be compared with the power and subtlety of the doctrine itself, clothed in the irony and eloquence of a writer such as Hobbes.

SIX: SOME TOPICS CONSIDERED

(1) *The Criticism of Hobbes.* Most great philosophers have found some defenders who are prepared to swallow everything, even the absurdities; but Hobbes is an exception. He has aroused admiration in some of his readers, horror in others, but seldom affection and never undiscriminating affection. Nor is it surprising that this should be so. He offended against taste and interest, and his arrogance invited such a consequence. He could not deny himself the pleasure of exaggeration, and what were remembered were his incautious moments, and the rest forgotten. His doctrines, or some of them, have received serious attention and criticism from the time when they first appeared; but his critics have for the most part been opponents, and his few defenders not conspicuous for their insight into his meaning. On the whole it remains true that no great writer has suffered more at the hands of little men than Hobbes.

His opponents divide themselves into two classes; the emotional and the intellectual. Those who belong to the first are concerned with the supposed immoral tendencies of his doctrines; theirs is a practical criticism. The second are concerned with the theoretical

[103] *L.*, p. 364.

cogency of his doctrines; they wish to shed light and sometimes succeed in doing so.

With the critics of the first class we need not greatly concern ourselves, though they still exist. They find in Hobbes nothing but an apostle of atheism, licentiousness and despotism, and express a fitting horror at what they find. The answers to *Leviathan* constitute a library, its censors a school in themselves. Pious opinion has always been against him, and ever since he wrote he has been denounced from the pulpit. Against Hobbes, Filmer defended servitude, Harrington liberty, Clarendon the church, Locke the Englishman, Rousseau mankind and Butler the Deity. And a writer of yesterday sums up Hobbes's reflections on civil philosophy as 'the meanest of all ethical theories united with unhistorical contempt for religion to justify the most universal of absolutisms'. No doubt some responsibility for all this attaches to Hobbes himself; he did not lack caution, but like all timid men he often chose the wrong occasion to be audacious. It is true that his age excused in Spinoza what it condemned in Hobbes; but then Spinoza was modest and a Jew, while Hobbes was arrogant and enough of a Christian to have known better. And that the vilification of Hobbes was not greater is due only to the fact that Machiavelli had already been cast for the part of scapegoat for the European consciousness.

The critics of the second class are more important, because it is in and through them that Hobbes has had his influence in the history of ideas. They, also, are for the most part his opponents. But, in the end, if Hobbes were alive today he would have some reason to complain (as Bradley complained) that even now he must 'do most of his scepticism for himself'. For his critics have shown a regrettable tendency to fix their attention on the obvious errors and difficulties and to lose sight of the philosophy as a whole. There has been a deplorable over-confidence about the exposure of faults in Hobbes's philosophy. Few accounts of it do not end with the detection of a score of simple errors, each of which is taken to be destructive of the philosophy, so that one wonders what claim Hobbes has to be a philosopher at all, let alone a great one. Of course there are inconsistencies in his doctrines, there is vagueness at critical points, there is misconception and even absurdity, and the detection of these faults is legitimate and useful criticism; but niggling of this sort will never dispose of the philosophy. A writer like Bentham may fall by his errors, but not one such as Hobbes. Nor is this the only defect of his critics. There has been failure to consider his civil philosophy in the context of the history of political philosophy, which has obscured the fact that Hobbes is not an outcast but, in purpose though not in doctrine, is an ally of Plato, Augustine and Aquinas. There has been failure to detect the tradition to which his civil philosophy belongs, which has led to the misconception that it belongs to none and is without lineage or progeny. And a large body of criticism has been led astray by attention to superficial similarities which appear to unite Hobbes to writers with whom, in fact, he has little or nothing in common.

The task of criticism now is to make good some of these defects. It is not to be expected that it can be accomplished quickly or all at once. But a beginning may be made by reconsidering some of the vexed questions of the civil philosophy.

(2) *The Tradition of Hobbes.* Hobbes's civil philosophy is a composition based upon two themes, Will and Artifice. The individual who creates and becomes the subject of civil authority is an *ens completum*, an absolute will. He is not so much a 'law unto himself' as free from all law and obligation which is the creature of law. This will is absolute because it is not conditioned or limited by any standard, rule or rationality and has neither plan nor end to determine it. This absence of obligation is called by Hobbes, natural right. It is an original and an absolute right because it derives directly from the character of will and not from some higher law or from Reason. The Proximity of several such individuals to one another is chaos. Civil association is artificial, the free creation of these absolute wills, just as nature is the free creation of the absolute will of God. It is an artifice that springs from the voluntary surrender of the unconditional freedom or right of the individual, and consequently it involves a replacement of freedom by law and right by obligation.[104]

---

[104] *L.*, ch. xxi.

In the creation of civil association a sovereignty corresponding to the sovereignty of the individual is generated. The Sovereign is the product of will, and is himself representing the wills of its creators. Sovereignty is the right to make laws by willing. The Sovereign, therefore, is not himself subject to law, because law creates obligation, not right. Nor is he subject to Reason, because Reason creates nothing, neither right nor obligation. Law, the life of civil association, is the command of the Sovereign, who is the Soul (the capacity to will), not the head, of civil association.[105]

Now, two things are clear about such a doctrine. First, that its ruling ideas are those that have dominated the political philosophy of the last three hundred years. If this is Hobbes's doctrine, then Hobbes said something that allied him to the future. And secondly, it is clear that this doctrine is a break-away from the great Rational-Natural tradition of political philosophy which springs from Plato and Aristotle and found embodiment later in the Natural Law theory. That tradition in its long history embraced and accommodated many doctrines, but this doctrine of Hobbes is something it cannot tolerate. Instead of beginning with right, it begins with law and obligation, it recognizes law as the product of Reason, it finds the only explanation of dominion in the superiority of Reason, and all the various conceptions of nature that it has entertained exclude artifice as it is conceived by Hobbes. For these reasons it is concluded that Hobbes is the originator of a new tradition in political philosophy.[106]

But this theory of Hobbes has a lineage that stretches back into the ancient world. It is true that Greek thought, lacking the conception of creative will and the idea of sovereignty, contributed a criticism of the Rational-Natural theory which fell short of the construction of an alternative tradition: Epicurus was an inspiration rather than a guide. But there are in the political ideas of Roman civilization and in the politico-theological ideas of Judaism strains of thought that carry us far outside the Rational-Natural tradition,

[105] *L.*, pp. 8, 137.
[106] Strauss, *op. cit.*, ch. viii.

and which may be said to constitute beginnings of a tradition of Will and Artifice. Hobbes's immediate predecessors built upon the Roman conception of *lex* and the Judaic-Christian conception of will and creation, both of which contained the seeds of opposition to the Rational-Natural tradition, seeds which had already come to an early flowering in Augustine. And by the end of the middle ages this opposition had crystallized into a living tradition of its own. Hobbes was born into the world, not only of modern science, but also of medieval thought. The scepticism and the individualism, which are the foundations of his civil philosophy, were the gifts of late scholastic nominalism; the displacement of Reason in favour of will and imagination and the emancipation of passion were slowly mediated changes in European thought that had gone far before Hobbes wrote. Political philosophy is the assimilation of political experience to an experience of the world in general, and the greatness of Hobbes is not that he began a new tradition in this respect but that he constructed a political philosophy that reflected the changes in the European intellectual consciousness which had been pioneered chiefly by the theologians of the fifteenth and sixteenth centuries. *Leviathan*, like any masterpiece, is an end and a beginning; it is the flowering of the past and the seed-box of the future. Its importance is that it is the first great achievement in the long-projected attempt of European thought to re-embody in a new myth the Augustinian epic of the Fall and Salvation of mankind.

(3) *The Predicament of Mankind.* In the history of political philosophy there have been two opposed conceptions of the source of the predicament of man from which civil society springs as a deliverance: one conceived the predicament to arise out of the nature of man, the other conceived it to arise out of a defect in the nature of man. Plato, who went to what he believed to be the nature of man for the ground and structure of the *polis*, is an example of the first. And Spinoza, with his insistence on the principle that nothing in nature must be attributed to a defect of it,[107] adheres, in his different convention, to the same project of deducing civil society from

---

[107] Spinoza, *Ethica*, Pars, III, Praefatio.

'the very condition of human nature'.[108] For Augustine, on the other hand, the predicament arises from a defect in human nature, from sin. Where does Hobbes stand in this respect? The widely-accepted interpretation of Hobbes's view is that, for him, the predicament springs from the egoistical character of man and that therefore it is vice and depravity that create the chaos. Moreover, it is a genuinely original depravity, for the Fall of man (or anything to take its place) is no part of Hobbes's theory. But when we look closer, what was distinguished as egoism (a moral defect) turns out to be neither moral nor a defect; it is only the individuality of a creature shut up, without hope of immediate release, within the world of his own imagination. Man is, by nature, the victim of solipsism; he is an *individua substantia* distinguished by incommunicability. And when this is understood, we are in a position to accept Hobbes's own denial of a doctrine of the natural depravity of man;[109] and he appears to take his place, on this question, beside Plato and Spinoza, basing his theory on the 'known natural inclinations of mankind'.[110] But not without difficulty. First, the striving after power which is characteristic of the human individual may, in Hobbes's view, be evil; it is so when it is directed by Pride. And Pride is so universal a defect in human nature that it belongs to the constitutive cause of the predicament. And, if by interpreting it as illusion Hobbes deprives Pride of moral significance, it still remains a defect. And since Pride (it will be remembered) is the Augustinian interpretation of the original sin, this doctrine of Hobbes seems to approximate his view to the conception of the predicament as springing from, not nature, but defect in nature. But secondly, the predicament for Hobbes is actually caused, not by an internal defect in human nature, but by something that becomes a defect when a man is among men. Pride in one may inhibit felicity, but it cannot produce chaos. On this point, then, I think our conclusion must be that Hobbes's conception of the natural man (apart from his defects) is such that a predicament requiring a deliverance is created

[108] Spinoza, *Tractatus Politicus*, §4.
[109] *E.W.*, II, xvi–xvii; *L.*, pp. 97, 224, 480.
[110] *L.*, p. 554.

whenever man is in proximity to man, and that his doctrine of Pride and the unpermissible form of striving after power only increases the severity of the predicament.

(4) *Individualism and Absolutism.* Individualism as a gospel has drawn its inspiration from many sources, but as a reasoned theory of society it has its roots in the so-called nominalism of late medieval scholasticism, with its doctrines that the nature of a thing is its individuality, that which makes it *this* thing, and that both in God and man will is precedent to reason. Hobbes inherited this tradition of nominalism, and more than any other writer passed it on to the modern world. His civil philosophy is based, not on any vague belief in the value or sanctity of the individual man, but on a philosophy for which the world is composed of *individuae substantiae*. This philosophy, in Hobbes, avoided on the one hand atomism (the doctrine that the individual is an indestructible particle of matter) and on the other hand universalism (the doctrine that there is but one individual, the universe), and involved both Hobbes and his successors in the conception of a scale of individuals in which the individuality of sensations and images was preserved while the individuality of the man was asserted. The human being is first fully an individual, not in respect of self-consciousness, but in the activity of willing.[111] Between birth and death, the self as imagination and will is an indestructible unit, whose relations with other individuals are purely external. Individuals may be collected together, may be added, may be substituted for one another or made to represent one another, but can never modify one another or compose a whole in which their individuality is lost. Even reason is individualized, and becomes merely the reasoning of an individual without

---

[111] Briefly, it may be said that the doctrine that sprang from the reflections of medieval philosophical thinkers distinguished two elements in personality, a rational element and a substantial element. The standard definition of *persona* was that of Boëthius—'the individual substance of a rational nature'. In later medieval thought this definition suffered disruption. Emphasis upon the rational element in personality resulted, finally, in the Cartesian doctrine of the primacy of cognition and of self-consciousness as the true ground of personality. While emphasis upon the substantial element made the most of the opposition between personality and rationality and resulted in what may be called the romantic doctrine of personality with its assertion of the primacy of will—the person is that which is separate, incommunicable, eccentric or even irrational. This second emphasis was the work of the late medieval nominalists, and it is the emphasis that is dominant in Hobbes.

power or authority to oblige acceptance by others: to convince a man is not to enjoy a common understanding with him, but to displace his reason by yours.[112] The natural man is the stuff of civil association which, whatever else it is, is an association that can comprehend such individuals without destroying them. Neither before nor after the establishment of civil association is there any such thing as the *People*, to whom so much previous theory ascribed sovereignty. Whatever community exists must be generated by individual acts of will directed upon a single object, that is, by agreement: the essence of agreement is, not a common will (for there can be no such thing), but a common object of will. And, since these individual wills are in natural opposition to one another, the agreement out of which *civitas* can spring must be an agreement not to oppose one another, a will not to will. But something more is required; merely to agree not to will is race suicide. The agreement must be for each to transfer his right of willing in some specific respect, to a single artificial Representative, who is thenceforth authorized to will and to act in place of each individual. There is in this association no concord of wills, no common will, no common good; its unity lies solely in the singleness of the Representative, in the *substitution* of his one will for the many conflicting wills.[113] It is a collection of individuals united in one Sovereign Representative, and in generation and structure it is the only sort of association that does not compromise the individuality of its components.

Now, the common view is that though Hobbes may be an individualist at the beginning, his theory of civil association is designed precisely to destroy individualism. So far as the generation of civil association is concerned, this is certainly not true. To authorize a representative to make a choice for me does not destroy or compromise my individuality; there is no confusion of wills, so long as it is understood that my will is in the authorization of the representative and that the choice he makes is not mine, but his on my be-

---

[112] *L.*, p. 33.
[113] *L.*, pp. 126, 167.

half. Hobbes's individualism is far too strong to allow even the briefest appearance of anything like a general will.[114]

Nor is the effect generated, the Leviathan, a designed destruction of the individual; it is, in fact, the *minimum* condition of any settled association among individuals. The Sovereign is absolute in two respects only, and neither of them is destructive of individuality: first, the surrender of natural right to him is absolute and his authorization is permanent and exclusive; and secondly, there is no appeal from the legitimacy of his command. The natural right surrendered is the unconditional right, on all occasions, to exercise one's individual will in the pursuit of felicity.[115] Now, an absolute right, if it is surrendered at all, is necessarily surrendered absolutely: Hobbes refused the compromise which suggests that a part of the right had to be sacrificed, not because he was an absolutist in government, but because he knew a little elementary logic. But to surrender an absolute right to do something on all occasions, is not to give up the right of doing it on any occasion. For the rest, Hobbes conceives the Sovereign as a law-maker and his rule, not arbitrary, but the rule of law. And we have already seen that law as the command of the Sovereign holds within itself a freedom absent from law as Reason or custom: it is Reason, not Authority, that is destructive of individuality. And, of course, the silence of the law is a further freedom; when the law does not speak the individual is sovereign over himself.[116] What, indeed, is excluded from Hobbes's *civitas* is not the freedom of the individual, but the independent rights of spurious 'authorities' and of collections of individuals such as churches, which he saw as the source of the civil strife of his time.

It may be said, then, that Hobbes is not an absolutist precisely because he is an authoritarian. His scepticism about the power of reasoning, which applied no less to the 'artificial reason' of the Sovereign than to the reasoning of the natural man, together with the

---

[114] Thus, Hobbes does not say that the criminal *wills* his own punishment, but that he is the *author* of his own punishment. *L.*, p. 167.

[115] *L.*, p. 99.

[116] *L.*, p. 163; cf. Aristotle, *Nic. Eth.*, V, xi, 1.

rest of his individualism, separate him from the rationalist dictators of his or any age. Indeed, Hobbes, without being himself a liberal, had in him more of the philosophy of liberalism than most of its professed defenders.[117] He perceived the folly of his age to lie in the distraction of mankind between those who claimed too much for Authority and those who claimed too much for Liberty. The perverse authoritarians were those who forgot, or never understood, that a moral authority derives solely from an act of will of him who is obliged, and that, since the need for authority springs from the passions of men, the authority itself must be commensurate with what it has to remedy, and who therefore claimed a ground for authority outside the wills and desperate needs of mortal men. The perverse libertarians were those whose illusions led them to cling to a natural right in religion which was destructive of all that was achieved by the surrender of the rest of natural right.[118] *Autres temps, autres folies*: if Hobbes were living today he would find the universal predicament appearing in different particulars.

(5) *The Theory of Obligation.* Under the influence of distinctions we are now accustomed to make in discussing questions of moral theory, modern critics of Hobbes have often made the mistake of looking for an order and coherence in his thoughts on these questions which is foreign to the ideas of any seventeenth-century writer. Setting out with false expectations, we have been exasperated by the ambiguity with which Hobbes uses certain important words (such as, obligation, power, duty, forbid, command), and have gone on, in an attempt to understand his theory better than he understood it himself, to interpret it by *extracting* from his writings at least some consistent doctrine. This, I think, is the error that lies in attributing to him a theory of civil obligation in terms of self-interest; which is an error, not because such a theory cannot be extracted from his writings, but because it gives them a simple

---

[117] Hobbes stood in contrast to both the rationalist and the 'social instinct' ethics of his contemporaries, and was attacked by representatives of both these schools. The rationalists nurtured the doctrines of anti-liberalism. And it was Richard Cumberland with his 'social instinct' and later Adam Smith with his 'social passions' who bewitched liberalism by appearing to solve the problem of individualism when they had really only avoided it.

[118] *L.*, p. 337; *E.W.*, VI, 190.

formality which nobody supposes them to possess. Even if we confine ourselves to *Leviathan*, we are often met with obscurity and
ambiguity; but Hobbes is a writer who encourages the expectation
of consistency, and the most satisfactory interpretation will be that
which gives as coherent a view as is consistent with all of what
Hobbes actually wrote.

Hobbes begins with the natural right of each man to all things.
Now, this right is always at least as great as a man's power to enjoy
it; for, when power is sufficient a man acts,[119] and nothing that a
man does can exceed what he has a natural right to do. It follows
that power and natural right are equal to one another only when
the power is irresistible.[120] This is so with God, in whom right and
power are equal because his power is as absolute as his right.[121]
But it is not so with men; for, in the unavoidable competition, a
man's power, so far from being irresistible, is merely equal to the
power of any other man. Indeed, his natural right, which is absolute, must be vastly greater than his power which, in the circumstances, is small because it is uncertain. It appears, then, that
while natural right is absolute, power is a variable quality. Natural
right and the power to enjoy it are, therefore, two different considerations; neither is the cause of the other, and even where (as in
God) they are equal, they are still not identifiable with one another.
Might and Right are never the same thing.

According to Hobbes, for a man to be 'obliged' is for him to be
bound, to be constrained by some external impediment imposed,
directly or indirectly, by himself. It is to suffer some specific self-
inflicted diminution of his freedom which may be in respect of his
right to act or of both his right and his power to act. And in this
connection to do and not to do are alike to act.

First, then, were a man to be constrained from willing and performing a certain action because he judged its likely consequences
to be damaging to himself, he would suffer no external constraint
and therefore could not properly be said to be 'obliged' to refrain

[119] *E.W.*, I, 128. Power is another name for cause, act for effect.
[120] *Elements of Law*, p. 56.
[121] *L.*, p. 276.

from this action. Here the so-called constraint is internal, a combination of rational judgement and fear, which is aversion from something believed to be hurtful. Neither his right to do what he wills to do nor his power to do it have suffered any qualification: he remains 'governed by his own reason'. Thus, no man may be said to be 'obliged' to act rationally so long as rationality is understood in terms of theorems about the likely consequences of actions; and fear, even if it is fear of being thwarted by the power of another man, is, as we have seen, a reason for acting or refraining from a particular action, not an external constraint upon conduct. Secondly, were a man to will to perform an action which he is unable to perform from his own lack of power to do so (e.g. to lift a weight beyond his capacity to lift), he could not properly be said to be 'obliged' to refrain from the action. He is deprived of nothing: his right to will remains intact and he never had the power he lacks. And thirdly, a man prevented by the power (and not merely the fear of the power) of another from performing an action he has willed and is otherwise able to perform, or one compelled by another to move in a manner he has not chosen to move, is certainly constrained, and his freedom is in some specific respect diminished. But here the constraint is solely in respect of this power; it leaves unimpaired his right to do as he wills. He is deprived of one of the qualities of a free man, the exercise of his ability to do as he wishes. But, although the constraint here is certainly external and although his freedom is substantially diminished, this constraint and this diminution are not self-imposed and consequently he cannot properly be said to be 'obliged' to do what he is compelled to do or to desist from what he is prevented from doing.

In order to be obliged, then, or (avoiding the confusion of common speech) in order to have an obligation, a man must himself perform an action which obligates him: there is, strictly speaking, 'no obligation on any man, which ariseth not from some act of his own'.[122] This act must be one which acknowledges or imposes constraint upon his unconditional right to do whatever he wills and

---

[122] *L.*, p. 166.

has power to do, thus diminishing his natural freedom. The constraint imposed or acknowledged must be limited and specific: to surrender his right completely would be to obliterate himself and there would be nothing left to be obligated. That is, the act must be a surrender not of the right but of the unconditionality of the right. Further, if (as it must be) this constraint is to be external it cannot arise from merely putting-by the unconditionality of the right; it must be the giving up of whatever is given up to another who then has the right to enjoy it. And lastly, an obligation undertaken cannot lapse merely by a failure to fulfil it; it can be ended only in an agreement that it shall be terminated or (if it is temporary) in reaching its natural terminus—a promise fulfilled.

Now, since to undertake an obligation is always to perform a voluntary act of self-denial, it must always be done in the hope of acquiring some benefit. No man can voluntarily 'despoil' himself of any part of his unconditional right knowing that it will be to his disadvantage. And the only 'good' any man can recognize is the satisfaction of his wants and the avoidance of that greatest of all dissatisfactions, death. It is to this end that men bind themselves, undertake duties and become capable of injustice or injury to others which are the outcomes of not observing obligations. Thus, they make promises to one another and enter into agreement of mutual trust, designing thereby to make more secure the satisfaction of their wants. These obligations are genuine; they are voluntary undertakings which, on that account, *ought* not to be made void by those who undertake them. Nevertheless, the situation of one who accepts a promise or one who is the first performer in an agreement of mutual trust, remains hazardous, for the *strength* of the bonds of obligation lies not in themselves but in the fear of the evil consequences of breaking them. And, in the circumstances, these evil consequences are nothing more than what lies within the power of the party bilked to impose and the fear of them is, therefore, not notably compelling.

But there is a way in which human beings may acquire less transitory obligations, although these also are the outcome of voluntary actions. If the theorems of natural reason about prudent

conduct (theorems such as 'honesty is, on the whole, the best policy') were to be recognized as the *laws* of a God, and if further this
God were to be recognized as their God and they to lie within the
jurisdiction of these rules, they would have acknowledged their conduct to be subject to these rules and would have obligated themselves to observe them. In this situation they are alike bound by a
known external impediment to the exercise of their unconditional
right to do what each wills and has power to do. In a voluntary act
of acknowledgement they would have submitted themselves to the
rule of divine commands. They have not authorized God to make
rules for their guidance and they have not endowed him with power
to enforce these rules, but they know that he exists, that he is a
law-giver and omnipotent, and they have acknowledged themselves
to be his Subjects. Henceforth the reason why, for example, they
ought to keep the agreements they have undertaken is not merely
that they ought not 'to make void voluntary acts of their own' but
that God has ruled that agreements made ought to be kept. And the
advantage they hope to gain from this acknowledgement is the benefit of the approval of the ruler of the universe and perhaps also
'reward in heaven' for obeying his commands. What they have
handed over in this acknowledgement is the right of each to rule
himself according to his own natural reason. But they remain free
to disobey these divine laws and, so far as life on earth is concerned, with a fair chance of impunity. This God is omnipotent,
but he has no agents on earth equipped with power to enforce penalties for disobedience. This obligation, and transitory obligations
such as those which arise from making promises to private persons, may be said to be examples of pure but imperfect 'moral' obligation. Nothing is given up save the right of a man to govern his
own conduct; nothing is provided save a bare rule of conduct.

What, then, is *civil* obligation? Like all other obligations, it
arises from a voluntary act. This act is a notional covenant between
many in which the right of each to govern himself by his own reason is surrendered and a sovereign Actor (the occupant of an artificially created office) is authorized to exercise it on their behalf; that
is, to declare, to interpret and to administer rules of conduct which

the covenanters pledge themselves in advance to obey. The persons concerned are under no obligation to make any such agreement among themselves; they are merely instructed to do so by reason and fear. Thus, civil obligation is a 'moral' obligation; it arises from a genuine surrender of *right*. Furthermore, it comprehends all other moral obligation. It is true that the subjects of a civil sovereign may have acknowledged themselves to be obligated to the laws of a God known to them by their natural reason and even to one whose will is also revealed in prophetic utterances (Scripture). But first, a civil subject cannot know where his duty lies if he understands himself to be obligated by two possibly divergent sets of laws; and secondly, God has not himself provided an authoritative apparatus (a court of law) for deciding the meaning of his laws in contingent circumstances, and while this is so the obligations they entail remain imperfectly specified; what they mean is almost anybody's guess. Consequently, on both these counts, it falls to the civil sovereign to specify his subjects' obligations; he must assimilate divine to civil law and he must provide an official interpretation of the meaning in contingent circumstances of all the rules which govern his subjects' conduct. And there is something more which distinguishes civil obligation. In addition to binding themselves each to surrender his right to govern himself, the covenanters who thus create a *civitas* pledge themselves to use all their strength and power on behalf of the civil sovereign; that is, they obligate themselves not only in respect of their right to govern themselves, but in respect also of the use of their power. This, then, is the unique characteristic and special virtue of civil obligation and civil association: a subject obligated both in respect of his right to act and his power to act, and an association equipped with known and authoritative rules of conduct which cannot be breached with impunity.

(6) *Civil Theology.* Long before the time of Hobbes the severance of religion from civil life, which was one of the effects of early Christianity, had been repealed. But the significant change observable in the seventeenth century was the appearance of states in which religion and civil life were assimilated to one another as closely as the universalist tradition of Christianity would permit. It

was a situation reminiscent at least of the ancient world, where religion was a communal *cultus* of communal deities. In England, Hooker had theorized this assimilation in the style of a medieval theologian; it was left to Hobbes to return to a more ancient theological tradition (indeed, a pagan tradition) and to theorize it in a more radical fashion.

In the later middle ages it had become customary to divide Theology, the doctrine concerning divine things, into a part concerned with what is accessible by the light of natural reason (and here the doctrine was largely Aristotelian in inspiration), and a part concerned with what is known only through the revelation of Scripture. Theology, that is, was both Rational and Revealed. This way of thinking had sprung, by a long process of mediation, from the somewhat different view of the *genera theologiae* that belonged to the late Roman world for which the contrast was between Rational Theology (again largely derived from Aristotle) and Civil Theology.[123] This last was the consideration of the doctrines and beliefs of religions actually practised in civil communities. It was not concerned with philosophic speculation or proof, with first causes or the existence of God, but solely with the popular beliefs involved in a religious *cultus*. It is to this tradition that Hobbes returned. Of course, the immediate background of his thought was the political theology of the late middle ages and the Reformation; and, of course, Scripture was the authoritative source to which he went to collect the religious beliefs of his society. And it is not to be supposed that he made any conscious return to an earlier tradition, or that his way of thinking was unique in his generation. What is suggested is that he has more in common with the secular theologians of the Italian Renaissance than with a writer such as Erastus, and that he treats the religion of his society as he finds it in the Scriptures, not in the style of a Protestant theologian, but rather in the style of Varro.

Hobbes's doctrine runs something like this. Religious belief is something not to be avoided in this world, and is something of the greatest practical importance. Its generation is from fear arising

---

[123] Augustine, *De Civitate Dei*, Bk. VI.

out of the unavoidable limits of human experience and reasoning. There can be no 'natural knowledge of man's estate after death',[124] and consequently there can be no natural religion in the accepted meaning of the term. Natural religion implies a universal natural Reason; but not only is reasoning confined to what may be concluded from the utterances of the senses, but it is never more than the reasoning of some individual man. There is, then, first, the universal and necessary lack of knowledge of things beyond the reach of sense; secondly, innumerable particular expressions of this lack of knowledge in the religious fears of human beings; and thirdly, the published collection in the Christian Scriptures of the fears of certain individuals, which has become the basis of the religious idiom of European civilization. And the result is confusion and strife; confusion because the Scriptures are at the mercy of each man's interpretation, strife because each man is concerned to force his own fears on other men or on account of them to claim for himself a unique way of living.

To those of Hobbes's contemporaries for whom the authority of medieval Christianity was dead, there appeared to be two possible ways out of this chaos of religious belief. There was first the way of natural religion. It was conceived possible that, by the light of natural Reason, a religion, based upon 'the unmoveable foundations of truth',[125] and supplanting the inferior religions of history, might be found in the human heart, and receiving universal recognition, become established among mankind. Though their inspiration was older than Descartes, those who took this way found their guide in Cartesian rationalism, which led them to the fairyland of Deism and the other fantasies of the *saeculum rationalisticum*, amid the dim ruins of which we now live. The other way was that of a civil religion, not the construction of reason but of authority, concerned not with belief but with practice, aiming not at undeniable truth but at peace. Such a religion was the counterpart of the sovereign civil association. And civil philosophy, in its project of giving this

[124] *L.*, p. 113.
[125] Herbert of Cherbury, *De Veritate*, p. 117.

civil association an intellectual foundation, could not avoid the responsibility of constructing a civil theology, the task of which was
to find in the complexities of Christian doctrine a religion that
could be an authorized public religion, banishing from civil association the confusion and strife that came from religious division.
This was the way of Hobbes. He was not a natural theologian, the
preconceptions of natural theology and natural religion were foreign to his whole philosophy; he was a civil theologian of the old
style but in new circumstances. For him, religion was actual religious beliefs, was Christianity. He was not concerned to reform
those beliefs in the interest of some universal, rational truth about
God and the world to come, but to remove from them the power to
disrupt society. The religion of the seventeenth century was, no less
than the religion of any other age, a religion in which fear was a
major constituent. And Hobbes, no less than others of his time—
Montaigne and Pascal, for example—felt the impact of this fear; he
died in mortal fear of hell-fire. But whereas in an earlier age Lucretius conceived the project of releasing men from the dark fears of
their religion by giving them the true knowledge of the gods, no
such project could enter the mind of Hobbes. That release, for him,
could not come from any knowledge of the natural world; if it came
at all it must be the work of time, not reason. But meanwhile it was
the less imposing task of civil theology to make of that religion
something not inimical to civilized life.

(7) *Beyond Civility*. Political philosophy, I have suggested, is
the consideration of the relation between civil association and eternity. The *civitas* is conceived as the deliverance of a man observed
to stand in need of deliverance. This, at least, is the ruling idea of
many of the masterpieces of political philosophy, *Leviathan* among
them. In the Preface to the Latin edition Hobbes says: 'This great
Leviathan, which is called the State, is a work of art; it is an artificial man made for the protection and salvation of the natural man,
to whom it is superior in grandeur and power'. We may, then, enquire of any political philosophy conceived on this plan, whether
the gift of civil association to mankind is, in principle, the gift of
salvation itself, or whether it is something less, and if the latter,

what relation it bears to salvation. The answers to these questions will certainly tell us something we should know about a political philosophy; indeed, they will do more, they will help us to determine its value.

When we turn to make this enquiry of the great political philosophies, we find that, each in its own convention, they maintain the view that civil association is contributory to the fulfilment of an end which it cannot itself bring about; that the achievement in civil association is a tangible good and not, therefore to be separated from the deliverance that constitutes the whole good, but something less than the deliverance itself. For both Plato and Aristotle civil association is not man's highest activity, and what is achieved in it must always fall short of the best life, which is a contemplative, intellectual life. And the contribution of the *civitas* to the achievement of this end is the organization of human affairs so that no one who is able may be prevented from enjoying it.[126] For Augustine the *justitia* and *pax* that are the gifts of civil association are no more than the necessary remedy for the immediate consequences of the original sin; they have a specific relation to the justice of God and the *pax coelestis*, but they cannot themselves bring about that 'perfectly ordered union of hearts in the enjoyment of God and one another in God'.[127] For Aquinas a *communitas politica* may give to man a natural happiness, but this, while it is related to the supernatural happiness, is not itself more than a secondary deliverance from evil in the eternal life of the soul. And Spinoza, who perhaps more completely than any other writer adheres to the conception of human life as a predicament from which salvation is sought, finds in civil association no more than a second-best deliverance, giving a freedom that cannot easily be dispensed with, but one not to be compared with that which belongs to him who is delivered from the power of necessity by his knowledge of the necessary workings of the universe.[128]

---

[126] Plato, *Republic*, 614 *sq.*; Aristotle, *Nic. Eth.*, X, vii–ix.
[127] Augustine, *De Civitate Dei*, xix, 13.
[128] Spinoza, *Ethica*, Pars, V.

Now, in this matter Hobbes is perhaps more suspect than any other great writer. This alleged apostle of absolutism would, more than others, appear to be in danger of making civil association a hell by conceiving it as a heaven. And yet there is little justification for the suspicion. For Hobbes, the salvation of man, the true resolution of his predicament, is neither religious nor intellectual, but emotional. Man above all things else is a creature of passion, and his salvation lies, not in the denial of his character, but in its fulfilment. And this is to be found, not in pleasure—those who see in Hobbes a hedonist are sadly wide of the mark—but in Felicity, a transitory perfection, having no finality and offering no repose. Man, as Hobbes sees him, is not engaged in an undignified scramble for suburban pleasures; there is the greatness of great passion in his constitution. The restless desire that moves him is not pain,[129] nor may it be calmed by any momentary or final achievement;[130] and what life in another world has to offer, if it is something other than Felicity, is a salvation that has no application to the man we know.[131] For such a man salvation is difficult; indeed what distinguishes Hobbes from all earlier and most later writers is his premise that a man is a moving 'body', that human conduct is inertial, not teleological movement and that his 'salvation' lies in 'continual success in obtaining those things which a man from time to time desires'. And certainly civil association has no power to bring this about. Nevertheless, what it offers is something of value relative to his salvation. It offers the removal of some of the circumstances that, if they are not removed, must frustrate the enjoyment of Felicity. It is a negative gift, merely making not impossible that which is sought. Here, in civil association, is neither fulfilment nor wisdom to discern fulfilment, but peace, the only condition of human life that can be permanently established. And to a race condemned to seek its perfection in the flying moment and always in the one to come, whose highest virtue is to cultivate a clear-sighted vision of the consequences of its actions, and whose greatest need

---

[129] Locke, *Human Understanding*, II, xxi, 32.
[130] Aquinas, *Summa Theologica*, II, i, 1. Q. 27. 1.
[131] *L.*, p. 48.

(not supplied by nature) is freedom from the distraction of illusion, the Leviathan, that *justitiae mensura atque ambitionis elenchus*, will appear an invention neither to be despised nor over-rated. 'When the springs dry up, the fish are all together on dry land. They will moisten each other with their dampness and keep each other wet with their slime. But this is not to be compared with their forgetting each other in a river or a lake'.

The "Introduction to *Leviathan*" first appeared in the 1946 Blackwell edition of *Leviathan* edited by Oakeshott. It was subsequently revised slightly and included in his *Hobbes on Civil Association*. It is new to this edition of *Rationalism in Politics*. Reprinted by permission from *Hobbes on Civil Association*. ©1975 by Basil Blackwell, Oxford, England.

The moral life in the writings
of Thomas Hobbes

ONE

The moral life is a life *inter homines*. Even if we are disposed to look for a remote ground (such, for example, as the will of God) for our moral obligations, moral conduct concerns the relations of human beings to one another and the power they are capable of exerting over one another. This, no doubt, spills over into other relationships—those with animals, for example, or even with things —but the moral significance of these lies solely in their reflection of the dispositions of men towards one another. Further, the moral life appears only when human behaviour is free from natural necessity; that is, when there are alternatives in human conduct. It does not require that a specific choice should be made on each occasion, for moral conduct may be habit; it does not require that each occasion should find a man without a disposition to behave in a certain manner; and it does not require that on any occasion the range of choices should be unlimited. But it does require the possibility of choice, and we may perhaps suppose that specific choices of some sort (though not necessarily the choice of *this* action) have been made at some time even though they have become lost and super-seded in a settled disposition. In other words, moral conduct is art, not nature: it is the exercise of an acquired skill. But the skill here is not that of knowing how to get what we want with the least ex-penditure of energy, but knowing how to behave as we *ought* to be-have: the skill, not of desiring, but of approving and of doing what is approved.

All this is, of course, well known. Every moralist has perceived a gap between the ascertained inclinations of human beings and what ought to be done about them. But there is something else to be observed, namely, that what we ought to do is unavoidably con-nected with what in fact we are; and what we are is (in the connec-tion) what we believe ourselves to be. And a moralist who fails to recognize this is apt to fall into absurdity. What Hume complained of was not the attempt to ascertain the connection between moral and factual propositions but the hasty and unsatisfactory manner in which this was done. It was the acute Vauvenargues who de-tected that it was only by the subterfuge of inventing a 'virtu incom-patible avec la natur de l'homme' that Le Rochefoucauld was able to announce coldly that 'il n'y avait aucun virtue'. Indeed, the idioms of moral conduct which our civilization has displayed are distin-guished, in the first place, not in respect of their doctrines about how we *ought* to behave, but in respect of their interpretations of what in fact we are.

There are, I believe, three such idioms, which I shall denote: first, the morality of communal ties; secondly, the morality of indi-viduality; and thirdly, the morality of the common good.

In the morality of communal ties, human beings are recognized solely as members of a community and all activity whatsoever is un-derstood to be communal activity. Here, separate individuals, capa-ble of making choices for themselves and inclined to do so, are un-known, not because they have been suppressed but because the circumstances in which they might have appeared are absent. And here, good conduct is understood as appropriate participation in the unvarying activities of a community. It is as if all the choices had already been made and what ought to be done appears, not in general rules of conduct, but in a detailed ritual from which divergence is so difficult that there seems to be no visible alternative to it. What ought to be done is indistinguishable from what is done; art appears as nature. Nevertheless, this is an idiom of *moral* conduct, because the manner of this communal activity is, in fact, art and not nature; it is the product, not (of course) of design, but of numbers, long-forgotten choices.

In the morality of individuality, on the other hand, human beings are recognized (because they have come to recognize themselves in this character) as separate and sovereign individuals, associated with one another, not in the pursuit of a single common enterprise, but in an enterprise of give and take, and accommodating themselves to one another as best they can: it is the morality of self and other selves. Here individual choice is pre-eminent and a great part of happiness is connected with its exercise. Moral conduct is recognized as consisting in determinate relationships between these individuals, and the conduct approved in that which reflects the independent individuality understood to be characteristic of human beings. Morality is the art of mutual accommodation.

The morality of the common good springs from a different reading of human nature, or (what is the same thing) the emergence of a different idiom of human character. Human beings are recognized as independent centres of activity, but approval attaches itself to conduct in which this individuality is suppressed whenever it conflicts, not with the individuality of others, but with the interests of a 'society' understood to be composed of such human beings. All are engaged in a single, common enterprise. Here the lion and the ox are distinguished from one another, but there is not only one *law* for both, there is a single approved condition of circumstance for both: the lion shall eat straw like the ox. The single approved condition of human circumstances is called 'the social good', 'the good of all', and morality is the art in which this condition is achieved and maintained.

Perhaps a deeper review of the history of European morals would disclose other general moral dispositions to be added to these, and perhaps my descriptions of those I have noticed are unnaturally precise, ideal extrapolations of what has actually been felt; but I have no doubt that dispositions of these kinds have appeared, and (without ever quite superseding one another) they have followed one another during the last thousand years of our history, each in turn provoking moral reflection appropriate to itself.

TWO

In considering the writings of a moralist the first thing to be ascertained is, then, the understanding he has of the nature of human beings. And in Hobbes we may recognize a writer who was engaged in exploring that idiom of the moral life I have called the morality of individuality. Nor is it at all remarkable that this should be so. It is only a very poor moralist who invents for himself either virtues or a version of human nature; both precepts and his reading of human character he must take from the world around him. And, since the emergent human character of western Europe in the seventeenth century was one in which a feeling for individuality was becoming pre-eminent—the independent, enterprising man out to seek his intellectual or material fortune, and the individual human soul responsible for its own destiny—this unavoidably became for Hobbes, as it was for his contemporary moralists, the subject matter of moral reflection. For Hobbes (or for any other moralist in the seventeenth and eighteenth centuries) to have undertaken to explore either the morality of communal ties or the morality of the common good would have been an anachronism. What, then, distinguishes Hobbes from his contemporaries is not the idiom of the moral life he chose to explore, but the precise manner in which he interpreted this current sentiment for individuality and the doctrine of moral conduct he associated with it, or purported to deduce from it. And if it is the enterprise of every philosopher to translate current sentiments into the idiom of general ideas and to universalize a local version of human character by finding for it some rational ground, this enterprise was fortified in Hobbes by his notion of philosophy as the science of deducing the general causes of observed occurrences. His concern was with both men and things; but he was content to allow a certain looseness in the connection between the two,[1] and unlike Spinoza, who presents us with a universe composed of metaphysical individualities (man being only a special case of a universal condition), Hobbes's starting-point as a moralist was with unique *human* individuality; and, as he understood it, his first business was to rationalize *this* individuality by displaying its 'cause', its components and its structure.

Hobbes's complex image of human character was settled upon what he calls 'two most certain postulates of human nature', namely, the postulate of 'natural appetite' or passion, and the postulate of 'natural reason'.[2] It was an image which, in various idioms, had haunted European reflection for many centuries, and though its most familiar idiom is Christian, it is traceable in the Latin thought of pagan antiquity. It is displayed in the lines of the sixteenth century poet, Fulke Greville:

> *O wearisome condition of humanity,*
> *Born to one law and to another bound,*
> *Vainly begot and yet forbidden vanity,*
> *Created sick, commanded to be sound,*
> *What meaneth nature by these diverse laws,*
> *Passion and Reason, self-division's cause.*

But, whereas the poet is content to compose an image, the philosopher's task is to resolve its incoherence and to make it intelligible.

Any abridgment of Hobbes's carefully pondered and exceedingly complicated image of human nature is hazardous, but to follow all its intricacies is impossible now. To be brief—at least as compared with Hobbes himself—he understood a human being to be a bodily structure characterized by internal movements. There is, first, what he called *vital* movement, the involuntary movement which is identified with being alive and which is exemplified in the circulation of the blood and in breathing. This bodily structure, however, exists in an environment to which it is sensitive, and its contacts with this environment are felt either to assist its vital movements or to

---

[1] *English Works* (Molesworth), II, xx.
[2] *E.W.*, II, vii.

impede them. Experiences friendly to vital movement are pleasures and are recognized as good; those which are hostile to it are pains and recognized as evil. Thus, pleasure and pain are our own introspective awareness of being alive; and we prefer pleasure to pain because we prefer life to death. Further, what we prefer we endeavour to bring about. We endeavour to experience those contacts which promote our vital movements and to avoid those which hinder them; and these endeavours are understood by Hobbes as incipient movements towards and away from the components of our environment, movements which he calls respectively appetites and aversions.

In general, for Hobbes, this account of being alive applied both to human beings and to animals, and some of it, perhaps, to other organisms also: an original endowment of vital movement stimulated or hindered by contacts with an environment, and a primordial aversion from death. But at this point Hobbes distinguished between human beings and other organisms. An animal, for example, may feel pleasure and pain, but its vital movements are affected only by an environment with which it is in immediate contact, its appetites and aversions are movements of like and dislike only in relation to what is present, and its hunger is the hunger of the moment.[3] But human beings have other endowments which amplify the range of their appetites and aversions. The chief of these are memory and imagination. Human beings are capable of storing up their experiences of pleasure and pain and of recollecting their causes at a later time; and, in addition to their inescapable environment of objects, they surround themselves with a world of imagined experiences, and they are capable of desiring what is not present except in imagination. Their appetites are inventive and selfconsciously pursued, and they are capable of voluntary movements for the achievement of their imagined ends and not merely of reflex responses to whatever happens to constitute their environment. To the simple passions of desire and love, of aversion and hate and of joy and grief, are added hope and despair, courage and anger, am

---

[3] *Leviathan* (Pogson Smith), p. 82.

bition, repentance, covetousness, jealousy and revenge. They desire not only an environment presently favourable to their vital movements, but a command over that environment which will ensure its friendliness in the future; and the end they seek, Felicity, is not properly-speaking, an end, but merely 'continual success in obtaining those things which a man from time to time desireth'.[4] They are, however, restless and ever unsatisfied, not merely because the world is continually provoking them to fresh responses, but because the appetite of an imaginative creature is essentially unsatisfiable. They have 'a restless desire for power after power which ceaseth only in death', not because they are driven to seek ever 'more intensive delights', but because they cannot be assured of the power to live well which they have at present without the acquisition of more.

Moreover, as Hobbes understood it, although men and animals are alike in their self-centredness, the characteristic difference between them lies in the competitive nature of human appetite and passion: every man wishes to out-do all other men. 'Man, whose Joy consisteth in comparing himself with other men, can relish nothing but what is eminent'.[5] Human life, consequently, is a race which has 'no other goal, nor other garland, but being foremost'; Felicity is 'continually to outgo the next before'.[6] Indeed, the greatest pleasure of a human being, what most of all stimulates the vital movement of his heart, is the consciousness of his own power; the spring of his natural appetite is not what the present world offers him, but his desire for precedence, his longing to be first, for glory and to be recognized and honoured[7] by other men as pre-eminent. His supreme and characteristic passion is Pride; he wishes above all else to be convinced of his own superiority. And so strong is this desire that he is apt to try to satisfy it in make-believe, if (as is usually the case) actual circumstances deny it to him. Thus, pride may degenerate into vain glory (the mere supposition of glory 'for

[4] *L.*, p. 48.
[5] *L.*, p. 130.
[6] *Elements of Law*, I, ix, 21.
[7] To 'honour' a man is to esteem him to be of great power. *E.W.*, IV, 257.

delight in the consequences of it'); and in the illusions of vain glory he loses ground in the race for precedence.[8]

The passion of pride has, however, a partner; namely, fear. In animals, fear may be understood as merely being affrighted, but in man it is something much more important. Any creature of imagination engaged in maintaining his superiority over others of his kind must be apprehensive of not being able to do so. Fear, here, is not merely being anxious lest the next pleasure escape him, but dread of falling behind in the race and thus being denied felicity. And every such dread is a reflection of the ultimate fear, the fear of death. But, whereas animals may fear anything which provokes aversion, with men the chief fear (before which all others are of little account) is fear of the other competitors in the race. And whereas with animals the ultimate dread is death in any manner, the ultimate fear in man is the dread of violent (or untimely)[9] death at the hand of another man; for this is dishonour, the emblem of all *human* failure. This is the fear which Hobbes said is the human passion 'to be reckoned with'; its spring is not a mere desire to remain alive in adverse circumstance, nor is it a mere aversion from death, least of all from the pain of death; its spring is aversion from shameful death.

Human life is, then, a tension between pride and fear; each of these primary passions elucidates the character of the other, and together they define the ambivalent relationship which men enjoy with one another. They need one another, for without others there is no precedence, no recognition of superiority, no honour, no praise, no notable felicity; nevertheless every man is the enemy of every man and is engaged in a competition for superiority in which he is unavoidably apprehensive of failure.[10]

---

[8] *Elements*, I, ix, I; *L.*, pp. 44, 77.

[9] *L.*, p. 100.

[10] This is the 'warre of every man, against every man' (*L.*, p. 96), understood by Hobbes to be a permanent condition of universal hostility. It is, of course, a mistake to suppose that Hobbes invented this image of 'natural' human relations (it goes back at least to Augustine, who took the story of Cain and Abel to be the emblem of it), what he did was to rationalize it in a new manner, detaching it from 'sin'. Further, Hobbes distinguished this condition from another, also called 'warre', where hostility is both intermittent and particular and which he recognized as a means by which a condition of peace (a *civitas*) might be established and defended, which the 'warre of every man against every man' could never be.

So much, then, for the postulate of 'natural appetite' and its entailments in human disposition and conduct. But there is a second postulate, that of 'natural reason'.

'Reason', 'rational' and 'reasoning' are words which, in Hobbes's vocabulary, signify various human powers, endowments and aptitudes which, though they are related to one another, are not identical. In general, they are words which stand for powers which distinguish men, not from one another, but from animals. Human beings are different from beasts in respect of having two powers which may be recognized as, at least, intimations of rationality. First, they are able to regulate their 'Traynes of Thoughts' in such a manner as, not merely to perceive the cause of what has been imagined, but, 'when imagining any thing whatsoever, [to] seek all the possible effects, that can be produced by it; that is to say, [to] imagine what [they] can do with it, when [they] have it'.[11] In other words, human processes of thinking have a scope and an orderliness denied to those of beasts because in them sensation is supplemented by reasoning. This, it seems, is a natural endowment. Secondly, human beings have the power of Speech;[12] and speech is the transference of the 'Trayne of our Thoughts into a Trayne of Words'.[13] This power is a special endowment received from God ('the first author of Speech') by Adam when he was taught by God how to name such creatures as were presented to his sight; and it is the condition of that uniquely human power of 'reasoning', the power of putting words together in a significant manner and of composing arguments. Nevertheless, the power of Speech has to be learned afresh by each generation, and a child becomes recognizable as a 'Reasonable Creature' only when it has 'attained the use of Speech'.[14]

The first use of words is as *'Markes, or Notes* of remembrance' and to register the consequences of our thoughts.[15] But they may

[11] *L.*, p. 20.
[12] *L.*, ch. iv.
[13] *L.*, p. 24.
[14] *L.*, p. 37.
[15] *L.*, p. 25.

be used also to communicate with other men; to communicate both information and desires. Beasts, it is true, have some means of communicating their desires to one another; but, not having the use of words, they are unable to communicate (what, because of the narrowness of their imaginations, they have not got), namely, those long-term, considered enterprises which in human beings are properly called 'wills and purposes'. Their power of communication, and consequently the agreement they may have with one another, is 'natural' or instinctive.[16] Among men, on the other hand, communication is by means of the artifice of words. By these means they can (among much else) 'make known to others [their] wills and purposes, that [they] may have the mutual help of one another'.[17] Speech, then, is the ground of such mutual understanding as human beings enjoy among themselves; and this mutual understanding is the ground of any agreement they may have with one another in the pursuit of their desires. Indeed, as Hobbes understands it, Speech itself (as a means of communication) is based upon agreement—agreement about the significance of words.

Generally speaking, agreement between human beings appears only in specific agreements, and these may be of three different sorts. Sometimes it happens that a man, wanting what another man has and is willing to part with if he is recompensed, an exchange may be agreed upon and concluded on the spot, as with buying and selling with ready money. This is a situation described by Hobbes as one in which the thing and the right to the thing are transferred together.[18] And however mistrustful one may be of the man with whom one makes such a bargain, the only disappointment one may suffer is the disappointment to which every buyer is liable, namely, finding that what he has bought turns out to be different from what he has expected it to be. On other occasions, however, the right may be transferred before the thing itself is handed over, as when for a sum of money paid an undertaking is given to deliver tomorrow what has been purchased, or when a man agrees

---

[16] L., p. 130 sq.
[17] L., p. 25.
[18] L., p. 102.

to do a week's work for payment to be received at the end of the week. Such an agreement is called a Pact or Covenant, one party promising and the other performing and waiting for the promise to be fulfilled. In other words, Covenant is an agreement entailing credit. And this element of credit is supremely characteristic of the third kind of agreement; what Hobbes calls 'covenants of mutual trust'. These are Covenants in which neither party 'presently performs', but both agree to perform later. And it is in respect of these that 'reason' gives its more unmistakable warning and in which the true predicament of men in a state of nature is revealed.

Human beings, then, on account of the scope of their imaginations (embracing the future as well as the present), and on account of their powers of speech, are recognizable as contract—and—covenant-making creatures: their agreement is not 'natural' but executed in 'artificial' agreements.[19] Moreover, since agreements may be recognized as endeavours to modify the condition of suspicion and hostility which is their natural circumstance, and therefore to modify the fear that this condition entails, human beings have, in general, a sufficient motive for entering into them. But the regrettable fact is that the relief given by the otherwise most useful sort of agreement (that is, Pacts or Covenants of mutual trust) is uncertain and apt to be evanescent. For in these one party must perform first, before the other keeps his part of the bargain, and the risk of him who is to be the second performer not keeping his promise (either because it may not then be in his interest to do so, or, more probably, because 'ambition' and 'avarice' have intervened) must always be great enough to make it unreasonable for any man to consent to be the first performer. Thus, while such covenants may be entered into, reason warns us against being the first to execute them,[20] and therefore against entering into them except as second performers. In short, if 'reason' merely enabled human beings to communicate and to make covenants with one another, it must be recognized as a valuable endowment but insufficient to resolve the tension be-

[19] *L.*, p. 131. Covenants, of course, are not possible between men and beasts; but they are also impossible without an intermediary with God. *L.*, p. 106.

[20] *L.*, p. 131.

tween pride and fear. This, however, is not the limit of its usefulness: these 'rational' powers also reveal the manner in which the
defects of covenanted agreements may be remedied and make possible the emancipation of the human race from the frustrations of
natural appetite.

'Reason', here, as Hobbes understood it, is not an arbitrary imposition upon the passionate nature of man; indeed, it is generated
by the passion of fear itself. For fear, in human beings, is active
and inventive; it provokes in them, not a mere disposition to re-
treat, but 'a certain foresight of future evil' and the impulse to 'take
heed' and to provide against what is feared. 'They who travel carry
their swords with them, . . . and even the strongest armies, and
most accomplished for fight, [yet] sometimes parley for peace, as
fearing each other's power, and lest they might be overcome'.[21] In
short, fear of the mischances that may befall him in the race awak-
ens man from his dreams of vain glory (for any belief in continuous
superiority is an illusion) and forces upon his attention the true
precariousness of his situation.

His first reaction is to triumph by disposing of his immediate
enemy, the one next before him in the race for precedence, but 'reason' rejects this as a short-sighted triumph—there will always remain others to be disposed of and there will always remain the uncertainty of being able to dispose of them. And besides, to dispose
of an enemy is to forgo recognition of one's own superiority, that is,
to forgo felicity.[22] What has to be achieved is a permanent release
from fear of dishonourable death; and reason, generated by fear
and pronouncing for the avoidance of the threat of death as the
condition of the satisfaction of any appetite, declares for an agreed
modification of the race for precedence, that is, for a condition of
peace. The consequence of natural appetite is pride and fear; the
'suggestion' and promise of reason is peace. And peace, the product
of the mutual recognition of a common enemy (death) is to be
achieved only in a condition of common subjection to an artificially

[21] E.W., II, 6 fn.
[22] Cf. L., pp. 549–50.

created sovereign authority, that is, in the *civitas*.[23] There, under a civil law made and enforced by a Common Power authorized to do so, Covenants lose their uncertainty and become 'constant and lasting', and the war of every man against every man is brought to an end. The endeavour for peace is natural, begotten by human reason upon human fear; the condition of peace is a contrivance, designed (or discerned) by reason and executed in an agreement of 'every man with every man' in which each surrenders his 'right to govern himself' to a 'common authority'.[24]

To survive, then, is seen to be more desirable than to stand first; proud men must become tame men in order to remain alive. Yet, if we accept this as Hobbes's solution of the predicament of natural man, incoherence remains. Human life is interpreted as a tension between pride (the passion for pre-eminence and honour) and fear (the apprehension of dishonour) which reason discerns how to resolve. But there are difficulties.

First, the resolution suggested is one-sided: fear is allayed but at the cost of Felicity. And this is a situation to be desired only by a creature who fears to be dishonoured more than he desires to be honoured, a creature content to survive in a world from which both honour and dishonour have been removed—and this is not exactly the creature Hobbes had been describing to us. In the end, it appears, all that reason can teach us is the manner in which we may escape fear, but a man compact of pride will not be disposed to accept this low-grade (if gilt-edged) security as the answer to his needs, even if he believes that to refuse it entails almost inevitable dishonour. In short, either this is a solution appropriate to the character of a more commonplace creature, one who merely desires 'success in obtaining those things which a man from time to time desireth',[25] who wants to prosper in a modest sort of way and with as little hindrance and as much help as may be from his fellows, and for whom survival in this condition is more important than Joy; or Hobbes was guilty of defining human Felicity in such a

---

[23] See p. 344, note.
[24] *L.*, pp. 131–2.
[25] *L.*, p. 48.

manner that it is inherently impossible to be experienced by human beings as he understands them, guilty of the solecism of making the conditions of Felicity a bar to its attainment.

And secondly, we may, perhaps, inquire why, on Hobbes's reading of the situation, pride and fear should not be allowed to remain without any attempt to resolve the tension between them. No doubt, when reason speaks it may legitimately claim to be heard; for reason, no less than passion belongs to 'nature'. But if (as Hobbes understood it) the office of reason is that of a servant, revealing the probable causes of events, the probable consequences of actions and the probable means by which desired ends may be attained, whence comes its authority to determine a man's choice of conduct? And if no such authority may be attributed to it, are we constrained to do more than to take note of its deliverances and then choose (with our eyes open) what we shall do? A prudent man, one set upon survival, will not easily be argued out of his prudence, and he may like to support himself with the opinion that he is acting 'rationally'; but he may suddenly find his prudence deprived of its value when he sees in another (who has chosen the risky enterprise of glory) the 'Joy' he has himself foregone. He will be reminded that there is such a thing as folly; and his gilt-edged security may seem a shade less attractive, a shade less adequate to human character.[26] Perhaps, even, he may dimly discern that

> There is no pleasure in the world so sweet
> As, being wise, to fall at folly's feet.

At all events (though, as we shall see, Hobbes is unjustly accused of ignoring these considerations), we may, perhaps, suspect that in seeming here to recommend the pursuit of peace and the rejection of glory as 'rational' conduct, he was, as on some other occasions, being forgetful of his view that 'reason serves only to convince the truth (not of fact, but) of consequence'[27] and was taking improper

---

[26] But against this may be set the fact that in the *civitas* there is still some opportunity for competition and taking risks; all that we are deprived of is the 'joy' of success in utterly unprotected imprudence.

[27] *L.*, p. 292, etc.

advantage of that older meaning of 'reason' in which it was recognized to have the qualities of a master or at least of an authoritative guide.

THREE

As it first appears, the condition of peace is merely a conclusion of natural reason. Awakened from the make-believe of vain glory and inspired by the fear of shameful death, 'reason' not only reveals to men the connection between survival and peace, but also 'suggesteth' the means by which this condition may be achieved and discerns its structure, which Hobbes called 'the convenient articles of peace'.[28] With the first (the means of achievement) we are not now concerned, but a consideration of the second discloses what Hobbes meant by 'peace'. There are, in all, nineteen of these articles and together they outline a condition in which the struggle for precedence is superseded, not by co-operative enterprise, but by mutual forebearance. This array of articles, said Hobbes, may, however, be 'contracted into an easy sum, intelligible even to the meanest capacity, that is, *Do not to another, which thou wouldest not have done to oneself*'.[29] The negative form of the maxim reveals the idiom of the moral life which Hobbes was exploring, but he interprets it (as Confucius did before him) as an injunction to have consideration for others and to avoid partiality for oneself.[30]

But a transformation has taken place. The conditions of peace, first offered to us as *rational theorems* concerning the nature of shameful-death-avoiding conduct (that is, as a piece of prudential wisdom), now appear as *moral obligation*. Clearly (on Hobbes's assumptions) it would be foolish, in the circumstances, not to declare for peace and not to establish it in the only manner in which it can be established; but, somehow, it has also become a dereliction of duty not to do so. Nor is this change of idiom inadvertent. For Hobbes leaves us in no doubt that he properly understood the na-

[28] *L.*, p. 98.
[29] *L.*, p. 121; *E.W.*, IV, 107.
[30] *Analects*, xv, 23.

ture of moral conduct and the difference between it and merely prudent or necessary conduct.

It is to be observed, however, that in Hobbes's vocabulary the words 'good' and 'evil' had (as a rule) no moral connotation. 'Good' merely stood for what is desirable, that is, for whatever may be the object of human appetite; 'evil' signified whatever is the object of aversion. They are, therefore, redundant words which merely repeat what is already signified in words such as 'pleasurable' and 'painful'. When Hobbes said: 'Reason declares peace to be good', he did not mean that all men *ought* to promote peace, but only that all sensible men will do so.[31] And when he said: 'Every man desires his own good and his own good is peace', he could not conclude that every man *ought* to endeavour peace,[32] but only that a man who does not do so is 'contradicting himself'.[33] There is, it is true, something that Hobbes calls a 'precept of reason', and even a 'rule of reason' or a 'law of reason' or a 'dictate of reason', thus making it appear that what is rational is, on that account, somehow obligatory. But all the examples he gives make it clear that a 'precept of reason' is only a hypothetical precept and not the equivalent of a duty. Temperance, he says, 'is a precept of reason, because intemperance tends to sickness and death';[34] but temperance cannot be a duty unless to remain alive and well is a duty, and Hobbes is clear that these are 'rights' and therefore not duties. And when he writes of the laws of Nature in general as 'dictates of Reason' he makes clear that he means 'sayings' or 'pronouncements' of reason, and *not* 'commands'.[35]

But the word 'justice' has a moral connotation, and it was the word Hobbes most often used when he was writing in the normative idiom: to behave morally is to do just actions, and to be a virtuous man is to have a just disposition. Nevertheless, although to behave justly is to be identified with the performance of certain

---

[31] *E.W.*, II, 48; V, 192.

[32] In Hobbes's idiom it is meaningless to say that a man ought to *desire* anything, though there are occasions when he falls into this way of speaking. Cf. *L.*, p. 121.

[33] Cf. *L.*, pp. 101, 548; *E.W.*, II, 12, 31.

[34] *E.W.*, II, 49.

[35] *L.*, p. 122 *sq.*

actions and with refraining from others, the identification calls for some subtlety. A man's duty is to have 'an unfeigned and constant endeavour'[36] to behave justly; what counts, in the first place, is the endeavour and not the external achievement. Indeed, a man may do what, on the surface, is a just action, but because it is done by chance or in pursuance of an unjust endeavour he must be considered, not to be doing justice, but merely not to be guilty; and, conversely, a man may do an injurious action, but if his endeavour is for justice, he may be technically guilty but he has not acted unjustly.[37] But it must be understood, first, that for Hobbes 'endeavour' is not the same as 'intention': to 'endeavour' is to perform actions, to make identifiable movements, and it is, therefore, possible for others to judge of a man's 'endeavour' where it might be difficult to be confident about his intention. And secondly, while it seems to me doubtful whether Hobbes held there to be an obligation to be a just man, duty is fulfilled only where a man both acts justly (that is, makes movements which constitute 'endeavouring justice') and acts guiltlessly (that is, avoids doing injury).

Now, as Hobbes understood it, the object of moral endeavour is peace; what we already know to be a rational endeavour is now declared to be the object of just endeavour. Or, to amplify this definition a little, just conduct is the unfeigned and constant endeavour to acknowledge all other men as one's equal, and when considering their actions in relation to oneself to discount one's own passion and self-love.[38] The word 'unfeigned' was, I think, intended to indicate that this endeavour is not moral endeavour unless it is pursued for its own sake and not, for example, in order to avoid punishment or to win an advantage for oneself. And the word 'endeavour' meant not only always to intend peace, but always to act in such a manner that peace is the probable consequence of our action.

The precept we have before us is, then, that 'every man *ought* to endeavour peace', and our question is, What reason or justifica-

---

[36] *L.*, p. 121.
[37] *E.W.*, II, 32; IV, 109.
[38] *L.*, pp. 118, 121.

tion did Hobbes provide for this delineation of moral conduct? Why ought a man unfeignedly endeavour to keep his word, to accommodate himself to others, not to take more than his share, not to set himself up as a judge in his own cause, not display hatred and contempt towards others, to treat others as his equals, and to do everything else that pertains to peace?[39] How did Hobbes bridge the gap between men's natural inclinations and what ought to be done about them? And with this question we reach the obscure heart of Hobbes's moral theory. For, not only is an answer to it the chief thing we should look for in the writings of any moralist, who normally takes his precepts from current moral opinion and himself contributes only the reasons for believing them to be true; but also, in the case of Hobbes, it is the question which his commentators have had most trouble in discovering the answer to, though some of them have pressed their conclusions upon us and dismissed those of others with remarkable arrogance. Hobbes was usually so much more concerned with elucidating adequate motives or 'causes' for what is alleged to be just conduct than with finding adequate reasons for calling it just, that those who seek an answer to our question are forced to use all their ingenuity.

FOUR

There are three current readings of Hobbes's answer to this question which deserve consideration because, though none is (I believe) entirely satisfactory, each has been argued acutely and carefully and none is without plausibility.[40]

1. The first account runs something like this:[41]

Every man must either endeavour 'the preservation of his own nature', or endeavour something more than this, for example, to be first in the race. To endeavour nothing at all is impossible: 'to have no desire is to be dead'. Now every man, in all circumstances, has

---

[39] *L.*, ch. xv.

[40] In all, of course, there are many more than three.

[41] L. Strauss, *The Political Philosophy of Hobbes*.

the right to endeavour 'the preservation of his own nature';[42] in doing so he is acting justly. And in no circumstances has any man the right to endeavour more than this (for example by indulging in useless cruelty or by desiring to be first); if he seeks what is superfluous to 'the preservation of his own nature',[43] his endeavour is unreasonable, reprehensible and unjust because it is an endeavour for his own destruction. But to endeavour to preserve his own nature, we have seen, is precisely, to endeavour peace; and to endeavour more than this is to endeavour war and self-destruction. Therefore a man is just when he endeavours peace, and unjust when he endeavours war. Every man has an obligation to be just, and (in principle) he has no other obligation but to endeavour peace. In short, duty is identified with dispositions and actions which are 'rational' in the sense of not being 'self-contradictory'. And Hobbes, it is said, found support for this position in the observation that the endeavour of a man to preserve his own nature has the approval of conscience, and the endeavour to do more than this is disapproved by conscience: the feeling of guiltlessness and of guilt attach themselves respectively to each of these endeavours. Thus, activity which springs from fear of shameful death and is designed to mitigate that fear alone has the approval of conscience and is obligatory.

Now, there can be no doubt that this is moral doctrine in so far as it is an attempt to elucidate a distinction between natural appetite and permissible appetite; it does not assimilate right to might or duty to desire. Moreover, it is a doctrine which identifies moral conduct with prudentially rational conduct: the just man is the man who has been tamed by fear. But if Hobbes has said no more than this, he must be considered not to have said enough. And, in any case, he did say something more and something different.

In the first place, the answer given here to the question, why ought all men to endeavour peace? itself provokes a question: we want to know why every man has an obligation only to endeavour to preserve his own nature. The whole position rests upon the belief

[42] *L.*, p. 99.
[43] *E.W.*, II, 45n; *L.*, p. 116 *sq.*

that Hobbes thought every man had an *obligation* to act in such a manner as not to risk his own destruction, whereas what Hobbes said is that every man has a *right* to preserve his own nature and that a right is neither a duty nor does it give rise to a duty of any sort.[44] Secondly, an interpretation of Hobbes which represents him as saying that dutiful conduct is rational conduct in the sense of being 'consistent' or non-self-contradictory conduct, and that it is dutiful because it is rational in this (or any other) sense, must be considered wide of the mark. There are occasions when Hobbes appealed to the principle of 'non-contradiction' in order to denote what is desirable in conduct;[45] but, it is safe to say, he distinguished clearly between merely rational conduct and obligatory conduct. On no plausible reading of Hobbes is the Law of Nature to be considered obligatory because it represents rational conduct. Thirdly, this interpretation does not recognize moral conduct as the disinterested acknowledgment of all others as one's equal which Hobbes took to be fundamental for peace; on this showing, all endeavours for peace, however interested, would be equally just. And lastly, there is in this account a confusion between the cause of conduct alleged to be just and the reason for thinking it just. For the apprehension of shameful death and the aversion from it are not reasons why we have an obligation to endeavour peace; they are the causes or motives of our doing so. And if 'reason' is added (as Hobbes added it) as a mediator between fear and pride, we have still not made our escape from the realm of causes into the realm of justifications, because 'reason' for Hobbes (except where he is being unmistakably equivocal) has no prescriptive force. In short, if Hobbes said no more than this he must be considered not to have had a moral theory at all.

2. There are, however, other interpretations of Hobbes's views on this matter, which run on different lines. And we may consider next what is, perhaps, the simplest of all the current accounts. It goes as follows:

[44] *L.*, p. 99.
[45] E.g. *E.W.*, II, 12, 31; *L.*, pp. 101, 548.

According to Hobbes, all moral obligation derives from *law*; where there is no law there is no duty and no distinction between just and unjust conduct, and where there is law in the proper sense there is an obligation to obey it upon those who come under it if there is also an adequate motive for obeying it. Now, law properly speaking (we are told) is 'the command of him, that by right hath command over others';[46] or (in a more ample description) 'law in general, . . . is command; nor a command of any man to any man; but only of him whose command is addressed to one formerly obliged to obey him'.[47] And a law-maker in the proper sense is one who has acquired this antecedent authority to be obeyed by being given it, or by being acknowledged to have it, by those who are to be subject to his commands, 'there being no obligation on any man, which ariseth not from some act of his own'.[48] This act of authorization or acknowledgment is a necessary condition of genuine law-making authority. In other words, there can be no such thing, for Hobbes, as a 'natural', unacquired, authority to make law.[49] To this, two other condition of obligation are added: law in the proper sense can issue from a 'law-maker' only when those who are obliged by it know him as the author of the law, and when they know precisely what he commands. But these conditions are, in fact, entailed in the first condition; for, no subject could know himself to be a subject without this act of authorization or acknowledgment, and it would be impossible to perform such an act and at the same time be ignorant of who the law-maker is and what he commands.

In short, it is unmistakably Hobbes's view that law is something made and that it is binding solely on account of having been made in a certain manner by a law-maker having certain characteristics; and that obligation springs only from law. Or, in other

---

[46] *L.*, p. 123.

[47] *L.*, pp. 203, 406; *E.W.*, II, 49.

[48] *L.*, pp. 166, 220, 317, 403, 448; *E.W.*, II, 113, 191; IV, 148.

[49] Those passages in which Hobbes seems inclined to recognize mere Omnipotence as authority to make law are not to be excluded from this condition. Omnipotence, no less than any other authoritative characteristic, is something accorded; he only is Omnipotent who is admitted or acknowledged to be so or who has been expressly accorded unlimited power. And this is true of God (except where the name God denotes merely a First Cause) no less than of men, for 'God' is a name to which men have agreed to accord a certain significance. *L.*, pp. 282, 525.

words, no command is inherently (that is, merely on account of what it commands or on account of the reasonableness of what it commands) or self-evidently binding; its obligatoriness is something to be proved or rebutted, and Hobbes told us what evidence is relevant for this proof or rebuttal. This evidence is solely concerned with whether or not the command is law in the proper sense, that is, whether or not it has been made by one who has authority to make it.

Now the proposition that the law of the *civitas* is law in the proper sense was, for Hobbes, not an empirical but an analytic proposition;[50] *civitas* is defined as an artificial condition of human life in which there are laws which are known to have been made by a law-maker who has acquired the authority to make them by being given it by those who are subject to him,[51] and in which what is commanded is known, and in which there is an authentic interpretation of what is commanded. And further, those who are subject to these laws have an adequate motive for their subjection. All the conditions for law in the proper sense are satisfied by civil law. Consequently (it is argued by those who defend this reading of Hobbes's writings) Hobbes's settled view was that civil laws are unquestionably obligatory, and their obligatoriness springs not from their being a reflection of some other 'natural' law which carries with it 'natural' duties, but solely from the character of their maker and the manner in which they have been made, promulgated and interpreted. The question, Why am I morally bound to obey the commands of the sovereign of my *civitas*? (which, for Hobbes, is the important question) requires no other answer than, Because I, in agreement with others in a similar plight to myself, and with a common disposition to make covenants, having 'authorized' him, know him indubitably to be a law-giver and know his commands as laws properly speaking.[52] Furthermore (it is argued), not only are the laws of a *civitas* laws in the proper sense, but, in a *civitas*, they

---

[50] Cf. *L.*, p. 443.

[51] This is true both in respect of sovereigns whose authority is by Acquisition and those who acquire it by Institution (*L.*, p. 549 *sq.*). And it is taken by Hobbes to have been true also of the ancient 'Kingdom' of the Jews (*L.*, ch. 35).

[52] *L.*, pp. 131, 135, 166, 220, 317.

are, for Hobbes, the only laws which have this character. Neither the so-called 'laws' of a church, nor the so-called Laws of Nature, are, in a *civitas*, laws in the proper sense unless and until they have been made so by being promulgated as civil laws.[53] Indeed, it is Hobbes's view that there is no law that is law properly speaking which is not a 'civil' law in the sense of being the command of a civil sovereign: God's laws are laws in the proper sense only where God is a civil sovereign exercising his sovereignty through agents. The civil sovereign does not, of course, 'make' the Laws of Nature as rational theorems about human preservation, but he does, in the strictest sense, 'make' them laws in the proper sense.[54] It may, for example, be accounted reasonable to render unto God (where God is *not* a civil sovereign) the things that are God's and unto Caesar the things that are Caesar's, but, according to Hobbes, this does not become a duty until these respective spheres are defined, and, in both cases, the definition is a matter of civil law. No doubt in a *civitas* a subject may retain the relics of a Natural Right, but a natural right, according to Hobbes, is not an obligation and has nothing whatever to do with a man's duties.

On this reading of Hobbes's thoughts on moral obligation, there remains the question whether or not he thought that men who are not subjects of a properly constituted civil sovereign and who therefore have no duties under a civil law nevertheless have duties as well as rights. And this question resolves itself into the question, Where there is no civil law, is there a law which is law in the proper sense? This is an interesting question, but for two reasons it is not a highly important question for those who read Hobbes in the manner we are now considering. First, Hobbes is understood to be writing, not for savages, but for men who belong to a *civitas*; his project is to show what *their* obligations are and whence they arise, and if he has given a reason for believing that civil law is binding and is the only law that is binding, he does not need to do more than this. And secondly (on the interpretation we

---

[53] *L.*, pp. 205, 222, 405, 406, 469.
[54] *L.*, p. 437.

are now considering) there can be no question of the obligations of civil law being derived from or being in any way connected with, another law, even if that other 'law' were found, in circumstances other than those of the *civitas*, to be law in the proper sense and to impose duties upon all mankind: in a *civitas* the *only* law in the proper sense is civil law. The core of this interpretation is the belief that, for Hobbes, the *civitas* constituted not a useful addition to human life, but a transformation of the natural conditions of human life. However, the consideration of Hobbes's thoughts on obligations imposed by a law other than civil law is more appropriate in connection with another interpretation of his moral theory for which this question is central.

In the interpretation we are now considering, then, what *causes* human beings to enter into the agreement by which the civil sovereign is constituted and authorized is their fear of destruction which has been converted into a rational endeavour for peace; but they have no obligation to do so. Their *duty* to endeavour peace begins with the appearance of civil law, a law properly so-called and the only one of its kind, commanding this endeavour.

This interpretation (like any other) depends upon a certain reading of important passages in Hobbes's writings, and without calling attention to all the relevant passages it may be noticed, first, that it relies upon what must be recognized as the only intelligible reading of the passage in *Leviathan* where Hobbes maintains what may be called the sovereignty of civil law;[55] and secondly, it entails understanding the expression 'whose command is addressed to one formerly obliged to obey him'[56] (used by Hobbes to define the lawgiver in the proper sense) to signify 'one who has already covenanted to set him up, or who has otherwise recognized him, or acknowledged him as a sovereign law-maker'. This, I believe, in spite of the weakening of the word 'obliged' that it involves, is the most plausible reading of this expression.[57] But this reading is not without difficulties and we shall have to consider another reading of it the

[55] *L.,* p. 205.
[56] *L.,* p. 203.
[57] Cf. Pollock, *An Introduction to the History of the Science of Politics,* p. 65.

acceptance of which would go far to make this interpretation of Hobbes's moral theory untenable.

To this interpretation there are three main objections. First (it is observed), if the only obligation of the subject in a *civitas* is to perform the duties imposed by the law-maker whom he had (by covenant or acknowledgment) authorized, and if it is based solely upon the fact that they are genuine duties because the civil law is undoubtedly law in the proper sense and applies to the subject in a *civitas*, what, if anything, binds him to go on observing the acknowledgment or covenant which authorizes the law-maker to make law? Has he a duty to continue this acknowledgment, in so far as it can be separated from the duty to obey the laws? If not, does not Hobbes's account of moral obligation hang suspended for want of an answer to a pertinent question? And if he has such a duty, must not there be a law in the proper sense, other than civil law, which imposes it? This must be recognized as a formidable objection, but in the view of those whose views we are now considering, it is not unanswerable; indeed, there are two possible answers. First, it may be contended that there is little in Hobbes (except what is obscure or equivocal, e.g., *L.*, p. 110) to suggest that he held the making of the Covenant (besides being a prudent act) was also a moral obligation, and that 'keeping the covenant' and 'obeying the law' were not inseparable activities; and if there is a duty to obey the law (which there is), then there is a constructive duty to keep and protect the covenant.[58] But, secondly, if it is conceded that for there to be a duty to 'keep the covenant' there must be a law imposing this duty and it cannot be the civil law itself, then, since on this interpretation there is no such 'other' law in the proper sense (i.e. no law which is *not* based on the acknowledgment of the ruler by the subject) to be found in Hobbes's writings, we must conclude that for Hobbes there was no specific duty to keep the covenant. And why should there be? Neither Hobbes's moral theory nor any other is to be reckoned defective because it does not show every desirable action to be also a duty. For Hobbes duty is

[58] Cf. *E.W.*, II, 31; *L.*, 101, 548.

always (directly or indirectly) the activity of endeavouring peace, and to endeavour peace *is* a duty only when there is a law commanding it. To make and keep the covenant (or the acknowledgment) in which the *civitas* is set up are activities of endeavouring peace. But if, in this respect, they are eligible to become duties, it is not necessary for them to be duties; and, if they are not duties (for lack of a law commanding them) they are not, on that account, unintelligible. They are for Hobbes (on this reading) acts of prudence which are reasonable and desirable to be performed on condition that others perform them, or acts of 'nobility' which make no conditions. It is, of course, true that, for Hobbes, it could never be a duty to act against one's own interest (that is, to endeavour the war of all against all), but it does not follow from this that endeavouring peace must always be a duty. In short, if Hobbes is understood to have said that there is a duty to obey the law of the *civitas* because, for the subjects of a *civitas*, it is law in the proper sense, but that there is no separate duty to make and keep the covenant or acknowledgment which sets up the civil sovereign, he is not being understood to have said anything inherently absurd: he is merely being recognized to have said that there is a proper use for the word 'duty', but that what holds the *civitas* together is not 'duty' (except, for example, the duty imposed by a law against treason) but either self-interest instructed by reason, or the nobility which is too proud to calculate the possible loss entailed in obedience to a 'sovereign' who lacks power to enforce his commands.[59]

The second objection is as follows: it is alleged that, for Hobbes, rational behaviour is endeavouring peace, and that this becomes a duty if and when it is commanded by law in the proper sense. Further, since civil law *is* law in the proper sense and the only law in the proper sense (owing its propriety not to its being a reflection of some other, superior and equally proper law, but solely to the man-

---

[59] In the Conclusion of *Leviathan* (p. 548) Hobbes added a twentieth Law of Nature, namely, 'that every man is bound by Nature, as much as in him lieth, to protect in Warre, the Authority, by which he himself is protected in time of Peace'. And he explains that this is so because not to act in this way would be self-contradictory. But to demonstrate self-consistency, is not to demonstrate duty: and the conduct which is here asserted to be self-consistent becomes a duty only when there is a law in the proper sense imposing it, and for members of a *civitas* such a law must be a civil law.

ner in which it has been made, published and authentically interpreted) and commands its subjects to endeavour peace, these have
a duty (which persons in other circumstances have not) of 'endeavouring peace'. But (it is objected) this is not an accurate account of the situation. What, even for Hobbes, the civil law commands is not merely that a man shall 'endeavour peace' but that he
shall perform specific actions and refrain from others: it is no defence for the law-breaker to say, 'I am endeavouring peace', if he
neglects to do what the law commands or does what it forbids. The
answer to this objection is, however, that, for Hobbes, 'endeavouring peace' was always performing specific acts (and not merely having peaceful intentions or a generally peaceful disposition); to be
disposed in a certain direction is to make movements in that direction. And, while reason acquaints all but madmen and children
with the general pattern of acts which may be expected to promote
a peaceful condition of human life, it is the province of law to decide what acts, in specific circumstances, are necessary to a condition of peace and to impose them as duties.[60] When 'endeavouring
peace' is a *duty*, it is always the duty of obeying a law, and a law is
always a set of specific commands and prohibitions. Hence, the
duty of endeavouring peace is indistinguishable from the duty of
performing the acts prescribed by law: a man cannot at the same
time 'endeavour peace' and do what the law forbids, though he may
do so by actions which the law does not require him—by being benevolent, for example. But his *duty* to 'endeavour peace' is a duty to
obey the law, that is, to be both just and guiltless.

The third objection is that Hobbes is often to be found writing
about 'natural laws' and writing about them as if he considered
them to be laws in the proper sense and capable of imposing a 'natural obligation' upon all men to endeavour peace, and any account
of Hobbes's moral theory which ignores this is implausible. This,
again, is not easily to be disposed of. It is true that Hobbes repeat-
edly and clearly asserted that Natural Laws are not properly speaking laws at all except where they appear as the commands of a law-

[60] *L.*, p. 136.

giver *who owes his authority to a covenant or an acknowledgment*; apart from this, they are only 'qualities which dispose men to peace and order', 'dictates', 'conclusions' or 'theorems' of natural reason 'suggesting' the conduct which belongs to a condition of peace and therefore the rational (but not the moral) foundation of the *civitas*.[61] But these assertions are partnered by others capable of being interpreted to mean that the Laws of Nature themselves impose obligations upon all men (rulers included), and even that the obligations of the subject to obey the laws of his *civitas* derives from the duty he has under one or more of these natural laws.[62] However, since the view that Hobbes believed Natural Law to be law in the proper sense and to be the source of all moral obligation is the central theme of the third important account of Hobbes's moral theory, the force of this objection to this account will best be considered in that connection.

3. This third interpretation begins at the same place as the one we have just considered.[63] It recognizes that, for Hobbes, all moral obligation derives from a law of some sort: where there is authentic law there is, on that account, duty; where there is no law there is no duty. Consequently, endeavouring peace can be shown to be a duty upon all men if there is a valid and universally applicable law commanding it. So far, I think there can be no serious disagreement about what Hobbes thought. But it is now contended that the Law of Nature itself and without further qualification is, in Hobbes's view, a valid, universal and perpetually operative law imposing this duty upon all men. Every interpreter of Hobbes recognizes that what Hobbes called the Laws of Nature and what he called 'the convenient articles of peace' are, in respect of content, the same thing and that they are the 'suggestions' or conclusions of reason about the preservation of human life. What is asserted now is that Hobbes also believed them to be laws in the proper sense; namely, that their author is known and that he has acquired an

[61] *L.*, pp. 97, 122, 205, 211, etc.; *E.W.*, II, 49–50, etc.

[62] *L.*, pp. 99, 110, 203, 121, 273, 258–9, 363; *E.W.*, II, 46, 47, 190, 200.

[63] H. Warrender, *The Political Philosophy of Hobbes*; J.M. Brown, *Political Studies*, Vol. I, No. I; Vol. II, No. 2.

antecedent right to command, that they have been published and are known, that there is an authentic interpretation of them and that those who have a duty to obey have a sufficient motive for doing so. And the conclusion suggested is that endeavouring peace was, for Hobbes, an obligation laid upon all men by a Law of Nature and that any further obligation there may be to obey the laws of the *civitas*, or to obey covenanted commands, derives from this natural and universal obligation.[64]

Now, it is not to be denied that there are expressions and passages in Hobbes's writings which appear to be designed to make us believe that this is his view, but before we accept them at their face value we must consider in detail whether Hobbes also held the beliefs which are for him certainly entailed in this view. And if we find this not to be the case, it may be thought that these passages are eligible for some other interpretation, or that we must be content to have detected what, on any reading, is a notable incoherence in his writings.

The direction of our first inquiry is unmistakable. Since, according to Hobbes, the obligation a law imposes is due not to the law itself but to its author,[65] who must not only be known as its author but known also to have a right to command, our first inquiry must be: Did Hobbes believe the Law of Nature to have an author known as such to all mankind? And if so, who did he think was its author and in what manner did he think this author was known to be the maker of this law? And, together with this, we may appropriately consider what thoughts Hobbes's writings disclose about the right of this author to make this law. The answer urged upon us in the interpretation we are now considering is that Hobbes unmistakably believed the Law of Nature to have an author

---

[64] There are further subtleties in some versions of this interpretation which I do not propose to consider here because, whether or not they can be shown to be components of Hobbes's view of things, they do not affect the main point. For example, the suggestion that the *civitas* is a condition in which the obligation to endeavour peace (already imposed by a Natural Law) is 'validated'. Clearly, this suggestion is cogent only when it is believed that, for Hobbes, the Law of Nature is law in the proper sense. Our main concern is with the question: Is the Law of Nature, by itself and without qualification of circumstances or persons, law in the proper sense and capable of imposing upon all mankind the duty of 'endeavouring peace'?

[65] E.g. *E.W.*, II, 191 *sq.*

who is naturally known to all men as such; that this author is God himself; and that his right to legislate derives, not from his having created those who should obey his commands, but from his Omnipotence.[66] The Law of Nature, it is contended, is law in the proper sense; it is binding upon all men in all circumstances because it is known to be the command of an Omnipotent God.

The first difficulty which stands in the way of our accepting this interpretation is that it must remain exceedingly doubtful (to say the least) whether Hobbes thought that our natural knowledge includes (or could possibly include) a knowledge of God as the author of imperative laws for human conduct. He reasoned thus about the word 'God': divinities appear first as projections of human fear consequent upon our frequent ignorance of the causes of the good and ill fortunes which befall us, but the notion of 'one God, Infinite and Omnipotent' derives, not from our fears, but from our curiosity about 'the causes of natural bodies, their several virtues and operations': in tracing these causes backwards we unavoidably 'come to this, that there must be one First Mover; that is a First, and Eternal cause of all things; which is that which men mean by the name of God'.[67] It is this God, then, a necessary hypothesis, of whom we may be said, in the first place, to have natural knowledge. And in virtue of the Omnipotence of this God (his 'rule' as a First Cause being inescapable and absolute) we may speak of him as 'King of all the earth', and we may speak of the earth as his natural Kingdom and everything on earth as his natural subject; but if we do speak in this manner, we must recognize that we are using the words 'King' and 'Kingdom' in only a metaphorical sense.[68]

Nevertheless, the name God may also be used with another signification in which he may be said to be a 'King' and to have a natural Kingdom and natural subjects in the proper meaning of these

---

[66] This excludes two otherwise possible views. First, that it is a duty to conform to the Law of Nature because it is self-evidently rational or because it is axiomatically obligatory: there is, I think, no plausible reading of Hobbes in which the Law of Nature is recognized to be obligatory except in respect of its authorship. And secondly, that the Law of Nature is obligatory on account of its authorship, but that the author is not God. For this third interpretation of Hobbes's theory, God is essential.

[67] L., p. 83.

[68] L., pp. 90, 314 sq.

expressions: he is a genuine ruler over those 'that believe that there is a God that governeth the world, and hath given Praecepts, and propounded Rewards and Punishments to Mankind'.[69] But, about this there are two observations to be made. First, these beliefs fall short of natural knowledge, which is confined (in this connection) to the necessary hypothesis of God as the Omnipotent First Cause;[70] the 'providential' God is no less a 'projection' of human thought than the God who is the First Cause, but whereas the First Cause is a projection of human reason, the providential God is a projection of human desire.[71] And secondly, since these beliefs about a 'providential' God are avowedly *not* common to all mankind,[72] God's natural subjects (i.e. those who have an obligation to obey his commands) are those only who have acknowledged a 'providential' God concerned with human conduct and who hope for his rewards and fear his punishments. (And it may be remarked here, in passing, that this circumstance qualifies the distinction Hobbes was apt to make between God's natural subjects and his subjects by covenant: the only proper understanding of the expression 'Kingdom of God' is when it is taken to signify 'a Commonwealth, instituted (by the consent of those who were to be subject thereto) for their Civil Government'.[73]) The law which the subjects of this God are bound to obey is the Law of Nature;[74] they have a duty always to endeavour peace. Others, it is true, may feel the weight of this law, may find themselves in receipt of pleasure for following its precepts or pain for not doing so, but these have no moral obligation to obey

---

[69] *L.*, pp. 274, 314. This is a necessary condition, but (as we shall see shortly) the necessary and sufficient condition is that they should not only 'believe' in a God of this sort, but that they should have acknowledged him as *their* ruler.

[70] According to Hobbes we have no natural knowledge of God's nature, or of a life after death. *L.*, 113.

[71] *L.*, p. 525.

[72] *L.*, p. 275. This is not because some men are atheists. An 'atheist', according to Hobbes, is an ill-reasoner who fails to arrive at the hypothesis of a First Cause and is only inferentially a man who does not believe in a 'providential' God concerned with human conduct. Hobbes recognizes various classes of person in this respect—Atheists; those who recognize a First Cause but do not believe in a providential God; the insane and the immature; and those who recognize a First Cause and believe in a 'providential' God. It is only those who compose the last of these classes who are obliged by the Law of Nature.

[73] *L.*, p. 317, etc. But *E.W.*, II, 206, should be noticed.

[74] *L.*, p. 276.

it and this pleasure is not a reward and this pain is not a punishment.

It would appear, then, that according to Hobbes, God as the author of a law imposing the duty of endeavouring peace, is the ruler, not of all mankind, but only of those who acknowledge him in this character and therefore know him as its author; and this acknowledgment is a matter of 'belief', not of natural knowledge.[75] It is a loose way of talking to say that Hobbes anywhere said that we are obliged by the Laws of Nature because they are the Laws of God; what he said is that we would be obliged by them if they were laws in the proper sense, and that they are laws in the proper sense only if they are known to have been made by God.[76] And this means that they are laws in the proper sense only to those who know them to have been made by God. And who are these persons? Certainly not all mankind; and certainly only those of mankind who have acknowledged God to be maker of this law. The proposition, then, that Hobbes thought the Law of Nature to be law in the proper sense and to bind all mankind to an endeavour for peace, cannot seriously be entertained, whatever detached expressions (most of them ambiguous) there may be in his writings to support it.[77]

But further, if it is clear that even God's so-called 'natural subjects' can have no natural knowledge of God as the author of a universally binding precept to endeavour peace, it is clear also that Hobbes did not allow them to have any other sort of knowledge of God as the author of a Law of Nature of this kind. He expressly affirmed that if they claim to know God as the author of a law imposing the duty of endeavouring peace on all mankind by means of 'Sense Supernatural' (or 'Revelation', or 'Inspiration') their claim must be disallowed:[78] whatever else 'Sense Supernatural' might acquaint a man with, it cannot acquaint him with a universal law or with God as the author of a universal law. Nor can 'Prophecy' supply what 'natural knowledge' and 'Sense Supernatural' have failed

[75] Cf. *L.*, p. 300.
[76] *L.*, p. 403.
[77] E.g. *L.*, pp. 315, 363.
[78] *L.*, p. 275.

to supply. It is true that by 'Faith' a man may know God as the author of a law, but what 'Faith' can show us is not God as the author of a 'Natural Law' imposing duties on all men, but God as the author of a 'Positive Law' enjoining duties only upon those who by indirect covenant have acknowledged him as their ruler and have authorized him by their consent. In short, only where the endeavour for peace is enjoined by a positive law does it become a duty, this law alone being law in the proper sense as having a known author; and this law is binding only upon those who know its author.

The question, Did Hobbes think the Law of Nature to be law in the proper sense in respect of having a known author? resolves itself into the question, Who among mankind, because they know God as the author of a precept to endeavour peace, did Hobbes think to be bound to obey this precept? And in answering this question, we have found that Hobbes's much advertised distinction between God's 'natural subjects' and his subjects by covenant or acknowledgment is not as firmly based as we at first supposed: God's only 'Kingdom', in the proper sense, is a *civitas* in which God is owned as the author of the *civil* law. And the same conclusion appears when we consider the related question, By what authority does God impose this obligation? In the interpretation of Hobbes's writings we are now considering the authority of God over his so-called 'natural subjects' is said to derive from his Irresistible Power and consequently to be an authority to make law for all mankind.[79] But this cannot be so, whatever Hobbes seems to have said in these passages and elsewhere. Omnipotence or Irresistible Power is the characteristic of God as 'the First, and Eternal Cause of all things', but this God is not a lawmaker or a 'ruler', and we have been warned that to speak of him as a 'King' and as having a 'Kingdom' is to speak metaphorically. The God who appears as, in the proper sense, a 'ruler' (the imposer of authentic obligations) is not the 'ruler' of everybody and everything in the world, but only of 'as many of mankind as acknowledge his Providence'. It is in their ac-

---

[79] *L.*, pp. 90, 276, 315, 474, 551; *E.W.*, II, 209; VI, 170.

knowledgment of him as their ruler that he comes to be known as the author of law properly speaking; this acknowledgment is the necessary 'act' from which all obligation 'ariseth' because it is the act without which the ruler remains unknown.[80] Not Omnipotence, then, but a covenant or an acknowledgment is the spring of God's authority to make laws in the proper sense.

Now, besides having a known author, the Law of Nature, if it is to be law in the proper sense, must have two other characteristics; namely, it must be known or knowable by those who are obliged to obey it (that is, it must have been in some manner 'published' or 'declared'), and there must be an 'authentique interpretation' of it. Did Hobbes think that the Law of Nature has these characteristics?

In regard to the first, the interpretation of Hobbes we are now considering appears to be in no difficulty: it relies upon Hobbes's statements that the Law of Nature is declared by God to his natural subjects in the 'Dictates of Natural Reason' or of 'Right Reason'; that it is known in this manner 'without other word of God'; and that a sufficient knowledge of it is available even to those whose power of reasoning is not very conspicuous.[81] But, it may be asked how can a man know 'by the Dictates of Right Reason' that the endeavour for peace is a command emanating from a proper authority, and therefore imposing upon him a duty to obey, when 'Reason' (being, according to Hobbes, the power of discerning the probable cause of given occurrences or the probable effects of given actions or movements serving 'to convince the truth (not of fact, but) of consequence')[82] can neither itself supply, nor be the means of ascertaining, categorical injunctions? How can God 'declare his laws' (as *laws* and not merely as theorems) to mankind in 'the Dictates of Natural Reason'? And the answer to these inquiries is clear: nobody holding Hobbes's views about the nature of 'reason' could possibly hold God to be able to do anything of the sort. And if God cannot do this, then the whole idea of the Law of Nature being law in the proper sense and imposing duties on all mankind be-

[80] *L.*, pp. 97, 166, 317.
[81] *L.*, pp. 225, 275, 277, 554.
[82] *L.*, p. 292; *E.W.*, I, 3.

cause it is known and known to be the Law of God, collapses. No doubt there are occasions when Hobbes encourages us to think that he thought the Law of Nature was naturally known, *as a law in the proper sense* imposing upon all mankind the duty of endeavouring peace; he was not above speaking of 'natural duties'[83] (though he refused to recognize the expression 'natural justice'),[84] and we shall have to consider later why he encourages us to think in this manner. But there is also no doubt that, according to his own understanding of 'Reason', all that he may legitimately think is that the Law of Nature *as a set of theorems about human preservation* is known to all mankind in this manner.[85] In default, then, of evidence from the writings of Hobbes other than these unmistakably equivocal references to 'natural reason', we must conclude that the Law of Nature is not law in the proper sense, and that the duty to endeavour peace is not naturally known either to all mankind or even to God's so-called 'natural subjects'. What *is* known is the duty to endeavor peace when it is recognized as imposed by the positive law of God upon those who by indirect covenant have acknowledged his authority to impose this duty; it is known to them because it has been published to them either in the 'propheticall' word of God, or in the positive law of the *civitas;* and in the *civitas* 'prophecy' and the command of the Sovereign are not to be distinguished, for the Civil Sovereign is 'God's prophet'.[86]

The third characteristic of law in the proper sense is the existence of an 'authentique interpretation' of its meaning;[87] and this the Law of Nature manifestly lacks unless it is supplied by some

[83] *L.*, p. 277.

[84] *E.W.*, II, vi.

[85] *L.*, p. 286. The expression 'Right Reason' belongs to a well-established view of things in which it was supposed that 'reason', a 'divine spark', could acquaint mankind with at least some of its moral duties, but it is a view of things which Hobbes on most occasions is concerned expressly to deny. For Hobbes 'our natural reason' is 'the undoubted word of God' (*L.*, p. 286), but what it conveys is hypothetical information about causes and effects, not categorical information about duties; and there is even some inconsistency in his use of the expression '*our* reason'—'reason', properly speaking, is, for him, the power of reasoning, i.e. of drawing warrantable conclusions. The appearance, then, of this expression 'Right Reason' in Hobbes's writings is a signal to the attentive reader to be on his guard and to suspect equivocation.

[86] *L.*, p. 337.

[87] *L.*, pp. 211 *sq.*, 534; *E.W.*, II, 220.

positive and acknowledged authority, such as a civil sovereign or a 'prophet' instructed by God and acknowledged by his followers:[88] God himself cannot be the interpreter of the Law of Nature any more than he can be the interpreter of his Scriptural 'word'. In short, for Hobbes, there can be no interpreter or interpretation of the Law of Nature which is at once 'natural' or 'uncovenanted' and 'authentique'. It is true that the 'natural reason' or the 'conscience' of private men may be represented as interpreters of the Law of Nature,[89] but they cannot be thought to supply an 'authentique' interpretation of it as a law. When each man is his own interpreter, not only is it impossible to exclude the partiality of passion (and conscience, in the end, is only a man's good opinion of what he has done or is inclined to do), but the obligation of the law thus interpreted ceases to be a universal obligation to endeavour peace and becomes, at most, an obligation upon each man to obey his own *bona fide* version of the law—which is not enough. A law which may be different for each man under 'it' is not a law at all but merely a multiplicity of opinions about how the legislator (in this case, God) wishes us to behave.[90] There is, in fact, no law where there is no *common* authority to declare and interpret it.[91] Nor does it mend matters to suggest that each man is responsible to God for the *bona fide* character of his interpretation: this responsibility could only apply to that fraction of mankind who believed in a providential God concerned with human conduct.

The inquiry provoked by the interpretation of Hobbes's writings we are now considering has led us to the view that the question, Has the Law of Nature, according to Hobbes, the necessary and sufficient characteristics of a law in the proper sense binding all mankind to the duty of endeavouring peace? Or (in another form) Is the duty of endeavouring peace a 'natural', uncovenanted duty, binding

---

[88] *L.,* pp. 85, 317.

[89] *L.,* p. 249.

[90] Cf. *L.,* pp. 453, 531, 534. Compare Hobbes's rejection of 'writers' and 'books of Moral Philosophy' as authentic interpreters of the civil law (*L.,* p. 212). An 'authentique' interpretation must be single and authoritative, and without an interpretation there is no known law and therefore no law and no duty.

[91] *L.,* p. 98.

upon all men? must be answered in the negative. But this inquiry has also suggested that perhaps the more relevant questions are, In what circumstances did Hobbes think the Law of Nature acquires these characteristics? and, To whom is the endeavour for peace not only a rational course of conduct for those intent upon survival but a morally binding injunction? For, although Hobbes said much that pushes our thoughts in another direction, it seems clear that for him the Law of Nature possessed these characteristics only in certain circumstances and imposed duties only upon certain persons. In general, these circumstances are those in which to endeavour peace has become a rule of positive law, human or divine; and, in general, the persons bound are those only who know the author of this law and have acknowledged his authority to make it.[92] This seems to correspond with what I take to be Hobbes's deepest conviction about moral duties; namely, that there can be 'no obligation upon any man which ariseth not from some act of his own'.[93] But the bearing of this principle is not that, for Hobbes, the choice of him who is obliged creates the duty, but that where there has been no choice (covenant or acknowledgment) there is no known law-giver and therefore no law in the proper sense and no duty. And it is a principle which seems to me to exclude the possibility of 'natural' (that is, uncovenanted) duties. The necessary 'act' may be the acknowledgment of God in the belief in a 'providential' God concerned with human conduct; but, for those who live in a *civitas*, it is the act which creates and authorizes the civil sovereign because, for such persons, there are no duties which do not reach them as the commands of this sovereign.

---

[92] Hobbes, it is well known, distinguished between two classes of obligation — *in foro interno* and *in foro externo*. This distinction has been elucidated with great care and subtlety by Mr Warrender, but it will be agreed that it is subsidiary to the question we are now concerned with, namely; What, in Hobbes's view, are the necessary conditions of obligation of any sort? Consequently I do not propose to go into it here. It may, however, be remarked that Mr Warrender's view that Hobbes held that, *in the State of Nature*, the Laws of Nature bind always *in foro interno*, and *in foro externo* not always (Warrender, p. 52; *L.*, p. 121), is not quite convincing. What Hobbes must be understood to be saying is that the Laws of Nature, *where they are laws in the proper sense*, oblige always *in foro interno* and *in foro externo* not always. Is it not going further than the text warrants to interpret 'always' as meaning 'in all conditions of human life', including the State of Nature?

[93] *L.*, pp. 314, 317, 403, 448.

There may be other and more obscure thoughts to be taken into account, but it seems to me certain that Hobbes thought that, whatever may or may not belong to other conditions of human circumstance, the *civitas* is unquestionably a condition in which there is a law in the proper sense[94] (namely, the civil law), in which this law is the only law in the proper sense, and in which it is the duty of all subjects to endeavour peace. The reading of Hobbes in which this covenanted duty derives from a 'natural' duty, imposed antecedently upon all mankind by an independent and perpetually operative Law of Nature, ignores so many of Hobbes's conclusions about God, 'reason', human knowledge, 'the signification of words' and the conditions of moral obligation, that what it explains is little compared with what it leaves unaccounted for, and cannot be accepted as a satisfactory account. And besides these fundamental discrepancies, perhaps the most fertile source of the misunderstanding reflected in this interpretation is the confusion (for which Hobbes is responsible) between what he said about the 'Laws of Nature' as 'theorems concerning what conduceth to the conservation and defence' of mankind (namely, their availability to natural reason and their unquestionable intelligibility to even the meanest intellect) and what he said about them as morally binding injunctions—the confusion between reason which teaches and laws which enjoin.

FIVE

It is safe to say that every interpretation of Hobbes's moral theory leaves something that Hobbes wrote imperfectly accounted for. But it is reasonable to distinguish between those interpretations which conflict with some (perhaps, many and repeated) detached statements in the writings, and those which conflict with what may, perhaps, be considered the structural principles of Hobbes's view of things, though it is difficult to decide where to draw the line. Of the interpretations we have before us, the first seems to me the least

---

[94] *L.*, p. 443.

possible to accept, and the second (in which duty is understood to be an endeavour for peace according to the laws of the *civitas*) to be the most plausible because it conflicts least with what I take to be the structural principles of Hobbes's philosophy. Nevertheless, it must be acknowledged that Hobbes's statements about 'natural' duties imposed by a Natural Law (which are the central theme of the third interpretation) are not to be regarded as mere inadvertencies. It is true that they are inconsistent with some of Hobbes's most cherished principles, but they are far too numerous to be merely ignored; indeed, Mr Warrender has shown that, if they are abstracted from the whole, they are capable of composing together a tolerably complete moral theory. The situation we have on our hands (as I understand it) is, then, a set of philosophical writings in which there appear (not side by side, but almost inextricably mixed) a theory of moral obligation at once original and consistent with the other philosophical novelties to be found in them, and another account of moral obligation the vocabulary and general principles of which are conventional (though there are original touches of detail); and anyone disposed to find the one more significant than the other[95] may be expected to offer a more plausible explanation of the presence of what he finds less significant than that it springs merely from the confusion of Hobbes's thoughts. No doubt there is confusion at some points, but the presence of these two theories of obligation cannot be taken as an example of mere confusion.

Our question, in general, is: Why did Hobbes, in an enterprise designed to elucidate the ground and character of the obligations entailed in living in a *civitas*, run together two strikingly different (and at some points contradictory) accounts of moral obligation? And, in detail, our puzzle is to account for the discrepancies which appear in his writings of which the following are a brief selection.

---

[95] Besides the other reasons I have already stated for finding less to object to in the first of these two than the second, as an interpretation of Hobbes's writings, some weight may perhaps be given to the fact that Hobbes believed what he had written on the subject of moral obligation would appear offensively eccentric to his contemporaries (e.g., *L.*, p. 557), and he could scarcely have believed this if his theory were of the character Mr Warrender attributes to it.

1. He tells us that in nature 'every man has a right to everything; even to another's body', a right to govern himself according to his own judgment, 'to do anything he liketh', and to preserve himself in any manner that he finds expedient.[96] And he tells us that in nature every man has a 'natural' obligation to endeavour peace, imposed by a Natural Law which is the command of an omnipotent God.

2. He tells us that 'Reason' 'serves only to convince the truth (not of fact, but) of consequence',[97] that it deals only in hypothetical propositions about causes and effects, that its business in human conduct is to suggest fit means for achieving desired ends, and that nothing is obligatory on account of being reasonable; but he tells us also that the Laws of Nature, as laws and not merely as hypothetical conclusions about human preservation, are made known to us in 'the dictates of natural reason'.[98]

3. He tells us that, by means of reason, we may know God as the author of a moral law; and he tells us also that by reason we can know nothing whatever about God as the author of a moral law (or about his rewards and punishments in another life), but may know God only as a First Cause.

4. He tells us that 'our obligation to civil obedience . . . is before all civil law',[99] and suggests that it is a 'natural' and universal obligation and derives from it an obligation not to rebel against the civil sovereign; but elsewhere he denies the universality of this 'natural' obligation and specifies a class of person to whom it applies and makes it rest upon a covenant or an acknowledgment.

5. He asserts the independent *authority* of both Natural Law and Scripture, the one based on reason and the other on revelation, but elsewhere he tells us that, as members of a *civitas*, the *authority* of Natural Law derives from the imprimatur of the civil sovereign and that the precepts of Scripture are what the civil sovereign says they are.

[96] *L.*, p. 99.
[97] *L.*, p. 292, etc.
[98] *L.*, p. 275, etc.
[99] *E.W.*, II, 200.

6. He uses the word 'precept' of reason as an alternative to the expression 'general rule' of reason[100] to describe the first Law of Nature in an account which ends by denying that the prescriptive character of Natural Law has anything to do with its reasonableness.[101]

7. He uses the expression 'natural Laws' both when he means to denote the hypothetical conclusions of human reason about human self-preservation and to denote obligations imposed by God upon those who believe in a providential God and obligations alleged to be imposed by God upon all men except atheists(?), lunatics and children. This is a manner of speaking which is almost a confession of a design to confuse.

8. He says that a sovereign (without qualification) is obliged by the Law of Nature to 'procure the safety (and welfare) of the people' and must 'render an account thereof to God, the Author of the Law, and to none but him';[102] but, on his own showing (and apart from numerous other difficulties), this is at best true of a sovereign who belongs to that class of person who believes in a providential God concerned with human conduct, a class which (in Hobbes's writings) it is exceedingly difficult to distinguish from that of Christian believers.

9. He makes great play with a distinction between 'God's natural kingdom' and his 'natural subjects', and then tells us that the word 'kingdom' and the word 'subject' are merely metaphorical expressions in default of the 'artifice' of a 'covenant'.

10. He distinguishes between 'the first Founders, and Legislators of Commonwealths among the Gentiles'[103] who, in order to promote civil obedience and peace, encourage their subjects to believe the civil law has divine sanction, and the situation (as among the ancient Jews) where 'God himself' is said to establish a kingdom by covenant; but he ignores the fact that all that he has said about God and human imagination brands the expression 'God himself'

[100] *L.*, p. 100.
[101] *L.*, p. 122.
[102] *L.*, p. 258.
[103] *L.*, pp. 89–90.

as meaningless: God 'is' what he is believed or 'dreamed' to be, and he 'does' what he is believed or 'dreamed' to do.

Some commentators have believed themselves to have satisfactorily resolved some of these examples of discrepancy without having to resort to a general explanation, and perhaps the most notable of these resolutions is that attempted by Mr Warrender in respect of *Leviathan* p. 205.[104] But even that cannot be considered successful. He finds in this passage a *reductio ad absurdum* of natural-law theory which he conjectures Hobbes could not have intended, and he rejects what must be recognized as the literal meaning of the passage because he cannot bring himself to believe that Hobbes (who certainly both asserts and denies them elsewhere) could have concurred with its entailments. But whatever success or lack of success commentators have had in resolving some of the more superficial discrepancies of Hobbes's writings, there remains a core of discrepancy impervious to this kind of treatment, and we are provoked to seek a general explanation more plausible than mere native confusion of mind, careless reasoning and a propensity to exaggeration.

Hobbes's writings on civil obedience (and *Leviathan* in particular) may be taken to have a twofold purpose. It would appear that his project was to display a theory of obligation consistent with the tenets of his general philosophy and with his reading of human nature; and also to show his contemporaries where their civil duties lay and why they lay there, in order to combat the confusion and anarchical tendencies of current thought and conduct.[105] The first of these enterprises is an exercise in logic, and it is appropriately conducted in the vocabulary which Hobbes had made his own. The second, on the other hand, could not be successful unless it were

---

[104] Warrender, p. 167.

[105] If we distinguish (as we may) between an account of the dispositions and actions alleged to be morally obligatory and a doctrine designed to display the reason why whatever is believed to be obligatory is so, it may be observed, first, that, in so far as Hobbes was engaged in recommending new duties (which he is loth to do, *E.W.*, II, xxii), they were not inventions of his own but were the duties inherent in the emerging conditions of a modern State where governing is recognized as a sovereign activity; and secondly, that the two enterprises upon which Hobbes was (on this reading of him) engaged, conflict (where they do conflict) not notably in respect of the duties recognized but in respect of the reason given for their being duties.

framed in the idiom and the vocabulary of current political theory and thus present a doctrine whose novelties (if any) were assimilated to current prejudices about moral conduct. Now, as it turned out, these two enterprises (which in a more conventional writer might have been run together without notable discrepancy) conflicted with one another, not in matters of peripheral importance but in matters of central importance. Hooker, in an earlier generation, had found it possible to expound a doctrine of civil obedience, not very unlike Hobbes's more conventional theory, by making a few adjustments in the current natural-law theory, and Hobbes may be read (in one of his moods) as attempting the same sort of enterprise, though his adjustments were more radical and did not escape giving offence. But no conceivable adjustment of this conventional natural-law doctrine could result in an account of civil obligation even remotely compatible with his general philosophy. In short, if we have to choose between an explanation of the more important discrepancies in Hobbes's writing in terms of mere confusion or an explanation in terms of artful equivocation, I think the probability lies with the latter.

And if we do settle for an explanation of this sort, which recognizes Hobbes to have two doctrines, one for the initiated (those whose heads were strong enough to withstand the giddiness provoked by his scepticism) and the other for the ordinary man who must be spoken to in an idiom and a vocabulary he is accustomed to, and to whom novelties (both in respect of duties and in respect of their grounds) must be made to appear commonplaces, we are not attributing a unique and hitherto unheard of character to *Leviathan*. Numerous other writers on these topics (Plato, for example, Machiavelli and even Bentham) were the authors of works which contain at once, and imperfectly distinguished from one another, an esoteric and an exoteric doctrine; and the view that matters of this sort (indeed, political questions generally) are 'mysteries' to be discussed candidly and directly only with the initiated goes back to the beginnings of political speculation and was by no means dead in the seventeenth century.

I do not suppose that this account of Hobbes's thoughts on obligation will commend itself to everyone, and in the nature of the
case it cannot be demonstrated to be true. But what appears to me
probable is that the discrepancies in Hobbes's writings are of a
character to require some such general explanation.

SIX

Our study of Hobbes has reached some conclusions which most
readers will find difficult to avoid. It seems clear that he believed
that a rational disposition in human beings was to be indentified
as an endeavour for peace. And peace meant acknowledging all
others as our equal, keeping our promises, not displaying contempt
and hatred and not endeavouring to out-do all others in order to
have the elation of being recognized to occupy first place. This manner of living is suggested by reason, which also suggests the means
by which it may be instituted and maintained: it is the *civitas*. The
reward of its accomplishment is emancipation from the constant
fear of violent and shameful death at the hands of other man. And,
so far, the sufficient *cause* or *motive* for endeavouring peace is
found in fear of shameful death: fear prompts reason and reason
discloses what must be done to avoid the circumstances which generate fear.

We have looked further to find if Hobbes had anything to say in
support of his view that this endeavour is, in fact, not only reasonable, but also just—that is, morally obligatory. Here, we have observed, first, that Hobbes was certainly capable of distinguishing
between the sufficient causes for human conduct and the reasons
which may be given in justification of it. And further, we have observed the sort of reason which Hobbes considered adequate; namely, the existence of a law in the proper sense commanding this endeavour. Beyond this, there lies a region difficult to map. And the
best an explorer can do is to determine what he thinks to be its
more significant features and to give his reasons for preferring
these to others. And this is what I have done. But there is still
something more to be said.

The morality we have seen Hobbes to be defending is the morality of the tame man. It is still true that the greatest stimulus to the vital movement of the heart is the elation generated by being continuously recognized to be superior. But this greatest good must be foregone: pride, even when it does not degenerate into vain-glory, is too dangerous a passion to be allowed, even if its suppression somewhat dims the brilliance of life.

But, in the writings of Hobbes there is another line of argument, not extensively elaborated, but enough to push our thoughts in a different direction. In this line of thought the just disposition is still recognized to be an endeavour for peace and what is sought is still emancipation from the fear of violent and shameful death at the hands of other men, but the desired condition is to be attained, not by proud man, awakened by fear, surrendering his pride and becoming (by covenant) tame man, but by the moralization of pride itself. How can this happen?

Let us suppose a man of the character Hobbes supposed all men to be: a man unavoidably his own best friend and (on account of his weakness) subject to the fear of finding himself shamed and dishonoured and even killed. But let us also suppose that the preponderant passion of this man remains pride rather than fear; that he is a man who would find greater shame in the meanness of settling for mere survival than in suffering the dishonour of being recognized a failure; a man whose disposition is to overcome fear not by reason (that is, by seeking a secure condition of external human circumstances) but by his own courage; a man not at all without imperfections and not deceived about himself, but who is proud enough to be spared the sorrow of his imperfections and the illusion of his achievements; not exactly a hero, too negligent for that, but perhaps with a touch of careless heroism about him; a man, in short, who (in Montaigne's phrase) 'knows how to belong to himself', and who, if fortune turned out so, would feel no shame in the epitaph:

Par delicatesse
J'ai perdu ma vie.

Now, a man of this sort would not lack stimulus for the vital movement of his heart, but he is in a high degree self-moved. His endeavour is for peace; and if the peace he enjoys is largely his own unaided achievement and is secure against the mishaps that may befall him, it is not in any way unfriendly to the peace of other men of a different kind. There is nothing hostile in his conduct, nothing in it to provoke hostility, nothing censorious. What he achieves for himself and what he contributes to a common life is a complete alternative to what others may achieve by means of agreement inspired by fear and dictated by reason; for, if the unavoidable endeavour of every man is for self-preservation, and if self-preservation is interpreted (as Hobbes interprets it), not as immunity from death but from the fear of shameful death, then this man achieves in one manner (by courage) what others may achieve in another (by rational calculation). And, unlike others, he not only abstains from doing injury but is able to be indifferent to having to suffer it from others. In short, although this character looks, at first sight, much more like the *âme forte* of Vauvenargues than anything we might expect to find in Hobbes, there is nothing in it which conflicts with Hobbes's psychology, which, in fact, identifies differences between men as differences in their preponderant passions and can accommodate the man in whom pride occupies a greater place than fear.

Indeed, it is a character which actually appears in Hobbes's writings, and is, moreover, recognized there as just character. 'That which gives to human actions the relish of justice,' he says, 'is a certain Nobleness or Gallantness of courage (rarely found), by which a man scorns to be beholden for the contentment of life, to fraud or breach of promise. This justice of Manners, is that which is meant, where justice is called a virtue.'[106] He recognized that a man may keep his word, not merely because he fears the consequences of breaking it, but from 'a glory or pride in appearing not to need to break it'.[107] He identified magnanimity with just conduct

[106] *L.*, p. 114.
[107] *L.*, pp. 108; cf. p. 229.

that springs from 'contempt' of injustice, and recognized that men are sometimes prepared to lose their lives rather than suffer some sorts of shame.[108] And the only hindrance to our recognizing this as a genuinely Hobbesian character is the general assertion that Hobbes always used the word 'pride' in a derogatory sense.[109]

But this assertion is, in fact, too sweeping. It is, of course, true that Hobbes sometimes used the word 'pride' in a derogatory sense to indicate one of the three passions pre-eminent in causing strife;[110] but he also identified it with generosity, courage, noble-ness, magnanimity and an endeavour for glory,[111] and he distin-guished it from 'vain-glory', which is always a vice because it entails illusion and strife without the possibility of felicity.[112] In short, Hobbes (who took the conception 'pride' from the Augustinian tra-dition of moral and political theology) recognized the twofold mean-ing which the word has always carried. Pride, in that tradition, was the passion to be God-like. But it was recognized that this may be either the endeavour to put oneself in the place of God, or the en-deavour to imitate God. The first is a delusive insolvence in which a Satanic self-love, believing itself to be omnipotent, is not only the last analysis of every passion but the only operative motive, and conduct becomes the imposition of oneself upon the world of men and of things. This Hobbes, like every other moralist, recognized as a vice and an absolute bar to a peaceful condition of human cir-cumstance: it is the pride which provokes a destroying nemesis, the pride which Heraclitus said should be put out even more than a fire. But, as Duns Scotus said, there is no vice but it is the shadow of a virtue; and in the second manner of being God-like, self-love appears as self-knowledge and self-respect, the delusion of power over others is replaced by the reality of self-control, and the glory of the invulnerability which comes from courage generates magna-nimity and magnanimity, peace. This is the *virtue* of pride whose

[108] *E.W.*, II, 38.
[109] Strauss, p. 25.
[110] *L.*, pp. 57, 128, 246.
[111] *L.*, p. 96.
[112] *L.*, pp. 44, 77.

lineage is to be traced back to the nymph Hybris, the reputed mother of Pan by Zeus; the pride which is reflected in the *megalopsychos* of Aristotle and at a lower level in the wise man of the Stoics; the *sancta superbia* which had its place in medieval moral theology; and which was recognized by Hobbes as an alternative manner to that suggested by fear and reason of preserving one's own nature and emancipating oneself from the fear of shameful death and from the strife which this fear generates.

Nor is this idiom of the character of the just man without its counterpart in the writings of other moralists of the same general disposition as Hobbes. Spinoza, considering the same problem as Hobbes, indicated two alternative escapes into peace from the competitive propensities of human nature; the one generated by fear and prudential foresight which results in the law and order of the *civitas*, and the other the escape offered by the power of the mind over the circumstances of human life. And Hume, taking pride and humility (which, like Hobbes, he identified with fear)[113] as the simple passions, equally self-centred, recognized both as generators of virtue, but 'self-esteem' as the generator of the 'shining virtues'— courage, intrepidity, magnanimity, and the endeavour for the sort of glory in which 'death loses its terrors' and human life its contentiousness. But whereas Hume found the merit of pride as the motive for just conduct not only in its 'agreeableness' (identifying it with pleasure and humility with frustration) but also in its superior 'utility',[114] the question we have to ask ourselves about Hobbes is, Why did he not pursue this line or argument further? Why did he deny utility to pride and conclude that, in the end, 'the passion to be reckoned with is fear'?

And to this question Hobbes himself provided a clear answer, an answer less fully elaborated than Spinoza's but in principle the same: it is not because pride does not provide an adequate motive for a successful endeavour for peace, but because of the dearth of noble characters. 'This,' he says, 'is a generosity too rarely to be

---

[113] *Elements*, I, ix, 2.
[114] *Treatise*, II, i and iii; *Enquiries*, §263; *Essays*, xvi; The Stoic.

found to be presumed, especially in pursuers of wealth, command and sensual pleasure; which are the greatest part of Mankind.'[115] In short, Hobbes perceived that men lack passion rather than reason, and lack, above all, *this* passion. But where it is present, it is to be recognized as capable of generating an endeavour for peace more firmly based than any other and therefore (even in the *civitas*, where it is safe to be just) the surest motive for just conduct. Indeed, it seems almost to have been Hobbes's view that men of this character are a necessary cause of the *civitas*; and certainly it is only they who, having an adequate motive for doing so, may be depended upon to defend it when dissension deprives the sovereign of his power. And he saw in Sidney Godolphin the emblem of this character.[116] Nevertheless, even here Hobbes displays his disposition to be more interested in the causes or motives of just conduct than in the reasons for believing that we have an obligation to endeavour peace: 'pride' does not supply a reason, it is only a possible alternative cause.

There is, perhaps, one further observation to be made. Fear of shameful death, provoking reason to suggest the convenient articles of peace and the manner in which they may become the pattern of human life, generates the morality of the tame man, the man who has settled for safety and has no need of nobility, generosity, magnanimity or an endeavour for glory in order to move him to behave justly. And, in so far as this was Hobbes's view, he has been recognized as the philosopher of a so-called 'bourgeois' morality. But this is an idiom of the moral life which, in spite of Hobbes's individualistic reading of human nature, seems to intimate and point towards the notion of a 'common good'. It seems to suggest a single approved condition of human circumstances for all conditions of men, and morality as the art in which this condition is achieved and maintained. But there are qualifications to be noticed which tend to confirm the view that, with Kant and others, he was pre-eminently a philosopher of the morality of individuality. First,

---

[115] *L.*, p. 108.
[116] *L.*, Dedication, p. 548; *Vita* (1681), 240.

Hobbes was primarily concerned with motives for obeying civil law; he is less concerned with what a man might otherwise do with his life than with the minimum conditions in which the endeavour for peace could be the pattern of conduct for even the least well-disposed man. These minimum conditions are that there shall be one *law* for the lion and the ox and that both should have known and adequate motives for obeying it. And this, while perhaps intimating the disposition which generated the morality of the 'common good', does not itself entail it. And secondly, Hobbes had this other mood, in which pride and self-esteem are recognized to supply an adequate motive for endeavouring peace, and in this mood he was unmistakably a philosopher of the morality of individuality. This idiom of morality is 'aristocratic'; and it is neither inappropriate nor unexpected to find it reflected in the writings of one who (though he felt constrained to write for those whose chief desire was to 'prosper') himself understood human beings as creatures more properly concerned with honour than with either survival or prosperity.

NOTE TO P. 307

The precise manner in which Hobbes believed a *civitas* may be 'caused', or may be imagined to emerge, lies to one side of the subject of this essay, but it is an interesting topic, attractive if for no other reason than because of its difficulty and I propose to consider it briefly.[117]

Hobbes's position is that unless something is done to change his natural condition, no man is secure against the natural 'covetousness, lust, anger and the like' of his fellows and (consequently) has nothing better to look forward to than a nasty and brutish existence, frustrated and full of contention. Even in this state of nature, men (it is true) are capable of making contracts, agreements, covenants, etc., with one another, but these, so far from substan-

---

[117] In the following account I have had the advantage of suggestions kindly offered me by Mr J.M. Brown, who nevertheless must not be held responsible for the blunders it may still contain.

tially modifying the condition of insecurity, are themselves infected with this insecurity. And this is specially the case with covenants of mutual trust. For in these, one of the covenanters must perform his part of the bargain first, but he who does so risks being bilked; indeed, the risk that he whose part it is to be the second performer will not keep his promise (not necessarily because it may be against his interest to do so, but because 'avarice' and 'ambition' are apt to triumph over reason) must always be great enough to make it unreasonable for any man to consent to be a first performer. Thus, while in these conditions contracts may be made and executed, and even covenants of mutual trust, they always entail a risk which no reasonable man will take and they offer no extensive or reliable modification of the war of all men against all men.

This situation, however, would be transformed if there were a 'common power' acknowledged by all men to have the authority to compel the keeping of covenants; and Hobbes's question is: How may such a 'common power' be imagined to be 'caused' and what must be its character?

The only manner in which such a 'common power' may be erected, he tells us, is for every man to covenant with every man to transfer his natural *right* to govern himself and to preserve his own nature, and to relinquish his natural *power* (such as it is) to secure the fulfilment of his own desires, to one man or an assembly of men, and to 'acknowledge himself to be the author of whatsoever he that so beareth their person, shall act, or cause to be acted, in those things which concern the common peace and safety; and therein to submit their wills, every one to his will, and their judgments, to his judgment'.

Now, accepting for the moment the conclusion, namely, that those who have put themselves in this situation will enjoy what they seek to enjoy, peace, what we have to consider is the intelligibility of the process by which it is reached. Certain difficulties appear. The covenant by means of which this common power is purported to be established is unmistakably what Hobbes calls a covenant of mutual trust, and it is made by men in a state of nature, consequently (unless we are given some cogent reason for thinking otherwise) it cannot be supposed to be exempt from the considerations which make all such covenants unreasonably risky undertakings for the first performer and therefore not to be relied upon by reasonable men. It is true that its terms are different from the terms of any other covenant of mutual trust; but how can its terms (that is, *what* is promised) transform a covenant of a kind in which it is unreasonably risky to be the first performer into one in which the risk (if any) is not unreasonable? It is true, also that it is (what not all other covenants of mutual trust are) a covenant to which many are parties; but, since there is no reason why an ordinary covenant of mutual trust should not be of this sort, and if it were so, there is no reason why it should be less reasonable to suspect non-performance on the part of at least some of the participants, the multilateral character of this covenant does not appear to distinguish it to any advantage. And further, Hobbes's words often seem to suggest that the mere entering into this covenant, the mere 'signing' of it (so to speak), generates the 'common power', and it is not easy to understand how this can be so.

But if we go again to what Hobbes wrote we may, perhaps, find him to be saying something that avoids these difficulties. This would, I think, be so if we were to interpret him as follows:

There will be 'peace' and a condition in which covenants will be lasting and constant, only if there is a Sovereign to enforce peace and to compel the keeping of covenants. This Sovereign, in order to perform his office, must have *authority* (that is, right), and he must have *power*. The only way in which he can be imagined to acquire authority is by means of a covenant of the sort already described, and in order to have authority nothing more than this covenant is needed. Therefore such a covenant (or something like it) may be recognized as a necessary 'cause' of a *civitas*. And, further, it may, perhaps, also be recognized as empirically necessary as a means of generating the *power* required by the Sovereign, because it is hardly to be imagined that a number of individuals will in fact acknowledge his authority in the acts and dispositions of obedience which constitute his power unless they have covenanted to do so. Nevertheless, the covenant by itself is not the sufficient cause of a *civitas;*

it gives authority, but it merely promises power. The necessary and sufficient cause of a Sovereign possessed of the authority and the power required to establish a condition of 'peace' is a covenant of this sort combined with a sufficiently widespread disposition (displayed in overt acts) to observe its terms; for the Sovereign's power is only the counterpart of his subjects' disposition to obey. And consequently, we are provoked to look in Hobbes's account for some argument which will convince us that it is reasonable to expect that this covenant, unlike others made in the state of nature, will be kept. For, perhaps with some colour of paradox, it now appears that the power necessary to establish peace and to compel the keeping of covenants is generated not by making the covenant but only in the process of keeping it, that is, in dispositions and acts of obedience. In short, we have been convinced that it must always be unreasonable to be the first performer in an ordinary covenant of mutual trust in the state of nature, and what Hobbes has now to demonstrate to us is that it is not unreasonable for any man to be the first performer in *this* covenant of mutual trust. And it may be observed, at once, that this condition of affairs cannot be made to spring from there being a power to compel those who are to be the second performers to keep their promises, because what we are seeking is an intelligible explanation of how such a power can be 'errected'.

Now, on this question Hobbes seems to have made his position doubly secure. He undertakes to show us: first, that it is reasonable to be the first performer in this covenant even if there is no reasonable expectation that the other covenanters will keep their promises; and further, that there is in fact a reasonable expectation that a significant number of covenanters will keep their promises, and that in the case of *this* covenant (unlike that of ordinary covenants) this is enough to make it not unreasonable to be a first performer.

First, a party to this covenant is, to be sure, taking some risk if he obeys a Sovereign authority who is unable to compel the obedience of the other parties and if he has no reasonable expectation that they also will obey. Nevertheless, it is not an unreasonable risk because what he stands to lose is insignificant compared with what he stands to gain, and because, in fact, unless someone is the first performer in this covenant the 'common power' necessary to peace can never come into existence.[118] This is a cogent argument; it observes a relevant distinction between the covenant to authorize the exercise of sovereign authority and other covenants of mutual trust, and it points out the entailment of this in respect of the reasonableness of being a first performer in this covenant; but most readers of Hobbes will look for something to fortify it. And, at least without going against anything he wrote, this may be found in the following considerations.

One of the important differences between the covenant to acknowledge the authority of a Sovereign and thus endow him with power and any other covenant of mutual trust is that it may be effectively fulfilled even if all the parties do *not* behave as they have promised to behave. In an ordinary covenant of mutual trust between two the first performer is not requited unless the other keeps his word when his time comes. And this is true, also, in an ordinary covenant of mutual trust (one concerned with goods and services) in which there are many participants; the first performer, and each other performer, is deprived of something significant unless *all* the participants perform. But in this covenant among many to obey a Sovereign authority, the first performer, and each other willing performer, loses nothing if, instead of all performing, only some do so—as long as those who do are sufficient in number to generate the power necessary to compel those who are not disposed to obey. And while it may be unreasonable to expect that ambition and avarice will distract none of the parties to this covenant from keeping their promise to obey, it is not unreasonable to expect that a sufficient number will be immune from this distraction. Thus, there is a feature in this covenant which distinguishes it from all others and makes it not unreasonable to be a first performer; and every party to it is potentially a first performer. But, since what is sought by all reasonable men and what is counted upon by a first

---

[118] Perhaps, for the generation of the *civitas*, it is necessary to assume a man, not 'reasonable', but proudly careless of the consequences of being the first for peace; if so, there is some authority in Hobbes for this assumption.

performer in this covenant is a durable condition of peace, the position is, perhaps, better understood as one in which it is not unreasonable to be a first performer and to go on performing because it is not unreasonable to expect that enough of the other parties will themselves voluntarily perform for enough of the time to generate enough power in the sovereign to force those who on any particular occasion may not be disposed to obey. For, the reasonableness of being a first performer does not depend upon his having a reasonable expectation that there will be a permanent body of particular persons who will always be disposed to requite his trust in them; it will suffice if he has a reasonable expectation that at any particular time there will be enough who are so disposed. The clouds of avarice, ambition and the like sweep over the sky and their shadows fall upon this man and now upon that; no single man can be depended upon to keep the covenant all the time and upon every occasion. But this is not necessary; it is enough if enough may on any occasion be reasonably depended upon to endow by their willing obedience the sovereign with enough power to terrify into obedience those who on that occasion are not disposed to obey.

The argument, then, seems to run, briefly, as follows: Natural reason warns us against being the first performer in all ordinary covenants of mutual trust; and it tells us, also, that it is in our interest to seek peace and it suggests the manner in which peace may emerge. The necessary condition of peace is a Sovereign at once authoritative and powerful. The authority of this Sovereign can derive only from a covenant of mutual trust of every man with every man in which they transfer to him their natural right to govern themselves and in which they own and acknowledge all his commands in respect of those things which concern the common peace and safety as if they were their own. But the power of this Sovereign to enforce his commands derives only from those who have thus covenanted to obey actually obeying. A start must be made somewhere, and it must be shown to be a reasonable beginning. Is it not reasonable to expect that, having been reasonable enough to have made the covenant, enough men at any one time will be reasonable enough (that is, will be free enough from avarice and ambition and the like to recognize where their interest lies) to be disposed to keep it? And if this is so, it becomes a not unreasonable risk for any man to be the first performer. And every party to this covenant is a potential first performer. 'This is the generation of that great Leviathan ... to which we owe under the Immortal God, our peace and defence.'

It must be acknowledged, however, that this account shows not that it is undeniably reasonable to be a first performer in this covenant to set up a sovereign authority (or even that it is undeniably not unreasonable to be such), but only that the risk entailed here is far more reasonable (or far less unreasonable) than the risk entailed in an ordinary covenant of mutual trust. And since, as I understand it, what Hobbes is seeking is a demonstration of reasonableness and not merely the probability of superior reasonableness, I must suspect that this account is either faulty or incomplete. To what extent the supposition of a man (such as Hobbes understood Sidney Godolphin to have been) careless of the consequences of being bilked as the first performer in this covenant, a man of 'pride' and not of 'reason', supplies what is lacking, the reader must decide for himself.

"The Moral Life in the Writings of Thomas Hobbes" was a lecture given at the University of Nottingham. It was first published in the original edition of *Rationalism in Politics*.

Logos and telos

All readers of Hobbes are aware that he counted himself an opponent of Aristotle. 'I believe', he wrote in *Leviathan*, 'that scarce anything can be more absurdly said in natural Philosophy, than that which is called Aristotle's *Metaphysiques*, nor repugnant to Government than much of what is said in his *Politiques*; nor more ignorant than a great part of his *Ethiques*'. And his writings elsewhere echo these sentiments. But most readers suspect this announcement of rejection (although it is qualified) to be somewhat exaggerated and we have had our suspicion confirmed by numerous writers (Brandt, Strauss, Peters, Warrender etc.) who point to various Aristotelian ingredients deeply imbedded in Hobbes's thought. This, however, does not satisfy Professor Spragens who has set himself the task of exploring what he believes to be the systematic (not merely sporadic or incidental) relationship between 'the Aristotelian model of the world' and that of Thomas Hobbes. He suggests that Hobbes accepted the 'underlying framework' of the Aristotelian model but transformed it by substituting ideas of his own for each of its component concepts, and he contends that when this transformation is understood in detail it 'goes a long way toward resolv-

351

ing some of the apparent paradoxes of Hobbes's thought and its relation to the Aristotelian tradition'.

This thesis is not seriously disputed and Professor Spragens's
task is not to demolish contrary views but to make us understand
the systematic relationship between Hobbes and Aristotle more
thoroughly. The reader will have to put up with some fashionable
talk about paradigms and 'paradigm transformation' and he will
quickly perceive that for Professor Spragens there is no worthwhile
distinction to be made between physics and metaphysics. But he
should persevere; what follows is not vitiated by these eccentricities. In three chapters Hobbes's acceptance of the Aristotelian universe as an homogeneous order composed of things in motion and
his transformation of the Aristotelian concepts of homogeneity, of
motion and of things is unfolded with care and candour. Where Aristotle finds teleological change, movement in which a potential is
actualized and governed always by its preordained destination (its
final cause), Hobbes found only continuous incidental movement,
motion composing an endless chain of purposeless collisions ('there
is no cause of motion except a body continuous and moved'),
change which is the deflection of a moving body and (in the last
resort) is always and only change of place—in short, a universe not
composed of finite, teleological changes but of infinite inertial
movement. Where Aristotle found the world to be composed of substance and motion, the identity of each distinguishable thing being
its share in 'substance', and motion being change in which this
identity is confirmed and explored, Hobbes found only 'bodies'
('things placed') moving in respect of their impacts upon one another, the universe being 'the Aggregate of all Bodies'. And where
Aristotle understood the cosmos to be not only composed of various
finite identities each seeking its own destiny but to be itself a system exhibiting a single 'principle of motion and change' and free
from notable teleological cross-purposes, Hobbes understood the
movements of its component bodies to be mere occurrences caused
by earlier occurrences, and 'mere nature' to be without any purposive coherence.

All this is carefully set out; and if one allows for some exaggeration in pointing up the contrasts and overlooks a valiant (but not, I think, successful) attempt to specify Aristotelian 'substance', it is illuminating. But there is more to come. Professor Spragens makes it the starting point of his second thesis which concerns Hobbes's theory of civil association and, incidentally, Aristotle's theory of *polis*-life.

He holds that, in principle and certainly with Aristotle and Hobbes, the aim of a 'political theory' is to display human association (and particularly civil association) in its relation to a cosmology; that to do so presented no problem to Aristotle for whom political association was at once 'natural' and *logistikon* because *logos* was inherent in 'nature'; that Hobbes, premising the absence of *logos* from 'nature', encountered serious difficulties which some of his commentators have regarded as fatal and from which others have sought to rescue him, usually by denying that the premise is Hobbesian; that, when properly understood, there is a close relationship between his cosmological 'model' and his civil philosophy but that (contrary to his own view of the matter) it is analogical, not implicatory.

This is a complicated and contentious thesis; and I cannot help thinking that Professor Spragens would have found himself obliged to modify it if, in addition to his careful elaboration of the Aristotelian–Hobbesian contrasts, teleological change/inertial motion, and substance/body, he had given us a comparable chapter on Reason/Reasoning devoted to Aristotelian and Hobbesian man. Of course he does not neglect the topic, but he allows it to be overshadowed by biology and physics and consequently it never emerges that, in spite of significant differences, both these writers regard human conduct as an intelligent engagement and human association as transactions of agreement or disagreement, and that the differences between their cosmological 'models' is not the difference between a universe instinct with *logos* and one from which *logos* has been excluded.

The contrast we are offered is, briefly, as follows. For Aristotle man is a part of 'nature'. This means that human conduct is teleological, aimed at achieving the 'excellence' potential and common to all human beings. Association in this enterprise is 'natural' to human beings and *polis*-life is such association. For Hobbes, also, man is part of 'nature'. But this means that he is merely a body among bodies, tied to the wheel of inertial motion, devoid of any quality of 'becoming', without any common substantive excellence (potential or otherwise) to achieve, perpetually liable to be inhibited or deflected by other equally powerful moving bodies, each impelled by an insatiable appetite to keep on the move and aware only of a *summum malum*—stoppage (death)—which, unlike Aristotelian excellence, is divisive and not integrative. Human conduct is 'behaviour' and 'nature' (here, human nature) is red in tooth and claw. There is nothing in this 'nature', from which *logos* has been excluded, to portend a release from this condition, but its contentiousness may, perhaps, be 'contained' by an artifice. Civil association is such a containment and it is founded upon fear of ill-success in the satisfaction of appetite; that is, inertial motion.

But, although neither of these accounts, so far as it goes, is exactly incorrect, both, I think, are inadequate. This is an attenuated Aristotle and a sadly foreshortened Hobbes.

Professor Spragens insists that in the Aristotelian universe 'everything that moved naturally moved in the same way', that there were 'no lines of differentiation among different characteristic modes of behaving in different forms of life', that the *logos* in 'nature' was a uniform principle of teleological change, and consequently that physics and politics belong to the same universe of discourse. But this insistence upon uniformity is overdone. Human conduct, for Aristotle, displayed *logos* in virtue of being deliberate, of being in terms of educated and understood choices, and not on account of being (like all activity) teleological. The 'incontinent' man was not an 'accident', like a monster; he was one who had himself made wrong choices. Human association was not like that of bees and ants; it was in terms of words which had meanings and of agreements, disagreements and compromises. And *polis*-life, association expressly concerned with the achievement of human excellence, was an engagement of deliberation and persuasion which Aristotle recognized as an historic human achievement of self-understanding and practice, differentiated even from other modes of human association, such as 'tribal' life. In short, human excellence was not the outcome of a process like that in which an acorn (barring accidents) matured into an oak tree; it was the outcome of a procedure which had to be learned. Not only was the condition itself unique to human beings as the excellence of anything is unique to its kind, but it was sought in a unique engagement of selfconscious self-enactment. Indeed, there is room for doubt whether, in the end, human excellence (the 'purpose' human beings are joined in seeking) was, for Aristotle, anything more substantial than this deliberative self-enactment, and whether the good *polis* was anything more than that which had the constitution best disposed for deliberating and reaching genuinely common decisions about what to do in contingent situations.

The decisive feature of Hobbes's universe is the exclusion of Aristotelian *telos* and with it any notion either that human beings might naturally be joined in seeking a common human excellence or that there might be for any man a conclusion to his activity, a condition of rest which he might seek and recognize as his *summum bonum*. Human conduct is each man seeking continuous success in satisfying an endless succession of wants; ill-success is evil, and the greatest evil is the termination of his endeavour, death. Nevertheless, human beings are distinguished from other moving bodies in respect of the selfconsciousness of this enterprise, of their ability to time and to calculate their moves and to converse with one another not by making noises but in words which have agreed meanings. They act and respond to actions and they are inventive of wants; they have imagination and live much of their lives in the future. And unlike the relationship of a tree to the earth in which it grows, men are related to one another in terms of understood conditions. None of this escapes Professor Spragens, but he contends that Hobbes accommodates it in his cosmology by reducing it (without remainder) to inertial motion: the model is that of heavy bodies falling. For Hobbes there is nothing uniquely human. This cannot, I think, be sustained.

There are, then, human purposes or at least deliberate responses to situations; but since there is no uniting purpose the endeavours of each man are likely to be thwarted by those of others. Men may be intermittent (though necessarily unreliable) co-operators, they make promises and sometimes keep them, but they are certainly not natural friends. Indeed, their condition is the most exasperating of all conditions—that of natural enemies and unavoidable partners. They are engaged in an interminable race devoid of rules and the emblem of the satisfaction of all wants is to be and to remain ahead of all other contestants. But this sought-after position of superiority is not only relative to the inferiority of that of others; its worth lies in the 'glory' which accompanies it and this 'glory' lies only in the acknowledgement of others. A human being, for Hobbes, is not merely a body with an urge for self-preservation: he certainly 'shuns death' as the greatest of evils but his wants are not confined to death-avoidance. The human 'state of nature' is a profoundly 'social' condition. And I emphasize this because Professor Spragens considers it to be a condition of total disorder and disassociation because it lacks Aristotelian *telos*.

The natural condition of human beings is, however, one of net dissatisfaction: an undeniable urge to be, to remain and to be recognized to be first and fear of ill-success always exceeding hope of success. And the question to which Hobbes addresses himself is, How may the perils, the insecurities and the disasters inherent in this condition be abated?

Professor Spragens describes Hobbes's intellectual situation as follows: (1) Since there is 'no human content' to Hobbes's cosmology because it assumes 'that the entire natural order including man moves in fundamentally the same way' (inertial motion, not teleological change) it can provide no answer to this uniquely human predicament; (2) nevertheless this cosmology did provide Hobbes with an 'organizational paradigm' which resonates and is reflected in his answer—that is, in what Professor Spragens calls Hobbes's 'political theory'.

The first of these contentions I find puzzling, and not only on account of a suggestion of incoherence. As I understand Hobbes the predicament he is considering is uniquely human although the condition it generates is, in some respects, common to all moving bodies; it calls for an answer in terms of uniquely human conduct. But I cannot understand how this can be so for Professor Spragens's Hobbes who is alleged to have accommodated human beings and human conduct in the universe by reducing emotion, memory, imagination, will, choice, speech, deliberation, agreement and disagreement, reasoning and even selfconsciousness to 'appetite' and 'aversion'—words which stand for that inertial motion which is common to all bodies whatsoever; and the universe is merely the aggregate of such bodies. 'Man, as a natural creature, is no different' from any other moving body. His 'natural tendency' is the 'universal tendency of nature', the impulse to keep moving; and he is nothing but this tendency. Who, then, is this other man whom the universe is alleged not to accommodate, the man who can devise a cosmology and perhaps a civil order, and where may we expect to meet him? He is, of course, 'nature's most Excellent work', rational man. And Professor Spragens errs only in not allowing Hobbes's cosmology to contain intelligent movement; perhaps on account of some confusion between *telos* and *logos*.

In his second contention, however, he is on the other tack, concerned with the resources of a cosmology which recognizes only universal and homogeneous inertial movement, not in respect of their incapacity to provide the conceptual structure of the notional condition in which the perils and insecurities of rational man's natural condition are abated, but in respect of their capacity to do so. Here he has some interesting observations, but they do not carry him very far mainly because he never holds clearly before himself the exact character of the civil condition which constitutes this abatement. For example, human fear of being thwarted in the satisfaction of wants he takes (plausibly enough) to be an exhibition of inertial motion, and he notices that Hobbes not unreasonably conjectures that this fear is a motive second to none for seeking an abatement of 'natural' insecurity. But he exaggerates its place in Hobbes's theory of civil association, calling it not merely the 'impetus' for the establishment of this condition, but the 'cause' of it.

The decision to seek 'peace' instead of 'glory' may be taken from a variety of motives and Hobbes thinks 'fear' is the most compelling of these; but neither fear nor any other emotion is capable of *devising* civil association. It will not appear unless it is deliberately devised, and human beings must be shewn to be intellectually, not merely emotionally, capable of this invention. I think it is fair to say that Hobbes's cosmology excludes one mode of association; namely, that in which the human beings concerned surrender themselves to a *telos* and are joined in terms of the pursuit of a single substantive purpose. But the device Hobbes sets before his readers, that of association in terms of the recognition of the authority of rules of conduct, has no counterpart in a universe composed of bodies characterized solely by inertial motion.

Hobbes's exploration of this mode of association is intricate but it turns upon the assumption that human beings are what they believe themselves to be and are bound (that is, subject to authority) only when they bind themselves. Those who believe themselves to be subject to a natural law in virtue of recognizing the authority of God its author might be supposed to have a head start of others who entertain no such belief. They recognize themselves to have natural obligations which might be turned into civil laws. And Hobbes examines their situation at length. But he did not think that association in terms of the authority of a positive civil law depended upon any such belief. He conceived it possible for a set of human beings themselves to erect and authorize a law-making authority. Indeed, he had understood them to be, even in the 'state of nature', well aware of rules and rule-making; they converse with one another in words and to use a language is, for him, to be party to a covenant in which meanings (that is, rules) are agreed. What was lacking and what might abate their insecurity was an identifiable rule-maker, exactly specified rules, a procedure of adjudication and the assurance that rules cannot be breached with impunity. These are the features of civil association. And while this condition is possible to human beings who are not joined in seeking a common excellence and who have no *summum bonum* in which to rest, it could not be devised and 'erected' by bodies tied to the wheel of inertial motion. And, of course, what Professor Spragens calls 'politics' and Hobbes calls civil association is anything but inertial motion; it is, precisely, an abatement of the competition to satisfy wants. Whether or not the 'erection' of *civitas* is properly to be described in terms of inertial motion, its operation is certainly not this.

"Logos and Telos" first appeared as a review of *The Politics of Motion: the World of Thomas Hobbes* by Thomas Spragens, Jr. in *Government and Opposition*, Volume 9, Number 2, 1974. It is new to this edition of *Rationalism in Politics*.

PART FOUR

Reflections on modern politics

The masses in
representative democracy

ONE

The course of modern European history has thrown up a character whom we are accustomed to call the 'mass man'. His appearance is spoken of as the most significant and far-reaching of all the revolutions of modern times. He is credited with having transformed our way of living, our standards of conduct and our manners of political activity. He is, sometimes regretfully, acknowledged to have become the arbiter of taste, the dictator of policy, the uncrowned king of the modern world. He excites fear in some, admiration in others, wonder in all. His numbers have made him a giant; he proliferates everywhere; he is recognized either as a locust who is making a desert of what was once a fertile garden, or as the bearer of a new and more glorious civilization.

All this I believe to be a gross exaggeration. And I think we should recognize what our true situation is in this respect, what precisely we owe to this character, and the extent of his impact, if we understood more clearly who this 'mass man' is and where he has come from. And with a view to answering these questions, I propose to engage in a piece of historical description.

It is a long story, which has too often been made unintelligible by being abridged. It does not begin (as some would have us understand) with the French Revolution or with the industrial changes of the late eighteenth century; it begins in those perplexing centuries which, because of their illegibility, no historian can decide whether they should properly be regarded as a conclusion or a preface, namely the fourteenth and fifteenth centuries. And it begins, not with the emergence of the 'mass man', but with an emergence of a very different kind, namely, that of the human individual in his modern idiom. You must bear with me while I set the scene for the entry of the character we are to study, because we shall mistake him unless we prepare ourselves for his appearance.

TWO

There have been occasions, some of them in the distant past, when, usually as a consequence of the collapse of a closely integrated manner of living, human individuality has emerged and has been enjoyed for a time. An emergence of this sort is always of supreme importance; it is the modification not only of all current activities, but also of all human relationships from those of husband, wife and children to those of ruler and subject. The fourteenth and fifteenth centuries in western Europe were an occasion of this kind. What began to emerge, then, was conditions so preeminently favourable to a very high degree of human individuality, and human beings enjoying (to such a degree and in such numbers) the experience of 'self-determination' in conduct and belief, that it overshadows all earlier occasions of the sort. Nowhere else has the emergence of individuals (that is, persons accustomed to making choices for themselves) either modified human relationships so profoundly, or proved so durable an experience, or provoked so strong a reaction, or explained itself so elaborately in the idiom of philosophical theory.

Like everything else in modern Europe, achievement in respect of human individuality was a modification of medieval conditions of life or thought. It was not generated in claims and assertions on behalf of individuality, but in sporadic divergencies from a condition of human circumstance in which the opportunity for choice was narrowly circumscribed. To know oneself as the member of a family, a group, a corporation, a church, a village community, as the suitor at a court or as the occupier of a tenancy, had been, for the vast majority, the circumstantially possible sum of self-knowledge. Not only were ordinary activities, those concerned with getting a living, communal in character, but so also were decisions, rights and responsibilities. Relationships and allegiances normally sprang from status and rarely extricated themselves from the analogy of kinship. For the most part anonymity prevailed; individual human character was rarely observed because it was not there to be observed. What differentiated one man from another was insignificant when compared with what was enjoyed in common as members of a group of some sort.

This situation reached something of a climax in the twelfth century. It was modified slowly, sporadically and intermittently over a period of about seven centuries, from the thirteenth to the twentieth century. The change began earlier and went more rapidly in some parts of Europe than in others; it penetrated some activities more readily and more profoundly than others; it affected men before it touched women; and during these seven centuries there have been many local climaxes and corresponding recessions. But the enjoyment of the new opportunities of escape from communal ties gradually generated a new idiom of human character.

It emerged first in Italy: Italy was the first home of the modern individual who sprang from the break-up of medieval communal life. 'At the close of the thirteenth century', writes Burckhardt, 'Italy began to swarm with individuality; the ban laid upon human personality was dissolved; a thousand figures meet us, each in his own special shape and dress.' The *uomo singolare*, whose conduct was marked by a high degree of self-determination and a large number of whose activities expressed personal preferences, gradually detached himself from his fellows. And together with him appeared, not only the *libertine* and the *dilettante*, but also the *uomo unico*, the man who, in the mastery of his circumstances, stood alone and was a law to himself. Men examined themselves and were not dismayed by their own want of perfection. This was the character which Petrarch dramatized for his generation with unmatched skill and unrivalled energy. A new image of human nature appeared— not Adam, not Prometheus, but Proteus—a character distinguished from all others on account of his multiplicity and of his endless power of self-transformation.

North of the Alps, events took a similar course, though they moved more slowly and had to contend with larger hindrances. In England, in France, in the Netherlands, in Spain, in Switzerland, in Poland, Hungary and Bohemia, and particularly in all centres of municipal life, conditions favourable to individuality, and individuals to exploit them, appeared. There were few fields of activity untouched. By the middle of the sixteenth century they had been so firmly established that they were beyond the range of mere suppression: not all the severity of the Calvinist *régime* in Geneva was sufficient to quell the impulse to think and behave as an independent individual. The disposition to regard a high degree of individuality in conduct and in belief as the condition proper to mankind and as the main ingredient of human 'happiness', had become one of the significant dispositions of modern European character. What Petrarch did for one century, Montaigne did for another.

The story of the vicissitudes of this disposition during the last four centuries is exceedingly complex. It is a story, not of steady growth, but of climaxes and anti-climaxes, of diffusion to parts of Europe at first relatively ignorant of it, of extension to activities from which it was at first excluded, of attack and defence, of confidence and of apprehension. But, if we cannot pursue it in all its detail, we may at least observe how profoundly this disposition imposed itself upon European conduct and belief. In the course of a few hundred years, it was magnified into an ethical and even into a metaphysical theory, it gathered to itself an appropriate understanding of the office of government, it modified political manners and institutions, it settled itself upon art, upon religion, upon industry and trade and upon every kind of human relationship.

In the field of intellectual speculation the clearest reflection of this profound experience of individuality is to be seen in ethical theory. Almost all modern writing about moral conduct begins with the hypothesis of an individual human being choosing and pursuing his own directions of activity. What appeared to require explanation was not the existence of such individuals, but how they could come to have duties to others of their kind and what was the nature of those duties; just as the existence of other minds became a problem to those who understood knowledge as the residue of sense experience. This is unmistakable in Hobbes, the first moralist of the modern world to take candid account of the current experience of individuality. He understood a man as an organism governed by an impulse to avoid destruction and to maintain itself in its own characteristic and chosen pursuits. Each individual has a natural right to independent existence: the only problem is how he is to pursue his own chosen course with the greatest measure of success, the problem of his relation to 'others' of his kind. And a similar view of things appeared, of course, in the writings of Spinoza. But even where an individualistic conclusion was rejected, this autonomous individual remained as the starting point of ethical reflection. Every moralist in the seventeenth and eighteenth centuries is concerned with the psychological structure of this assumed 'individual': the relation of 'self' and 'others' is the common form of all moral theory of the time. And nowhere is this seen more clearly to be the case than in the writings of Kant. Every human being, in virtue of not being subject to natural necessity, is recognized by Kant to be a Person, an end in himself, absolute and autonomous. To seek his own happiness is the natural pursuit of such a person; self-love is the motive of the choices which compose his conduct. But as a rational human being he will recognize in his conduct the universal conditions of autonomous personality; and the chief of these conditions is to use humanity, as well in himself as in others, as an end and never as a means. Morality consists in the recognition of individual personality whenever it appears. Moreover, personality is so far sacrosanct that no man has either a right or a duty to promote the moral perfection of another: we may promote the 'happiness' of others, but we cannot promote their 'good' without destroying their 'freedom' which is the condition of moral goodness.

In short, whatever we may think of the moral theories of modern Europe, they provide the clearest evidence of the overwhelming impact of this experience of individuality.

But this pursuit of individuality, and of the conditions most favourable to its enjoyment, was reflected also in an understanding of the proper office of government and in appropriate manners of governing and being governed, both modifications of an inheritance from the Middle Ages. We have time only to notice them in their most unqualified appearance, namely, in what we have come to call 'modern representative democracy'. This manner of governing and being governed appeared first in England, in the Netherlands and in Switzerland, and was later (in various idioms) extended to other parts of Western Europe and the United States of America. It is not to be understood either as an approximation to some ideal manner of government, or as a modification of a manner of government (with which it has no connection whatever) current for a short while in certain parts of the ancient world. It is simply what emerged in Western Europe where the impact of the aspirations of individuality upon medieval institutions of government was greatest.

The first demand of those intent upon exploring the intimations of individuality was for an instrument of government capable of transforming the interests of individuality into rights and duties. To perform this task government required three attributes. First, it must be single and supreme; only by a concentration of all authority at one centre could the emergent individual escape from the communal pressures of family and guild, of church and local community, which hindered his enjoyment of his own character. Secondly, it must be an instrument of government not bound by prescription and therefore with authority to abolish old rights and create new: it must be a 'sovereign' government. And this, according to current ideas, means a government in which all who enjoyed rights were partners, a government in which the 'estates' of the realm were direct or indirect participants. Thirdly, it must be powerful—able to preserve the order without which the aspirations of individuality could not be realized; but not so powerful as itself to constitute a new threat to individuality. In an earlier time, the recognized methods of transforming interests into rights had been judicial; the 'parliaments' and 'councils' of the middle ages had been pre-eminently judicial bodies. But from these 'courts of law' emerged an instrument with more emphatic authority to recognize new interests by converting them into new rights and duties; there emerged legislative bodies. Thus, a ruler, and a parliament representative of his subjects, came to share the business of 'making' law. And the law they made was favourable to the interests of individuality: it provided the detail of what became a well-understood condition of human circumstance, commonly denoted by the word 'freedom'. In this condition every subject was secured of the right to pursue his chosen directions of activity as little hindered as might be by his fellows or by the exactions of government itself, and as little distracted by communal pressures. Freedom of movement, of initiative, of speech, of belief and religious observance, of association and disassociation, of bequest and inheritance; security of person and property; the right to choose one's own occupation and dispose of one's labour and goods; and over all the 'rule of law': the right to be ruled by a known law, applicable to all subjects alike. And these rights, appropriate to individuality, were not the privileges of a single class; they were the property of every subject alike. Each signified the abrogation of some feudal privilege.

This manner of governing, which reached its climax in the 'parliamentary' government which emerged in England and elsewhere in the late eighteenth and early nineteenth centuries, was concurrently theorized in an understanding of the proper office of government. What had been a 'community' came to be recognized as an 'association' of individuals: this was the counterpart in political philosophy of the individualism that had established itself in ethical theory. And the office of government was understood to be the maintenance of arrangements favourable to the interests of individuality, arrangements (that is) which emancipated the subject from the 'chains' (as Rousseau put it) of communal allegiancies, and constituted a condition of human circumstance in which the intimations of individuality might be explored and the experience of individuality enjoyed.

Briefly, then, my picture is as follows. Human individuality is an historical emergence, as 'artificial' and as 'natural' as the landscape. In modern Europe this emergence was gradual, and the specific character of the individual who emerged was determined by the manner of his generation. He became unmistakable when the habit appeared of engaging in activities identified as 'private'; indeed, the appearance of 'privacy' in human conduct is the obverse of the desuetude of the communal arrangements from which modern individuality sprang. This experience of individuality provoked a disposition to explore its own intimations, to place the highest value upon it, and to seek security in its enjoyment. To enjoy it came to be recognized as the main ingredient of 'happiness'. The experience was magnified into an ethical theory; it was reflected in manners of governing and being governed, in newly acquired rights and duties and in a whole pattern of living. The emergence of this disposition to be an individual is the pre-eminent event in modern European history.

THREE

There were many modest manners in which this disposition to be an individual might express itself. Every practical enterprise and every intellectual pursuit revealed itself as an assemblage of opportunities for making choices: art, literature, philosophy, commerce-industry and politics each came to partake of this character. Nevertheless, in a world being transformed by the aspirations and activities of those who were excited by these opportunities, there were some people, by circumstance or by temperament, less ready than others to respond to this invitation; and for many the invitation to make choices came before the ability to make them and was conse-

quently recognized as a burden. The old certainties of belief, of occupation and of status were being dissolved, not only for those who
had confidence in their own power to make a new place for themselves in an association of individuals, but also for those who had
no such confidence. The counterpart of the agricultural and industrial *entrepreneur* of the sixteenth century was the displaced la-
bourer; the counterpart of the *libertine* was the dispossessed believer. The familiar warmth of communal pressures was dissipated for
all alike—an emancipation which excited some, depressed others.
The familiar anonymity of communal life was replaced by a personal
identity which was burdensome to those who could not transform it
into an individuality. What some recognized as happiness, appeared to others as discomfort. The same condition of human circumstance was identified as progress and as decay. In short, the
circumstances of modern Europe, even as early as the sixteenth
century, bred, not a single character, but two obliquely opposed
characters: not only that of the individual, but also that of the 'individual *manqué*'. And this 'individual *manqué*' was not a relic of a
past age; he was a 'modern' character, the product of the same dissolution of communal ties as had generated the modern European
individual.

We need not speculate upon what combination of debility, ignorance, timidity, poverty or mischance operated in particular
cases to provoke this character; it is enough to observe his appearance and his efforts to accommodate himself to his hostile environment. He sought a protector who would recognize his predicament,
and he found what he sought, in some measure, in 'the government'. From as early as the sixteenth century the governments of
Europe were being modified, not only in response to the demands
of individuality, but in response also to the needs of the 'individual
manqué'. The 'godly prince' of the Reformation and his lineal de-
scendant, the 'enlightened despot' of the eighteenth century, were
political inventions for making choices for· those indisposed to
make choices for themselves; the Elizabethan Statute of Labourers
was designed to take care of those who were left behind in the
race.

The aspirations of individuality had imposed themselves upon conduct and belief and upon the constitutions and activities of governments, in the first place, as demands emanating from a powerful and confident disposition. There was little attempt to moralize these demands, which in the sixteenth century were clearly in conflict with current moral sentiment, still fixed in its loyalty to the morality of communal ties. Nevertheless, from the experience of individuality there sprang, in the course of time, a morality appropriate to it—a disposition not only to explore individuality but to approve of the pursuit of individuality. This constituted a considerable moral revolution; but such was its force and vigour that it not only swept aside the relics of the morality appropriate to the defunct communal order, but left little room for any alternative *to itself*. And the weight of this moral victory bore heavily upon the 'individual *manqué*'. Already outmanoeuvred in the field (in conduct), he now suffered a defeat at home, in his own character. What had been no more than a doubt about his ability to hold his own in a struggle for existence, became a radical self-distrust; what had been merely a hostile prospect, disclosed itself as an abyss; what had been the discomfort of ill-success was turned into the misery of guilt.

In some, no doubt, this situation provoked resignation; but in others it bred envy, jealousy and resentment. And in these emotions a new disposition was generated: the impulse to escape from the predicament by imposing it upon all mankind. From the frustrated 'individual *manqué*' there sprang the militant 'anti-individual', disposed to assimilate the world to his own character by deposing the individual and destroying his moral prestige. No promise, or even offer, of self-advancement could tempt this 'anti-individual'; he knew his individuality was too poorly furnished to be explored or exploited with any satisfaction whatever. He was moved solely by the opportunity of complete escape from the anxiety of not being an individual, the opportunity of removing from the world all that convicted him of his own inadequacy. His situation provoked him to seek release in separatist communities, insulated from the moral pressure of individuality. But the opportunity he sought appeared fully when he recognized that, so far from being alone, he belonged to the most numerous class in modern European society, the class of those who had no choices of their own to make. Thus, in the recognition of his numerical superiority the 'anti-individual' at once recognized himself as the 'mass man' and discovered the way of escape from his predicament. For, although the 'mass man' is specified by his disposition—a disposition to allow in others only a replica of himself, to impose upon all a uniformity of belief and conduct that leaves no room for either the pains or the pleasures of choice—and not by his numbers, he is confirmed in this disposition by the support of others of his kind. He can have no friends (because friendship is a relation between individuals), but he has comrades. The 'masses' as they appear in modern European history are not composed of individuals; they are composed of 'anti-individuals' united in a revulsion from individuality. Consequently, although the remarkable growth of population in Western Europe during the last four hundred years is a condition of the success with which this character has imposed itself, it is not a condition of the character itself.

Nevertheless, the 'anti-individual' had feelings rather than thoughts, impulses rather than opinions, inabilities rather than passions, and was only dimly aware of his power. Consequently, he required 'leaders': indeed, the modern concept of 'leadership' is a concomitant of the 'anti-individual', and without him it would be unintelligible. An association of individuals requires a ruler, but it has no place for a 'leader'. The 'anti-individual' needed to be told what to think; his impulses had to be transformed into desires, and these desires into projects; he had to be made aware of his power; and these were the tasks of his leaders. Indeed, from one point of view, 'the masses' must be regarded as the invention of their leaders.

The natural submissiveness of the 'mass man' may itself be supposed to have been capable of prompting the appearance of appropriate leaders. He was unmistakably an instrument to be played upon, and no doubt the instrument provoked the *virtuoso*. But there was, in fact, a character ready to occupy this office. What was required was a man who could at once appear as the image and the master of his followers; a man who could more easily make choices for others than for himself; a man disposed to mind other people's business because he lacked the skill to find satisfaction in minding his own. And these, precisely, were the attributes of the 'individual *manqué*', whose achievements and whose failures in respect of individuality exactly fitted him for this task of leadership. He was enough of an individual to seek a personal satisfaction in the exercise of individuality, but too little to seek it anywhere but in commanding others. He loved himself too little to be anything but an egoist; and what his followers took to be a genuine concern for their salvation was in fact nothing more than the vanity of the almost selfless. No doubt the 'masses' in modern Europe have had other leaders than this cunning frustrate who has led always by flattery and whose only concern is the exercise of power; but they have had none more appropriate—for he only had never prompted them to be critical of their impulses. Indeed, the 'anti-individual' and his leader were the counterparts of a single moral situation; they relieved one another's fustrations and supplied one another's wants. Nevertheless, it was an uneasy partnership: moved by impulses rather than by desires, the 'mass man' has been submissive but not loyal to his leaders: even the exiguous individuality of the leader has easily aroused his suspicion. And the leader's greed for power has disposed him to raise hopes in his followers which he has never been able to satisfy.

Of all the manners in which the 'anti-individual' has imposed himself upon Western Europe two have been pre-eminent. He has generated a morality designed to displace the current morality of individuality; and he has evoked an understanding of the proper office of government and manners of governing appropriate to his character.

The emergence of the morality of the 'anti-individual', a morality, namely, not of 'liberty' and 'self-determination', but of 'equality' and 'solidarity' is, of course, difficult to discern; but it is already clearly visible in the seventeenth century. The obscurity of its beginnings is due in part to the fact that its vocabulary was at first

that of the morality of the defunct communal order; and there can
be little doubt that it derived strength and plausibility from its deceptive affinity to that morality. But it was, in fact, a new morality,
generated in opposition to the hegemony of individuality and calling for the establishment of a new condition of human circumstance reflecting the aspirations of the 'anti-individual'.

The nucleus of this morality was the concept of a substantive
condition of human circumstance represented as the 'common' or
'public' good, which was understood, not to be composed of the various goods that might be sought by individuals on their own account, but to be an independent entity. 'Self-love', which was recognized in the morality of individuality as a legitimate spring of
human activity, the morality of the 'anti-individual' pronounced to
be evil. But it was to be replaced, not by the love of 'others', or by
'charity' or by 'benevolence' (which would have entailed a relapse into the vocabulary of individuality), but by the love of 'the community'.

Round this nucleus revolved a constellation of appropriate
subordinate beliefs. From the beginning, the designers of this morality identified private property with individuality, and consequently connected its abolition with the condition of human circumstances appropriate to the 'mass man'. And further, it was
appropriate that the morality of the 'anti-individual' should be radically equalitarian: how should the 'mass man', whose sole distinction was his resemblance to his fellows and whose salvation lay in
the recognition of others as merely replicas of himself, approve of
any divergence from an exact uniformity? All must be equal and
anonymous units in a 'community'. And, in the generation of this
morality, the character of this 'unit' was tirelessly explored. He was
understood as a 'man' *per se*, as a 'comrade', as a 'citizen'. But the
most acute diagnosis, that of Proudhon, recognized him as a 'debt-
or'; for in this notion what was asserted was not only the absence of
distinction between the units who composed the 'community' (all
are alike 'debtors'), but also a debt owed, not to 'others' to but to
the 'community' itself: at birth he enters into an inheritance which
he had played no part in accumulating, and whatever the magni-

tude of his subsequent contribution, it never equals what he has enjoyed: he dies necessarily insolvent.

This morality of the 'anti-individual', the morality of a *solidarité commune*, began to be constructed in the sixteenth century. Its designers were mostly visionaries, dimly aware of their purposes, and lacking a large audience. But a momentous change occurred when the 'anti-individual' recognized himself as the 'mass man', and perceived the power that his numerical superiority gave him. The recognition that the morality of the 'anti-individual' was, in the first place, the morality not of a sect of aspirants, but of a large ready-made class in society (the class, not of the 'poor', but of those who by circumstance or by occupation had been denied the experience of individuality), and that in the interests of this class it must be imposed upon all mankind, appears unmistakably first in the writings of Marx and Engels.

Before the end of the nineteenth century, then, a morality of 'anti-individualism' had been generated in response to the aspirations of the 'mass man'. It was, in many respects, a rickety construction: it never achieved a design comparable to that which Hobbes or Kant or Hegel gave the morality of individuality; and it has never been able to resist relapse into the inappropriate concepts of individuality. Nevertheless it throws back a tolerably clear reflection of the 'mass man', who by this means became more thoroughly acquainted with himself. But we are not concerned with its merits or defects, we are concerned only to notice it as evidence of the power with which the 'mass man' has imposed himself on modern Europe over a period of about four centuries. 'Anti-individuality', long before the nineteenth century, had established itself as one of the major dispositions of the modern European moral character. And this disposition was evident enough for it to be recognized unequivocally by Sorel, and to be identified by writers such as Nietzsche, Kierkegaard and Burckhardt as the image of a new barbarism.

From the beginning (in the sixteenth century) those who exerted themselves on behalf of the 'anti-individual' perceived that his counterpart, a 'community' reflecting his aspirations, entailed a

'government' active in a certain manner. To govern was understood
to be the exercise of power in order to impose and maintain the
substantive condition of human circumstance indentified as 'the
public good'; to be governed was, for the 'anti-individual', to have
made for him the choices he was unable to make for himself. Thus,
'government' was cast for the rôle of architect and custodian, not of
'public order' in an 'association' of individuals pursuing their own
activities, but of 'the public good' of a 'community'. The ruler was
recognized to be, not the referee of the collisions of individuals, but
the moral leader and managing director of 'the community'. And
this understanding of government has been tirelessly explored over
a period of four and a half centuries, from Thomas More's *Utopia* to
the Fabian Society, from Campanella to Lenin. But the leaders who
served the 'mass man' were not merely theorists concerned to make
his character intelligible in a moral doctrine and in an understanding of the office of government; they were also practical men who
revealed to him his power and the manner in which the institutions of modern democratic government might be appropriated to
his aspirations. And if we call the manner of government that had
been generated by the aspirations of individuality 'parliamentary
government', we may call the modification of it under the impact of
the 'mass man', 'popular government'. But it is important to understand that these are two wholly different manners of government.

   The emergent individual in the sixteenth century had sought
new rights, and by the beginning of the nineteenth century the
rights appropriate to his character had, in England and elsewhere,
been largely established. The 'anti-individual' observed these rights,
and he was persuaded that his circumstances (chiefly his poverty)
had hitherto prevented him from sharing them. Hence the new
rights called for on his behalf were, in the first place, understood as
the means by which he might come to participate in the rights won
and enjoyed by those he thought of as his better placed fellows. But
this was a great illusion; first, because in fact he had these rights,
and secondly because he had no use for them. For the disposition
of the 'mass man' was not to become an individual, and the enterprise of his leaders was not to urge him in this direction. And what,

in fact, prevented him enjoying the rights of individuality (which were as available to him as to anyone else) was not his 'circumstances' but his character—his 'anti-individuality'. The rights of individuality were necessarily such that the 'mass man' could have no use for them. And so, in the end, it turned out: what he came to demand were rights of an entirely different *kind*, and of a kind which entailed the abolition of the rights appropriate to individuality. He required the right to enjoy a substantive condition of human circumstance in which he would not be asked to make choices for himself. He had no use for the right to 'pursue happiness'—that could only be a burden to him: he needed the right to 'enjoy happiness'. And looking into his own character he identified this with Security—but again, not security against arbitrary interference in the exercise of his preferences, but Security against having to make choices for himself and against having to meet the vicissitudes of life from his own resources. In short, the right he claimed, the right appropriate to his character, was the right to live in a social protectorate which relieved him from the burden of 'self-determination'.

But this condition of human circumstances was seen to be impossible unless it were imposed upon all alike. So long as 'others' were permitted to make choices for themselves, not only would his anxiety at not being able to do so himself remain to convict him of his inadequacy and threaten his emotional security, but also the social protectorate which he recognized as his counterpart would itself be disrupted. The Security he needed entailed a genuine equality of circumstances imposed upon all. The condition he sought was one in which he would meet in others only a replica of himself: what he was, everybody must become.

He claimed this condition as a 'right', and consequently he sought a government disposed to give it to him and one endowed with the power necessary to impose upon all activities the substantive pattern of activity called 'the public good'. 'Popular government' is, precisely, a modification of 'parliamentary government' designed to accomplish this purpose. And if this reading is correct, 'popular government' is no more intimated in 'parliamentary government' than the rights appropriate to the 'anti-individual' are intimated in the rights appropriate to individuality: they are not complementary but directly opposed to one another. Nevertheless, what I have called 'popular government' is not a concrete manner of government established and practised; it is a disposition to impose certain modifications upon 'parliamentary government' in order to convert it into a manner of government appropriate to the aspirations of the 'mass man'.

This disposition has displayed itself in specific enterprises, and in less specific habits and manners in respect of government. The first great enterprise was the establishment of universal adult suffrage. The power of the 'mass man' lay in his numbers, and this power could be brought to bear upon government by means of 'the vote'. Secondly, a change in the character of the parliamentary representative was called for: he must be not an individual, but a *mandataire* charged with the task of imposing the substantive condition of human circumstances required by the 'mass man'. 'Parliament' must become a 'work-shop', not a debating assembly. Neither of these changes was intimated in 'parliamentary government'; both, in so far as they have been achieved, have entailed an assembly of a new character. Their immediate effect has been twofold: first, to confirm the authority of mere numbers (an authority alien to the practice of 'parliamentary government'); and secondly, to give governments immensely increased power.

But the institutions of 'parliamentary government' proved to have only a limited eligibility for conversion into institutions appropriate to serve the aspirations of the 'mass man'. And an assembly of instructed delegates was seen to be vulnerable to a much more appropriate contrivance—the *plébiscite.* Just as it lay in the character of the 'mass man' to see everyman as a 'public official', an agent of 'the public good', and to see his representatives not as individuals but instructed delegates, so he saw every voter as the direct participant in the activity of governing: and the means of this was the *plébiscite.* An assembly elected on a universal adult suffrage, composed of instructed delegates and flanked by the device of the *plébiscite* was, then, the counterpart of the 'mass man'. They gave him exactly what he wanted: the illusion without the reality of choice; choice without the burden of having to choose. For, with universal suffrage have appeared the massive political parties of the modern world, composed not of individuals but of 'anti-individuals'. And both the instructed delegate and the *plébiscite* are devices for avoiding the necessity for making choices. The 'mandate' from the beginning was an illusion. The 'mass man', as we have seen, is a creature of impulses, not desires; he is utterly unable to draw up instructions for his representative to follow. What in fact has happened, whenever the disposition of 'popular government' has imposed itself, is that the prospective representative has drawn up his own mandate and then, by a familiar trick of ventriloquism, has put it into the mouth of his electors: as an instructed delegate he is not an individual, and as a 'leader' he relieves his followers of the need to make choices for themselves. And similarly, the *plébiscite* is not a method by which the 'mass man' imposes his choices upon his rulers; it is a method of generating a government with unlimited authority to make choices on his behalf. In the *plébiscite* the 'mass man' achieved final release from the burden of individuality: he was told emphatically what to choose.

Thus, in these and other constitutional devices, and in less formal habits of political conduct, was generated a new art of politics: the art, not of 'ruling' (that is, of seeking the most practicable adjustments for the collisions of 'individuals'), nor even of maintaining the support of a majority of individuals in a 'parliamentary' assembly, but of knowing what offer will collect most votes and making it in such a manner that it appears to come from 'the people'; the art, in short, of 'leading' in the modern idiom. Moreover, it is known in advance what offer will collect the most votes: the character of the 'mass man' is such that he will be moved only by the offer of release from the burden of making choices for himself, the offer of 'salvation'. And anyone who makes this offer may confidently demand unlimited power; it will be given him.

The 'mass man', as I understand him, then, is specified by his character, not by his numbers. He is distinguished by so exiguous an individuality that when it meets a powerful experience of individuality it revolts into 'anti-individuality'. He has generated for himself an appropriate morality, an appropriate understanding of the office of government, and appropriate modifications of 'parliamentary government'. He is not necessarily 'poor', nor is he envious only of 'riches'; he is not necessarily 'ignorant', often he is a member of the so-called *intelligentsia*; he belongs to a class which corresponds exactly with no other class. He is specified primarily by a moral, not an intellectual, inadequacy. He wants 'salvation'; and in the end will be satisfied only with release from the burden of having to make choices for himself. He is dangerous, not on account of his opinions or desires, for he has none: but on account of his submissiveness. His disposition is to endow government with power and authority such as it has never before enjoyed: he is utterly unable to distinguish a 'ruler' from a 'leader'. In short, the disposition to be an 'anti-individual' is one to which every European man has a propensity; the 'mass man' is merely one in whom this propensity is dominant.

FOUR

Of the many conclusions which follow from this reading of the situation the most important is to dispose of the most insidious of our current political delusions. It has been said, and it is commonly believed, that the event of supreme importance in modern European history is 'the accession of the masses to complete social power'. But that no such event has taken place is evident when we consider what it would entail. If it is true (as I have contended) that modern Europe enjoys two opposed moralities (that of individuality and that of the 'anti-individual'), that it enjoys two opposed understandings of the office of government, and two corresponding interpretations of the current institutions of government, then, for the 'mass man' to have won for himself a position of undisputed sovereignty would entail the complete suppression of what, in any reading, must be considered the strongest of our moral and political dispositions and the survival of the weakest. A world in which the 'mass man' exercised 'complete social power' would be a world in which the activity of governing was understood *solely* as the imposition of a single substantive condition of human circumstance, a world in which 'popular government' had altogether displaced 'parliamentary government', a world in which the 'civil' rights of individuality had been abrogated by the 'social' rights of anti-individuality—and there is no evidence that we live in such a world. Certainly the 'mass man' has emerged and has signified his emergence in an appropriate morality and an appropriate understanding of the office of government. He has sought to transform the world into a replica of himself, and he has not been entirely unsuccessful. He has sought to enjoy what he could not create for himself, and nothing he has appropriated remains unchanged. Nevertheless, he remains an unmistakably derivative character, an emanation of the pursuit of individuality, helpless, parasitic and able to survive only in opposition to individuality. Only in the most favourable circumstances, and then only by segregating him from all alien influences, have his leaders been able to suppress in him an unquenched propensity to desert at the call of individuality. He has imposed himself emphatically only where the relics of a morality of communal ties survived to make plausible his moral and political impulses. Elsewhere, the modifications he has provoked in political manners and moral beliefs have been extensive, but the notion that they have effaced the morality of individuality and 'parliamentary government' is without foundation. He loves himself too little to be able to dispose effectively of the only power he has, namely, his numerical superiority. He lacks passion rather than reason. He has had a past in which he was taught to admire himself and his antipathies; he has a present in which he is often the object of the ill-concealed contempt of his 'leaders'; but the heroic future forecast him is discrepant with his own character. He is no hero.

On the other hand, if we judge the world as we find it (which includes, of course, the emergence of the 'mass man') the event of supreme and seminal importance in modern European history remains the emergence of the human individual in his modern idiom. The pursuit of individuality has evoked a moral disposition, an understanding of the office of government and manners of governing, a multiplicity of activity and opinion and a notion of 'happiness', which have impressed themselves indelibly upon European civilization. The onslaught of the 'mass man' has shaken but not destroyed the moral prestige of individuality; even the 'anti-individual', whose salvation lies in escape, has not been able to escape it. The desire of 'the masses' to enjoy the products of individuality has modified their destructive urge. And the antipathy of the 'mass man' to the 'happiness' of 'self-determination' easily dissolves into self-pity. At all important points the individual still appears as the substance and the 'anti-individual' only as the shadow.

"The Masses in Representative Democracy" was first published in *Freedom and Serfdom: An Anthology of Western Thought*, Albert Hunold (editor), in 1961. It is new to this edition of *Rationalism in Politics*. Reprinted by permission from *Freedom and Serfdom*, edited by Albert Hunold. ©1961 by D. Reidel Publishing Co., Dordrecht, Holland.

The political economy
of freedom

The work of the late Professor Henry C. Simons of the University of Chicago will be well known to students of economics, and they will not need their attention called to this collection of some of his more important essays.[1] To others, however, it may be supposed that his name will be unknown. But, in spite of the fact that he is neither a brilliant nor a popular writer, he has something for the general reader; and though much of what he says has the USA for its immediate background, he has something in particular for the English reader. And I propose in this review to recommend him as a writer who should not be neglected by anyone interested in the way things are going. As an economist, Simons was concerned particularly with problems of banking, currency and monetary policy, but (like his teacher and colleague at Chicago, Professor F. H. Knight,[2] who has built up so distinguished a school of economic studies at that university) he was well aware that in every discussion of a special problem and in every proposal of economic policy

[1] *Economic Policy for a Free Society.* University of Chicago Press and Cambridge University Press, 1948.
[2] F. H. Knight, *Ethics of Competition* (1935), and *Freedom and Reform* (1947).

there lies an often undisclosed preference for a society integrated in one way rather than another. And in order to make his preferences in this matter secure against superstition, he went to some trouble to bring them out into the open and to put them in order. They do not amount to anything so elaborate as a political philosophy, indeed he claims for them only the title of 'a political *credo*'; there is nothing pretentious in this attempt to hold 'economics' and 'politics' together. And it is successful mainly because it is not merely one project among others but represents the permanent habit of his mind. It is true there are a couple of essays in this volume directed expressly to the investigation of political ends and means, but the bulk of them is concerned with special economic problems and he never fails to show how his proposed solution is related to the wider context of the type of society he believes to be desirable. To those anxious to find out where they stand in these matters he offers not only a lucid, if fragmentary, account of his own preferences, but also a profound insight into the compatibility or incompatibility of different economic expedients with different forms of social integration.

Needless to say, Simons does not pretend to invent a political *credo* for himself: he is without the vanity of those who refuse to be convinced of their own honesty of purpose until they have made a desert of their consciousness before beginning to cultivate it for themselves. His pride is in belonging to a tradition. He speaks of himself as 'an old-fashioned liberal', and he allies himself with a line of predecessors which includes Adam Smith, Bentham, Mill, Sidgwick as well as de Tocqueville, Burckhardt and Acton. This strikes one as being a trifle uncritical; the historical nuance is missed. But it is nothing to worry about. Simons was a generous-minded man where the work of others was concerned, accepting gratefully what was offered and providing the critical subtleties for himself. If he was a liberal, at least he suffered from neither of the current afflictions of liberalism—ignorance of who its true friends are, and the nervy conscience which extends a senile and indiscriminate welcome to everyone who claims to be on the side of 'progress'. We need not, however, disturb ourselves unduly about the label he tied on to his *credo*. He calls himself a liberal and a democrat, but he sets no great store by the names, and is concerned to resolve the ambiguity which has now unfortunately overtaken them. It is to be expected, then, that much of what Simons has to say will seem at once familiar and unpardonably outmoded. It will seem familiar, not because it has been unduly chewed over in recent years, but because the leaders of fashion, the intellectual dandies of the Fabian Society, preserved it in their hastily composed syllabus of errors. And it will seem outmoded because of the disapproval of these eccentric arbiters. The great merit of this book, however, is the opportunity it gives to 'this sophisticated generation', which knows all the answers but is sadly lacking in education, to consider for itself what it has been told to reject as mere superstition.

Simons finds in its 'emphasis on liberty' the 'distinctive feature' of the tradition with which he allies himself; he believes in liberty. And this at once will raise a presumption against him. For to be a genuine libertarian in politics is to belong to a human type now sadly out of fashion. Other loves have bewitched us; and to confess to a passion for liberty—not as something worth while in certain circumstances but as the *unum necessarium*—is to admit to a disreputable naïvety, excusable only where it makes a desire to rule. Liberty has become the emblem of frivolous or of disingenuous politics. But the damage which libertarian politics have suffered from open and from hidden enemies is not irreparable; after all, their cunning is only circuitous folly and will find them out. It is self-appointed friends who have often shown themselves more dangerous. We must be clear, they say, about what we mean by 'freedom'. First, let us define it; and when we know what it is, it will be time enough to seek it out, to love it and to die for it. What is a free society? And with this question (proposed abstractly) the door opens upon a night of endless quibble, lit only by the stars of sophistry. Like men born in prison, we are urged to dream of something we have never enjoyed (freedom from want) and to make that dream the foundation of our politics. We are instructed to distinguish between 'positive' and 'negative' freedom, between the 'old' and the 'new' freedom, between 'social', 'political', 'civil', 'economic' and 'personal' freedom; we are told that freedom is the 'recognition of necessity'; and we are taught that all that matters is 'inner freedom' and that this is to be identified with equality and with power: there is no end to the abuse we have suffered. But a generation which has stood so long on that doorstep, waiting for the dawn, that 'le silence éternel de ces espaces infinis' has begun to unnerve it, should now be ready to listen to a more homely message. And anyone who has the courage to tell it to come in and shut the door may perhaps be given a hearing. This at least is what I understand Simons to be saying to us. The freedom which he is to inquire into is neither an abstraction nor a dream. He is a libertarian, not because he begins with an abstract definition of liberty, but because he has actually enjoyed a way of living (and seen others enjoy it) which those who have enjoyed it are accustomed (on account of certain precise characteristics) to call a free way of living, and because he has found it to be good. The purpose of the inquiry is not to define a word, but to detect the secret of what we enjoy, to recognize what is hostile to it, and to discern where and how it may be enjoyed more fully. And from this inquiry will spring, not only a closer understanding of what we actually enjoy, but also a reliable criterion for judging the proposed abstract freedoms which we are urged to pursue. For a proposed freedom which manifestly could not be achieved by means of the kind of arrangements which secure to us the freedom we now enjoy will reveal itself as an illusion. Moreover, we must refuse to be jockeyed into writing 'freedom', in deference to the susceptibilities of, say, a Russian or a Turk who has never enjoyed the experience (and who, consequently, can think only in abstractions), because any other use of the English word would be misleading and eccentric. *Freedom*, in English, is a word whose political connotation springs as directly from our political experience as the connotations of ἐλευθερία, *libertas* and *liberté* spring respectively from quite different experiences.

What, then, are the characteristics of our society in respect of which we consider ourselves to enjoy freedom and in default of which we would not be free in our sense of the word? But first, it must be observed that the freedom we enjoy is not composed of a number of independent characteristics of our society which in aggregate make up our liberty. Liberties, it is true, may be distinguished, and some may be more general or more settled and mature than others, but the freedom which the English libertarian knows and values lies in a coherence of mutually supporting liberties, each of which amplifies the whole and none of which stands alone. It springs neither from the separation of church and state, nor from the rule of law, nor from private property, nor from parliamentary government, nor from the writ of *habeas corpus*, nor from the independence of the judiciary, nor from any one of the thousand other devices and arrangements characteristic of our society, but from what each signifies and represents, namely, the absence from our society of overwhelming concentrations of power. This is the most general condition of our freedom, so general that all other conditions may be seen to be comprised within it. It appears, first, in a diffusion of authority between past, present and future. Our society is ruled by none of these exclusively. And we should consider a society governed wholly by its past, or its present, or its future to suffer under a despotism of superstition which forbids freedom. The politics of our society are a conversation in which past, present and future each has a voice; and though one or other of them may on occasion properly prevail, none permanently dominates, and on this account we are free. Further, with us power is dispersed among all the multitude of interests and organizations of interest which comprise our society. We do not fear or seek to suppress diversity of interest, but we consider our freedom to be imperfect so long as the dispersal of power among them is incomplete, and to be threatened if any one interest or combination of interests, even though it may be the interest of a majority, acquires extraordinary power. Similarly, the conduct of government in our society involves a sharing of power, not only between the recognized organs of government, but also between the Administration and the Opposition. In short, we consider ourselves to be free because no one in our society is allowed unlimited power—no leader, faction, party or 'class', no majority, no government, church, corporation, trade or professional association or trade union. The secret of its freedom is that it is composed of a multitude of organizations in the constitution of the best of which is reproduced that diffusion of power which is characteristic of the whole.

Moreover, we are not unaware that the balance of such a society is always precarious. 'The history of institutions,' says Acton, 'is often a history of deception and illusions.' Arrangements which in their beginnings promoted a dispersion of power often, in the course of time, themselves become over-mighty or even absolute while still claiming the recognition and loyalty which belonged to them in respect of their first character. To further liberty we need to be clear-sighted enough to recognize such a change, and energetic enough to set on foot the remedy while the evil is still small. And what more than anything else contributes to this clear-sightedness is relief from the distraction of a rigid doctrine which fixes upon an institution a falsely permanent character, and then (when the illusion is at last recognized) calls for a revolution. The best institutions, of course, are those whose constitution is both firm and self-critical, enjoying their character as the repository of a beneficial fragment of power but refusing the inevitable invitation to absolutism. And though these are few, it is perhaps permissible to number among them the hitherto existing parties of English politics.

It might be thought (by those who have not enjoyed the experience of living in such a society, and who can therefore think of it only in the abstract) that a society of this sort could be saved from disintegration only by the existence at its head of some overwhelming power capable of holding all other powers in check. But that is not our experience. Strength we think to be a virtue in government, but we do not find our defence against disintegration either in arbitary or in very great power. Indeed, we are inclined to see in both these the symptoms of an already advanced decay. For overwhelming power would be required only by a government which had against it a combination so extensive of the powers vested in such a variety of different individuals and interests as to convict the government of a self-interest so gross as to disqualify it for the exercise of its proper function. Normally, to perform its office (which is to prevent coercion) our government requires to wield only a power greater than that which is concentrated in any one other centre of power on any particular occasion. Consequently it is difficult to excite in us the belief that a government not possessed of overwhelming power is on that account a weak government. And we consider that our freedom depends as much upon the moderation of the power exercised by government as upon the proper and courageous use of that power when necessity arises.

But further, our experience has disclosed to us a method of government remarkably economical in the use of power and consequently peculiarly fitted to preserve freedom: it is called the rule of law. If the activity of our government were the continuous or sporadic interruption of the life and arrangements of our society with arbitrary corrective measures, we should consider ourselves no longer free, even though the measures were directed against concentrations of power universally recognized to be dangerous. For not only would government of this kind require extraordinary power (each of its acts being an *ad hoc* intervention), but also, in spite of this concentration of governmental power, the society would be without that known and settled protective structure which is so important a condition of freedom. But government by rule of law (that is, by means of the enforcement by prescribed methods of settled rules binding alike on governors and governed), while losing nothing in strength, is itself the emblem of that diffusion of power which it exists to promote, and is therefore peculiarly appropriate to a free society. It is the method of government most economical in the use of power; it involves a partnership between past and present and between governors and governed which leaves no room for arbitrariness; it encourages a tradition of resistance to the growth of dangerous concentrations of power which is far more effective than any promiscuous onslaught however crushing; it controls effectively, but without breaking the grand affirmative flow of things; and it gives a practical definition of the kind of limited but necessary service a society may expect from its government, restraining us from vain and dangerous expectations. Particular laws, we know, may fail to protect the freedom enjoyed in our society, and may even be destructive of some of our freedom; but we know also that the rule of law is the greatest single condition of our freedom, removing from us that great fear which has overshadowed so many communities, the fear of the power of our own government.

Of the many species of liberty which compose the freedom we enjoy, each amplifying and making more secure the whole, we have long recognized the importance of two: the freedom of association, and the freedom enjoyed in the right to own private property. A third species of liberty is often set beside these two: freedom of speech. Beyond question this is a great and elementary form of freedom; it may even be regarded as the key-stone of the arch of our liberty. But a key-stone is not itself the arch, and the current exaggeration of the importance of this form of liberty is in danger of concealing from us the loss of other liberties no less important. The major part of mankind has nothing to say; the lives of most men do not revolve round a felt necessity to speak. And it may be supposed that this extraordinary emphasis upon freedom of speech is the work of the small vocal section of our society and, in part, represents a legitimate self-interest. Nor is it an interest incapable of abuse; when it is extended to the indiscriminate right to take and publish photographs, to picket and enter private houses and cajole or blackmail defenceless people to display their emptiness in foolish utterances, and to publish innuendos in respect of those who refuse to speak, it begins to reveal itself as a menace to freedom. For most men, to be deprived of the right of voluntary association or of private property would be a far greater and more deeply felt loss of liberty than to be deprived of the right to speak freely. And it is important that this should be said just now in England because, under the influence of misguided journalists and cunning tyrants, we are too ready to believe that so long as our freedom to speak is not impaired we have lost nothing of importance—which is not so. However secure may be a man's right to speak his thoughts, he may find what is to him a much more important freedom curtailed when his house is sold over his head by a public authority, or when he is deprived of the enjoyment of his leasehold because his landlord has sold out to a development company, or when his membership of a trade union is compulsory and debars him from an employment he would otherwise take.

The freedom of association enjoyed in our society has created a vast multitude of associations so that the integration of our society may be said to be largely by means of voluntary associations; and on this account we consider our freedom extended and made more secure. They represent a diffusion of power appropriate to our notion of freedom. The right of voluntary association means the right to take the initiative in forming new associations, and the right to join or not to join or to quit associations already in existence: the right of voluntary association is also a right of voluntary dissociation. And it means also the duty of not forming or joining any association designed to deprive, or in effect depriving, others of the exercise of any of their rights, particularly that of voluntary association. This duty is not to be thought of as a limitation of the right; the right, like all rights, is without any limits except those provided by the system of rights to which it belongs and those inherent in its own character: this duty is merely the negative definition of the right. And when we consider the full nature of the right, it is clear that its exercise can be hostile to what we know as our freedom only when it leads to that which in fact denies its own character—a 'compulsory-voluntary' association. A 'compulsory-voluntary' association is a conspiracy to abolish our right of association; it is a concentration of power actually or potentially destructive of what we call freedom.

It will be agreed that, from one point of view, property is a form of power, and an institution of property is a particular way of organizing the exercise of this form of power in a society. From this point of view distinctions between different kinds of property scarcely appear; certainly all categorical distinctions are absent. Personal and real property, chattels, property in a man's own physical and mental capacities and property in the so-called means of production, are all, in different degrees, forms of power, and incidentally spring from the same sources, investment, inheritance and luck. In every society an institution of property is unavoidable. The ideally simplest kind of institution is that in which all proprietary right is vested in one person who thereby becomes despot and monopolist, his subject being slaves. But, besides being the least complex, this institution is, to our way of thinking, the most hostile to freedom. We have, perhaps, been less successful, from the point of view of freedom, in our institution of property than in some of our other arrangements, but there is no doubt about the general character of the institution of property most friendly to freedom: it will be one which allows the widest distribution, and which discourages most effectively great and dangerous concentrations of this power. Nor is there any doubt about what this entails. It entails a right of private property—that is, an institution of property which allows to every adult member of the society an equal right to enjoy the ownership of his personal capacities and of anything else obtained by the methods of acquisition recognized in the society. This right, like every other right, is self-limiting: for example, it proscribes slavery, not arbitrarily, but because the right to own another man could never be a right enjoyed equally by every member of society. But in so far as a society imposes external limits, arbitrarily excluding certain things from private ownership, only a modified right of private property may be said to prevail, which provides for less than the maximum diffusion of the power that springs from ownership. For what may not be owned by any individual must nevertheless be owned, and it will be owned, directly or indirectly, by the government, adding to governmental power and constituting a potential threat to freedom. Now, it may happen that a society determines to withdraw from the possibility of private ownership certain things not inherently excluded by the right of private property itself, and there may be good reason for taking this course. But it should be observed that whatever benefits may flow from such an arrangement, the increase of liberty as we understand it is not among them. The institution of property most favourable to liberty is, unquestionably, a right to private property least qualified by arbitrary limits and exclusions, for it is by this means only that the maximum diffusion of the power that springs from ownership may be achieved. This is not mere abstract speculation; it is the experience of our society, in which the greatest threats to freedom have come from the acquisition of extraordinary proprietary rights by the government, by great business and industrial corporations and by trade unions, all of which are to be regarded as arbitrary limitations of the right of private property. An institution of property based upon private property is not, of course, either simple or primitive; it is the most complex of all institutions of property and it can be maintained only by constant vigilance, occasional reform and the refusal to tinker. And it is instructive to observe how closely many of the private property rights which we all regard as inseparable from freedom are bound up with other private property rights which it is now the custom erroneously to consider hostile to freedom. That a man is not free unless he enjoys a proprietary right over his personal capacities and his labour is believed by everyone who uses freedom in the English sense. And yet no such right exists unless there are many potential employers of his labour. The freedom which separates a man from slavery is nothing but a freedom to choose and to move among autonomous, independent organizations, firms, purchasers of labour, and this implies private property in resources other than personal capacity. Wherever a means of production falls under the control of a single power, slavery in some measure follows.

With property we have already begun to consider the economic organization of society. An institution of property is, in part, a device for organizing the productive and distributive activity of the society. For the libertarian of our tradition the main question will be how to regulate the enterprise of making a living in such a way that it does not destroy the freedom he prizes. He will, of course, recognize in our institution of private property a means of organizing this enterprise wholly friendly to liberty. All monopolies, or near monopolies, he knows as impediments to that liberty, and the greatest single institution which stands between us and monopoly is private property. Concerning monopolies he will have no illusions; he will not consider them optimistically, hoping that they will not abuse their power. He will know that no individual, no group, association or union can be entrusted with much power, and that it is mere foolishness to complain when absolute power is abused. It exists to be abused. And consequently he will put his faith only in arrangements which discourage its existence. In other words, he will recognize that the only way of organizing the enterprise of getting a living so that it does not curtail the freedom he loves is by the establishment and maintenance of effective competition. He will know that effective competition is not something that springs up of its own accord, that both it and any alternative to it are creatures of law; but since he has observed the creation (often inadvertently) by law of monopolies and other impediments to freedom, he will not think it beyond the capacity of his society to build upon its already substantial tradition of creating and maintaining effective competition by law. But he will recognize that any confusion between the task of making competition effective and the task (to be performed by effective competition itself) of organizing the enterprise of getting a living and satisfying wants will at once be fatal to liberty as he knows it. For to replace by political control the integration of activity which competition (the market) provides is at once to create a monopoly and to destroy the diffusion of power inseparable from freedom. No doubt the libertarian, in this matter, will have to listen to the complaint that he has neglected to consider the efficiency with which his economic system produces the goods; how shall we reconcile the conflicting claims of freedom and efficiency? But he will have his answer ready. The only efficiency to be considered is the most economical way of supplying the things men desire to purchase. The formal circumstances in which this may be at its maximum is where enterprise is effectively competitive, for here the entrepreneur is merely the intermediary between consumers of goods and sellers of services. And below this ideal arrangement, the relevant comparison is not between the level of efficiency attainable in an improved (but not perfected) competitive economy and the efficiency of a perfectly planned economy, but between an improved competitive economy and the sort of planned economy (with all its wastefulness, frustration and corruption) which is the only practical alternative. Everything, in short, that is inimical to freedom—monopoly, near monopoly and all great concentrations of power—at the same time impedes the only efficiency worth considering.

This outline of the political faith of a libertarian in the English tradition will be thought to lack something important unless there is added to it at least a suggestion of the end or purpose which informs such a society. It belongs, however, to some other tradition to think of this purpose as the achievement of a premeditated utopia, as an abstract ideal (such as happiness or prosperity), or as a preordained and inevitable end. The purpose of this society (if indeed it may be said to have one) is not something put upon it from the outside, nor can it be stated in abstract terms without gross abridgment. We are not concerned with a society which sprang up yesterday, but with one which possesses already a defined character and traditions of activity. And in these circumstances social achievement is to perceive the next step dictated or suggested by the character of the society in contact with changing conditions and to take it in such a manner that the society is not disrupted and that the prerogatives of future generations are not grossly impaired. In place of a preconceived purpose, then, such a society will find its guide in a principle of *continuity* (which is a diffusion of power between past, present and future) and in a principle of *consensus* (which is a diffusion of power between the different legitimate interests of the present). We call ourselves free because our pursuit of current desires does not deprive us of a sympathy for what went before; like the wise man, we remain reconciled with our past. In the obstinate refusal to budge, in the pure pragmatism of a plebiscitary democracy, in the abridgment of tradition which consists in merely doing what was done 'last time', and in the preference for the short-cut in place of the long way round that educates at every step, we recognize, alike, the marks of slavery. We consider ourselves free because, taking a view neither short nor long, we are unwilling to sacrifice either the present to a remote and incalculable future, or the immediate and foreseeable future to a transitory present. And we find freedom once more in a preference for slow, small changes which have behind them a voluntary consensus of opinion, in our ability to resist disintegration without suppressing opposition, and in our perception that it is more important for a society to move together than for it to move either fast or far. We do not pretend that our decisions are infallible; indeed, since there is no external or absolute test of perfection, infallibility has no meaning. We find what we need in a principle of change and a principle of identity, and we are suspicious of those who offer us more; those who call upon us to make great sacrifices and those who want to impose upon us an heroic character.

Now, though none of these characteristics is fully present in our society at this time, none is wholly absent. We have experienced enough of it over a sufficiently long period of time to know what it means, and from that experience has sprung our notion of freedom. We call ourselves free because our arrangements approximate to this general condition. And the enterprise of the libertarian in politics will be to cultivate what has already been sown, and to avoid the fruitless pursuit of proposed freedoms which could not be secured by the only known method of achieving freedom. Policy will not be the imagination of some new sort of society, or the transformation of an existing society so as to make it correspond with an abstract ideal; it will be the perception of what needs doing now in order to realize more fully the intimations of our existing society. The right conduct of policy, then, involves a profound knowledge of the character of the society, which is to be cultivated, a clear perception of its present condition, and the precise formulation of a programme of legislative reform.

The present condition of our society is exceedingly complex; but, from the point of view of the libertarian, three main elements may be distinguished. There is, first, a widespread and deplorable ignorance of the nature of the libertarian tradition itself, a confusion of mind in respect of the kind of society we have inherited and the nature of its strength and weakness. With eyes focused upon distant horizons and minds clouded with foreign clap-trap, the impatient and sophisticated generation now in the saddle has dissolved its partnership with its past and is careful of everything except its liberty. Secondly, owing to the negligence of past generations, there is an accumulated mass of maladjustment, of undispersed concentrations of power, which the libertarian will wish to correct because it threatens liberty, and which others also may wish to correct for less cogent reasons. Thirdly, there is the contemporary mess, sprung from the attempts of men ignorant of the nature of their society to correct its maladjustments by means of expedients which, because they are not inspired by a love of liberty, are a threat to freedom both in failure and in success.

The two great, mutually exclusive, contemporary opponents of libertarian society as we know it are collectivism and syndicalism. Both recommend the integration of society by means of the erection and maintenance of monopolies; neither finds any virtue in the diffusion of power. But they must be considered mutually exclusive opponents of a free society because the monopoly favoured by syndicalism would make both a collective and a society of free men impossible.

Collectivism in the modern world has several synonyms; it stands for a managed society, and its other titles are communism, national socialism, socialism, economic democracy and central planning. But we will continue to call it collectivism, this being its least emotive name. And we will assume that the problem of imposing a collectivist organization upon a society which enjoys a high degree of freedom has been successfully solved—that is, we will assume that the necessary contemporary *consensus* has been achieved. This is not a tremendous assumption, because (paradoxically enough) collectivism appears most readily to us as a remedy for elements in our society which are agreed to be impediments to freedom. What the libertarian is concerned to investigate is the compatibility of collectivist organization with freedom as he knows it. To be brief, collectivism and freedom are real alternatives—if we choose one we cannot have the other. And collectivism can be imposed upon a society educated in a love of freedom with an appearance of not destroying *continuity*, only if men forget their love of liberty. This, of course, is not a new idea, it is how the matter appeared to observers, such as de Tocqueville, Burckhardt and Acton, when the character of modern collectivism was in process of being revealed.

Neglecting the more scandalous charges which may be brought against collectivism in action, let us consider only the defects (from the point of view of liberty) inherent in the system. The opposition of collectivism to freedom appears first in the collectivist rejection of the whole notion of the diffusion of power and of a society organized by means of a multitude of genuinely voluntary associations. The cure proposed for monopoly is to create more numerous and more extensive monopolies and to control them by force. The organization to be imposed upon society springs from the minds of those who compose the government. It is a comprehensive organization; loose ends, uncontrolled activities must be regarded as the product of incompetence because they unavoidably impair the structure of the whole. And great power is required for the over-all control of this organization—power sufficient not merely to break up a single over-mighty concentration of power when it makes its appearance, but to control continuously enormous concentrations of power which the collectivist has created. The government of a collectivist society can tolerate only a very limited opposition to its plans; indeed, that hard-won distinction, which is one of the elements of our liberty, between opposition and treason is rejected: what is not obedience is sabotage. Having discouraged all other means of social and industrial integration, a collectivist government must enforce its imposed order or allow the society to relapse into chaos. Or, following a tradition of economy in the use of power, it will be obliged to buy off political opposition by favouring groups able to demand favours as the price of peace. All this is, clearly, an impediment to freedom; but there is more to follow. In addition to the rule of law, and often in place of it, collectivism depends for its working upon a lavish use of discretionary authority. The organization it imposes upon society is without any inner momentum; it must be kept going by promiscuous, day-to-day interventions—controls of prices, licences to pursue activities, permissions to make and to cultivate, to buy and to sell, the perpetual readjustment of rations, and the distribution of privileges and exemptions—by the exercise, in short, of the kind of power most subject to misuse and corruption. The diffusion of power inherent in the rule of law leaves government with insufficient power to operate a collectivist society. It will be observed, further, that collectivism involves the abolition of that division of labour between competitive and political controls which belongs to our freedom. Competition may, of course, survive anomalously and vestigially, in spite of policy; but, in principle, enterprise is tolerated only if it is not competitive, that is, if it takes the form of syndicates which serve as instruments of the central authorities, or smaller businesses which a system of quotas and price controls has deprived of all elements of risk or genuine enterprise. Competition as a form of organization is first devitalized and then destroyed, and the integrating office it performs in our society is incorporated in the functions of government, thus adding to its power and involving it in every conflict of interest that may arise in the society. And with the disappearance of competition goes what we have seen to be one of the essential elements of our liberty. But of all the acquisitions of governmental power inherent in collectivism, that which comes from its monopoly of foreign trade is, perhaps, the most dangerous to liberty; for freedom of external trade is one of the most precious and most effective safeguards a community may have against excessive power. And just as the abolition of competition at home draws the government into (and thus magnifies) every conflict, so collectivist trading abroad involves the government in competitive commercial transactions and increases the occasions and the severity of international disharmony. Collectivism, then, is the mobilization of a society for unitary action. In the contemporary world it appears as a remedy for the imperfect freedom which springs from imperfect competition, but it is a remedy designed to kill. Nor is this surprising, for the real spring of collectivism is not a love of liberty, but war. The anticipation of war is the great incentive, and the conduct of war is the great collectivizing process. And large-scale collectivism is, moreover, inherently warlike; the condition of things in which it is appropriate in the end makes its appearance. It offers a double occasion for the loss of liberty—in the collectivist organization itself and in the purpose to which that organization is directed. For though collectivism may recommend itself as a means to 'welfare', the only 'welfare' it is capable of pursuing—a centralized, national 'welfare'—is hostile to freedom at home and results in organized rivalry abroad.

Collectivism is indifferent to all elements of our freedom and the enemy of some. But the real antithesis of a free manner of living, as we know it, is syndicalism. Indeed, syndicalism is not only destructive of freedom; it is destructive, also, of any kind of orderly existence. It rejects both the concentration of overwhelming power in the government (by means of which a collectivist society is always being rescued from the chaos it encourages), and it rejects the wide dispersion of power which is the basis of freedom. Syndicalism is a contrivance by means of which society is disposed for a perpetual civil war in which the parties are the organized self-interest of functional minorities and a weak central government, and for which the community as a whole pays the bill in monopoly prices and disorder. The great concentrations of power in a syndicalist society are the sellers of labour organized in functional monopoly associations. All monopolies are prejudicial to freedom, but there is good reason for supposing that labour monopolies are more dangerous than any others, and that a society in the grip of such monopolies would enjoy less freedom than any other sort of society. In the first place, labour monopolies have shown themselves more capable than enterprise monopolies of attaining really great power, economic, political and even military. Their appetite for power is insatiable and, producing nothing, they encounter none of the productional diseconomies of undue size. Once grown large, they are exceedingly difficult to dissipate and impossible to control. Appearing to spring from the lawful exercise of the right of voluntary association (though as monopolistic associations they are really a denial of that right), they win legal immunities and they enjoy popular support however scandalous their activity. Enterprise monopolies, on the other hand (not less to be deplored by the libertarian), are less dangerous because they are less powerful. They are precariously held together, they are unpopular and they are highly sensitive to legal control. Taken separately, there is no question which of the two kinds of monopoly is the more subversive of freedom. But in addition to its greater power, the labour monopoly is dangerous because it demands enterprise monopoly as its complement. There is a disastrous identity of interest between the two kinds of monopoly; each tends to foster and to strengthen the other, fighting together to maximize joint extractions from the public while also fighting each other over the division of the spoils. Indeed, the conflict of capital and labour (the struggle over the division of earnings) is merely a sham fight (often costing the public more than the participants), concealing the substantial conflict between the producer (enterprise and labour, both organized monopolistically) and the consumer. Syndicalism, then, has some claim to be considered the pre-eminent adversary of freedom, but it is not less the enemy of collectivism. A collectivist government faced with numerous functional minorities each organized monopolistically with power to disrupt the whole plan of production unless its demands are met and each (when not making large demands) keeping the civil war going by means of promiscuous little hindrances to the orderly conduct of business, would be the easy victim of blackmail. And if the collectivist government derived its political strength from highly syndicalist labour organizations, its desperate position would be that of a victim of blackmail in a society which had not made the activity an offence. Of all forms of society, a collectivist society is least able to deal with the disruptive potentialities of syndicalism.

Where collectivism and syndicalism have imposed themselves upon societies which enjoy a libertarian tradition they appear as mutually exclusive tendencies (sometimes anomalously in alliance with one another) threatening achieved freedom. But to the libertarian who still has faith in his tradition, the chief danger lies, not in the possibility that either will establish itself exclusively, but in their joint success in hindering a genuinely libertarian attack upon the accumulated maladjustments in our society and upon our real problems. That attack is certainly long overdue, and the delay must not be attributed entirely to the popularity of these pseudo-remedies. Libertarian society has not been entirely idle in the past fifty years; liberty has been extended by the correction of many small abuses. But the general drift of reform in this country has too often been inspired by vaguely collectivist motives. Liberty has been lost inadvertently through the lack of a clearly formulated libertarian policy of reform.

However, Simons now comes forward with such a policy. He is not the first to do so, but no friend of freedom will fail to benefit by reflecting upon what he has to say. Nobody could be less complacent about the present state of liberty than Simons; and his proposals are not only libertarian, they are in many respects (as he points out) more radical than the projects of the collectivists. A planner who aims at change by means of promiscuous intervention and the use of discretionary authority, while destroying liberty, does less for reform than a libertarian who would extend and consolidate the rule of law. Simons calls his policy a 'positive programme for *Laissez Faire*', mainly because it aims at making competition effective wherever effective competition is not demonstrably impossible, at re-establishing a diffusion of power now deeply compromised by monopolies of all sorts, and at preserving that division of labour between competitive and political controls which is the secret of our liberty. But, both in England and in America, the policy he proposed in 1934 would now in part be a programme of *laissez faire* in the historical sense—a programme of removing specific restrictions upon competition which have established themselves not by default but by the activity of collectivists. Nevertheless, his proposals have, of course, nothing whatever to do with that imaginary condition of wholly unfettered competition which is confused with *laissez faire* and ridiculed by collectivists when they have nothing better to say. As every schoolboy used to know, if effective competition is to exist it can do so only by virtue of a legal system which promotes it, and that monopoly has established itself only because the legal system has not prevented it. To know that unregulated competition is a chimera, to know that to regulate competition is not the same thing as to interfere with the operation of competitive controls, and to know the difference between these two activities, is the beginning of the political economy of freedom.

The libertarian, then, finds the general tendency towards a policy of collectivism a hindrance; but the unavoidable (and exceedingly uneconomical) collectivism which sprang up in libertarian societies engaged in a war of survival is recognized as an evil not without compensation. The believer in collectivism naturally looks upon war as an opportunity not to be missed, and the demobilization of society is no part of his programme. But to those who believe in liberty and yet remain hesitant about demobilization, Simons addresses some wise words: 'If wars are frequent, victories will probably go to those who remain mobilized . . . [But] if there are vital, creative forces to be released by demobilization—by return to a free society —the nation may thereby gain enough strength to compensate handsomely for the risks involved.' Every man, whom war took away from his chosen vocation, returned to it with pent-up energies ready to be released; and what is true of an individual may here be true also of an economy. Demobilization offered an opportunity for the springing up of a revitalized and more effectively competitive economy (an opportunity of which the collectivists deprived us), which would have made us more able to withstand future wars. There is a potential gain, if it can be harvested, for a society with a libertarian tradition, in the successive shocks of mobilization and demobilization. And just as a civilian will fight better (for he has something to fight for) if in the intervals of peace he is permitted to be a civilian (and not kept bumming around in an industrial army), so an economy which is, in peace, allowed to stretch itself and flex its limbs will be found, when it is mobilized for war, to possess superior stamina to one kept permanently mobilized.

The main principles of the policy are simple, and we have already noticed them. First, private monopoly in all its forms is to be suppressed. This means the establishment and maintenance (by means of the reform of the law which gives shape to the world of business and industry) of effective competition wherever effective competition is not demonstrably impossible: a genuine 'socialization' of enterprise in place of the spoof 'socialization' of the collectivist. The monopolies and the monopolistic practices to be destroyed are monopolies of labour. Restraint of trade must be treated as a major crime. In respect of enterprise, the absurd powers of corporations must be reduced. 'There is simply no excuse,' says Simons, 'except with a narrow and specialized class of enterprise, for allowing corporations to hold stock in other corporations—and no reasonable excuse (the utilities apart) for hundred-million-dollar corporations, no matter what form their property may take. Even if the much advertised economies of gigantic financial combinations were real, sound policy would wisely sacrifice these economies to preservation of more economic freedom and equality.' The corporation is a socially useful device for organizing ownership and control in operating companies of size sufficient to obtain the real economies of large-scale production under unified management; but the corporation law which has allowed this device to work for the impediment of freedom is long overdue for reform. In respect of labour, the problem of reducing the existing or threatened monopolies and monopoly practices is more difficult. The best one may hope, perhaps, is that labour monopolies, if not fostered and supported by the law, will cease to grow and even decline in power. And if we deal intelligently with other, easier problems, it is to be expected that this problem will become less intractable by progress in other directions.

Secondly, undertakings in which competition cannot be made to work as the agency of control must be transferred to public operation. Now the difference between this policy and that of the collectivist should be observed. There is, in the first place, a difference of emphasis. The collectivist would, in the end, take over every undertaking the 'nationalization' of which does not offer insuperable technical difficulties; the libertarian would create a government-controlled monopoly only when monopoly of some sort is unavoidable. The collectivist favours monopolies as an opportunity for the extension of political control; the libertarian would break up all destructible monopolies. And the ground of this emphasis is clear. To the libertarian all monopolies are expensive and productive of servility. While the collectivist welcomes and sees his opportunity in a society in which (owing to growth of population and changes in the technique of production) enterprise tends to become gigantic even when the law does not encourage undue size, the libertarian sees in this tendency a threat to freedom which must be warded off (and can be warded off) by the appropriate legal reforms. And from this difference of emphasis springs all the other differences: the disinclination to create monopolies where there are none (in education, for example), the disposition to reduce and to simplify all monopolies taken over so that they may contribute as little as possible to the power of government, the strongest legal discouragement to the appearance of syndicalist tendencies within these monopolies, and the recognition that the effect of all such proposals upon the power of government is as important as their effect upon 'society'. In short, the political economy of freedom rests upon the clear acknowledgment that what is being considered is not 'economics' (not the maximization of wealth, not productivity or the standard of life), but *politics*, that is, the custody of a manner of living; that these arrangements have to be paid for, are a charge upon our productive capacity; and that they are worth paying for so long as the price is not a diminution of what we have learned to recognize as liberty.

The third object of this economic policy is a stable currency, maintained by the application of fixed and known rules and not by day-to-day administrative tricks. And that this belongs to the political economy of freedom needs no argument: inflation is the mother of servitude.

Politics is not the science of setting up a permanently impregnable society, it is the art of knowing where to go next in the exploration of an already existing traditional kind of society. And in a society, such as ours, which has not yet lost the understanding of government as the prevention of coercion, as the power which holds in check the overmighty subject, as the protector of minorities against the power of majorities, it may well be thought that the task to which this generation is called is not the much advertised 'reconstruction of society' but to provide against the new tyrannies which an immense growth in population in a wantonly productivist society are beginning to impose; and to provide against them in such a manner that the cure is not worse than the disease.

"The Political Economy of Freedom" first appeared in *Cambridge Journal*, Volume II, 1949.

On being conservative

The common belief that it is impossible (or, if not impossible, then so unpromising as to be not worth while attempting) to elicit explanatory general principles from what is recognized to be conservative conduct is not one that I share. It may be true that conservative conduct does not readily provoke articulation in the idiom of general ideas, and that consequently there has been a certain reluctance to undertake this kind of elucidation; but it is not to be presumed that conservative conduct is less eligible than any other for this sort of interpretation, for what it is worth. Nevertheless, this is not the enterprise I propose to engage in here. My theme is not a creed or a doctrine, but a disposition. To be conservative is to be disposed to think and behave in certain manners; it is to prefer certain kinds of conduct and certain conditions of human circumstances to others; it is to be disposed to make certain kinds of choices. And my design here is to construe this disposition as it appears in contemporary character, rather than to transpose it into the idiom of general principles.

The general characteristics of this disposition are not difficult to discern, although they have often been mistaken. They centre upon a propensity to use and to enjoy what is available rather than to wish for or to look for something else; to delight in what is present rather than what was or what may be. Reflection may bring to light an appropriate gratefulness for what is available, and consequently the acknowledgment of a gift or an inheritance from the past; but there is no mere idolizing of what is past and gone. What is esteemed is the present; and it is esteemed not on account of its connections with a remote antiquity, nor because it is recognized to be more admirable than any possible alternative, but on account of its familiarity: not, *Verweile doch, du bist so schön,* but, *Stay with me because I am attached to you.*

If the present is arid, offering little or nothing to be used or enjoyed, then this inclination will be weak or absent; if the present is remarkably unsettled, it will display itself in a search for a firmer foothold and consequently in a recourse to and an exploration of the past; but it asserts itself characteristically when there is much to be enjoyed, and it will be strongest when this is combined with evident risk of loss. In short, it is a disposition appropriate to a man who is acutely aware of having something to lose which he has learned to care for; a man in some degree rich in opportunities for enjoyment, but not so rich that he can afford to be indifferent to loss. It will appear more naturally in the old than in the young, not because the old are more sensitive to loss but because they are apt to be more fully aware of the resources of their world and therefore less likely to find them inadequate. In some people this disposition is weak merely because they are ignorant of what their world has to offer them: the present appears to them only as a residue of inopportunities.

To be conservative, then, is to prefer the familiar to the unknown, to prefer the tried to the untried, fact to mystery, the actual to the possible, the limited to the unbounded, the near to the distant, the sufficient to the superabundant, the convenient to the perfect, present laughter to utopian bliss. Familiar relationships and loyalties will be preferred to the allure of more profitable attachments; to acquire and to enlarge will be less important than to keep, to cultivate and to enjoy; the grief of loss will be more acute than the excitement of novelty or promise. It is to be equal to one's own fortune, to live at the level of one's own means, to be content with the want of greater perfection which belongs alike to oneself and one's circumstances. With some people this is itself a choice; in others it is a disposition which appears, frequently or less frequently, in their preferences and aversions, and is not itself chosen or specifically cultivated.

Now, all this is represented in a certain attitude towards change and innovation; change denoting alterations we have to suffer and innovation those we design and execute.

Changes are circumstances to which we have to accommodate ourselves, and the disposition to be conservative is both the emblem of our difficulty in doing so and our resort in the attempts we make to do so. Changes are without effect only upon those who notice nothing, who are ignorant of what they possess and apathetic to their circumstances; and they can be welcomed indiscriminately only by those who esteem nothing, whose attachments are fleeting and who are strangers to love and affection. The conservative disposition provokes neither of these conditions: the inclination to enjoy what is present and available is the opposite of ignorance and apathy and it breeds attachment and affection. Consequently, it is averse from change, which appears always, in the first place, as deprivation. A storm which sweeps away a copse and transforms a favourite view, the death of friends, the sleep of friendship, the desuetude of customs of behaviour, the retirement of a favourite clown, involuntary exile, reversals of fortune, the loss of abilities enjoyed and their replacement by others—these are changes, none perhaps without its compensations, which the man of conservative temperament unavoidably regrets. But he has difficulty in reconciling himself to them, not because what he has lost in them was intrinsically better than any alternative might have been or was incapable of improvement, nor because what takes its place is inherently incapable of being enjoyed, but because what he has lost was something he actually enjoyed and had learned how to enjoy and what takes its place is something to which he has acquired no attachment. Consequently, he will find small and slow changes more tolerable than large and sudden; and he will value highly every appearance of continuity. Some changes, indeed, will present no difficulty; but, again, this is not because they are manifest improvements but merely because they are easily assimilated: the changes of the seasons are mediated by their recurrence and the growing up of children by its continuousness. And, in general, he will accommodate himself more readily to changes which do not offend expectation than to the destruction of what seems to have no ground of dissolution within itself.

Moreover, to be conservative is not merely to be averse from change (which may be an idiosyncrasy); it is also a manner of accommodating ourselves to changes, and activity imposed upon all men. For, change is a threat to identity, and every change is an emblem of extinction. But a man's identity (or that of a community) is nothing more than an unbroken rehearsal of contingencies, each at the mercy of circumstances and each significant in proportion to its familiarity. It is not a fortress into which we may retire, and the only means we have of defending it (that is, ourselves) against the hostile force of change is in the open field of our experience; by throwing our weight upon the foot which for the time being is most firmly placed, by cleaving to whatever familiarities are not immediately threatened and thus assimilating what is new without becoming unrecognizable to ourselves. The Masai, when they were moved from their old country to the present Masai reserve in Kenya, took with them the names of their hills and plains and rivers and gave them to the hills and plains and rivers of the new country. And it is by some such subterfuge of conservatism that every man or people compelled to suffer a notable change avoids the shame of extinction.

Changes, then, have to be suffered; and a man of conservative temperament (that is, one strongly disposed to preserve his identity) cannot be indifferent to them. In the main, he judges them by the disturbance they entail and, like everyone else, deploys his resources to meet them. The idea of innovation, on the other hand, is improvement. Nevertheless, a man of this temperament will not himself be an ardent innovator. In the first place, he is not inclined to think that nothing is happening unless great changes are afoot and therefore he is not worried by the absence of innovation: the use and enjoyment of things as they are occupies most of his attention. Further, he is aware that not all innovation is, in fact, improvement; and he will think that to innovate without improving is either designed or inadvertent folly. Moreover, even when an innovation commends itself as a convincing improvement, he will look twice at its claims before accepting them. From his point of view, because every improvement involves change, the disruption entailed has always to be set against the benefit anticipated. But when he has satisfied himself about this, there will be other considerations to be taken into the account. Innovating is always an equivocal enterprise, in which gain and loss (even excluding the loss of familiarity) are so closely interwoven that it is exceedingly difficult to forecast the final up-shot: there is no such thing as an unqualified improvement. For, innovating is an activity which generates not only the 'improvement' sought, but a new and complex situation of which this is only one of the components. The total change is always more extensive than the change designed; and the whole of what is entailed can neither be foreseen nor circumscribed. Thus, whenever there is innovation there is the certainty that the change will be greater than was intended, that there will be loss as well as gain and that the loss and the gain will not be equally distributed among the people affected; there is the chance that the benefits derived will be greater than those which were designed; and there is the risk that they will be off-set by changes for the worse.

From all this the man of conservative temperament draws some appropriate conclusions. First, innovation entails certain loss and possible gain, therefore, the onus of proof, to show that the proposed change may be expected to be on the whole beneficial, rests with the would-be innovator. Secondly, he believes that the more closely an innovation resembles growth (that is, the more clearly it is intimated in and not merely imposed upon the situation) the less likely it is to result in a preponderance of loss. Thirdly, he thinks that an innovation which is a response to some specific defect, one designed to redress some specific disequilibrium, is more desirable than one which springs from a notion of a generally improved condition of human circumstances, and is far more desirable than one generated by a vision of perfection. Consequently, he prefers small and limited innovations to large and indefinite. Fourthly, he favours a slow rather than a rapid pace, and pauses to observe current consequences and make appropriate adjustments. And lastly, he believes the occasion to be important; and, other things being equal, he considers the most favourable occasion for innovation to be when the projected change is most likely to be limited to what is intended and least likely to be corrupted by undesired and unmanageable consequences.

The disposition to be conservative is, then, warm and positive in respect of enjoyment, and correspondingly cool and critical in respect of change and innovation: these two inclinations support and elucidate one another. The man of conservative temperament believes that a known good is not lightly to be surrendered for an unknown better. He is not in love with what is dangerous and difficult; he is unadventurous; he has no impulse to sail uncharted seas; for him there is no magic in being lost, bewildered or shipwrecked. If he is forced to navigate the unknown, he sees virtue in heaving the lead every inch of the way. What others plausibly identify as timidity, he recognizes in himself as rational prudence; what others interpret as inactivity, he recognizes as a disposition to enjoy rather than to exploit. He is cautious, and he is disposed to indicate his assent or dissent, not in absolute, but in graduated terms. He eyes the situation in terms of its propensity to disrupt the familiarity of the features of his world.

TWO

It is commonly believed that this conservative disposition is pretty deeply rooted in what is called 'human nature'. Change is tiring, innovation calls for effort, and human beings (it is said) are more

apt to be lazy than energetic. If they have found a not unsatisfactory way of getting along in the world, they are not disposed to go
looking for trouble. They are naturally apprehensive of the unknown and prefer safety to danger. They are reluctant innovators,
and they accept change not because they like it but (as Rochefoucauld says they accept death) because it is inescapable. Change
generates sadness rather than exhilaration: heaven is the dream of
a changeless no less than of a perfect world. Of course, those who
read 'human nature' in this way agree that this disposition does
not stand alone; they merely contend that it is an exceedingly
strong, perhaps the strongest, of human propensities. And, so far
as it goes, there is something to be said for this belief: human circumstances would certainly be very different from what they are if
there were not a large ingredient of conservatism in human preferences. Primitive peoples are said to cling to what is familiar and to
be averse from change; ancient myth is full of warnings against innovation; our folklore and proverbial wisdom about the conduct of
life abounds in conservative precepts; and how many tears are shed
by children in their unwilling accommodation to change. Indeed,
wherever a firm identity has been achieved, and wherever identity is
felt to be precariously balanced, a conservative disposition is likely
to prevail. On the other hand, the disposition of adolescence is often predominantly adventurous and experimental: when we are
young, nothing seems more desirable than to take a chance; *pas de
risque, pas de plaisir.* And while some peoples, over long stretches
of time, appear successfully to have avoided change, the history of
others displays periods of intense and intrepid innovation. There
is, indeed, not much profit to be had from general speculation
about 'human nature', which is no steadier than anything else in
our acquaintance. What is more to the point is to consider current
human nature, to consider ourselves.

    With us, I think, the disposition to be conservative is far from
being notably strong. Indeed, if he were to judge by our conduct
during the last five centuries or so, an unprejudiced stranger might
plausibly suppose us to be in love with change, to have an appetite
only for innovation and to be either so out of sympathy with our-

selves or so careless of our identity as not to be disposed to give it any consideration. In general, the fascination of what is new is felt far more keenly than the comfort of what is familiar. We are disposed to think that nothing important is happening unless great innovations are afoot, and that what is not being improved must be deteriorating. There is a positive prejudice in favour of the yet untried. We readily presume that all change is, somehow, for the better, and we are easily persuaded that all the consequences of our innovating activity are either themselves improvements or at least a reasonable price to pay for getting what we want. While the conservative, if he were forced to gamble, would bet on the field, we are disposed to back our individual fancies with little calculation and no apprehension of loss. We are acquisitive to the point of greed; ready to drop the bone we have for its reflection magnified in the mirror of the future. Nothing is made to outlast probable improvement in a world where everything is undergoing incessant improvement: the expectation of life of everything except human beings themselves continuously declines. Pieties are fleeting, loyalties evanescent, and the pace of change warns us against too deep attachments. We are willing to try anything once, regardless of the consequences. One activity vies with another in being 'up-to-date': discarded motor-cars and television sets have their counterparts in discarded moral and religious beliefs: the eye is ever on the new model. To see is to imagine what might be in the place of what is; to touch is to transform. Whatever the shape or quality of the world, it is not for long as we want it. And those in the van of movement infect those behind with their energy and enterprise. *Omnes eodem cogemur*: when we are no longer light-footed we find a place for ourselves in the band.[1]

Of course, our character has other ingredients besides this lust for change (we are not devoid of the impulse to cherish and preserve), but there can be little doubt about its pre-eminence. And, in these circumstances, it seems appropriate that a conservative disposition should appear, not as an intelligible (or even plausible) al-

---

[1] 'Which of us,' asks a contemporary (not without some equivocation), 'would not settle, at whatever cost in nervous anxiety, for a febrile and creative rather than a static society?'

ternative to our mainly 'progressive' habit of mind, but either as an unfortunate hindrance to the movement afoot, or as the custodian of the museum in which quaint examples of superseded achievement are preserved for children to gape at, and as the guardian of what from time to time is considered not yet ripe for destruction, which we call (ironically enough) the amenities of life.

Here our account of the disposition to be conservative and its current fortunes might be expected to end, with the man in whom this disposition is strong last seen swimming against the tide, disregarded not because what he has to say is necessarily false but because it has become irrelevant; outmanoeuvred, not on account of any intrinsic demerit but merely by the flow of circumstance; a faded, timid, nostalgic character, provoking pity as an outcast and contempt as a reactionary. Nevertheless, I think there is something more to be said. Even in these circumstances, when a conservative disposition in respect of things in general is unmistakably at a discount, there are occasions when this disposition remains not only appropriate, but supremely so; and there are connections in which we are unavoidably disposed in a conservative direction.

In the first place, there is a certain kind of activity (not yet extinct) which can be engaged in only in virtue of a disposition to be conservative, namely, activities where what is sought is present enjoyment and not a profit, a reward, a prize or a result in addition to the experience itself. And when these activities are recognized as the emblems of this disposition, to be conservative is disclosed, not as prejudiced hostility to a 'progressive' attitude capable of embracing the whole range of human conduct, but as a disposition exclusively appropriate in a large and significant field of human activity. And the man in whom this disposition is pre-eminent appears as one who prefers to engage in activities where to be conservative is uniquely appropriate, and not as a man inclined to impose his conservatism indiscriminately upon all human activity. In short, if we find ourselves (as most of us do) inclined to reject conservatism as a disposition appropriate in respect of human conduct in general, there still remains a certain kind of human conduct for which this disposition is not merely appropriate but a necessary condition.

There are, of course, numerous human relationships in which a disposition to be conservative, a disposition merely to enjoy what they offer for its own sake, is not particularly appropriate: master and servant, owner and bailiff, buyer and seller, principal and agent. In these, each participant seeks some service or some recompense for service. A customer who finds a shopkeeper unable to supply his wants either persuades him to enlarge his stock or goes elsewhere; and a shopkeeper unable to meet the desires of a customer tries to impose upon him others which he can satisfy. A principal ill-served by his agent, looks for another. A servant ill-recompensed for his service, asks for a rise; and one dissatisfied with his conditions of work, seeks a change. In short, these are all relationships in which some result is sought; each party is concerned with the ability of the other to provide it. If what is sought is lacking, it is to be expected that the relationship will lapse or be terminated. To be conservative in such relationships, to enjoy what is present and available regardless of its failure to satisfy any want and merely because it has struck our fancy and become familiar, is conduct which discloses a *jusqu'aubutiste* conservatism, an irrational inclination to refuse all relationships which call for the exercise of any other disposition. Though even these relationships seem to lack something appropriate to them when they are confined to a nexus of supply and demand and allow no room for the intrusion of the loyalties and attachments which spring from familiarity.

But there are relationships of another kind in which no result is sought and which are engaged in for their own sake and enjoyed for what they are and not for what they provide. This is so of friendship. Here, attachment springs from an intimation of familiarity and subsists in a mutual sharing of personalities. To go on changing one's butcher until one gets the meat one likes, to go on educating one's agent until he does what is required of him, is conduct not inappropriate to the relationship concerned; but to discard friends because they do not behave as we expected and refuse to be educated to our requirements is the conduct of a man who has altogether mistaken the character of friendship. Friends are not concerned with what might be made of one another, but only with the enjoyment of one another; and the condition of this enjoyment is a ready acceptance of what is and the absence of any desire to change or to improve. A friend is not somebody one trusts to behave in a certain manner, who supplies certain wants, who has certain useful abilities, who possesses certain merely agreeable qualities, or who holds certain acceptable opinions; he is somebody who engages the imagination, who excites contemplation, who provokes interest, sympathy, delight and loyalty simply on account of the relationship entered into. One friend cannot replace another; there is all the difference in the world between the death of a friend and the retirement of one's tailor from business. The relationship of friend to friend is dramatic, not utilitarian; the tie is one of familiarity, not usefulness; the disposition engaged is conservative, not 'progressive'. And what is true of friendship is not less true of other experiences—of patriotism, for example, and of conversation—each of which demands a conservative disposition as a condition of its enjoyment.

But further, there are activities, not involving human relationships, that may be engaged in, not for a prize, but for the enjoyment they generate, and for which the only appropriate disposition is the disposition to be conservative. Consider fishing. If your project is merely to catch fish it would be foolish to be unduly conservative. You will seek out the best tackle, you will discard practices which prove unsuccessful, you will not be bound by unprofitable attachments to particular localities, pieties will be fleeting, loyalties evanescent; you may even be wise to try anything once in the hope of improvement. But fishing is an activity that may be engaged in, not for the profit of a catch, but for its own sake; and the fisherman may return home in the evening not less content for being empty-handed. Where this is so, the activity has become a ritual and a conservative disposition is appropriate. Why worry about the best gear if you do not care whether or not you make a catch? What matters is the enjoyment of exercising skill (or, perhaps, merely passing the time),[2]

---

[2] When Prince Wen Wang was on a tour of inspection in Tsang, he saw an old man fishing. But his fishing was not real fishing, for he did not fish in order to catch fish, but to amuse himself. So Wen Wang wished to employ him in the administration of government, but he feared his own ministers, uncles and brothers might object. On the other hand, if he let the

and this is to be had with any tackle, so long as it is familiar and is not grotesquely inappropriate.

All activities, then, where what is sought is enjoyment springing, not from the success of the enterprise but from the familiarity of the engagement, are emblems of the disposition to be conservative. And there are many of them. Fox placed gambling among them when he said that it gave two supreme pleasures, the pleasure of winning and the pleasure of losing. Indeed, I can think of only one activity of this kind which seems to call for a disposition other than conservative: the love of fashion, that is, wanton delight in change for its own sake no matter what it generates.

But besides the not inconsiderable class of activities which we can engage in only in virtue of a disposition to be conservative, there are occasions in the conduct of other activities when this is the most appropriate disposition; indeed there are few activities which do not, at some point or other, make a call upon it. Whenever stability is more profitable than improvement, whenever certainty is more valuable than speculation, whenever familiarity is more desirable than perfection, whenever agreed error is superior to controversial truth, whenever the disease is more sufferable than the cure, whenever the satisfaction of expectations is more important than the 'justice' of the expectations themselves, whenever a rule of some sort is better than the risk of having no rule at all, a disposition to be conservative will be more appropriate than any other; and on any reading of human conduct these cover a not negligible range of circumstances. Those who see the man of conservative disposition (even in what is vulgarly called a 'progressive' society) as a lonely swimmer battling against the overwhelming current of circumstance must be thought to have adjusted their binoculars to exclude a large field of human occasion.

In most activities not engaged in for their own sake a distinction appears, at a certain level of observation, between the project undertaken and the means employed, between the enterprise and the tools used for its achievements. This is not, of course, an abso-

old man go, he could not bear to think of the people being deprived of his influence. *Chuang Tzu.*

lute distinction; projects are often provoked and governed by the tools available, and on rarer occasions the tools are designed to fit a particular project. And what on one occasion is a project, on another is a tool. Moreover there is at least one significant exception: the activity of being a poet. It is, however, a relative distinction of some usefulness because it calls our attention to an appropriate difference of attitude towards the two components of the situation.

In general, it may be said that our disposition in respect of tools is appropriately more conservative than our attitude towards projects; or, in other words, tools are less subject to innovation than projects because, except on rare occasions, tools are not designed to fit a particular project and then thrown aside, they are designed to fit a whole class of projects. And this is intelligible because most tools call for skill in use and skill is inseparable from practice and familiarity: a skilled man, whether he is a sailor, a cook or an accountant, is a man familiar with a certain stock of tools. Indeed, a carpenter is usually more skilful in handling his own tools than in handling other examples of the kind of tools commonly used by carpenters; and the solicitor can use his own (annotated) copy of Pollock on *Partnership* or Jarman on *Wills* more readily than any other. Familiarity is the essence of tool using; and in so far as man is a tool using animal he is disposed to be conservative.

Many of the tools in common use have remained unchanged for generations; the design of others has undergone considerable modification; and our stock of tools is always being enlarged by new inventions and improved by new designs. Kitchens, factories, workshops, building sites and offices disclose a characteristic mixture of long-tried and newly invented equipment. But, be that how it may, when business of any kind is afoot, when a particular project has been engaged in—whether it is baking a pie or shoeing a horse, floating a loan or a company, selling fish or insurance to a customer, building a ship or a suit of clothes, sowing wheat or lifting potatoes, laying down port or putting up a barrage—we recognize it to be an occasion when it is particularly appropriate to be conservative about the tools we employ. If it is a large project, we put it in charge of a man who has the requisite knowledge, and we expect him to engage subordinates who know their own business and are skilled in the use of certain stocks of tools. At some point in this hierarchy of tool-users the suggestion may be made that in order to do this particular job an addition or modification is required in the available stock of tools. Such a suggestion is likely to come from somewhere about the middle of the hierarchy: we do not expect a designer to say 'I must go away and do some fundamental research which will take me five years before I can go on with the job' (his bag of tools is a body of knowledge and we expect him to have it handy and to know his way about it); and we do not expect the man at the bottom to have a stock of tools inadequate for the needs of his particular part. But even if such a suggestion is made and is followed up, it will not disrupt the appropriateness of a conservative disposition in respect of the whole stock of tools being used. Indeed, it is clear enough that no job would ever get done, no piece of business could ever be transacted if, on the occasion, our disposition in respect of our tools were not, generally speaking, conservative. And since doing business of one sort or another occupies most of our time and little can be done without tools of some kind, the disposition to be conservative occupies an unavoidably large place in our character.

The carpenter comes to do a job, perhaps one the exact like of which he has never before tackled; but he comes with his bag of familiar tools and his only chance of doing the job lies in the skill with which he uses what he has at his disposal. When the plumber goes to fetch his tools he would be away even longer than is usually the case if his purpose were to invent new or to improve old ones. Nobody questions the value of money in the market place. No business would ever get done if, before a pound of cheese were weighed or a pint of beer drawn, the relative usefulness of these particular scales of weight and measurement as compared with others were threshed out. The surgeon does not pause in the middle of an operation to redesign his instruments. The MCC does not authorize a new width of bat, a new weight of ball or a new length of wicket in the middle of a Test Match, or even in the middle of a cricket season. When your house is on fire you do not get in touch with a fire-prevention research station to design a new appliance; as Disraeli pointed out, unless you are a lunatic, you send for the parish fire-engine. A musician may improvise music, but he would think himself hardly done-by if, at the same time, he were expected to improvise an instrument. Indeed, when a particularly tricky job is to be done, the workman will often prefer to use a tool that he is thoroughly familiar with rather than another he has in his bag, of new design, but which he has not yet mastered the use of. No doubt there is a time and a place to be radical about such things, for promoting innovation and carrying out improvements in the tools we employ, but these are clearly occasions for the exercise of a conservative disposition.

Now, what is true about tools in general, as distinct from projects, is even more obviously true about a certain kind of tool in common use, namely, general rules of conduct. If the familiarity that springs from relative immunity from change is appropriate to hammers and pincers and to bats and balls, it is supremely appropriate, for example, to an office routine. Routines, no doubt, are susceptible of improvement; but the more familiar they become, the more useful they are. Not to have a conservative disposition in respect of a routine is obvious folly. Of course, exceptional occasions occur which may call for a dispensation; but an inclination to be conservative rather than reformist about a routine is unquestionably appropriate. Consider the conduct of a public meeting, the rules of debate in the House of Commons or the procedure of a court of law. The chief virtue of these arrangements is that they are fixed and familiar; they establish and satisfy certain expectations, they allow to be said in a convenient order whatever is relevant, they prevent extraneous collisions and they conserve human energy. They are typical tools—instruments eligible for use in a variety of different but similar jobs. They are the product of reflection and choice, there is nothing sacrosanct about them, they are susceptible of change and improvement; but if our disposition in respect of them were not, generally speaking, conservative, if we were disposed to argue about them and change them on every occasion, they would rapidly lose their value. And while there may be rare occasions when it is useful to suspend them, it is pre-eminently appropriate that they should not be innovated upon or improved while they are in operation. Or again, consider the rules of a game. These, also, are the product of reflection and choice, and there are occasions when it is appropriate to reconsider them in the light of current experience; but it is inappropriate to have anything but a conservative disposition towards them or to consider putting them all together at one time into the melting-pot; and it is supremely inappropriate to change or improve upon them in the heat and confusion of play. Indeed, the more eager each side is to win, the more valuable is an inflexible set of rules. Players in the course of play may devise new tactics, they may improvise new methods of attack and defence, they may do anything they choose to defeat the expectations of their opponents, except invent new rules. That is an activity to be indulged sparingly and then only in the off-season.

There is much more that might be said about the relevance of the disposition to be conservative and its appropriateness even in a character, such as ours, chiefly disposed in the opposite direction. I have said nothing of morals, nothing of religion; but perhaps I have said enough to show that, even if to be conservative on all occasions and in all connections is so remote from our habit of thought as to be almost unintelligible, there are, nevertheless, few of our activities which do not on all occasions call into partnership a disposition to be conservative and on some occasions recognize it as the senior partner; and there are some activities where it is properly master.

THREE

How, then, are we to construe the disposition to be conservative in respect of politics? And in making this inquiry what I am interested in is not merely the intelligibility of this disposition in any set of circumstances, but its intelligibility in our own contemporary circumstances.

Writers who have considered this question commonly direct our attention to beliefs about the world in general, about human beings in general, about associations in general and even about the universe; and they tell us that a conservative disposition in politics can be correctly construed only when we understand it as a reflection of certain beliefs of these kinds. It is said, for example, that conservatism in politics is the appropriate counterpart of a generally conservative disposition in respect of human conduct: to be reformist in business, in morals or in religion and to be conservative in politics is represented as being inconsistent. It is said that the conservative in politics is so by virtue of holding certain religious beliefs; a belief, for example, in a natural law to be gathered from human experience, and in a providential order reflecting a divine purpose in nature and in human history to which it is the duty of mankind to conform its conduct and departure from which spells injustice and calamity. Further, it is said that a disposition to be conservative in politics reflects what is called an 'organic' theory of human society; that it is tied up with a belief in the absolute value of human personality, and with a belief in a primordial propensity of human beings to sin. And the 'conservatism' of an Englishman has even been connected with Royalism and Anglicanism.

Now, setting aside the minor complaints one might be moved to make about this account of the situation, it seems to me to suffer from one large defect. It is true that many of these beliefs have been held by people disposed to be conservative in political activity, and it may be true that these people have also believed their disposition to be in some way confirmed by them, or even to be founded upon them; but, as I understand it, a disposition to be conservative in politics does not entail either that we should hold these beliefs to be true or even that we should suppose them to be true. Indeed, I do not think it is necessarily connected with any particular beliefs about the universe, about the world in general or about human conduct in general. What it is tied to is certain beliefs about the activity of governing and the instruments of government, and it is in terms of beliefs on these topics, and not on others, that it can be made to appear intelligible. And, to state my view briefly before elaborating it, what makes a conservative disposition in politics intelligible is nothing to do with a natural law or a providential order, nothing to do with morals or religion; it is the observation of our current manner of living combined with the belief (which from our point of view need be regarded as no more than an hypothesis) that governing is a specific and limited activity, namely the provision and custody of general rules of conduct, which are understood, not as plans for imposing substantive activities, but as instruments enabling people to pursue the activities of their own choice with the minimum frustration, and therefore something which it is appropriate to be conservative about.

Let us begin at what I believe to be the proper starting-place; not in the empyrean, but with ourselves as we have come to be. I and my neighbours, my associates, my compatriots, my friends, my enemies and those who I am indifferent about, are people engaged in a great variety of activities. We are apt to entertain a multiplicity of opinions on every conceivable subject and are disposed to change these beliefs as we grow tired of them or as they prove unserviceable. Each of us is pursuing a course of his own; and there is no project so unlikely that somebody will not be found to engage in it, no enterprise so foolish that somebody will not undertake it. There are those who spend their lives trying to sell copies of the Anglican Catechism to the Jews. And one half of the world is engaged in trying to make the other half want what it has hitherto never felt the lack of. We are all inclined to be passionate about our own concerns, whether it is making things or selling them, whether it is business or sport, religion or learning, poetry, drink or drugs. Each of us has preferences of his own. For some, the opportunities of making choices (which are numerous) are invitations readily accepted; others welcome them less eagerly or even find them burdensome. Some dream dreams of new and better worlds: others are more inclined to move in familiar paths or even to be idle. Some are apt to deplore the rapidity of change, others delight in it; all recognize it. At times we grow tired and fall asleep: it is a blessed relief to gaze in a shop window and see nothing we want; we are grateful for ugliness merely because it repels attention. But, for the most part, we pursue happiness by seeking the satisfaction of desires which spring from one another inexhaustably. We enter into relationships

of interest and of emotion, of competition, partnership, guardian-
ship, love, friendship, jealousy and hatred, some of which are more
durable than others. We make agreements with one another; we
have expectations about one another's conduct; we approve, we are
indifferent and we disapprove. This multiplicity of activity and variety of opinion is apt to produce collisions: we pursue courses which
cut across those of others, and we do not all approve the same sort
of conduct. But, in the main, we get along with one another, sometimes by giving way, sometimes by standing fast, sometimes in a
compromise. Our conduct consists of activity assimilated to that of
others in small, and for the most part unconsidered and unobtru-
sive, adjustments.

Why all this should be so, does not matter. It is not necessarily
so. A different condition of human circumstances can easily be
imagined, and we know that elsewhere and at other times activity
is, or has been, far less multifarious and changeful and opinion far
less diverse and far less likely to provoke collision; but, by and
large, we recognize this to be our condition. It is an acquired condition, though nobody designed or specifically chose it in preference
to all others. It is the product, not of 'human nature' let loose, but
of human beings impelled by an acquired love of making choices for
themselves. And we know as little and as much about where it is
leading us as we know about the fashion in hats of twenty years'
time or the design of motor-cars.

Surveying the scene, some people are provoked by the absence
of order and coherence which appears to them to be its dominant
feature; its wastefulness, its frustration, its dissipation of human
energy, its lack not merely of a premeditated destination but even of
any discernible direction of movement. It provides an excitement
similar to that of a stock-car race; but it has none of the satisfaction of a well-conducted business enterprise. Such people are apt to
exaggerate the current disorder; the absence of plan is so conspicuous that the small adjustments, and even the more massive arrangements, which restrain the chaos seem to them nugatory; they
have no feeling for the warmth of untidiness but only for its inconvenience. But what is significant is not the limitations of their pow-

ers of observation, but the turn of their thoughts. They feel that there ought to be something that ought to be done to convert this so-called chaos into order, for this is no way for rational human beings to be spending their lives. Like Apollo when he saw Daphne with her hair hung carelessly about her neck, they sigh and say to themselves: 'What if it were properly arranged.' Moreover, they tell us that they have seen in a dream the glorious, collisionless manner of living proper to all mankind, and this dream they understand as their warrant for seeking to remove the diversities and occasions of conflict which distinguish our current manner of living. Of course, their dreams are not all exactly alike; but they have this in common: each is a vision of a condition of human circumstance from which the occasion of conflict has been removed, a vision of human activity co-ordinated and set going in a single direction and of every resource being used to the full. And such people appropriately understand the office of government to be the imposition upon its subjects of the condition of human circumstances of their dream. To govern is to turn a private dream into a public and compulsory manner of living. Thus, politics becomes an encounter of dreams and the activity in which government is held to this understanding of its office and provided with the appropriate instruments.

I do not propose to criticize this jump to glory style of politics in which governing is understood as a perpetual take-over bid for the purchase of the resources of human energy in order to concentrate them in a single direction; it is not at all unintelligible, and there is much in our circumstances to provoke it. My purpose is merely to point out that there is another quite different understanding of government, and that it is no less intelligible and in some respects perhaps more appropriate to our circumstances.

The spring of this other disposition in respect of governing and the instruments of government—a conservative disposition—is to be found in the acceptance of the current condition of human circumstances as I have described it: the propensity to make our own choices and to find happiness in doing so, the variety of enterprises each pursued with passion, the diversity of beliefs each held with the conviction of its exclusive truth; the inventiveness, the change-fulness and the absence of any large design; the excess, the over-activity and the informal compromise. And the office of government is not to impose other beliefs and activities upon its subjects, not to tutor or to educate them, not to make them better or happier in another way, not to direct them, to galvanize them into action, to lead them or to co-ordinate their activities so that no occasion of conflict shall occur; the office of government is merely to rule. This is a specific and limited activity, easily corrupted when it is com-bined with any other, and, in the circumstances, indispensable. The image of the ruler is the umpire whose business is to adminis-ter the rules of the game, or the chairman who governs the debate according to known rules but does not himself participate in it.

Now people of this disposition commonly defend their belief that the proper attitude of government towards the current condi-tion of human circumstances is one of acceptance by appealing to certain general ideas. They contend that there is absolute value in the free play of human choice, that private property (the emblem of choice) is a natural right, that it is only in the enjoyment of diversi-ty of opinion and activity that true belief and good conduct can be expected to disclose themselves. But I do not think that this dispo-sition requires these or any similar beliefs in order to make it intel-ligible. Something much smaller and less pretentious will do: the observation that this condition of human circumstance is, in fact, current, and that we have learned to enjoy it and how to manage it; that we are not children *in statu pupillari* but adults who do not consider themselves under any obligation to justify their preference for making their own choices; and that it is beyond human experi-ence to suppose that those who rule are endowed with a superior wisdom which discloses to them a better range of beliefs and activi-ties and which gives them authority to impose upon their subjects a quite different manner of life. In short, if the man of this disposi-tion is asked: Why ought governments to accept the current diversi-ty of opinion and activity in preference to imposing upon their sub-jects a dream of their own? it is enough from him to reply: Why not? Their dreams are no different from those of anyone else; and if it is boring to have to listen to dreams of others being recounted, it is insufferable to be forced to re-enact them. We tolerate monomaniacs, it is our habit to do so; but why should we be *ruled* by them? Is it not (the man of conservative disposition asks) an intelligible task for a government to protect its subjects against the nuisance of those who spend their energy and their wealth in the service of some pet indignation, endeavouring to impose it upon everybody, not by suppressing their activities in favour of others of a similar kind, but by setting a limit to the amount of noise anyone may emit?

Nevertheless, if this acceptance is the spring of the conservative's disposition in respect of government, he does not suppose that the office of government is to do nothing. As he understands it, there is work to be done which can be done only in virtue of a genuine acceptance of current beliefs simply because they are current and current activities simply because they are afoot. And, briefly, the office he attributes to government is to resolve some of the collisions which this variety of beliefs and activities generates; to preserve peace, not by placing an interdict upon choice and upon the diversity that springs from the exercise of preference, not by imposing substantive uniformity, but by enforcing general rules of procedure upon all subjects alike.

Government, then, as the conservative in this matter understands it, does not begin with a vision of another, different and better world, but with the observation of the self-government practised even by men of passion in the conduct of their enterprises; it begins in the informal adjustments of interests to one another which are designed to release those who are apt to collide from the mutual frustration of a collision. Sometimes these adjustments are no more than agreements between two parties to keep out of each other's way; sometimes they are of wider application and more durable character, such as the International Rules for the prevention of collisions at sea. In short, the intimations of government are to be found in ritual, not in religion or philosophy; in the enjoyment of orderly and peaceable behaviour, not in the search for truth or perfection.

But the self-government of men of passionate belief and enterprise is apt to break down when it is most needed. It often suffices to resolve minor collisions of interest, but beyond these it is not to be relied upon. A more precise and a less easily corrupted ritual is required to resolve the massive collisions which our manner of living is apt to generate and to release us from the massive frustrations in which we are apt to become locked. The custodian of this ritual is 'the government', and the rules it imposes are 'the law'. One may imagine a government engaged in the activity of an arbiter in cases of collisions of interest but doing its business without the aid of laws, just as one may imagine a game without rules and an umpire who was appealed to in cases of dispute and who on each occasion merely used his judgment to devise *ad hoc* a way of releasing the disputants from their mutual frustration. But the diseconomy of such an arrangement is so obvious that it could only be expected to occur to those inclined to believe the ruler to be supernaturally inspired and to those disposed to attribute to him a quite different office—that of leader, or tutor, or manager. At all events the disposition to be conservative in respect of government is rooted in the belief that where government rests upon the acceptance of the current activities and beliefs of its subjects, the only appropriate manner of ruling is by making and enforcing rules of conduct. In short, to be conservative about government is a reflection of the conservatism we have recognized to be appropriate in respect of rules of conduct.

To govern, then, as the conservative understands it, is to provide a *vinculum juris* for those manners of conduct which, in the circumstances, are least likely to result in a frustrating collision of interests; to provide redress and means of compensation for those who suffer from others behaving in a contrary manner; sometimes to provide punishment for those who pursue their own interests regardless of the rules; and, of course, to provide a sufficient force to maintain the authority of an arbiter of this kind. Thus, governing is recognized as a specific and limited activity; not the management of an enterprise, but the rule of those engaged in a great diversity of self-chosen enterprises. It is not concerned with concrete persons, but with activities; and with activities only in respect of their propensity to collide with one another. It is not concerned with moral right and wrong, it is not designed to make men good or even better; it is not indispensable on account of 'the natural depravity of mankind' but merely because of their current disposition to be extravagant; its business is to keep its subjects at peace with one another in the activities in which they have chosen to seek their happiness. And if there is any general idea entailed in this view, it is, perhaps, that a government which does not sustain the loyalty of its subjects is worthless; and that while one which (in the old puritan phrase) 'commands for truth' is incapable of doing so (because some of its subjects will believe its 'truth' to be error), one which is indifferent to 'truth' and 'error' alike, and merely pursues peace, presents no obstacle to the necessary loyalty.

Now, it is intelligible enough that any man who thinks in this manner about government should be averse from innovation: government is providing rules of conduct, and familiarity is a supremely important virtue in a rule. Nevertheless, he has room for other thoughts. The current condition of human circumstances is one in which new activities (often springing from new inventions) are constantly appearing and rapidly extend themselves, and in which beliefs are perpetually being modified or discarded; and for the rules to be inappropriate to the current activities and beliefs is as unprofitable as for them to be unfamiliar. For example, a variety of inventions and considerable changes in the conduct of business, seem now to have made the current law of copyright inadequate. And it may be thought that neither the newspaper nor the motor-car nor the aeroplane have yet received proper recognition in the law of England; they have all created nuisances that call out to be abated. Or again, at the end of the last century our governments engaged in an extensive codification of large parts of our law and in this manner both brought it into closer relationship with current beliefs and manners of activity and insulated it from the small adjustments to circumstances which are characteristic of the operation of our common law. But many of these Statutes are now hopelessly out of date. And there are older Acts of Parliament (such as the Merchant Shipping Act), governing large and important departments of activity, which are even more inappropriate to current circumstances. Innovation, then, is called for if the rules are to remain appropriate to the activities they govern. But, as the conservative understands it, modification of the rules should always reflect, and never impose, a change in the activities and beliefs of those who are subject to them, and should never on any occasion be so great as to destroy the *ensemble*. Consequently, the conservative will have nothing to do with innovations designed to meet merely hypothetical situations; he will prefer to enforce a rule he has got rather than invent a new one; he will think it appropriate to delay a modification of the rules until it is clear that the change of circumstances it is designed to reflect has come to stay for a while; he will be suspicious of proposals for change in excess of what the situation calls for, of rulers who demand extra-ordinary powers in order to make great changes and whose utterances are tied to generalities like 'the public good' or 'social justice', and of Saviours of Society who buckle on armour and seek dragons to slay; he will think it proper to consider the occasion of the innovation with care; in short, he will be disposed to regard politics as an activity in which a valuable set of tools is renovated from time to time and kept in trim rather than as an opportunity for perpetual re-equipment.

All this may help to make intelligible the disposition to be conservative in respect of government; and the detail might be elaborated to show, for example, how a man of this disposition understands the other great business of a government, the conduct of a foreign policy; to show why he places so high a value upon the complicated set of arrangements we call 'the institution of private property'; to show the appropriateness of his rejection of the view that politics is a shadow thrown by economics; to show why he believes that the main (perhaps the only) specifically economic activity appropriate to government is the maintenance of a stable currency. But, on this occasion, I think there is something else to be said.

To some people, 'government' appears as a vast reservoir of

power which inspires them to dream of what use might be made of it. They have favourite projects, of various dimensions, which they sincerely believe are for the benefit of mankind, and to capture this source of power, if necessary to increase it, and to use it for imposing their favourite projects upon their fellows is what they understand as the adventure of governing men. They are, thus, disposed to recognize government as an instrument of passion; the art of politics is to inflame and direct desire. In short, governing is understood to be just like any other activity—making and selling a brand of soap, exploiting the resources of a locality, or developing a housing estate—only the power here is (for the most part) already mobilized, and the enterprise is remarkable only because it aims at monopoly and because of its promise of success once the source of power has been captured. Of course a private enterprise politician of this sort would get nowhere in these days unless there were people with wants so vague that they can be prompted to ask for what he has to offer, or with wants so servile that they prefer the promise of a provided abundance to the opportunity of choice and activity on their own account. And it is not all as plain sailing as it might appear: often a politician of this sort misjudges the situation; and then, briefly, even in democratic politics, we become aware of what the camel thinks of the camel driver.

Now, the disposition to be conservative in respect of politics reflects a quite different view of the activity of governing. The man of this disposition understands it to be the business of a government not to inflame passion and give it new objects to feed upon, but to inject into the activities of already too passionate men an ingredient of moderation; to restrain, to deflate, to pacify and to reconcile; not to stoke the fires of desire, but to damp them down. And all this, not because passion is vice and moderation virtue, but because moderation is indispensable if passionate men are to escape being locked in an encounter of mutual frustration. A government of this sort does not need to be regarded as the agent of a benign providence, as the custodian of a moral law, or as the emblem of a divine order. What it provides is something that its subjects (if they are such people as we are) can easily recognize to be valuable; indeed, it is something that, to some extent, they do for themselves in the ordinary course of business or pleasure. They scarcely need to be reminded of its indispensability, as Sextus Empiricus tells us the ancient Persians were accustomed periodically to remind themselves by setting aside all laws for five hair-raising days on the death of a king. Generally speaking, they are not averse from paying the modest cost of this service; and they recognize that the appropriate attitude to a government of this sort is loyalty (sometimes a confident loyalty, at others perhaps the heavy-hearted loyalty of Sidney Godolphin), respect and some suspicion, not love or devotion or affection. Thus, governing is understood to be a secondary activity; but it is recognized also to be a specific activity, not easily to be combined with any other, because all other activities (except the mere contemplation of the scene) entail taking sides and the surrender of the indifference appropriate (on this view of things) not only to the judge but also to the legislator, who is understood to occupy a judicial office. The subjects of such a government require that it shall be strong, alert, resolute, economical and neither capricious nor over-active: they have no use for a referee who does not govern the game according to the rules, who takes sides, who plays a game of his own, or who is always blowing his whistle; after all, the game's the thing, and in playing the game we neither need to be, nor at present are disposed to be, conservative.

But there is something more to be observed in this style of governing than merely the restraint imposed by familiar and appropriate rules. Of course, it will not countenance government by suggestion or cajolery or by any other means than by law; an avuncular Home Secretary or a threatening Chancellor of the Exchequer. But the spectacle of its indifference to the beliefs and substantive activities of its subjects may itself be expected to provoke a habit of restraint. Into the heat of our engagements, into the passionate clash of beliefs, into our enthusiasm for saving the souls of our neighbours or of all mankind, a government of this sort injects an ingredient, not of reason (how should we expect that?) but of the

irony that is prepared to counteract one vice by another, of the rail-
lery that deflates extravagance without itself pretending to wisdom,
of the mockery that disperses tension, of inertia and of scepticism:
indeed, it might be said that we keep a government of this sort to
do for us the scepticism we have neither the time nor the inclination to do for ourselves. It is like the cool touch of the mountain
that one feels in the plain even on the hottest summer day. Or, to
leave metaphor behind, it is like the 'governor' which, by controlling
the speed at which its parts move, keeps an engine from racketing
itself to pieces.

It is not, then, mere stupid prejudice which disposes a conservative to take this view of the activity of governing; nor are any
highfalutin metaphysical beliefs necessary to provoke it or make it
intelligible. It is connected merely with the observation that where
activity is bent upon enterprise the indispensable counterpart is
another order of activity, bent upon restraint, which is unavoidably
corrupted (indeed, altogether abrogated) when the power assigned
to it is used for advancing favourite projects. An 'umpire' who at
the same time is one of the players is no umpire; 'rules' about
which we are not disposed to be conservative are not rules but in-
citements to disorder; the conjunction of dreaming and ruling generates tyranny.

FOUR

Political conservatism is, then, not at all unintelligible in a people
disposed to be adventurous and enterprising, a people in love with
change and apt to rationalize their affections in terms of 'progress'.[3] And one does not need to think that the belief in 'progress' is
the most cruel and unprofitable of all beliefs, arousing cupidity
without satisfying it, in order to think it inappropriate for a government to be conspicuously 'progressive'. Indeed, a disposition to be

---

[3] I have not forgotten to ask myself the question: Why, then, have we so neglected what is
appropriate to our circumstances as to make the activist dreamer the stereotype of the modern politician? And I have tried to answer it elsewhere.

conservative in respect of government would seem to be pre-eminently appropriate to men who have something to do and something to think about on their own account, who have a skill to practise or an intellectual fortune to make, to people whose passions do not need to be inflamed, whose desires do not need to be provoked and whose dreams of a better world need no prompting. Such people know the value of a rule which imposes orderliness without directing enterprise, a rule which concentrates duty so that room is left for delight. They might even be prepared to suffer a legally established ecclesiastical order; but it would not be because they believed it to represent some unassailable religious truth, but merely because it restrained the indecent competition of sects and (as Hume said) moderated 'the plague of a too diligent clergy'.

Now, whether or not these beliefs recommend themselves as reasonable and appropriate to our circumstances and to the abilities we are likely to find in those who rule us, they and their like are in my view what make intelligible a conservative disposition in respect of politics. What would be the appropriateness of this disposition in circumstances other than our own, whether to be conservative in respect of government would have the same relevance in the circumstances of an unadventurous, a slothful or a spiritless people, is a question we need not try to answer: we are concerned with ourselves as we are. I myself think that it would occupy an important place in any set of circumstances. But what I hope I have made clear is that it is not at all inconsistent to be conservative in respect of government and radical in respect of almost every other activity. And, in my opinion, there is more to be learnt about this disposition from Montaigne, Pascal, Hobbes and Hume than from Burke or Bentham.

Of the many entailments of this view of things that might be pointed to, I will notice one, namely, that politics is an activity unsuited to the young, not on account of their vices but on account of what I at least consider to be their virtues.

Nobody pretends that it is easy to acquire or to sustain the mood of indifference which this manner of politics calls for. To rein-in one's own beliefs and desires, to acknowledge the current shape of things, to feel the balance of things in one's hand, to tolerate what is abominable, to distinguish between crime and sin, to respect formality even when it appears to be leading to error, these are difficult achievements; and they are achievements not to be looked for in the young.

Everybody's young days are a dream, a delightful insanity, a sweet solipsism. Nothing in them has a fixed shape, nothing a fixed price; everything is a possiblity, and we live happily on credit. There are no obligations to be observed; there are no accounts to be kept. Nothing is specified in advance; everything is what can be made of it. The world is a mirror in which we seek the reflection of our own desires. The allure of violent emotions is irresistible. When we are young we are not disposed to make concessions to the world; we never feel the balance of a thing in our hands—unless it be a cricket bat. We are not apt to distinguish between our liking and our esteem; urgency is our criterion of importance; and we do not easily understand that what is humdrum need not be despicable. We are impatient of restraint; and we readily believe, like Shelley, that to have contracted a habit is to have failed. These, in my opinion, are among our virtues when we are young; but how remote they are from the disposition appropriate for participating in the style of government I have been describing. Since life is a dream, we argue (with plausible but erroneous logic) that politics must be an encounter of dreams, in which we hope to impose our own. Some unfortunate people, like Pitt (laughably called 'the Younger'), are born old, and are eligible to engage in politics almost in their cradles; others, perhaps more fortunate, belie the saying that one is young only once, they never grow up. But these are exceptions. For most there is what Conrad called the 'shadow line' which, when we pass it, discloses a solid world of things, each with its fixed shape, each with its own point of balance, each with its price; a world of fact, not poetic image, in which what we have spent on one thing we cannot spend on another; a world inhabited by others besides ourselves who cannot be reduced to mere reflections of our own emotions. And coming to be at home in this commonplace world quali-fies us (as no knowledge of 'political science' can ever qualify us), if we are so inclined and have nothing better to think about, to en-gage in what the man of conservative disposition understands to be political activity.

"On Being Conservative" was originally a lecture given at the University of Swansea in 1956. It was first published in the original edition of *Rationalism in Politics*.

Talking politics

Politics is not concerned with anything or everything which it may come into a man's head to want and to contend for but with the consideration of the arrangements and rules which give shape to an association of human beings. The vocabulary of political discourse is composed of words and expressions used to diagnose situations alleged to call for redress in an official response, to identify the shapes of the features and characteristics of a state or alternative more desirable shapes, to express and to recommend beliefs, doctrines, or dispositions alleged to be important in formulating political proposals; or to denote allegiances to considerations of general desirability in respect to the arrangements of a state. In short, it is a vocabulary that purports to express the conflicts, the tensions, and the alignments of political belief and design which are characteristic of modern states.

And it is of this political vocabulary, its fortunes, its virtues and its vices, its use and its abuse, that I wish to speak.

It is, of course, a European vocabulary. For although states, or approximations of them, are now spread about the world, they are all European inventions. Some of the expressions of this vocabulary have been appropriated from the distant past, words first invented and used in relation to long defunct associations thought to be in some sense the precursors of modern states—an ancient Greek *polis*, a biblical 'nation', a Roman or a Persian empire, or a medieval realm or patrimonial estate. Others are words from common discourse given expressly political meanings. And others again are inventions of our own designed to characterize emergent political persuasions or allegiances; although even the most time-bound of these expressions—Tory, Jacobin, Confederate, Whig—are apt to be generalized and as universals long outlive the circumstances of their invention.

We have, then, an extensive political vocabulary at our disposal: nouns and adjectives. We are not uninventive, but we use what we have economically, often preferring an old word even if this entails muddling the conversation by endowing it with an unfamiliar meaning. This vocabulary includes such expressions as: democracy, consent, consensus, power, freedom, the common interest, radical, progressive, liberal, conservative, a Bill of Rights, the rule of law, Right, Left, Center, totalitarian, equality, justice, toleration, and so on.

It may be supposed that many of these expressions were invented in order to distinguish and declare beliefs or dispositions and thus to make the political engagements less of a battle in the dark; but nobody could mistake them for scientific expressions. Indeed, we must allow them some degree of crudity; political discourse, concerned with persuasion, can never be a very refined engagement. But our language of politics is a vernacular that for long enough has been at the disposal, not only of scrupulous users (like Tocqueville, Madison, or Burke), but of anyone who wishes to persuade others of the virtue of a belief or the merits of a political response, and in these circumstances it has suffered grievous corruption.

First, there is the confusion, born of inadvertence, in which political discourse degenerates into artless muddle: a preference for the vague and indeterminate, for words that may be invested with multiple meanings and turned into all-purpose expressions. What may now be meant by the word 'liberal' is anyone's guess. 'Progressive' and 'reactionary' are models of ambiguity. And who knows whether the famous phrase 'of the people' is an objective genitive or merely a vague anticipation of the more explicit phrases that follow it? Then there is the perversion that occurs when any of these expressions is abridged into a slogan: relatives transformed into absolutes, 'free speech' and laissez-faire (which emerged as pleas for release from specific inhibiting conditions) turned into empty unconditional claims. We look for a thought and find only a worn-out, sapless incantation. For, in achieving the status of a battlecry, a political expression surrenders its place in a living language of political discourse and becomes a piece of bric-a-brac, like a notice-board displayed for sale in a second-hand shop: Beware of the Dog. There is no dog, and although the notice-board could hardly have been made unless there were people with dangerous dogs, it is in the shop to be bought by anyone who takes a fancy to it, for its decorative value or to stop a hole to keep the wind away: detente, 'democracy in danger', 'minority rights', 'majority rule'. Then again, these expressions are available to be used artfully, to distract attention or to direct it elsewhere—like the ugly mask of a dancer that says, 'My beauty is not my only virtue', and either speaks truly or lies, but divulges little. For fraud has been added to muddle, doubletalk to inadvertence and oversophistication. Novel projects are labeled with familiar names that belong to a wholly different universe of discourse, and ancient enormities are revived in modern forms and given false names in an effort to make them acceptable. An arbitrary redistribution of wealth is called 'taxation', a calculated debauch of the currency is called 'inflation', the exercise of 'lordship' by rulers is called 'socialization', servility packaged with benefits announces itself as 'the New Freedom', and a group whose confessed intention is to 'smash capitalism' is called 'a coalition of moderates'.

Now, none of this is surprising; it is what may happen to any vernacular in the hands of optative users, especially when their desires concern the alteration of the common arrangements of an association where, as the ancient Chinese sardonically remarked, 'the rectification of names' is an important consideration. And we may think we have not erred so greatly in this matter as some others. But there is one misfortune common to us all.

A modern state, as it emerged (whenever and wherever it might be in the last five hundred years), was observed to have certain constituent characteristics that, although not unique to this kind of association, appeared there more distinctly than elsewhere. These naturally became the focus of political attention. Political deliberation was concerned to understand them, to suggest for each an allegedly desirable shape corresponding to current beliefs. And the language of politics reflected these engagements. But, although nothing has since happened to depose them from this position of central importance, our language of politics has now become so elaborate and so confused that these great themes have got lost in its complications. We imagine that we are addressing ourselves to a succession of newly emergent beliefs and situations, each calling for an official response, but—distracted by their purported novelty and confused by a lot of new words and expressions (most of them devoid of any precise meaning)—we remain unaware that we are all the time concerned with these central themes and fatally confused about which of them we are considering. In short, political discourse has become so thickly orchestrated that we are unable to distinguish, or even to hear, the melodies which are the heart of the matter.

Let me remind you of them.

TWO

A modern state, as it emerged from a medieval realm, a patrimonial estate, a military protectorate, or a collection of colonial settlements, had three distinct features that it has never lost: an office of authority, an apparatus of power, and a mode of association. Each was in the making, not out of nothing but out of current beliefs and by the imposition of an allegedly more desirable shape upon what happened to be there. And this making and remaking has gone on ever since. In the history of some states there have been short pauses when one or another of these features seemed to acquire a temporarily acceptable shape, but nowhere has the shape of any of them become unquestionably fixed. Politics, the consideration of the shapes of these features in terms of their desirability, which one optimistic *Federalist* writer thought might be done once and for all, has been a continuous and unremitting engagement.

First, the office of authority. A state is an association of human beings constituted in the only manner in which such an association may be constituted; namely, in the acknowledgment of the authority of its rules and arrangements. And here, where these rules and arrangements are eligible to be changed and none is immune from amendment, this acknowledgment is the recognition of the authority of the office in whose custody they lie and of the procedures by which they may be changed and come to be prescribed. And by the acknowledgment of authority I do not mean approval of what is prescribed or the recognition of power to enforce prescriptions; I mean the recognition of an antecedent right to prescribe. This recognition is given in virtue of the shape or constitution of the office and not at all in virtue of the quality of its enactments or of their outcomes. When on the eve of the battle of Agincourt the soldier Bates said in conversation with his fellows, 'We know enough, if we know we are the King's subjects', he, briefly, acknowledged the authority of a King-shaped office of rule and recognized an obligation that perhaps he might not always adequately discharge but that he could not deny without declaring himself quit of the realm. We may think we are more sophisticated than this man of long ago, but we are not; we merely have different beliefs about what is authoritative and are more muddled about them.

A modern state, then, emerged with the appearance of an office of rule and the acknowledgment of its authority. This office was a status, identified by a name, together with rules specifying the conditions of its proper occupation. Often there was such an office and occupant ready to hand (a medieval king or a grand duke), but even so they had to get their authority accepted in the new circumstances; and since authority is always an endowment by those whom it obligates, they were not always or rapidly successful in doing so. Otherwise, an office and the conditions of its occupation had to be invented. King-shaped offices were qualified by being incorporated with representative assemblies or abolished in favor of other constitutional shapes. Some of these have been the outcome of careful deliberation in which the shape emerged from beliefs about authority, others have been hasty and non-durable contrivances. But everywhere they have had to win recognition; everywhere, late or soon, they have met with denial of their authority in rebellion or civil war; nowhere have they survived without change. Such changes make up a state's constitutional history which, at bottom, is the history of a succession of beliefs about authority.

In early days this was the most important theme of political reflection and its importance has not diminished. We tinker with it continuously, wondering whether some change in electoral law or some extension of the franchise might not constitute a more acceptably authoritative office of rule. We wear ourselves out by continually starting again from scratch. And by far the larger part of our political vocabulary is concerned with this theme. But the authority of an office of rule remains always a delicate matter of current belief. It must be able to survive a rainy day, it must be proof against disapproval and ridicule of the performances of the office and it cannot be bought with good works; it

hangs like a drop of dew
Upon a blade of grass.

The most substantial expressions of the fluctuating beliefs that endow an office of rule with authority are actual constitutional shapes in all their detail, but we have never in this matter given up the use of somewhat vague general expressions—as if the ingredient of myth they bring with them were necessary for our peace of mind. Thus, an office of rule is said to be authoritative because it is 'democratic' or 'republican' or 'parliamentary' or 'liberal'. We are familiar with the expression 'majority rule', and according to *Pravda* the government of Russia is a 'revolutionary-democratic dictatorship'.

These expressions belong properly to our vocabulary of authority. They describe, somewhat vaguely, the shape of an office of rule and at the same time they purport to give reasons for attributing or not attributing authority to it. When Henry Grattan, in 1790, said, 'Rank majorities may give a nation law, but rank majorities cannot give law authority', he was not denying that the expression 'majority rule' stood for a belief about authority, he was asserting that it did not stand for an acceptable belief about authority. But these expressions are soft and often difficult to construe. They reflect our chronic irresolution about the terms upon which we are willing to attribute authority to an office of rule and they impose a ramshackle character upon most modern states.

Moreover, our irresolution in this matter has bred obliquity. Our vocabulary of authority has been usurped to serve another, quite different, purpose. Its expressions have become ambiguous by having imposed upon them meanings which are concerned not at all with the authority of an office of rule but with its propensity to favor certain interests. The word 'democracy', for example, is made to stand for a 'method' of governing distinguished by its probable products, a 'utilitarian device', a piece of machinery designed, not to express certain beliefs about authority but to fabricate rules and arrangements that promote certain interests. According to Madison, the superiority of what he called a 'republican' over a 'democratic' office of government lay in its capacity to control the factious inclinations of human beings. For Bentham, the virtue of universal suffrage and the other constitutional arrangements he favored was not that they were the terms upon which an office of rule might be more decisively recognized to have authority but that they were plausible devices for promoting a substantive condition of things called the greatest happiness. And the constitution of an office of rule is now commonly considered merely in terms of its propensity to promote what some party or faction wishes to see promoted. When your electoral prospects are dim, propose a change in the electoral rules.

The muddle and chicanery which this abuse of our vocabulary of authority has imposed upon political discourse is not negligible. In prising loose our authority-words from their proper concern and attaching them elsewhere, it has generated a fatal indifference to the authority of an office of rule and has persuaded many that the principle of association in a state is to be sought not in the authority of its government but in a consensual approval of its performances—which, of course, in a modern state is always lacking.

THREE

The second feature of a state is the apparatus of governing annexed to the office of rule. The consideration here is not authority but power.

The word 'power' in a political vocabulary stands, properly, for a human relationship. It means the ability to procure with certainty a wished-for response in the substantive conduct of another. And, since it is a relationship of human beings, and thus depends upon both the ability and the disposition of the respondent to make the wished-for response, this certainty can never be absolute and power can never be irresistible.

The considerations in terms of which the wished-for response is sought are the beliefs of the respondent about the consequences to himself of compliance or noncompliance to the demand. Thus, there is a relationship of power between one who makes a demand threatening the respondent with some harmful consequence if he does not comply, and a respondent who fears the threatened consequence both because of his aversion from it and because he believes there are the resources and the intention to implement the threat; or between one whose demand is joined with the promise of a satisfaction, and a respondent who is so far unwilling to forgo it that he regards it as an otherwise unobtainable necessity and who believes there are the resources and the intention to provide it. And since fear of injury or want elevated into need are the conditions of a power relationship, he who neither fears anything nor needs anything cannot be drawn into it.

Power, then, is categorically distinguished from authority. To have power does not, itself, endow a man or an office with authority; to be acknowledged to have authority does not, itself, endow a man or an office with power; and to recognize the power behind a demand, although it may be a good reason for complying with what is demanded, cannot be a reason for acknowledging an obligation to do so. Thus, a well-informed blackmailer and his fearful subject may be said to stand to one another in a transitory relationship of power.

In a modern state there is a carefully assembled, durable apparatus of power annexed to the office of authority. Its ingredients do not themselves entail a relationship of power. They are the procedures, inventions, devices, machines, and contrivances of all sorts which in modern times have greatly increased our information about what is going on and the certainty with which it may be controlled—which, for the most part, is at the disposal of anyone who can afford to use it for the satisfaction of his wants. They compose an apparatus of power when they are mobilized and deployed to exact, under threat of injury or disadvantage, specific performances from assignable agents.

But where, as in a modern state, such an apparatus is annexed to an office of authority, both its ingredients and its employment are subject to conditions. The only legitimate use of this apparatus is to enforce subscription to the rules and arrangements to which the associates are already obligated to subscribe; and the threatened disadvantageous consequences are penalties and not merely injuries. In short, what turns a person into a subject of this apparatus of power is not merely his fears or needs but his failure to fulfil an obligation. And in a state this apparatus is the only power that the associates may legally invoke for the protection of themselves or be required to submit to. What it adds to an association constituted in the acknowledgment of the authority of an office of rule is the assurance, or at least the expectation, that obligations cannot be breached with impunity.

Nevertheless, this apparatus of power has always been regarded with immense suspicion and has been the subject of continuous political concern; that is, concern about the desirability of its components and the manner in which it is exercised. And we are equipped with a vocabulary that enables us to identify these components and debate these desirabilities. The first consideration, of course, is that the apparatus of power should be indissolubly linked with the office of authority; the situation where this is not so is called a 'tyranny'. The second consideration is that this link between power and authority should be preserved exactly and in all its detail: the consideration that an apparatus of power is liable to corruption and the desirability of avoiding this mischief. Thirdly, this apparatus has been inspected for what, in the change of moral opinion, may be recognized as excess both in its procedures of investigation and in the penalties it exacts. For it is well known that certainty in detecting delinquency and totally effective penalties may be achieved at too great a moral cost. And lastly, it may be considered, not in relation to its authority, but in respect to its being commensurate with the engagements of a government. These are all themes proper to political reflection and they have been explored continuously in relation to a modern state. But, alas, muddle has intervened. 'Power' is now the most abused word in our language of politics.

For long enough now for it to have achieved a sort of orthodoxy, we have had urged upon us the doctrine that ruling is the exercise of power and that a state is an association constituted by an apparatus of power. A few of the proponents of this doctrine have tried to persuade us that 'power' here is not even a human relationship, such as that between a potentate with wants to satisfy and fearful or needy subjects, but is merely the stimulation of behaviour, like an electric shock and the commensurate muscular twitch it causes. But this is easily recognized as the very worst of modernistic rot: even torturers seek something more from their victims (a confession or an admission) than the evidence of suffering pain.

But even where this apparatus is properly understood as setting up a relationship of demand and contingent response, the doctrine that ruling is the exercise of power is a half-baked affair. It allows only an inquiry into the source of this power, the effect of its exercise, and the acceptability of this effect. Having no place for the idea of authority, it is unable to recognize the difference between legitimate and illegitimate power; and it has become the occasion for the now common confusion that obscures, and often denies, the difference between being robbed and being fined for a failure to fulfil an obligation. And where being robbed and being fined or taxed, where being kidnapped and being gaoled are understood only in terms of the exercise of power, where a gangster and a policeman, a murderer and an executioner are recognized solely as repositories of power, they become indistinguishably objectionable, or the second is thought to be even more reprehensible than the first. We are then on the way to the fashionable doctrine that robbing and ruling are alike unacceptable exertions of power, a doctrine that lies behind some the the sillier political pronouncements and some of the more eccentric pleadings we now hear in courts of law.

Nor is the confusion resolved when the doctrine that identifies ruling with the exercise of power is merely qualified by a smuggled-in reference in authority. The office of rule in a modern state cannot be understood as merely the authorized custodian and operator of an apparatus of power, and a state cannot be persons associated merely in the recognition of the legitimacy of this apparatus. Before all else, this office is that of a prescriber of rules of conduct; the relationship set up with its subjects is not a power relationship of compulsion and obedience but a relationship of authority and obligation. And its authority to enforce the fulfilment of obligations derives from its authority to prescribe them.

Thus, ruling may properly be identified with the exercise of power only where the conduct enforced is understood *not* to be the fulfilment of obligations but compliance with the demands of merely powerful persons, a purported 'dominant class' or the operators of a *coup d'état;* that is, where the ruler is identified as a 'tyrant'. And ruling may be properly identified with the exercise of legitimate power only where there is a lingering belief that the obligations thus enforced do not derive from the authority of the office of rule but from God or Nature. This is the fanciful doctrine of the Declaration of Independence, in which governments are said to exist merely to *secure* rights that they have not themselves the authority to prescribe, and where the 'consent' of subjects can legitimize nothing more than the apparatus of power which is necessary to provide that security.

The apparatus of power in a modern state, then, provides plenty for us to think about, but our exploration of this theme has been more than a little muddled.

FOUR

The third feature of a modern state is its character as an association of human beings. Here, the consideration is neither authority nor power but the relationship of the associates to one another and the engagements of the office of rule.

For two or more persons to compose an association is for them to be related to one another in terms of some recognized conditions of association that they may make for themselves or accept ready-made. These conditions may be displayed in somewhat vague customs of conduct, they may be spelled out in a rule-book, or they may be declared in an acknowledged common purpose. Thus, associates are never whole persons. They are *personae;* that is, persons in their relation to one another in terms of some specified conditions: brothers, partners in business, colleagues, playmates, comrades, friends, and so on. No one such relationship can exhaust the associational potentialities of any man; there can be no unconditional human relationship (that is, persons related but not by particular conditions); and there is no *ensemble* in which all relationships coalesce in the sense that our common use of the word 'society' suggests. If the word 'social' is used to denote a relationship, it must be some particular relationship distinguished from all others. To investigate the character of a state as an association is, then, to consider the mode of association it constitutes and the *persona* that these particular conditions of relationship impose upon the associates.

Now, the conditions that constitute a state as an association are the actual obligations prescribed by its office of authority. Consequently, an inquiry into the character of such an association is an inquiry, not into the beliefs that give authority to this office, but into the obligations it uses its authority to prescribe, and into the *persona* that these obligations actually impose upon those who are subject to its rule. In other words, it is an inquiry into the engagements of government; and, if the word 'citizen' may stand for the *persona* concerned, it is an investigation of this *persona* and not of any other that other relationships may generate.

This, then, is the third great theme of political reflection in regard to a modern state, distinguished and continuously explored since the sixteenth century. And since a modern state has never ceased to be recognized as an association in the making, attention has always been directed to the sort of association it might be made to become no less than to what it may be perceived to be. But the exploration of this theme has been sadly hindered by confusion.

First, it is usually conducted in terms of the vocabularies of authority or of power; but in this connection these words are meaningless. To say, for example, that the conditions of association are or should be 'democratic' is absurd. The word 'democracy' denotes, not the engagements of a government, but a belief in which an office of rule is recognized to have authority; there are no 'democratic' rules of relationships. And the obligations in terms of which 'citizens' are associated cannot be characterized by the power to enforce them. Secondly, this inquiry has been almost obliterated by drivel about something called 'society', a fanciful total of unspecified relationships which only a simpleton would think of identifying with a state.

Nevertheless, over the years two tolerably distinct (and many very indistinct) doctrines have emerged about the character of a state as an association of human beings—both, of course, concerned not only with what a state may be perceived to be but also with what it might be made to become.

In the first of these doctrines a state is presented to us as an association of human beings related to one another in terms of their joint pursuit of some recognized substantive purpose. The associates are obligated to engage in this common enterprise, the custodian of which is the office of authority. What is here attributed to a state, or is said to be what a state may or should be made to become, is a well-known mode of association: that in which a Many becomes One in virtue of a common substantive engagement. Let me briefly sketch its general character before considering it in relation to a state.

The central feature is the uniting purpose in terms of which the associates are related to one another. This purpose must be known to the associates and it must be a substantive condition of things to be procured or an interest in such a condition of things to be promoted. But, since pursuing such a purpose necessarily means responding to emergent situations by choosing to do *this* rather than *that* in the hope of procuring a wished-for outcome favourable to the achievement of the purpose, those who are associated in this manner are related to one another not only in recognizing their joint purpose but in making such choices (or acknowledging them as their own choices) and in performing such actions. It is association in terms of substantive conduct instrumental to the purpose concerned. If such an association has rules for the conduct of the associates, then these also are instrumental rules whose desirability lies in their propensity to promote, or at least not to hinder, the pursuit of the purpose. The government of such an association is a managerial engagement and the *persona* it imposes upon the associates is that of servants of the purpose.

This is a familiar mode of association; it is hardly surprising that a state should have invoked this understanding of itself and that inquiry concerned with a state as an association should have been directed to the specification of the purpose of interest attributable to it.

There were serious difficulties with this particular view and they have not diminished. A state as it emerged in the sixteenth century was a supremely miscellaneous collection of communities without a common history, language, or law, divided from one another ethnically, in customs, and often in religious beliefs. And the states that have since emerged all over the globe are no different in this respect. As an emergent association, a state certainly was not a Many become One in virtue of thinking the same thoughts and having a common substantive purpose, and there was little to suggest that it might be made to become so. Michel de l'Hôpital had no illusions about sixteenth century France in this respect, and Madison had none about the United States of America.

But the belief that this is what a state might or should be made to become was not without circumstantial nourishment. Some modern states emerged from patrimonial estates and thus started life as enterprise associations of a sort; the governments of all modern states have a by no means recessive ingredient of 'lordship', ill-distinguished from their office as rulers, which entailed ownership and a managerial engagement; and in more recent times the mission of creating a communal solidarity has been attributed to the office of authority. Modern history is littered not only with visions, in various idioms, of a state as a purposive association, but also with projects to impose this character upon a state.

This undertaking appeared first in a religious idiom, with the state understood as a solidarity in terms of religious belief and the substantive conduct that went with it. Its high point was late sixteenth century Geneva, and there are still states that affect the character of religious communities. But this idiom of solidarity is reflected now, first, in the vision of a state as an association constituted (at least in part) in the enjoyment of a carefully guarded orthodoxy of beliefs about this and that and in propagating this orthodoxy in the world at large; and secondly, in the view that the ties of association in a state are not quite what they should be unless they include a consensus of belief about certain important matters other than the authority of its government—what Tocqueville called 'an independent convergence of outlook', citizens joined in thinking the same thoughts and loving the same things.

The so-called 'enlightened' rulers of the eighteenth century understood themselves to be the guardians of a comprehensive 'national interest' with a mission to harness their subjects' activities to its promotion and to educate them in the parts they should play. And while these rulers leant heavily upon their characters as, in part, seigneurial lords, some of their constitutional successors have aspired to become 'democratic' managers of 'the social development of the nation'. It is now four centuries since there was laid before us in all its detail the vision of a state as a development corporation, its members related to one another as 'workers' in a collective undertaking devoted to the maximum exploitation of its resources and managed by a board of directors; where 'law' is the instrumental rules of a corporate enterprise and where 'politics' (if any) is contention about who gets what, when and how, urging upon the managers some marginally different 'alternative' purpose, and voting them into office on the rare occasion when they are not *coup d'étatistes*. This is the idiom of a state as a purposive association that has now become most familiar to us.

But grandiose constructions of this sort (never quite matching the prospect) are not the only products of this vision of a state as a corporate enterprise; it has displayed itself also in temporary expedients to promote affluence or diminish poverty and in bursts of missionary zeal toward the world at large, and it has acquired a seductively confused vocabulary in which to recommend itself.

It intrudes wherever a state is thought of as associates related in terms of common substantive aims of 'goals', a comprehensive 'national interest' or 'National Idea'; where the *persona* attributed to the citizen is that of the servant of a 'national program' or the follower of an inspired 'leader'; where the engagement attributed to government is that of 'articulating the national values', 'defining the national goals', 'marshaling the national will', or 'transforming society'. And this vision intrudes, of course, when a state is at war, and all the more decisively when the war is thought of as a crusade.

Words such as organic, authoritarian, collectivist, and totalitarian are often used to describe a state thus understood. And all the old words such as 'liberal', 'progressive', 'democratic', 'dictatorial' are corrupted still further in its service. The condition of things aimed at, the 'national goal', is variously described, the favorite expression now being something called 'social justice' (that is, a preferred distribution of goods). The relationship it establishes between the associates is commonly called 'social' (that is, relationship in terms of the satisfaction of substantive wants), and the 'lordship' that has here devoured rulership is said to be 'planning' or 'management' or 'leadership'. It was this vision of the character of a state that Tocqueville pointed to, without approval, when he said in 1848: 'You must understand that the passions of men, from being political, have now become social.'

In the other, somewhat older, doctrine the mode of association attributed to a state is relationship in terms of non-instrumental rules of conduct, called 'the law'. And by calling these rules 'non-instrumental' I mean that they are not rules that specify a practice or routine purporting to promote the achievement of a substantive purpose. They are more like (although they are not exactly like) the rules of a game which are directions, not about how to win but about how to play, or the rules of public debate, which do not tell a speaker what to say and are wholly indifferent to any particular conclusion. These non-instrumental rules specify and prescribe, not choices to be made or actions to be performed, but conditions to be subscribed to in choosing and acting. Like all other rules they exist in advance of conduct, but they are incapable of initiating action or utterance. Association here is not in terms of the projected or the actual outcome of what is done, but in terms of formal conditions to be subscribed to in doing. If the word 'civility', or indeed the word 'justice', were taken to stand for the general character of these conditions of conduct, then a state thus understood would be recognized as a 'civil association' or association in terms of 'just' conduct. And since the injunction to act 'civilly' or 'justly' is not an injunction to perform any substantive action whatever, a state, in this understanding of it, is a moral and not a purposive association.

Persons thus associated may be otherwise assumed to be agents seeking the satisfaction of their various wants and related to some others in all or any of the ways in which human beings may be related; but in *persona civica* they exist and are related solely in respect to their obligations to observe the conditions prescribed in these non-instrumental rules of conduct. They have no common substantive purpose, but they have a common concern.

This, then, is a distinct mode of association—relationship in terms of obligations to subscribe to non-instrumental rules of conduct that are indifferent to the success or to the failure of the substantive enterprises being pursued. The engagements of the office of rule in such an association and the apparatus of power annexed to it will reflect this mode of association. They will be neither managerial nor conciliatory of interests. Ruling here has no ingredient of 'lordship', and rules can perform their office only because they have no substantive interest of their own and are indifferent to the substantive interests of their subjects. They are custodians of the rules that constitute this mode of association. And politics in such a state, concerned with deliberating, from the standpoint of their desirability, the civil obligations imposed upon the conduct of the associates, cannot be concerned with who gets what, when and how, because these rules are not awards of advantage or disadvantage. It cannot be the consideration of the propensity of these rules to promote or hinder the achievement of a common substantive purpose; there is none.

A rule of civil association is desirable in respect to the accuracy with which it reflects, or does not affront, the moral imagination of the associates when it is directed to what they have learned to distinguish as a relationship not of moral perfection but of civility or justice. There are, in this matter, no absolute standards; this moral imagination, concerned with civil obligations, is all there is. Nevertheless, this political engagement to deliberate the rules that spell out an acceptable image of civility is the most difficult of all human engagements simply because it has no place for the consideration of what is most readily considered, namely, interests.

Now, this mode of association attributed to a state, or said to be what a state should be made to become, is grossly misunderstood and misdescribed both by those who think it is a desirable mode of association for a state and those who do not. For the most part, we know it now only in the parodies it has evoked.

The use of the word 'democracy' to describe it is an elementary mistake; this word properly denotes neither a mode of association nor the engagements of a government but its constitutional shape. But the description of civil association as relationship in terms of the enjoyment of 'rights' is as profoundly misleading as it is common, even where 'rights' are not confused with allocations of substantive satisfactions.

The rules of civil association specify and prescribe, as exactly as may be, the obligations to be subscribed to in doing and speaking. What they remove from the scene is not choice of what to do or to say but a notional unconditional choice. The associates are related in the recognition of their obligation to observe these conditions. And it cannot be otherwise. Nevertheless, this sort of association is often said to be relationship not in terms of obligations but in the enjoyment of 'rights'. But what can these 'rights' be? They cannot be the fanciful unconditionals ('liberty' or 'the pursuit of happiness') because it is precisely this unconditionality of conduct that the obligation to subscribe to conditions removes. They cannot denote the postulate of human agency (choice); this can neither be assured nor taken away by rules of conduct and without it rules of conduct are meaningless. Nor can they be exemptions from obligations, although this is often what they are made to appear. These 'rights' are in fact the totally unspecifiable obverse of civil obligations—the right to 'privacy', to a fair trial, or the newly announced 'basic right to reproduce'—that become determinate and lose their deceptive appearance of being unconditionals only when they are specified in a collection of exactly described obligations. The language of rights is the language of pretended unconditionals and misdescribes the terms of civil association.

Further, it is commonly said that, in contrast to that of a purposive association, the government of a civil association is notably 'inactive', indisposed to 'intervene' in the conduct of its subjects, or permitted to do so only to a 'limited' extent. Such an association is called a 'minimal' state. But to distinguish between these two modes of association in terms of different amounts of 'interference' by their governments is a total misrepresentation, making the distinction appear to be one of degree and not of mode, and distracting our attention from the political choice they offer us. Wherever our preference lies, it is unscrupulous or foolish to describe the first merely as a more thoroughly organized version of the second, and the second as only a diminished or 'moderate' version of the first.

And again, a state understood as a civil association is frequently described by its friends as a 'free enterprise' or 'private enterprise' association, and is identified by its detractors with something called 'capitalism' and denigrated as the 'anarchy of laissez-faire'. But civil association is not relationship in terms of the pursuit of any enterprise whatever, 'public' or 'private'. The *persona civica* is not that of a bargainer for the satisfaction of wants; it is a subject of obligations. And 'capitalism', if it means anything, denotes a strategic device for satisfying wants and the relationships concerned in that enterprise. Only a state that is itself an enterprise can properly be called a 'capitalist' state, and only in that context can this word have a political meaning. And surely it is time we gave up the ludicrous notions that the phrase laissez-faire ever stood for unconditional conduct and that what is needed to turn anarchy into order is not the recognition of some non-instrumental rules of conduct but the appointment of a manager.

Finally, the saddest of all the misunderstandings of a state as a civil association: that in which it is properly presented as association in terms of non-instrumental conditions imposed upon conduct and specified in general rules from whose obligations no associate and no conduct is exempt, but defended as the mode of association more likely than any other to promote and to go on promoting the satisfaction of our diverse and proliferant wants. Prosperity may be the likely contingent outcome of civil association, but to recommend it in these terms is to recommend something other than civil association.

FIVE

It is the mark of all intelligent discourse that it is about something in particular. When it loses itself in a morass of cross-purposes in which utterances slide by one another it may be recalled by asking, What are we supposed to be talking about? And thus it is with politics. Political talk is inevitably concerned with local and transitory situations, but it will not go far before one of those haunting words is uttered (democracy, freedom, rights, justice) and we become aware that we are talking about a state—that strange association of human beings, of debatable character, at once supremely artificial and supremely inartistic, that nevertheless constitutes a specific human relationship and endows its otherwise miscellaneous components with a specific *persona*, whatever it may be.

This talk has been going on a long time. It has at its disposal a large vocabulary that I think is now in a condition of considerable confusion; and a messy vocabulary presages a messy conversation. Very early the chief constitutive characteristics of a state were discerned to be an office of authority, an apparatus of power, and a mode of association clearly displayed in the engagements of its office of authority. All our political talk, whether it concerns air pollution, the busing of children to school, or whatever, is about one or another of these characteristics, postulating for it an alleged desirable shape. And most of its current mistiness comes from our failure to recognize that each is a distinct matter of consideration and to recognize which it is we are on any occasion concerned with.

In the emergence of a modern state the office of authority was, necessarily, the chief concern of political deliberation, and it has never ceased to be important. The question, In respect of what shape or constitution can we acknowledge this office to have an antecedent right to rule?, has nowhere received anything but an interim answer, and after years of close attention we have become impatient with it. We accept without misgiving the old vague words 'democratic', 'republican', etc. as good enough descriptions of the desirable shape, or we resort to meaningless expressions such as 'majority rules'. Or we dismiss the question as of no importance. But our current indifference to it has deeply corrupted the conduct of rulers and ruled alike, and goes far to account for the ramshackle character of most modern states.

The apparatus of power annexed to this office of authority has been relentlessly inspected and discussed, but the consideration given to it has become progressively more confused. Earlier generations were properly apprehensive lest it become detached from the office of authority and acquire a momentum of its own; standing armies were objects of suspicion and emergent so-called bureaucracies were regarded with mistrust. But we have now come to think of this apparatus merely in terms of our approval or disapproval of the outcome of its exercise: more power to it if it does what we want. We have argued ourselves into an inability to distinguish between power exercised in order to secure the fulfilment of obligations and power exerted to satisfy a want. We have even come to identify this apparatus with the office of government itself, and we seek to protect ourselves from it with the absurd device of a Bill of Rights.

But it is the third theme—the mode of association attributed to a state—that has now captured most of our attention. It is not a new theme—they were discussing it in the sixteenth century—but it is now our central concern. And how sadly confused is our handling of it. It is ill-distinguished from the other themes; often we do not get even to the point of recognizing that it concerns the particular relationship that human beings may have as members of a state. The modes of association that may be and have been attributed to a state are ill-specified and ill-distinguished from one another —or worse, they are mistaken for points on what is called the spectrum of political belief in this matter. The words in which we struggle to express this particular alignment of political belief are sadly inadequate. It is not a contrast between dictatorship and democracy (these are authority-words), or between Left and Right (these merely represent an insignificant squabble about the common purpose to be imposed upon a state already assumed to be a purposive association). The words Liberal and Conservative are already so overloaded with meanings that they must fail to be explicit here. And those who understand it in terms of Communism and Capitalism, collectivism and free enterprise, centralism and pluralism, merely add to the confusion by suggesting a substantive purpose for civil association. This alignment of political belief is not between those who value purposive association and those who do not, or between those who have a compassionate regard for their fellow men and those who have none; it concerns only the character of a *state* as an association of human beings.

We who (if I may presume) are disposed to elect for a state as a civil association have, perhaps, a harder task than our opponents, who are well served by the confusion into which political discourse has fallen. They have a ready response from those who are not averse from the warm embrace of even a compulsory *solidarité commune*, who are not dismayed when they find themselves bound to ends they have not chosen for themselves, particularly when (as part of the bargain) they are allocated a so-called 'social income' of unknown value. And perhaps we should not be so eager as we often are to disturb them. But the cooler virtues of civil association have much to recommend them, especially to those disposed to choose their own destinations even if they do not reach them. After all, this least burdensome of all human relationships in terms of obligations to subscribe to non-instrumental rules of conduct is the only kind of association that excludes no other and that mitigates conflict without imposing uniformity. And it is particularly appropriate to a state because it is the only morally tolerable form of compulsory association.

But if we are to make better known this most notable human invention, we must stop hiding behind such irrelevant expressions as 'democracy' and 'capitalism', and such ambiguous expressions as 'conservative' and 'moderate'; we must get to know, not only our opponents, but ourselves more exactly than we do at present; we must defend our position with reasons appropriate to it; and we must refuse to entangle ourselves with equivocal alliances.

There was once, so Schopenhauer tells us, a colony of porcupines. They were wont to huddle together on a cold winter's day and, thus wrapped in communal warmth, escape being frozen. But, plagued with the pricks of each other's quills, they drew apart. And every time the desire for warmth brought them together again, the same calamity overtook them. Thus they remained, distracted between two misfortunes, able neither to tolerate nor to do without one another, until they discovered that when they stood at a certain distance from one another they could both delight in one another's individuality and enjoy one another's company. They did not attribute any metaphysical significance to this distance, nor did they imagine it to be an independent source of happiness, like finding a friend. They recognized it to be a relationship in terms not of substantive enjoyments but of contingent considerabilities that they must determine for themselves. Unknown to themselves, they had invented civil association.

"Talking Politics" was originally given as an address in New York City under the auspices of *National Review* and first appeared in *National Review* on December 5, 1975. It is new to this edition of *Rationalism in Politics*. Reprinted by permission. ©1975 by *National Review*, Inc., 150 East 35th Street, New York, New York 10016.

PART FIVE

On the human condition

The tower of Babel

The project of finding a short cut to heaven is as old as the human race. It is represented in the mythology of many peoples, and it is recognized always as an impious but not ignoble enterprise. The story of the Titans is, perhaps, the most complicated of the myths which portray this *folie de grandeur*, but the story of the Tower of Babel is the most profound. We may imagine the Titans drawing back after the first unsuccessful assault to hear one of their number suggest that their programme was too ambitious, that perhaps they were trying to do too much and to do it too quickly. But the builders of the Tower, whose top was to reach to heaven, were permitted no such conference; their enterprise involved them in the babblings of men who speak, but do not speak the same language. Like all profound myths, this represents a project the fascination of which is not confined to the childhood of the race, but is one which the circumstances of human life constantly suggest and one which no failure can deprive of its attraction. It indicates also the consequences of such an enterprise. I interpret it as follows.

465

The pursuit of perfection as the crow flies is an activity both impious and unavoidable in human life. It involves the penalties of impiety (the anger of the gods and social isolation), and its reward is not that of achievement but that of having made the attempt. It is an activity, therefore, suitable for individuals, but not for societies. For an individual who is impelled to engage in it, the reward may exceed both the penalty and the inevitable defeat. The penitent may hope, or even expect, to fall back, a wounded hero, into the arms of an understanding and forgiving society. And even the impenitent can be reconciled with himself in the powerful necessity of his impulse, though, like Prometheus, he must suffer for it. For a society, on the other hand, the penalty is a chaos of conflicting ideals, the disruption of a common life, and the reward is the renown which attaches to monumental folly. *A mesure que l'humanité se perfectionne l'homme se dégrade.* Or, to interpret the myth in a more light-hearted fashion: human life is a gamble; but while the individual must be allowed to bet according to his inclination (on the favourite or on an outsider), society should always back the field. Let us consider the matter in application to our own civilization.

The activity with which we are concerned is what is called moral activity, that is, activity which may be either good or bad. The moral life is human affection and behaviour determined, not by nature, but by art. It is conduct to which there is an alternative. This alternative need not be consciously before the mind; moral conduct does not necessarily involve the reflective choice of a particular action. Nor does it require that each occasion shall find a man without a disposition, or even without predetermination, to act in a certain way: a man's affections and conduct may be seen to spring from his character without thereby ceasing to be moral. The freedom without which moral conduct is impossible is freedom from a natural necessity which binds *all* men to act alike. This does not carry us very far. It identifes moral behaviour as the exercise of an acquired skill (though the skill need not have been selfconsciously acquired), but it does not distinguish it from other kinds of art—from cookery or from carpentry. However, it carries us far enough for my purpose, which is to consider the *form* of the moral life, and in particular the form of the moral life of contemporary Western civilization.

In any manifestation of the moral life, form and content are, of course, inseparable. Nevertheless, neither can be said to determine the other; and in considering the form we shall be considering an abstraction which, in principle, is indifferent to any particular content, and indifferent also to any particular ethical theory. The practical question, What kinds of human enterprise should be designated right and wrong? and the philosophical question, What is the ultimate nature of moral criteria? are both outside what we are to consider. We are concerned only with the shape of the moral life. And our concern must be philosophical and historical, rather than practical, because neither a society nor an individual is normally given the opportunity of making an express choice of the form of a moral life.

The moral life of our society discloses a form neither simple nor homogeneous. Indeed, the form of our morality appears to be a mixture of two ideal extremes, a mixture the character of which derives from the predominance of one extreme over the other. I am not convinced of the necessary ideality of the extremes; it is perhaps possible that one, if not both, could exist as an actual form of the moral life. But even if this is doubtful, each can certainly exist with so little modification from the other that it is permissible to begin by regarding them as possible forms of morality. Let us consider the two forms which, either separately or in combination, compose the form of the moral life of the Western world.

TWO

In the first of these forms, the moral life is *a habit of affection and behaviour;* not a habit of reflective *thought,* but a habit of *affection and conduct.* The current situations of a normal life are met, not by consciously applying to ourselves a rule of behaviour, nor by conduct recognized as the expression of a moral ideal, but by acting in accordance with a certain habit of behaviour. The moral life in this form does not spring from the consciousness of possible alternative ways of behaving and a choice, determined by an opinion, a rule or an ideal, from among these alternatives; conduct is as nearly as possible without reflection. And consequently, most of the current situations of life do not appear as occasions calling for judgment, or as problems requiring solutions; there is no weighing up of alternatives or reflection on consequences, no uncertainty, no battle of scruples. There is, on the occasion, nothing more than the unreflective following of a tradition of conduct in which we have been brought up. And such moral habit will disclose itself as often in *not* doing, in the taste which dictates abstention from certain actions, as in performances. It should, of course, be understood that I am not here describing a form of the moral life which assumes the existence of a moral sense or of moral intuition, nor a form of the moral life presupposing a moral theory which attributes authority to conscience. Indeed, no specific theory of the source of authority is involved in this form of the moral life. Nor am I describing a merely primitive form of morality, that is, the morality of a society unaccustomed to reflective thought. I am describing the form which moral action takes (because it can take no other) in all the emergencies of life when time and opportunity for reflection are lacking, and I am supposing that what is true of the emergencies of life is true of most of the occasions when human conduct is free from natural necessity.

Every form of the moral life (because it is affection and behaviour determined by art) depends upon education. And the character of each form is reflected in the kind of education required to nurture and maintain it. From what sort of education will this first form of the moral life spring?

We acquire habits of conduct, not by constructing a way of living upon rules or precepts learned by heart and subsequently practised, but by living with people who habitually behave in a certain manner: we acquire habits of conduct in the same way as we acquire our native language. There is no point in a child's life at which he can be said to begin to learn the language which is habitually spoken in his hearing; and there is no point in his life at which he can be said to begin to learn habits of behaviour from the people constantly about him. No doubt, in both cases, what is learnt (or some of it) can be formulated in rules and precepts; but in neither case do we, in this kind of education, learn by learning rules and precepts. What we learn here is what may be learned without the formulation of its rules. And not only may a command of language and behaviour be achieved without our becoming aware of the rules, but also, if we have acquired a knowledge of the rules, this sort of command of language and behaviour is impossible until we have forgotten them as rules and are no longer tempted to turn speech and action into the applications of rules to a situation. Further, the education by means of which we acquire habits of affection and behaviour is not only coeval with conscious life, but it is carried on, in practice and observation, without pause in every moment of our waking life, and perhaps even in our dreams; what is begun as imitation continues as selective conformity to a rich variety of customary behaviour. This sort of education is not compulsory; it is inevitable. And lastly (if education in general is making oneself at home in the natural and civilized worlds), this is not a separable part of education. One may set apart an hour in which to learn mathematics and devote another to the Catechism, but it is impossible to engage in any activity whatever without contributing to this kind of moral education, and it is impossible to enjoy this kind of moral education in an hour set aside for its study. There are, of course, many things which cannot be learned in this sort of education. We may learn in this manner to play a game, and we may learn to play it without breaking the rules, but we cannot acquire a knowledge of the rules themselves without formulating them or having them formulated for us. And further, without a knowledge of the rules we can never know for certain whether or not we are observing them, nor shall we be able to explain why the referee has blown his whistle. Or, to change the metaphor, from this sort of education can spring the ability never to write a false line of poetry, but it will give us neither the ability to scan nor a knowledge of the names of the various metric forms.

It is not difficult, then, to understand the sort of moral education by means of which habits of affection and behaviour may be acquired; it is the sort of education which gives the power to act appropriately and without hesitation, doubt or difficulty, but which does not give the ability to explain our actions in abstract terms, or defend them as emanations of moral principles. Moreover, this education must be considered to have failed in its purpose if it provides a range of behaviour insufficient to meet all situations without the necessity of calling upon reflection, or if it does not make the habit of behaviour sufficiently compelling to remove hesitation. But it must not be considered to have failed merely because it leaves us ignorant of moral rules and moral ideals. And a man may be said to have acquired most thoroughly what this kind of moral education can teach him when his moral dispositions are inseverably connected with his *amour-propre*, when the spring of his conduct is not an attachment to an ideal or a felt duty to obey a rule, but his self-esteem, and when to act wrongly is felt as diminution of his self-esteem.

Now, it will be observed that this is a form of morality which gives remarkable stability to the moral life from the point of view either of an individual or of a society; it is not in its nature to countenance large or sudden changes in the kinds of behaviour it desiderates. Parts of a moral life in this form may collapse, but since the habits of conduct which compose it are never recognized as a system, the collapse does not readily spread to the whole. And being without a perceived rigid framework distinct from the modes of behaviour themselves (a framework, for example, of abstract moral ideals), it is not subject to the kind of collapse which springs from the detection of some flaw or incoherence in a system of moral ideals. Intellectual error with regard to moral ideas or opinions does not compromise a moral life which is firmly based upon a habit of conduct. In short, the stability which belongs to this form of the moral life derives from its elasticity and its ability to suffer change without disruption. First, there is in it nothing that is absolutely fixed. Just as in a language there may be certain constructions which are simply bad grammar, but in all the important ranges of expression the language is malleable by the writer who uses it and he cannot go wrong unless he deserts its genius, so in this form of the moral life, the more thorough our education the more certain will be our taste and the more extensive our range of behaviour within the tradition. Custom is always adaptable and susceptible to the *nuance* of the situation. This may appear a paradoxical assertion; custom, we have been taught, is blind. It is, however, an insidious piece of misobservation; custom is not blind, it is only 'blind as a bat'. And anyone who has studied a tradition of customary behaviour (or a tradition of any other sort) knows that both rigidity and instability are foreign to its character. And secondly, this form of the moral life is capable of change as well as of local variation. Indeed, no traditional way of behaviour, no traditional skill, ever remains fixed; its history is one of continuous change. It is true that the change it admits is neither great nor sudden; but then, revolutionary change is usually the product of the eventual overthrow of an aversion from change, and is characterstic of something that has few internal resources of change. And the appearance of changelessness in a morality of traditional behaviour is an illusion which springs from the erroneous belief that the only significant change is that which is either induced by selfconscious activity or is, at least, observed on the occasion. The sort of change which belongs to this form of the moral life is analogous to the change to which a living language is subject: nothing is more habitual or customary than our ways of speech, and nothing is more continuously invaded by change. Like prices in a free market, habits of moral conduct show no revolutionary changes because they are never at rest. But it should be observed, also, that because the internal movement characteristic of this form of the moral life does not spring from reflection upon moral principles, and represents only an unselfconscious exploitation of the genius of the tradition of moral conduct, it does not amount to moral self-criticism. And, consequently, a moral life of this kind, if it degenerates into superstition, or if crisis supervenes, has little power of recovery. Its defence is solely its resistance to the conditions productive of crisis.

One further point should, perhaps, be noticed: the place and character of the moral eccentric in this form of the moral life, when it is considered as the form of the moral life of a society. The moral eccentric is not, of course, excluded by this form of morality. (The want of moral sensibility, the hollowness of moral character, which seems often to inhere in peoples whose morality is predominantly one of custom, is improperly attributed to the customary form of their morality; its cause lies elsewhere.) We sometimes think that deviation from a customary morality must always take place under the direction of a formulated moral ideal. But this is not so. There is a freedom and inventiveness at the heart of every traditional way of life, and deviation may be an expression of that freedom, springing from a sensitiveness to the tradition itself and remaining faithful to the traditional form. Generally speaking, no doubt, the inspiration of deviation from moral habit is perfectionist, but it is not necessarily consciously perfectionist. It is not, in essence, rebellious, and may be likened to the sort of innovation introduced into a plastic art by the fortuitous appearance in an individual of a specially high degree of manual skill, or to the sort of change a great stylist may make in a language. Although in any particular instance deviation may lead the individual eccentric astray, and although it is not something that can profitably be imitated, moral eccentricity is of value to a society whose morality is one of habit of behaviour (regardless of the direction it may take) so long as it remains the activity of the individual and is not permitted to disrupt the communal life. In a morality of an habitual way of behaviour, then, the influence of the moral eccentric may be powerful but is necessarily oblique, and the attitude of society towards him is necessarily ambivalent. He is admired but not copied, reverenced but not followed, welcomed but ostracized.

THREE

The second form of the moral life we are to consider may be regarded as in many respects the opposite of the first. In it activity is determined, not by a habit of behaviour, but by *the reflective application of a moral criterion.* It appears in two common varieties: as *the selfconscious pursuit of moral ideals,* and as *the reflective observance of moral rules.* But it is what these varieties have in common that is important, because it is this, and not what distinguishes them from one another, which divides them from the first form of morality.

This is a form of the moral life in which a special value is attributed to selfconsciousness, individual or social; not only is the rule or the ideal the product of reflective thought, but the application of the rule or the ideal to the situation is also a reflective activity. Normally the rule or the ideal is determined first and in the abstract; that is, the first task in constructing an art of behaviour in this form is to express moral aspirations in words—in a rule of life or in a system of abstract ideals. This task of verbal expression need not begin with a moral *de omnibus dubitandum;* but its aim is not only to set out the desirable ends of conduct, but also to set them out clearly and unambiguously and to reveal their relations to one another. Secondly, a man who would enjoy this form of the moral life must be certain of his ability to defend these formulated aspirations against criticism. For, having been brought into the open, they will henceforth be liable to attack. His third task will be to translate them into behaviour, to apply them to the current situations of life as they arise. In this form of the moral life, then, action will spring from a judgment concerning the rule or end to be applied and the determination to apply it. The situations of living should, ideally, appear as problems to be solved, for it is only in this form that they will receive the attention they call for. And there will be a resistance to the urgency of action; it will appear more important to have the right moral ideal, than to act. The application of a rule or an ideal to a situation can never be easy; both ideal and situation will usually require intrepretation, and a rule of life (unless the life has been simplified by the drastic reduction of the variety of situations which are allowed to appear) will always be found wanting unless it is supplemented with an elaborate casuistry or hermeneutic. It is true that moral ideals and moral rules may become so familiar that they take on the character of an habitual or traditional way of *thinking* about behaviour. It is true also that long familiarity with our ideals may have enabled us to express them more concretely in a system of specific rights and duties, handy in application. And further, a moral ideal may find its expression in a type of human character—such as the character of the gentleman —and conduct become the imaginative application of the ideal character to the situation. But these qualifications carry us only part of the way: they may remove the necessity for *ad hoc* reflection on the rules and ideals themselves, but they leave us still with the problem of interpreting the situation and the task of translating the ideal, the right or the duty into behaviour. For the right or the duty is always to observe a rule or realize an end, and not to behave in a certain concrete manner. Indeed, it is not desired, in this form of the moral life, that tradition should carry us all the way; its distinctive virtue is to be subjecting behaviour to a continuous corrective analysis and criticism.

This form of the moral life, not less than the other, depends upon education, but upon an education of an appropriately different sort. In order to acquire the necessary knowledge of moral ideals or of a rule of life, we need something more than the observation and practice of behaviour itself. We require, first, an intellectual training in the detection and appreciation of the moral ideals themselves, a training in which the ideals are separated and detached from the necessarily imperfect expression they find in particular actions. We require, secondly, training in the art of the intellectual management of these ideals. And thirdly, we require training in the application of ideals to concrete situations, in the art of translation and in the art of selecting appropriate means for achieving the ends which our education has inculcated. Such an education may be made compulsory in a society, but if so it is only because it is not inevitable. It is true that, as Spinoza says,[1] a substitute for a perfectly trained moral judgment may be found in committing a rule of life to memory and following it implicitly. But, though this is as far as some pupils will get, it cannot be considered to be the aim of this moral education. If it is to achieve its purpose, this education must carry us far beyond the acquisition of a moral technique; and it must be considered to have failed in its purpose if it has not given

---

[1] *Ethica*, V, x.

both ability to determine behaviour by a selfconscious choice and an understanding of the ideal grounds of the choice made. Nobody can fully share this form of the moral life who is not something of a philosopher and something of a self-analyst: its aim is moral behaviour springing from the communally cultivated reflective capacities of each individual.

Now, a moral life in which everyone who shares it knows at each moment exactly what he is doing and why, should be well protected against degeneration into superstition and should, moreover, give remarkable confidence to those who practise it. Nevertheless, it has its dangers, both from the point of view of an individual and from that of a society. The confidence which belongs to it is mainly a confidence in respect of the moral ideals themselves, or of the moral rule. The education in the ideals or in the rule must be expected to be the most successful part of this moral education; the art of applying the ideals is more difficult both to teach and to learn. And together with the certainty about how to *think* about moral ideals, must be expected to go a proportionate uncertainty about how to *act*. The constant analysis of behaviour tends to undermine, not only prejudice in moral habit, but moral habit itself, and moral reflection may come to inhibit moral sensibility.

Further, a morality which takes the form of the selfconscious pursuit of moral ideals is one which, at every moment, calls upon those who practise it to determine their behaviour by reference to a vision of perfection. This is not so much the case when the guide is a moral rule, because the rule is not represented as perfection and constitutes a mediation, a cushion, between the behaviour it demands on each occasion and the complete moral response to the situation. But when the guide of conduct is a moral ideal we are never suffered to escape from perfection. Constantly, indeed on all occasions, the society is called upon to seek virtue as the crow flies. It may even be said that the moral life, in this form, demands an hyperoptic moral vision and encourages intense moral emulation among those who enjoy it, the moral eccentric being recognized, not as a vicarious sufferer for the stability of a society, but as a leader and a guide. And the unhappy society, with an ear for every call, certain always about what it ought to *think* (though it will never for long be the same thing), in action shies and plunges like a distracted animal.

Again, a morality of ideals has little power of self-modification; its stability springs from its inelasticity and its imperviousness to change. It will, of course, respond to interpretation, but the limits of that response are close and severe. It has a great capacity to resist change, but when that resistance is broken down, what takes place is not change but revolution—rejection and replacement. Moreover, every moral ideal is potentially an obsession; the pursuit of moral ideals is an idolatry in which particular objects are recognized as 'gods'. This potentiality may be held in check by more profound reflection, by an intellectual grasp of the whole system which gives place and proportion to each moral ideal; but such a grasp is rarely achieved. Too often the excessive pursuit of one ideal leads to the exclusion of others, perhaps all others; in our eagerness to realize justice we come to forget charity, and a passion for righteousness has made many a man hard and merciless. There is, indeed, no ideal the pursuit of which will not lead to disillusion; *chagrin* waits at the end for all who take this path. Every admirable ideal has its opposite, no less admirable. Liberty or order, justice or charity, spontaneity or deliberateness, principle or circumstance, self or others, these are the kinds of dilemma with which this form of the moral life is always confronting us, making us see double by directing our attention always to abstract extremes, none of which is wholly desirable. It is a form of the moral life which puts upon those who share it, not only the task of translating moral ideals into appropriate forms of conduct, but also the distracting intellectual burden of removing the verbal conflict of ideals before moral behaviour is possible. These conflicting ideals are, of course, reconciled in all amiable characters (that is, when they no longer appear as ideals), but that is not enough; a verbal and theoretical reconciliation is required. In short, this is a form of the moral life which is dangerous in an individual and disastrous in a society. For an individual it is a gamble which may have its reward when undertaken within the limits of a society which is not itself engaged in the gamble; for a society it is mere folly.

FOUR

This brief characterization of what appear to be two forms of the moral life, while perhaps establishing their distinction or even their opposition, will have made us more doubtful about their capability of independent existence. Neither, taken alone, recommends itself convincingly as a likely form of the moral life, in an individual or in a society; the one is all habit, the other all reflection. And the more closely we examine them, the more certain we become that they are, not forms of the moral life at all, but ideal extremes. And when we turn to consider what sort of a form of the moral life they offer in combination, we may perhaps enjoy the not illusory confidence that we are approaching more nearly to concrete possibility, or even historical reality.

In a mixture in which the first of these extremes is dominant, the moral life may be expected to be immune from a confusion between behaviour and the pursuit of an ideal. Action will retain its primacy, and, whenever it is called for, will spring from habit of behaviour. Conduct itself will never become problematical, inhibited by the hesitations of ideal speculation or the felt necessity of bringing philosophic talent and the fruits of philosophic education to bear upon the situation. The confidence in action, which belongs to the well-nurtured customary moral life, will remain unshaken. And the coherence of the moral life will not wait upon the abstract unity which the reflective relation of values can give it. But, in addition, this mixed form of the moral life may be supposed to enjoy the advantages that spring from a reflective morality—the power to criticize, to reform and to explain itself, and the power to propagate itself beyond the range of the custom of a society. It will enjoy also the appropriate intellectual confidence in its moral standards and purposes. And it will enjoy all this without the danger of moral criticism usurping the place of a habit of moral behaviour, or of moral speculation bringing disintegration to moral life. The education in moral habit will be supplemented, but not weakened, by the education in moral ideology. And in a society which enjoyed this form of the moral life, both habit and ideology might be the common possession of all its members, or moral speculation might in fact be confined to the few, while the morality of the many remained one of the habit of behaviour. But, in any case, the internal resources of movement of this form of morality would be supplied by both its components: to the potential individual eccentricity which belongs to a traditional morality would be added the more consciously rebellious eccentricity which has its roots in the more precisely followed perfectionism of a morality of ideals. In short, this form of the moral life will offer to a society advantages similar to those of a religion which has taken to itself a theology (though not necessarily a popular theology) but without losing its character as a way of living.

On the other hand, a morality whose form is a mixture in which the second of our extremes is dominant will, I think, suffer from a permanent tension between its component parts. Taking charge, the morality of the selfconscious pursuit of ideals will have a disintegrating effect upon habit of behaviour. When action is called for, speculation or criticism will supervene. Behaviour itself will tend to become problematical, seeking its self-confidence in the coherence of an ideology. The pursuit of perfection will get in the way of a stable and flexible moral tradition, the naïve coherence of which will be prized less than the unity which springs from selfconscious analysis and synthesis. It will seem more important to have an intellectually defensible moral ideology than a ready habit of moral behaviour. And it will come to be assumed that a morality which is not easily transferable to another society, which lacks an obvious universality, is (for that reason) inadequate for the needs of the society of its origin. The society will wait upon its self-appointed moral teachers, pursuing the extremes they recommend and at a loss when they are silent. The distinguished and inspiring visiting preacher, who nevertheless is a stranger to the way we live, will displace the priest, the father of his parish. In a moral life constantly or periodically suffering the ravages of the ar-

mies of conflicting ideals, or (when these for the time have passed)
falling into the hands of censors and inspectors, the cultivation of
a habit of moral behaviour will have as little opportunity as the
cultivation of the land when the farmer is confused and distracted
by academic critics and political directors. Indeed, in such a mixture (where habit of behaviour is subordinate to the pursuit of ideals) each of the components is unavoidably playing a role foreign to
its character; as in a literature in which criticism has usurped the
place of poetry, or in a religious life in which the pursuit of theology offers itself as an alternative to the practice of piety.

These, however, must be counted incidental, though grave,
imperfections in this mixture of extremes in the moral life; the
radical defect of this form is the radical defect of its dominant extreme—its denial of the poetic character of all human activity. A
prosaic tradition of thought has accustomed us to the assumption
that moral activity, when analysed, will be found to consist in the
translation of an idea of what ought to be into a practical reality,
the transformation of an ideal into a concrete existence. And we
are accustomed, even, to think of poetry in these terms; first, a
'heart's desire' (an idea) and then its expression, its translation into words. Nevertheless, I think this view is mistaken; it is the su-
perimposition upon art and moral activity generally of an inappropriate didactic form. A poem is not the translation into words of a
state of mind. What the poet says and what he wants to say are not
two things, the one succeeding and embodying the other, they are
the same thing; he does not know what he wants to say until he
has said it. And the 'corrections' he may make to his first attempt
are not efforts to make words correspond more closely to an already formulated idea or to images already fully formed in his
mind, they are renewed efforts to formulate the idea, to conceive
the image. Nothing exists in advance of the poem itself, except perhaps the poetic passion. And what is true of poetry is true also, I
think, of all human moral activity. Moral ideals are not, in the first
place, the products of reflective thought, the verbal expressions of
unrealized ideas, which are then translated (with varying degrees
of accuracy) into human behaviour; they are the products of

human behaviour, of human practical activity, to which reflective thought gives subsequent, partial and abstract expression in words. What is good, or right, or what is considered to be reasonable behaviour may exist in advance of the situation, but only in the generalized form of the possibilities of behaviour determined by art and not by nature. That is to say, the capital of moral ideals upon which a morality of the pursuit of moral ideals goes into business has always been accumulated by a morality of habitual behaviour, and appears in the form of abstract ideas only because (for the purposes of subscription) it has been transformed by reflective thought into a currency of ideas.[2] This view of the matter does not, of course, deprive moral ideals of their power as critics of human habits, it does not denigrate the activity of reflective thought in giving this verbal expression to the principles of behaviour; there is no doubt whatever that a morality in which reflection has no part is defective. But it suggests that a morality of the pursuit of moral ideals, or a morality in which this is dominant, is not what it appears at first sight to be, is not something that can stand on its own feet. In such a morality, that which has power to rescue from superstition is given the task of generating human behaviour —a task which, in fact, it cannot perform. And it is only to be expected that a morality of this sort will be subject to sudden and ignominious collapse. In the life of an individual this collapse need not necessarily be fatal; in the life of a society it is likely to be irretrievable. For a society is a common way of life; and not only is it true that a society may perish of a disease which is not necessarily fatal even to those of its members who suffer from it, but it is also true that what is corrupting in the society may not be corrupting in its members.

[2] For example, Jên (consideration for others) in the Confucian morality was an abstraction from the filial piety and respect for elders which constituted the ancient Chinese habit of moral behaviour. The activity of the Sages, who (according to Chuang Tzu) *invented* goodness, duty and the rules and ideals of moral conduct, was one in which a concrete morality of habitual behaviour was sifted and refined; but, like too critical anthologists, they threw out the imperfect approximations of their material and what remained was not the reflection of a literature but merely a collection of masterpieces.

FIVE

The reader, knowing as much as I about the form of the moral life of contemporary Christendom, will not need to be told where all this is leading. If what I have said is not wide of the mark, it may perhaps be agreed that the form of our morality is that of a mixture in which the morality of the selfconscious pursuit of moral ideals is dominant. The moral energy of our civilization has for many centuries been applied mainly (though not, of course, exclusively) to building a Tower of Babel; and in a world dizzy with moral ideals we know less about how to behave in public and in private than ever before. Like the fool, our eyes have been on the ends of the earth. Having lost the thread of Ariadne, we have put our confidence in a plan of the labyrinth, and have given our attention to interpreters of the plan. Lacking habits of moral behaviour, we have fallen back upon moral opinions as a substitute; but, as we all know, when we reflect upon what we are doing we too often conclude that it is wrong. Like lonely men who, to gain reassurance, exaggerate the talents of their few friends, we exaggerate the significance of our moral ideals to fill in the hollowness of our moral life. It is a pitiless wedding which we have celebrated with our shadowy ideal of conduct. No doubt our present moral distraction (which is now several centuries old) springs partly from doubts we have in respect of the ideals themselves; all the effort of analysis and criticism has not yet succeeded in establishing a single one of them unquestionably. But this is not the root of the matter. The truth is that a morality in this form, regardless of the quality of the ideals, breeds nothing but distraction and moral instability. Perhaps it is a partial appreciation of this which has led some societies to give an artificial stability to their moral ideals. A few of these ideals are selected, those few are turned into an authoritative canon which is then made a guide to legislation or even a ground for the violent persecution of eccentricity. A moral ideology is established and maintained because this appears the only means of winning the necessary moral stability for the society. But in fact it is no remedy; it merely covers up the corruption of consciousness, the moral distraction inherent in morality as the selfconscious pursuit of moral ideals. However, it serves to illustrate the truth that the one kind of society which must of necessity be the enemy of profitable moral eccentricity is the society whose moral organization springs from the pursuit of ideals; for the moral life of such a society is itself nothing better than an arbitrary selection of moral eccentricities.

Now, I am not contending that our morality is wholly enclosed in the form of the selfconscious pursuit of moral ideals. Indeed, my view is that this is an ideal extreme in moral form and not, by itself, a possible form of morality at all. I am suggesting that the form of our moral life is dominated by this extreme, and that our moral life consequently suffers the internal tension inherent in this form. Certainly we possess habits of moral behaviour, but too often our selfconscious pursuit of ideals hinders us from enjoying them. Self-consciousness is asked to be creative, and habit is given the role of critic; what should be subordinate has come to rule, and its rule is a misrule. Sometimes the tension appears on the surface, and on these occasions we are aware that something is wrong. A man who fails to practise what he preaches does not greatly disturb us; we know that preaching is in terms of moral ideals and that no man can practise them perfectly. This is merely the minor tension be-tween ideal and achievement. But when a man preaches 'social jus-tice' (or indeed any other ideal whatsoever) and at the same time is obviously without a habit of ordinary decent behaviour (a habit that belongs to our morality but has fortunately never been idealized), the tension I speak of makes its appearance. And the fact that we are still able to recognize it is evidence that we are not wholly at the mercy of a morality of abstract ideals. Nevertheless, I do not think that anyone who has considered the matter will be disposed to deny that we are for the most part dominated by this morality. It is not our fault; we have been given little or no choice in the matter. It is, however, our misfortune. And it may be relevant, in conclusion, to consider briefly how it has come about.

On this subject, the history of European morals, I have nothing new to say; I can only direct attention to what is already well known. The form of contemporary western European morality has come to us from the distant past. It was determined in the first four centuries of the Christian era, that momentous period of our history when so much of our intellectual and emotional outlook began to emerge. It would, of course, be absurd to suggest that European morality sprang from some new species of seed first sown in that period; what, if anything, was new at that time was the mixture of seed which was at the disposal of those generations, to be sown, cultivated and sown once more until its characteristic fruit became fixed. It was an age of moral change. In that Greco-Roman world the old habits of moral behaviour had lost their vitality. There were, no doubt, men who were good neighbors, faithful friends and pious citizens, whose confidence in the customs that determined their conduct was still unshaken; but, in general, the impetus of moral habit of behaviour seems to have been spent—illustrating, perhaps, the defect of a form of morality too securely insulated from the criticism of ideals. It was, in consequence, an age of intense moral self-consciousness, an age of moral reformers who, unavoidably, preached a morality of the pursuit of ideals and taught a variety of dogmatic moral ideologies. The intellectual energy of the time was directed towards the determination of an ideal, and the moral energy towards the translation of that ideal into practice.[3] Moral selfconsciousness itself became a virtue;[4] genuine morality was identified with the 'practice of philosophy'.[5] And it was thought that for the achievement of a good life it was necessary that a man should submit to an artificial moral training, a moral gymnastic, *ás,hsi.*; learning and discipline must be added to 'nature'. The age, of course, was able to distinguish between a man who attained to a merely intellectual appreciation of moral ideals and one who was successful in the enterprise of translating ideal into conduct, but it was common ground that the moral life was to be achieved only, as Philo said, 'by reading, by meditation and by the calling to mind of noble ideals'. In short, what the Greco-Roman world of this

---

[3] Epictetus, *Diss.*, i, 4 and 30.
[4] *Ibid.*, 2, 10.
[5] *Dio Chrysostom*, ii, 239.

period had to offer was a morality in which the selfconscious pursuit of moral ideals was pre-eminent.

And our inheritance from that other great source of our moral inspiration, from early Christianity, was of a similar character: indeed it is not an inheritance which in this matter can be securely separated from that of the ancient world as a whole. In the earliest days, to be a Christian was to be a member of a community animated by a faith and sustained by a hope—faith in a person and hope for a coming event. The morality of these communities was a custom of behaviour appropriate to the character of the faith and to the nature of the expectation. It was a way of living distinguished in its place and time by the absence from it of a formulated moral ideal; and it was a way of living departure from which alone involved the penalty of exclusion from the community. And further, it was a way of living which admitted, but did not demand, extremes of behaviour, counsels of perfection. The nearest thing to a moral ideal known to these communities was the ideal of charity; the nearest thing to a moral rule was the precept to love God and one's neighbour. It was a morality which found its characteristic verbal expression in the phrase, τοὺς τρόπους, κυριου, the custom of the Lord. But over these earliest Christian communities, in the course of two centuries, there came a great change. The habit of moral behaviour was converted into the selfconscious pursuit of formulated moral ideals—a conversion parallel to the change from faith in a person to belief in a collection of abstract propositions, a creed. This change sprang from a variety of sources; from a change in the circumstances of the Christian's life, from the pressure of the alien intellectual world in which the Christian was set down, from the desire to 'give a reason for the hope' that animated him, from the necessity of translating the Christian way of life into a form in which it could be appreciated by those who had never shared the original inspiration and who, having to learn their Christianity as a foreign language, needed a grammar. The urge to speculate, to abstract and to define, which overtook Christianity as a religion, infected also Christianity as a way of moral life. But, whatever was the impulse of the change, it appears that by the middle of the

third century there existed a Christian morality in the familiar form
of the selfconscious pursuit of moral ideals, and by the time of St
Ambrose the *form* of this morality had become indistinguishable
from that of the morality of the surrounding world, a morality of
virtues and vices and of the translation of ideals into actions. A
Christian morality in the form of a way of life did not, of course,
perish, and it has never completely disappeared. But from this time
in the history of Christendom a Christian habit of moral behaviour
(which had sprung from the circumstances of Christian life) was
swamped by a Christian moral ideology, and the perception of the
poetic character of human conduct was lost.

I do not wish to suggest that either the selfconscious morality
of the Greco-Roman world at the beginning of our era, or the
change which overtook Christian morality in the second and third
centuries, was avoidable. The one was merely the filling of the vacu-
um left by the collapse of a traditional morality, and as for the other
—perhaps, in order to convert the world, a morality must be reduced to the easily translatable prose of a moral ideal, must be defined and made intellectually coherent, even though the price is a
loss of spontaneity and confidence and the approach of the danger
of obsession. The fact, however, remains that the moral inheritance
of western Europe, both from the classical culture of the ancient
world and from Christianity, was not the gift of a morality of habitual behaviour, but of a moral ideology. It is true that, in the course
of centuries, this moral form went some way towards being recon-
verted into a morality of habit of behaviour. Such a conversion is
certainly possible when moral ideals become familiar and, finding
expression in customs and institutions which exert a direct pressure upon conduct, cease to be mere ideals. And it is true, also,
that the invading barbarians contributed a morality of custom rather than of idea. Nevertheless, modern European morality has never
been able to divest itself of the form in which it first emerged. And
having once committed the indiscretion of formulating itself in the
abstract terms of moral ideals, it was only to be expected that its
critics (who have never for long been silent) should seize upon
these, and that in defending them against attack they should be-

come rigid and exaggerated. Every significant attack upon Christian morality (that of Nietzsche, for example) has been mistaken for an attack upon the particular moral ideals of Christian life, whereas whatever force it possessed derived from the fact that the object of attack was a morality of ideals which had never succeeded in becoming a morality of habit of behaviour.

The history of European morals, then, is in part the history of the maintenance and extension of a morality whose form has, from the beginning, been dominated by the pursuit of moral ideals. In so far as this is an unhappy form of morality, prone to obsession and at war with itself, it is a misfortune to be deplored; in so far as it cannot now readily be avoided, it is a misfortune to be made the best of. And if a morality of ideals is now all, or at least the best, of what we have, it might seem an injudicious moment to dwell upon its defects. But in order to make the best of an unavoidable situation, we need to know its defects as well as feel its necessity. And what at the present time stands between us and the opportunity (such as it is) of surmounting our misfortune is not our sense of the difficulty of doing so, but an erroneous inference we have drawn from our situation—the belief, which has slowly settled upon us, encouraged by almost all the intellectual tendencies of recent centuries, that it is no misfortune at all, but a situation to be welcomed. For the remarkable thing about contemporary European morality is not merely that its form is dominated by the selfconscious pursuit of ideals, but that this form is generally thought to be better and higher than any other. A morality of habit of behaviour is dismissed as primitive and obsolete; the pursuit of moral ideals (whatever discontent there may be with the ideals themselves) is identified with moral enlightenment. And further, it is prized (and has been particularly prized on this account since the seventeenth century) because it appears to hold out the possibility of that most sought-after consummation—a 'scientific' morality. It is to be feared, however, that in both these appearances we are sadly deceived. The pursuit of moral ideals has proved itself (as might be expected) an untrustworthy form of morality, the spring neither of a practical nor of a 'scientific' moral life.

The predicament of Western morals, as I read it, is first that our moral life has come to be dominated by the pursuit of ideals, a dominance ruinous to a settled habit of behaviour; and, secondly, that we have come to think of this dominance as a benefit for which we should be grateful or an achievement of which we should be proud. And the only purpose to be served by this investigation of our predicament is to disclose the corrupt consciousness, the self-deception which reconciles us to our misfortune.

"The Tower of Babel" was first published in *Cambridge Journal*, Volume II, 1948. It should not be confused with the paper of the same name which appeared in Oakeshott's *On History and Other Essays* (1983).

The voice of poetry in the
conversation of mankind

ONE

There are philosophers who assure us that all human utterance
is in one mode. They recognize a certain variety of expression,
they are able to distinguish different tones of utterance, but they
hear only one authentic voice. And there might be something to be
said for this view if we were considering some primordial condition
of the race when death was close, when leisure was scarce, and
when every utterance (even religious rites and magical spells) may
be supposed to have had a practical bearing. But it is now long
since mankind has invented for itself other modes of speaking. The
voice of practical activity may be the commonest to be heard, but it
is partnered by others whose utterance is in a different idiom. The
most notable of these are the voices of 'poetry' and of 'science'; but it
would seem that, more recently, 'history' also has acquired, or has
begun to acquire, an authentic voice and idiom of its own. In these
circumstances the task of discerning a singleness in human utterance has become more difficult. Nevertheless, the view dies hard
that Babel was the occasion of a curse being laid upon mankind

from which it is the business of the philosophers to deliver us, and a disposition remains to impose a single character upon significant human speech. We are urged, for example, to regard all utterances as contributions (of different but comparable merit) to an inquiry, or a debate among inquirers, about ourselves and the world we inhabit. But this understanding of human activity and intercourse as an inquiry, while appearing to accommodate a variety of voices, in fact recognizes only one, namely, the voice of argumentative discourse, the voice of 'science', and all others are acknowledged merely in respect of their aptitude to imitate this voice. Yet, it may be supposed that the diverse idioms of utterance which make up current human intercourse have some meeting-place and compose a manifold of some sort. And, as I understand it, the image of this meeting-place is not an inquiry or an argument, but a conversation.

In a conversation the participants are not engaged in an inquiry or a debate; there is no 'truth' to be discovered, no proposition to be proved, no conclusion sought. They are not concerned to inform, to persuade, or to refute one another, and therefore the cogency of their utterances does not depend upon their all speaking in the same idiom; they may differ without disagreeing. Of course, a conversation may have passages of argument and a speaker is not forbidden to be demonstrative; but reasoning is neither sovereign nor alone, and the conversation itself does not compose an argument. A girl, in order to escape a conclusion, may utter what appears to be an outrageously irrelevant remark, but what in fact she is doing is turning an argument she finds tiresome into a conversation she is more at home in. In conversation, 'facts' appear only to be resolved once more into the possibilities from which they were made; 'certainties' are shown to be combustible, not by being brought in contact with other 'certainties' or with doubt, but by being kindled by the presence of ideas of another order; approximations are revealed between notions normally remote from one another. Thoughts of different species take wing and play round one another, responding to each other's movements and provoking one another to fresh exertions. Nobody asks where they have come from or on what authority they are present; nobody cares what will become of them when they have played their part. There is no sympo-siarch or arbiter; not even a doorkeeper to examine credentials. Eve-ry entrant is taken at its face-value and everything is permitted which can get itself accepted into the flow of speculation. And voices which speak in conversation do not compose a hierarchy. Conversation is not an enterprise designed to yield an extrinsic profit, a contest where a winner gets a prize, nor is it an activity of exegesis; it is an unrehearsed intellectual adventure. It is with con-versation as with gambling, its significance lies neither in winning nor in losing, but in wagering. Properly speaking, it is impossible in the absence of a diversity of voices: in it different universes of dis-course meet, acknowledge each other and enjoy an oblique relation-ship which neither requires nor forecasts their being assimilated to one another.

This, I believe, is the appropriate image of human intercourse —appropriate because it recognizes the qualities, the diversities, and the proper relationships of human utterances. As civilized human beings, we are the inheritors, neither of an inquiry about ourselves and the world, nor of an accumulating body of informa-tion, but of a conversation, begun in the primeval forests and ex-tended and made more articulate in the course of centuries. It is a conversation which goes on both in public and within each of our-selves. Of course there is argument and inquiry and information, but wherever these are profitable they are to be recognized as passages in this conversation, and perhaps they are not the most captivating of the passages. It is the ability to participate in this conversation, and not the ability to reason cogently, to make discov-eries about the world, or to contrive a better world, which distin-guishes the human being from the animal and the civilized man from the barbarian. Indeed, it seems not improbable that it was the engagement in this conversation (where talk is without a conclu-sion) that gave us our present appearance, man being descended from a race of apes who sat in talk so long and so late that they wore out their tails. Education, properly speaking, is an initiation into the skill and partnership of this conversation in which we learn to recognize the voices, to distinguish the proper occasions of utterance, and in which we acquire the intellectual and moral habits appropriate to conversation. And it is this conversation which, in the end, gives place and character to every human activity and utterance. I say, 'in the end', because, of course, the immediate field of moral activity is the world of practical enterprise, and intellectual achievement appears, in the first place, within each of the various universes of discourse; but good behaviour is what it is with us because practical enterprise is recognized not as an isolated activity but as a partner in a conversation, and the final measure of intellectual achievement is in terms of its contribution to the conversation in which all universes of discourse meet.

Each voice is the reflection of a human activity, begun without premonition of where it would lead, but acquiring for itself in the course of engagement a specific character and a manner of speaking of its own: and within each mode of utterance further modulation is discernible. There is, then, no fixed number to the voices which engage in this conversation, but the most familiar are those of practical activity, of 'science' and of 'poetry'. Philosophy, the impulse to study the quality and style of each voice, and to reflect upon the relationship of one voice to another, must be counted a parasitic activity; it springs from the conversation, because this is what the philosopher reflects upon, but it makes no specific contribution to it.

This conversation is not only the greatest but also the most hardly sustained of all the accomplishments of mankind. Men have never been wanting who have had this understanding of human activity and intercourse, but few have embraced it without reserve and without misgiving, and on this account it is proper to mention the most notable of those who have done so: Michel de Montaigne. For the most part, however, the conversation has survived in spite of our notions about the education of the young which seem to become more and more remote from this understanding of human activity and intercourse.[1] Moreover, in some of the voices there are in-

---

[1] Here is a passage from the reflections of an Eton master (William Cory) who understood education as a preparation for participation in conversation: At school 'you are not engaged so much in acquiring knowledge as in making mental efforts under criticism. . . . A certain amount of knowledge you can indeed with average faculties acquire so as to retain; nor need

nate tendencies towards barbarism which make it difficult to sustain.

Each voice is at once a manner of speaking and a determinate utterance. As a manner of speaking, each is wholly conversable. But the defect to which some of the voices are liable is a loosening (even a detachment) of what is said from the manner of its utterance, and when this takes place the voice appears as a body of conclusions reached (dogmata), and thus, becoming eristic, loses its conversability. 'Science', for example, is a manner of thinking and speaking represented (and always on the verge of being misrepresented) in an encyclopædia of knowledge. The voice of philosophy, on the other hand, is unusually conversable. There is no body of philosophical 'knowledge' to become detached from the activity of philosophizing: hence Hume's perception of the supremely civilizing quality of philosophical reflection, and hence the difficulty which both men of science and of business have in understanding what philosophy is about and their frequent attempts to transform it into something more familiar to themselves. But further, the conversation may not only be destroyed by the intrusion of the eristic tendencies of the voices; it may suffer damage, or even for a time come to be suspended, by the bad manners of one or more of the participants. For each voice is prone to *superbia*, that is, an exclusive concern with its own utterance, which may result in its identifying the conversation with itself and its speaking as if it were speaking only to itself. And when this happens, barbarism may be observed to have supervened.

The image of human activity and intercourse as a conversation will, perhaps, appear both frivolous and unduly sceptical. This understanding of activity as composed, in the last resort, of inconsequent adventures, often put by for another day but never conclud-

you regret the hours you spend on much that is forgotten, for the shadow of lost knowledge at least protects you from many illusions. But you go to a great school not so much for knowledge as for arts and habits; for the habit of attention, for the art of expression, for the art of assuming at a moment's notice, a new intellectual position, for the art of entering quickly into another person's thoughts, for the habit of submitting to censure and refutation, for the art of indicating assent or dissent in graduated terms, for the habit of regarding minute points of accuracy, for the art of working out what is possible in a given time, for taste, discrimination, for mental courage and mental soberness. And above all you go to a great school for self-knowledge.'

ed, and of the participants as playfellows moved, not by a belief in the evanescence of error and imperfection but only by their loyalty and affection for one another, may seem to neglect the passion and the seriousness with which, for example, both scientific and practical enterprises are often pursued and the memorable achievements they have yielded. And the denial of a hierarchical order among the voices is not only a departure from one of the most notable traditions of European thought (in which all activity was judged in relation to the *vita contemplativa*), but will seem also to reinforce the scepticism. But, although a degree of scepticism cannot be denied, the appearance of frivolity is due, I think, to a misconception about conversation. As I understand it, the excellence of this conversation (as of others) springs from a tension between seriousness and playfulness. Each voice represents a serious engagement (though it is serious not merely in respect of its being pursued for the conclusions it promises); and without this seriousness the conversation would lack impetus. But in its participation in the conversation each voice learns to be playful, learns to understand itself conversationally and to recognize itself as a voice among voices. As with children, who are great conversationists, the playfulness is serious and the seriousness in the end is only play.

In recent centuries the conversation, both in public and within ourselves, has become boring because it has been engrossed by two voices, the voice of practical activity and the voice of 'science': to know and to contrive are our pre-eminent occupations. There have, of course, been ups and downs in this respect; but what transformed the situation was the appearance in the seventeenth century of an unmistakable disposition in favour of a division of the intellectual world between these two masters, a disposition which has since asserted itself more and more unmistakably. And on many occasions all that there is to be heard is the eristic tones of the voice of science in conference with that modulation of the voice of practical activity *we* call 'politics'.[2] But for a conversation to be

[2] The assimilation of 'politics' to practical activity is characteristic (though not exclusively so) of the history of modern Europe, and during the last four centuries it has become increasingly complete. But in ancient Greece (particularly in Athens) 'politics' was understood as a 'poetic' activity in which speaking (not merely to persuade but to compose memorable

appropriated by one or two voices is an insidious vice because in the passage of time it takes on the appearance of a virtue. All utterance should be relevant; but relevance in conversation is determined by the course of the conversation itself, it owes nothing to an external standard. Consequently an established monopoly will not only make it difficult for another voice to be heard, but it will also make it seem proper that it should not be heard; it is convicted in advance of irrelevance. And there is no easy escape from this *impasse*. An excluded voice may take wing against the wind, but it will do so at the risk of turning the conversation into a dispute. Or it may gain a hearing by imitating the voices of the monopolists; but it will be a hearing for only a counterfeit utterance.

To rescue the conversation from the bog into which it has fallen and to restore to it some of its lost freedom of movement would require a philosophy more profound than anything I have to offer. But there is another, more modest, undertaking which is perhaps worth pursuing. My proposal is to consider again the voice of poetry; to consider it as it speaks in the conversation. That this is an opportune enterprise no one interested in the conversation will doubt. It is true that the voice of poetry has never been wholly excluded; but it is often expected to provide no more than an entertainment to fill in the intervals of a more serious discussion, and the fact that it has fallen to imitating the voices of politics and science may be taken as a sign of the difficulty it now has in getting a hearing in its own character. And if what is now needed is some relief from the monotony of a conversation too long appropriated by politics and science, it may be supposed that an inquiry into the quality and significance of the voice of poetry may do something in this interest. But is not merely opportune, it is also 'philosophical': for, the consideration of poetry becomes philosophical when poetic imagining is shown to have, not a necessary place, but a specific place in the manifold of human activities. At all events, anyone fond of reflection who has found delight in listening to the voice of poetry is unprotected against the inclination to meditate upon the nature of that

verbal images) was pre-eminent and in which action was for the achievement of 'glory' and 'greatness'—a view of things which is reflected in the pages of Machiavelli.

delight; and if he gives way to the impulse to put his meditations in order, he is only doing his best to understand the quality of the voice and its relationship to the other voices. And if that best is good enough, he may say something worthwhile on behalf of poetry.

Yet expectations should be limited. Neither the poet nor the critic of poetry will find very much to his purpose in what I have to say. The poet is, of course, sovereign over himself and his own activity. And the concern of the critic is to quicken the hearing we give to the voice of poetry and to explore the qualities of a poem. In this it is not a bad thing to be something of a philosopher; philosophic reflection may perhaps hinder the critic from asking irrelevant questions and from thinking and speaking about poems in an inappropriate manner, and this (though it does not carry us very far) is something not to be despised.[3] But he requires other qualifications, and the critic who swims too strongly in this sea is apt soon to find himself out of sight of his object. For philosophy here is concerned merely with the domain of the poetic and with enlarging our understanding of the voice of poetry as it speaks in a conversation which it may from time to time command but in which it is never alone.

TWO

As I understand it, the real world is a world of experience within which self and not-self divulge themselves to reflection. No doubt this distinction is ambiguous and unstable: it is difficult (if not impossible) to find anything which, in principle, belongs exclusively to either side of the partnership. But on any occasion, although uncertainty may remain at the edges, we do not hesitate to make this distinction. And what on any occasion is recognized as self is recognized on account of its separating itself from a present not-self: self and not-self generate one another.

[3] The connoisseurship of the poetic with which philosophical reflection has endowed some critics (Coleridge, for example, or Geoffrey Scott in *The Architecture of Humanism*), in others appears as an unreflective (but, of course, not unacquired) habit and aptitude of thinking and saying the appropriate kind of things about works of art. Max Beerbohm's dramatic criticism is an example of this.

The self appears as activity. It is not a 'thing' or a 'substance' capable of being active; it is activity. And this activity is primordial; there is nothing antecedent to it. It may display varying degrees of strength or weakness; it may be lively or lethargic, attentive or wandering; it may be educated or relatively naïve; but there is no condition of rest or passivity to be overcome before it can begin. Thus, it is inappropriate to think of this self as a room, either furnished, or empty, or on the way to being furnished; properly speaking, it is only skilful or clumsy, wakeful or sluggish. Further, on every occasion this activity is a specific mode of activity; to be active but with no activity in particular, to be skilful but with no particular skill, is as impossible to the self as not to be active at all.

I shall call this activity 'imagining': the self making and recognizing images, and moving about among them in manners appropriate to their characters and with various degrees of aptitude. Thus sensing, perceiving, feeling, desiring, thinking, believing, contemplating, supposing, knowing, preferring, approving, laughing, crying, dancing, loving, singing, making hay, devising mathematical demonstrations, and so on, each is, or has its place in, an identifiable mode of imagining and moving about in an appropriate manner among images of a certain kind. And although we may not be always (or even often) aware of the universe of discourse to which our imagining on any occasion belongs, imagining is never unspecific (though it may in fact be confused) because it is always governed by the considerabilities which belong to a particular skill.

The not-self, then, is composed of images. But these images are not 'given' or 'presented' to the self; they are not independent existences caught as they swim by in the net of an expectant or an indifferent self. And they are not this because they are not anything at all out of relation to a self: and self is activity. Images are made. Nevertheless, self and not-self, imagining and image, are neither cause and consequent nor consciousness and its contents: the self is constituted in the activity of making and moving among images. Further, these images are not made out of some other, less-defined material (impressions of *sensa*), for no such material is available. Nor are they representations of other existences, images of 'things';

for example: what we call a 'thing' is merely a certain sort of image recognized as such because it behaves in a certain manner and responds to our questioning appropriately. Again, although images may often be vague and indefinite in appearance, they are always specific in character; that is, they correspond to a specific mode of imagining which may be discerned (if we wish to discern it) by ascertaining what sort of questions are relevant to be asked about its images: there is no image eligible to have all sorts of inquiries relevantly made about it. And finally, an image is never isolated and alone; it belongs to the world or field of images which on any occasion constitutes the not-self.

This activity of imagining, then, is neither the φαντασία of Aristotle, nor is it the 'original fancy' of Hobbes, nor is it what Coleridge called 'primary imagination', nor is it the 'blind but indispensable link' between sensation and thought which Kant calls imagination. It is not generic activity, preceding and providing the materials for special activities; in all its appearances it is governed by specific and ascertainable considerabilities. It is not a condition of thought; in one of its modes it is thought.

THREE

What I have called the conversation of mankind is, then, the meeting-place of various modes of imagining; and in this conversation there is, therefore, no voice without an idiom of its own: the voices are not divergencies from some ideal, non-idiomatic manner of speaking, they diverge only from one another. Consequently, to specify the idiom of one is to discern how it is distinguished from, and how it is related to the others. And since the most familiar partners to the voice of poetry are the voices of practical activity and of 'science', I should begin by saying something about these.

Practical activity is the commonest manner of imagining; we absolve ourselves from it with difficulty and we easily relapse into it. In it the self is making, recognizing, and moving about among images of a certain sort. And the aspect of practical imagining which calls first for our attention is its character as desire and aversion: the world of practice is the world *sub specie voluntatis,* and its constituents are images of pleasure and pain.[4] Desiring, of course, is not the cause of activity in a hitherto inactive self; we do not first 'have a desire' which causes us to move from a condition of rest to one of movement: desiring is merely being active in a particular manner, reaching out one's hand to pick a flower, or feeling in one's pocket for a coin. Nor do we first have a desire and then set about finding the means to satisfy it: our desires are known only in the activity of desiring, and to desire is to seek a satisfaction. Much of the time, no doubt, we act like automatons, imagining not by making specific choices but by habit; but in practical activity these habits are habits of desire and aversion. The enterprise, so far, in practical activity is to fill our world with images of pleasure.

But further, what is sought in desiring is not merely images of pleasure, but images of pleasure recognized to be 'facts'; and this presupposes a distinction between 'fact' and 'not-fact'. Even a world of make-believe images presupposes this distinction, for make-believe is attaching the character of 'fact' to what is nevertheless recognized to be 'not-fact' in order to enjoy the pleasure which this ideal attachment affords. Nor are 'not-facts' to be identified as illusions; illusion is mistaking 'fact' for 'not-fact', or 'not-fact' for 'fact'.

As I understand it, the distinction between 'fact' and 'not-fact' is a distinction between different kinds of images and not a distinction between something that is not an image and a mere image. And consequently we are sometimes uncertain whether or not to recognize an image as 'fact', and when we are doubtful we have questions we are accustomed to ask ourselves in order to reach a conclusion. Nevertheless, a reflective decision of this sort is often unnecessary, and it would indeed be impossible were we not familiar with a world of images in which 'fact' and 'not-fact' were already recognized. The self does not awake to a world of undetermined images and then begin to distinguish some of them as 'facts'; the recognition of 'fact' is not an activity which, in general, supervenes

---

[4] My view is not that practical activity appears *first* as desire and aversion, or that it can ever be identified with desire and aversion, but merely that desire and aversion are always present.

upon a more primitive image-making activity, it is one which has
no specified beginning, one in which we are constantly engaging
without much reflection, and, though we may educate ourselves in
this respect, we never lack the equipment for the engagement.
Moreover, images recognized as 'facts' are not all recognized as the
same sort of 'fact'. And the determinants of 'practical fact' are, generally speaking, pragmatic: image is 'fact' if by regarding it as 'fact'
(pleasurable or painful) the desiring self is preserved for further activity. Death, the cessation of desire, is the emblem of all aversion.
In short, there is *scientia* in practical activity, but it is *scientia
propter potentiam.*

In practical activity, then, every image is the reflection of a desiring self engaged in constructing its world and in continuing to
reconstruct it in such a manner as to afford it pleasure. The world
here consists of what is good to eat and what is poisonous, what is
friendly and what is hostile, what is amenable to control and what
resists it. And each image is recognized as something to be made
use of or exploited. 'We must have have spent three hours,' says a
writer, recalling a visit to the Owen Falls, Lake Victoria, 'watching
the waters and revolving plans to harness and bridle them. So
much power running to waste, such a coign of vantage unoccupied,
such a lever to control the natural forces of Africa ungripped cannot
but vex and stimulate the imagination.' This is not a poetic image
such as Keats imagined—

> *The moving waters at their priest-like task*
> *Of pure ablution round earth's human shores—*

nor is it a 'scientific' image; it is a practical image.

But to be practically active is to be a self among selves (*inter
homines esse*). Nevertheless, the relationship of selves to images
recognized as other selves is not, in the first place, different from
their relationship to images recognized as 'things'—though it is
more difficult to manage. Another self is known as the consumer of
what I produce, the producer of what I consume, one way or another the assistant in my projects, the servant of my pleasure. That is
to say, the desiring self admits the 'fact' of other selves, but refuses

to recognize them as selves, refuses to recognize their subjectivity: activity is acknowledged only in respect of the use that may be made of it. Each self inhabits a world of its own, a world of images related to its own desires; solitariness, the consequence of its inability in this activity to recognize other selves as such, is intrinsic, not accidental. The relations between such selves is an unavoidable *bellum omnium contra omnes.*

The skill in desire and aversion is knowing how to preserve the practical self from dissolution, the skill in which 'fact' at the appropriate level is recognized, illusion is escaped, and pleasure rather than pain experienced. And it belongs to this skill to seek to accomplish its object with the least possible expenditure of energy: to be economical in this respect is itself to place a greater distance between the desiring self and death, and therefore to conserve energy is not a work of supererogation. The mere expenditure of energy (for the enjoyment of it) is foreign to the desiring self, which recognizes only the satisfaction of accomplishment or the mortification of failure. But if this economy is appropriate on all occasions, it will be pre-eminently so when the desiring self encounters another self. For, of all practical images, another self is the least tractable and offers the greatest opportunity for wasted energy and the most conspicuous occasion for defeat. To bind another self to one's desires calls for exceptional skill. Force or peremptory command may in some circumstances suffice to convert another self to my purposes, but this will rarely be the most certain or the most economical manner of achieving my ends. It will more often happen that failure is avoided only by an acknowledgment of the subjectivity of the other self which involves taking into alliance what refuses to be treated as a slave; that is, by offering a *quid pro quo* which is itself a recognition of subjectivity.[5] Such an alliance may be of short duration, or it may have the greater degree of permanence which belongs to a settled manner of behaviour or an instituted procedure friendly to a common measure of self-maintenance in the activity of desiring.

---

[5] An image recognized merely as a 'thing' neither demands nor requires a *quid pro quo* for its use.

There should, however, be no misunderstanding about the limits of this alliance, limits set, not circumstantially, but by the character of the desiring selves. It rests upon a merely *de facto* admission of the subjectivity of the selves concerned; not to make this admission is a form of illusion which may hinder successful activity. The desiring selves enter into no obligation, recognize no right; they admit the subjectivity of other selves only in order to make use of it for their own ends. It is, therefore, a disingenuous recognition of subjectivity; the *bellum omnium contra omnes* carried on by other means.

But the world of practical activity is not only the world *sub specie voluntatis*, it is also the world *sub specie moris*: it is composed not merely of images of desire and aversion but also of images of approval and disapproval.

Approving is not the same activity as desiring, and disapproval is not to be identified with aversion. For example, death is the emblem of all aversion, but not of all disapproval: we must always be averse from our own death, but there are circumstances in which we may not disapprove of it and we may act accordingly. Nevertheless, practical activity without the recognition of both these dimensions remains an abstraction. One may indeed suppose a man able, perhaps, to perceive in the activity of others the operation of these moral categories but regarding them as no more than a guide to the help or hindrance he may expect from such selves in the satisfaction of his own desires;[6] but it is an image which remains a mere image and refuses to qualify as 'fact'. Sometimes approving seems to coincide with the activity of desiring: the spectator at the Owen Falls (although he says nothing about it) clearly entertained no doubt at all about the propriety of his images of desire. On other occasions approval and disapproval are apt to appear as critics of desire and aversion, operative in an *actus secundus*. But however they appear, images of approved or disapproved desire or aversion are known only in the activities of ap-

---

[6] The character of the revolutionary as he appears in Bakunin's *The Catechism of a Revolutionary* is an attempt to portray such a man; but even here what appears is not a man divested of morality but one whose approvals and disapprovals are rather eccentric.

proving or disapproving. And when the dimensions of approval and disapproval are acknowledged, practical imagining is recognized as an activity whose object is to fill our world with images both desired and approved.

This moral attitude is concerned with the relations between selves engaged in practical activities. The merely desiring self can go no further than a disingenuous recognition of other selves; in the world *sub specie moris*, on the other hand, there is a genuine and unqualified recognition of other selves. All other selves are acknowledged to be ends and not merely means to our own ends: I may employ their skill, but it is also recognized to be proper (not merely necessary) that I should pay for it. And, as Hobbes observed, a man achieves this moral attitude if 'when weighing the actions of other men with his own, they seem too heavy, to put them in the other part of the balance, and his own in their place, that his own passions and self-love, may add nothing to the weight'.[7] In other words, selves in moral activity are equal members of a community of selves: and approval and disapproval are activities which belong to them as members of this community. The moral skill in practical activity, the *ars bene beatique vivendi*, is knowing how to behave in relation to selves ingenuously recognized as such.

In general, then, moral activity may be said to be the observation of a balance of accommodation between the demands of desiring selves each recognized by the others to be an end and not a mere slave of somebody else's desires. But this general character appears always as a particular balance, and one 'morality' differs from another in respect of the level at which this balance is struck and in respect of the quality of the equilibrium. In a 'puritan' morality, for example, the level of the autonomy of selves and the quality of the equilibrium appears in a readiness to be scandalized, a refusal to deviate a hair's breadth from the settled point of balance and an exclusion of any disposition to allow the range of sympathy to extend itself.

[7] *Leviathan*, Chapter 15.

The utterances of the self in practical activity are, for the most part, actions; it reveals itself in conduct. But in the course of moving about among the images of the practical world we also speak words, sometimes by way of commentary on what we are doing, sometimes to add force or a more precise definition to what we are doing or looking for others to do. The character and purport of this speech is appropriate to the needs of the practical self. It is the means by which we engage the attention of other selves; it allows us to identify and describe images of desire and approval, to explain, argue, instruct and negotiate; to advise, exhort, threaten and command; to pacify, encourage, comfort and console. By means of this language we communicate our desires, aversions, preferences, choices, requests, approvals and disapprovals; we make promises and acknowledge duties; we confess hopes and fears; we signify forgiveness and penitence.

The language in which the business of practical life is conducted is a symbolic language. Its words and expressions are so many agreed signs which, because they have relatively fixed and precise usages, and because they are non-resonant, serve as a medium for confident communication. It is a language that has to be learned by imitation. In themselves, the sound (the manner in which they are pronounced) and the shape (the manner in which they are spelled) of these words are insignificant so long as they are recognizable. On many occasions other signs, gestures or movements may be substituted for words, and words have the advantage over these signs only in the finer distinctions they may express. Moreover, these other signs (nodding, smiling, frowning, beckoning, shrugging the shoulders, etc.) are themselves symbols; they also have to be learnt, and they may have different significations in different societies. In using these words and signs, then, we do not seek to enlarge their meaning, or to set going a procession of linguistic reverberations; indeed, this language is like a coinage, the more fixed and invariable the value of its components, the more useful it is as a medium of exchange. In short, speaking here is expressing or conveying images and is not itself image-making. If I say, 'I am sad', I am not seeking to add a fresh *nuance* to the word 'sad'; I expect the word to be understood without quibble or difficulty, and I expect as a reply not, 'What do you mean?', but 'What's happened?' or, 'Cheer up'. If I say, 'Put it in the bucket', my remark may puzzle a child who does not know what the word 'bucket' signifies; but an adult, practised in this symbolic language, may be expected to reply, for example, 'Where is the bucket?' A conjunction of such symbols is insignificant when they stand for images which do not cohere—like, 'boiling ice', or 'liquid trees'; and if I want to deceive somebody in this language I do so by using the wrong word. The *clichés* of the business-man's letter are unobjectionable, indeed they are to be preferred to elegance because they are familiar and more genuinely symbolic. So far as this sort of language is concerned there would be an unquestionable advantage if a single set of symbols were current throughout the world: a 'basic' language of this sort, understood by all, is both possible and desirable. And again, it is not unreasonable that rulers should regard it their duty to see that goods offered for sale are not wrongly described: at least, from the nature of the language, it is a duty possible to be performed, for every word has its proper reference or signification.

This, then, is practical activity, and this is the nature of practical language, and the idiom of the voice of practice. Its talk is not only of bullocks; it may convey endearments as well as information; it may argue as well as command: and it may move alike among conceptional and visual images. But the discourse of practice—the discourse which takes place between selves in practical activity and which the voice of practice brings to the conversation—is always conditioned by its concern with images of desire and aversion, approval and disapproval, and by the particular level of 'fact' and 'not-fact' it recognizes.

FOUR

On our first encounter with it, as school-boys, 'science' appears as an encyclopædia conveying information about the world fascinatingly different from what we would otherwise suppose to be the case. The image of a stationary earth is replaced by that of a sta-

tionary sun, iron dissolves into arrangements of electrons and pro-
tons, water is revealed to be a combination of gases and the concept of undulations in the air of various dimensions takes the
place of the images of sounds. And we are introduced to other
images which have no counterparts in our familiar world, the concepts (for example) of velocity, of inertia, and of latent heat. These
are the 'wonders of science'. And with them we enter a world whose
images are not images of desire and aversion and provoke neither
approval nor disapproval, a world where 'fact' and 'not-fact' are distinguished, but on some other principle than the pragmatic principle of the world of practical activity. *Scientia,* the recognition of
'fact' and 'not-fact', we were already acquainted with, but hitherto
it had been *scientia propter potentiam*—knowing how to get what
we want, how to contrive a world of approved and pleasure-giving
images. This, on the other hand, appeared to be a different kind of
scientia: the world understood in respect of its independence of
our hopes and desires, preferences and ambitions, a world of
images which some other creature, differently constituted, with
different desires, dwelling in a different part of the universe (an
inhabitant of Mars, for example), could share with us if his attention were given the same sort of twist and came to be governed by
the same considerabilities; and a world which a blind man could
enter as easily and move about in as freely as one who could see.
Moreover, this world of 'science' was revealed not only to be composed of images independent of our practical concerns but also to
be a system of conceptional images related to one another consequentially and claiming universal acceptance as a rational account
of the world we live in. Thus, *scientia* came to be understood, not
as an array of marvellous discoveries, nor as a settled doctrine
about the world, but as a universe of discourse, a way of imagining
and moving about among images, an activity, an inquiry not specified by its current achievements but by the manner in which it was
conducted. And its voice was heard to be not (as we had first supposed) the didactic voice of an encyclopædia, but a conversable
voice, one speaking in an idiom of its own but capable of participating in the conversation.

Scientific investigation, the activity of being a scientist, is mankind in search of the intellectual satisfaction which comes from constructing and exploring a rational world of related concepts in which every image recognized to be relevant 'fact' in the idiom of this inquiry is given a place and an interpretation. Its impulse is not to make a world, each of whose component images is welcome on account of the pleasure it gives or the moral approval it evokes, but to make a rational world of consequentially arranged conceptual images. The 'natural world' of the scientist is an artefact no less than the world of practical activity; but it is an artefact constructed on a different principle and in response to a different impulse. And, properly speaking, *scientia* is what happens when we surrender ourselves to this impulse for rational understanding; it exists only where this impulse is cultivated for its own sake unhindered by the intrusion of desire for power and prosperity, and only the shadow of it appears where the products of this engagement (the discoveries about the world) are what is valued, and are valued only for what can be contrived from them. Of course, desire and approval and even the expectation of pleasure have their place in the generation of this activity, but they do not enter into the structure of this universe of discourse as they do into the structure of the practical universe: pleasure is not the warrant of valid achievement, it is not even the *ratio cognoscendi* of valid achievement, but only the self-congratulation which comes with the belief that one has been successful in this intellectual undertaking.

It is not to be supposed that the self in scientific activity begins with a premeditated purpose, a ready-made method of inquiry, or even with a given set of problems. The so-called 'methods' of scientific investigation emerge in the course of the activity and they never take account of all that belongs to a scientific inquiry; and in advance of scientific thought there are no scientific problems. Even the principle of the 'rationality of nature' is not a genuine presupposition; it is merely another way of describing the impulse from which *scientia* springs. All that exists in advance of scientific inquiries is the urge to achieve an intellectually satisfying world of images. Thinking *becomes* scientific in a process similar to that in which some universities, which began as seminaries for training would-be teachers of an already settled doctrine, deserted their original sectarian character and became societies of scholars distinguished not by a doctrine held in common but by their manner of engaging in learning and teaching. But the emancipation which specifies *scientia* is not an emancipation from a dogma; it is an emancipation from the authority of practical imagining. It is a false theory of scientific knowledge which understands it as the most economical arrangement of the images of practical imagining—not because economy of concepts is a vice in scientific theory, but because its images are not those of the world of practice. The mark of the scientist is, then, his power of moving freely within current scientific theory (for this is where he begins), of perceiving the ambiguities and incoherencies which reveal its irrationality, of speculating upon and making guesses about directions of profitable advance, of distinguishing what is important from what is trivial and of pursuing his conjectures in such a manner as to produce significant and unambiguous conclusions. And in this respect, every detailed piece of scientific investigation is a microcosm of the manner in which the grander and more general scientific theories are explored and elucidated.

In practical activity each self seeks its own pleasure: *chacun est un tout à soi-même, car, lui mort, le tout est mort pour soi.*[8] But this pursuit of pleasure involves accommodation to other selves, and consequently practical activity is at least intermittently co-operative and calls for a certain level of communication between selves. *Scientia*, on the other hand, is essentially a co-operative enterprise. All who participate in the construction of this rational world of conceptual images of invoking universal acceptance are as if they were one man, and exactness of communication between them is a necessity. Indeed, *scientia* may be said to be itself the mutual understanding of one another enjoyed by those who know how to participate in the construction of this world of images. Scientists do their cumulative best to inform us about the world but *scientia* is the

[8] Pascal, *Pensées*, 457.

activity, not the information, and the principle of this activity is the exclusion of whatever is private, esoteric, or ambiguous. And in response to this requirement of exactness of communication images become measurements according to agreed scales, relationships are mathematical ratios, and positions are indicated by numerical coordinates: the world of science is recognized as the world *sub specie quantitatis*.

The voice of science, then, is not essentially didactic; it is a conversable voice, but the language it speaks is a more severely symbolic language even than that of practice, and the range of its utterance is both narrower and more precise. Whereas words in practical activity are often only slightly more subtle and more easily transmissible alternatives to gestures (words and gestures being alike symbolic) and may be legitimately used both to proclaim and to conceal thoughts, words in scientific utterance are more precisely symbolic, and when they can be refined no further, they give place not to gestures but to technical expressions, to signs and mathematical symbols which can be more exactly assembled and are more exactly related to one another because they have been purged of the last vestiges of ambiguity. Symbols are like chessmen: they stand for what can be done with them according to known rules, and the rules which govern the use of mathematical symbols are more strict than those which govern the use of words; indeed, some statements made in mathematical symbols are incapable of being translated into words. The idiom of scientific utterance has superficial similarities and correspondences to that of practical utterance: both, for example, recognize a distinction between 'fact' and 'not-fact'; in neither is speaking itself image-making; whereas the one must be argumentative, the other may be so; and in both, knowledge, opinion, conjecture, and supposition are severally recognized. But the similarities are only superficial. 'Fact' and 'not-fact' are, in each activity, differently determined; and *scientia* is conditioned throughout by its impulse to construct a rational world of consequentially related conceptual images, an impulse which constitutes a different universe of discourse from that of practice.

FIVE

By 'poetry' I mean the activity of making images of a certain kind and moving about among them in a manner appropriate to their character. Painting, sculpting, acting, dancing, singing, literary and musical composition are different kinds of poetic activity. Of course, not everyone who lays paint upon canvas, who chisels stone, or moves his limbs rhythmically, or opens his mouth in song, or puts pen to paper in verse or prose, speaks in the idiom of poetry, but only those who engage in these and similar operations in a certain manner.[9] The voice of poetry is one which speaks in the idiom of this activity. How shall we specify it?

Let me recall a manner of being active different from that in either practice or science, but nevertheless not unfamiliar. I will call it 'contemplating', or 'delighting'. This activity, like every other, is making images of a certain sort and moving among them in an appropriate manner. But these images, in the first place, are recognized to be mere images; that is to say, they are not recognized either as 'fact' or as 'not-fact', as 'events' (for example) to have taken place or not to have taken place. To recognize an image as 'fact', or to ask oneself the question: Is that 'fact' or 'not-fact'?, is to announce oneself to be engaged in some other manner of activity than contemplation—a practical, a scientific, or an historical manner. Nor is it enough to say: 'This image may or may not be 'fact', but in contemplating it I ignore the possibility of its factual character.' For images are never neutral, eligible to be considered in this or that manner: they cannot divest themselves of the considerabilities which determine their character and they are always the partners of a specific kind of imagining. Where imagining is 'contemplating', then, 'fact' and 'not-fact' do not appear. And consequently these images cannot be recognized as either 'possible' or 'probable', as illusions or as make-believe images, because all these categories look back to a distinction between 'fact' and 'not-fact'.

Further, images in contemplation are merely present; they provoke neither speculation nor inquiry about the occasion or condi-

[9] Aristotle, *Poetics*, i, 7–8; ix, 2.

tions of their appearing but only delight in their having appeared. They have no antecedents or consequents; they are not recognized as causes or conditions or signs of some other image to follow, or as the products or effects of one that went before; they are not instances of a kind, nor are they means to an end; they are neither 'useful' nor 'useless'. Contemplative images may have connections with one another, but they have no history: if they had a history they would be historical images. In practical activity an image may be said to be impermanent because it is always a temporary resting-place in a necessarily endless process which is concluded only in death; it is a step in the execution of a policy or a project; it is something to be made use of, to be improved or transformed. And the same is true of the conceptual images of scientific theory, which are recognized as having entailments and logical connections, which are often kept ready for use as tools of inquiry for the appropriate occasion when it arises, and are capable of improvement. The images which partner contemplation, on the other hand, have the appearance of being both permanent and unique. Contemplation does not use, or use-up or wear-out its images, or induce change in them: it rests in them, looking neither backwards nor forwards. But this appearance of being permanent is not to seem durable instead of transitory; like any other image, the image which partners contemplation may be destroyed by inattention, may be lost, or may decompose. It is permanent merely because change and destruction are not potential in it; and it is unique because no other image can fill its place.

Moreover, the image in contemplation is neither pleasurable nor painful; and it does not attract to itself either moral approval or disapproval. Pleasure and pain, approval and disapproval are characteristics of images of desire and aversion, but the partner of desire and aversion is incapable of being the partner of contemplation.

Nevertheless, it is not to be supposed that some superior 'reality' or importance may properly be attributed to the images of contemplative imagining. And in this connection I must distinguish what I mean by contemplation from another, and perhaps more familiar, notion. Some writers (whose manner of thinking has impressed itself deeply upon our intellectual habits) understand contemplation as an experience in which the self is partnered, not by a world of unique but transitory images, but by a world of permanent essences: to contemplate is to 'behold' the 'universals' of which the images of sense, emotion, and thought are mere copies. And consequently, for these writers contemplation is the enjoyment of a special and immediate access to 'reality'. It seems probable that Plato held some such view as this; Spinoza appears to have attributed this character to what he calls *scientia intuitiva*;[10] and Schopenhauer found in *Kontemplation* a union of the self with *species rerum*.[11] And I do not think there can be any serious doubt about how Plato, at least, arrived at this conception of contemplation (Θεωρία). Activity, both human and divine, he understood as fabrication, the activity of a craftsman; and 'to make' was to copy, reproduce, or imitate an ideal model in the transitory materials of space and time. Consequently, activity was understood to entail, as a first step, a 'vision' of the archetype to be copied; and this experience he called Θεωρία. Thus, contemplation (this immediate experience, not of images, but of the real εἶδος) emerged by supposing the activity of a craftsman to have been arrested before the work of copying had been begun. And in the Platonic conspectus the voice of Θεωρία was acknowledged to be supreme in the conversation of mankind on account of its release from the concerns of craftsmanship, which were considered to be servile because they were apt to be repetitive and in any case were understood to be those of a merely imitative image-maker.

For many centuries in the intellectual history of Europe, contemplation, understood as a purely receptive experience of real entities, occupied the highest place in the hierarchy of human experiences, scientific inquiry being recognized as, at best, preparatory to it, and practical engagements as mere distractions. In recent times, however, not only has it been demoted from this position of

---

[10] *Ethica*, ii, 40; v, 25–38.
[11] *Die Welt als Wille und Vorstellung*, §34.

supremacy (by a philistine concern with useful knowledge), but it has even been called in question by the re-emergence of an understanding of activity which has no place for it. The Platonic understanding of activity as copying ideal models (and therefore entailing a 'vision' of the models to be copied) has been overshadowed by a concept of 'creative' activity[12] which, having no place for ideal models or for images recognized as mere copies of these models, has no place either for this kind of contemplation. But there are difficulties inherent in this notion of Θεωρία which this reversal of its historic fortunes only imperfectly discloses. It need not be doubted that Θεωρία reflects some observed condition of human experience, but it may be questioned whether the reflection is as faithful as it should be; and I do not myself know where to place an experience released altogether from modality or a world of 'objects' which is not a world of images and is governed by no considerabilities. Moreover, to make an experience of this sort supreme seems to entail a belief in the pre-eminence of inquiry, and of the categories of 'truth' and 'reality', a belief which I would wish to avoid. But be that how it may, this is not the notion of contemplation I am now exploring. Contemplation, as I understand it, is activity and it is image-making; and the images of contemplative imagining are distinguished from those of both scientific and practical imagining, not by reason of their 'universality', but on account of their being recognized as individuals and neither as concretions of qualities any of which might appear elsewhere (as both coal and wood may be recognized for their combustibility or two men may be compared in respect of their mastery of a particular skill), nor as signs or symbols of something else. And I am disposed to think that this is all that can, in the end, survive of the Platonic conception of Θεωρία.

Since images in contemplation are different in character from those which partner both practical and scientific activity, the organization of these images will also be different. The coherence of the images of the practical world (organized by such distinctions as pleasurableness and painfulness, approval and disapproval, 'fact'

---

[12] Cf. M. Foster, *Mind*, October 1934.

and 'not-fact', expected and unexpected, chosen and rejected) springs from their being the creatures of desire; and the world of scientific images has communicable intelligibility as the principle of its order. In what fashion are the images of contemplation organized, and in what manner does the contemplating self move among them?

The world in which the self awakes in contemplation may be dark and its images indistinct, and in so far as the activity verges upon lethargy what appears will be a mere sequence of images, one following another in lazy association, each entertained for its moment of delight but none held or explored. This, however, is the nadir of contemplation, from which the contemplative self rises when one image (because of the pre-eminent delight it offers) becomes the focus of attention and the nucleus of an activity in which it is allowed to proliferate, to call up other images and be joined with them and to take its place in a more extended and complex composition. Nevertheless, this composition is not a conclusion; it is only another image of the same sort. In this process images may generate one another, they may modify and fuse with one another, but no premeditated achievement is pursued. The activity here is clearly not inferential or argumentative. Since there is no problem to be solved, no hypothesis to be explored, no restlessness to be overcome, no desire to be satisfied, or approval to be won, there is no 'This, therefore That', no passage from image to image in which each movement is a step in an elucidation or in the execution of a project. And since what is sought is not an *exit* from this labyrinth of images, a guide of any kind would be out of place. At every turn what impels the activity and gives it whatever coherence it may possess, is the delight offered and come upon in this perpetually extending partnership between the contemplating self and its images.

Contemplating, then, is a specific mode of imagining and moving about among images, different from both practical and scientific imagining. It is an activity of making and entertaining mere images. In practice and in science 'activity' is undeniable. In the one there is a need to be satisfied, a thirst to be quenched, and satiety is always followed by want; there may be weariness, but there is no rest. And in the other there is a corresponding restlessness appropriate to its idiom; every achievement in the exploration of the vision of a wholly intelligible world of images being merely a prelude to fresh activity. But since in contemplation there is neither research for what does not appear nor desire for what is not present, it has often been mistaken for inactivity. But it is more appropriate to call it (as Aristotle called it) a non-laborious activity —activity which, because it is playful and not businesslike, because it is free from care and released from both logical necessity and pragmatic requirement, seems to participate in the character of inactivity. Nevertheless, this appearance of leisureliness (σχολή) is not an emblem of lethargy; it springs from the self-sufficiency enjoyed by each engagement in the activity and by the absence of any premeditated end. At whatever point contemplation is broken off it is never incomplete. Consequently, the 'delight' which I have coupled with contemplation is not to be thought of as a reward which follows upon the activity, as wages follow work, as knowledge follows upon scientific research, as release follows death or an injection of opium; 'delighting' is only another name for 'contemplating.'

Every mode of imagining is activity in partnership with images of a specific character which cannot appear in any other universe of discourse; that is, each mode begins and ends wholly within itself. Consequently, it is an error (though a common one) to speak of a manner of imagining as the 'conversion', or 'transformation', or 'reconstruction' either of a supposed unspecified image or of an image belonging to a different universe of discourse. An unspecified image is only another name for a nonentity; and the images of one universe of discourse are not available (even as raw materials) to a different mode of imagining. For example, the word 'water' stands for a practical image; but a scientist does not first perceive 'water' and then resolve it into H_2O: *scientia* begins only when 'water' has been left behind. To speak of H_2O as 'the chemical formula for water' is to speak in a confused manner: H_2O is a symbol the rules of whose behaviour are wholly different from those which govern the symbol 'water'. And similarly, contemplative activity is never the 'conversion' of a practical or a scientific image into a contemplated image;

its appearance is possible only when practical and scientific imagining have lost their authority.

Nevertheless, it is clear that one mode of imagining may give place to and supersede another, and the relationship between these different universes of discourse will be illuminated if we understand how this may come about. Of all the modes of imagining practical activity is unmistakably the commonest among adult human beings—and understandably so, for the avoidance of death is the condition of any sort of activity. Departures from this activity have always the appearance of excursions into a foreign country; and this is pre-eminently so with contemplation, which can never be expected to be more than an intermittent activity. How is the passage from practice to contemplation made? In general, it would seem that any occasion which interrupts the affirmative flow of practical activity, any lessening of the urgency of desire, any softening of the wilfulness of ambitions, or anything that blunts the edge of moral appraisal offers an invitation to contemplative activity to make its appearance. Contemplation is not itself lethargic, but it may find its opportunity when practical activity becomes lethargic. An image which the desiring self has failed to make its own (if it does not become an image of aversion) is, so to speak, ready to be superseded by an image of contemplative delight. Disenchantment, or the more permanent detachment which belongs to a practical attitude of 'fatalism', commonly induce (or perhaps are only other names for) lethargy in practice which contains an intimation of the leisureness which belongs to contemplation. Moreover, a practical image which has been circumstantially loosened from its world and is framed apart (such as a house no longer habitable, or a ship no longer seaworthy, or unrequited love) or an image that has an ambiguously practical character (such as a loaf of bread in paint, a man in stone, a friend or a lover) constitutes a momentary interruption of practical activity, and contemplation may flow in to take its place. Indeed, any practical image which, from the unfamiliar circumstances of its appearance, induces wonder may open a door upon the world of contemplation, so long as wonder does not pass into curiosity (*scientia*). And it would seem that contemplation may supervene more easily when the practical image is a memory-image. For, in regard to experiences remembered, desire and aversion are apt to be less clamorous, approval and disapproval less insistent, and even the urge to distinguish between 'fact' and 'not-fact' is diminished; though, of course, a memory and a memory contemplated are images that belong to different universes of discourse. In short, and in general, although no image can ever survive outside its proper universe of discourse, diminished or interrupted activity in one mode may generate an opportunity for the appearance of another. And those who would enjoy the difficult delights of contemplation must be ready to enter by whatever door chance or circumstance may open to them.

SIX

I have recalled this manner of being active because, as I understand it, poetic imagining is contemplative activity. I do not mean that poetic imagining is one species among others of contemplative imagining; I mean that the voice of contemplation is the voice of poetry and that it has no other utterance. And just as activity in practice is desiring and obtaining, and activity in science is inquiring and understanding, so poetry is contemplating and delighting.[13]

That the activity in poetry is imagining, making and moving about among images, is so little to be questioned that even those who do not accept my view that *all* activity (except symbolic utterance) is imagining are not likely to deny it. But, in my view, poetry appears when imagining is contemplative imagining; that is, when images are not recognized either as 'fact' or as 'not-fact',[14] when

[13] I have said that I am inclined to think that what I mean by 'contemplation' is all that can survive in the Platonic conception of Θεωρία. This belief may now be restated as the belief that what Plato described as Θεωρία is, in fact, aesthetic experience but that he misdescribed it and attributed to it a character and a supremacy which it is unable to sustain. By understanding 'poetry' as a craft, and craft as an activity of imitating ideal models, he followed a false scent which led him to the unnecessary hypothesis of non-image-making, 'wordless' experience, namely, that of 'beholding' the ideal models to be copied. Nevertheless, the platonic Θεωρία, if it were admitted to be image-making, would direct our attention to an activity of image-making which would not be 'copying' and whose images would not be 'representations'.

[14] And therefore neither as 'illusions' nor as images of 'make-believe'.

they do not provoke either moral approval or disapproval, when they are not read as symbols, or as causes, effects, or means to ulterior ends, but are made, remade, observed, turned about, played with, meditated upon, and delighted in, and when they are composed into larger patterns which are themselves only more complex images and not conclusions. A poet arranges his images like a girl bunching flowers, considering only how they will appear together. He has to do only with images to which such arrangement is appropriate; the bunch is only another image of the same sort; and the style and diction which distinguishes him from other poets lies in the character of the images he is apt to delight in and in the manner in which he is disposed to arrange them. And it is with 'style' in this sense that the critic (as distinct from the philosopher) is concerned.

Thus, any scene, shape, pattern, pose or movement in the visible or audible world, any action, happening or event or concatenation of events, any habit or disposition exhibited in movement or speech, any thought or memory is a poetic image if the manner in which it is imagined is what I have called 'contemplating'. But certain images—scenes, shapes, poses, movements, etc.—are more readily and more unmistakably recognized as poetic images because of the circumstances in which they appear: they positively provoke a contemplative attitude rather than any other because of their resistance to being read symbolically. Such images we call works of art: for example, Donatello's David, Seurat's La Grande Jatte, Mozart's *Figaro*, the nurse in *Romeo and Juliet*, Moby Dick the Whale, Anna Karenina, Lord Randall of the ballad, *Paradise Lost*, a pose or a phrase of movement of Nijinski, an entrance of Rachel, Tom Walls' leer, or verbal images such as

O sea-starved hungry sea

Earth of the slumbering and liquid trees

And man is such a marigold

Goe, and catche a falling starre,
  Get with child a mandrake roote,
Tell me, where all past yeares are,
  Or who cleft the Divels foot . . .

Of course, none of these and similar shapes, sounds, movements, characters, verbal constructions, etc., is incapable of being
imagined in an unpoetic manner. A piece of sculpture may be considered indecent, a painting may be an object of worship, Uncle
Mathew's verdict on the nurse in *Romeo and Juliet* ('dismal bitch')
shows him to have been imagining in the idiom of practice, and
almost any verbal construction (a metaphor, for example) may be
used for its 'aptness' as an oratorical device to persuade a listener
of the truth of a proposition or to embellish an otherwise commonplace statement. A work of art is merely an image which is protected in an unusual degree from being read (that is, imagined) in an
unpoetic manner, a protection it derives from its quality and from
the circumstantial frame within which it appears.[15] This quality is
perhaps less likely to be mistaken in the images of some arts than
in those of others. A musical image is more secure than a pictorial
image; and the poetic character of a verbal image may sometimes
be intimated by its practical incoherence. And further, a word or a
verbal construction may have a recognized home in more than one
universe of discourse: 'the French Revolution' for Blake was a poetic image, for de Tocqueville it represented an historical image, for
Napoleon a practical image; the word 'democracy' for some people
represents a quasi-scientific image, for many it signifies a practical
image (the symbol of a condition desired and to be approved), for
de Tocqueville it stood for an historical image, but for Walt Whit-
man it was a poetic image. In short, the character of an image is
revealed in its behaviour, in the sort of statements which can relevantly be made about it and in the sort of questions which can
relevantly be asked about it.

Let us suppose that the activity in poetry is not 'contemplating', but is some version of practical or scientific activity. It would

---

[15] The frame provided, for example, by a theatre, or a picture gallery, or a concert hall, or
the covers of a book.

then be relevant to ask certain questions about an image recognized to be a poetic image: we might consider whether it was 'fact' or 'not-fact' and what sort of 'fact' or 'not-fact' it was. We might ask, in respect of Donatello's David: Was David (whoever he was) of these proportions? was he accustomed to wearing a hat of this sort, or did he wear it only on the occasions when he was posing for the sculptor? Of Anna Karenina we might relevantly ask: Is it a fact that she said these words on this occasion, or has Tolstoy misreported what she actually said? Of Hamlet we might inquire: What was his normal bed-time? Of Marlowe's Tamburlaine we should at once be sceptical; How does he come to be speaking English, or is Marlowe translating for our benefit from the Scythian tongue? Of *Paradise Lost* we might inquire, in respect of many passages: What part of the country is being described to us? or: What was the date of Adam's death? Of a performance of *Figaro* we might ask: How close a resemblance has the singer's voice to that of the real Barbarina? And so on.

But we need only to suppose these and other inquiries in the same idiom in order to recognize that they are misconceived. What Anna said on any occasion could not have been misreported by Tolstoy because she is incapable of speaking any words which he has not put into her mouth. Hamlet never went to bed; he exists only in the play, he is a poetic image composed of the words and actions which Shakespeare gave him, and beyond these he is nothing. Rachel did not 'imitate' the words and actions, or 'resemble' the character or appearance of a living or once living person, she divested herself of her own practical self and became (on a stage) a poetic image in which movement and speech were combined.[16] Corot could not misreport a landscape because he was not making a report at all, he was making a poetic image. Donatello's David is not an 'imitation' King David as a boy; it is not even an imitation of a model: a sculptor's model is not a person, but a pose. A photograph (if it purports to record an event) may 'lie', but a poetic image can never 'lie' because it does not affirm anything. These images—

---

[16] Drama is not 'acting' or 'make-believe acting', it is 'playing at acting'.

shapes, scenes, movements, characters, verbal constructions—do not belong to a universe of discourse in which 'fact' and 'not-fact' can be distinguished; they are fictions. And these stories and descriptions in paint or words or stone or the movements of dance are stories of fictitious events and scenes; they are fables. And on this account, also, they are neither illusions nor make-believe images, nor are they images made in an activity of pretending; for, illusion, make-believe, and pretence are all impossible without a reference to 'fact'. Anna was not a suicide; Othello was not a murderer; Daisy Miller was not a silly girl who died of the *perniciosa*—she was never, in that sense, alive; she is a phantom. Indeed, even to speak of these images in the past tense is to speak inappropriately about them; they do not belong to the world of practical time and space. And further, moral approval or disapproval are alike inapplicable to these images; they are not people who inhabit or who have ever inhabited the practical world of desire and enterprise, and consequently their 'conduct' cannot be either 'right' or 'wrong' nor their dispositions 'good' or 'bad'. The Cenci, according to the chronicle, was a disagreeable and ill-mannered family, but the poetic image of Beatrice in Shelley's drama is an emblem neither of good nor of bad behaviour; she is a tragic fiction, ineligible for either approval or disapproval. And the fact that we are held back from approving or disapproving of the 'conduct' and character of, for example, Anna Karenina, Lord Jim, or the Duchessa Sanseverina, as they come to us in the pages of books, is evidence of our recognition of their unmistakably poetic quality. Nor, finally, are poetic images capable of giving either pleasure or pain. Pleasure and pain are the partners of desiring, but here desire and aversion are absent: what in the practical world would be pleasurable or painful situations in poetry are alike delightful.

In short, painters, sculptors, writers, musical composers, actors, dancers, and singers, when they are poets, are not doing *two* things—observing, thinking, remembering, hearing, feeling, etc., and then 'expressing' or making analogues, imitations, or reproductions of what they have seen, heard, remembered, felt, etc., in the practical world, and doing it well or ill, correctly or incorrectly—

they are doing *one* thing, imagining poetically. And the images they make behave in the manner of images which are the counterparts of contemplative imagining. There are, of course, many inquiries we may properly make about these images, inquiries designed to elicit their qualities and in the course of which we may educate ourselves in the activity of delighting; but here we are concerned only to observe that inquiries appropriate to practical, scientific or historical images are not appropriate to poetic images.

Nevertheless, there are false beliefs about poetic imagining and poetic images which die hard. Some people find poetic images unintelligible unless they can be shown to be in some sense 'true' or representations of 'truth', and the obvious difficulties which face such a requirement are circumvented by means of a concept of 'poetic truth', a special kind of 'truth' usually believed to be more profound than other manifestations of 'truth'. There is, further, a disposition to understand poetic imagining as an activity (superior to other activities) in which 'things are seen as they really are', poets being thought to have a special gift in this respect, not enjoyed by other people. Again, there are people who do not understand how poetic imagining can be anything other than 'expressing' or 'conveying' or 'representing' experiences which the poet has himself enjoyed and wishes others to enjoy also; and these 'experiences' are often thought of as 'emotions' or 'feelings'. And finally, it is commonly believed that all poetic imagining is an attempt to make images which have a special quality named 'beauty'. But all these and similar beliefs are, I think, misleading, and none of them can survive investigation; and I am certain that they must be erroneous if (as I believe) poetic imagining is what I have called 'contemplating'.

The notion of 'poetic truth' has this much to be said for it: it recognizes that whatever 'truth' a poetic image may represent, it is not practical, scientific, or historical truth. That is to say, it belongs to the view that to charge a poetic image with practical impossibility, scientific solecism, or historical anachronism is as much out of the nature of things as to accuse a cabbage of theft. But, properly speaking, 'truth' concerns propositions, and while practical statements may constitute propositions and scientific and historical statements always do so, poetic images are never of this character. And I do not myself understand how the concept 'truth' applies to poetic images such as

> O sea-starved hungry sea

> Fair maid, white and red,
> Comb me smooth, and stroke my head;
> And every hair a sheave shall be,
> And every sheave a golden tree.

or to Anna Karenina, or a movement of Nijinski on the stage, or a tune of Rossini or to Bellini's St Francis. None of these purports to be an affirmation of 'fact'; and, indeed, a world of images from which 'fact' or 'not-fact' are alike absent is not a world whose constituents are properly to be qualified by such epithets as 'true' and 'erroneous', 'veracious' or 'false' or 'mistaken'.

And when, further, it is said that poetic imagining is 'seeing things as they really are', that what distinguishes a poet is the 'precision' of his observation, we seem to have been inveigled back into a world composed, not of images but of cows and cornfields, midinettes and May mornings, graveyards and Grecian urns which may be observed with varying degrees of accuracy but which otherwise owes nothing to imagining. Or, if this is not what is intended, then it would appear that poetic imagining is being presented to us (after the manner of Plato and his followers) as insight into the 'permanent essences' of the things of a phenomenal world and is, on that account, 'seeing things as they really are'. But either way, what is being said in these invocations of 'truth' and 'reality' may perhaps be recognized either as a denial of the interdependence between the self and its images, or as a somewhat confused representation of the mistaken belief that all modes of imagining and moving about among images are properly to be understood as contributions to an inquiry into the nature of the real world. Nor are these difficulties avoided in the more modest claim that poetic imagining is seeing 'things' as they are when perception is unclouded by the preoccupations of desire, approval, curiosity, or inquiry. As I understand it, the poet is not saying anything at all about 'things'[17] (that is, about images belonging to a world of discourse other than that of poetry). He is not saying, 'This is what these persons, objects and events (the return of Ulysses, Don Juan, sunset on the Nile, the birth of Venus, the death of Mimi, modern love, a cornfield (Traherne), the French Revolution) really were or are', but 'In contemplation I have made these images, read them in their own character, and seek in them only delight'. In short, when you know what things are really like you can make no poems.

And yet, no doubt, there are still some misgivings to be allayed. Even if we agree that poetic imagining is not properly described as seeing 'things' such as May mornings and graveyards 'as they really are', there are less improbable versions of this view which ought to be considered. Are you proposing (I shall be asked) to throw overboard also the theory of poetic imagining in which it is understood to be experiencing feelings or emotions and in which poetic images are understood to be the 'expressions' of such experiences? And I must confess that my answer is: 'Yes, that is exactly what I am proposing to do, but not without consideration.'

Of course it will readily be understood that I am unable to recognize poetic imagining as a 'communication' of an emotional experience designed to evoke this experience in others, for that would give it an unequivocally practical character. And Ode to Dejection is not an attempt to excite dejection in the reader; an Ode to Duty is not an attempt to make us feel dutiful, any more than a tragic situation in a play is one designed to give us pain. Nor (without inconsistency) can I accept the view that in a poetic image an emotional experience is simply 'expressed',[18] for here also the activity would be unmistakably practical and not contemplative, and the image a symbol; a large part of our practical activity consists in expressing

---

[17] Nor about 'aspects' of 'things'.

[18] The other words commonly used in this connection have each a different *nuance*, but they are all alike unsatisfactory: convey, communicate, represent, exhibit, display, embody, perpetuate, describe, find an objective correlative for, incarnate, make immortal, etc. The least objectionable perhaps is the most time-worn: imitate. This recognizes the fictitious character of the poetic image, but it errs in suggesting an activity of copying and the presumption of something to be copied.

our emotions in conduct and words. But beyond these there is another and perhaps more plausible theory. It is to be found explicitly in the writings of Wordsworth,[19] but other writers (Sir Philip Sidney and Shelley) seem also to hold it, and it is among the more common current theories. It runs as follows: poetry begins with an emotional experience undergone by the poet himself (anger, for example, or love, or dejection, or loss of faith), this emotional experience is then contemplated, and from this activity of contemplation a poetic image is generated which is an 'expression' of an analogue of the original emotional experience and consequently may be expected to give us what Sidney[20] calls 'a more familiar insight' into the experience.

There are several objections to this theory, the spring of which is, I think, the belief that poetry must be supposed to provide information or instruction of some sort. It requires the poet himself to have undergone the emotional experience with which poetic imagining is said to begin. And, perhaps as a corollary, the poet is presented to us in this theory as pre-eminently a man of feeling or emotion.[21] But in order to contemplate an emotion (if the expression may be allowed to pass) it is clearly not necessary to have undergone it; indeed, it would seem that the spectator-like mood of contemplation would be more likely to establish itself if the emotion had *not* been experienced. In this respect, then, the theory makes a necessity of what is no more than an unlikely possibility. Further, the theory attributes to the poet the activity of contemplating an emotion being undergone—and this is an impossibility. An emotion is a practical image, and as such it cannot belong to the contemplative world of discourse. It is only when feelings are 'imaginary' (in the sense of not being felt) that they may become the stuff of a poetic image.[22] And it is fair to say that some of the exponents of

---

[19] 'Observations prefixed to the second edition of *Lyrical Ballads*.'

[20] Sidney, *Apologie for Poetrie.*

[21] Shelley, *A Defense of Poetry*; or Wordsworth: 'poetry is the spontaneous overflow of powerful feelings'.

[22] It is a profound saying that 'all sorrows can be borne if you can put them into a story', but what it means is that all sorrows can be borne if we can succeed in substituting poetic images in their place.

this theory have had misgivings on this point. In Wordsworth's account, what is contemplated is a 'recollected emotion';[23] and Sidney speaks of passions that are somehow not passions at all—not felt, but 'seen through'. But misgivings are not enough; and Wordsworth's do not carry him very far, for he insists that the poetic image appears only when contemplative tranquillity has given place to another emotion 'kindred to that which was before the subject in contemplation', and is itself the expression of an emotion which 'does actually exist in the mind'. Moreover, in this theory a distinction is made between the image generated and the experience contemplated; the one is said to 'express' the other. But, as I understand it, a poetic utterance (a work of art) is not the 'expression' of an experience, it *is* the experience and the only one there is. A poet does not do *three* things: first experience or observe or recollect an emotion, then contemplate it, and finally seek a means of expressing the results of his contemplation; he does one thing only, he imagines poetically. Painting a picture, composing a verbal image, making a tune are themselves the activities of contemplation which constitute poetic imagining.[24] The notion that there are poets who unfortunately, because of the want of some technical accomplishment, are unable to 'express themselves', that is, write poetry or paint pictures or dance, is a false notion: there are no such people. There are poets (that is, people capable of creating and moving about among poetic images), and there are people capable of recognizing a work of art in its proper character.[25]

---

[23] Memories seem to be a fruitful spring of poetic images because in remembering (if we succeed in escaping the mood of nostalgia) we are already halfway released from the practical world of desire and emotion. But even here, what can be contemplated is not an actual and recognized memory, but an abstraction—a memory not identified as 'fact' and one divorced from space and time. Poetry is not the daughter of memory but its stepdaughter. Cf. Eckermann, *Gesprache mit Goethe*, 28 March 1831.

[24] The changes poets are apt to make in their work are not, strictly speaking, 'corrections'— that is to say, attempts to improve the 'expression' of an already clear mental image; they are attempts to imagine more clearly and to delight more deeply. And the 'studies' which painters often make which later may become components of a larger and complex composition (e.g. Seurat's studies for La Grande Jatte) are not hypotheses being tried out; each is itself a snatch of poetry, an image which may or may not become part of a more complex image.

[25] If these objections are not conclusive against the theory, there is another which it is, perhaps, not irrelevant to mention. It is noticeable that in respect of what are recognized to be some of the most unmistakable works of art it is anybody's guess what the emotion was

The theory, indeed, breaks down conspicuously when set against even the most plausible example. If this were a satisfactory account of any poetic image, surely it should be so of Keats's *Ode to Melancholy*. And yet, quite clearly, this poem could have been composed by a man of sanguine temperament who never himself felt the touch of melancholy; clearly, also, it is not designed to excite melancholy in the reader (or, if that were its design, it fails signally); and it cannot be said to tell us what melancholy 'really is'. Indeed, it is only when we are misled by the title of the poem (which, in a work of art, is never of any significance;[26] poets always know poems by their first lines, and in composition they never begin with a 'subject' but always with a poetic image) that we get the misleading notion that this poem is 'about melancholy' in anything like the same sense as this essay is 'about poetry'. In fact, this poem is a complex of images made in an activity of contemplation (but not the contemplation of the emotion symbolized in the word 'melancholy'), which neither 'expresses' melancholy nor gives us 'a more familiar insight' into melancholy, but which allows us an opportunity for contemplative delight.

The activity in poetic imagining, then, is not an activity in which something is 'expressed', or 'conveyed', or 'mimicked', or 'copied', or 'reproduced', or 'exhibited'; there is no undifferentiated 'primary imagination'[27] to supply it with materials, nor have other

---

that the poet sought to 'express'. What emotion is expressed in *Anna Karenina?* in Botticelli's Birth of Venus? in *Figaro?* in St Paul's Cathedral? in

Ah sunflower, weary of time,
That countest the steps of the sun?

Can it be that these poets, on these occasions, have been so incompetent as to leave us in doubt about what, in this view of things, was their main preoccupation?

[26] It may, however, be remarked that while the 'title' which a poet (or his editor) may give to a poem is usually to be understood merely as a means of identification and might (as often happens) be absent or be replaced by a number without loss, the titles of some poems may be recognized neither as mere identifications nor as (inevitably irrelevant) indications of what the poem is 'about', but as themselves poetic images and thus as a component of the poem itself, e.g., 'Sweeney among the Nightingales'. The table of contents of a book of musical compositions often (and appropriately) consists of the opening bars of the compositions themselves.

[27] Coleridge, *Biographia Literaria* (Everyman ed.), p. 159. Coleridge (after Kant) was disposed to understand that all experiencing is 'imagining', but what he calls 'primary imagination' is, in fact, 'primary' only in the sense that it is the mode of imagining we are most apt to engage in, namely, practical imagining.

modes of imagining anything it can make use of. It is the activity of being delighted in the entertainment of its own contemplative images. The patterns which these images may make together, the eligibility to become components of a more complex image, is not determined in advance. Sequences, patterns, correspondencies may give delight when they answer expectations, but only when they are poetic expectations; and they may give delight when they surprise by running wide of expectation, but only when it is poetic surprise. Nor may poetic imagining be said, with any significance, to be the pursuit of some absolute delight potential in these images. There is no 'true', or 'proper', or 'necessary' order or con-cretion of images to which approximation is being sought. Every poet is like the Spanish painter Orbaneja, of whom Cervantes tells us: when a bystander asked what he was painting, he answered, 'Whatever it turns out to be'. Consequently, 'beauty' (in the vocabu-lary of aesthetic theory, where I think it now properly belongs) is not a word like 'truth'; it behaves in a different manner. It is a word the use of which is to describe a poetic image which we are com-pelled to admire, not as we admire (with approval) a noble action, nor as we admire a thing well done (such as a mathematical dem-onstration), but on account of the pre-eminent delight it plants in the contemplative spectator.

Poetry, then, begins and ends as a language. But in the lan-guage of poetry, words, shapes, sounds, movements are not signs with preordained significances; they are not like chessmen behav-ing according to known rules or like coins having an agreed current value; they are not tools with specific aptitudes and uses; they are not 'conveyances' when what is to be conveyed exists already in thought or emotion. Nor is this a language full of synonyms where one sign may be substituted for another if it is apt to convey the same meaning, or where some other sort of sign (a gesture instead of a word) will often do as well. In short, it is not a symbolic lan-guage. In poetry words are themselves images and not signs for other images; imagining is itself utterance, and without utterance there is no image. It is a language without a vocabulary, and conse-quently one that cannot be learned by imitation. But if we were to call it (as I think it might properly be called) a metaphorical language we should at once go on to recognize the difference between metaphor in poetry and metaphor in a symbolic language. In a symbolic language metaphor is and remains a symbol. It may be a rhetorical expression designed to capture attention or to relieve (or to increase) the tension of an argument, or it may even be used in the interest of greater precision; but on all occasions it merely recognizes and makes use of natural or conventional correspondencies, and the aptness of the equivalence invoked is the condition of its effectiveness. Metaphors here are like counters which may carry an attractive design upon their face but it is a design which merely indicates (and does not constitute) their value: for 'son of Adam' read 'man', for 'golden meadow' read 'sunlit field of grass', for 'plum blossom' read 'chastity.'[28] In the language of poetry, on the other hand, metaphors are themselves poetic images, and consequently they are fictions. The poet does not recognize and record natural or conventional correspondencies, or use them to 'explore reality'; he does not invoke equivalencies, he makes images. His metaphors have no settled value; they have only the value he succeeds in giving them. Of course, as verbal expressions they are not immune from the infection of symbolism; any of them (and particularly the so-called 'consecrated' or 'archetypal' images) may relapse into being coins of fixed value, but when this happens they have merely ceased to be poetic images.[29] And to shuffle symbolic metaphors about, rearranging them into different patterns, is the activity which Coleridge contrasted with poetic imagining and called 'fancy'.[30] As in science there is no room for ambiguity, so in poetry there is no room for stereotypical images. What, therefore, has to be 'dissolved' before poetry can appear is not the images of a 'primary', non-modal manner of imagining but the authority of the symbolic language of practical activity and of the even more precisely symbolic language of science. The enemies of poetic imagining in music and in

[28] The so-called 'language of flowers' is a symbolic-metaphorical language of this sort.
[29] As in imitation period architecture, character acting or a good deal of Pre-Raphaelite poetry.
[30] Coleridge, *Biographia Literaria* (Everyman ed.), p. 160.

dancing are symbolic sounds and movements; the plastic arts emerge only when the symbolism of shapes is forgotten; and the symbolic language of practical activity offers a strong and continuous resistance to the appearance of poetry. There are periods in the history of every symbolic language when the symbolism is still inchoate and is consequently less hostile to poetry, and it would seem that this was the case in sixteenth-century England.[31] But, although no practical language ever becomes perfectly symbolic, the language of the twentieth century is more exactly so than that of the sixteenth century, and therefore constitutes a greater hindrance to poetic imagining. There are, however, still happily situated peoples, like the Irish, who have ready to be turned into poetry a language whose symbolism is archaic and therefore less apt to impose itself.

For those who understand poetic imagining as a naïve and a primordial activity, there is no puzzle about the historical ancestry of the poet. They recognize that a prosaic manner of thinking and speaking, one appropriate to the communication of 'scientific' knowledge, was an historic achievement, perhaps (so far as Europe was concerned) an invention of the Greeks of the classical age. They think of this as having been imposed upon a primordial mythological manner of thinking, which they identify with the poetic. And they go on to applaud or to disparage the invention as they feel inclined. This, however, I believe to be a mistaken view, and it is one which has had some unfortunate consequences in aesthetics: it has acquired a confused counterpart in fashionable psychological interpretations of poetic imagining. No doubt a mythological manner of thinking preceded what we recognize to be a 'scientific' manner; but its idiom was practical and religious rather than poetic, and it was something from which the poet no less than the scientist had to emancipate himself. It is only in a much later passage in European history that the effort of poetic imagination to free itself from the authority of 'scientific' thought became significant.

---

[31] Macaulay has some matchless pages on this subject at the beginning of his essay on Milton.

In ancient times two figures were recognized, each of which has his counterpart in the modern world. There was the seer, the teacher, often speaking in riddles, a figure of religious significance, a priest, a judge, perhaps a magician, whose person was sacrosanct and whose utterances were distinguished by their wisdom; and there was the entertainer, the gleeman, the singer of songs, who rehearsed familiar stories in familiar words and whose audience would tolerate no innovation. The historic progenitor of the poet has been found in each of these figures, and poetic activity has been interpreted accordingly; it has been confused with both wisdom and entertainment. But the poet whose activity I have been considering is a third person, without the wisdom of the seer and without the obligations of the entertainer. It is difficult to discern his counterpart in those ancient times: the man for whom the totem was neither an object of fear, of authority or of reverence, but an object of contemplation; the man for whom myth and magical spell and the cryptic utterances of the seer were not images of power or of wisdom but of delight. But whoever he was (perhaps the man who fashioned the totem-pole, who invented the verbal image of the spell or who translated historic event into myth), it may be supposed that his activity was as unacknowledged as that of the earliest thinkers who began to explore the entailments of a world recognized as 'natural' and not as the artifice or the avatar of a god; and certainly the mediations in which this specifically 'poetic' activity emerged from the acknowledged activities of these ancient societies are lost in obscurity.

That there have always been poets, and that there have always been 'works of art' in the sense in which I have used the expression, I see no reason to doubt; but the activity of the persons has not always been acknowledged and the character of the images as poetic images has often been obscured. And, although the general conditions of poetic imagining may be discerned in this emancipation from the authority of practical (particularly religious) imagining, the event may only rarely be detected. Properly speaking, it never took place in ancient Greece; a glimpse of it is to be found among the Romans; and subsequently in Europe it has been slowly and uncertainly achieved.[32] Here, not many centuries ago, what we may recognize as 'works of art' were recognized primarily as the servants of practical activity. Their office was understood to be decorative and illustrative, the embellishment of the kingly majesty, of religious observance and of the merchant's way of life. They were prized as expressions or evocations of piety, family pride and affection, respect for justice and deference to authority; as the means whereby the memory of notable persons and events were preserved, the faces of strangers made known to one another, true belief exhibited, and good behaviour taught. But emancipation, the recognition of these objects as images designed and fit for contemplative attention, did not spring from some new and unaccountable craving for release from the authority of practical imagining, and, of course, it did not immediately result in the production of works of an entirely different kind; it sprang from circumstantial changes which (giving a new context to what was already there) transformed it, and even provoked a disposition to make things appropriate to this context. Indeed, the mere lapse of time and ordinary forgetfulness played a considerable part in this emancipation: the survival of stories whose messages had been lost and of images whose 'meaning' had been forgotten, and the encounter with images (both verbal and plastic) from elsewhere whose symbolism was unknown. In the *Midsummer Night's Dream* and in the *Tempest*, for example, a whole world of images has been emancipated from their religious and practical significance and transformed into poetry: there are spells which do not bind, images which have lost their emotive power and figures who, having lost their place in both history and myth, acquire poetic character. And in respect of plastic invention, perhaps the most important circumstance mediating this change was the mere super-abundance of works eligible to be recognized as works of art. These, accumulated and deposited in the treasuries of princes, nobles, ecclesiastics, merchants, municipalities and corporations, their practical origin and occasion

---

[32] Of the East I hesitate to speak. But there is a significant anecdote of Chuang Tzu about Ch'ing, the chief carpenter of the Prince of Lu, whose description of the activity of being an artist is almost entirely in terms of what he had to forget.

unknown or forgotten, were detached from whatever practical use
or significance they might once have had and, in this manner,
framed apart in a new context, they became capable of provoking
contemplative attention—as in an earlier century the invading Romans were provoked to contemplative delight by the temples and
statues of Greece because for them they had no religious-symbolic
significance. And it is in similar circumstances that the poetic
qualities of icons and carpets, idols, buildings and utensils, seen
by eyes they were never made for or removed from their native context, have received recognition in our own times. The history of
modern art, from one point of view, is the story of the manner in
which human imagination has filled this context (itself the unde-
signed gift of historical circumstance) with appropriate images.
Nor is this true only of the plastic arts; the history of European
drama and of music tells the same story and displays the same
combination of contingency and invention responding to one another. And whatever in our current attitude runs counter to this—
our attention to the 'subject' of a poem or a picture; our disposition
to seek in poetry a guide to conduct; our confusion of poetry with
wisdom or with entertainment; our interest in the 'psychology' of
the poet; the difficulty we have of accepting the fictitious as such,
being disposed to interpret it as symbolic, or make-believe, or as
illusion, and so on—may be understood as a survival from bygone
times before poetry had emerged and had been recognized, or as a
revulsion from what is for us, historically, a comparatively new and
still imperfectly assimilated experience.

SEVEN

Every apology for poetry is an attempt to discern its place on the
map of human activity; every defence attributes to poetic imagining
a certain character and, in virtue of this character, a certain place
on the map. And it is to be expected that anyone who believes in
the pre-eminence of a particular mode of activity will be concerned
to discover the office of poetry in relation to that mode. Thus, since
it is now commonly believed that practical enterprise and moral en-

deavour are the pre-eminently proper occupations of mankind, we are not surprised when we find that the commonest apology for poetry is a vindication of it in respect of these occupations. An inquiry into the relation of art to society is understood to be an inquiry into its relation to a society of men engaged in practical activity: what is the 'function' of poetry in the social order? Some of the writers who steer this course, having no great opinion of poetic imagining, understand it to be a regrettable distraction from the proper business of living; at best it is a holiday excursion from which a man might hope to return to work rested and perhaps with renewed energy. Others, however, recognize poetry to be a profitable servant of practical endeavour, apt to perform a variety of useful tasks. The office of poetry, we are informed by these writers, is to tell us how we ought to live or to provide us with a particular kind of criticism of our conduct; it is to record and disseminate a scale of moral values; it is to give a special kind of moral education in which good emotions are not merely described and recommended but actually awakened in us; it is to promote emotional health and sanity; it is to cure a corrupt consciousness and to 'attune us to existence'; it is to reflect the structure and operation of the 'society' in which it appears;[33] it is to comfort the miserable, to strike terror into sinners, or merely to provide 'music while you work'. In a more profound view (Schiller's), the 'social value' of art is recognized to lie in the relief it offers from the uniformities and rigidities of a life narrowly concentrated upon practical endeavour. And in a notorious piece of hyperbole poets have been called 'the unacknowledged legislators of the world'.[34]

Those writers, on the other hand, who believe inquiry about ourselves and the world we inhabit to be the pre-eminently proper occupation of mankind are appropriately concerned to interpret the office of poetry in relation to *scientia*. The problem of art and socie-

---

[33] Writers who take this view recognize *Provençale* love poetry of the twelfth century, not as a new direction of contemplative attention but as a reflection of a change in human sentiment, not as an event in the history of poetry but as an event in the history of morals.

[34] Perhaps, instead of hyperbole we should recognize this as merely a reflection of the manifold character of Apollo. Cf. Bacon, *Advancement of Learning*, I; Vico, *Scenza Nuova*, II, §615.

ty is the problem of its place in a society of men engaged in scientific investigation. Apologists in this idiom have, perhaps, the harder
task; but they have not been dilatory in undertaking it. Here again,
there are writers who find in poetic imagining merely a distraction
from the engagements of *scientia*, and who find in the non-symbol-
ic language of poetry only a worthless instrument of scientific communication. These are the abolitionists: they have a notable pedigree and they have flourished among us since the seventeenth
century. But they are partnered by writers who claim for poetic imagining the power of 'seeing things as they really are', who recognize poetry as a record and repository of knowledge about the
world, and who understand it in such a manner as to attribute to it
the power and the office of giving us 'a clear and impartial awareness of the nature of the world'. And there are even some people
who discern in the very process of scientific inquiry and discovery a
component which they identify as poetic imagining.

So far as I am concerned, an apology for poetry in either of
these idioms is misconceived; although some of the things said in
this manner may not be ill-observed or untrue.[35] Having chosen
their course, those who think in this manner understand everything merely in respect of the help or hindrance it offers them in
reaching their destination. Their inquiry is not concerned with ascertaining the place of poetry on the map of human activity; it is
concerned only with the subordinate relation of poetry to the feature on the map which happens to interest them most. But, as I
understand it, the only apology for poetry worth considering is one
which seeks to discern the place and quality of the voice of poetry
in the conversation of mankind—a conversation where each voice
speaks in its own idiom, where from time to time one voice may
speak louder than others, but where none has natural superiority,
let alone primacy. The proper context in which to consider poetic
utterance, and indeed every other mode of utterance, is not a 'society' engaged in practical enterprise, nor one devoted to scientific inquiry; it is this society of conversationists.

---

[35] For example, Schiller's thoughts on the usefulness of a 'useless' activity.

Each voice in this conversation, from one point of view, represents an emancipation from the conditions which determine the idiom of each of the others. *Scientia* is an 'escape' from the *scientia propter potentiam* of practice, and practical activity is an 'escape' from scientific 'fact'. Consequently, if we speak of poetic imagining as a form of 'escape' (recognizing contemplation as an 'escape' from desiring, approving, contriving and inquiring) we are saying no more than that it moves in a universe of discourse differently constituted from that of any other kind of imagining; we are saying no more than what may properly be said of both practice and science. And the note of deprecation which obtrudes itself when poetic imagining is said to be an 'escape' merely advertises an imperfect understanding of the conversation. *Of course*, from one point of view, poetry is an 'escape'; not escape (as is sometimes supposed) from the perhaps unmanageable or frustrating practical life of a poet, but from the considerabilities of practical activity. But there is nothing sacrosanct about practical enterprise, moral endeavour, or scientific inquiry that 'escape' from them is to be deplored. Indeed, these are inherently burdensome activities from which we may properly seek release; and it is a tiresome conversation in which only these voices are heard. In poetry, then, a self which desires and suffers, which knows and contrives, is superseded by a self which contemplates, and every backward glance is an infidelity at once difficult to avoid and fatal in its consequences. Nevertheless, in order to participate in the conversation a voice must not only speak in its own idiom, it must also be capable of being understood; and we should consider how it is possible for the voice of poetry to be heard and understood in conversation with partners of so different a character.

There is I think, no mystery in the common understanding enjoyed by the voices of science and practical activity. Although the idioms in which they speak are different, there is a counterpart in practice to many of the features of the scientific universe of discourse: the images of both practice and of science are apt to be arranged consequentially, in both activities there is a recognition of 'fact' and 'not-fact', and the language of both is a symbolic language. But, as I have described it, there would appear to be little or no possibility of common understanding between the voice of poetry and the other voices in the conversation: its utterance points to no conclusion, it recognizes neither 'fact' nor 'not-fact' and its language is not a language of signs. And this remoteness of poetic utterance no doubt accounts for the disposition to assimilate it somehow or other to the idioms of science and of practice. Most poets (even when we do not make the mistake of attributing to them the opinions they put into the mouths of their characters) have some thoughts about the world in general and about the conduct of life, and when we listen to these thoughts the voice of poetry seems to acquire an intelligibility which it otherwise lacks. Shakespeare's 'view of life' may appear to us profound, or we may find it as unsatisfactory as Johnson found it,[36] but whatever our conclusion we seem, by considering it, to have drawn the voice of poetry into the conversation and given it a place it would otherwise be without. But it is an illusion; we have caught merely what is unpoetic—the theology of Dante, the perishable religious convictions of Bunyan, the verisimilitude of Ingres, the dated 'pessimism' of Hardy, the pseudo-scientific speculations of Goethe, the patriotism of Chopin —and the poetic image itself has slipped through our net and escaped into its proper element. Or again, it may be conjectured that to be brought up (like French boys and girls) on Racine is an education in desire and approval remarkably different from that which English boys and girls derive from being brought up on Shakespeare; but, whether the difference is profound or superficial, it does not spring from the different poetic qualities of these writers. And yet, just as Plato discerned in the desiring soul a shadowy counterpart of reason (which he called 'temperance') enabling it not to behave rationally but to hear the voice of reason and to submit to its rule, we may, I think, find in practical activity itself intimations of contemplative imagining capable of responding to the voice of poetry.

---

[36] *Preface to Shakespeare.*

In the common relationships of practical activity—those of producer and consumer, master and servant, principal and assistant—each participant seeks some service or recompense for service, and if it is not forthcoming the relationship lapses or is terminated. And this is the case also in the relationship of partners in an enterprise, and even in that of comrades where attachment is circumstantial and springs from a common occupation, interest, belief, or anxiety. In the world *sub specie voluntatis* we normally reject what is not to our liking; and in the world *sub specie morum* we normally reject what proves itself to be irrational or imperfect. But there are relationships, still unmistakably practical, where this is not so. It is not so, for example, in love and in friendship. Friends and lovers are not concerned with what can be made out of each other, but only with the enjoyment of one another. A friend is not somebody one trusts to behave in a certain manner, who has certain useful qualities, who holds acceptable opinions; he is somebody who evokes interest, delight, unreasoning loyalty, and who (almost) engages contemplative imagination. The relationship of friends is dramatic, not utilitarian. And again, loving is not 'doing good'; it is not a duty; it is emancipated from having to approve or to disapprove. Its object is individual and not concretion of qualities: it was for Adonis that Venus quit heaven. What is communicated and enjoyed is not an array of emotions—affection, tenderness, concern, fear, elation, etc.—but the uniqueness of a self. But while there is nobody incapable of being loved, there is nobody who singles himself out as pre-eminently proper to be loved. Neither merit nor necessity has any part in the generation of love; its progenitors are chance and choice—chance, because what cannot be identified in advance cannot be sought; and in choice the inescapable practical component of desire makes itself felt.[37] In short, the world *sub specie amoris* is unmistakably the world of practical activity; there is desire and frustration, there is moral achievement and failure, there is pleasure and pain, and death (of one kind or another) is both a possibility and is recognized as the *summum malum*. Nevertheless,

[37] Hence St Augustine's difficulty in understanding how God can be said to 'love' man. *De Doct. Christ.* i, 34.

the image in love and friendship (what is created in these manners of imagining) is, more than in any other engagement in practical imagining, 'whatever it turns out to be'. If these are not properly speaking contemplative activities, they are at least ambiguously practical activities which intimate contemplation and may be said to constitute a connection between the voices of poetry and practice, a channel of common understanding. And, no doubt, it is on this account that fictitious persons in fictitious love are the most familiar of all poetic images.

Further, there is, perhaps, in 'moral goodness' (as distinguished from 'virtuous conduct', 'excellence of character', or the engagement in 'good works') a release from the deadliness of doing and a possibility of perfection, which intimates poetry. For here is a private and self-sufficient activity, not accommodated to the world, emancipated from place or condition, in which each engagement is independent of what went before and of what may come after, in which no man is ineligible to engage on account of ignorance or inexpertness in judging the probable consequences of actions, or (as Kant says) by reason of some special disfavour of destiny or by the niggardly endowment of a step-motherly Nature,[38] and in which success is entirely independent of 'usefulness' or external achievement.

Moreover, a poetic utterance (a work of art) is itself often an ambiguous image. Its place in the practical world—in respect of occupying space, being desirable, having a price, and so on—may make it liable to be misread. And there are some works of art—buildings, for example—which may be said to be intrinsically ambiguous because they demand to be considered not only as poetic images but also from the point of view of their durability and the manner in which they satisfy a practical need. But the opportunities which works of art (some more so than others) give for the neglect of their poetic character may also be an oblique means of getting themselves recognized in their poetic character. Our attention may be attracted to a work of art, in the first place, for some entire-

---

[38] *Grundlegung zur Metaphysik der Sitten*, 394.

ly extraneous reason—because it seems to represent something in the practical world which is familiar to us or of special interest, because it supplies us with a piece of historical information we have been seeking, because some detail catches our fancy, or merely because it is the work of a friend or an acquaintance—but having, in this manner, been lured into looking or listening, the mood of contemplation may supervene and its proper character as a poetic image may, suddenly or gradually, come to impose itself upon us. And even this entrance to the world of poetry is not to be despised.

And again, the recollections of childhood may constitute the connection sought. Everybody's young days are a dream, a delightful insanity, a miraculous confusion of poetry and practical activity in which nothing has a fixed shape and nothing has a fixed price. 'Fact' and 'not-fact' are still indistinct. To act is to make a bargain with events; there are obscure longings, there are desires and choices, but their objects are imperfectly discerned; everything is 'what it turns out to be'. And to speak is to make images. For, although we spend much of our early years learning the symbolic language of practical intercourse (and when we learn a foreign tongue it is always learnt as a symbolic language), this is not the language with which we begin as children. Words in everyday use are not signs with fixed and invariable usages; they are poetic images. We speak an heroic language of our own invention, not merely because we are incompetent in our handling of symbols, but because we are moved not by the desire to communicate but by the delight of utterance. And however immersed we may become in practical or scientific enterprise, anybody who recollects the confusion it was to be young will have a ready ear for the voice of poetry.

It is, then, not impossible to understand how the voice of poetry should be able to make itself heard in a conversation apt, as it now is, to be dominated by the voices of practice and of science. Nevertheless, as I understand it, poetic imagining brings to the conversation a unique utterance, not to be assimilated to any other. Its voice is pre-eminently conversable. In both scientific and practical imagining utterance and voice, *what* is said and *how* it is said, doctrine and activity, are distinguishable and may become separated from one another; in poetry this is impossible. A poetic image is not a symbol; since it 'expresses' nothing, there can be no tension between imagining and utterance. Moreover, the relationship between poetic images is itself a conversational relationship; they neither confirm nor refute one another, they merely evoke one another and join, not to compose a premeditated conclusion, but to compose another and more complex image of the same kind. Further, poetry has nothing to teach us about how to live or what we ought to approve. Practical activity is an endless battle for noble or for squalid but always for illusory ends, a struggle from which the practical self cannot escape and in which victory is impossible because desire can never be satisfied: every attainment is recognized to be imperfect, and every imperfection has value only as an incipient perfection which is itself an illusion. And even 'forgiveness' is only an emblematic break in the chain of the fatality of doing; every action, even those that are forgotten, is irreparable. Poetic activity has no part in this struggle and it has no power to control, to modify, or to terminate it. If it imitates the voice of practice its utterance is counterfeit. To listen to the voice of poetry is to enjoy, not a victory, but a momentary release, a brief enchantment. And perhaps, obliquely, it is to enjoy something more. Having an ear ready for the voice of poetry is to be disposed to choose delight rather than pleasure or virtue or knowledge, a disposition which will reflect itself in practical life in an affection for its intimations of poetry.

Nevertheless, we must expect to listen for this voice more often than we hear it. Poetic imagining has frequently been recognized as a 'visitation'; but while this has been taken as an emblem of its superior status, even of its divine inspiration, properly understood it is testimony only of the unavoidable transience of contemplative activity:

> All things can tempt me from this craft of verse:
> One time it was a woman's face, or worse—
> The seeming needs of my food-driven land;
> Now nothing but comes readier to the hand
> Than this accustomed toil. When I was young,
> I had not given a penny for a song

Did not the poet sing it with such airs
That one believed he had a sword upstairs;
Yet would be now, could I but have my wish,
Colder and dumber and deafer than a fish.

But it is a wish that can have only an intermittent fulfilment. In short, there is no *vita contemplativa*; there are only moments of contemplative activity abstracted and rescued from the flow of curiosity and contrivance. Poetry is a sort of truancy, a dream within the dream of life, a wild flower planted among our wheat.

"The Voice of Poetry in the Conversation of Mankind" first appeared in a short book of the same name published by Bowes and Bowes in 1959.

Index

This book is set in Bookman, a typeface in
the Egyptian family, characterized by open
counters and sturdy serifs. This version
has been adapted for contemporary
typesetting from the original nineteenth-century
design produced at the Miller & Richards
foundry as a boldface for their Old Style Antique.
It is lighter and more refined than the
original but retains its easy legibility.

*Printed on paper that is acid-free and meets
the requirements of the American National
Standard for Permanence of Paper for Printed
Library Materials, Z39.48-1992.* ∞

Editorial services by Custom Editorial Productions, Inc., Cincinnati, Ohio

Index by Primary Sources Research, Chevy Chase, Maryland

Book Design by Binns & Lubin, New York, New York

Typography by Alexander Typesetting, Inc., Indianapolis, Indiana

Printed and bound by Edwards Brothers, Inc., Ann Arbor, Michigan